Folk Law

Edited by Alison Dundes Renteln and Alan Dundes

Folk Law

Essays in the Theory and Practice of
Lex Non Scripta

Volume I

The Univers

The University of Wisconsin Press
114 North Murray Street
Madison, Wisconsin 53715

©1994 Alison Dundes Renteln and Alan Dundes
All rights reserved

Published in paperback by the University of
Wisconsin Press in 1995

First published in hardcover by Garland Publishing, Inc.,
in 1994, as Volume 7 of Garland Folklore Casebooks

2   4   5   3   1

Printed in the United States of America

Library of Congress Cataloging-in-Publication Data

Folk law : essays in the theory and practice of Lex non scripta /
edited by Alison Dundes Renteln and Alan Dundes.
    p. cm.
Includes bibliographical references.
ISBN 0-299-14344-9 (pbk.)
1. Customary law. I. Dundes Renteln, Alison. II. Dundes, Alan.
[K282.F65 1995]
340.5—dc20   94-812

To Carolyn Dundes,
Mother and Wife

Contents

Introduction   xiii

What Is Folk Law?   1

The Concept of Folk Law in Historical Context:
   A Brief Outline   5
G.C.J.J. van den Bergh

Custom in Classical Roman Law   33
A. Arthur Schiller

Custom as a Source of Law in India   49
M.P. Jain

Some Realism About Customary Law—The West
   African Experience   83
Gordon R. Woodman

Customary Law: A Confusing Fiction   111
J.P.B. de Josselin de Jong

The Common Law and Legal Theory   119
A.W.B. Simpson

An Approach to Customary Law   141
Alan Watson

Pioneers in the Study of Folk Law   159

Results and Task of Legal Ethnology in Europe   161
Ernő Tárkány-Szücs

Indigenous and Foreign Influences on the Early
   Russian Legal Heritage   187
Samuel Kucherov

Main Trends in German Ethnological Jurisprudence and Legal Ethnology *Rüdiger Schott*	201
Methods and Theories of Dutch Juridical-Ethnological Research in the Period 1900 to 1977 *A.K.J.M. Strijbosch*	231
Aspects of the Controversy on Customary Law in India *C. van Vollenhoven*	251
African Legal Tradition: J.M. Sarbah, J.B. Danquah, N.A. Ollennu *Irina Sinitsina*	263
The Ascertainment of Folk Law	283
Methods of Legal Research into Customary Law *A.N. Allott*	285
The Judicial Ascertainment of Customary Law in British Africa *A.N. Allott*	295
The Problem of Reducing Customary Laws to Writing *T.O. Elias*	319
The Recording of Customary Law: Some Problems of Method *Simon Roberts*	331
Ascertainment of Customary Law: Problems and Perspectives with Special Reference to Zambia *Muna Ndulo*	339
The Conversion of Customary Law to Written Law *Obeid Hag Ali*	351
The White Man's Burden: *Ersatz* Customary Law and Internal Pacification in South Africa *Robert J. Gordon*	367

Contents

The Expression of Folk Law in Folklore, Symbol, and Ritual — 395

Folklore Research and Legal History in the German Language Area — 397
Hermann Baltl

Traces of Ancient Germanic Law in a German Game-Song — 407
Paul G. Brewster

Legal Folklore of Children — 417
A.F. Chamberlain

The Role of Proverbs in a Nigerian Judicial System — 421
John C. Messenger, Jr.

Property Distribution by Lot in Present-Day Greece — 433
Harry L. Levy

Symbols in Customary Law — 439
Durica Krstić

A Note on the Bedouin Image of 'Adl as Justice — 455
Clinton Bailey

Furniture Arrangement as a Symbol of Judicial Roles — 459
John N. Hazard

The "Ordeal of Water" in Nineteenth-Century Thailand — 467
Carl Bock

The Euro-American Trial as Expiatory Oral Ordeal — 473
Theodor Reik

Codes of Folk Law — 483

Mesopotamian Laws and the Historian — 485
Albrecht Goetze

Biblical and Cuneiform Law Codes — 495
Raymond Westbrook

Tibetan Folk-Law — 513
Shih-Yü Yü Li

The Nature of Malay Customary Law *Joseph Minattur*	539
Customs Connected with Homicide in Morocco *Edward Westermarck*	569

Volume II

Cases of Folk Law	599
Trouble-Cases and Trouble-less Cases in the Study of Customary Law and Legal Reform *J.F. Holleman*	601
Injury and Liability in African Customary Law in Zambia *A.L. Epstein*	625
Witchcraft and the Law *Roger Howman*	637
White Man's Law Among Filipino Tribesmen *R.F. Barton*	655
The Legal Process in a Village in North India: The Case of Maya *R.S. Freed*	671
The Litigious Daughter-in-Law: Family Relations in Rural Russia in the Second Half of the Nineteenth Century *Beatrice Farnsworth*	689
Pigs and Positivism *Hendrik Hartog*	711
Folk Law in Conflict	751
"Civilized" Law and "Primitive" Peoples *L.C. Green*	753
Conflicts of Western and Non-Western Law *R.D. Kollewijn*	775

The Conflict of Laws in Africa *E.G. Unsworth*	795
The Inarticulate Premise *Robert B. Seidman*	805
The *Otieno* Case: African Customary Law Versus Western Jurisprudence *Roy Carleton Howell*	827
Legal Recognition and Protection of Minority Customs in a Plural Society in England *Alec Samuels*	845
Culture and Culpability: A Study of Contrasts *Alison Dundes Renteln*	863

International Folk Law	881
François Gény's Doctrine of Customary Law *Peter E. Benson*	883
What Constitutes Custom in International Law? *Nirmala Naganathan*	897
Unwritten International Law *Rudolf Bernhardt*	915
Soviet Theory of the Legal Nature of Customary International Law *Richard J. Erickson*	939
The Myth of Customary International Law *N.C.H. Dunbar*	961
The Enforceability of Customary Norms of Public International Law *Steven M. Schneebaum*	983
Custom as a Source of International Law of Outer Space *Vladlen S. Vereshchetin and Gennady M. Danilenko*	1003

Customary Law: From "Universal" in a European System to "Regional" in a World System   **1019**
Allan Rosas

Suggestions for Further Reading in Folk Law   **1033**

Introduction

Folk law is a socially defined group's orally transmitted traditional body of obligations and prohibitions, sanctioned or required by that group, binding upon individuals or subsets of individuals (e.g., families, clans) under pain of punishment or forfeiture. Folk law is known by a bewildering number of terms, including customary law, unwritten law, common law, indigenous law, living law, primitive law, etc. It is normally studied by members of various academic disciplines such as historians, philosophers, sociologists, anthropologists, and classicists; but in our view, the subject of folk law falls at the intersection of two disciplines in particular, namely, jurisprudence and folklore.

It was in the above mentioned context that a happy collaboration was initiated between a specialist in jurisprudence and a folklorist. We have sought to put together under one cover some of the most interesting essays written about folk law. Our intention was to facilitate the serious study of folk law, not only by students of jurisprudence and folklore, but by anyone curious about the subject matter. It is our impression that folk law tends to be neglected by both law school curricula and by folklore institutes. While folk or customary law might be taught occasionally at some law schools, it is not offered at the vast majority of law schools. Similarly, while introductory textbooks on folklore commonly include coverage of folk medicine, folk law is rarely if ever even mentioned.

We have divided the essays somewhat arbitrarily into eight sections. The first set of essays is concerned with the definition of folk law. We have tried to select articles representing diverse points of view with examples of folk law drawn from different societies. The second section is historically oriented. It seeks to demonstrate how the study of folk law began in various locales. The third group of papers treats what is usually termed in the literature as "the ascertainment" of folk law, referring to the fieldwork and recording techniques utilized to identify *bona fide* folk law as such. We tended to choose essays dealing with African folk law for this section since most of the theoretical writing about "ascertainment" has been by Africanists. (This is part of a general difficulty we encountered throughout the volume inasmuch as more has been written about African folk law than about the folk law of any other area.)

The fourth section is quite a novel one, we think. It concerns the expression of folk law in other folkloristic forms, e.g., folksong. Also covered are symbolic representations of folk law as well as ritual forms of folk law. The fifth set of essays concerns the rule-approach to folk law, as manifested, for example, in the study of purported codes of folk law. This is in contrast to the sixth group of papers which gets down to cases. The case approach to folk law (as opposed to the rule-approach) seems to be preferred by anthropologists who encounter specific cases, e.g., disputes, in the course of carrying out their fieldwork.

The penultimate section discusses one of the most fascinating aspects of the study of folk law: conflict of laws. As a result of centuries of imperialism and colonialism, not to mention large-scale immigration movements of various peoples, we find situations all over the world involving some form of legal pluralism. By this we mean that two or more distinct legal systems are in effect for the same population. In such instances, the question inevitably arises as to which legal system takes precedence. It is precisely this issue, for example, in colonial Africa, which encouraged the investigation and in some cases codification of folk or customary law in the first place. Suppose what is mandated by folk law is deemed a criminal offense by the colonial legal system imposed from without. Such conflicts demonstrate the inevitable relativity and arbitrariness of many elements of legal systems.

The final section of the volume is concerned with the role of folk law in international law. Just as there may be conflict of laws *within* a given country which has to contend with legal pluralism, so there may be conflict of laws between two sovereign states. Is there an ascertainable body of international folk law that should take precedence over the law of individual states? And if there is not, should there not be created, by some international body, folk law or its equivalent, by treaty or agreement, some means of dealing with the issues of protecting space exploration or a deteriorating ozone layer? With this set of essays, we hope to show that the study of folk law, far from being an esoteric branch of jurisprudence or folkloristics, is right on the front line of contemporary problems in international law.

For those readers whose appetites for folk law may have been whetted by the essays we have selected, we have appended a relatively small set of suggestions for further reading. It turns out there are literally hundreds if not thousands of books and essays written on folk law. Many are written in the local languages of the countries where the folk law exists. We have generally limited ourselves to materials written in English, French, and German. Even with that self-imposed limitation, we hope that we have given a fair introduction to the scope of folk law with

Introduction

respect to what it is, how it has been studied, and why it is relevant to the modern world.

Although American legal scholars tend to be unfamiliar with the voluminous scholarship on folk law, there is considerable interest in the subject across the globe. For instance, the international membership list of the Commission on Folk Law and Legal Pluralism based in Nijmegen, the Netherlands, attests to the worldwide concern with customary law. Particularly strange is the fact that even though the common law is itself a form of customary law, legal practitioners and scholars in common-law nations, e.g., the United States, sometimes seem not to have the slightest inkling of what folk law is.

In many disputes in which folk law is the central issue, the conflict is one between the state and an indigenous population. Often the dispute involves conflicting state or "official" law and folk law, and at stake may be legal practices that are crucial for the maintenance of group identity. Groups that seek to employ folk law often lack substantial political power and must request that it be recognized by the dominant culture in that society. Furthermore, they must also prove its existence. It is, therefore, difficult to avoid acknowledging that implicit in debates about folk law is a struggle for power between a group lacking any real bargaining power and the elites associated with the state.

Groups that adhere to folk law are not in power in the larger society. If their law is recognized, it will be at the discretion of those in power. Even where nations have attained independence and theoretically need no longer be influenced by the West, they may, nevertheless, follow a Western model. For example, as will be clear in chapter 3, which deals with the ascertainment of folk law, questions about what folk law is are usually framed from the vantage point of the colonial power. The African Restatement project is a clear example of this bias insofar as the natives do not need to have the law restated; they already know what their law requires.

On the one hand, nations have sometimes concluded that it was to their advantage to study and allow the practice of customary law because it might afford them greater control over the local population (see Gordon essay). On the other hand, practices that were in accordance with folk law but which were viewed as "repugnant" might officially be abolished. One interesting question is why attempts to crush folk law have so often failed.

Another normative issue that arises in the context of debates about the "validity" of folk law concerns gender equality. Those who wish to have folk law recognized in some cases seek to perpetuate patriarchal customs. In response, women may challenge the use of customary law inasmuch as its continued recognition will force them to remain in positions of inferior status. So there are those who would advocate the abolition of some types of folk law.

In this work we do not take a position on the validity of folk law. But we would argue that it is essential to study and understand a phenomenon so pervasive in the world and one that has such important political implications.

With the inclusion of more than fifty separate essays, it was simply not possible to avoid some repetition of subject matter. We have tried to keep such overlap at a minimum. We should also confess that our organizational categories are not watertight. Some of the essays in the "Cases of Folk Law" section do discuss folk law in conflict just as some of the essays in the "Folk Law in Conflict" section do discuss individual cases. But overall we feel that we have adequately sampled the voluminous scholarship devoted to folk law and we believe we have brought together under one cover essays from a remarkable variety of published sources sufficient to encourage courses and seminars in folk law at law schools and graduate schools or to supplement the reading materials available for pre-law courses at the undergraduate level. It is also our hope that this volume might stimulate further research in folk law all over the world.

Folk Law

of Cinderella or the flood myth. In this way, folklore differs from so-called high culture and mass culture. We know who wrote Faulkner's novels and we know who wrote the Tarzan adventures. The same holds for law. With modern written legislation, we usually know the individual or group of individuals who penned the first draft of the Declaration of Independence or a particular law. But with folk law, the maxim or axiom simply comes as "given" within a folk group.

Historically, what has happened is that as each group becomes literate, it continues at the same time to retain some elements of the oral culture that preceded the invention or borrowing of writing. So the most literate society on the face of the earth is bound to have some form of folk law. What we really have is a continuum. In a society without writing, everything is orally transmitted. In theory, all the law in such a society would be folk law. In a society with a written language, there will usually be at least two sets of laws: written law and unwritten or folk law. Typically, the written law is given priority over unwritten law, but that is not always the case. We may assist the reader in understanding unwritten law, the subject of this entire volume, by giving a series of oppositions:

oral	written
flexible (variation)	fixed
anonymous	known author
old	new
primitive	civilized
folk	elite
peasant	aristocrat
rural	urban

Lex non scripta is often defined in terms of the left hand column, where *lex scripta*, in contrast, is characterized by the right hand column.

From the above discussion, we hope it is clear that there has always been folk law and that there will continue to be folk law no matter how much written legislation is enacted. The earliest written human records that we have from centuries past all attest to the existence of folk law.

Finally, we should indicate that we prefer the term folk law to customary law because we find the adjective "customary" to be confusing. Custom is a standard genre of folklore and it would include many kinds of traditional behavior that have nothing whatever to do with law. The bridesmaid's catching the bride's wedding bouquet is a custom, but it is not a law as such; a gentleman's rising from his seat when a lady

G.C.J.J. VAN DEN BERGH

The Concept of Folk Law in Historical Context: A Brief Outline

Since all human societies have some form of folk law and this has undoubtedly been the case since the emergence of early man, the reader may begin his or her odyssey into the realm of folk law by perusing this first essay in the volume which consists of an erudite but succinct historical survey of folk law, concentrating principally upon Western countries. Beginning with classical Greece and Rome, G.C.J.J. van den Bergh, Professor of History of Law, University of Utrecht, provides an admirable overview of the development of European interest in folk law.

For other useful surveys, see Paul Vinogradoff, "Customary Law," in G.C. Crump and E.F. Jacob, eds., The Legacy of the Middle Ages *(Oxford: The Clarendon Press, 1926), pp. 287–319; Munroe Smith, "Customary Law: Roman, Mediaeval and Modern Theories," in his* A General View of European Legal History *(New York: Columbia University Press, 1972), pp. 269–309; W. Ullmann, "Bartolus on Customary Law,"* Juridical Review, *52 (1940), 265–283; Harold J. Berman, "The Background of the Western Legal Tradition in the Folklaw of the Peoples of Europe,"* University of Chicago Law Review, *45 (1978), 553–597. For earlier considerations of so-called "living folk law," see W. Van Der Vlugt, "Levend Volksrecht,"* De Gids, *59 (3) (1895), 11–58 and J. Van Kuyk, "Levend Volksrecht,"* Tijdschrift voor Rechtsgeschiedenis, *1 (1918–1919), 1–44, 267–297.*

For one of the many attempts to distinguish clearly between custom and law, see Wolfgang H. Lindig, "Recht und Sitte: Einige Bermerkungen zu einem rechtsethnologischen Problem," Baessler-Archiv, *N.F. 8 (1960), 247–255. For an excellent survey of the concept of legal custom, see John Gilissen,* La Coutume *(Turnhout, Belgium: Brepols, 1982). Gilissen is one of the leading twentieth-century scholars of legal customs. For a valuable consideration of the relevance of customary law in canonical law, see Merlin Joseph Guilfoyle,* Custom: An

---

Reprinted from Keebet von Benda-Beckmann and Fons Strijbosch, eds., *Anthropology of Law in the Netherlands: Essays on Legal Pluralism*, Verhandelingen van het Koninklijk Instituut voor Taal-, Land- en Volkenkunde 116 (Dordrecht: Foris Publications, 1986), pp. 67–89. Reprinted by permission of the Koninklijk Institute voor Taal-, Land- en Volkenkunde, Leiden, The Netherlands.

Historical Synopsis and Commentary *(Washington, D.C.: The Catholic University of America, 1937).*

See also Felix Speiser, "Sitte, Brauch, und Recht," Schweizerisches Archiv für Volkskunde 43 (1946), 73–90 and Paul Bohannan, "The Differing Realms of the Law" in Law and Warfare: Studies in the Anthropology of Conflict *(Garden City, New York: The Natural History Press, 1967), pp.43–56.*

Folk Law as Customary Law

The historian must begin his tale somewhere, although in history there are no proper beginnings. This is just as true for the history of ideas. The quest for the originator of an idea is hopeless, because strictly speaking truly new ideas are hardly ever born, all being cast in a matrix of existing concepts. Traditional distinctions are transformed in modern theories, and more often than not it seems impossible to determine anything more precise than a wide 'zone of transition'. The same goes for the concept of folk law.[1]

The word does not seem to be much older than the nineteenth century, but the idea is cast in the mould of age-old distinctions, on the one hand between written and unwritten law, which played an important role in Greek philosophy, on the other hand between law and custom, *lex* and *consuetudo*, which medieval legal theorists found in the heritage of Roman law. Folk law is essentially customary law, says Savigny (1814: 14) who very nearly invented the term.

Written and Unwritten Law

It would go much too far to discuss here the Greek origins of the distinction between written and unwritten law with all its philosophical ramifications. Although, for us, customary law and unwritten law are often nearly synonymous, the Greek concept of *nomoi agrafoi* had originally little to do with our concept of customary law. The *nomoi agrafoi* are innate 'laws', natural law in a most elementary and not exclusively juristic sense (RE I (1893) 889; Hirzel 1900). Naturally, educated Romans, as the jurists were, were familiar with these Greek concepts. Ulpian (2nd century) puts the Greek distinction of written and unwritten law at the opening of his textbook for beginners (D 1.1.6.1., Ulp. 1 Inst.), though hardly for systematizing purposes (cf. Thomas 1963: 48; Kaser 1978: 105, 118; so already Pernice 1899: 163).

Some link between Greek and Roman concepts seems to have been contemplated already by Cicero (Part. or. 37.130), but it is mainly because Justinian's (527–565) textbook for beginners, following that of Ulpian, linked the Greek distinction of written and unwritten law with the Roman division of law and custom, that both distinctions seem near synonyms to us (but see Lauria 1967: 80; Nörr 1969: 358).

Custom in Roman Law

The Roman concept of law was quite different from our own (cf. Horak 1969: 31 ff; Nörr 1969: 355, Flume 1975: 22; Kaser 1978: 119). Our idea of law is based on a formalized, binary concept of validity: a rule is either valid or not. And valid rules can only be produced by a limited number of legitimate 'sources'. For the Romans (as for all peoples who did not fall victim to the *mos geometricus*) there was a wide range of shades of validity between the two extremes. If they ever developed something like a theory of the sources of law (they did not even have a technical term for the concept), it had not quite the same status it has in our legal theory (cf. Nörr 1969: 360; Bleicken 1975: 358; Kaser 1978: 105). Still it seems justified to start with the observation that the traditional Roman catalogue of the 'sources' of law as given by the jurists Gaius (Gai 1.2) and Papinian (D 1.1.7) does not mention custom at all.[2] Justinian added it to the list, superimposing on it the division of written and unwritten law[3], with express reference to the Greeks (I 1.2.3). In I 1.2.9 the *ius ex non scripto* is defined in this way:

> "From the unwritten comes the law which is sanctioned by use, because long lasting customs, which are approved of by agreement of those who are used to them, resemble laws."

Justinian, stressing long-established use as a source of law, may seem to come near the modern concept of *'die normative Kraft des Faktischen'* (Jellinek), but this was not the main element in the Roman idea of customary law.

What was said about the Roman concept of validity can also be put in another way. They did not understand law—as we jurists are used to do—to be a complete and cohesive system of valid normative propositions (cf. Nörr 1969: 360; Weber 1922: 398), emanating from either law or custom (cf. Land 1899: 3; Flume 1975: 7; Gilissen 1981: 237). For them all law applied to a specific political community (cf. Brie 1899: 19), it was correlated with specific institutions (cf. Nörr 1969: 358), it was based in the last resort on authority and tradition. All law consisted of the public pronouncements of bodies or persons vested with authority by tradition: laws of the *populus*, decisions of the *plebs*, opinions of the Senate, constitutions of the *princeps*, edicts of the magistrates, *responsa* of the jurists. The first in this list, and the model for all, was the *lex publica* established by consensus of the *populus Romanus* (cf. Bleicken 1975; Kaser 1978: 110 f). And the last of the list, the opinions of jurists, were the intermediary between pronouncement and application for all others (cf. Thomas 1963: 42 f; Nörr 1972: 48; Flume 1975: 14). Pomponius expresses the Roman attitude clearly: "How much law could there be in society if there were not those who could direct it?" (D 1.2–2.13).

Although there were a number of institutions whose origins the Romans were not able to trace back to such a public pronouncement (cf. Thomas 1963: 40 f; Kaser 1978: 110 f), e.g., *patria potestas* or prohibition of donations between man and wife[4], they ascribed these to the *mores maiorum*. But here also there is no generalized idea of enduring custom prominent (but see Kaser 1978: 111), although naturally this is not lacking in any definition of custom.[5] Here again it is rather the principle of authority that seems decisive: the *maiores*, the *patres* had authority and what they did therefore had force of law. Festus defines *mos* as *institutum patrium*, ordinance or institution of the fathers.[6] The Romans referred to *mores* mainly as the origin of institutions believed to be uniquely Roman (cf. Kaser 1978: 111). This reflects the idea that *mores* were the basis of Rome's greatness and their decay the cause of its decline (cf. Ranft 1957: 382). This is a far cry from the modern concept of customary law.

As the Romans never divorced the idea of law from that of a political community—and, of course, primarily their own *civitas*—they seem to have perceived the foreign legal practices obtaining in their expanding empire rather more as fact than as law.[7] For political reasons they may have found it prudent not to ignore such facts, but no legal principle seems to have been involved. A distinction of custom and customary law is not found in Roman sources (cf. Flume 1975: 34). The Roman attitude toward foreign legal systems—of which they seem to have known very little indeed—was on the whole pragmatic, and the jurists never seem to have developed a comprehensive theory of customary law. The bare outline of such a theory is found, though, in D 1.3.32, a fragment standing in the name of the great classical jurist Salvius Julianus, living in the time of Hadrian (117–138). The old question whether this whole fragment can be attributed safely to that famous jurist seems to be answered in the positive now by many Romanists.[8]

However that may be, the theory is rather ingenious. It seems to be connected with the relation of *populus* and *princeps*, and with the status of the last as lawgiver. Naturally, in the traditional republican catalogue of law no mention was made of the pronouncements of the princeps. So at some time during the principate the list must have been expanded (cf. Kaser 1978: 107). Gaius firmly states that there was never any doubt that the constitutions of the princeps have force of law (Gai 1.5; see also Pap. D 1.1.7 pr.; Ulp. D 1.4.1.1), but this only serves to arouse the suspicion that at some period there actually had been a discussion, if not about the binding force itself, at least about the question of how it could be construed juridically. And Justinian himself testifies to the fact that the classical jurists did discuss the question whether an interpretation of law given by the princeps had binding force (C 1.14.12).

Apparently the lawgiving power of the princeps was construed by some jurists to follow from the *lex regia* or *lex de imperio*, the law by which the Roman people transferred formally all its powers to the princeps, or at least gave him *tribunicia potestas* (cf. Berger 1953: 550). This construction may have been somewhat academic; it is found in elementary textbooks (cf. Gai. 1.5; D 1.4.pr. and 1 (Ulp. 1 Inst.); Inst. 1.2.6) and in two constitutions of Justinian dating from 529 and 533 one of which concerns the reform of the law curriculum (C 1.14.12; C 1.17.7 = Const. deo auctore). Now it seems to me that this theory — or should one say ideology — is alluded to in D 1.3.32.1: "Leges nulla alia ex causa nos teneant, quam quod iudicio populi receptae sunt . . . ".[9] If the validity of all laws rests on popular consent, then also the *tacitus consensus* of the people expressed without writing *rebus ipsis et factis*, must have force of law too. Whether this ingenious theory was dogmatically correct is another matter (see Pernice 1899: 158 ff).

Since in this theory of customary law the *populus* plays an important part, we should be careful to assess the meaning of that word. The various meanings of 'people' and *'volk'* will be discussed later, but it is necessary to stress here that, for the Romans, *populus* had a different connotation. Primarily it meant the Roman *'Staatsvolk'* which is mentioned also in the formula SPQR: *Senatus Populusque Romanus*. *Populus* here does not mean the inhabitants of the territory of a state: it *is* the state, or shall we say the main constitutional body. So in my view Julian's theory of customary law does not depart from the Roman idea that all law is the rule of a political community, consisting of the pronouncements of persons or bodies vested with authority by tradition. Also in the concept of *tacitus consensus populi*[10] it is not so much the force of habit as the authority of the *populus Romanus* which gives custom the force of law. Of course the unspoken will of the people as a rule could only be ascertained when the fact of enduring usage[11] was proved, e.g., by a contradictory judgement (cf. Ulp. D 1.3.34) but pace Brie (1899: 12) we should not be led to believe that *consensus* and *consuetudo* were two separate factors in the making of customary law. As far as the length of usage was concerned, the Romans were never specific about either period or proof (cf. Pissard 1910: 10 ff; Flume 1975: 34).

Julian does not present us with a universally valid or fully developed theory of customary law (cf. Kaser 1978: 113). Roman jurists hardly ever aimed at construing such theories. When the principate developed into absolute monarchy with superior power, the idea of the people as lawgiver just faded away and, with it, the idea of the force of habit—which as I said never was lacking in definitions of custom—must have gained prominence. Justinian stressed it and it may not be without reason that he replaced *consensus populi* by *consensus utentium*.[12]

At this point the theory of customary law begins to break away from the traditional Roman concept of law. If there is to be some authority behind the binding force of custom, it cannot be that of the *populus* any more. In the Middle Ages it will be replaced by tacit consent of the ruling superior.

Law and Custom in Justinian's Codification

In Justinian's codification, too, the possibility of conflicts between law and custom seems to present itself as a legal problem. In C 8.52(53).2 (319) it is said that custom cannot abrogate *ratio*[13] or *lex*, and Nov. 134.1 (556) states that bad inventions cannot be legitimized by long standing custom. It is not clear when actually the Romans began to see conflicts of law and custom as legal problems.[14] This can hardly have been the case already in the classical *formula*-process. The *formula* instructed the judge precisely about the facts that were disputed as well as about the law that was to apply when the facts were proved, but it left him completely free as regards the means by which to reach a decision. Naturally Roman administrators met with local customs in the provinces, but the question how to deal with them was a question of policy, not of law. Claudius (41–54) allows a tribe to keep to its long standing usage *beneficio meo* (cf. Flume 1975: 24) and when Pliny the Younger asks Trajan's (98–117) decision concerning a custom in Bithynia contravening a law imposed by the Romans (Plin. ep. X, 114, 115), the emperor's decision seems rather pragmatic (cf. Flume 1975: 28).

I tend to think that conflicts between law and custom became legal problems only in the *cognitio*-process, especially after the Constitutio Antoniniana of 212 had made nearly all inhabitants of the empire Roman citizens. In the *cognitio*-process judges were no longer private citizens acting as one-man-jury, precisely instructed by the parties and the praetor with regard to the law that was to apply if the facts were proved. Now they were public servants, having to decide for themselves what law was applicable in the case at hand. Obviously the Constitutio Antoniniana could not overnight change the law by which all peoples of the empire were living (cf. Mitteis 1891: 5; Kaser 1939: 81; 1971: 196 note 20; 1978: 116). From that time at the latest, therefore, Roman judges could be confronted with Roman citizens invoking non-Roman law on their behalf.[15] This is, I think, the decisive point (cf. Thomas 1963: 50 f). The question is not whether the Romans were familiar with a general notion of law-and-custom—quite obviously they were—nor whether they theorized about the legitimation of customary law—clearly they hardly ever contemplated such theories. The right question to ask is when problems of law-and-custom (apart from being a matter of rhetoric) became inevitably problems of law in a Roman court. In my opinion this would have happened in the third century at the latest.

According to another theory, though, from the days of Constantine (324–337), when absolute monocracy had established itself firmly and many traditional Roman attitudes were revolutionized (cf. Wieacker, cited by Kop 1980: 42), the emperor's attitude towards customary law changed. But perhaps such general explanations are overdone altogether. The few surviving texts in which the emperor denies legal force to custom are fragments, and in most cases we are unable to reconstruct the context in which they were issued precisely. They may have concerned cases in which particularly urgent interests of the state were at issue, like a community claiming immunity from taxation without being able to produce a written privilege to that effect; or a matter in which the emperor actually meant to legislate for the whole empire.[16]

Law and Custom in Medieval IUS Commune and Later

However that may be, the justinianic codification failed to provide later generations of learned jurists with a clear answer to the question, which should prevail, if custom should conflict with law.[17] The answers provided by medieval scientific jurisprudence, whether civil or canonical, were on the whole rather hostile towards customary law (cf. Brie 1899: 62 ff; Pissard 1915: 12; Gierke 1915: 188). For that hostility the jurists may have had political as well as professional reasons which cannot be discussed here. Medieval glossators found a much discussed antimony between D 1.3.32.1 and I 1.2.11 on the one hand, and C 8.52(53).2 on the other. To the solution of that antimony—which naturally had a bearing on contemporary political theory as well—much discussion was spent, without leading to an overall *communis opinio* (cf. Brie 1899: 96 ff). The record of the debate is found in some very extensive glosses.[18]

The glossators sought a solution for the antimony in a series of distinctions which still form part of our legal heritage, e.g., between general and particular law or custom, earlier and subsequent law, compulsory and complementary law. In the view of the glossators consensus was less important than enduring use (cf. Brie 1899: 111). It seems to have been in canon law mainly that *ratio* was made the touchstone of customary law (cf. Brie 1899: 67 ff; Ranft 1957: 388; cf. Köbler 1969: 360) and more precise criteria were developed with regard to duration: legitimate prescription during a specific period—usually forty years—had to be proved. Gratianus (ca. 1140) presents us a logical system of rules (Decretum Grat. D. 11). A custom has force of law if it does not contradict positive law, but it is invalid if it is not *rationabilis*, that is, not in accordance with the rules of divine or natural law, reason or equity.[19] This is the root of the repugnancy clause, which, in various formulations, is nearly universally applied by European colonists from the sixteenth century till our day (cf. Gilissen 1962: 32; Derrett 1963: 117; Hooker 1975: 61; Sohier 1949: 19 ff; Strijbosch 1980: 28). Actually, the term *consuetudo repugnans* is already used by fourteenth-century legists.

Already in early times the church had been confronted with various monastic customs, but especially when the pope rose to secular power and the hierarchical model of the church prevailed, the fight against local custom gained momentum. It did no harm to indulge in the symbolic transfer of a clod of earth, if that was deemed necessary to make sure of the possession of donated lands for the church.[20] But Innocentius III (1198–1216) writes to the bishop of Poitiers, that the custom to ask all people present at a moot—lettered and unlettered, wise and unwise alike—what the decision should be, is *minus rationabilis* and therefore should not be indulged in.[21] In ecclesiastical matters the bishop has authority to pronounce sentence on his own. Here the new, hierarchical and unitarian concept of law confronts the 'Germanic' idea of people gathering in a moot to decide what the law is to be. This is one of those instances by which the pope sets an example, to be followed by secular princes in due course.

In the tradition of civil and canon law *consuetudo* is hardly an independent source of law any more. As a legitimation for its binding force *tacitus consensus superioris* is replacing that of the people.[22] Its force being dependent on the consent of the sovereign, it only obtains as long as it is not at variance with written law, that is, mainly where law is absent (*cum deficit lex*). Therefore, legislation can put an end to custom at any time. From the twelfth century onwards customary law is pushed back step by step. Lawgivers no doubt only pretended to suppress *bad* customs (cf. Gilissen 1962: 31 ff). But that remained greatly a matter of arbitrary definition. Law recording, though facilitating the appeal to customary law by lifting the burden of proof, in the end often had the same effect as legislation (cf. Gilissen 1962:33; Kroeschell 1977: 378). Custom may only fill the gaps left by legislators. In legal practice the theory of customary law developed into a rigid restrictive doctrine.

As a rule, the existence of a valid custom (as far as not being recorded or notorious) cannot be presumed, but must be proved by the party invoking it on his behalf (see, e.g., Menochius 1587: VI.14.14; 1609: 32, 65; 251,19; et al.). Proof is often so difficult as to be nearly impossible (see e.g. Menochius 1587: II.8.8; 1609: 8.16; Mascardus 1584: 423; Glück 1867: 476; Gilissen 1962: 30); its technicalities (period, quality and number of conclusive facts, quality and number of witnesses) are complicated and disputed. And even if duly proved, a custom may be denied validity for not being *rationabilis*.[23] In fourteenth-century France a definition of customary law would come quite near Holmes' well-known definition of law: it is what the courts will do, that is, acknowledge as having done before (see Pissard 1910: 97).

Naturally this picture applies only for the general trend. There were considerable differences in various territories, as well as branches of the law. Brie (1905) denies that German jurists of the Reception period (end XV to mid XVII) were hostile to customary law. His argument is neither wholly consistent, nor convincing. But he is right in stressing that in Germany the main opposition was not law against custom, but learned *ius commune* against particularistic law, whether customary or statutory. Naturally political power is the primary issue. Attempts at codification had only limited scope and little influence. More important factors were to what degree a sovereign succeeded in making the law his prerogative, and to what degree academic jurists, trained in the civil and canon law tradition of hostility towards customary law, gained predominance in the legal system. For that matter, sovereign and jurists often entered into a very successful alliance, although naturally they never succeeded altogether in preventing new customs arising out of new developments in society and commerce. From the fifteenth century the rising nation-states stepped in with growing success, with legislation and other measures. On the whole customary law gradually became a matter of secondary importance, although its binding and even derogatory force (based on tacit consent of the sovereign) remained accepted theoretically (cf. Kosters 1912: 27).

Customary Law in the Colonies

The civil and canon law tradition also determined in great measure how Europeans in the era of colonial expansion confronted indigenous law. Although a comprehensive history of that confrontation is yet unwritten, and we must reckon with important differences in attitude towards indigenous law in various colonial administrations (cf. Hooker 1975), some general lines seem to stand out. In the first part of the colonial era, which lasted well into the eighteenth century and in some cases into the beginning of the nineteenth, commercial companies governed the colonies. Their general policy was not to interfere in native affairs, unless specific commercial interests were at stake. If it was stated firmly in Calvin's case of 1608[24] that ". . . if a Christian king should conquer the kingdom of an infidel . . . the laws of that infidel are abrogated," this was hardly a practicable line of action. Indigenous and European courts as a rule existed side by side, and only in exceptional cases did European courts apply native law (see, e.g., Hooker 1975:251), until, after the middle of the eighteenth century, colonial administrations began to reorganize the administration of justice and in some cases even to contemplate codification of native law (cf. Hooker 1975:61,252). This development, mirroring the ideals of the era of Enlightenment, was concomitant with the transition of colonial government from company to state. But when indigenous law was applied, it was always under the restrictions of the classical doctrine, which is expressed, e.g., by Raffles, proclaiming in 1814 in Java, that "a judge shall be guided in his decisions by existing native laws and ancient customs, provided the same be not decidedly at variance with the universal and acknowledged principles of natural justice" (cf. Jaspan 1965:225).[25] The application of this vague rule implied a great deal of arbitrariness (cf. Gilissen 1962: 32; Hooker 1975: 133).

And besides, there remained the problems of proof we have already met. Whereas native courts were supposed to know indigenous law, in European courts it often had (and in post-colonial state courts still has) to be specially pleaded as a matter of fact (cf. Hooker 1975: 136). The Privy Council only made an exception for notorious custom. This well-known exception, which applied everywhere in Europe, goes back on canon law.[26] It meant that, as a rule, the courts only took judicial notice of customs that were established by a series of previous judicial decisions (cf. Hooker 1975:137). This is completely in accordance with medieval doctrine, which was constructed on Ulpian's incidental suggestion that a provincial governor, confronted with an appeal to local custom, should investigate in the first place whether the custom was confirmed by a contradictory judgment (D 1.3.34; Ulp. 4. de off. proconsulis; cf. Pissard

1910: 11 ff). The same idea may be still behind Ter Haar's theory that adat is what obtains in decisions, primarily of the courts (cf. Hooker 1975: 293; Strijbosch 1980: 68 ff).

All in all indigenous customary law remained in a subservient position. When native courts were integrated in a national legal system, or indigenous law was applied by European courts, the outcome inevitably was something quite different: a new, 'hybrid' legal system. If custom was proved it did not have to be applied, and if it was applied this often involved distortion (see, e.g., Hooker 1975: 217; David 1973: 587 f).

Decline and Resurrection of Customary Law

In Europe, the eighteenth century was the nadir of customary law theory. In natural law thinking neither tradition nor enduring usage could prevail against reason (cf. Kosters 1912: 34f). The great codifications (among which one must count the numerous written constitutions) were pushing back customary law to a marginal position (cf. Pissard 1910: 187; Gény 1919: I,36,318; Van Apeldoorn-Leyten 1972: 103). If the first commentators of the new codes still left some room for customary law, legal theory became even more negative with the ascent of legalism. In the liberal bourgeois ideology of the nineteenth century, which identified law with the state, the privilege of labelling anything as 'law' was restricted to a limited number of institutions. If the people could make law at all, they could do so only through those institutions. Custom had no independent status; it was valid only as far as the law referred to it.[27]

The only fundamental, theoretical opposition against this set of ideas came from the Historical School in Germany. According to Savigny (1779–1861) all law originated from the customs and beliefs of the people, and when gradually the undifferentiated functions of the people were distributed over various orders of society, the jurists inherited the legal function. It was by their work, not by legislation that the law developed. Folk law was essentially the law of the nation, which was not identical with either *populus* or state.[28] Law was not one with the state, and customary law was regaining a position of its own besides legislation in the theory of the sources of law. Law and custom were often regarded, as even in present day legal theory (cf. Flume 1975: 7; Van Apeldoorn-Leyten 1972: 64, 97 ff; Bellefroid 1927: 2; Gény 1919: 238; Land 1899: 3) as the main, if not the sole sources of all law. Along the lines set out by Savigny, Puchta (1828; 1837) developed a new theory of customary law. Although this was heavily criticized by later-nineteenth-century legalists and positivists, it had a lasting effect on continental legal thinking. Since then customary law, or folk law, as it is often called since Savigny, has been regarded as non-state law, that is, law not emanating from state organs ('non-state' may assume other meaning too, see below). This idea, by the way, did not necessarily imply that defendants of customary law adopted a pluralistic theory of law; application and enforcement of customary law remained totally dependent on state organs. Therefore, it is not surprising that customary law, while honoured in theory, was ignored in practice; the whole theory primarily had an ideological function (cf. Kamphuisen 1935: 2; Nörr 1969: 365).

The age-old debate between state law and customary law is resuscitated, but now with reversed positions; it is no longer emerging state law against existing custom, but surviving custom in a world nearly completely dominated by state law. Every statement theoretically recognizing customary law is invariably followed by an enumeration of its disadvantages, e.g., its uncertainty. The people—of which the *vulgus*, ordinary people, form the most numerous part—is not the *Staatsvolk* of the Roman republic, but the sum total of the subjects of a state. From this context came the concept of folk law used by Ludwig Mitteis (1859–1921) as a tool of analysis. He proposed the thesis that in the eastern provinces of the Roman Empire, besides official law, there existed in practice a great deal of folk law, which could be reconstructed from papyri and other sources that were little known until then (cf. Mitteis 1891). This concept of folk law was practically identical with the idea of 'living law' in the sociology of law of Mitteis's contemporary Eugen Ehrlich (1862–1922). It was again the same notion which a decennium before had given birth to the notion of 'vulgar law', with which Brunner (1840–1915) designated the living Roman law in the western part of the former Roman empire in the fourth, fifth and sixth centuries (cf. Kop 1980). It may have been the experience of legal pluralism in the multi-national Austrian empire which influenced Brunner and Ehrlich, who were Austrians, as well as Mitteis who taught in Vienna; but their common frame of mind must have been shaped mainly by the theory of the reception of Roman law in the Middle Ages then dominant: the expansion of a technically superior, foreign, written legal system 'from above' against tenacious if unsuccessful resistance 'from below' (cf. Vinogradoff 1925: 21; see also Ullmann 1966: 20 f). Mitteis (1891: 4) expressly concludes from this model of the medieval reception that developments in the Roman Empire must have taken the same course. Even in the life of legal systems natural selection and survival of the fittest came to be the leading principles.

The Evolutionistic Paradigm

All the same, all these theories from the history of law remain well within a monistic concept of law. State law is the predominant reality and the inexorable aim of evolution. If it leaves room for other forms of law, these must be either 'survivals' *(Volksrecht)* or 'phenomena of decay' *(Vulgarrecht)*. Customary law is believed to have flourished mainly in early and primitive societies, and if it lives on in modern society it remains dependent on state organs for its application and enforcement. Anything short of that would at once be labelled and condemned as taking the law into one's own hand.

The concept of 'survivals' is prominent, too, in the work of Henry Sumner Maine (1822–1888), who, like his contemporary Johann Jacob Bachofen (1815–1887), combined the research attitude towards law of Montesquieu with the teachings of Savigny (except for the mystical *Volksgeist*), and inaugurated the comparative study of law as a cultural phenomenon on the basis of data from ancient history and contemporary ethnology. *Ancient Law* and *Das Mutterrecht* both appeared in 1861 and are considered now as the starting point of historic-comparative jurisprudence, a line of research which proved fruitful in history as well as in anthropology of law (cf. Stone 1949: 451 ff; Krader 1966: 3 ff; Stein 1980: Wesel 1980). All scholars active in the field of ethnological-historical jurisprudence (Maine, Vinogradoff, Maitland, Pollock, Kovalevsky, Post, Kohler, etc.) though greatly differing in theoretical outlook and highly critical of each other, shared some basic postulates (adapted from Krader 1966: 9):

1. The law has evolved from implicit and loose rules to explicit and fixed rules; customary law precedes codes, unwritten written law.
2. The law derives from folk custom and is not invented by legislators; early folk custom is an unspecified whole of law, religion, morals, etc.
3. Law is not an autonomous system, but a function of society, even when jurists develop it into a special skill.
4. The study of law is a means to understand society and the study of society is indispensable to understand law.

It need hardly be stressed that, on the whole, neither legal science nor the law curriculum was ever completely reformed in conformity with these postulates. The position of customary law in the nineteenth century is like that of the Historical School itself. The intellectual influence of the school in the first half of the nineteenth century was enormous, but with regard to its political aims it had no enduring success. Codification went on in the various German states as well as in other parts of Europe, and finally, after the establishment of the new German empire in 1870 the work on the civil code (*Bürgerliches Gesetzbuch*) began, which came into force on January 1, 1900. Customary law remained in a marginal position. In some cases the only reason preventing governments from suppressing native law was the belief that natives were not civilized enough to share the blessings of 'ordinary law' (cf. Holleman 1956: 238; Verloren van Themaat 1968). French colonial policy aimed consistently at assimilation, that is, forced evolution towards French standards of civilisation (cf. Gilissen 1962: 28; Hooker 1975: 198). In the German colony, which is now Togo, customary law was acknowledged in theory but often suppressed in practice (cf. Van Rouveroy van Nieuwaal 1979: 146; 1980: 33). Maybe only in Indonesia was there a drive for the recognition of adat law as law, which was accepted as official government policy in 1928 (cf. Strijbosch 1980: 32). What was new here, was the intention of turning the 'soft view of law' (cf. Krader 1966: 14) of scholarly comparative jurisprudence into an effective legal policy with distinct ethnical overtones. Adat law was to be acknowledged as law in its own right. This included a formal abolition by statute, already in 1920, of the repugnancy clause (cf. Strijbosch 1980: 28 note 6). Admittedly, all this did not make adat law exempt from the inflexible course of evolution. Adequate description of adat law was eventually directed by the ideal to make it into a scientific system of law (cf. Strijbosch 1980: 69, 172). The models of development of law in countries of the third world were, and still are, copied mainly from the history of law of continental Europe.

The recognition of living law and adat law eventually led to a breach with the prevailing monistic concept of law, and the acceptance of a pluralism of law in developing countries which in its turn gave reason to question the validity of evolutionary theories, as well as the traditional, monolithic picture of law in modern nation states. A theory of legal pluralism is in the making.[29] For the time being it is again a soft view of law.

In Search for a Theory

If we try to assess the present situation with the foregoing survey (which is by no means exhaustive) in mind, I think some lines can be drawn. It is evident to what extent the division of law and custom, as it took shape in the civil and canon law tradition, still forms the matrix of our perception of the problem of folk law. On the other hand we cannot discuss the problem in the same way as our ancestors, because of the historical and sociological experience accumulated in the meantime. The four basic postulates sketched above have in large measure lost their meaning as a result of ongoing research. It may be open to discussion whether "any scheme of universal legal evolution must be rejected" (Stein 1980: 104; in similar sense MacCormack 1969: 159; but see Wesel 1980: 75 ff). But certainly such a scheme can no longer build on simplistic binary concepts like law-custom, written-unwritten law, state-folk law. There are no 'pure' legal systems of either a primitive or developed type. All systems we know of, whether from history or anthropology, are complex wholes of various interacting forces. The problem, how to make the postulated interdependence of legal and social development explicit, remains unsolved and it helps little to label law a 'semi-autonomous' system. 'Customary law' itself is an ambiguous concept (cf. J.P.B. de Josselin de Jong 1948; Gilissen 1962: 24; P.E. de Josselin de Jong 1980: 134). If we restrict ourselves to its meaning of 'non-state law', it may either mean law which has not emanated from state institutions, or a legal system of a non-state (familial, territorial or professional) community. So indeed 'customary law' may include the ordinance of (forgotten) lawgivers (cf. Gilissen 1962: 25, Tárkány-Szücs 1980: 198) and codes may be regarded the depository of customary law.

The uses of writing prove to be so diversified as to make writing a useless criterion for classifying a type of law (cf. Van den Bergh 1964: 81). Not everything called customary law is unwritten (cf. De Smidt 1960: 90); e.g., Balinese adat is often laid down in written regulations (cf. Prins 1962: 166). Neither is every law written (cf. Gilissen 1953: 264; Genicot 1977: 12). The binding force of Roman law itself (the *ius scriptum* par excellence) in the Middle Ages was based on custom, not statutory enactment. The greater part of unwritten law now obtaining in the Netherlands, e.g., with regard to building contracts, is to be found in standard clauses and court records, just as it was in the Middle Ages. It is precisely one of the tasks of present day jurisprudence to reassess critically the value of these traditional concepts. Maybe it is presumptuous to think that a more sophisticated theory of law can do away outright with such concepts as law/custom or written/unwritten. The force of tradition might prove too strong for that. But then at least we should care to strive for better operational definitions of them.

Analysis of 'Folk Law'

In view of that necessity I should like to conclude with some remarks on the term 'folk law' itself. The founders of the Commission on Folk Law and Legal Pluralism have had some trouble in labelling the field of study, because for some reason or other traditional terms like customary law, unwritten law, primitive law, or tribal law no longer seemed satisfactory. After discussion, folk law was adopted in the end, although evidently this term has its disadvantages too.

In the first place, it seems plausible that the term folklaw or *Volksrecht* is just about as ambiguous as customary law:

1. It may point to the *origin* of a rule, an institution, a legal system. For Savigny (1814) *Volksrecht* is the law emanating from the people, not made by lawgivers. Beseler (1843), followed, e.g., by, Van Vollenhoven (1918), adapted this idea and saw *Volksrecht* (as against *Juristenrecht*, lawyer's law) as national (German) law, based on popular consciousness not custom and gradually corrupted and suppressed by the bad custom of jurist's law. Sohm (1871) and Brunner (1887) define *Volksrecht* (as against *Königsrecht*, the law of the king, for the Frankish period) as the law made and applied with the cooperation of the people (cf. Kroeschell 1972: 84). Mitteis (1891) calls *Volksrecht* (as against *Reichsrecht*) the living law not emanating from the Roman empire and existing beside official law. (For 'legal folk custom' see Tárkány-Szücs 1980: 202).

2. It may point to the *form* of a rule, an institution, a legal system. Folk law has not been subjected to analytical procedures of conceptualization, definition, deduction and rule-formulation (science, jurist's law, codification). It is not a system of abstract concepts and normative propositions but of perceptible, formal acts and words, natural institutions, symbols, symbolic procedures and objects, proverbs, etc. (cf. Savigny 1814: 9 ff; Mitteis-Lieberich 1974: 13).

3. It may point to the *content* of a rule, an institution, a legal system. Law (with language, morals, etc.) being part of the culture of an ethnic unit, is supposed to show the characteristic features of that unit: " . . . so entspricht dem deutschen Volk ein deutsches Recht, wie eine deutsche Sprache" (Puchta 1841: I, 15). Folk law is mixed up with religion, magic, morals, etc. (cf. e.g., Mitteis-Lieberich 1974: 12). The law of kinship-based societies without government shows features not found in the legal system of states, viz. the paradigm of litigation is not 'enforcement of right' but 'reconciliation' (cf. MacCormack 1971; Strijbosch 1980: 170).

4. It may point to the *scope of application* of a rule, an institution, a legal system. *Volksrecht* (as against *Landrecht*, the law of the land) is ruled by the principle of personality, that is, it only applies to the members of the respective tribe *(Stammesrecht)*, not to everybody living in a territory (cf. Schroder and Von Kunssberg 1922: 246). Adat law in Indonesia applies only on the basis of membership of an indigenous group, excluding Europeans, Arabs, Chinese and Indians (cf. Strijbosch 1980: 26).

Now in the heyday of historicism the causal relation between origin, form, content and scope of application was accepted as unproblematic.

Therefore it may have been no problem to mix up these notions in the concept of folk law, even if it suggested much more than could be ascertained. But today, after the decline of the evolutionistic universal history and the ascent of structuralism, it would be begging the question to do the same (in similar sense Tárkány-Szücs 1980: 204). From its creation *Volksrecht* has been a contradictory term which, apart from having distinct ideological overtones, largely takes its meaning from the concepts with which it is paired (*Gesetzesrecht, Rechtswissenschaft, Juristenrecht, Königsrecht, Reichsrecht, Landrecht*), which does not make it very well suited for use as an analytical term.

The Concept of 'Folk'

Secondly, the work *volk* has an extremely wide spectrum of meanings, not to mention its rather nasty recent connotations. If we leave these out for the moment, I think we can roughly discern the following fields of meaning.

1. *Populus*. The word 'people' somehow seems to be associated often with the state, either as the *Staatsvolk* of the Roman republic, as the inhabitants of a state with regard to their government ('the British people'), or even as a community striving for the establishment of a separate state ('the Palestinian people'). The word has often assumed a contradictory meaning, when people and sovereign (or government or state) are seen as opposing conceptions. This opposition is expressed in extreme form in the idea of sovereignty of the people, but it also plays a role in Savigny's conception of *Volksrecht* and in Mitteis's opposition of *Reichsrecht* and *Volksrecht*. But *volk* may also mean all people sharing a common language, beliefs, traditions, etcetera, which may range from a tribe to something as big and elusive as 'the English-speaking peoples'.

2. *Vulgus*. The masses, ordinary people. This is the 'lower' and more numerous class of the population (especially in highly industrialized countries, because it is often not so striking in other parts of the world), which in the nineteenth century, and to some extent even now, forms the main subject of study of folklore and *Volkskunde*. This connotation has played some part too in the formation of the concepts of vulgar law, and of *Volksrecht* in Mitteis' sense. In the nineteenth century it was a widespread belief that the lower strata of society, not affected by higher culture, remained primitive and were, therefore, comparable with the primitives studied by ethnology.

3. *Natio*. This concept originally had a rather loose sense. The Holy Roman Empire of the German nation comprised Germanic countries

on both sides of the Alps. The *natio germanica* of medieval universities might comprise either all students from north of the Alps (in Italy), or from north of the Loire (in France), or again those who spoke Germanic languages. In an analogous sense some people formerly used to speak about the Dutch nation or people, including Flanders and South-Africa, and nowadays one speaks about the 'Deutsche Nation,' including both Germanies, or the 'Arabic nation'. But since the nineteenth century, nation was used mainly as a synonym for people, meaning the people forming a nation-state, or the state itself (the United Nations).

Conclusions

It will be very clear, that if we want to use folk law as an analytical concept, we must be very critical about all these implied connotations, and define it operationally in such a way as to disassociate it from them as far as possible. For one thing, with the concept of folk law we acknowledge our plight—knowingly or not—of a binary way of thinking which has haunted the social sciences from their beginning and which perhaps has more to do with a European experience of fundamental social change between roughly speaking, 1750 and 1880, than with social reality elsewhere in the world (status-contract, *Gemeinschaft-Gesellschaft, Staat-Volk*, cultured-primitive, pre-industrial-industrial, tribal-urban, etc.). And it may be no more than begging the question to say, that we do not believe in the reality of those concepts, but simply use them as analytical concepts or ideal types. But it is difficult to transcend our own experiences, which have moulded the very language in which we discuss social phenomena. Still it is one of the fundamental rules of the science-game, that we should strive for just that as best as we can.

Notes

1. Folk law as a branch may be regarded as something different from anthropology of law as a field of research in anthropology, although it seems hard to define in a precise way. But anyway I do not intend to describe the history of anthropology of law in this article. The literature on customary law is immense. For the historical part Brie 1899 is unsurpassed, although naturally a bit outdated in its general historical outlook, as well as in its method of treating the sources. As regards law-and-custom in the ancient world, see Gaudemet 1964. For the early Middle Ages see Köbler 1969; and see Van den Bergh 1984. For a brief survey with further literature see also Krause 1970. I thank professor Feenstra for his valuable suggestions.

2. Cf. Thomas 1963: 48. Naturally they should not be taken as theoretical statements, but as simple enumerations for practical purposes, maybe as a guideline for judges (cf. Savigny 1840: I, 106). Custom is mentioned by rhetorical writers (Cic. top. 5.28; Auct. ad Herenn. 2.13.19; Quint. inst. orat. 12.3.6) but these texts, of which only Cicero's list shows some similarity with those of the jurists, reflect Greek theories of rhetoric and cannot be taken to represent the legal point of view. Besides, only Cicero speaks of Roman law ('*ius civile*'), the others of law in general. But see Lauria (1967: 47), who states without so much as an attempt at justification that the ideas of Roman jurists are to be explained by Greek theories of rhetoric, poetics and philosophy.

3. Not only the distinction written/unwritten but the whole scheme may have been taken from Ulpian (D. 1.1.6.1) but that cannot be ascertained; neither does the palingenesia give a clue (see Lenel 1889).

4. See D. 1.6.8 pr.; D. 24.1.1; other examples D. 27.10.1 pr.; D. 28.6.2 pr.; D. 29.2.8 pr.

5. See, e.g., Varro in Serv. ad Verg. (Bruns 1909: II, 79); Ulp. reg. 4; in Cod. Theod. the words '*vetustas*' and '*antiquitas*' are used.

6. Bruns 1909: II, 79; cf. Isidor. Etym. 5.3 (Bruns 1909: II, 80). On these texts see Bleicken 1975: 353, 359, 394.

7. Cf. Thomas 1963: 44; Flume 1975: 28, 33, 34. But see Nörr 1969: 359. Naturally we must be on our guard against false implications from this statement. Firstly, to say that the Romans had no binary concept of validity is tantamount to saying that they did not distinguish sharply between law and fact. Secondly, by holding that the Romans saw foreign law rather as fact than as law, we do not mean to imply modern dogmatic conclusions grafted on that distinction, e.g., that custom had to be proved as any other fact (cf. Hooker 1975: 136; Strijbosch 1980: 40, 62, 127). In Roman sources there seems to be only one (albeit very influential) statement on proof of legal custom (cf. Ulp. D. 1.3.34; Pissard 1910:11).

8. Until recently most Romanists believed with Schulz that the fragment was interpolated, see, e.g., Thomas 1963: 44 ff; Gaudemet 1964: 29; Schmiedel 1966: 45–52; and again Flume 1975: 32, all with further literature. But see now Nörr 1967:359 f; 1969: 356; Kaser 1971: 196; 1978: 112 f; Waldstein 1976: 366 f; 1981: 122 n. 82; Wacke 1976: 455. Strangely enough the discussion still seems to focus on the question, whether the fragment is either classical, or interpolated by Justinian's compilers (Kaser 1978: 113 note 74). If we deny with Stuhff (1966: 52), Schmiedel (1966: 65) and Nörr (1967: 460) a link between *consuetudo*-doctrine and vulgar law, the possibility of (early or later) postclassical adaptation before Justinian's time, which Lombardi (1952: 46 with note 107), Thomas (1963: 46, 49) and I (1969:345) suggested earlier, cannot be dismissed out of hand. The statement that the theory of customary law in D 1.3.32.1 fits well with the ideology of the principate (cf Nörr 1967: 460; Wacke 1976: 455) is too generic to be acceptable without question. For instance, the ideology of the principate under Augustus and Tiberius is quite different from that of the Severans (see Wieacker 1978: 250). Steinwenter (1930: 422), on the other hand believed that the political argumentation of D 1.3.2.1 was to be expected from republican rather than from imperial jurists. Such general statements are hardly convincing,

if they are not accompanied by a qualified attempt at justification. The idea of *consensus populi* on which the argument of D 1.32.1 hinges, is certainly not republican, see Gaudemet 1964: 18 f.

9. The statement cannot, in my opinion, be taken to mean that all law is based on popular consent, because then it would be evidently false. But there was a widespread belief in antiquity that all law should be, cf. note 10.

10. Which is found, e.g., in Gai 3.82; D 1.3.32; D 1.3.35; Ulp. reg. 4; I I.2.11; Gell. 20.10.9; see Thomas 1963: 46; Van den Bergh 1969: 346; Kosters 1912: 28.

11. See especially Ulp. reg. 4: *Mores sunt tacitus consensus populi longa consuetudine inveteratus.*

12. I 1.2.9. But in I 1.2.11 *consensus populi* is used again. On the other hand one might argue that *populus* in I 1.2.11 is to be interpreted in the light of I 1.2.9, which would take its pregnant meaning away.

13. The vexed question whether *ratio* in this context means *ratio utilitatis* (public policy) or *ratio iuris* (legal principle, natural law, reasonableness, equity or what?) cannot be decided, see Brie 1899: 31.

14. Julian already says in D 1.3.32 pr. that customs (meaning provincial customs) are to be followed where there is no written law, and the formula *cum deficit lex* is in Tertullian as well as in Isidor. But these words are used only to give a general idea of the field where custom applies. Should they be taken to mean—as was assumed in later ages—that custom had only subsidiary force and applied where there was no law, they would contradict the statement of Julian at the end of D 1.3.32.1 viz. that custom can derogate law. See Brie 1899: 2ff. Taking the contradiction as an argument for interpolation is to beg the question.

15. Cf. Van den Bergh 1969: 346; Thomas 1963: 501 also stresses the importance of the Constitutio Antoniniana (though giving a slightly different picture of the development), but rather seems to place the creation of a theory of customary law in the middle of the fourth century. This leaves some two ages of legal development to be accounted for. But any attempt at a more precise date is guesswork.

16. E.g. D 47.12.3.5: . . . *quia generalia sunt rescripta et oportet imperialia statuta suam vim optinere et in omni loco valere.* This text, by the way, is not concerned with a conflict between law and custom, but between imperial and municipal laws.

17. The same question was read in other writers who were important in transmitting the heritage of Antiquity to the Middle Ages, e.g., Isidor, who defines custom as: "*ius quoddam moribus institutum, quod pro lege suscipitur cum deficit lex*". With another text of Isidor Gratian opens the paragraph on customary law in the Decretum (D. 11.1). On the meaning of the words *cum deficit lex* see also note 14.

18. Glo *abrogentur* ad D 1.3.32; glo *imitatur* ad I 1.2.9 and other glosses.

19. Decret. Grat. D 1, 1–5; D 8, 2 and 3; Extra 1.4. See Brie 1899: 67 ff; Krause 1970: 1677.

20. Extra 1.4.2 of Innocentius III (1198–1216).

21. Extra 1.4.3.
22. Already Irnerius seems to base the authority of customary law on tacit approval of the emperor, see Brie 1899: 113 ff. In this context it seems interesting to note the historical argument ascribed to Pillius and Irnerius in the gloss *abrogentur* ad D 1.3.32.1: In the time that this fragment (that is, the fragment of Julian) was written, the people had the power to give the law; therefore it was abrogated by its opposite custom. But now (that is, in Irnerius's time) both are done only by the emperor. See also Voet 1698: 1.3.37; Glück 1867: 449 ff.
23. Some jurists, for that matter, apply the same standard to laws: ". . . *si iniqua esset et ratione careret lex, legis nomen non obtineret*". (Menochius 1587: II.1.5). But see Voet 1698: I.3.23:" . . . *judicis sit, secundum legem, non vero de legis iustitia vel iniustitia iudicare*".
24. 7 Rep. 17 Lord Coke, cited after Holleman 1956: 233 note 1; cf. Maddock 1980: 7.
25. See also Hooker 1975: 61, 130, 252; Maddock 1980: 7. The formula 'justice, equity and good conscience' shows a remarkable change of meaning. According to Derrett (1963: 148), in South East Asia it did not operate as a repugnancy clause, but as a guideline for judges in cases not covered by statute or case law. In Africa, on the other hand, it became a repugnancy clause.
26. Extra 2.21.3; cf. Voet 1698: I.3.32; Glück 1867: 476, with literature; Pissard 1910: 16.
27. See e.g. *Allgemeines Bürgerliches Gesetzbuch* of 1811, para. 10; *Wet Algemene Bepalingen* of 1826, para. 3.
28. See Savigny 1814: 161. Savigny developed his theory of *Volksrecht* also in order to save the position of (Romanistic) legal science as the common law for the whole of the German nation, that is, including the Austrian countries.
29. For literature see Van den Bergh 1982.

Standard Abbreviations

For readers not familiar with the standard abbreviations used, the following references may be relevant. For the standard abbreviations of classical authors and their works see e.g. Lewis and Short, *Latin Dictionary*, p. vii ff. RE = Pauly-Wissowa's *Real-Encyclopädie der classischen Altertumswissenschaft*, 1893–. For legal sources the following standard abbreviations are used. D(igestia), C(odex) and I(nstitutiones) are parts of the *Corpus Iuris Civilis* (stereotype edition by Kruger, Mommsen Schöll and Kroll, Berlin 1872 and later). The Cod(ex) Theod(osianus) is an older collection of imperial constitutions. Other abbreviations are of names of classical Roman jurists and their works: Ulp(ian), Gai(us) Jul(ianus), Pap(inian), Paul(us), *Inst(itutiones), De off(icio) proc(onsulis), Reg(ulae). Decret(um) Grat(iani)* and *(Liber) Extra* are parts of the *Corpus*

Iuris Canonici. Medieval glosses on the *Corpus Iuris Civilis* are cited with *glos* and the word(s) in the relevant text to which they are connected.

References

Apeldoorn, L.J. van, Leyten, J.
1972   *Inleiding tot de studie van het Nederlandse recht*, Zwolle: Tjeenk Willink.

Bellefroid, J.H.P.
1927   *De bronnen van het stellig recht en haar onderlinge verhoudingen*, Nijmegen: Dekker en Van de Vegt.

Berger, A.
1953   *Encyclopedic Dictionary of Roman Law*, Philadelphia: American Philosophical Society.

Bergh, G.C.J.J. van den
1964   *Themis en de Muzen; de functie van de gebonden vormen in het recht*, Haarlem: Tjeenk Willink.
1969   'Legal Pluralism and Roman Law,' *The Irish Jurist* 4:338–350. (French version in: J. Gilissen (ed.), *Le Pluralisme Juridique*, pp. 89–103, Brussels 1972: Editions de l'Université.)
1982   *Wet en gewoonte; historische grondslagen van een dogmatisch geding*, Deventer: Kluwer.

Beseler, G.
1843   *Volksrecht und Juristenrecht*, Leipzig: Weidmann.

Bleicken, J.
1975   *Lex publica; Gesetz und Recht in der römischen Republik*, Berlin: Springer.

Brie, S.
1899   *Die Lehre vom Gewohnheitsrecht; eine historisch-dogmatische Untersuchung*, Vol. I, Geschichtliche Grundlegung (*Bis zum Ausgang des Mittelalters*), Breslau: Marcus.
1905   'Die Stellung der Deutschen Rechtsgelehrten der Rezeptionszeit zum Gewohnheitsrecht,' in: *Festgabe Felix Dahn I, Deutsche Rechtsgeschichte*, pp. 129–164, Breslau: Marcus.

Bruns, C.
1909   *Fontes Iuris Romani Antiqui*, 7th print, Tübingen: Mohr.

David, R.
1973   *Les Grands Systèmes de Droit Contemporains*, 5th ed., Paris: Dalloz.

Derrett, J.D.M.
1963   'Justice, Equity and Good Conscience,' in: J.N.D. Anderson (ed.), *Changing Law in Developing Countries*, pp. 114–153, London: Allen & Unwin.

Flume, W.
1975   *Gewohnheitsrecht und römisches Recht*, (Rheinland-Westfälische Akademie der Wissenschaften, Geisteswissenschaftliche Vorträge G 201), Opladen: Westdeutscher Verlag.

Gaudemet, J.
1964 'L'Autorité de la Loi et de la Coutume dans l'Antiquité,' in: *Rapports Généraux au VIe Congrès International de Droit Comparé*, pp. 9–37, Brussels: Bruylant.

Genicot, L.
1977 *La Loi*, (Typologie des Sources du Moyen Age, Fasc. 22), Turnhout: Brepols.

Gény F.
1919 *Méthode d'Interprétation et Sources du Droit Positif*, 2 vols., 2nd print, Paris: Librairie générale de droit et de jurisprudence.

Gierke, O.
1915 'Grundzüge des deutschen Privatrechts,' in: F. Holtzendorf and J. Kohler (eds.), *Enzyklopädie der Rechtswissenschaft*, Vol I, pp. 175–202, 7th print, München: Duncker & Humblot.

Gilissen, J.
1953 'Loi et Coutume,' *Tijdschrift voor Rechtsgeschiedenis* 21:257–296.
1962 'La Rédaction des Coutumes dans le Passé et dans le Présent; Essai de Synthèse', in: J. Gilissen (ed.), *La Rédaction des Coutumes dans le Passé et dans le Présent*, pp. 15–61, Brussels: Editions de l'Université.
1964 'La Loi et la Coutume dans l'Histoire du Droit depuis le Haut Moyen Age, in: *Rapports Généraux au VIe Congrès International de Droit Comparé*, pp. 53–101, Brussels, Bruylant.
1981 *Historische inleiding tot het recht*, Antwerpen: Kluwer.

Glück, C.F.
1867 *Ausführliche Erlaütterung der Pandecten nach Hellfeld; ein Commentar* I, 2nd print, Erlangen: Palm & Enke.

Hirzel, R.
1900 'Agraphos nomos,' *Abhandlungen königlichen Saechsische Gesellschaft der Wissenschaften* 20:1–98.

Holleman, F.D.
1956 'The Recognition of Bantu Customary Law in South Africa,' in: *The Future of Customary Law in Africa*, pp. 232–256, Leiden: Universitaire Pers.

Hooker, B.
1975 *Legal Pluralism; an Introduction to Colonial and Neo-colonial Laws*, London: Oxford University Press.

Horak, F.
1969 *Rationes Decidendi; Entscheidungsbegründigungen bei den älteren römischen Juristen bis Labeo*, Vol. I, Aalen: Scientia.

Jaspan, M.A.
1965 'In Quest for New Law: the Perplexities of Legal Syncretism in Indonesia,' *Comparative Studies in Society and History* 7:252–265.

Josselin de Jong, J.P.B. de
1948 'Customary Law; a Confusing Fiction,' *Mededelingen van de Koninklijke Vereeniging Indisch Instituut* 80: 3.

Josselin de Jong, P.E. de
1980 'Gewohnheit, Recht und Gewohnheitsrecht,' in: W. Fikentscher (ed.), *Entstehung und Wandel rechtlicher Traditionen*, pp. 121–141, Freiburg-München: Alber.

Kamphuisen, P.W.
1935 *Gewoonterecht*, Den Haag: Nijhoff.

Kaser, M.
1939 'Mores maiorum und Gewohnheitsrecht,' *Zeitschrift der Savigny - Stiftung für Rechtsgeschichte, rom. Abt., 59:52–101*.
1971 *Das römische Privatrecht I*, 2nd print, München: Beck.
1978 'Zur Problematik der Römischen Rechtsquellenlehre,' in:*Festschrift für Werner Flume*, Vol I, 101–125, Köln: Schmidt.

Köbler, G.
1969 'Zur Frührezeption der Consuetudo in Deutschland', *Historisches Jahrbuch* 89:337–371.

Kop, P.C.
1980 *Beschouwingen over het zgn. "Vulgaire' Romeinse Recht*, Den Haag: Universitaire Pers Leiden.

Kosters, J.
1912 *De plaats van gewoonte en volksovertuiging in het privaatrecht*, Arnhem: Gouda Quint.

Krader, L.
1966 'Introduction,' in: L. Krader (ed.), *Anthropology and Early Law*, pp. 3–16, New York: Basic Books.

Krause, H.
1970 'Gewohnheitsrecht,' in: *Handwörterbuch zur deutschen Rechtsgeschichte*, Vol. I, col. 1675–1684, Berlin: Schmidt.

Kroeschell, K.
1972 *Deutsche Rechtsgeschichte I (bis 1250)*, Reinbek bei Hamburg: Rowohlt.
1977 'Rechtsaufzeichnung und Rechtswirklichkeit; das Beispiel des Sachsenspiegels', in: P. Classen (ed.), *Recht und Schrift im Mittelalter*, pp. 349–380, Sigmaringen: Thorbecke.

Land N.K.F.
1899 *Inleiding tot de verklaring van het Burgerlijk Wetboek*, Haarlem: Bohn.

Lauria M.
1967 *Jus, Visioni romane e moderne*, Napoli: l'Arte Tipografica.

Lenel, O.
1889 *Palingenesia Iuris Civilis*, Anastatic reprint, Graz: Akademische Druck- und Verlagsanstalt, 1960.

Lombardi, G.
1952 'Sul Titolo 'Quae Sit Longa Consuetudo' (8. 51 53) nel Codice Giustinianeo', *Studia et documenta historiae et iuris* 18: 21–87.

MacCormack, G.
1969 'Haegerstroems Magical Interpretation of Roman Law,' *The Irish Jurist* 4: 153-167.
1971 'Roman and African Litigation,' *Tijdschrift voor Rechtsgeschiedenis* 39: 221–255.

Maddock, K.
1980 *Anthropology, Law and the Definition of Aboriginal Rights to Land*, Publikaties over Volksrecht VI, Nijmegen: Instituut voor Volksrecht.

Mascardus, J.
1584 *Conclusiones Probationum Omnium . . .* The edition used is Frankfurt/Main:Feyerabend, 1585. The figure cited is the number of the conclusion.

Menochius, J.
1587 *De Praesumptionibus, Conjecturis, Signis et Indiciis Commentaria.* The edition used is Geneva: De Tournes, 1724. The figures refer to the book, the conclusion and the relevant paragraph in the conclusion.
1609 *Consilia Sive Responsa.* The edition used is Frankfurt/Main: Sumptibus Wechelianorum, 1628. Figures refer to number and paragraph of advice.

Mitteis, L.
1891 *Reichsrecht und Volksrecht in den östlichen Provinzen des römischen Kaiserreichs*, Leipzig: Teubner.

Mitteis, H. and H. Lieberich
1974 *Deutsche Rechtsgeschichte*, 13th print, München: Beck.

Nörr, D.
1967 Review of Schmiedel, 1966 and Stuhff, 1966, *Zeitschrift der Savigny-Stiftung für Rechtsgeschichte, rom. Abt.* 84:454–466.
1969 'Zur Entstehung der Gewohnheitsrechtliche Theorie,' in: *Festschrift für W. Felgenträger*, pp. 353–367. Göttingen: Schwartz.
1972 *Divisio und Partitio; Bemerkungen zur römischen Rechtsquellenlehre und zur antiken Wissenschaftstheorie*, Berlin: Schweitzer.

Pauly-Wissowa
1893 *Real-Encyclopädie der classischen Altertumswissenschaft*, Stuttgart: Druckenmüller.

Pernice, A.
1899 'Zum römischen Gewohnheitsrechte' *Zeitschrift der Savigny-Stiftung fur Rechtsgeschichte, rom. Abt.* 20: 127–171.

Pissard, H.
1910 *Essai sur la Connaissance et la Preuve des Coutumes en Justice dans l'Ancien Droit Francais et dans le Système Romano-Canonique*, Paris: Rousseau.

Prins, J.
1962 'The Study of 'Adat Recht' (Adat Law)—the Work of Van Vollenhoven and his Disciples,' in: J. Gilissen (ed.), *La Rédaction des Coutumes dans le Passé et dans le Présent*, pp. 165-184. Brussels: Editions de l'Université.

Puchta G. F.
1828; 1837 *Das Gewohnheitsrecht*, 2 Vols., Erlangen: Palm.
1841 *Cursus der Institutionen I*. The edition used is the 10th, edited by P. Kruger, Leipzig: Breitkopf und Härtel, 1893.

Ranft, J.
1957 'Consuetudo' in: Th. Klauser (ed.), *Reallexikon für Antike und Christentum III*, col. 379-390, Stuttgart: Hiersemann.

Rouveroy van Nieuwaal, Emile van
1979 'Unité ou Diversité du Droit; Bases Juridiques du Droit Coutumier au Togo,' *Verfassung und Recht im Uebersee* 12: 143-158.
1980 'Bases Juridiques du Droit Coutumier au Togo dans l'Epoque Coloniale Allemande (1884-1914),' *Verfassung und Recht im Uebersee* 13: 27-35.

Savigny, F.C. von
1814 *Vom Beruf unserer Zeit für Gesetzgebung und Rechtswissenschaft*, Heidelberg: Mohr u. Zimmer.
1840 *System des heutigen römischen Rechts I*, Berlin: Veit.

Schmiedel, B.
1966 *Consuetudo im klassischen und nachklassischen römischen Recht*, Graz-Köln: Böhlau.

Schroder, R. and E. von Kunssberg
1922 *Lehrbuch der deutschen Rechtsgeschichte*, 6th print, Berlin: De Gruyter.

Smidt, J.Th. de
1960 'Le Problème de la Rédaction des Droits Coutumiers: Interêt, Difficultés, Méthodes,' in *Rapports Généraux au V. Congres International de Droit Comparé*, Vol I, pp. 89-101. Brussels: Bruylant.

Sohier, A.
1949 *Traité Elémentaire de Droit Coutumier du Congo Belge*, Brussels: Larcier.

Stein, P.
1980 *Legal Evolution: The Story of an Idea*, Cambridge: University Press.

Steinwenter, A.
1930 'Zur Lehre vom Gewohnheitsrecht,' in *Studi Bonfante II*, pp. 421-440, Milano: Treves.

Stone, J.
1949 *The Province and Function of the Law*, Sydney: Associated General Publications.

Strijbosch, A.K.J.M.
1980 *Juristen en de studie van volksrecht in Nederlands Indië en anglofoon Afrika*, Publikaties over Volksrecht VII, Nijmegen: Instituut voor Volksrecht.

Stuhff, G.
1966 *Vulgarrecht im Kaiserrecht, Weimar*: Böhlau.

Tárkány-Szücs, E.
1980 'Collecting Legal Folk Customs in Hungary,' *Acta Ethnographica Academiae Scientiarum Hungaricae* 29: 181–205.

Thomas, J.A.C.
1963 'Custom and Roman Law,' *Tijdschrift voor Rechtsgeschiedenis* 31: 39–53.

Ullmann, W.
1966 *Principles of Government and Politics in the Middle Ages*, 2nd ed., London: Methuen.

Verloren van Themaat, R.
1968 'Die bepaling van Rigting by die Regsopleiding van die Bantoe,' *Tydskrif vir hedendaagse Romeins-Hollandse Reg* 31: 40–57.

Vinogradoff, P.
1925 *Custom and Right*, Instituttet for Sammenlignende Kulturforskning, Serie A, III, Oslo: Aschehoug.

Voet, J.
1968 *Commentarius ad Pandectas I*. The edition used is Geneva: Cramer, 1757. The figures cited refer to the book, title (chapter) and paragraph.

Vollenhoven, C. van
1918, 1931, 1933
Het adatrecht van Nederlandsch-Indië, 3 Vols, Leiden: Brill.

Wacke, A.
1976 Review of Flume, 1975, *Juristenzeitung* 1976: 455.

Waldstein, W.
1976 Review of Flume, 1975, *Zeitschrift der Savigny-Stiftung für Rechtsgeschichte, rom. Abt.*, 93:358–369.
1981 'Gewohnheitsrecht und Juristenrecht in Rom,' in: M. Harder and G. Thielmann (eds.), *De Iustitia et Iure; Festgabe für Ulrich von Lübtow zum 80. Geburtstag*, pp. 105–127. Berlin: Duncker & Humblot.

Weber, M.
1922 *Wirtschaft und Gesellschaft*. The edition used is the Studienausgabe of the 5th print, Tübingen: Mohr, 1972.

Wesel, U.
1980 *Der Mythos vom Matriarchat; über Bachofens Mutterrecht und die Stellung von Frauen in frühen Gesellschaften*, Frankfurt/Main: Suhrkamp.

Wieacker, F.
1978 'Zur Ideologie der römischen Juristen; vom Gebrauch aktueller Erklärungsmodelle in der heutigen Romanistik,' in: *Festschrift für Werner Flume*, Vol I, 233–254, Köln: Schmidt.

A. ARTHUR SCHILLER

Custom in Classical Roman Law

As the preceding essay makes abundantly clear, the concept of custom or folk law was a matter of some concern in Roman times. One of the finest overviews of the role of custom in Roman law was written by Professor A. Arthur Schiller (1902–1977) who taught at Columbia Law School for some forty-five years. For a list of his many publications, see Roger S. Bagnall and William V. Harris, eds., Studies in Roman Law in Memory of A. Arthur Schiller *(Leiden: E.J. Brill, 1986), pp. ix–xiv.*

For additional discussions of custom in Roman Law, see J. Gaudemet, *"Coutume et raison en droit romain,"* Revue Historique de droit francais et étranger, *17 (1938), 141–170; J.A.C. Thomas, "Custom and Roman Law,"* Tijdschrift voor Rechtsgeschiedenis, *31 (1963), 39–53; Burkhard Schmiedel,* Consuetudo im Klassischen und nach-klassischen romischen Recht *(Graz: H. Bohlaus, 1966); G.C.J.J. van den Bergh, "Legal Pluralism and Roman Law,"* The Irish Jurist, *4 (1969), 338–350; Lucio Bove,* La consuetudine in diritto romano *(Napoli: E. Jovene, 1971). For a sample of the voluminous literature devoted to the continuing influence of Roman law, see Hessel E. Yntema, "Roman Law and Its Influence on Western Civilization,"* Cornell Law Quarterly, *39 (1949), 77–88; Edward D. Re, "The Roman Contribution to the Common Law,"* Fordham Law Review, *29 (1950), 447–494.*

One of the interesting theoretical issues discussed by Professor Schiller in the portion of his paper entitled "Can custom abrogate statute?" is what happens when a legislated statute is traditionally ignored or not enforced by a people. For other considerations of this matter, see J.R. Philip, "Some Reflections on Desuetude," The Juridical Review, *43 (1931), 260–267; Arthur E. Bonfield, "The Abrogation of Penal Statutes by Nonenforcement,"* Iowa Law Review, *49 (1964), 389–440; J.A.C. Thomas, "Desuetudo,"* Revue Internationale des Droits de L'Antiquité, *3ᵉ serie, 12 (1965), 469–483; Abraham Harari, "Desuetude,"* Journal of Jewish Studies, *25 (1974), 101–113; and Hector MacQueen, "Desuetude, the Cessante Maxim and Trial by Combat in Scots Law,"* Journal of Legal History, *7 (1986), 90–97. Perhaps the most comprehensive treatment of the question is to be found*

Reprinted from *Virginia Law Review*, 24 (1938), 268–282, with permission.

in *Athanassios Vamvoukos*, Termination of Treaties in International Law: The Doctrines of Rebus Sic Stantibus and Desuetude *(Oxford: Clarendon Press, 1985). For desuetude, see pp. 217-303.*

Introduction*

In any treatment of the problems of jurisprudence, the subject of legal custom and customary law must occupy a fairly significant position. The Anglo-American writer in such a discussion frequently turns to that other of the world's great legal systems, the Roman law. And, in the opinion of the author, many of the most renowned writers have presented a somewhat misleading view of Roman customary law. They have failed to emphasize the fact that the Roman law, even limiting the use of that term to the legal system of the Roman people from the time of the foundation of Rome to the rule of Justinian (c. 754 B. C. to 527/65 A. D.), nevertheless existed for some twelve hundred years and had naturally, in the course of that time, passed through several stages of development. The position of customary law in the so-called classical period (roughly 150 B. C. to 235 A. D.), the period in which the Roman law reached its greatest heights, might well differ from the understanding of customary law in the pre-classical as well as in the post-classical periods. Allen,[1] though calling attention to the long duration of the Roman law, nevertheless discusses custom without much regard to

---

*Note—This paper, in somewhat altered form, was read before the Riccobono Seminar of Roman Law at the October, 1937, meeting.

Abbreviations employed herein are: Brie = Brie, Die Lehre vom Gewohnheitsrecht (Breslau 1899); C. = Codex Iustinianus, ed. P. Krueger, in Corpus Iuris Civilis, vol. II (ed. stereo. 10, Berlin 1929); D = Iustiniani Digesta, ed. Mommsen—Krueger, in Corpus Iuris Civilis, vol. I (ed. stereo. 15, Berlin, 1929), the matter in parentheses following the Digest citation being the name of the jurist, the book and title of the work, from which the Justinianian extract was taken; G. = Gaius, Institutiones, ed. Seckel—Kuebler (7th ed., Leipzig 1935); Inst. = Iustiniani Institutiones, ed. Krueger, in Corpus Iuris Civilis, vol. I (ed. stereo. 15, Berlin 1929); Kniebe = Kniebe, Zur Lehre vom römischen Gewohnheitsrecht in vorjustinianischer Zeit (Diss. Freiburg 1908); P. = Paulus, Sententiae ad filium, in Riccobono—Baviera—Ferrini, Fontes iuris romani antejustiniani (Florence 1909), pp. 261-344; RE = Paulys Real-Encyclopädie der classischen Altertumswissenschaft, ed. by Wissowa—Kroll (Stuttgart 1894–date); Recueil Gény = Recueil d'études sur les sources du droit en l'honneur de François Gény, 3 vols. (Paris n. d.); Studi Bonfante = Studi in onore di Pietro Bonfante nel XL anno d'insegnamento, 4 vols. (Milano 1930); SZ = Zeitschrift der Savigny-Stiftung für Rechtsgeschichte, romanistische Abteilung (Weimar 1880–date).Translations of the sources by the author; papyri references in note 56 and abbreviations of classical writers throughout are standard, see Greek and Latin dictionaries.

historical sequence and mingles statements of Cicero, Ulpian and Justinian in the development of his points. Vinogradoff, in a short discussion,[2] maintains that customary law of the Justinianian period reflects that of the classical epoch. Munroe Smith[3] treats the subject historically, yet regards customary law from beginning to end as nothing more than case-law.

The citation of authorities need not be augmented. The generally approved opinion is that the Roman law of custom is that which is expressed in the Corpus Iuris (the compilation at Justinian's order). Therein are to be found definitions of the customary law and an enumeration of the elements essential to the establishment of legal custom, both of which factors were taken over into mediaeval canonical and civil law and were subsequently developed in modern jurisprudence. It is the contention of the author that there is a vast difference between the idea of customary law in the classical period and that of post-classical and Justinianian times, and that a study of the opinions of the jurists and non-legal writers of the classical age deserves further attention.[4] This study, therefore, is directed to customary law and legal custom in the times of Cicero, Varro, Quintilian, and Labeo, Gaius, Ulpian and the remainder of the jurists, and any consideration of pre-classical and post-classical sources is merely by way of comparison or as an indication of historical evolution.

Ius Non Scriptum

In his Topica (5.28) Cicero makes the statement that "the civil law (*ius civile*) is to be found in statutes, resolutions of the senate, judgments, authority of the learned in the law, edicts of the magistrates, custom and *aequitas*." Other rhetorical writers of classical times likewise consider custom as one of the 'sources' or fonts of the law.[5] This equivalence of custom with statute, or with *senatus consultum*, etc., flows necessarily from the rhetorical distinction between written law (*ius scriptum*), e. g. statutes, resolutions of the senate, and unwritten law (*ius non scriptum*), e. g. custom, authority of the learned in the law. To the Roman philosophers and rhetorical writers the term *ius scriptum* served, in the main, to designate the statutory law, the term *ius non scriptum* the customary law of a particular people, naturally, in most instances, of the Romans. The Roman distinction is based upon the Greek differentiation of *nomos eggraphos* and *nomos agraphos*, written law and unwritten law, which goes back to Aristotle.[6] This distinction, however, was normally used to depict a very different contrast than among the Roman orators, namely, the positive law of a particular people (*nomos eggraphos*) as opposed to natural law (*nomos agraphos*).[7] Only in exceptional cases did the Greeks employ the latter term for the unformed positive law of a particular people.[8] When the Roman philosophers came to borrow the Greek terms, inasmuch as they already possessed a Latin equivalent of the term for natural law, namely, *ius gentium*, they restricted *nomos agraphos* or, in Latin, *ius non scriptum*, to the exceptional Greek usage, that is, to customary law.[9]

This general concept of *ius non scriptum*, customary law, so familiar to Roman philosophical writers of the classical period, remains a learned, theoretical generalization as far as the Roman jurists are concerned, of no practical import and of no vital interest.[10] In no case do the jurists identify custom as one of the sources of the law; custom is not, therefore, of the same status as statute, jurist's *responsum*, etc. There seems to be no doubt but that the development of the concept of *ius non scriptum* among legal authorities is to be dated in post-classical times.[11]

The General Concept of Customary Law

Classical writers, both legal and non-legal, made use of a number of technical terms that may be translated by the word 'custom'. Among the most frequent were *mos*[12] and *mores*,[13] used to denote the age-old customary origin of legal principles. Both Cicero and the jurists, when relating public law or private law rules back to the *mos maiorum*, 'custom of our ancestors', or to *mores*, 'usage', wish to ascribe ancient origin to legal principles for which no statutory basis was known. Another term, not differing materially in content from the above, is *consuetudo*,[14] the earliest known usage of which is in the *lex Antonia de Termessibus* of 71 B. C.[15] Numerous other terms are to be found which need not be enumerated here.[16] The problem is, what did these terms actually mean to the jurists?

Nineteenth century continental legal scholarship, partly on the basis of the materials in the Roman sources, and partly on theoretical speculation, built up theories of customary law which vitally influenced modern legal systems and modern jurisprudence generally. Savigny,[17] and more particularly Puchta,[18] early lights of the so-called Historical School, in accord with their universal doctrine that law exists within the consciousness of the people (*'Volksbewusstsein'*), saw in custom just as in every other 'source' of the law, merely the expression of the inner legal persuasion of the populace. To quote Puchta:[19] "Customary law exists and is valid for the same reason that a popular conviction exists, in the last analysis for the same reason that peoples exist." The views of these representatives of the Historical School were attacked by numerous writers in the latter part of the nineteenth and early twentieth century,[20] and were finally superseded by the theory that custom served as the factual basis of legal principles in many instances, and that such body of principles made up the customary law.

Brie,[21] perhaps the most thorough expounder of this later theory, extracted from the extant source materials and stressed the two elements essential for the legal recognition of custom, namely, long-continuing usage of customary practice, and tacit consent or general agreement. He discusses a host of passages[22] which on their face seems to bear out his view, although as far as the classical jurists are concerned, only Julian,[23] if the passage is genuine, specifically enumerates the two essential elements. The classical jurists do speak of the 'consensus' of those using a practice,[24] but they mean thereby the external expression of the popular will, in other words 'legal custom', not 'customary law'. It is the rhetoricians and the Byzantine jurists who shift from this view to that of 'tacit' consent or *conventio*, 'general agreement', thereby equalizing custom and statute as sources of the law, specifying the elements necessary for each, and granting validity to both by reason of the sovereignty of the people. It seems, nevertheless, that the majority of modern opinion accepts the position outlined by Brie, and holds that the classical jurists recognized customary law and defined the elements necessary thereto.[25]

At the turn of the century, however, Pernice[26] urged that the classical jurists did not know the concept 'customary law' per se; custom from which law may derive, yes, but not the general concept of the rhetoricians.[27] Ehrlich, in 1902,[28] held that the only customary law that the Romans knew was that introduced and developed by the jurists, in other words, the *ius civile*. The genuinity of the Julian passage (D. 1.3.32) was attacked by many.[29] Finally, in 1932, at the third German legal historians' congress, Schulz posed the problem: Did the classical Roman law know customary law?[30] His answer was in the negative. He distinguished between customary law, that is, the general legal norms which, without action on the part of the state, might be binding upon a judge, and legal custom, which does not result in a legal rule unless and until adopted. From his examination of the sources, he alleged that interpolation could be discovered in those passages in which the general concept was decisive, while the subject matter of the remaining passages was legal custom.[31] Lively discussion followed the reading of Schulz's paper;[32] he found supporters and opponents but I am convinced that he was correct, and that much of the divergency there and elsewhere expressed is due to the faulty analysis of the concept 'customary law', a matter into which I cannot enter.[33]

Legal Custom in Classical Times

The fact that the classical law did not know 'customary law' does not mean that custom, legal custom, did not play an extensive role in classical Rome. All admit that in pre-classical times most of the law was customary in origin; the XII Tables are nothing more than a codification of such law, with perhaps a few legislative innovations.[34] And even in classical times some of the law was of this nature. But it is to be noted that only five situations in the private law have been discovered which are described as being of customary origin.[35] Firstly, the prohibition of marriage between closely related persons,[36] secondly, the possibility of pupillary (minor children) substitution in inheritance,[37] thirdly, the invalidity of gifts between spouses,[38] fourthly, the approval of a tutor for the obligations of his ward,[39] and fifthly, the solidary (complete) liability of a plurality of bankers in the transaction of *expensilatio*, the literal contract by entries in the account books.[40]

This apparent absence of legal rules of customary law, as far as the private law is concerned, means, however, that if legal custom became a part of the classical law, it is to be found within the other well-known spheres of the law, namely, the *ius civile*, the *ius gentium*, the *ius honorarium*; and such, indeed, is the case. According to Ehrlich,[41] the *ius civile*, the law introduced by the jurists, was nothing more than customary law, and is to be contrasted with the *ius sacrum*, the religious customary law, and the *ius publicum*, primarily statute law.[42] Furthermore, it is to be noted that those legal principles which were described, in the paragraph above, as having originated in custom, are elsewhere said to be of the *ius civile*.[43] Modern scholars are wont to hold that a considerable portion of the *ius civile* is legal custom introduced by the jurists, even if they do not take the extreme view of the concept *ius civile* that Ehrlich presents.[44]

The *ius gentium* contains perhaps even more of customary flavor, especially that portion which found its expression in the edict of the praetor, in that law of the praetorian office known as the *ius honorarium*. There is close connection between *consuetudo* and the praetorian edict; when the law-making faculty of the praetor began to be recognized, the edict became the chief embodiment of the fixed customary law, now defined in the terms of a newer *ius gentium*.[45] Conversely, *consuetudo* was not law except insofar as affirmed, proclaimed and protected by the praetor.[46] The fullest picture of legal custom within the praetorian law and the *ius gentium* is given by Pernice.[47] Attention may here be called to the praetor's emphasis on blood relationship whereby primitive customary ideas were converted into legal rules, or to the *iudicium rei uxoriae* (action on dotal property) which is customary in origin but for the most part developed by the praetor, or to the edict fixing the liability of seamen, innkeepers and stablemen, which is not borrowed but native Roman law, and not an emergency measure[48] but praetorian recognition of customary usage. In similar fashion, Pernice sees in the adaptation of certain contracts to peregrine (foreign) use, such as the *stipulatio* (formal promise) or the literal contract, the infiltration of legal custom into the *ius gentium*. When it is realized from how many different sources the *ius gentium* developed, it must be accepted that customary usage, particularly business practice, played a most significant part.

Local Custom and Mos Iudiciorum

Up to the present the discussion has been upon Roman, that is, city-Rome law. What was the position of custom in the local, primarily provincial law, of the classical times? Scholars are now inclined to consider the majority of passages at the close of Digest 1.3, that portion known as '*De longa consuetudine*', which incidentally has afforded the major portion of the materials for the view that customary law as such existed in classical as well as post-classical times; this portion of the Digest many scholars now maintain contains passages which in their original scope dealt with local, not imperial, law.[49] So Julian in Digest 1.3.32 was concerned with municipal liturgies under the *lex Papia et Poppaea*; D. 1.3.33–34 are extracts from Ulpian's work on the provincial governor and therefore refer to provincial practice; the use of local custom in the interpretation of statutes was the subject matter of Paul, Digest 1.3.36, and Calistratus, Digest 1.3.38; Paul, Digest 1.3.37, has to do with *consuetudo civitatis*, the custom of a particular local government. Consequently, these classical jurists were dealing with local or popular law, '*Volksrecht*', to use the expression of the eminent scholar Ludwig Mitteis, who first treated of the major problem of the interrelation of the imperial or state law (*Reichsrecht*) and the local or provincial law (*Volksrecht*).[50] There are many other passages in the sources which speak of *mos* or *consuetudo regionis, civitatis, provinciae*,[51] and in this category is also to be placed the well-known constitution of Constantine, C. 8.52.2 of 319 A. D.[52] This passage reads: "The authority of custom and long-continuing usage is not to be taken lightly, but it is not to prevail to the extent of overcoming either reason or statute." This pronouncement may indicate that the rule was otherwise in the period before the *constitutio Antoniniana* of 212 A. D., by which citizenship was granted to practically all throughout the whole empire.[53] The actual position of customary law in the provinces in classical times, how far it supplemented, amended or even abrogated city-Rome law, is however, far from settled.⁵⁴

With local custom is probably to be tied up *mos iudiciorum*, 'custom of the courts'; this expression is fairly frequent in the sources, though somewhat rare in classical times.⁵⁵ It has reference to constant court practice, not precedent in the strict sense of the term, and its authority as a subsidiary source of law is recognized in a rescript of Severus which Callistratus (Digest 1.3.38) presents; to quote, "Our emperor Severus rescripted that where doubts occur in statutes, custom or the authority of constant decisions to the same effect ought to have the force of statute." In provincial practice the citation of precedents involving customary usage was quite frequent, as the Greco-Egyptian papyri conclusively show,⁵⁶ whereas this practice is unknown for classical Rome.⁵⁷ So the whole question of *mos iudiciorum* may be one of provincial law as far as the jurists are concerned,⁵⁸ a view which would indicate that the constitutions of the early third century, in which the phrase *mos iudiciorum* is most often found, were all rescripts of the emperors directed to the provinces.⁵⁹

Can Custom Abrogate Statute?

This study may be concluded with the discussion of a topic upon which modern scholars are practically evenly divided pro and con, namely, the abrogation of a statute by reason of customary law, spoken of as 'desuetude of the law'. Those scholars who hold that, in classical times, statutes might be abrogated by reason of non-use point, first and foremost, to the famous passage of Julian which bears directly upon the point.⁶⁰ To this passage are added the number of legal institutions which the jurists declare have disappeared by reason of customary nonuse, among others the rules provided for in the second chapter of the *lex Aquilia*,⁶¹ and the succession of *gentiles* to an inheritance.⁶² Two well-known letters in the Pliny-Trajan correspondence⁶³ are taken by some as evidence of the fact that custom might abrogate statute.⁶⁴ C. 8.52.2, discussed supra, which apparently qualifies the view expressed by Julian is said to be limited to provincial law by some of these writers, or is held to be an expression of the post-classical point of view.⁶⁵ All in all, a great number of scholars hold that desuetude may abrogate a statute in both classical and post-classical times.⁶⁶

On the other hand, there are those who declare that non-use could not abrogate a statute in classical times. Pernice⁶⁷ long since pointed out that although a statute might be, to all practical purposes, forgotten, it was within the power of a magistrate to resuscitate it at any time.

Such is the case of the *lex Genucia* on usury, which, unused for more than a century, the praetor Asellio attempted to revive, but he was murdered for his pains.[68] Such is also the case in the Pliny-Trajan letters[69] in which an unused statute was revived by the emperor.[70]

But the chief attack has been directed against the classicality of the Julian passage, most brilliantly by Steinwenter and Solazzi. The former[71] demonstrates that the concluding portion of the passage, which has to deal with desuetude, is in direct contrast to classical law. No case of such abrogation is known, and though to all practical purposes repeal might be the result of non-use (which incidentally is not the same as use), in the formal sense there was no such doctrine. Only if custom was a source of law, of like status to statute, *senatus consultum*, etc., could such a holding be possible. It has been shown above that *consuetudo* and *lex* were not of equal status among the jurists; such equivalence is, in the main, a school-doctrine of post-classical times. According to Steinwenter, nothing beyond the first sentence of D. 1.3.32.1 is genuinely Julian, and perhaps even a part of this is gloss. Certainly the portion we are here concerned with was not written by the jurist, but is the work of a post-classical glossator. As a matter of fact, Steinwenter considers the passage as it stands does not even represent the views of Justinian.[72]

Solazzi, in a paper read at about the same time as that submitted by Steinwenter,[73] comes to substantially the same conclusions. He introduces further evidence that custom could not abrogate statute,[74] and he attempts a reconstruction of the Julian passage which makes the non-use of unwritten law the chief subject-matter of the quotation.[75] The writer is of the opinion that Steinwenter and Solazzi have proved the case, and enrolls himself with those who hold that in classical times custom could not abrogate statute.[76]

Conclusion

It is left to the reader whether there are not substantially significant differences between the customary law of the Justinianian epoch and subsequent ages and that of classical times. In the latter it has been shown that custom is not an independent source of law, that there is no general concept of customary law, that no requisites for the validity of custom are set forth, that few private law rules are attributed to customary origin, that custom is practically completely absorbed in other spheres of law, that the possible importance of customary law in the provinces is at variance with the situation in city-Rome, and that custom could not abrogate statute. With these factors in mind, is it correct to speak to the customary law of the Romans, without specifying that the reference is to the Roman law of the post-classical period, a period which is generally considered an age of decadence as far as law is concerned, when compared to the classical era.

Notes

1. *Law in the Making* (2nd ed., Oxford 1930), pp. 38–45. On p. 38, note 1, he states that he is "concerned with the juristic theory (so far as formulated) of custom in classical Roman Law," yet much of the theory that he presents is post-classical in origin.

2. The Problem of Customary Law in his *Collected Papers*, vol. 2 (Oxford 1928), 411 at pp. 415–17.

3. Customary Law, in his *A General View of European Legal History* (New York 1927), 269 at pp. 291–96, 299–306.

4. It may be noted that continental writers are more familiar with the distinctions between the law of classical and post-classical times, due to the wider penetration of studies upon the Roman law.

5. Auctor ad Herennium 2.13.19; Quintilian, Inst. orat. 12.3.6. See generally discussion by Kniebe, *op. cit.*, pp. 28–42.

6. *Rhetorica* 1.10.1368b: "Law is either special or general. I mean by special law that which is written governing a particular community, by general all that unwritten said to be recognized everywhere."

7. *Cf.* Weiss, *Griechisches Privatrecht* (Leipzig 1923), vol. 1, pp. 73–74 with further references.

8. An instance is Aristotle, *Rhetorica* 1.13.1373b; Pernice, in SZ 22 (1901) pp. 82–88, clearly demonstrates that this and some other instances are exceptional.

9. *Cf.* Pernice, *loc. cit. supra* n.8; Steinwenter, *Mores*, in RE 16 (1935), col. 295. Note also the interesting passage in Cicero, *Part. orat.* 37.130: "But there are other divisions of law, those things which are written and those which without writing are upheld by the *ius gentium* or the customs of our ancestors."

10. Such a passage as D. 1.1.6.1 (Ulpian I inst.): "Now this law of ours exists either by writing or without writing, as the Greeks say, 'of laws, some are written (*eggraphoi*), some are unwritten (*agraphoi*)'", is either interpolated, so Perozzi, *Instituzioni di diritto romano*, vol. 1 (2nd ed., Roma 1928), p. 42, note 2, or mere repetition of current rhetorical thought.

11. Perozzi, *loc. cit. supra* n. 10, alleges that the distinction *ius scriptum—ius non scriptum* in the writings of classical jurists is everywhere interpolated, but it would seem more correct to say that the jurists knew, but did not emphasize, the distinction, so Jörs—Kunkel, Wenger, *Römisches Recht* (2nd ed., Berlin, 1935), pp. 1–2.

12. *E. g.* D. 4.6.26.2 (Ulpian 12 ed.); D. 29.2.8 pr. (Ulpian 7 Sab.); D. 48.9.9 pr. (Modest. 12 pand.); Cicero, *De leg.* 2.10.23.

13. *E. g.* D. 1.7.34 (Paul 11 quaest.); D. 23.2.8 (Pomp. 5 Sab.); D. 1.3.32 pr. (Julian 84 dig.).

14. von Velsen, in SZ 21 (1900) 73, at pp. 128–36, holds that in early Roman law *consuetudo* equalled *actiones*, the third element of Pomponius' trichotomy of *lex, ius civile* and *actiones*; *contra*, and rightly so, Kniebe, *op. cit.*, pp. 19–27.

15. Bruns, *Fontes iuris romani antiqui* (7th ed., Tübingen 1909), No. 14, tablet II, lines 18–22. Among other instances are Cicero, in Verrem II 4.55.122; D. 1.3.33 (Ulpian 1 off. procons.); D. 48.22.16 (Marcian).

16. Consult Brie, *op. cit.*, pp. 6–12; Kniebe, *op. cit.*, pp. 11–18.

17. *System des heutigen römischen Rechts*, vol. 1 (Berlin 1840), sects. 8, 25, 27.

18. *Das Gewohnheitsrecht* (Erlangen 1828/37).

19. In his review of the work of an early critic, von Beseler, Volksrecht und Juristenrecht quoted by Ehrlich, *Fundamental Principles of the Sociology of Law*, trans. by Moll (Cambridge 1936), p. 448.

20. Note Jhering, *Geist des römischen Rechts*, vol. 2 (6th ed., Leipzig 1921), pp. 29–34; later Ehrlich, *op. cit. supra* n. 19, pp. 442–61, which is a masterly exposition of both sides of the question.

21. The Roman law portion, *op. cit.*, pp. 1–58.

22. Among them may be noted Cicero, *De inven.* 2.22.67; Varro, in Servius' commentary on Virgil's Aeneid, 7.601; Quintilian, *Inst. orat.*, 5.10.13; Julian, in D. 1.3.32; Hermogenianus, in D. 1.3.35; Ulpian, in the *Regulae* 1.4; finally Justinian, in the *Inst.* 1.2.9.

23. Hermogenianus and Ulpian Regulae, as well as Justinian, are of course, post-classical.

24. *Cf.* Steinwenter, in *Studi Bonfante*, vol. 2 (Milano 1930), 421 at pp. 424–25.

25. Buckland, *Text-Book of Roman Law* (2nd ed., Cambridge 1932), p.52; Kübler, *Geschichte des Römischen Rechts* (Leipzig 1925); pp. 127–28; Girard, *Manuel élémentaire de droit romain* (8th ed., Paris 1929), p. 55; *cf.* Windscheid, *Lehrbuch des Pandektenrechts*, vol. I (9th ed., Frankfurt 1906), Section 15, with further references p. 76, note*.

26. In SZ 22 (1901), pp. 59–61.

27. Of the same opinion Lambert, *Etudes de droit commun législatif*, vol. 1 (Paris 1903), pp. 693–717.

28. *Beiträge zur Theorie der Rechtsquellen* (Berlin 1902), pp. 42–47.

29. References in *Index Interpolationum*, ed. Levy—Rabel, vol. 1 (Weimar 1929), col. 7, and supp. 1 (Weimar 1929), col. 3.

30. His paper and the discussion thereon summarized in SZ 53 (1933), pp. 641–43.

31. Schulz itemized six groups of sources: 1. passages which are general statements of the 'sources' of the law do not mention customary law, and the reference to the unwritten law, as in D. 1.1.6.1, even if genuine, is intended to mean the *ius gentium*; 2. statements on the point whether customary law can set aside statute are not trustworthy (see *infra*); 3. passages in which custom or business practice is utilized for the interpretation of legal transactions are instances of legal custom, not customary law; 4. legal custom, also, is involved in the administrative provisions which are alleged to have originated in customary

practice. *e. g.* the governor must always enter his province by the same roads, D. 1.16.4.5; 5. passages in which customary law is said to be the decisive factor are interpolated, if the subject matter is private law, and if public law only a very few are genuine, *e. g.* that communal liturgical duties are determined by *consuetudo*, D. 26.7.32.6; and 6. passages in which legal rules are said to be based on *mores* have reference to *mores* as moral practice, which is not identical with custom, *e. g.* women cannot be *iudices*, D. 5.1.12.2.

32. Among others, Rabel, taking into consideration pre-classical law, would distinguish between 'legally relevant' and 'legally irrelevant' custom rather than between 'customary law' and 'legal custom'; Schönbauer, who denied the non-genuinity of the passages referred to in 5, note *supra*, declared that customary law could not originate in the absolute empire nor could it arise in the law schools, therefore it must have been known to the classical jurists, even though the theory was not greatly developed by them; Levy alleged that the Romans had practically nothing else but customary law, for instance, the validity of the edict of the praetor depended upon customary law rather than statute, indeed the whole constitutional make-up of the Republic can only be understood on the basis of customary law; Niedermeyer would distinguish city-Rome from provincial law, customary law being absent from the former in classical times, but present in the latter; Schwarz compared Roman law with the English common law, which eighteenth century English juristic thought considered as being customary law, a view now generally obsolete. The reader will note that many of these points are dealt with in the discussion, *infra*.

33. *Cf.* for example, the position of Smith, *op. cit. supra* note 3, at pp. 299–306, that customary law is nothing more than case-law, with the views of Pernice, or of Schulz.

34. Voigt, *Römische Rechtsgeschichte*, vol. 1 (Leipzig 1892), p. 19; Kipp, *Geschichte der Quellen, des römischen Recht*s (4th ed., Leipzig 1919), pp. 19–20.

35. These instances noted by Pernice, in SZ 20 (1899), pp. 151–52; by Brie, *op. cit.*, p. 37, note 25; and by Steinwenter, in RE 16 (1935), col. 293. In the field of public law there are considerably more situations which the jurists designated as having customary origin, *e. g.* the inability of women and slaves to be *iudices*, the delegation of *iurisdictio*, even such a significant situation as the magistrate's reliance on the advice of the senate has no statutory basis, so Schönbauer, in SZ 47 (1927), pp. 288–89. Further cases in the public law by Pernice, in SZ 20 (1899), p. 149; Steinwenter, *loc. cit.*

36. D. 23.3.39.1 (Paul 6 ad Plaut.); D. 23.2.8 (Pomp. 5 ad Sab.).

37. D. 28.6.2 pr. (Ulpian 6 ad Sab.).

38. D. 24.1.1 (Ulpian 32 ad Sab.). Alibrandi, in *Opere Giuridiche e storiche*, vol. 1 (Roma 1896), pp. 593–603, declares that Ulpian is mistaken and that the rule is based on Augustan legislation; *cf.* also Thayer, *Lex Aquilia—On Gifts between Husband and Wife* (Cambridge 1929), p. 127.

39. D. 29.2.8 pr. (Ulpian 7 ad Sab.)

40. Auctor ad Herennium 2.13.19.

41. Die Tatsachen des Gewohnheitsrechts, in *Die feierliche Inauguration des Rektor*s * * * Universität Czernowitz (Czernowitz 1906), pp. 55–56.

42. Similarly Biondi, Prospettive romanistiche, in *Pubblicazioni della Università Cattolicà del Sacro Cuore*, serie II, vol. 37 (Milano 1933), pp. 32–33, speaks of the *ius civile* as a law essentially customary.

43. *Cf.* P. 2.19.3 with D. 23.2.39.1 on prohibition of marriage; D. 41.2.1.4 (Paul 54 ad ed.) with D. 24.1.1 on invalidity of gifts between spouses.

44. Collinet, in *Recueil Gény*, vol. 1 (Paris n. d.), p. 24, declares that custom, in the widest sense of the term, includes within itself the adoption into the *ius civile* of the institutions or formulas found in the science of the jurists, *'doctrine'* in the modern continental terminology.

45. Greenidge, *Legal Procedure of Cicero's Time* (Oxford 1901), pp. 91–93.

46. Costa, *Storia delle fonti del diritto romano* (Torino 1909), pp. 42–43. According to Costa only with the compilation of the edict under Hadrian could custom assume an independent character.

47. *Zum römischen Gewohnheitsrechte*, in SZ 20 (1899) 127, at pp. 128–42.

48. As Dernburg, *System des Römischen Rechts*, vol. 2 (8th ed., Berlin 1912), pp. 625–26, would have it.

49. Puchta, Pernice, Ehrlich, references by Steinwenter, in *Studi Bonfante*, vol. 2 p. 429; *contra*, Vinogradoff, *loc. cit. supra* note 2.

50. *Reichsrecht und Volksrecht in den östlichen Provinzen des römischen Kaiserreichs* (Leipzig 1891).

51. *E. g.* D. 50.17.34 (Ulpian 45 and Sab.),? interpolated; D. 26.7.7.10 (Ulpian 35 ad ed.); D. 33.10.7.1 (Celsus 19 dig.); D. 50.13.1.10 (Ulpian 8 omn. trib.); C. 4.65.8 (231 A. D.)

52. Mitteis, *op. cit. supra* note 50, pp. 161–65.

53. For other interpretations of C. 8.52.2, see Scialoja, in his *Studi Giuridici*, vol 1 (Roma 1933), pp. 39–47, 302–16.

54. Generally on local custom, see Kniebe, *op. cit.*, pp. 75–80; Steinwenter, in RE 16 (1935), col. 290 with further references.

55. D. 50.13.1.10 (Ulpian 8 omn. trib.); C. 4.19.2 (215 A. D.); C. 2.12.10 (227 A. D.); C. 4.50.3 (228 A. D.).

56. *E. g.* P. Oxy. VI 889.25–30; BGU I 15.9–11; P. Oxy. II 237.VII.17–18.

57. Brie, *op. cit.*, pp. 52–58.

58. Brie, *loc. cit. supra* note 57, contends that *mos iudiciorum* refers only to imperial rescripts and does not mean court usage; Allen, *op. cit. supra* note 1, pp. 119–20, suggests that it refers chiefly to points of procedure and often means no more than 'by due process of law'; Strachan-Davidson, *Problems of the Roman Criminal Law*, vol. 1 (Oxford 1912), pp. 79–80, holds that the pronouncements of inferior judges may come in as evidence of the prevalence of custom and general agreement.

59. See generally, Steinwenter, in RE 16 (1935), col. 292.

60. D. 1.3.32.1 (Julian 84 dig.): "Immemorial custom is not unreasonably observed as a statute, and this is the law which is described as established by usage. For since statutes themselves bind us for no other reason than because they have been accepted by the judgment of the people, so properly those things which the people approve without any writing, bind all; what difference does it make whether the people declares its will by vote, or by acts and conduct

themselves? Wherefore rightly it is taken that statutes are abrogated not only by the voice of the legislator, but also by the tacit consent of all through desuetude.

61. D.9.2.27.4 (Ulpian 18 ad ed.); but Pernice, Krüger, Jörs declare that this passage is Tribonianian interpolation, references in *Index Interpolationum*, ed. Levy—Rabel, vol. 1, col. 115, and supp. 1, col. 149.

62. G. 3.17.

63. Translated *infra* note 69.

64. So Kipp, *op. cit. supra* note 34, p. 23, who declares that it is within the power of the emperor to recognize or deny recognition to custom, and the mere fact that Trajan reiterates the Bithynian provincial ordinance does not necessarily mean that non-use cannot repeal a statute; *contra*, Jörs—Kunkel—Wenger, *loc. cit. supra* note 11.

65. Smith, *op. cit. supra* note 3, pp. 269—70; Jolowicz, *Historical Introduction to the Study of Roman Law* (Cambridge 1932), p. 360. Scialoja, *loc. cit. supra* note 53, however, considers that C. 8.52.2 is the reverse of the Julian passage, namely, *consuetudo* cannot resist a statute which abrogates it; a view not generally accepted.

66. In addition to those above cited, most recently Riccobono, *Corso di diritto romano*, pt 2 (Milano 1933/34), pp. 310–17; Buckland—McNair, *Roman Law and Common Law* (Cambridge 1936), pp. 15–16.

67. In SZ 20 (1899), pp. 149–50.

68. Appian, Bell. civ. 1.54; see generally Klingmüller, in RE 6 (1909), cols. 2192–94.

69. Pliny, *Epis.* 10.114–15: "Pliny to Trajan, emperor: 'The *lex Pompeia*, Sir, allows the Bithynian city-states to grant citizenship to whomsoever they will, provided these persons do not belong to any of the (other) city-states which are in Bithynia. The same law specifies the causes for which the censors may expel any member of the senate. Certain of the censors accordingly, have inquired of me whether they ought to expel one who was (a citizen) of another state. But I thought it necessary to consult you as to what you think ought to be done, not only because the statute, though it forbids a foreign citizen to be admitted, does not order a senator to be expelled for this reason, but also because I am informed by others that there are several senators (in this situation) in other states, and it will result in that many men and many states will be thrown into confusion by that part of the statute, which for a long time has had no effect by a certain (common) consent. I have appended the titles of the law to this letter.'

"Trajan to Pliny: 'You might reasonably, my dear Pliny, be doubtful what ought to be your answer to the censors consulting you, whether they might elect into the senate citizens of other states yet of the same province. For the authority of the statute (on the one hand) and long-continuing custom contrary to the statute (on the other) might place you in a quandary. I think the proper mean to be that we should make no change as to what is past but let those (senators) elected remain, of whatever state they are citizens, although contrary to the statute, but in the future the lex Pompeia is to be observed; for it we wish to extend its force retroactively, this must needs result in great confusion.'"

70. In accord with the view of Pernice are Weiss, *Grundzüge der römischen Rechtsgeschichte* (Reichenberg 1936), p. 18; Steinwenter, in RE 16 (1935), cols. 295–96.

71. Zur Lehre vom Gewohnheitsrechte, in *Studi Bonfante*, vol. 2, pp. 419–40.

72. He makes this point by a comparison of D. 1.3.32.1 with the writings of scholiasts contemporary with Justinian, references, *op. cit. supra* note 71, p. 438, notes 109–11.

73. La desuetudine della legge, in *Archivio Giuridico*, vol. 102 (Modena 1929), pp. 3–27.

74. For example, Tertullian, de corona 4, says: "Custom, even in civil cases, is recognized as a statute, provided a statute is lacking."

75. D. 1.3.32.1 according to Solazzi: "There is not unreasonably observed as a statute that which is called the law established by usage. Since statutes themselves bind us for no other reason than because they have been accepted by the judgment of the people, so properly those laws which the people has approved, should be binding. Wherefore it is correctly held that law established by usage is annulled not only by the vote of the people, but also by reason of desuetude through the tacit consent of all." This version is to be compared with the passage as it stands in the Digest, see *supra* note 60.

76. See also, Siber, *Römisches Recht*, vol. 1 (Berlin 1925), p. 30; recently, Jörs—Kunkel—Wenger, *op. cit., supra* note 11, p. 2, note 6; Schulz, *Principles of Roman Law* (Oxford 1936), pp. 14–15.

M.P. JAIN

Custom as a Source of Law in India

Folk law is to be found in every country in the world. In some countries there are dozens of different ethnic or religious groups, each of which has its own distinct system of folk law. India provides an excellent example of such a country. Not only are there critical differences between Hindu and Muslim legal customs, but all of the many linguistic and ethnic groups have their own folk laws as well.

In the following useful survey of folk law in India, M.P. Jain, Professor of Law at Banaras Hindu University and author of Outlines of Indian Legal History *(Bombay: N.M. Tripathi, 1966), even discusses differences in the folk law of individual families. Although the author, perhaps with some justification, tends to feel that the multitudinous variety of folk laws has had a negative divisive effect upon India as a whole, his scholarly documentation of this variety suggests that folk law is likely to continue to be important for decades to come.*

For representative samples of the vast literature devoted to folk law in India, see W.H. Rattigan, "Customary Law in India," The Law Magazine and Review, *4th Series, 10 (1884–1885), 1–18; Scripati Charan Roy,* Customs and Customary Law in British India *(Calcutta: Hare Press, 1911); Julius Jolly,* Hindu Law and Customs *(Calcutta: Greater India Society, 1928); George Rankin, "Custom and the Muslim Law in British India,"* Transactions of the Grotius Society, *25 (1939), 89–118; K. Ishwaran, "Customary Law in Village India,"* International Journal of Comparative Sociology, *5 (1964), 228–243; R. Deb, et al., "Patterns of Criminal Justice Amongst Some Tribes,"* Journal of the Indian Law Institute, *12 (1970), 205–236; Marc Galanter, "The Aborted Restoration of 'Indigenous' Law in India,"* Comparative Studies in Society and History, *14 (1972), 53–70; R.S. Khare, "Indigenous Culture and Lawyer's Law in India,"* Comparative Studies in Society and History, *14 (1972), 71–96; B.S. Sinha, "Custom and Customary Law in Indian Jurisprudence,"* Indian Socio-Legal Journal *(1976), 83–97.*

In any scheme of teaching Jurisprudence custom has an important place as a source of law. Indian teachers generally introduce this topic to their

---

Reprinted from *Jaipur Law Journal*, 3 (1963), 96–130.

students through English and sometimes Continental materials. Even the Indian authors on Jurisprudence refer mainly to foreign materials and not to Indian materials. There is, however, a rich material in Indian social and legal history which can more appropriately be made use of in explaining the place of custom in society. A growing use of this material will help to focus attention on some of the main problems of new India. This paper is a brief attempt at noticing some of this Indian material.

I

Western Jurists

In the evolution of human society, it appears to be beyond doubt that custom arose first, law came later. Law denotes a more definitive organisation of human society with some kind of power structure established. Customs arise whenever a few human beings come together, as no association of human beings can exist permanently without adopting consciously or unconsciously, some definite rules governing reciprocal rights and obligations.[1] It also looks to be axiomatic that, to start with, law was built upon custom.[2] One example which immediately comes to mind is that of the English common law which in its origin was built upon custom[3] and which later absorbed into itself the customs of the mercantile community to give to the common law world the modern Mercantile Law.[4] The Twelve Tables of Rome were based upon customs of the people.[5]

Custom is regarded as a source of law by the Western jurists, though they assign importance to it to a varying degree depending upon their approach and outlook. Austin having defined 'law' as the command of a political superior or definite human authority addressed to political inferiors and enforced by a penalty or sanction, held that custom becomes a law only when it receives judicial or legislative recognition.[6] This excludes from the pale of law those customs which exist with all the force of law but have not come before the courts unlike those which through accident have come before the courts and have been recognised there. The rigours of Austin's theory have been mitigated by other Analytical Jurists following Austin. Holland, though practically adopting Austin's definition of law, nevertheless, holds that courts do not *proprio motu* for the time make custom a law, that they merely decide as a fact that there exists a legal custom about which there might have been some question up to that time, just as there might be about the meaning and interpretation of an Act of Parliament, and the observance of a custom is not the cause of law; but is evidence of its existence.[7] Courts give operation to customs not prospectively from the date of such recognition, but also retrospectively; so far implying that custom was law before it received the stamp of judicial authentication. Allen also disagrees with Austin's thesis. He regards custom as "self-contained, self-sufficient, and self-justified law" and says that the function of the court is "declaratory rather than constitutive".[8] When a custom is proved in a court by satisfactory evidence, the function of the court is merely to declare the custom operative law. Thus custom does not derive its inherent validity from the authority of the Court. The difficulty in the way of accepting this view is the veto which a court wields to declare a custom invalid on the ground of unreasonableness.

The Historical Jurists attached a much greater importance to custom. They held that all early law was customary, and that the function of legislation is limited to supplementing and redefining custom. According to Savigny, the real basis of all positive law is to be found in the general consciousness of people (*Volksgeist*). The source of law is not the command of the sovereign, not even the habits of a community, but the 'instinctive sense of right possessed by every race'. Since this consciousness is invisible, it is to be discovered by the external acts which manifest itself in usages, manners and customs. Custom is thus evidence of law whose real source lies deeper in the minds of men. As a necessary consequence it follows that custom, as the external evidence of law in the abstract, possesses the force of law before it is received by the courts, and not as a result of this process.[9] According to Savigny, the acts required for the establishment of customary law ought to be plural, uniform and constant. They may be judicial decisions, but these are not indispensable for its establishment, although some have thought otherwise; the authors of the acts must have performed them with the consciousness that they spring from a legal necessity.[10] Of course, the flaw in this theory is that there are customs which are not based on an instinctive sense of right in the community as a whole, but on the interests of a strong minority, for example, slavery. Though it is also true that not all customs are consciously created, growth of much customary law is not the result of conscious thought, but of tentative practice.

The fact, however, remains that for those on whom a custom operates, it is binding by itself whether or not the stage ever comes when it is debated or discussed in a court. In the consciousness of the followers of the custom, it has a obligatory force. Take the examples of India; here for long before the advent of the British, customs were observed by the people, and were enforced not by the courts but by the village or community *panchayats*; the Government did not interfere with the prevalent norms. When the British system of Justice came, these very customs came to be pleaded before the courts which enforced them. In such a situation, custom did not become effective for the first time after judicial recognition. It was there already in full force, the difference was that instead of the *panchayats* it came to be enforced by the courts. Thus the Analytical Theory does not very much fit the Indian condition.

II

Hindu View of Custom

Custom has always been given a very important place as a source of law by the Hindu Jurists. Two views have prevailed regarding the relative value of custom *vis-a-vis* the *sruti* and *smriti*. The *Dharmashastra* writers subordinated customs to *sruti* and *smriti* which were given a higher authority. Thus, according to Gautam, *dharmas* (customs) of countries, castes and families, which are not opposed to *Vedic* scriptures, are authoritative and binding. Manu and Yajnavalkya declare that sources of *Dharma* are *sruti*, *smriti* and *sadachara* in that order. Apararka held the view that a custom repugnant to any 'clear' text of '*Vedas*' is to be rejected. Mitakshara, Dayabhaga, Mayukha also place custom as subordinate to *sruti* and *smriti*. This, however, was not the unanimity of opinion. There were dissenting voices against the view of subordinating custom. Visvarupa, Medhatithi favour the view that prescriptions of *smritis* (and even of *sruti*) need not be observed when they are vehemently condemned by the people (e.g. *niyoga*, though sanctioned by the texts, are, nevertheless, abhorred by custom).[11] In one text of the *Manusmriti* itself, there is a hint to regard custom as superior to everything. According to it, *smritis* themselves embody practices of the people current in their days: *Achara* is transcendental law, and so are the practices declared in the *Veda* and *smriti*; therefore, a twice born person desirous of his own welfare should always make efforts to follow it.[12] The *Arthasastra* writers, e.g., Kautilya, held that usages and customs were of equal authority as evidence of law; and in case of conflict between them, the former must be taken to be of greater force as being actually observed in practice.

Whatever theory the *Dharmashastra* writers propounded of the validity of custom, the fact remains that customs have played a very important role as a material source of ancient Hindu law. The process of integrating custom with the law has always been going on; the Hindu Jurists were liberal in their attitude towards recognising and accepting them, *e.g.*, the eight forms of marriage were recognised by *Dharmashastra* writers even though some of the forms were highly objectionable. To start with, the *dharmasutra* tried to bring the text of the *sruti* in conformity with the customs prevailing in the contemporary society at the time they were composed. Then the *smritis* drew heavily on the customs of the people for whom they were designed. That largely explains why so many various *Dharmashastras* came into being, and why they differed from each other. When the *smritis* failed to satisfy the growing needs and changing conditions of the people, the commentaries adapted the *smriti*-law, by the process of interpretation, to bring in it the customs which had taken roots in the contemporary society. What the commentaries did was to take up an old text of the *Dharmashastra* and interpret it in such a manner that it came in harmony with social mores and customs of the people. As the Privy Council has stated, "The Digest subordinates in more that one place the language of texts to custom and approved usage".[13] It is how, starting with the same texts as the base, two major schools of Hindu law developed in India, and that one of them came to have four sub-schools.[14] It may also be pointed out that the process was not entirely one-sided; while customs were recognised, it would also be correct to say that customs also, to some extent, were modified and supplemented by the opinions of the Hindu Jurists.

In Sanskrit, the word for custom is *sadachar*. The exact import of *sadachar* has been shifting from age to age and among commentators. In the earliest days, *achara* to be followed was that observed or declared by *brahmans* who were learned in the *Vedas*, and were highly moral and selfless (*sistas*). This standard gave a kind of choice or freedom to a particular jurist to be selective in accepting or recognising custom. If there was any custom which he thought was immoral or anti-social, he could discourage it by calling it as being not consonant to good conduct. Gradually, this harsh standard came to be relaxed so much so that every usage, having no visible secular purpose, came to be looked upon as binding and, lastly, the usages even of the *sudras* came to be enforced by the king.

From Gautama, Manu, Brahaspati etc., it follows that the customs and usages of which account is to be taken are those of districts (*desa* or *janpada*), towns and villages, castes, families, guilds, corporations or groups (*gana, sreni, sangh, naigam, varga*).

III

Muslim View of Custom

The two principal sources of the Islamic law are the *Koran*, as containing the word of God, and the *hadis* or traditions, being the inspired utterances of the Prophet and precedents derived from his acts. Next important sources are: *ijma*, the consensus of opinion amongst the learned; *urf* or custom; and *qiyas*, the analogical deductions from the first three.

There is no doubt that, during his life time, the Prophet himself recognised the force of customary law. He either gave his express sanction to certain pre-Islamic usages prevalent amongst the Arabs, or suffered such usages to continue without expressing disapprobation. His companions, after his death, recognised many customs which were not inconsistent with the teaching of the Islamic faith. The *hadis* contained, to a large extent, the customary law of pre-Islamic Arabia. In *Koran*, there is not much of law. Hence the rule that it must be read in conjunction with the customs then in vogue. It is thus clear that in its formative stages the Muslim law drew a good deal from the customs prevailing in Arabia. When, however, the principles of the law became settled, custom was relegated to an inferior position. Though the Muslim Jurists continued to recognise custom as a source of law on the principle "treat whatever the people generally consider to be good for themselves as good in the eye of God", nevertheless, it is now relegated to an inferior position, coming after *ijma*, i.e., it is considered inferior to the *Koran*, the *hadis* and *ijma*, but superior to *qiyas*. Hence, according to the strict rule of Muslim law, a custom opposed to the principles derived from the former sources is illegal. The conditions laid down for the validity of custom, under the Muslim law are: first, it must be generally prevalent in the country; second, it must not be merely a local usage in a village or a town, though it need not be ancient or immemorial; third, it must be an established course of conduct, not merely a practice on a few occasions; and, fourth, custom being essentially territorial, it cannot affect the law in other lands, and as it is confined to a particular period it cannot affect the custom in another age.[15]

IV

Custom in the Modern Indian Legal System

What place was given to custom in the scheme of administration of justice in India during the British period? The Englishmen were very particular in leaving the personal laws of the people undisturbed as much as possible and this attitude characterised the whole of the British period. In 1781, the Act of the settlement passed to remove defects from the Regulating Act, 1773, directed the Supreme Court at Calcutta to decide 'matters arising out of inheritance and succession to land and goods', and matters of 'contract and dealing between party and party', 'by the laws and usages of Muhammadans', in the case of Muhammadans

Custom as a Source of Law in India

and 'by the laws and usages of the Gentoos' in case of the Gentoos. Provisions on the same lines were made for other Presidency towns and were repeated from time to time with slight verbal[16] variations.

As to the *mofussil* area, *i. e.*, the territories beyond the Presidency towns, the starting point is 1772, when for the first time, Warren Hastings created an *adalat* system in Bengal, Bihar and Orissa. The *adalats* were directed to decide all cases of inheritance, marriage, caste and other religious usages and institutions according to the laws of the *Koran* with respect to the Muhammadans and the laws of the *Shaster* with respect to the Hindus.[17] In 1781, this provision was supplemented by a provision to the effect that in all cases for which no specific directions were given, the *adalats* were to act according to justice, equity and good conscience.[18] Practically the same was repeated in S.37 of the Bengal, Agra and Assam Civil Courts Act of 1887 where Muhammadan law and Hindu law were substituted for 'the law of the *Koran* and the law of the *Shaster*' respectively. No mention was made in this provision of custom. Warren Hastings had supposed that the Hindus and Muslims were governed by their religious or sacerdotal texts; he failed to appreciate that more than these texts, the local and personal usages had come to play an important role in the lives of the people. In course of time, better knowledge came to prevail amongst the British administrators regarding the Indian conditions, and then custom came to be given its due importance. Thus in 1827, when Monstuart Elphinstone legislated for the territories annexed to the Bombay Presidency, Regulation IV of 1827, in S.26, deviated from the Bengal model by giving precedence to custom; it laid down that "the law to be observed in the trial of suits shall be Acts of Parliament and regulations of Government applicable to the case; in the absence of such Acts and regulations, the usage of the country in which the suit arose; if none such appears, the law of the defendant, and, in the absence of specific law and usage, justice, equity and good conscience alone". In S. 16 of the Madras Civil Courts Act, 1873, it was laid down that to decide any question regarding succession, inheritance, marriage or caste, or religious institution, "the Muhammadan law... and the Hindu law..., any custom (if such there be) having the force of law and governing the parties or property concerned, shall form the rule of decision...".

The above provisions did not follow a uniform pattern insofar as the question of the relative position of custom *vis-a-vis* the personal law (as contained in the religious books) was concerned. Except the Bombay Regulation, all other provisions left the question vague. Only the Bombay Regulation clearly assigned precedence to custom over the personal law. The Madras provision did mention 'custom' but did not explicitly give any precedence to it over rules of personal law. The Bengal provision did not mention custom at all. Courts were thus confronted with the question: in case of conflict between the custom and the written text of law, what was to be followed? Insofar as the Hindus were concerned, the courts, taking note of the great importance given to custom in the ancient India, ruled early that "under the Hindoo system of law, clear proof of usage will outweigh the written text of the law", which came to mean that if a custom is proved to be established on a point of Hindu law, then the courts are bound to follow it even though it may be inconsistent with some express text in the *Dharmashastras* or the commentaries[19]. The point was made still more specific in *Neelkisto Deb v. Beerchunder*[20] where it was said that where custom was proved to exist it would oust the general law, which, however, will regulate all outside the custom. The courts in laying down that immemorial usage is transcendental law have depended on the text of Manu which has been quoted above[21]. This judicial approach to custom in the area of Hindu law, even though not in conformity with the orthodox approach, was yet in conformity with the genius of the law which always gave a high regard to custom.

The position of custom in the area of Muslim law remained doubtful for quite some time. The difficulty arose because, traditionally, the Muslim Jurists placed custom at a low level of priority. Early in the day, the Bombay Supreme Court was called upon to decide,[22] with reference to the Bombay Presidency town, whether Khojas and Cutchi Memons, who were Muslim by religion, but who followed the Hindu customs of inheritance and succession, should be governed by their customs or by the orthodox Muslim law. Referring to the expression 'laws and usages' of the Muslims in the clause referring to the Presidency towns, Perry, C.J., refused to read it as meaning the application of the *Koran* only to the Muslims without regard to their usages. He pointed out that the clause in question was framed on political grounds solely, and without reference to orthodoxy, or the purity of any religious belief. The underlying purpose of the clause was to give the benefit of their laws to the people of India. The effect of the clause was not to adopt the text of the *Koran* as law any further than it has been adopted in the laws and usages of the Muhammadans; and if any class of Muhammadans are found to be in possession of any usage which was otherwise valid as a legal custom, and which did not conflict with any express law of the English Government, they were just as much entitled to the protection of this clause as the most orthodox *sunni*.

It has been already mentioned that the rule of decision (S. 37 of the Act of 1887) for Bengal, Bihar and Orissa, did not mention 'custom' as a source of law. It, therefore, remained a matter of doubt whether in case of Muslims, custom could prevail in derogation to the Muslim law in this territory.[23] As late as 1904, the Allahabad High Court held in *Jammya* v. *Diwan*[24] that a family custom among Muslims excluding daughter from inheritance could not be proved as the provision did not provide an opening to custom as against the Muslim law. This view had been held by the courts previously for, as early as 1866, in *Surmust Khan* v. *Kadir Dad Khan*,[25] the same view was propounded. It may be mentioned that this attitude of the court was due to the low place allotted to custom traditionally by the Muslim Jurists. So far as the Hindus were concerned, the same provision was interpreted differently and custom was given a high place in the scheme of law because of the high place traditionally allotted to custom by the Hindu Jurists. It was only when the Allahabad ruling came before the Privy Council for review in *Mohd. Ismail* v. *Lala Sheomukh*[26], that custom got the precedence over the Muslim law and was made legally enforceable even in derogation to the orthodox Muslim law.[27]

A special reference need be made to Punjab which is preeminently a land of customary law. Neither the sacred books of the Hindus nor those of the Muslims have made much of an impact on the rural life of the Punjab and people are mostly governed by their customary law. In the pre-British times, these customs were enforced by the village or tribal *panchayats or jirgas*. On the annexation of Punjab by the British in 1849, the Governor-General, while constituting the Board of Administration, gave assurance to the people; that the "native institutions and practices shall be upheld as far as they are consistent with the distribution of justice to all classes". Soon after, directions were issued that the *lex loci* or "local customs which had been obeyed by any tribe or sect" will be enforced.[28] Section 5 of the Punjab Laws Act, 1872,[29] expressly directed the courts to observe any custom applicable to the parties concerned which is not contrary to justice, equity and good conscience, and has not been altered or abolished by law, or declared by competent authority to be void, in deciding questions regarding succession, marriage, special property of women, betrothal, divorce, dower, adoption, guardianship, minority, bastardy, family relations, wills, legacies, gifts, partitions of any religious usage or institution. Custom was thus made the first rule of decision. It was at one time held by the courts in Punjab that the effect of this provision was to make custom the primary law of the Punjab in relation to the matters specified in that section and to cast upon anyone alleging that he was governed by personal law the burden of so proving. Bringing out the implications of the above provision, the Privy Council has stated in *Abdul Hussein* v. *Sona Dero*[30] that the section raises no presumption that the parties are to be governed by custom rather than by personal law which must be applied unless the custom is proved. The clause put the custom in the forefront as the rule of decision: the legislature has recognised the fact that in Punjab, customs largely govern the people. But, before a custom may be enforced, it must be established by the ordinary processes of evidence.[31] A person asserting the custom has to prove it before the courts can apply it.

There is no such thing in Punjab as a 'general custom'. Custom there is mainly tribal, and even with the same tribe, it may vary from locality to locality. Each tribe has its own customs and in the Punjab there are many tribes. Origins of the tribes differ; even with the tribes of the same origin, local and social conditions have greatly differed resulting in varying customs. There is thus no single body of customary or tribal law common to the whole of Punjab.[32] While the custom in Punjab is mainly agricultural, even the urban people are not completely free from it.[33]

Customs prevail in Oudh, mainly in the matter of succession and they have figured before the courts from time to time both among Hindus and Muslims.[34] In Oudh Laws Acts, 1876, S. 3, a provision similar to the Punjab provision has been enacted. Similarly, S. 27 of the N.W.F.P. Reg. VII of 1901 made an equivalent provision giving custom precedence over the personal laws. The Central Provinces Laws Act, 1875, did the same thing.[35] On the Malabar Coast, Maramakatayam law of inheritance in which descent is traced in the female line, a person's heirs being the children of his sister, came to be judicially recognised on the basis of custom.[36]

The Kumaon Hills constitute another tract of land where customs preponderate. Among others, the hills are inhabited by people known as Khasis who have stuck to their customs on various points which are at variance with the Mitakshara. On the coast of Malabar, people known as Mopalas, who are Muslims by religion, follow not the orthodox system of Muslim law but the Hindu law known as Marumukkthayam or matriarchal system and their customs have been applied by the courts.

It may however be mentioned that the clauses giving precedence to custom, did not have much of any special significance, for even without them, custom would have been preferred over the personal law as was held by the Privy Council in the *Moottu Ramalinga Case*. To some extent, these clauses did away with the doubt, in the area of Muslim law, regarding the relative position of custom *vis-a-vis* the personal law, but even here the Privy Council's verdict had gone in favour of the custom.

V

Kinds of Customs Enforced

From the above it is clear that during the British Period, the customs came to be given a pre-eminent place as a rule of decision. This happened as a result of statutory provisions, or where these were deficient, by the judicial interpretation. The courts accepted and applied customs of all types, *e.g.*, tribal, communal, sectarian, local, family etc.

Most of the customs brought before the courts are tribal, communal or sectarian, *i.e.*, those which apply to a particular caste, community, or group residing in a particular territorial area.[37] A few examples may be noted here ; Customs in Punjab, Malabar coast, Kumaon hills are all of this category.[38] Apart from these, courts have recognised several miscellaneous customs of various groups. The Kamma community in Andhra has a custom of affiliating a son-in-law and giving him a share in the property; this adoption known as *illatom* adoption has been recognised by the Court.[39] The Jain community, irrespective of its various sects in which it is divided, has a custom that a widow can make an adoption without the consent of her husband (except in Madras and Punjab).[40] Recently, the Supreme Court in *Munnalal* v. *Raj Kumar*[41] reviewed the large number of cases having a bearing on this point and sustained the custom as one prevailing in the Jain community as such irrespective of the locality where they may reside or the sect in which they are divided. Another custom of Jains recognised by the courts is that a widow has full power to alienate the self-acquired property of her deceased husband.[42] A custom prevails among the Chetti inhabitants of a few villages in Madura District whereby when a husband during the life of his wife marries another wife, he sets aside a portion of his property for the first wife's maintenance (called *moopu*) and the rest of the property is divided in two parts, each part going to the sons of each wife.[43] Nairs in South Malabar have peculiar usages. Some of them have been judicially established. Amongst them, polyandry was legally recognised, and descent or property was through females. Adoption of females with the family when necessary to preserve it was also recognised.[44]

A family custom is one which applies to a particular family only. At an early stage in the evolution of the Indian legal system, doubt had been entertained by the courts on the question whether a family custom, different from a local custom, could be regarded as legally enforceable. In *Tarachand* v. *Reeb Ram*[45] the Judges of the Madras High Court referred to the jurisprudential theories and said that they all referred to customary law, antagonistic to the general law, to be established by evidence of the acts of a single family confessedly subject to the general law.[46] In *Basvantrav v. Mantappa*,[47] the Bombay High Court refused to give effect to a family custom saying that "it would be a dangerous doctrine that any petty family is at liberty to make a law for itself, and thus to set aside the general law of the country". But this view could not remain in force very long. From the very beginning, the trend of the Privy Council was different. In *Soorendranath v. Mst. Heeramonee*,[48] a family was held to have retained the mithila law even though it migrated from there, and had been residing in Bengal, for generations. In *Abraham v. Abraham*,[49] the Privy Council had definitely accepted the possibility of a Christian family, converted from Hindu or Muslim religion, to have its law. These cases made the Bombay and Madras views regarding the efficacy of a family custom completely untenable and so the courts changed their opinions.[50]

In a number of cases, too many to recount here, family customs have been applied by the courts. A family of *jats* migrated from Delhi to U.P. in 1858. It was held that according to customs applied to *jats* in Delhi, adoption of an orphan was valid and that the family must be presumed to have carried this custom with it to U.P. and so it must be applied to it.[51] Impartibility of estates is a creature of custom and it has been enforced in a large number of cases as a family custom.[52] In certain cases where impartibility of zamindari has been sustained because of a family custom, a right to maintenance in certain members of the family has also been recognised because of the family custom.[53] An interesting institution created by custom, prevalent among certain families in certain parts of the country, is that of a 'composite family', i.e., two or more families agree to live and work together, pool their resources, throw their gains and labour into the joint-stock, shoulder the common risks, utilise the resources of the units indiscriminately for the purposes of the whole family.[54] A Jain family became Vashnabs, but even then the Jain custom was applied to it and it was held that change in religion did not affect the laws and customs by which the personal rights and status of the members of the family were governed.[55] A family custom governing succession of a Muslim family in Oudh has been upheld by the Privy Council.[56]

Commenting upon the legal enforceability of a family custom of succession, the Privy Council stated in *Shiba Prasad Singh v. Prayag Kumari*,[57] that "a Hindu family, no doubt, cannot by agreement between its members make a custom for itself of succession to family property at variance with the ordinary law. But where a family is found to have been governed as to its property by a customary rule of succession different from that of the ordinary law, that custom is itself law. The rule of succession in such a case is recognised by the state as part of the law of the family, though it is no more than the result of a course of conduct of individual subjects of the state constituting the family".

It has been held judicially that a family custom is capable of being destroyed by disuse.[58]

A local custom is one which is binding on all persons in the local area where it prevails. A few examples of such customs can be found in the Indian case-law, though it will be seen that they are few as compared to the tribal or family customs which have been noticed above. Another point to note is that while customs in India in the area of family relations and succession to property are either tribal or communal or family, the local customs are more of a secular nature and do not affect family relations or succession; they create other rights. One of the most widely spread customs in several parts of India is the right of pre-emption. Pre-emption is essentially a Muslim concept and the Muhammadan law deals with it in detail. But in certain areas of India, the right of pre-emption came to be recognised as prevailing amongst the non-Muslims also as a matter of custom.[59] It has also been held that the rules of Muhammadan law of pre-emption would apply to non-Muslims also except insofar as such ruch rules are modified.

Section 18 of the Indian Easements Act stipulates that an easement may be acquired by custom. It has thus been held that a right of privacy may be established as a customary easement in a locality.[60] Rights not amounting to easements have been recognised by the courts as customary rights. Thus the right of pasturage in the land of another,[61] right to bury dead on another's,[62] right to worship, right to hold festivals, right to remove earth from a portion of a field,[63] right to a village pathway,[64] have all been judicially conceded. In a number of cases, the Calcutta High Court has held that a fluctuating body of persons cannot acquire a customary right in the nature of a profit-a-prendre.[65] Patna High Court disagrees with this view.[66] But Bombay High Court has held that members of a village are not a fluctuating body.[67]

VI

Requisites of a Valid Custom

A custom is a rule which in a particular family or in a particular district, has, from long usage, obtained the force of law. It is not that each and every custom can be legally enforced. A custom to be legally recognisable and enforceable must fulfil several requisites, *viz.*, it must be ancient, certain and reasonable, and, being in derogation of the general rules of law, must be construed strictly.[68] A neat formulation of a valid custom is contained in the Hindu Marriage Act and the Hindu Succession Act wherein it is said that the expression 'custom' and 'usage' signify any rule which, having been continuously and uniformly observed for a long time obtained the force of law among Hindus in any local area, tribe, community, group or family: Provided that the rule is certain and not unreasonable or opposed to public policy.[69]

One of the attributes of an enforceable custom is that it should be certain and not vague; that the course of conduct upon which the custom rests must not be left in doubt but be proved with certainty.[70] The reason behind this rule is simple to understand. If one is left in doubt as to what the custom is, he cannot apply it.[71] If a custom is vague, the courts cannot be definite about its content and so cannot give effect to it.

A custom to be valid must be ancient.[72] The Royal Court in England laid down the rule that country custom was only valid if immemorial. It could not be transferred from one country to another, nor could it be changed. At first, immemoriality must have referred to the actual memory of any person living, since, in the first centuries after the Conquest, law was preserved by oral tradition. Later, it was necessary to prove that there was no record of any different rule. The problem can be illustrated by an important case in 1346 (Y.B. 20, Ewd. III). The Prince of Wales held a court at Macclesfield which tried a plea of covenant on simple contract. The defendant demanded judgment "saying that, by the common law used in the country of Cheshire and elsewhere throughout the whole realm of England no one need answer any claim of covenant without a special deed testifying to that covenant". The plaintiff claimed a contrary custom at the Eyres of Macclesfield. The King's Bench held that there was no such custom, since the Eyres had first been held in the time of Edward I, "after the time of memory". As records were maintained in writing, the Central courts appear gradually to have limited customs to those recognised when the earliest records started, or not contradicted since that time. They fixed on the year 1189 (Throne of Richard I, from which date the earliest rolls of the King's Bench are available) as the beginning of legal memory, an appropriate date as most royal court rolls start about that time.[73]

But the expression 'immemorial origin' in India does not have the same sense as in England. Though in the beginning, the Privy Council appeared to be of the view that a custom should be ancient,[74] the judicial attitude somewhat softened later. The Allahabad High Court frankly stated, "We cannot in these provisions apply the principles of the English Common Law, that a custom is not proved if it is shown not to be immemorial. To apply such a principle... would be to destroy many customary rights of modern growth in villages and other places. It would be inexpedient... to attempt to prescribe any such period".[75] In one case, the Calcutta High Court held that a right of pasturage being enjoyed for 40 years was not immemorial and hence not customary.[76] In fact, the general view taken by the Calcutta High Court is that either 1773 A.D. or 1793 A.D. is the date for treating a custom which has been in existence as immemorial.[77] The Bombay High Court has taken the view that if within the last 20 years, there have occurred a number of instances in which the alleged custom has been recognised, the presumption arises of immemorial usage.[78] In *Mt. Subhani* v. *Nawab*,[79] the Privy Council held that in India it is not of the essence of the rule that the custom to be binding must be ancient and its antiquity must be carried back to a period beyond the memory of man—still less, that it is ancient in the English technical sense.[80] It depends upon the circumstances of each case what antiquity must be established before the custom can be accepted. What is necessary to be proved is that the usage has been acted upon in practice for such a long time as to show that it has, by common consent, been submitted to as the established governing rule of the particular locality. In the instant case, a custom proved to be in existence over a period of nearly 30 years was held legally enforceable. The Privy Council has held that customary law, if found to exist in 1880, must be taken to have the ordinary attribute of a custom that it is ancient.[81]

The Supreme Court of India has stated that a custom derives its force from the fact that by long usage it has obtained the force of law, but the English rule that a custom to be legal and binding must have been used so long that the memory of man runneth not to the contrary should not be strictly applied to Indian conditions. All that is necessary to prove is that the usage has been acted upon in practice for such a long period and with such invariability as to show that it has, by common consent, been submitted to as the established governing rule of a particular locality.[82]

The Andhra High Court has held that a custom being in existence for 40 years, is an enforceable custom.[83] The Calcutta High Court has held recently that the rule of legal memory does not apply to custom in India,[84] even though it is proved or assumed that the law was otherwise previously; proof of existence of a custom for 50 years is enough to give it validity of law, even though it is proved that previous to that period a different state of things existed.[85] In *Bari* v. *Tukaram*,[86] the Court held legally enforceable as a customary right, a right to remove earth from a portion of a field which right had been enjoyed for the last 30 years. In *Bhiku* v. *Sheoram*,[87] a right enjoyed for 20 years by kumhars to take earth from a portion of a field was held valid as a customary right.

From the above, it is clear that there is no uniform rule regarding the time factor for which a custom must have been in operation before it is legally recognised. The minimum period for this purpose appears to be 20 years. But the High Courts differ in their approach on this point. Now, the definition of custom adopted by the Hindu legislation says 'for a long period' instead of 'immemorial', which denotes that the English rule has not been adopted, but as 'long period' has not been defined, uncertainty as to what that is continues in the views of the various High Courts.

A custom should not be unreasonable.[88] It should not be against reason, but the reason referred to here "is not to be understood as meaning every unlearned man's reason but artificial and legal reason warranted by authority of law", and, further, "it is sufficient if no good legal reason can be assigned against it".[89]

Examples of customs held unreasonable by the courts are not many.[90] One or two examples of unreasonable customs may be considered here. A custom of total remission of rent on the ground that a certain portion of the land was subject to inundation resulting in the destruction of crops, the extent of such destruction not being specific, has been held to be unenforceable in law both because it is unreasonable and uncertain.[91] A right of pasturage over the land of another may be regarded as unreasonable if it completely deprives the owner of his right to the lands. It is not possible to deprive the owner of his land completely. In the instant case, right of pasturage was being enjoyed on swampy land. Later the land became fit for cultivation. The Court held that a part of the land may be given on rent so long as sufficient land was left for pasturage for those who are entitled to it and that no such right can be claimed over the whole of the land.[92] It has been held that it is the usage which makes the law, and not the reason of the thing for it cannot be said that a custom is founded on reason, though an unreasonable custom is void;[93] for no reason, even the highest whatsoever, would make a custom or law. The circumstance that the reason for the custom has subsequently been found to be wrong cannot affect its validity. It is no requirement of a valid custom that it should be deducible from any accepted principle of law. A right having been established 50 years ago and which has not been shown to have since been denied or disputed in any decided case cannot be overthrown on the strength of recently expounded theories regarding its basis.[94]

A custom should not be immoral or opposed to public policy or against justice, equity and good sense.[95] There is, however, no fixed test to judge the morality or otherwise of a custom. In *Gopi* v. *Jaggo*,[96] the Privy Council allowed a custom which recognised and sanctioned remarriage of a woman who had been abandoned and deserted by her husband.

According to the custom, desertion by the husband dissolved the marriage tie leaving the woman free to re-marry. In *Nanee Tara Naikin* v. *Allarakia Soomar*,[97] the Bombay High Court had recognised the custom of adoption of girls by the dancing girls. But the judicial view changed. In *Mathura Naikin* v. *Esu Naikin*,[98] the Court held the custom to be immoral, for the profession of dancing girls was immoral, and adoption by them of girls was designed to perpetuate this profession. But in matters of succession, *dasis* (dancing girls) have been held to be governed by their customs and a custom excluding married *dasis* from inheritance to another *dasis* has been judicially accepted.[99]

Following customs regarding divorce have been held to be immoral; a custom permitting a woman to desert her husband at her pleasure and marry again without his consent,[100] a custom by which the marriage tie could be dissolved by either husband or wife against the wish of the divorced party on payment of a sum money.[101]

There was nothing immoral in a custom permitting divorce by mutual agreement.[102] In certain cases it has been held that unless both the parties had specifically agreed, a divorce granted by a caste *panchayat* would be against public policy and could not be enforced by the courts.[103] The Madras High Court has recently held the proposition to be too wide.[104]

A custom abhorrent to decency or morality however long practised and recognised by a community cannot be enforced by the courts. Thus a custom permitting marriage with daughter's daughter was held immoral.[105]

It is under this heading, that the courts exercise a kind of 'censorial' power on the customs.

VII

Proof of a Custom

Before the advent of the British period, the customs of the people were mostly unwritten and unrecorded and were enshrined in the 'unexpressed consciousness of the people' and were enforced by the village *panchayat*. With the coming in of the British methods and forms of administration of justice, it became necessary and imperative to establish customs in the courts before they could be enforced. It thus became necessary to ascertain the customs and record them in writing. No longer could the custom remain in the consciousness of the people.

The first important principle laid down by the courts in a large number of cases is that a party alleging that he is governed by a custom must specifically allege the same and prove its existence;[106] there is no presumption that a particular person or class of persons is governed by a custom and the onus to prove it rests on him who alleges it.[107] This principle is followed strictly so much so that even in those areas, like Punjab and Oudh, where the statutes give preference to customs over the personal law of the party concerned, there is no presumption that a custom exists; it must be alleged and proved.[108] The Privy Council has stated[109] that what is required before an alleged custom can receive the recognition of the courts, and so acquire legal force, is satisfactory proof of usage so long and invariably acted upon in practice as to show that it has, by common consent, been submitted to as the established governing rule of the particular family, class or district of the country.

The custom must be established by clear and unambiguous proof, by cogent and satisfactory evidence. In the absence of such an evidence the court cannot come to a conclusion whether any custom is really operative or what is its content and scope. But, at the same time, the Privy Council has made it clear that rigorous and technical rules of proof, such as are insisted upon in England, are not required in India.[110]

A custom cannot be enlarged or extended by parity of reasoning, analogy or logical process.[111] One custom cannot be deduced from another. As the Supreme Court has stated: "Theory and custom are antithesis; custom cannot be a matter of mere theory but must always be a matter of fact. Thus a community living in one part of the country may have evolved a particular custom but from that it does not follow that the community living in another district is necessarily following the same custom".[112] In the Kamma Community in the Andhra Pradesh, there is a custom that if estrangement between wife and husband occurs, dowry and all presents given to the bride-groom by the bride's people at the time of the marriage must be handed back to the bride.[113] The Andhra High Court refused to extend it by the analogy to a situation when the bride died on the ground that there could be no greater estrangement than 'death'. But on evidence tendered the custom was held proved.[114] Thus a custom has to be established by evidence and not by *a priori* methods.

What the courts want is clear and unambiguous evidence with instances of the enforcement of the custom,[115] though it has also been laid down that proving of specific instances was not absolutely necessary at all times.[116] A family custom can be proved by establishing to the same group, *i.e.*, families having a common origin, and settled in the same part of the country.[117] A custom may be proved by general evidence as to its existence by members of the tribe or family who would naturally be cognizant of its existence, and its exercise without controversy.[118] This may be said to be the effect of Ss. 48 and 49 of the Evidence Act.[119]

Decisions of courts regarding a custom are relevant under S.42 of the Indian Evidence Act, though under that section they are not conclusive.[120] It has been held again and again that where a custom is repeatedly brought to the notice of the courts, the courts may hold that custom was introduced into the law and that no further proof was necessary of the custom in each case.[121] This is the effect of S.57 of the Evidence Act according to which nothing need be proved of which courts can take judicial notice. Therefore, a custom by repeated recognition by courts becomes entitled to judicial notice.[122]

Very great reliance has often been placed by the courts on *wajib-ul-arz* or *riwaz-i-am* for proof of customs. Those are village administration papers which were directed to be prepared by Regulation VII of 1822. These papers have been received in evidence under S.35 of the Indian Evidence Act which says that "An entry in any public or other official book, register, or record stating a fact in issue or relevant fact, and made by a public servant in the discharge of his official duties, or by any other person in performance of a duty specially enjoined by law of the country in which such book, register or record is kept, is itself a relevant fact. The *riwaz-i-am* is a public document or record and is admissible in evidence to prove the facts entered thereon subject to rebuttal.[123] The statements therein may be accepted even if unsupported by instances, as the Supreme Court has emphasized that "the fact that the entries therein are the result of careful research of persons who might also be considered to have become experts in these matters after an open public inquiry, has given them a value which should not be lightly underestimated.[124] Thus an entry in the *wajib-ul-arz* or *riwaz-i-am* may be given in evidence as a relevant fact because being made by a public officer, it contains an entry of a fact which is relevant.

These documents contain a record of customs prevalent in the villages in respect of whom they are prepared. The manner to prepare these papers with respect to custom appears to be that the officer recorded the statements of persons who were connected with the villages. Some of the persons whose evidence is taken may be the proprietors of villages who made statements declaring the existence of the custom in question.[125]

Entries in these documents constitute a *prima facie* evidence of the customs,[126] but it is not conclusive and it may be rebutted by other reliable evidence.[127] Also, the weight to be attached to the documents depends upon their intrinsic quality. As the Privy Council has stated, its weight may be very slight or may be considerable according to circumstances.[128] A *wajib-ul-arz*, as stated by the Privy Council in *Balgobind v. Badri Prasad*,[129] when properly used, affords most valuable evidence of custom and is much more reliable than oral evidence given after the event. On the other hand, as observed by the Privy Council in *Uman*

Parshad v. *Gandharp Singh*,[130] they at times contain statements which would appear to have been concocted by the persons making them in their own interest and are therefore to be disregarded, being worse than useless. With this precaution taken, the courts have depended on the records and decided a large number of cases on the bases of the entries therein of the customs without calling for any additional supporting evidence.[131] And they regard the record as more valuable and reliable than subsequent oral evidence given by the parties after a dispute as to custom has arisen. The evidentiary value of these documents can be shaken by showing that the officer preparing them neglected his duties or was misled in recording a custom. In *Uman Parshad.* v. *Gandharp Singh*,[132] the Privy Council refused to treat *wajib-ul-arz* as authoritative because it found that it was a concoction and was made at the instance of one of the parties to the dispute and that her views were entered in the record not as her views but as the official record of a custom. This, however, is an extreme case of its kind. Invariably, the courts follow these documents as evidencing custom and rarely has the basis or the authenticity of these documents ever been challenged. It may however be noted that courts have held that presumption in favour of customs as recorded in these documents would be weak where women are adversely affected as they have no opportunity to appear before revenue officers[133] and only a few instances would suffice to rebut it.

Further manuals of customary law in accordance with *riwaz-i-am* have been issued by authority for each district which stand on much the same footing as the *riwaz-i-am* itself as evidence of custom. Even if there be no evidence of instances, still for the custom mentioned in the manual of the customary law of the district, there is sufficient *prima facie* evidence of the existence of the custom, subject, of course, to rebuttal, and that it ought not to be held insufficient merely for want of instance.[134]

The inhabitants of the Kumaon Hills, known as Khasis, are governed by customs which are at variance with the Mitakshara on many points. As usual when any case came from this territory for decision, the court demanded strict proof of the custom and at times ignorant and simple people could not always muster sufficient proof to prove their customs. As a result, the people suffered injustice because many of their customs failed to get recognition at the hands of the courts. The U.P. Government felt that it was inequitable and imposing an impossible task to require the people of Kumaon, unsophisticated and uneducated as they were, to make them adduce proof to establish their customs and, therefore, it undertook to investigate and ascertain the customs of these people. In 1919, the Government appointed Shri Panna Lal, I. C. S., to make a collection of local customs of Kumaon and the result was the *Hindu Customary Law in Kumaon* published in 1920 by the authority of the

Government. This book has been held to be admissible in evidence in the courts under S. 35 of the Indian Evidence Act as it was compiled by making a local inquiry into the actual existing customs of the people.[135]

Besides the above-mentioned official attempts at ascertaining the customs of the people, some private attempts have been made in that direction. Based on the *riwaz-i-ams* and the judicial decisions, some treatises came to be prepared by scholars. One such book was brought out by Mr. William Rattigan in 1880 containing customs of the Punjab; it has run into several editions since its publication, and has assumed a great authority in matters of Punjab Customary Law, so much so that it has been noticed even by the Privy Council in *Mt. Subhani* v. *Nawab*,[136] as a book "of unquestioned authority in Punjab". This Digest of Customary Law has invariably been cited in judicial decisions. The Supreme Court has recently stated that the authoritative value of Rattigan's Compilation of Customary Law is now beyond controversy, having been recognised by the Punjab courts and even by the Privy Council.[137] But where there is a conflict between *riwaz-i-am* and Rattigan's Digest, the entries in the former ordinarily prevail. In Jammu and Kashmir, the High Court has referred to Sant Ram Dogra's *Code of Tribal Custom*.[138]

There is some difference of opinion in the judgments of the Privy Council itself over the question whether questions of the existence of an ancient custom are generally questions of law or are mixed questions of law and fact or simply of fact. In *Palaniappa Chetty* v. *Deivasikamony Pandara*[139], the Privy Council held it as a mixed question of law and fact. In several other cases, it held it to be a question of fact only.[139a]

VIII

Abrogation of Custom

While it was the settled policy of the British administration to preserve customs of the people in the administration of justice, there were certain forces which were working for their abrogation. One such effort, on a very big scale, was made through the Muslim Shariat Act, 1937, which abrogated custom applicable to Muhammadans and restored to them their personal law. Except agricultural land, all questions regarding intestate succession, special property of females, including personal property inherited or obtained under contract or gift or any other provision of personal law, marriage, dissolution of marriage, including *talaq, ila, zihar, lian, khula* and *mubarrat*, maintenance, dower, guardianship, gifts, trust and trust property, and *wakfs* (other than charities and charitable institutions and charitable and religious endowments) the rule of decision in cases where the parties are Muslims should be the Muslim Personal Law (Shariat).[140] Option was given to the Muslims to adopt the personal law in preference to their customary law in matters pertaining to adoption,[141] wills and legacies. The provisions of S. 2 are coercive, while those of S. 3 are persuasive. The reasons which were given to abrogate custom were 'uncertainty and the expense of ascertaining custom' and 'inadequate rights granted to women under the customary law as compared to the Muslim law'. It was pleaded that customary law was uncertain and indefinite whereas the Muslim personal law existed in the form of a veritable code and was too well-known to admit of any doubt or to entail any great labour in the shape of research, and so abolition of customs would ensure certainty and definiteness to the mutual rights and obligations of the public. This argument, of course, may not stand the test of scrutiny. But a much more sound reason to abrogate custom was that under it the position of women in matters of inheritance was inferior to that under the Muslim law. The general rule of intestate succession under custom was agnatic succession which excluded all females except a widow and daughter who were allowed a life interest or maintenance. The Muslim personal law accords a better position to women. The abrogation of customary law was a result of the agitation carried on by such bodies as the Jamiat-ul-Ulema-i-Hind, an organisation of Muslim religious men. Support was lent by many Muslim Women Organisations which condemned the customary law as adversely affecting their rights.

With a view to introducing uniformity in, and to liberalize, the law applicable to the Hindus, certain portions of it have been codified recently. By far and large, the effect of this legislation has been to reduce the importance of custom though it is not correct to say that custom has been completely abrogated. Some force is still given to customary law. Thus while S.4(a) of the Hindu Marriage Act, 1955, gives overriding effect to the Act, and abrogates a custom with respect to any matter for which the Act makes a provision, customs in respect of following matters have been left intact, *viz.*, recognition of marriage between parties within degrees of prohibited relationship, and *sapinda*ship,[142] rites and ceremonies regarding celebration of marriage,[143] divorces and thus a customary right to obtain dissolution of a Hindu marriage is not abrogated.[144]

Section 4 of the Hindu Succession Act, 1956, provides for the overriding effect of the Act in respect of matters dealt with by it. Any custom inconsistent with it is abrogated. The Act does not recognise impartibility except that created by *sanad* or government grant. Impartibility by custom has now been abrogated and succession to such property would now be regulated by the rules which apply to other property.[145] Custom regarding power of disposal is not abrogated; whether a person has power to dispose his property by will is a matter outside the Succession Act; it is to be decided by reference to custom.[146]

Similarly, S. 4 of the Hindu Adoptions and Maintenance Act, 1956, gives overriding effect to the Act. On two matters, however, customs have been saved: Adoption of a married person or of a person over 15 years of age, only if custom permits.

Concluding Remarks

The foregoing survey would show that, after the advent of the British in India, custom came to be given a place of honour in the administration of justice. A large volume of case-law arose in India having a bearing on custom. Custom came to play a very important part as a source of law; it took a place second only to the statutory law; custom was given preference over the religious laws of the parties. This was a reasonable and just approach for, in practice, the law of the *shastra* and the *shara* was not observed by the people in all its pristine purity and that all kinds of customs had ingrained themselves in the scheme of things. It was only just and equitable that the customs which people had been observing in practice be enforced rather than the theoretical law contained in the books; it would have been harsh with the people to force them to forego their customs in favour of the orthodox system of law.

All kinds of customs—family, local, tribal—came to be applied. Formally, the tests applied to adjudge the legal enforceability of a custom were the same as those laid down in England, but in their practical application, they were not rigidly enforced, and the courts showed a great amount of flexibility of approach and toleration towards customs. Thus about the qualification that a custom to be applicable should be antiquated, we have already seen the liberality of approach which the courts adopted towards this maxim in India, and, in a large number of cases, customs were enforced when there was evidence of their operation over a period of twenty years or so. This is not so in England where a custom must be in existence since 1189 A.D. Similarly, the courts, earlier in the day, declared that they would not insist upon technical methods of proof, and many customs were held proved even though the quantity and quality of evidence in support of them left something to desire.[147] Further, in England, there is nothing like a family or a tribal custom; there the custom is 'local' having the force of law in a particular locality. But in India, it is not so; here family customs came to be fully recognised and enforced. Similarly, the communal or tribal customs were enforced, whereas such would not be the case in England. It may be noted that a large mass of custom here is tribal or sectarian.

In England, the term 'usage' is used for a general line of conduct adopted by persons in a particular department of business life. In India, the term 'usage' has been used in a completely different sense. Usages accepted by the courts have had nothing to do with trade or commerce but covered all aspects of family relations. By and large, the term 'usage' has been used synonymously and interchangeably with custom. Bombay Regulation IV of 1827 speaks of the 'usage of the country', the Punjab Act, 1872, of the 'customs of the parties'. In the recent Hindu legislation, customs and usage have been defined in the same way. In some earlier cases, it was said that a custom is a usage of long standing,[148] but, in effect, it makes no difference, for in India the rule of immemorial antiquity does not operate, and a usage of twenty years standing even if it may not be characterised as custom, is followed nevertheless.

Another doctrine adopted in India, for which no parallel can be found in England, is that a family can renounce customs applicable to it and adopt other customs.[149] Another English rule was held not applicable to India which is that if a custom was alleged as applicable to a particular district, and the evidence tendered in its support proved that the rights claimed had been enjoyed by the people outside the district, the custom would fail.[150]

The looseness with which the English tests of a valid custom were applied in India had a good result in the formative stages of the judicial system, for, that way most of the customary law of the people was preserved. Even in matters of proof, the courts were not very technical or scrutinising.[151] Had those tests been rigidly applied, most of the customary law would have disappeared resulting in great injustice to the unsophisticated people; it would have created a great void in the judicial system because in the early British days the legislature was not active, did not enact laws in the area of private law, and judges had to decide cases, in the absence of law, by justice, equity and good conscience. In part, the judicial attitude of tolerance and indulgence to custom may be explained by the fact that the legislature being inactive, and there being no *lex loci* in the county, if customs were rejected on technical grounds, there would be no law to apply and the courts would be forced to invent principles to decide cases. Rather than resort to principles borrowed from a foreign Jurisprudence and unknown to people, it was better to enforce such customs as were available even though they might not fulfill all the rigours of English law. The judicial attitude was thus to some extent born out of necessity of the situation. This attitude towards custom did introduce an element of uncertainty and confusion as to the rights of individuals but that was for long the bane of the

Indian legal system, and this uncertainty was not so dangerous as would have arisen had the customs been abrogated and principles foreign to the people introduced.

Not only were customs recognised and legally enforced, a great effort was made to ascertain them and to reduce them in writing. It was done administratively, like compilation of *riwaz-i-am*, in addition to what happened judicially when a custom was held proved. Thus the customs which so long had been unwritten, and lived in the consciousness of the people, became certain and written. This made the system more definite, but it did, on the other hand, stereotype the customs; the element of flexibility and growth disappeared; customary law became rigid and lost its capacity of organic growth. Thereafter, the system could grow and be developed by legislation, and it was not the policy of the British administration to interfere with the personal laws of the people except when there was public opinion for it. To take an example, in the area of Muslim law, the Shariat Act was passed as a result of the demand of the Muslim people. This Act abrogated, to a large extent, custom modifying the Muslim law. In the area of Hindu law reformative legislation was undertaken from time to time as a result of public opinion, which abrogated custom as well as regarded Hindu law as backward. One difference of approach between Hindus and Muslims may however be underlined. Whereas custom was abrogated to restore orthodox Muslim personal law, there is no example where a custom was abrogated to restore a principle of *Dharmashastra*. Whatever changes were made were to reform Hindu law and to that extent, custom or text, whatever came in the way was abrogated. So much so, that through recent Hindu legislation, Hindu law has been codified and reformed and made uniform throughout the country, certain customs have been still preserved even at the cost of uniformity.

It appears that customs have had their heyday and they have practically exhausted their efficacy as law-creating agency. They have now ceased to act as a fruitful agency of law reform. It is difficult for new customs to get recognition from the courts. Their ascertainment has also led to their fixity. The future legal growth in India will be mostly due to legislation, and to some extent, judicial interpretation and precedent, though comparatively, the latter would be less important than the former. And, usually, when a new legislation is passed custom to that extent is abrogated as is depicted by the recent Hindu legislation. This trend, however, is in line with the developments which have taken place in every complex society, where the custom becomes less effective. The test of custom is continued observance and customs *ex hypothesi* cannot be suddenly created to meet a new problem. Custom is useful for situations which have already occurred, but cannot create a rule to deal with a future difficulty.

The predominance of custom makes the system less uniform; it varies from family to family, from region to region and from community to community. It places a double burden on the judiciary which has to decide not only questions of fact, but also to take evidence to decide the existence and content of the custom alleged to be applicable to the facts. Judicial proceedings thus become dilatory and time-consuming. It becomes expensive for the parties for they have to produce witnesses not only to testify to the facts of the case but also to custom. Till a custom is judicially accepted, its position remains vague and indefinite for no one can feel sure whether the custom would be accepted as valid or not. All these considerations point to one inevitable result—abrogation of custom and enactment of legislation instead. This has already been achieved to some extent. As time passes on, custom is bound to lose its pre-eminent position which it has enjoyed so long in India. It was inevitable till the legal system itself was in its formative stages. But when the legal system has achieved maturity, people have also become sophisticated and literate and, therefore, time is ripe for uniform legislation and abolition of custom. In every mature and developed system, custom plays a very minor role. Take the example of England. There is one other very important reason as to why custom should now be abrogated. Most of the customs are tribal and communal or sectarian, and so long as custom survives, these class distinctions are also bound to survive. It would lead to a better integration of the people, if the sense of separation of each community arising out of its distinctive customs were removed. As it happens, in every progressive society, custom ceases to play an important role after a stage of social evolution is reached which appears to have been reached in India. It may be that customs of certain tribes may have to be preserved for a little longer time, the Constitution seeks to do that with respect to certain very backward areas like NEFA and Nagaland. These people are in a backward state of evolution, and their modes should not be changed suddenly till they have reached a stage of evolution where they can assimilate new ideas and principles and give up their habitual and traditional patterns without much violence to their feelings and susceptibilities. But, as regards the rest of the people, these considerations do not prevail; and with them, no justification to keep their disparate customs appears to be imperative any longer.

Notes

1. Vinogradoff, *Collected Papers* 420. As Paton observes, "Indeed custom is coeval with the very birth of the community itself". *Jurisprudence* 143 (2nd ed. 1951). Even a primitive tribe may have a legal order long before it has developed a state. (1941) 55 *Harv. L. R.* 66–7.
2. 2 Newman, *Miscellaneous Lectures* 166; Spencer, *Study of Sociology* 108.
3. 1 Stephen's *Commentaries* 2, 19; 1 Pollock & Maitland, *History of English Law* 106, 183–8, 623 (2nd ed. 1952).
4. Paton, *Jurisprudence* 148 (2nd ed. 1961). "Mercantile Law, perhaps, provides one of the most interesting examples of custom". Keeton, *The Elementary Principles of Jurisprudence* 77, 81 (2nd ed. 1949).
5. Maine, *Ancient Law* 18 (1946)
6. According to Austin, nothing is entitled to the name 'Law' which does not possess all the attributes of state-created and state-enforced law and so, on this approach, logically, one shall have to say that customary law is not law at all, or that it is 'imperfect' or 'inchoate' law.
7. Holland, *The Elements of Jurisprudence* 53, 55, (8th ed. 1896).
8. Allen, *Law in the Making* 67, 125–151 (5th ed. 1951).
9. Keeton, *The Elementary Principles of Jurisprudence* 77 (2nd ed. 1949).
10. Kantorowicz, "Savigny and the Historical School of Law", (1937) 53 *L.Q.R.* 326. Thibaut seems to concede to each class of persons a power of establishing the law by their own will, but he mentions certain restrictions to narrow down the power materially. "Custom is, for the people that has established it, a mirror in which that people may recognise itself", says Puchta. To Puchta, custom was not only self-sufficient and independent of legislative authority but was a condition precedent, of all sound legislation.
11. Vrihaspati, Narada, Asahaya were in favour of unqualified acceptance of custom even when they were in conflict with the written laws. Some of the *smritis* underlined the significance of customs by saying that suppression of customs would give rise to resentment and rebellion.
12. Kane, *Hindu Customs and Modern Law* 33 (1950).
13. *Bhyah Ram Singh* v. *Bhyah Ugur Singh*, (1870) 13 M.I.A. 373, at 390.
14. As observed in *Muthukaruppa* v. *Sellathammal*, (1916) I.L.R. 39 Mad. 298, at 301, "The commentaries indicate an attempt to reconcile the text law with the actual usages of the people". In *Rutcheputty* v. *Rajunder*, (1839) 2 M.I.A. 132, the Privy Council has stated that different schools of law chiefly arose from the difference of local custom; the propounders of law interpreted the ancient texts in such a way as to make them harmonize with local usages, in other words, they had to harmonize the written with the unwritten. In *Balwant Rao* v. *Baji Rao*, (1921) I.L.R. 48 Cal. 30, at 41, the Privy Council said that "the commentators do not enact, they explain and are evidence of the congeries of customs which form the law". In *Jogdamba* v. *S.S.*, (1889) I.L.R. 16 Cal. 367, at 375 the Calcutta High Court remarked, "The truth is that commentaries and digests ... owe their binding force not to their promulgation by any sovereign authority, but to the respect due to their authors, and still more to the fact of their being in accordance with prevailing popular sentiment and practice. Their doctrines

may often have moulded usage, but still more frequently they have themselves been moulded according to prevailing usage of which they are only the recorded expression".

15. Abdur Rahim, *Muhammadan Jurisprudence* 55, 136, 137 (1958); Tyabji, *Principles of Muhammadan Law* 415 (3rd ed. 1940).

16. Jain, *Outlines of Indian Legal History* 115, 122 (1952).

17. *Supra* 16, at 64.

18. *Supra* 16, at 137.

19. *Collector of Madura* v. *Moottoo Ramalinga*, (1868) 12 M.I.A. 397, at 436; *Bhyah Ram Singh* v. *Bhyah Ugur Singh*, (1870) 13 M.I.A. 373, at 390.

20. (1869) 12 M.I.A. 523.

21. *Supra* note 12.

22. *Hirbae* v. *Sonabae*, 4 Ind. Dec. 100, 112.

23. As late as 1866, the Privy Council in *Jowala Buksh* v. *Dharum Singh*, (1866) 10 M.I.A. 511, at 538 stated: "Whether it is competent for a family converted from the Hindoo to the Mahomedan faith to retain for several generations Hindoo usages and customs, and by virtue of that retention to set up for itself a special and customary law of inheritance, is a question which, so far as their Lordships are aware, has never been decided. It is not absolutely necessary for the determination of this appeal to decide that question in the negative, and their Lordships abstain from doing so".

24. (1901) I.L.R. 23 All. 20. The High Court said that the terms of the provision in question were very positive and emphatic in terms that Muhammadan law was to be applied to the Muhammadans. The language of the provision was contrasted with S.5 of the Punjab Laws Act, 1872, which has been discussed below.

25. 1 F. B. Rulings, N. W. P. (1866), also, *Jowala Buksh* v. *Dharum Singh*, (1866) 10 M.I.A. 511, at 538.

26. 17 C.W.N. 97.

27. *Ali Asghar* v. *Collector of Bulandshahar*, (1917) I.L.R. 39 All. 574; *Mt. Jaffro* v. *Chatta*, 163 I. C. 650; *Roshan Ali Khan* v. *Chaudhri Asghar Ali*, (1929) 57 I.A. 29. In *Md. Ibrahim* v. *Shaik Ibrahim* A.I.R. 1922 P.C. 59, it was stated that in India "custom plays a large part in modifying the ordinary law, and it is now established that there may be a custom at variance even with the rules of Mahomedan Law, governing the succession in a particular community of Mahomedans".

28. Sir George Campbell, Lt. Governor of Bengal, who had served in Punjab earlier, observed in the Legislative Council that not one out of a hundred persons in the Punjab was governed by the strict provisions of the Hindu and Muhammadan law.

29. The section runs as follows : "In questions regarding succession, special property of females, betrothal, marriage, dower, adoption, guardianship, minority, bastardy, family relations, wills, legacies, gifts, partition, or any religious usage or institution, the rule of decision shall be—(a) any custom applicable to the parties concerned which is not contrary to justice, equity and good conscience, and has not been declared to be void by any competent authority, (b) the Mohammedan law, in cases where the parties are Hindus except insofar as such

law has been altered or abolished by legislative enactment, or is opposed to the provisions of this Act, or is modified by any such custom as is referred to in the preceding clause of this section".
30. (1917) 45 I.A. 10.
31. Also, *Vaishno Ditti* v. *Rameshri*, (1928) 55 I.A. 407, at 421; *Salig Ram* v. *Munshi Ram*, A.I.R. 1961 S.C. 1374.
32. *Ujagar* v. *Mst. Jeo*, A.I.R. 1959 S.C. 1041.
33. *Ramkishore* v. *Jainarayan*, (1921) 48 I.A. 405.
34. *Roshan Ali Khan* v. *Chaudhri Ashgar Ali*, (1929) 57 I.A. 29, at 33.
35. Section 5.
36. *Krishnan* v. *Sridevi*, (1889) I.L.R. 12 Mad. 512.
37. *Parandhamayya* v. *Navaratna Sikhamani*, A. I. R. 1949 Mad. 825; *Venkata Subba Rao* v. *Bhujangayya*, A.I.R. 1960 A.P. 412.
38. *Supra* note 28–36.
39. See *supra* note 37.
40. (1947) 74 I.A. 254; A.I.R. 1948 P.C. 177; *Sheo Singh Rai* v. *Mussumut Dakho*, (1878) 5 I.A. 87; *Chotay Lal Case*, (1878) 6 I.A. 15.
41. A.I.R. 1962 S.C. 1493.
42. *Sheo Singh Ral* v. *Mussumut Dakho*, (1876–1878) I. L. R. 1 All. 688; *Shimbhu Nath* v. *Gayan Chand*, (1894) I. L. R. 16 All, 379; *Chotay Lall* v. *Chunnoo Lall*, (1879) I.L.R. 4 Cal. 744, at 752.
43. *Palanjappa Chettiar* v. *Alayan Chetti*, (1921) 48 I.A. 539.
44. *Thiruthipalli Raman Menon* v. *Variangattil Palisseri Raman Menon*, (1900) 27 I.A. 231.
45. 3 Mad. H.C.R. 50.
46. The same view was reiterated in 6 Mad. H.C.R. 93.
47. 1 Bom. H.C.R., app. XLII.
48. (1868) 12 M.I.A. 81, at 91. To the same effect were the observations of the Privy Council in *Serumah* v. *Palathan*, 15 Cal. W. Rep. P.C. 4.
49. (1863) 9 M.I.A. 199. In this case the parties were left free to adopt the law. It was also seen that Thibaut supports the view that a family is capable of making an applicable custom.
50. *Shidhojiray* v. *Naikojiray*, 10 Bom. H. C. R., 228; *Bhau Nanaji Utpat* v. *Sundrabal*, 11 Bom. H.C.R.249. The Court held that the words usage of the country in Reg. IV of 1827 are sufficiently general to allow either of a very large or restricted application.
51. *Kunwar Basant Singh* v. *Kunwar Brij Raj Saran Singh*, (1935) 62 I.A. 180.
52. *Katama Natchiar* v. *Rajah of Shivagunga*, (1864) 9 M.I.A. 543; *Shiba Prasad Singh* v. *Prayag Kumari Debi*, (1932) 59 I.A. 331; *Baboo Gunesh Dutt Singh* v. *Maharaja Moheshur Singh*, (1855) 6 M.I.A. 154; *Mohesh Chunder Dhal* v. *Satrughan Dhal*, (1902) 29 I.A. 62, at 68; *Rawut Urjun Singh* v. *Rawut Ghunsiam Singh*, (1851) 5 M.I.A. 169. See, *Customs and Customary Law in British India*, 43–88 (1910).
53. *Rama Rao* v. *Raja of Pittapur*, (1918) 45 I.A. 148.
54. *Veerapa Naidu* v. *Nenkaiah*, A.I.R. 1961 A.P. 534.
55. *Manik Chand* v. *Jagat*, (1890) I.L.R. 17 Cal. 518
56. *Roshan Ali Khan* v. *Chaudhri Ashgar Ali*, (1929) 57 I.A. 29.

57. (1932) 59 I.A. 331.
58. *Soorendronath* v. *Heeramonee*, (1868) 12 M.I.A. 81, at 91; *Lekhraj Kunwar* v. *Harpal Singh*, (1911) 39 I.A. 10: *Rajkishen* v. *Ramjoy*, (1876) I.L.R. 1 Cal. 186; *Sarabjit* v. *Indarjit*, (1905) I.L.R. 27 All. 203; *Vannikone* v. *Vannichi Ammal*, (1928) I.L.R. 51 Mad. 1: *Baboo Beer Pertab Sahee* v. *Maharajah Rajender Pertab Sahee*, (1867) 12 M.I.A. 1.
59. *Audh Behari* v. *Gajadhar*, A.I.R. 1954 S.C. 417; *Sheo Kumar* v. *Smt. Sudama Devi*, A.I.R. 1962 Pat. 125; A.I.R. 1958 S.C. 838; *Bhimrao* v. *Patilbua Ramkishan*, A.I.R. 1960 Bom. 552. In view of Art. 19 (1)(f) of the Constitution, the law of pre-emption has been affected to some extent.
60. *Keshab Sahu* v. *Dasaratha Sahu*, A.I.R. 1961 Orissa 154.
61. *Bholanath Nundi* v. *Midnapore Zemindari Company Limited*, (1904) 31 I.A. 75.
62. *Ramzan Momin* v. *Dasrath Raut*, A.I.R. 1953 Pat. 138; *Mohidin* v. *Shivlingappa*, (1899) I.L.R. 23 Bom. 666.
63. *Bari w/o Rajeshwar* v. *Tukaram* A.I.R. 1959 Bom. 54.
64. *Narasappa* v. *Nanjappa*, A.I.R. 1955 Mys. 62.
65. *Arjun* v. *Manoranjam*, A.I.R. 1934 Cal. 461.
66. *Maharaj Bahadur* v. *Gandauri Singh*, A.I.R. 1917 Pat. 640.
67. *Bari w/o Rajeshwar* v. *Tukaram*, A.I.R. 1959 Bom. 54. The Court held in this case that the members of the Kumhar community living in a village did not form a 'fluctuating body.' The Privy Council's view, ref. *supra* 61, also supports this view.
68. *Ramalakshmi Ammal* v. *Sivanantha Perumal Sethurayar*, (1872) 14 M.I.A. 570; *Hurpurshad* v. *Sheo Dyal*, (1876) 3 I.A. 259; *Abdul Hussein Khan* v. *Bibi Sona Dero*, (1917) 45 I.A. 10: *Wolsanton Ltd.* v. *Newcastle Under-Lyme Corporation*, (1940) A.C. 860, at 876.
69. Section 3 (a) of the Hindu Marriage Act: S. 3 (1)(d) of the Hindu Succession Act.
70. *Subraya Pillai* v. *Srinivasa Pillai*, 3 Mad. H.C.R. 75, at 77. aff. by P. C. in *Rama* v. *Siva*, (1872) 14 M.I.A. 570. Also *Shidhojirav* v. *Naikojirav*, 10 Bom. H.C.R. 228, at 234.
71. *Chinnammal* v. *Varadarajulu*, (1892) I.L.R. 15 Mad. 307.
72. *Bholonath Nundi* v. *Midnapore Zemindary Company Limited*, (1904) 31 I.A. 75.
73. Lord Blakburn in *Dalton* v. *Angus* (1880–81) 6 A.C. 740, at 811; *Wolstanton Ltd.* v. *Newcastle Under-Lyme Corporation*, (1940) A.C. 860. The courts, however, have decided that in the case of an alleged custom it is sufficient to prove facts from which it may be presumed that the custom existed at that remote date and this presumption should in general be raised by evidence showing continuous user as of right going as far back as living testimony can go. This presumption is rebuttable. (1940) A.C 860, at 876.
74. *Hurpurshad* v. *Sheo Dyal*, (1876) 3 I. A. 259, at 285; *Ramalakshmi Ammal* v. *Sivanantha Perumal Sethurayar*, (1872) 14 M.I.A. 570, at 585–86.
75. *Kuar Sen* v. *Mamman*, (1895) I.L.R. 17 All. 87.
76. *Saladurjaman* v. *Oazaddin*, A.I.R. 1937 Cal. 46.

77. *Ambalika Dasi* v. *Aparna Dasi*, (1918) I.L.R. 45 Cal. 835, also *Nolin Behari* v. *Hari Pada Bhuia*, A.I.R. 1934 Supreme Cal. 452, *Jagmohan* v. *Srimati Monty*, Cases of Hindu Law 596 (1831). 1773 A.D. is the date when the Supreme Court was established in Calcutta; 1793 A.D. is the date when Cornwallis introduced his judicial plan for the administration of justice in the Provinces of Bengal, Bihar, and Orissa and made the permanent settlement of Bengal. Jain, *Outlines of Indian Legal History* 63, 74 (1952).
78. *Parshottam Ganpat* v. *Venichand Ganpat*, (1921) I.L.R. 45 Bom. 754.
79. (1940) 68 I.A. 1, at 31, A.I.R. 1941 P.C. 21.
80. *Baba Narayan* v. *Saboosa*, A.I.R. 1943 P. C. 111; *Lakshmidhar Mishra* v. *Rangalal*, A.I.R. 1950 P.C. 56; *Ramanand* v. *Suraj Prasad*, A.I.R. 1961 Pat. 101.
81. *Kunwar Basant Singh* v. *Kunwar Brij Raj Saran Singh*, (1935) 62 I.A. 180.
82. *Gokal Chand* v. *Parvin Kumari*, A.I.R. 1952 S.C. 231.
83. The case of *Kamma Community*, *infra* note 113; *Venkata Subba Rao* v. *Bhujangayya*, A.I.R. 1960 A.P. 412.
84. *Musammat Subhani* v. *Nawab*, (1940) 68 I.A. 1; *Rup Chand* v. *Jambu Parshad*, (1909) 37 I.A. 93.
85. *Biswanath* v. *Dhapu Devi*, A.I.R. 1960 Cal. 494.
86. A.I.R. 1959 Bom. 54.
87. A.I.R. 1928 Nag. 87.
88. It is from the canon law that the Western Jurists have imported the qualification that the custom must not be unreasonable.
89. *Ram Dhan Lal* v. *Radhe Sham*, 1951 S.C.J. 307, at 311.
90. In *Wolstanton Ltd.* v. *Newscatle Under-Lyme Corporation*, (1940) A.C. 860, the House of Lords held that a custom for the lord to get minerals beneath the surface of copyholds or customary freehold lands without making compensation for subsidence and damage to buildings, was not a reasonable custom.
91. *Shibnarain Mookerjee* v. *Bhutnath Guchait*, (1918) I.L.R. 45 Cal. 475.
92. *Saladurjaman* v. *Oazaddin*, A.I.R. 1937 Cal. 46; *Bholanath Nundi* v. *Midnapore Zemindary Company Limited*, (1904) 31 I.A. 75.
93. *Palaniappa Chettiar* v. *Chockalingam Chetti*, (1929) 57 M.L.J. 817; *Muharram Ali* v. *Barkat Ali*, (1930) I.L.R. 12 Lah. 286, following *Arthur* v. *Bokenham*, 88 E.R. 957.
94. *Thangavelu* v. *Court of Wards*, A.I.R. 1947 Mad. 38; *Chelladoral* v. *Chinnathambiar*, A.I.R. 1961 Mad. 42, at 46.
95. See Punjab Laws Act.
96. (1936) 63 I.A. 295.
97. Cited in the case mentioned in *infra* note 98.
98. (1880) I.L.R. 4 Bom, 545.
99. *Shanmugathammal* v. *Gomathi Ammal*, (1934) 67 M.L.J. 861.
100. *Narayan* v. *Laving*, (1878) I.L.R. 2 Bom. 140; *Uji* v. *Hathi*, (1870) 7 Bom. H.C. 133; *Venkata Krishnayya* v. *Lakshmi Narayana*, (1909) I.L.R. 32 Mad. 185.
101. *Keshav Hargovan* v. *Bai Gandi*, (1915) I.L.R. 39 Bom. 538.
102. *Sankaralingam* v. *Subban*, (1894) I.L.R. 17 Mad. 479; *Jina Magan* v. *Bai Jethi*, (1941) 43 Bom. L.R. 651

103. *Thangammal* v. *Gengayammal*, A.I.R. 1945 Mad. 308; *Keshav Hargovan* v. *Bai Gandi*, A.I.R. 1915 Bom. 107.
104. *Nallathangal* v. *Nainan Ambalam*, A.I.R. 1960 Mad. 179.
105. *Balusami* v. *Balakrishna*, A.I.R. 1957 Mad. 97. Such a custom prevailed amongst the Reddiar Community of Tirunelveli district.
106. *Abdul Hussein Khan* v. *Bibi Sona Dero*, (1917) 45 I.A. 10; *Charman Singh* v. *Gurdial Singh*, A.I.R. 1961 Punj. 301; *Ujagar Singh* v. *Mt Jeo*, A.I.R; 1959 S.C.1041, at 1048; *Gokal Chand* v. *Parvin Kumari*, A.I.R. 1952 S.C. 231; *Bhagwan Singh* v. *Bhagwan Singh*, (1899) 26 I.A. 153; *Chandika Bakhsh* v. *Muna Kuar*, (1902) 29 I.A. 70; *Rup Chand* v. *Jambu Parshad*, (1909) 37 I.A. 93; *Sahdeo Narain* v *Kusum Kumari*, (1922) 50 I.A. 58, at 62–64.
107. *D. B. Ghorpade* v. *Vijaysinhrao*, A.I.R. 1960 S. C. 1272; *Chotay Lall* v. *Chunnolal*, (1878) 6 I.A. 15.
108. *Fanindra Deb Raikat* v. *Rajeshwar Dass*, (1885) 12 I.A. 72, at 88; *Muhammad Ibrahim Rowther* v. *Shaikh Ibrahim Rowther*, (1922) 49 I.A. 119.
109. *Ramalakshmi Ammal* v. *Sivanantha Perumal Sethurayar*, (1872) 14 M.I.A.570 adopting the statement from *Subraya Pillai* v. *Srinivasa Pillai*, 3 Mad. H.C. 75.77; affirmed by the Bombay High Court in *Shidhojiray* v. *Naikojiray*, 10 Bom. H.C.R. 228, at 234.
110. *Roshan Ali Khan* v. *Chaudhri Asghar Ali*, (1929) 57 I.A. 29; *Sivananja* v. *Muthu Ramalingam*, 3 Mad. H. C. 75, 77; *Ramalakshmi Ammal*, v. *Sivanantha Perumal Sethurayar*, (1872) 14 M.I.A. 570, 585, 586; *Hurpurshad* v. *Sheo Dyal*, (1876) 3 I.A. 259, at 285.
111. *Mohd. Jan.* v. *Rafi-ud-din*, A.I.R. 1949 P.C. 70.
112. *Saraswathi Ammal* v. *Jagadambal*, A.I.R. 1953, S.C. 201.
113. *Parndhamayya* v. *Navaratna Sikhamani*, A.I.R. 1949 Mad. 825.
114. *Venkata Subba Rao* v. *Bhujangayya*, A.I.R. 1960 A.P. 412.
115. *Ramalakshmi Ammal* v. *Sivanantha Perumal Sethurayar*, (1872) 14 M.I.A. 570, at 585; *Muharram Ali* v. *Barkat Ali*, (1930) I.L.R. 12 Lah. 286; *Palaniappa Chettiar* v. *Chokalingam Chetti*, (1929) 57 M.L.J. 817.
116. *Ahmad Khan* v. *Channi Bibi*, (1925) 52 I.A. 379; *Mohesh Chunder Dhal* v. *Satrughan Dhal*, (1902) 29 I.A. 62; *Vaishno Ditti* v. *Rameshri*, (1928) 55 I.A. 407, at 421.
117. *Mohesh Chunder Dhal* v. *Satrughan Dhal*, (1902) 29 I.A. 62; *Roshan Ali Khan* v. *Chaudhri Asghar Ali*, (1929) 57 I.A. 29.
118. *Ahmad Khan* v. *Channi Bibi*, (1925) 52 I.A. 379; *Gokal Chand* v. *Parvin Kumari*, A.I.R. 1952 S.C. 231.
119. Section 48 runs as follows: "When the court has to form an opinion as to the existence of any general custom or right, the opinions, as to the existence of such custom or right of persons who would be likely to know of its existence if it existed, are relevant." Section 49 runs as: "When the court has to form an opinion as to the usages and tenets of any body of man or family, ... the opinions of persons having special means of knowledge therein, are relevant facts".
120. *Sundrabai* v. *Hanmant Gurnath*, (1932) I.L.R. 56 Bom. 298.

121. *Rama Rao* v. *Raja of Pittapur*, (1918) 45 I.A. 148; *Munnalal* v. *Raj Kumar*, A.I.R. 1962 S.C. 1493; *Krishnamurthi Ayyar* v. *Krishnamurthi Ayyar*, (1927) 54 I.A. 248; *Effuah Amissiah* v. *Effuah Krabah*, A.I.R. 1936 P.C. 147.
122. *Ujagar Singh* v. *Mst. Jeo*, A.I.R. 1959 S.C. 1041.
123. *Beg* v. *Allah Ditta*, (1916) 44 I.A. 89; *Abdul Hussein Khan* v. *Bibi Sona Dero*, (1917) 45 I.A. 10; *Ahmad Khan* v. *Channi Bibi*, (1925) 52 I.A. 379; *Kunwar Basant Singh* v. *Kunwar Brij Raj Saran Singh*, (1935) 62 I.A. 192; *Vaishno Ditti* v. *Rameshri*, (1928) 55 I.A. 407.
124. *Jau Kaur* v. *Sher Singh*, A.I.R. 1960 S.C. 1118.
125. *Rani Lekraj Kaur* v. *Baboo Mahpal Singh*, (1879) 7 I.A. 63, at 69.
126. *Muhammad Imam Ali Khan* v. *Sardar Husain Khan*, (1898) 25 I. A. 161; *Parbati Kunwar* v. *Chandarpal Kunwar*, (1909) 36 I.A. 125, at 135; *Thakur Nitrpal Singh* v. *Thakur Jai Singh Pal*, (1896) 23 I.A. 147; *Digambar Singh* v. *Ahmad Said Khan*, (1914) 42 I.A.10; *Balgobind* v. *Badri Prasad*, (1923) 50 I.A. 196; *Sheobaran Singh* v. *Kulsum-un-nissa*, (1927) 54 I.A. 204; *Jai Kaur* v. *Sher Singh*, A.I.R. 1960 S.C. 1118; *Salig Ram* v. *Munshi Ram*, A.I.R. 1961 S.C. 1374.
127. *Beg* v. *Allah Ditta*, (1916) 44 I.A.89.
128. *Muhammad Imam Ali Khan* v. *Sardar Husain Khan*, (1898) 25 I.A. 161.
129. (1923) 50 I.A. 196.
130. (1887) 14 I.A. 127.
131. *Thakur Nitrpal Singh* v. *Thakur Jai Singh Pal*, (1896) 23 I. A. 147; *Rani Lekraj Kaur* v. *Baboo Mahpal Singh*, (1879) 7 I. A. 63; *Bishwa Nath Singh* v. *Jugal Kishore*, (1923) 50 I.A. 179; *Balgobind* v. *Badri Prasad*, (1923) 50 I.A. 196.
132. (1887) 14 I.A. 134.
133. *Mt. Subhani* v. *Nawab*, A.I.R. 1941, P.C. 21; *Jai Kaur* v. *Sher Singh*, A.I.R. 1960 S.C. 1118; *Salig Ram* v. *Munshi Ram*, A.I.R. 1961 S.C. 1374.
134. *Abdul Hussein Khan* v. *Bibi Sona Dero*, (1917) 45 I.A. 10.
135. *Bihari* v. *Harlal*, (1935) I.L.R. 57 All. 430.
136. A.I.R. 1941 P.C. 21, at 23; (1940) 68 I.A. 1.
137. *Jai Kaur* v. *Sher Singh*, A.I.R. 1960 S.C. 1118.
138. *Aziz Dar* v. *Mt. Fazli*, A.I.R. 1960 J.K. 53.
139. (1917) 44 I.A. 147.
139a. *Mohesh Chunder Dhal* v. *Satrughan Dhal*, (1902) 29 I. A. 62; *Muhammad Kamil* v. *Imtiaz Fatima*, (1908) 36 I.A. 210; *Anant Singh* v. *Durga Singh*, (1910) 37 I.A. 191; *Raja of Ramnad* v. *Mangalam*, (1930) 57 I.A. 264; *Sundralingasawmi Kamaya Naik* v. *Ramasawmi Kamaya Naik*, (1899) 26 I.A. 55; *S. K. Wodeyar* v. *Ganapati*, A.I.R. 1935 Bom. 371.
140. To a limited extent, custom was abolished by the Cutchi Memons' Act. 1920. These people were governed by the Hindu law of inheritance and succession. This Act gave them an option to place themselves under the Muslim personal law by means of a declaration and thus abrogate custom.
141. Muslim law does not recognise adoption, but custom permits adoption in Punjab. *Nur* v. *Bhawan*, 162 I.C. 854.
142. Ss.5(iv) and 5(v).
143. S. 7.
144. S. 29(2).
145. *Chelladorai* v. *Chinnathambiar*, A.I.R. 1961 Mad. 42.

146. *Kaur Singh* v. *Jaggar Singh*, A.I.R. 1961 Punj. 489.

147. While generally that was the attitude, there are a few cases on record where the courts showed some intolerance towards some customs without any rational reason. One such case is *Gopalayyan* v. *Raghupatiayyan*, 7 Mad. H. C. 250. The Civil Judge found that among the *Brahmins* of the locality there prevailed a custom, 'uniform and uninterrupted', 'for the last 134 years', of adoption of sister's son. Nevertheless, the Madras High Court refused to accept the custom saying, "In the case of *Brahmins* it is impossible in any case to believe in the existence of a customary law of which no trace appears in any written authority of the place to which they belong".

148. In *Edward* v. *Sheikh Gozaffar Hussein*, 3 C.W.N. 21, the Court stated: "A long time must elapse before a custom can grow up; but this is not necessarily the case with respect to usage. There is a great difference between a 'custom' and 'usage' and that clearly the latter may be established in a much less period of time than a custom. We are not prepared to say how long a period must elapse before such a usage can grow up, but it can grow even in 12 years".

149. *Balwant Rao* v. *Baji Rao*, (1920) 47 I.A. 213; *Abraham* v. *Abraham*, (1863) 9 M.I.A. 199.

150. *Abdul Hussein Khan* v *Bibi Sona Dero*, (1917) 45 I.A.10.

151. In two cases, *Rup Chand* v. *Jambu Parshad*, (1909) 37 I.A. 93 (adoption of a married person amongst Jains) and *Chiman Lal* v. *Hari Chand*, (1913) 40 I.A. 156 (adoption completed merely by unequivocal declaration to that effect and treatment of the adoptee as adopted son) though the Privy Council was not satisfied with the evidence, as it was 'somewhat limited' in character and so cautioned against treating these cases as precedents for the future, did, nevertheless, apply custom to the instant situations at hand.

GORDON R. WOODMAN

Some Realism About Customary Law—
The West African Experience

In modern times, there has probably been more written about the subject of customary law in an African context than anywhere else in the world. For this reason, it makes sense to consider the African data in seeking an operational definition of folk law. The author, who holds an LL.B. (1961) and a Ph.D. (1966) from Cambridge University, is a Senior Lecturer on the Law Faculty of the University of Birmingham. After a discussion of techniques of determining customary law in courts as well as through legislation, the difficult task of definition is addressed in some detail.

For other attempts to define folk law on the basis of African data, see J.H. Driberg, "The African Conception of Law," Journal of Comparative Legislation and International Law, 16 (1934), 230–245; Max Gluckman, *"African Jurisprudence,"* The Advancement of Science, 18 (1962), 439–454; W. Twining, The Place of Customary Law in the National Legal Systems of East Africa *(Chicago: University of Chicago Press, 1963); C.M.N. White,* "African Customary Law: The Problem of Concept and Definition," *Journal of African Law, 9 (1965), 86–89; C. Ogwurike, "The Source and Authority of African Customary Law," University of Ghana Law Journal, 3 (1966), 11–20; Eugene Cotran, "The Place and Future of Customary Law in East Africa," in* East African Law Today, The British Institute of International and Comparative Law Commonwealth Law Series No. 5 *(London: The British Institute of International and Comparative Law, 1966), pp. 72–92; Alexander Nekam, "Aspects of African Customary Law,,"* Northwestern University Law Review, *62 (1967), 45–56; C.J.W. Fleming, "The Nature of African Customary Law in Central Africa," NADA, 10 (4) (1971), 93–102.*

Controversies over the proper, most accurate, or most useful definition of the word "law" have raised the question of the nature of "customary law." Those involved in the debate have usually been sociologists or

---

Reprinted from the *Wisconsin Law Review* (1969), 128–152, with permission. Copyright © 1969.

lawyers. It is understandable that experts with such diverse skills have been unable to reach agreement. Indeed, as will be suggested below, attempts by those trained in one discipline to accommodate the attitudes of those trained in the other have sometimes increased the confusion.

The principal source of divergence can be found in the failure to agree upon which facts should be central to the inquiry. On the one hand it is argued that one should look at the behavior of ordinary members of society, as does the sociologist, and seek to determine those rules of conduct which such members regard as legally binding. On the other hand it is argued that one should adopt the Holmesian approach to law, and look primarily to the courts (however these are defined) to find rules of law. As might be expected, such different approaches have produced different definitions of "law" and "customary law." This article will analyze some of these definitions with special reference to the situation in the modern states of Ghana and Nigeria.

Ghana and Nigeria are of special interest because their courts are of the Anglo-American type. The statutes that created these courts require them to apply, in a large proportion of cases, the "customary laws" of the peoples subject to their jurisdiction. As a result there exist in Ghana and Nigeria bodies of judicial decisions which supposedly set out principles of customary law. There also exist bodies of long-standing "custom" upon which the sociologist has concentrated. Thus the investigator of customary law many go either to the court records or to the villagers and townspeople. So rich is either source that he can quite easily restrict himself to one to the total exclusion of the other. Of course, there is strong disagreement, if only tacitly, as to which method is more likely to render the correct results.

It is contended in this article that the two approaches do not render the same results. Moreover, since what the courts regularly enforce as customary law is not necessarily what the sociologist fieldworker regards as customary law, it seems clear that either one definition will have to be discarded in favor of the other, or that each must give up any pretension to exclusive validity. It will be contended that the latter conclusion is preferable.

I. Customary Law in the Courts

The practice of the courts suggests why their customary law differs from the sociologists' customary law. It is clear that the divergence does not arise primarily from a different initial definition. The statutes do not provide the courts with a comprehensive definition of customary law or its statutory synonyms.[1] Those of some jurisdictions, such as Western

Nigeria,[2] provide no definition at all. Of those jurisdictions with statutes that do provide a definition, the Ghana definition is typical. It states:

> Customary law, as comprised in the laws of Ghana, consists of rules of law which by custom are applicable to particular communities in Ghana, not being rules included in the common law under any enactment providing for the assimilation of such rules of customary law as are suitable for general application.[3]

The positive part of the definition, the words "rules of law which by custom are applicable," is not very helpful as it does not answer the question of how a court is to distinguish between rules of law and rules of convention or morality.[4] The negative part of the definition, the "assimilation" provision, will be discussed later.

Nor have the courts themselves defined the term. On occasion some courts have suggested that their purpose is to enforce that which the sociologist would regard as customary law. Thus it was said in a recent Nigerian case that customary law was "a mirror of accepted usage."[5] Moreover, courts seek to apply the customs of the present day, not of the past,[6] and do not require such customs to have been in force for any minimum length of time, provided that they are well-established.[7] Thus there is no reason to assume that the courts have purposely set out to discover a customary law varying in substance from the customary law of the sociologists.

However, a court of law clearly cannot use the same methods of investigation as a sociologist. It is from differences in methods that divergent conclusions as to the nature of customary law are liable to be reached.

The legal rule for establishing customary law was laid down by the Privy Council in *Angu v. Attah*:[8]

> As is the case with all customary law, it has to be proved in the first instance by calling witnesses acquainted with the native customs until the particular customs have, by frequent proof in the courts, become so notorious that the courts will take judicial notice of them.[9]

This rule has two parts: first, that each rule of customary law be proved initially as a fact; second, that judicial notice be taken of a rule after frequent proof. Both will be discussed in turn, with special attention being paid to circumstances that can cause a divergence between what the courts, and what the sociologists, may respectively find to be customary law.

A. Methods of Proving Customary Law in the Courts

The most common method of proving customary law is that mentioned in *Angu*—the calling of expert witnesses. Expert witnesses are frequently chiefs or other traditional officeholders, part of whose duties it is to know the customs of their people. They are nearly always called by the parties, and the court is usually restricted to accepting or rejecting the evidence of custom put before it. Yet the courts have been aware of the danger of being misled. There have been cases where evidence has been rejected because the witness was unqualified,[10] or because only one witness was called.[11] The reports abound with comments such as: Now both these witnesses were called by the plaintiff and knew, of course, what evidence they were expected to give."[12] However, it is time-consuming and expensive to litigants for a court to demand more evidence. Thus courts have often considered it more expedient to decide cases on the basis of such material as is put before them, even if this means relying on dubious evidence. In the case last cited, for example, the court followed the evidence of the plaintiff's witnesses. In other cases courts have followed the evidence of a single expert witness.[13] In at least one case a court followed the evidence of a witness who was himself a party, even though such evidence favored his side.[14] Thus there is a significant possibility that courts will follow misleading expert evidence.

A second common method of proving customary law is through the use of authoritative textbooks.[15] Cases can be cited in which such books were relied upon in the absence of, or even in opposition to, other evidence of custom.[16] While these writings may generally provide reliable evidence of the custom of the peoples to which they refer, they have been followed in cases concerning different ethnic groups. Thus Sarbah's *Fanti Customary Laws* has been used in cases involving non-Fanti peoples.[17]

A third method arises from a qualification of the rule in *Angu v. Attah* to the effect that customary law need not be proved in those courts whose members are themselves required to possess expert knowledge. Rather, such courts may declare customary law from their own knowledge.[18] In the past, this qualification applied to all "native courts," but not to superior courts, apart from the Northern Nigeria Sharia Court of Appeal (which declares Moslem law from its own knowledge[19]). Since native courts are staffed by experts, their opinions on customary law are thought to be authoritative, and, therefore, are not easily disturbed on appeal. Thus, although the superior courts are often reluctant to accept local variations in general customs, they have accepted them when stated by native courts.[20] In theory the opinion of a native court as to customary law as expressed in one case could be used in a different case; but this has happened in one known instance. Perhaps this is because of insufficient research of court records.[21] However, despite the dicta suggesting that these decisions are authoritative, there have been cases where the superior courts have ignored native court opinions as to customary law. For example, one opinion was held to be too sweeping to be approved without authority.[22] Another was dismissed as "ridiculous."[23] Thus the superior courts do not consider native court opinions as to customary law to be invariably reliable.

As a fourth method courts sometimes sit with expert assessors, who advise them on questions of customary law.[24] However, the court's judgments do not often refer to such advice. Accordingly this does not seem to have been an important method of proof.

A fifth method, formerly used by the superior courts in Ghana, was to refer questions of customary law to referees, who would then make reports to native courts. However, this procedure was infrequently used, and when used the reports were not always accepted as reliable.[25]

A sixth method, the reliance upon previous decisions of the superior courts for evidence of custom, has been more commonly used. The rule in *Angu* suggests that decisions of the superior courts do not become probative until there are enough cases on a point so as to make it "notorious." In theory, a rule of customary law should be proved independently in each case. In practice, however, the courts have frequently referred to their previous decisions as evidence of custom even though insufficient in number to make the point notorious. Thus one finds decisions in which the court relied on a passage in a textbook, together with one previous case;[26] or in which a previous case was treated as giving additional weight to expert evidence.[27] On the other hand, such previous decisions are not binding, and can be outweighed by contrary evidence.[28] Nevertheless, they may carry considerable weight. Thus it has been held that a native court decision has no authority if there is a single decision of a superior court to the contrary.[29] The problem with this method is that it opens the possibility of perpetuating errors. If in one case a court accepts incorrect evidence of customary law, subsequent decisions are more likely to make the same mistake because of the weight accorded to the initial decision. Moreover, even if the initial decision is correct, its conclusions as to custom may be applied to a later case involving a different ethnic group with possibly different customs.[30]

B. Other Factors Affecting Judicial Conclusions on Customary Law

Several other factors seem to affect judicial conclusions on customary law, although they are not expressly approved, and may even be denied by some of the authorities. Among these are the court's own preconceptions about what the customary practice is. Although the rule in *Angu* clearly repudiates such reliance upon personal knowledge, a considerable number of Ghanaian cases, many of them comparatively recent, can be found in which judges have declared the customary law without any evidence or authority.[31] In Nigeria there appears to be a stronger insistence on the need for evidence before customary law can be declared.[32]

Closely related to such use of personal preconceptions is the use of logic to extend or discover rules of customary law—the use, expressly or implicitly, of the argument, "this must be the customary law, because in the circumstances it is the only logical possibility." Of course, this involves not simply the use of a logically necessary argument, but also an assumption about what is reasonable. For example, in *Bankole v. Tapo*[33] a claim was brought under Yoruba customary law against the individually-owned property of a deceased. The courts have held that under this law such property passes on intestacy to the family of the deceased. The plaintiffs sued on behalf of the family. However, it was shown that the deceased, during his lifetime, had given the property to his grandson. The court held that the rule of family inheritance did not apply to such property. The implied argument was simple: The rule of family inheritance applies only to property owned by the deceased at his death; this property had been disposed of by the deceased before his death; therefore, this property was not affected by the rule of family inheritance. However, the seeming inevitability of the argument conceals certain prejudices about the law of property. It was assumed (a) that a man was entitled to dispose of his individual property during his lifetime, and (b) that such dispositions remained effective after his death. There is no logical reason not to deny either of these propositions, and indeed the latter has been challenged in other cases dealing with Yoruba customary law.[34] It is not contended that the decision was wrong; the available evidence of customary practice is not conclusive, and the decision can be reconciled with the apparently contradictory evidence. The example is given simply to illustrate the contention that logical development of the courts' customary law could cause it to differ from the people's customary law.

Another example is the Ghanaian case, *Abude v. Onana V.*[35] Here it was necessary to determine the customary powers of a divisional council, a traditional council of elders of a community. In particular, questions were raised as to whether a section of the community could sue the council for an account of communal funds, and whether communal land could be alienated by a majority decision of the council. On the question of accountability the court, citing a case holding that a family head could not be sued for an account by a member of the family, held that there was sufficient evidence on record to preclude the action for an account, and moreover that such a result was reasonable because otherwise a dissentient group could, by constant litigation, paralyze the work of the council. It may be said in reply, firstly that the affairs of a chief's council do not have, as a logical necessity, to be governed by the same rules as the affairs of a family; secondly, that, in fact, the only evidence of custom on record was this case on the administration of family property;[36] and thirdly, that the courts have power to stop vexatious litigation. Also, the decision cited[37] concerned a different ethnic group, and was based solely on the authority of one textbook. On the question of alienation of communal land, the experienced trial judge had expressed doubt as to what the law was. The appeal court said simply: "Obviously, no council can possibly carry out its function if it should only perform its duties with the unanimous approval of all its members."[38] It may be replied that it is not absurd to suggest that communal land should normally be alienable only by unanimous consent. Land has always been a very important form of wealth in Ghana, and communal land was virtually inalienable in the past. Exceptions could still be allowed for special cases. Again, it is not contended that the appeal court's decision was demonstrably wrong, but only that it was not inevitably and "obviously" right.[39]

In cases where evidence has been scanty or totally unavailable, another factor has sometimes been determinative—where the onus of proof lay. As might be expected, the party relying on a proposition of customary law has the onus of proving it, and, indeed, this principle is incorporated in the evidence laws of Nigeria.[40] However, where both sides rely on propositions of customary law, the court must choose upon whom to place the onus. For example, in one case the parties agreed that land had been the subject of a gift at customary law. While the plaintiff argued that such gifts carried a right of reversion in the donor in the absence of express agreement to the contrary, the defendant argued that such gifts were prima facie absolute. The court placed the onus upon the plaintiff, decided that he had failed to discharge it, and held that his claim therefore failed. Clearly the court in this decision showed a preference for outright gifts, although gifts of land with a reversion in the donor have in practice been common in West Africa.[41] Again, the courts have sometimes, but not always, considered that if a custom was established for one ethnic group, this raised a presumption that it existed for another.[41a] Thus decisions as to where the onus lies seem sometimes to reflect the courts' personal knowledge or their ideas of what is reasonable.[42] Finally, in a few cases courts have accepted a view of customary law agreed upon by the parties, even though the courts were uncertain about its correctness.[43]

It would appear, therefore, that if a lawyer is attempting to predict a judicial decision on customary law he must examine how the customary practice can be proved in court, assess the weight which is likely to be given to the evidence, and take into account what are likely to be the court's own preconceptions about the existence and reasonableness of the custom.

C. *When Customary Law Becomes Notorious*

If the first part of the rule in *Angu v. Attah* stood alone, customary law would have to be proved in every case. However, the second part of the rule dispenses with the need for proof when a custom has by frequent proof become "notorious". This magnifies doubts already raised. For, as has been suggested above, it is possible in individual cases for a court to enforce as customary law a principle which is at variance with the customary practice. A reasonable interpretation of the second part of the rule in *Angu* suggests that if this happens several times, the courts will then be *compelled* to perpetuate the principle, and it will not be permissible to argue that the earlier decisions are wrong.[44] Thus the lawyer seeking to predict a court's decision will have to take into account previous decisions, not merely because they may be treated as relevant evidence, but also because they may in some cases be binding authority. It is thus necessary to consider how many decisions are needed for a rule to become notorious.

In 1940, the West African Court of Appeal held that a single decision upon a rule of custom, given in 1892, was insufficient to render the rule notorious.[45] However, in 1948, a decision of more recent date was followed by this court.[46] In 1959, the Ghana High Court held itself bound by a single decision of its own on customary law.[47] The law reports now contain many instances of decisions based on single cases, that in turn are not always based on overwhelming evidence.[48] While the Nigerian courts still express caution,[49] a similar trend can be seen in their decisions.[50]

However, although the courts appear to be moving towards the common law principles of precedent in customary law cases, few are explicit as to what is considered to be the minimum acceptable authority. Thus where a single decision is cited, it may be tacitly coupled with the court's own knowledge, so that in fact the court may be treating the previous decision as additional evidence, rather than as conclusive authority. Nevertheless, some cases do suggest that the courts sometimes approach previous decisions in customary law cases in much the same way as they approach previous decisions in common law cases.[51]

The second part of the rule in *Angu* is therefore liable to produce a further divergence between the courts' customary law and the sociologists' customary law. There have been instances where controversial points of customary law were settled by referring to one or a few decided cases that were in turn based on weak evidence. In a leading case of 1868,[52] for example, expert evidence was relied upon as the basis for the conclusion that under the Accra customary law of succession property passed to the matrilineal family of the deceased. This precipitated an argument as to the weight which should have been given to the expert evidence, with some writers contending that under Accra customary law, property passed to the patrilineal family, and others that it passed to the matrilineal family. In a leading case of 1916,[53] eight expert witnesses gave six different accounts of the custom. The court, nevertheless came to a conclusion about the custom. However, the law was unsettled until 1951, when the West African Court of Appeal in *Vanderpuye v. Botchway*[54] disapproved of certain dicta in the 1916 case, and laid down a different set of rules, apparently on the basis of another former decision. *Vanderpuye* has since been regarded as binding, and has been followed in a number of cases. These in turn have been regarded as adding further authority to the principle there laid down.[55]

Moreover, because previous decisions may be treated as binding authority, there is a further possibility that the courts might disregard local variations in customary practice. Further once a rule has been judicially recognized, it is liable to be applied to ethnic groups other than those whose customs were in issue in the decisive cases. Thus the Nigerian courts have sometimes held themselves bound by Ghanaian decisions on customary law, although there is no significant ethnic group common to both countries.[56] A fortiori, within each country there have been many more cases where decisions on the customary laws of certain ethnic groups have been regarded as authoritative in cases involving different groups.[57]

D. Legislative Developments

It is not certain whether the rule of *Angu v. Attah* still applies in Ghana. In 1960 a statute was enacted which reads: "Any question as to the existence or content of a rule of customary law is a question of law for the Court and not a question of fact."[58] The statute further provided that a court could hold an inquiry to ascertain the customary law if the submissions of the parties, reported cases, textbooks, and other appropriate sources did not settle the matter. It is submitted that this gives statutory approval to the practice of allowing judges to decide on the basis of their own knowledge, but at the same time retain their opportunity to receive evidence of custom if desired.[59]

Another development by the legislatures has increased the possibility of divergence between the courts' customary law and the sociologists' customary law. Machinery has been established in all parts of Ghana and Nigeria for the authoritative declaration or modification of customary law. For example, native authorities in Northern Nigeria are empowered to declare the customary law of their area or part of their area on any subject, and the governor can then direct this to be in force. These same authorities can also propose modifications in customary law, which the governor also can direct to be in force.[60] When such a declaration or modification is made, it is binding on the courts, which are thereafter required to treat it as part of the customary law, whether it is in accordance with customary practice or not. In Ghana there is the added provision that a rule of customary law may be declared, with or without modification, to be in force throughout Ghana. The courts are then required to treat the declaration as part of the common law, and not as customary law.[61]

Although these provisions have been little used, their effect has been significant. For example, a declaration by native authorities has been made of part of the customary law of testate succession for Akyem Abuakwa, Ghana, even though it quite possibly was not entirely consistent with the customary practice. Nevertheless it is clear that this declaration is binding on the courts.[62] Conversely, an attempt to alter the customary law, even though made by a traditional authority recognized by the people as having legislative power, will not be upheld by the courts if it fails to comply with the statutory requirements. For example, in 1948 the Ashanti (Ghana) Confederacy Council decided on a modification of the Ashanti law of succession. The Ashanti native courts gave effect to the decision, but were reversed on appeal by the superior courts on the ground that the consent of the Governor in Council, required by statute, had not been given.[63]

E. Arguments Supporting Judicial Methods of Determining Customary Law

The preceding discussion has attempted to show that the courts are likely to enforce as customary law rules different from those which a sociologist would include under the title.[64] It is difficult to find instances where it can be clearly demonstrated that this has in fact occurred, because insufficient sociological research has been done. However, a few possibilities may be mentioned.

A brief summary has been given of the way in which the courts settled the Accra customary law of succession. The legal authorities now hold that the Accra people follow a modified system of matrilineal succession. There is strong evidence, however, that this is contrary to the practice of the Accra people, causing one writer to go so far as to describe it as "a colossal pyramid of error."[65] Another example may be found in the law concerning pledges of land in Ghana. The courts have held that a creditor must be given possession of the land under a customary law pledge; if he is not given possession, the transaction cannot be a pledge, and will be regarded as an attempt to create a common law mortgage.[66] However, there is strong evidence that the people themselves have developed a form of customary pledge under which the creditor does not take possession.[67] A third example comes from Nigeria where the courts have held that a grant of family land by the head of the family without the other members' consent is not void, but is voidable at the instance of the other members.[68] However, sociologists' customary law probably knows nothing of the distinction between void and voidable grants.[69]

Before discussing the implications of this divergence, a few further comments on the above discussion seem desirable. It has been necessary to emphasize that the courts are likely to enforce rules which are not in fact "a mirror of accepted usage." This is not intended as a criticism of the courts. Rather it is intended only as a description of the existing situation. The authorities in Ghana and Nigeria are alone competent to decide whether this state of affairs ought to be altered. Certainly, arguments can be raised in favor of the present judicial methods. These arguments will be briefly stated, not in order to urge their acceptance, but merely because they may not be quite as apparent as those on the other side.

The courts cannot carry out sociological fieldwork. Their function is to resolve disputes expeditiously, without undue expense, and within the confines of a formal procedure. It is apparent, then, that they cannot carry out research with the thoroughness expected of a sociologist. Consequently, a certain degree of error about customary practices may perhaps be considered the price paid for the efficient functioning of the courts. Then too, the customary practice may not provide answers to particular problems raised in particular cases, problems which nevertheless must be resolved.

It would seem that the need to ascertain and declare customary law is urgent. Many uncertainties of litigation arise largely from the fact that in many areas a lawyer still cannot predict what the court will find to be the customary law. But once rules of customary law have been laid down in *binding* decisions, a prospective litigant can be more accurately advised. In this respect, the courts have made great progress in the last century, and particularly in the last 20 years. This progress might not have been possible if judges had been excessively cautious. For example, courts have been willing to disregard local variations in customs. In using textbooks and judicial decisions as evidence of customary law, in deciding where to impose the onus of proof, and in following notorious rules of customary law, courts have tended to discount the probability of differences between the customary laws of various ethnic groups. In their desire to achieve greater certainty, they may have wished to avoid the delay of proving every rule of customary law for every area in which there might have been local peculiarities.

Finally, it is arguable that the courts may sometimes be justified in deliberately departing from the customary practices. If a court imposes its own ideas of what is reasonable upon the customary law, it may be attempting to impose a progressive change on a way of life in need of reform. If customary law is to assist rather than impede social development, it may need the services of Mansfields rather than of Eldons, for as the Ghana Court of Appeal has said: "Stagnation of the law in a fast developing State should be regarded with abhorrence."[70] The courts seem to feel this particularly strongly in respect to local customary laws, in reference to which the following statement was made: "This court cannot allow local customs to override general principles and practice in these days of changing conditions."[71] Thus a multitude of local customary laws may, quite apart from the problem of ascertaining them, be considered undesirable in a developing nation where local rivalries and prejudices may be barriers to necessary change.

II. Some Proffered Definitions of Law and Customary Law: A Critique

With the above discussion in mind certain definitions of law and customary law will be evaluated.

Some Realism About Customary Law

Attempts have been made to define the law in terms of the attitudes or state of mind of the ordinary member of society—that a rule is a rule of law if the ordinary person regards it as binding upon him. Such definitions are common among sociologists, whose concern has been primarily to distinguish between those social norms of simple societies which are rules of law, and those social norms which are not. Thus Professor Gluckman defines law, for the purpose of his inquiry into the judicial process among the Barotse, as

> a set of rules accepted by all normal members of the society as defining right and reasonable ways in which persons ought to behave in relation to each other and to things, including ways of obtaining protection for one's rights.[72]

He distinguishes law thus defined from morality, for which he would apply this definition with the word "generous" substituted for the word "reasonable." Surprisingly, some lawyers have defined law in these terms. For example, Professor Elias proposes the following definition: "The law of a given community is the body of rules which are recognized as obligatory by its members."[73]

For the Ghanaian or Nigerian lawyer, such definitions are not only unhelpful, but also are misleading. A man goes to a lawyer not to find out what is socially acceptable, but to find out what the courts will do if he acts in a certain way, or to procure certain judicial action or inaction in response to a situation which has arisen. Thus, the lawyer's function is to assist the Holmesian "bad man"—the man who wishes to arrange his affairs with reference to possible judicial action.[74] For example, if an Accra man, contemplating the possibility of making a will, asks his lawyer what will happen if he dies intestate, he does not want to know what his relatives, or the people of Accra as a whole, would expect to happen; quite possibly he knows that better than the lawyer. Rather he wants to know who would be appointed to administer his estate, and who would be given his property in the event of litigation. Accordingly, the lawyer will not serve this client properly, if he investigates only what the people of Accra consider to be a reasonable way for relatives to behave. On the other hand, he will be serving his client properly if he tells him that, regardless of what anyone in Accra thinks, the courts will require the property distributed according to the rules of *Vanderpuye v. Botchway*.[75]

The position of a judge in such a case will be similar to that of the lawyer. If he ignores the law reports, and looks only, for example, to the body of rules which the Accra people recognize as obligatory, he will be making a revolutionary break with the well established practices of his profession. Although it is perhaps arguable that this would be desirable, any argument should focus upon the question of whether reform of the judicial process is desirable: it is not helpful to ignore the fact that this is the process through which such matters are now resolved.

Any attempt to disregard judicial practice in defining customary law is subject to similar criticism. It is surprising to find lawyers, albeit academic lawyers, overlooking this. For example, Professor Allott has written:

> The binding force of custom ultimately rests on the fact that it is habitually obeyed by those subject to it; if not fortified by established usage it is not law. But once custom has been codified or settled by judicial decision, its binding force depends on the statute or the doctrine of precedent; in short, it ceases to be customary law.[76]

Admittedly, Professor Allott later indicated that a divergence can occur between the law of the courts and that of the public; but it is submitted that this definition of customary law is open to question. As noted earlier, courts are required in large numbers of cases to apply customary law. Are they thus not entitled to apply in such cases, for example, the Akyem Abuakwa declaration on testate succession or the principles of *Vanderpuye*? Of course, they are not merely entitled, but consider themselves bound to apply them. Thus, what the courts regard as customary law is evidently not the same as Professor Allott's customary law.

A similar criticism may be made of Dr. Obi's definition, that customary law is "[a] rule (or body of rules) which the members of a given community recognize as binding on themselves, and which the courts will enforce if and when called upon to do so."[77] This definition excludes rules enforced by the courts if the people themselves do not regard them as binding. However, as suggested above, if a lawyer were to exclude such rules when advising clients, he would not be serving them well.

Other sociologists have sought to determine a definition by investigating, not only the state of mind of the people, but also the means by which social norms are enforced. Malinowski thus insisted that the law of primitive societies was distinguishable from their customs.[78] He contended that law could be distinguished by its binding nature, necessitated by "the natural mental trend of self-interest, ambition and vanity, set into play by a special social mechanism into which the obligatory actions are framed."[79] Rules of law tended to circumscribe men's natural tendencies, and thus required enforcement by the threat of sanctions. By contrast, customs were followed because men had no inclination to act otherwise.[80] The main objection which has been raised to this definition is that it fails to distinguish between the many different types of sanctions by which men might be made to obey rules, and as a result is over broad and vague.[81]

Attempts to refine this approach have therefore been concerned with defining more precisely the types of sanctions which distinguish of legal norm from other norms. The most detailed has been that of Professor Hoebel.[82] Hoebel begins with the argument of lawyers such as Holmes and Cardozo that norms become laws only after their regular enforcement by the courts. However, some of the societies with which Hoebel deals do not have formal court systems. But Hoebel argues that by expanding the concept of "courts," one would always be able to find courts in primitive societies. For example, he describes the Eskimo way of handling a recidivist murderer:

> Now arises the opportunity for some public-spirited man of initiative to perform a community service. He may undertake to interview, one after the other, all the adult males of the community to see if they agree that the killer had best be executed. If unanimous consent is given, he personally dispatches the murderer at the first opportunity, and no revenge may be taken on him by the murderer's relatives. Cases show that no revenge *is* taken.
> A community "court" has spoken and its judgment executed [sic].[83]

However, Hoebel contends that it is not essential to retain the concept of courts at all. What is the fundamental characteristic of law is the regular use of physical coercion in a socially-recognized manner as the means through which it is enforced.

> Hence we may say that privileged force, official authority, and regularity are the elements that modern jurisprudence teaches us we must seek when we wish to identify law.
> On this basis, for working purposes law may be defined in these terms: *A social norm is legal if its neglect or infraction is regularly met, in threat or in fact, by the application of physical force by an individual or group possessing the socially recognized privilege of so acting.*[84]

This definition appears to be all-embracing; it enables us to identify law in England by looking at the Supreme Court of Judicature and the other courts, but at the same time enables us to identify law in societies such as that of the Eskimos'. The question is how satisfactory is it for identifying customary law in Ghana and Nigeria today? On its face, it appears most helpful. The high courts and supreme courts regularly apply what they call customary law. These courts are recognized as having official authority, and their decisions are enforced by the application, in threat or in fact, of physical force by officers of the state. According to the definition, then, norms which are not so enforced are not legal.

Problems arise when one is confronted with statements outside the law reports to the effect that, for example, an Accra man's patrilineal family has a *right* to his property on his death intestate, or that a Ghanaian pledgee may not always have a *right* to possession of the land. Such statements perhaps may be dismissed by saying that they are not made in reference to legal rights, and that the rights to which they do refer are not regularly enforced by socially recognized authorities. However, is it justifiable to assume that the superior courts are invariably the only socially recognized authorities? Many people in these countries have no contact with the superior courts, being regulated in their daily lives by much nearer authorities. Accordingly there have been cases of socially approved killings of alleged witches, which killings the superior courts, of course, found to be illegal.[85] And a certain area of Nigeria was effectively ruled some years ago by the Odozi Obodo secret society, which enforced its own rules on the inhabitants, using capital punishment on occasion.[86] In addition there is at least one instance where socially recognized authorities of a Nigerian village prevented, by the threat of physical force, recourse to the state courts.[87] Certainly, these state courts would not have regarded such a norm as legal. Moreover, it is reasonable to assume that the published cases represent only the more extreme cases. Thus it seems apparent that there are other rules which are not only recognized by ordinary people as binding, but are effectively enforced, by the use or threat of physical force where necessary.

Even Hoebel's own examples are open to question on this score. The only West African society which he discusses is that of the Ashanti of Ghana.[88] Moreover, he expressly restricts this discussion to Ashanti law in the context of the state system as it existed before 1875, after which British domination began to be established.[89] Although such a restricted discussion might well preserve the clarity of his definition of law, the pointed implication of this is that the definition might not be so helpful with respect to twentieth-century Ashanti law. His discussion of the Eskimos is open to even more serious question. The description of Eskimo law is apparently intended to be comparatively up-to-date. But today the Eskimos are the subjects of the modern states of Canada, Denmark, the United States, and the Soviet Union. Under the laws of any of these states, as enforced by their respective organs of government including their courts, a killing such as the above described killing of a recidivist murderer would be a criminal offense.[90] If a lawyer in one of these countries is professionally concerned with a case involving such a killing, he would hardly be fulfilling his function if he shrugged it off by saying that it was lawful under a socially-recognized privilege. If the objection is made that this is carping criticism, because the Eskimos still live in almost complete isolation from the state machinery of these countries, it would be replied that, if they do, their situation is almost unique in the modern world, and therefore a definition which suits their case may not suit any other. Finally, it should be noted that even the Eskimos are now affected by the growing power of the modern state and may not long remain in self-governing independence.[91]

The difficulty with Hoebel's definition is that, although more narrow than that of Malinowski, it is still too broad and imprecise. Starting from the exactitude of Holmes and Cardozo, Hoebel has diluted their definition by substituting "socially recognized privilege" for "courts," and thereby has reintroduced the factor of people's mental attitude or state of mind. This may be satisfactory for societies where social recognition is accorded with comparative unanimity. Virtually everyone in England, for example, recognizes that the High Court may order the application of physical force to those who offend against the norms which that court enforces. We may also assume that all Eskimos recognized, at least before the advent of modern influences, that the killer of a recidivist murderer, in the circumstances described, had a privilege to act in this way. But in some societies, instances of social recognition may conflict. It is not invariably true that "within one community only one and not two compulsive orders can be valid at the same time."[92] In Ghana and Nigeria, for example, social recognition is accorded to the superior courts by one section of society, which includes of course those who operate the state powers of compulsion. But social recognition is also accorded—perhaps by a large number of people— to those who compel obedience to norms which are not accepted by the courts. Such a division is probably caused by the fact that these countries are in a transitional period. If so, it will undoubtedly be eliminated when the populations of Ghana and Nigeria accept the modern state's power of compulsion as the sole form of power to be given social recognition. But for the time being, social recognition is in the context of the societies of Ghana and Nigeria, an unduly vague concept.[93]

It could be said that there is also some vagueness in the term "courts." Although this is true, the individual institutions with a claim to the title can in modern societies be easily identified, the problem being simply to choose which will be regarded as courts for a particular purpose. The term "social recognition" on the other hand does not designate anything which is immediately visible or easily distinguishable. If one defines law in terms of courts, he may have to select between claims made on behalf of the Federal Supreme Court of Nigeria and claims made on behalf of the tribunal of the Odozi Obodo secret society. Yet both institutions are clearly identifiable. And since the professional legal practitioner has a right of audience before the former but not before the latter, he will probably find it convenient to exclude the latter from further consideration.

For the practicing lawyer, the best working definition of law still seems to be that of Holmes: "The prophecies of what the courts will do in fact, and nothing more pretentious, are what I mean by the law."[94] This suggests that the lawyer first examine the courts' records, in order to predict their future conduct. The result will be the discovery that in many areas of customary law it is quite clear what the courts will do, because the principles have already been laid down; in such cases, there will be no need to look any further. Some scholars, for example, Gray and Salmond, have insisted that there is no law at all in a particular situation until a court has acted.[95] However, it is submitted that to amend our definition to comply with this proposition, would be of little practical importance. Although conceivably such an amendment would be preferred, it should be noted that the lawyer advises his clients by prophetizing what the law will be if they go to court, rather than by telling them what the law is. The important point is that his advice will in both cases be based on a prediction of judicial action.

As might be expected, such a definition of law has led to an examination by writers such as Llewellyn and Frank of the extent to which judicial actions are in fact predictable. This article will not embark on such an examination with respect to customary law in Ghana and Nigeria; a challenge has already been made to one of the court's "paper-rules": that which says that the customary law enforced by the courts is "a mirror of accepted usage." It may well be, as Llewellyn argued with respect to American courts, that when one looks beyond the paper-rules, a certain degree of consistency may be found enabling the investigator to predict at least some of the courts' actions.[96] But further examination is necessary to confirm or refute this.

However a definition of law is needed by people other than the legal practitioner. The question then arises: Is the lawyer's definition of the law of assistance to the sociologist? Dr. Jeffreys, a lawyer with a sociological background, has argued that the sociologist is bound by the lawyer's definition: "The only persons who can define law are lawyers, not anthropologists, otherwise one is not *'ad idem'* on the subject as the lawyers say."[97] If by being *ad idem* the writer meant having the ability to understand each other, his contention seems incorrect. A person may find it convenient to define a word differently from the way I habitually define it, but we can still understand each other if each knows the other's definition. If being *ad idem* the writer means invariably using a word in the same sense, one may dispute the implication that it is necessarily desirable always to be *ad idem*. Moreover, even if one universal definition of law is necessary, by what right do the lawyers arrogate to themselves the power to determine it?[98]

It is submitted that the lawyer's definition may be just as misleading to the sociologist as the sociologist's to the lawyer. This proposition is illustrated in the work of Professor Evans-Pritchard on the Nuer.

> In a strict sense Nuer have no law. There are conventional compensations for damage, adultery, loss of limb, and so forth, but there is no authority with power to adjudicate on such matters or to enforce a verdict.[99]

Thus, as a result of accepting the lawyer's definition Evans-Pritchard was forced to conclude that if there were no courts there could be no law. Obviously this conclusion was unsatisfactory for his purposes because a few pages later he proceeded to speak of Nuer law, by giving law a different definition:

> We speak of "law" here in the sense which seems most appropriate when writing of the Nuer, a moral obligation to settle disputes by conventional methods, and not in the sense of legal procedure or of legal institutions.[100]

It is suggested that the difficulty encountered by Professor Evans-Pritchard need not have arisen; for the definition of law need not be confined to the "strict sense" accorded it by lawyers. As noted above, the sociologist, seeking to distinguish between social norms which are binding, and those which are merely moral, may quite properly designate the former as law, even if the society under investigation has no courts in the narrow, lawyer's sense. Thus, it helped to promote an understanding of certain aspects of Eskimo society to define law in Hoebel's terms. So also Gluckman's definition was useful for the purpose of examining all the facts which were part of the judicial process among the Barotse; although some rules were not enforced by the courts, they were nevertheless a source upon which judges drew in the process of decisionmaking.[101] A definition was therefore needed which would include these rules. It was argued above that Gluckman's definition is misleading to the Ghanaian or Nigerian lawyer. However, he himself was careful to point out that it was designed for a specific inquiry alone:

> This is a conventional treatment for purposes of analysis. I do not assert that it is illegitimate or wrong to use "law," or any of the [related] terms, with a different meaning. If anyone objects to my conventions, I can only reply that I have tried to be consistent in using them, and beg him to

confine himself to factual and analytical criticisms, and not to involve us in barren terminological dispute.[102]

It does not follow that we should abandon the attempt to define customary law for certain purposes merely because we have failed to find a definition suitable for all purposes. It is by now almost commonplace in jurisprudential thought to suggest that definition is often a question of choice, not of abstract logic—a recognition of what is most helpful, not a discrimination between truth and error.[103] The above discussion has attempted to show that one universally helpful definition cannot be found. We may now look briefly at the definitions most helpful for certain tasks.

III. Conclusion

It has been contended above that the legal practitioner should, for the purpose of advising his clients in customary law cases, or of persuading the courts to act in ways favorable to his clients in such cases, adopt Holmes' definition. The consequence will be that, if he finds in the law reports authority which he can be sure a court will follow, he need look no further. Sometimes, however, he will find that a point has not been settled. In such a case he must look for other evidence of what the court will do, or which may persuade it to act in a certain way. It has been seen that the courts apparently try to enforce the rules which ordinary people regard as binding. Although it has been contended above that in certain cases they have not in fact done this, it is possible that these cases are exceptions. More often than not, the sociologists' findings do seem to coincide with the courts' decisions. Therefore, to predict or influence the judicial action in a case where there is no authority, the lawyer should if possible carry out sociological investigation, and thus may find it necessary to use a sociologist's definition of law. However, he should remember that the object of the investigation is only to predict or influence what the court will do, and accordingly should bear in mind the problems involved in transferring a finding from the fieldworker's notebook to the court's judgment book.

The textbook writer and the researcher should adopt a similar approach if they wish their work to be of assistance to the legal profession. Thus, the first inquiry should be into the court records. If these yield clear authority, no further investigation is of practical value. Only if the court records are blank or equivocal, is it useful to refer to sociologists' works, or to carry out one's own fieldwork. If the lawyer does decide to carry out fieldwork, he should take care to learn the proper methods.

Sociological research requires a skill as technical as that of finding the *ratio decidendi* of a case, and one does not acquire the former skill by studying at a law school.

For a judge of the superior court the Holmesian definition may appear less useful. How does it help a judge in deciding a case to tell him that the law is a prediction of whatever he is going to do? The answer is, that judges usually try to follow the practice of their profession. They try to act predictably. Consequently, a judge will often employ the processes described above for ascertaining customary law. Thus a judge of the superior court should also look first to the court records for his authority, and may wish to look no further if they give a clear answer.

It has already been contended that it is not for the lawyer to tell the sociologist what definition he should adopt; there is a clear boundary between the two disciplines, and trespass by either party should be avoided. Rather, there is a need for friendly relations between these neighboring landowners.

All forms of social control are important to the student interested in social life. The work of lawyers may not always involve the most significant form of control. Malinowski wrote:

> The anthropological approach to law reveals better perhaps than any other that the law of order, the principles and rules kept because they are intrinsically related to cultural determinism in general, constitutes a legitimate subject for study. The whole domain of social control, as this has been named by Professor E.A. Ross, imposes itself on the work of the ethnographer and on his cogitations in jurisprudence, as strongly as it seems to have been alien and unpalatable to the lawyer-craftsman of the past and even of the present. This latter invariably thinks of law as that which starts when the jurisdicial machinery has to be mobilized.[104]

While this article does not accept Malinowski's definition of law as universally helpful, it does not intend to dispute the general importance of sociological research.

As a citizen, the lawyer should be concerned with the welfare of his country in matters outside his own technical competence. Similarly, if the law teacher is to assist his students to educate themselves fully, he must give them some insight into the relationship between the work of the courts and life outside. In teaching customary law he may be able to help them to think about what the proper relationship ought to be between the courts' customary law and the ordinary peoples' customary law.

To define law in terms of litigation is not to suggest that the lawyer should concern himself with nothing else. However, it is contended that these two types of customary law are two distinct entities. Knowledge of every aspect of society is valuable, but the craftsmanship of the lawyer does have a practical use, which it would be unrealistic to ignore. The lawyer and the sociologist may be neighboring landowners; they may even be able to cooperate to use their lands for the benefit of the community; but they are not joint tenants.

Notes

1. The term "customary law" is used in the statutes of Ghana, Western Nigeria, and Mid-Western Nigeria. The term "native law and custom," which was formerly in general use in British West Africa, is still used in the statutes of the Federal Territory of Lagos and Northern Nigeria. The terms "local custom" and "customary law" are both used in the statutes of Eastern Nigeria. However, the term "custom" is used in the evidence laws of all the regions of Nigeria and in the Federal Evidence Act, *Laws of Fed. of Nigeria* cap. 62 (1958).

2. The division of Nigeria into four regions and the Federal Territory of Lagos was in 1967 replaced by a division into twelve states. However, the old regional legislation is to remain in force until it is replaced by legislation of the new states. Therefore, it is more convenient to refer to the former division.

3. Interpretation Act of 1960, *Acts of Ghana* § 18(1).

4. See also a similar definition in the Federal Evidence Act § 2 *Laws of Fed. of Nigeria* cap. 62 (1958): "'custom' is a rule, which in a particular district, has, from long usage, obtained the force of law." This does not explain how a court decides whether a long-standing rule has or has not obtained the force of law. Identical definitions are found in: Evidence Act § 2, *Laws of E. Nigeria* cap. 49; Evidence Act § 2, *Laws of N. Nigeria* cap. 40 (1963). Similar definitions be found in: the Eastern Nigeria High Court Law § 2 cap. 61; Eastern Nigeria Magistrates' Courts Law § 2 cap. 82; Eastern Nigeria Customary Courts Law § 2 cap. 32. Other definitions are even less informative: see, *e.g.*, the High Court Law § 2, *Laws of N. Nigeria* cap. 49 (1963): "'native law and custom' includes Moslem law."

5. Owonyin v. Omotosho, [1961] 1 All Nigeria L.R. 304, 309.

6. *See* Lewis v. Bankole, [1929] 1 Nigeria L.R. 82, 84 (S. Nigeria 1908).

7. In Ghana, the courts have rejected earlier views to the contrary. In Welbeck v. Brown reported in J.M. Sarbah, *Fanti Customary Laws* 185 (1897), the majority of the court held that, as in England, a custom must have existed since 1189 to be enforceable by the court. The result would probably have been that no customs could have been enforced. In Mensah v. Wiaboe, [1921–25] Sel. Judg. Div. Cts. 170 (Ghana 1925), the court held that a custom must have existed since the institution of the Supreme Court in 1876. In Sasraku v. David, [1959] Ghana L.R. 7, 14, the Court of Appeal rejected this view also, holding: "Stagnation of the law in a fast developing state should be regarded with abhorrence."

8. [1874–1928] Privy Council Judg. 43 (Ghana 1916).

9. This rule is now contained in the Federal Evidence Act, § 14, *Laws of Fed. of Nigeria Cap.* 62 (1958) and in the evidence laws of the regions. In Ghana, it may have been altered in 1960.
10. *E.g.*, Adeseye v. Taiwo, 1 Sel. Judg. Fed. Sup. Ct. 84 (Nigeria 1956).
11. *E.g.*, Andre v. Agbebi, 10 Nigeria L.R. 79 (1931).
12. Ricardo v. Abal, 7 Nigeria L.R. 58, 59 (1926).
13. *See, e.g.*, Owoo v. Owoo, 11 Sel. Judg. App. W. Afr. 81 (Gold Coast 1945). *See* also Hannigan, "Native Custom, its Similarity to English Conventional Custom and its Mode of Proof," 1958 *J. Afr. L.* 101.
14. Baah v. Sackitey, [1948–51] D.C. (Land) 284 (1950).
15. On the question of which writings are authoritative under the Federal Evidence Act, see A. Park, *The Sources of Nigerian Law* 87–89 (1963). In Ghana, it has been suggested that the author must have been a legal practitioner (Krakue v. Krabah, Sup. Ct., [June 24, 1963], and must have died (Larbi v. Cato, [1960] Ghana L.R. 146, 153), although sociological research by living writers has been used (Ameoda v. Pordier, [1967] C.C. 122). In Nigeria, at least one case has relied on a book by a living person. Amoo v. Aidgun, [1957] W. Reg. Nigeria L.R. 55.
16. *See, e.g.*, Pappoe v. Kweku, [1923–25] Sel. Judg. Full Ct. 158 (Ghana 1924). *See also* Amoo v. Aidgun, [1957] W. Reg. Nigeria L.R. 55, involving a claim for an account by a customary law pledgor. The author's intention seems to have been misunderstood, with the result that the order compelling the pledgee to account was in opposition to the evidence relied upon by the author which indicated that pledges, in the absence of agreement, are not accountable. *Cf.* Woodman, "Developments in Pledges of Land in Ghanaian Customary Law," 1967 *J. Afr. L.* 8, 10.
17. Sarbah himself claimed that his book was an accurate description of the customary laws of all the Akan peoples, of which the Fanti are one. J.M. Sarbah, *supra* note 7, at title page, 3, 15. But it has been applied to the Ga, who are not Akan. *See, e.g.*, Addy v. Addy, Land Court (Accra Aug. 2, 1952).
18. Ababio v. Nsemfoo, 12 Sel. Judg. Ct. App. W. Afr. 127 (Ashanti 1946); Ehigie v. Ehigie, [1961] 1 All Nigeria L.R. 842. *Cf.* Fijabi v. Odumola, [1955–56] W. Reg. Nigeria L.R. 133.
19. Moslem law is classified in the statutes as a type of customary law. See *supra* note 4. Native courts were finally abolished in Ghana by the Courts Act of 1960, *Acts of Ghana*.
20. *See, e.g.*, Hutchison v. Essiabah, [1926–29] Sel. Judg. Full Ct. 83 (Ghana 1926).
21. The writer has come across only one case; Wutoh v. Gyebi, (1959) reported N. Ollennu, *Principles of Customary Land Law in Ghana* 193 (1962).
22. Asenso v. Nkyidwuo, [1956] 1 W. Afr. L.R. 243.
23. Akomea v. Biei, (1958) reported N. Ollennu, *supra* note 21, at 186, 189.
24. *See* A. Park, *supra* note 15, at 89–90, for the provisions in Nigeria. The institution no longer exists in Ghana.
25. *See, e.g.*, Nelson v. Ocansey, W. Afr. Ct. App. (March 11, 1950).
26. *See, e.g.*, Owiredu v. Moshie, 14 Sel. Judg. Ct. App. W. Afr. 11 (Gold Coast 1952); Suberu v. Sunmonu, 2 Sel. Judg. Fed. Sup. Ct. 33 (Nigeria 1957).

27. *E.g., In re* Beckley & Abiodun, 17 Nigeria L.R. 59 (1943).

28. *See, e.g.,* Captan v. Ankrah, 13 Sel. Judg. Ct. App. W. Afr. 151 (Gold Coast 1951), where expert evidence was preferred to the statement of customary law in Sackey v. Okantah, [1911–16] Div. & Full Ct. Judg. 88 (Ghana 1916) cited by the defendants.

29. Anane v. Mensah, [1959] Ghana L.R. 50.

30. Thus in the Ghana case, Golightly v. Ashrifi, 14 Sel. Judg. Ct. App. W. Afr. 676 (Gold Coast 1955), the court relied partly on two Nigerian decisions.

31. In Wiapa v. Solomon, Renner's Gold Coast R. 410 (Ghana 1905), the court held without evidence that hunting over vacant land gave the hunters no usufructuary title. In Jasi v. Tchum, [1911–16] Div. & Full Ct. Judg. 9 (Ghana 1911), Chief Justice Smyly indicated that he would have relied on his personal experience, had he had any on the point, where the expert witnesses were in conflict. In Asenso v. Nkyidwuo, 1 W. Afr. L.R. 243 (1956), the court, without authority or evidence, rejected the view of the native court. More recent cases of unsupported declarations of customary law are Fynn v. Kum, 2 W. Afr. L.R. 289 (1957); Boafo v. Staudt, (1958) reported N. Ollennu, *supra* note 21, at 183; Serwah v. Kesse, (1959) reported N. Ollennu id. at 201. See also Woodman, "The Scheme of Subordinate Tenures of Land in Ghana," 15 *Am. J. Comp. L.* 457 (1967) for a discussion of the judicial change of the rule on the alienability of the usufruct.

32. *See, e.g.,* the reassertion of the principle in Giwa v. Erinmilokun, [1961] 1 All Nigeria L.R. 294. Aileru v. Anibi, [1954] 20 Nigeria L.R. 46 (1952), may have been a case of a court's reliance on its own knowledge.

33. [1961] 1 All Nigeria L.R. 140.

34. *See, e.g.,* Dosunmu v. Dosunmu, 14 Sel. Judg. Ct. App. W. Afr. 527 (Lagos 1954).

35. 12 Sel. Judg. Ct. App. W. Afr. 102 (Gold Coast 1946).

36. This may be seen from a perusal of the judgment of the Divisional Court (Accra May 10, 1946).

37. Pappoe v. Kweku, [1923–25] Sel. Judg. Full Ct. 158 (Ghana 1924).

38. Abude v. Onano V. 12 Sel. Judg. Ct. App. W. Afr. 102, 105 (Gold Coast 1946).

39. A different class of examples consists of those cases in which the court's judgment against a party was on the ground that his allegations or evidence of customary law were self-contradictory. See, *e.g.,* Eze v. Igiliegbe, 14 Sel. Judg. Ct. App. W. Afr. 61 (S. Nigeria 1952).

40. *See* Federal Evidence Act, *Laws of Fed. of Nigeria* cap. 62 (1958); Evidence Laws of the Regions.

41. Giwa v. Erinmilokun, [1961] 1 All Nigeria L.R. 294. *Cf.* Coker v. Jinadu, [1958] L.L.R. 77. *See also* Kisseh v. Adabla [1961] Ghana L.R. 440 (plaintiff sued for partition of jointly owned land; the court held that the onus was on the defendant to show that customary law forbade partitioning).

41a. Cf. Antu v. Buedu [1926–29] Sel. Judg. Full Ct. 474 (Ghana 1929) (placing the onus on the party alleging a custom different from the "well-known general principle"); Fadire v. Abiri [1959] W. Reg. Nigeria L.R. 186 (placing the onus on the party alleging that the custom was the same as that judicially recognised for another area).

42. In Oloto v. Administrator-General, 12 Sel. Judg. Ct. App. W. Afr. 76 (Nigeria 1946), the court held that clear authority would be needed to establish the asserted proposition about customary law because it was so unreasonable. *See also* Odunsi v. Ojora, [1961] 1 All Nigeria L.R. 283.

43. *E.g.,* Okiji v. Adejobi, 5 Sel. Judg. Fed. Sup. Ct. 44 (Nigeria 1960).

44. It may still be possible to argue that the customary practice has changed since the earlier decision. See A. Allott, *Essays in African Law* 89–90 (1960); F. Bennion, *The Constitutional Law of Ghana* 411, 424–46 (1962). This would be different from arguing that the earlier decisions were wrong. If the contention is allowed, the onus of proof would be on the party alleging the change.

45. Larinde v. Afiko, 6 Sel. Judg. Ct. App. W. Afr. 108 (Nigeria 1940).

46. Acquah III v. Ababio, 12 Sel. Judg. Ct. App. W. Afr. 343 (Gold Coast 1948), following Yamuah IV v. Sekyi, 3 Sel. Judg. Ct. App. W. Afr. 57 (Gold Coast 1936).

47. Wutoh v. Gyebi, (1959) reported in N. Ollennu, *supra* note 21, at 193, 198.

48. Thus the decision in Owoo v. Owoo, 11 Sel. Judg. Ct. App. W. Afr. 81 (Gold Coast 1945), was based on the evidence of a single expert, which contradicted the view of the native court. The decision was the sole authority expressly relied upon in Ansah v. Sackey, 3 W. Afr. L.R. 325 (1958). However, in the later case the court may also have relied on its own knowledge of customary law.

49. *E.g.* Odunsi v. Ojora, [1961] 1 All Nigeria L.R. 283.

50. *E.g.* Ajoke v. Olateju, [1962] L.L.R. 137, 141, where a single case (from Ghana) was cited as authority for the proposition that a customary law caretaker of family property could be sued for an account by members of the family.

51. *E.g.* L.E.D.B. v. Tukur, [1963] L.L.R. 155, 160–61. There the court cited a 1957 case, holding that on the basis of the case "the legal position is clear." It held that part of the rule it applied was exemplified in a case decided in 1936. It then added that these cases must be distinguished from an earlier 1931 case; but if they could not be distinguished, then the 1931 case must be considered overruled by the 1957 case. The court also decided another point solely on the authority of the 1957 case. The influence of English doctrines of precedent on customary law in Western Nigeria has been noted by Ajayi, "The Interaction of English Law with Customary Law in Western Nigeria: II," 1960 *J. Afr. L.* 98, 100–03.

52. *See* J.M. Sarbah, *Fanti Customary Laws* 107–11 (1904); Sarbah, "Maclean and the Gold Coast Judicial Assessors," 9 *J. Afr. Soc'y* 349 (1910); Quartey-Papafio, "Law of Succession Among the Akras or Ga Tribes Proper of the Gold Coast," 10 *J. Afr. Soc'y* 64 (1910).

53. Sackey v. Okantah, [1911–16] Div. & Full Ct. Judg. 88 (Ghana 1916).

54. 13 Sel. Judg. Ct. App. W. Afr. 164 (Gold Coast 1951). The case relied upon by the court was Sackeyfio v. Tagoe, 11 Sel. Judg. Ct. App. W. Afr. 73 (Gold Coast 1945).

55. Thus it was followed without question and without further evidence in Amarfio v. Ayorkor, 14 Sel. Judg. Ct. App. W. Afr. 554 (Gold Coast 1954). In Acquaye v. Deedei, 3 W. Afr. L.R. 132 (1957), the court cited both Vanderpuye and Amarfio as authority.

56. *E.g.*, Awodiya v. Apoesho, [1959] W. Nigeria L.R. 221.

57. *E.g.*, Ifie v. Gedi, [1965] N.M.L.R. 457 (a Warri case in which the court relied entirely on Lagos decisions); Arthur v. Ayensu, 2 W. Afr. L.R. 357 (1957) (a Fanti case in which the court relied entirely on an Accra decision).

58. Courts Act of 1960, section 67, *Acts of Ghana* (now Courts Decree of 1966, *Nat. Lib. Coun. Decr.* 84, ¶ 65).

59. This is the view of F. Bennion, *supra* note 44, at 427; W. Harvey, *Law and Social Change in Ghana* 267–68 (1966). *Contra* Ollennu, "Judicial Precedent in Ghana," 2 *U. Gh. L.J.* 139, 157 (1966).

60. Northern Nigeria Native Authority Law Section 49, *Laws of N. Nigeria* Cap. 77 (1963).

61. Chieftancy Act of 1961, Sections 62–63, *Acts of Ghana*. The old provisions for the declaration and modification of customary law are still in force. *Id.* sections 58–61.

62. *See* K. Bentsi-Enchill, *Ghana Land Law* 200–01 (1964).

63. *E.g.*, Kosia v. Nimo, [1948–51] D.C. (Land) 239 (1950).

64. The contention has also been advanced in Hannigan, "The Impact of English Law Upon the Existing Gold Coast Custom and the Possible Development of the Resulting System," 8 *J. Afr. Adm.* 126 (1956).

65. Allott, "A Note on the Ga Law of Succession," 1953 *Bull. Sch. Oriental & Afr. Stud.* 164 *See also* R. Pogucki, *Gold Coast Land Tenure II*, at 37–41 (1955); K. Bentsi-Enchill, *supra* note 62, at 161–62 (referring to his experience as a practicing lawyer with Accra clients); N. Ollenu, *The Law of Testate and Intestate Succession in Ghana* 189–92 (1967).

66. Adjei v. Dabanka, 1 Sel. Judg. Ct. App. W. Afr. 63 (Gold Coast 1930).

67. *See* A. Allott, *supra* note 44, at 276–78, examples 2, 3 and 5; P. Hill, *The Gold Coast Cocoa Farmer* 77 (1956); K. Bentsi-Enchill, *supra* note 62, at 337–81. For a further account of the legal authorities on this point, see Woodman, *supra* note 16, at 20–21.

68. *E.g.*, Foko v. Foko, [1965] N.M.L.R. 3. *See also* Woodman, "A Note on Voidable Grants in Customary Law," 3 *Law in Soc'y* 59, 59–64 (1967).

69. *See* P. Lloyd, *Yoruba Land Law* 341–42 (1962). Nearly all the Nigerian cases on this point concerned Yoruba customary law.

70. Sasraku v. David, [1959] Ghana L.R. 7, 14.

71. Biei v. Akomea, 1 W. Afr. L.R. 174, 176 (1956).

72. M. Gluckman, *The Judicial Process Among the Barotse of Northern Rhodesia* 229 (1955). The author submits with respect that the words "and to things" could have been omitted because for legal purposes an individual's behavior can always be analysed in terms of its relationship to other persons.

73. T. Elias, *The Nature of African Customary Law* 55 (1956).

74. Holmes, "The Path of the Law," 10 *Harv. L. Rev.* 457, 460–01 (1897). Cf. H. Hart, *Concept of Law* 39 (1961). It is submitted that Professor Hart appropriately challenges Holmes' provocative description of the lawyer's client

as "the bad man." Nevertheless, for the purpose of considering the functions of the legal practitioner, it appears necessary to retain Holmes' basic reference to possible judicial action.

75. 13 Sel. Judg. Ct. App. W. Afr. 164 (Gold Coast 1951).

76. A. Allott, *supra* note 44, at 89.

77. S. Obi, *Modern Family Law in Southern Nigeria* 7 (1966).

78. This had been denied by several authors. *E.g.*, E. Hartland, *Primitive Law* 5, 213–14 (1924).

79. B. Malinowski, *Crime and Custom in Savage Society* 67 (1926).

80. The final form of his theory is presented in Malinowski, "A New Instrument for the Interpretation of Law—Especially Primitive," 51 *Yale L.J.* 1237 (1942). He agreed that the term "law" could be applied to other types of rules, but contended that rules of conduct requiring enforcement corresponded to "[*l*]*aw* as we use the term in our own society." *Id.* at 1243–44.

81. Hoebel, "Law and Anthropology," 31 *Va. L. Rev.* 835, 851 (1946).

82. E. Hoebel, *The Law of Primitive Man* 18–28 (1954). A similar approach, not worked out in such detail, is found in Radcliffe-Brown, "Sanction, Social," in 13 *Encyclopedia of the Social Sciences* 531 (1934).

83. E. Hoebel, *supra* note 82, at 25–26.

84. *Id.* at 28.

85. *See* Seidman, "Witch Murder and *Mens Rea:* A Problem of Society Under Radical Social Change," 28 *Mod. L. Rev.* 46 (1965).

86. Obodo v. The Queen, 4 Sel. Judg. Fed. Sup. Ct. 1 (Nigeria 1958). More details are provided in *General Report and Survey on the Nigerian Police Force for 1958*, at 14–15.

87. *See* M. Green, *Ibo Village Affairs* 103–04 (2nd ed. 1964).

88. E. Hoebel, *supra* note 82, at 211–54.

89. *Id.* at 212.

90. He describes other types of "lawful" killings. *Id.* at ch. 5.

91. Thus Hoebel mentions that today they are serviced by airplanes and steamships. *Id.* at 292.

92. Kelsen, "The Pure Theory of Law," 51 *L.Q. Rev.* 517, 534 (1935).

93. Two of the writers whose definitions are cited above, M. Gluckman, *supra* note 72, and T. Elias, *supra* note 73, relied on Goodhart's definition of law as "a rule of human conduct which is recognized as being obligatory." See Goodhart, "An Apology for Jurisprudence," in *Interpretations of Modern Legal Philosophies* 283, 288 (Sayre ed. 1947). Goodhart recognizes that "a rule may be regarded as obligatory by some and not by others," and that in such a case "there is no single answer to the question: Is it a law"? *Id.* at 290. This is the real point made in the present article. Later, however, he seems to propose a definition of "state law" requiring component rules to be recognized as obligatory by its members. *Id.* at 293. This appears to suffer from the same defect as the definitions mentioned above. See also Goodhart, "The Importance of a Definition of Law, 3" *J. Afr. Adm.* 106 (1951).

94. Holmes, *supra* note 74, at 460–61. See also B. Cardozo, *The Growth of the Law* 52 (1924).

95. J. Gray, *Nature and Sources of the Law* 82–108 (1909); J. Salmond, *Jurisprudence* 41–43 (11th ed. 1957).

96. K. Llewellyn, *The Common Law Tradition* (1960).

97. Jeffreys, Book Review, 9 *Afr. Stud.* 99 (1950). Jeffreys was criticizing Green for adopting Malinowski's definition.

98. The reply that lawyers can best define it because it is their subject of study begs the question of whether "law" really is their subject of study. If, as Jeffreys contends, "law" has only one meaning, it is possible that the lawyers may be misapplying the word.

99. E. Evans-Prichard, *The Nuer* 162 (1940).

100. *Id.* at 168. See also Evans-Pritchard, "The Nuer of the Southern Sudan," *African Political Systems* 272, 278, 293 (1940).

101. M. Gluckman, *supra* note 72, at 229.

102. *Id.* at 227. See also Gluckman, "African Jurisprudence," 18 *Advancement of Sci.* 439 (1962).

103. The "one proper meaning" approach led to Austin's exclusion of rules of customary law from the class of "laws properly so called," until they had been enforced by the courts and thus became tacit commands of the sovereign. The fallacy of this method is indicated by Williams, "International Law and the Controversary Concerning the Word 'Law,'" in *Philosophy, Politics and Society I*, at 134 (Laslett ed. 1956).

104. Malinowski, *supra* note 80, at 1249–50.

J.P.B. DE JOSSELIN DE JONG

Customary Law: A Confusing Fiction

Specialists in customary law may differ with respect to exactly how they define their terms, but few would argue that the concept of customary law is essentially meaningless and a prime candidate for the academic dustbin. One of those few is Dutch anthropologist J.P.B. de Josselin de Jong. In the following short paper, first presented in August 1948, in Brussels at the International Congress of Anthropological and Ethnological Sciences, he gives his reasons for his stance.

Scholars inquiring into the essentials of so-called "primitive law" generally take as their starting-point certain obvious characteristics of modern law and jurisprudence; codes, courts, organized sanctions. Apart from the question whether all these characteristics should be regarded as equally essential in this connection, it cannot be denied that the principle is sound. Law is not a natural phenomenon, independent of human society, but a phenomenon of culture of which we are conscious as members of our own, particular community, as participants of our own culture. In order to answer the question whether all human communities know "law" or what elements in other cultures correspond to our concept of "law," we cannot do without a clear notion of what exactly this concept means to us, here and now. Without aspiring at a definition which fully takes into consideration all aspects of the law-complex we may mention a few positive and negative characteristics about whose indispensableness there will probably be general agreement.

1. Law does not coincide with any other system of rules of conduct; 2. The differences between law and custom are of a formal and not of a material nature, the most obvious of these formal characteristics in our society being codification, organized force, jurisdiction; 3. The moral authority of law results from the conviction of its being indispensable rather than from the fear of sanctions; 4. Its regulating and administrative functions are no less important than its moral functions.

Reprinted from *Koninklijke Vereeniging Indisch Instituut*, Mededeling No. LXXX, Afd. Volkenkunde No. 29 (Amsterdam: Het Indisch Instituut, 1948), pp. 3–8; with permission.

Now it is mainly the formal characteristics just mentioned by which according to most older writers law differs from custom, which view implies that where these characteristics are lacking there is no law but only custom—or rather: there is no means for us to distinguish between law and custom. As Hartland put it: "customs that are fixed and generally obeyed are undistinguishable from law .... Primitive law is in truth the totality of custom of the tribe."[1] To Hartland primitive law really coincides with social organization in the most comprehensive sense of the word. In societies of this kind submission to custom functions as in our society does submission to law. Obviously Hartland had no reason to speak of "customary law" and in fact he did not, as far as I know.

C. van Vollenhoven and many others, however, did use the term in the sense of a system of law which does not fully correspond to our modern concept insofar as one or more of the above-mentioned formal characteristics are wanting. In the first volume of his *Het adatrecht van Nederlandsch-Indië (Customary law of the Netherlands East-Indies)*, published in 1918, Van Vollenhoven defined customary law as a body of uncodified rules of conduct which are enforced by sanctions. By "sanctions," of course, he meant organized sanctions, involving the existence of some organ, either an individual or a group, which has the power and authority to apply sanctions. This is meant when he and others define customary law or "adat-law" as "all customs that have legal consequences." To be sure, Van Vollenhoven realized that the dividing-line between law and customary law thus defined is rather vague. He himself, in fact, illustrated this lack of preciseness by means of significant examples. But he was not specially interested in the theoretical problem of the relation between custom and law: his primary concern was an administration of justice adapted as far as feasible to native custom and in view of this purpose a rough outline was both indispensable and sufficient. He evidently judged it necessary to emphasize the legal character of a large body of uncodified rules with a view to modern juridical misconceptions concerning this matter. With regard to the Indonesian field in particular he had to fight not only the reluctance to take native custom seriously, but also the tenacious mixing-up of adat and Mohammedan religious law. This may account for his preference for the term "adat-law."

In the period of 13 years between the first and second volumes of Van Vollenhoven's "Adatrecht" Malinowski, in his *Crime and Custom in Savage Society* (1926), sharply attacked what he considered to be the current ideas about the essence of "primitive law." He rejected the importance of formal characteristics, especially of organized sanction, as well as the conception of custom as the supreme regulating force, and he really identified primitive law with a system of social mechanisms built up roundabout the principle of reciprocity. I think it is superfluous to give a more detailed résumé of his theory: no doubt most of my hearers are familiar with it. Probably many anthropologists have experienced a similar mixed feeling of admiration and perplexity as I felt after reading his brilliant exposition. Perplexity, because, for all his profound and subtle analyses of all sorts of social interactions, the crucial problem what exactly is the difference between law and custom in Trobriand and similar societies was left unanswered. As W. Seagle has sharply formulated, this crucial problem is: "whether in the absence of political organization and of specific juridical institutions such as courts and codes, certain modes of conduct may be segregated from the general body of customs as at least incipiently legal".[2] It is true that Malinowski pretended having shown "that the rules of law form but one well-defined category within the body of custom" (p. 54), but it is not less true that this distinction was obviously based on contents, a quite arbitrary criterion, since law (I cite Seagle once more) "has no subject matter of its own."[3] What, according to Malinowski, may be termed Trobriand "civil law" are those rules of conduct which in modern society belong to "private law," while the rules of conduct "safeguarding life, property, and personality" are called by him "criminal law." And when, in his supplementary comment in the Introduction to H.J. Hogbin's book *Law and Order in Polynesia. A Study of Primitive Legal Institutions* (1934), he qualified law as "effective custom" or "the dynamism of custom," he really maintained his definition "by function and not by form" as he called it, contents, subject matter remaining his leading criterion.

It seems very strange indeed that Malinowski, while sharply criticizing the view that in societies lacking politically organized sanctions law and custom are one, custom reigning supreme, did not realize that his own description of the state of affairs in Trobriand society did not by any means refute the rejected view, but on the contrary confirmed it. For what else was this system of rights and duties governed by the principle of reciprocity than custom? This is not to say that his penetrating analysis of the dynamics of custom in Trobriand society has taught us nothing new. But owing to his over-emphasizing the functionalistic point of view and his disparaging all formal aspects, his own vision had become blurred and so, with regard to the central problem, we are left exactly where we were.

Nevertheless Malinowski's argument, expounded with his characteristic acumen and persuasiveness, has not failed to make a deep impression. Most writers dealing with the problem of primitive law after that have been taking great pains to work up his views in their own theories instead of analysing them critically and drawing their conclusions consistently. A few examples may suffice to illustrate the uncertainty and even confusion resulting from such efforts to work up contradictory arguments into a consistent whole.

We have seen that Van Vollenhoven in his first volume defined customary law as uncodified rules of conduct enforced by organized sanctions. In his second volume however, which appeared 5 years after Malinowski's *Crime and Custom*, he reverted to the problem and, without repeating his former definition, circumscribed customary law as "the mutual interaction between a normal custom and the other normal customs on one side and between normal customs and disturbing divergencies on the other side." "Even recommendation and disapproval," in his opinion, "are law and not just morals if they are indissolubly connected with command and prohibition in collective consciousness and behaviour . . . . . recommendation and disapproval are not vague notions in customary law" and he adduced examples of rules of conduct in which, as he expressed it, 'thus it happens', 'thus it is allowed', and 'thus it should be' coincide and which, though never confirmed by a judge, are generally respected. Only when somebody tries to violate this magical circle jurisdiction makes its appearance."[4] We see that, while the criterion of sanction is not abandoned altogether, a new element is introduced: the mutual interaction of normal customs enforced by recommendation and disapproval. Thereby the domain of customary law is really extended far—how far remains uncertain—beyond the limits indicated by his first definition, organized sanction being no longer the decisive factor.

A. S. Diamond, in his most useful and scholarly work *Primitive Law* (1935), after emphatically assenting to Malinowski's criticism of Hartland and expounding the principle of reciprocity, yet concludes that all those rules cannot be called "law," because "law" implies the existence of courts or "other communal organs for the purpose of laying down or enforcing any rules of civil law" and "special organs . . . . . . for the purpose of the settlement of disputes between members."[5] To my mind there appears to be some confusion in this argumentation. When one accepts Malinowski's functionalistic conception of the social mechanisms based on reciprocity as an argument against the absolute power of custom, one cannot at the same time reject their legal character.

Again, we meet with a similar lack of consistency in R. Thurnwald's "Werden, Wandel und Gestaltung des Rechtes im Lichte der Völkerforschung," which appeared in 1934 as the fifth volume of his admirable, encyclopaedic *Die menschliche Gesellschaft in ihren ethnosoziologischen Grundlagen*. The author deals briefly with the problem in his "Einleitung." "Mehr und mehr," he says, "hat die Einsicht Platz gegriffen, dasz das Recht eine Funktion der Lebensbedingungen und Geistesverfassung einer Gesellschaft ist, ein Regulativ für das Verhalten der Persönlichkeit innerhalb einer Gemeinde. Aus diesem Grunde hängt alles von der Art, der Zusammensetzung, der Tradition und der äusseren und inneren Situation dieser Gemeinde ab. Die 'Entstehung' der Rechtsnormen und ihre Fixierungsart spielt unter diesen Umständen eine untergeordnete Rolle".[6] After these rather non-committal pronouncements, however, he pursues: "Das Moment eines organisierten Zwanges hebt die Rechts-ordnung heraus gegenüber Brauch und Sitte"[7] and once more: "Besonders wichtig ist die Ausbildung einer anerkannten und institutionsmässigen Autorität im Innern eines Gemeindewesens"[8]. .... "Die Gewohnheit hat durch moralischen Anerkennung der leitenden Persönlichkeiten den Wert einer Sitte erhalten, und der anerkannte Zwang erhebt sie zum Recht"[9]. This definition sounds lucid enough: without organized force involving official authority there is no law, but "Brauch und Sitte" (Customs and manners). But then, quite unexpectedly, Malinowski's vision comes cropping up: "Wenn man aus allen Regelungen zwischen menschlichen Verhaltungsweisen .... den innersten Kern herauszuschälen sucht, so gelangt man zur Erkenntnis, dasz Reziprozität das ist, was die Wage des Rechts einspielen lässt".[10] Although this formulation is rather vague again we may consider it to suggest that, after all, it is not authority and organized force, but the dynamic principle of reciprocity which distinguishes law from custom. Further, Thurnwald, after mentioning the older view that there cannot be law without written codes and stating that this means degrading the so-called customary law (Gewohnheitsrecht) to something "gewissermassen nur halb Juristischen" gives this comment" "Diese Auffassung wird man mit gewissem Vorbehalten in der Tat nicht ganz Unrecht geben können."[11] This hesitating attitude is the more baffling as he himself, in his first chapter, has given a number of examples of uncodified, but explicitly established rules whose legal character cannot be doubted. It is evident, I think, that Thurnwald too has got entangled in the contradictory views of and intersecting approaches to the core of the matter which he tries to harmonize with each other.

These few examples, which could easily be multiplied, are sufficient to show that Malinowski's stimulating and provoking attack has created a good deal of confusion, especially with regard to the concept of customary law. Of course I do not mean to say that all vagueness concerning the real issue is to be traced back to Malinowski's theory. Marcel Mauss, for instance, in the over-succinct but profound chapter on "Phénomènes juridiques" in his *Manuel d'ethnographie* (1947), does not give evidence of having been strongly influenced by Malinowski, and yet he, too, has not succeeded in explaining what "customary law" really stands for. Apart from its succinctness, his argument may easily give rise to misunderstanding because his conception of law is a rather personal one, his terminology deviating accordingly. "Le droit," he says, "comprend l'ensemble des coutumes et des lois; comme tel, il constitue l'armature de la société, il est (citing Portalis) 'le précipité d'un peuple'; ce qui définit un groupe d'hommes, ce n'est ni sa religion, ni ses techniques, ni rien d'autre que son droit."[12] In accordance with this conception of law the whole of social, political, and family organization is classed with "phénomènes juridiques." However, within this very large domain of juridical phenomena in the widest sense of the word juridical rules and norms in a narrower sense are distinguished from non-juridical ones by means of formal and functional criteria. The function of all law, in this narrower sense, is an organizing one: "le droit est le moyen d'organiser le système des attentes collectives. . . . . . . Les phénomènes juridiques sont les phénomènes moraux organisés."[13] Considered from a formal point of view, law in modern society consists of a mixture of codified and uncodified rules of conduct, that is, of codified and customary law. In primitive society law is a mixture of formulated and unformulated rules, but the whole of it is termed "customary law." An important formal characteristic of all law is its preciseness: "il y a obligation juridique quand il y a terme précis de l'obligation et terme précis de l'infliction et de la peine."[14] The formulated rules of (primitive) customary law are to be found in proverbs, popular sayings, tales, myths, in short, in unwritten literature; the unformulated rules are to be deduced from collective reactions. (Primitive) customary law is to be looked for rather everywhere ("un peu partout"). Besides, in all these societies there are specialists who know those rules and who function as jurists, for instance, in collective consultations, when there is perfect consciousness of customary law with respect to concrete cases. It is a fiction that customary law is rigorously fixed and unchangeable: on the contrary, it is through customary law that social life adjusts itself more or less consciously to changing conditions.

In this argument customary law stands for: 1. uncodified rules of conduct or modes of behaviour taken into account by modern jurisprudence; 2. formulated or unformulated rules of conduct or modes of behaviour or a mixture of both in primitive society: in fact, it has become practically meaningless.

After all that has been written about primitive law since Henry Maine's *Ancient law* it should be clear by now that the essential problem of the relation between phenomena of law and phenomena of custom has been obscured again and again by gathering all dubious cases into a separate category which is neither law nor custom but a certain "tertium quid" which does not require a sharp definition. And it should also be clear that the "vitium originis" is the neglecting of the formal aspects of law of which Malinowski's theory is an outstanding example. This does not mean, however, as has been intimated already by Seagle, that we should cling dogmatically to modern forms of juridical procedure and authority. When Radcliffe Brown states: "The term (law) is. . . . usually confined to 'social control through the systematic application of the force of politically organized society'" and then informs us that in his article "the field of law will therefore be regarded as coterminous with that of organized legal sanction,"[15] this statement is acceptable as a kind of working-hypothesis or a convenient starting-point. Radcliffe Brown himself, indeed, did not pretend it to be more. But when, after an analysis of the Ifugao system, he concludes: "The Ifugao thus have an organized system of justice, which, however, does not constitute a system of law in the narrow sense of the term since there is no judicial authority," some of us may wonder whether this case does not prove that the preliminary definition has been too narrow after all. However this may be, Brown's instructive survey certainly shows that it will be very difficult to give a definition of the cultural phenomenon of law sufficiently narrow to exclude custom and sufficiently wide to allow for the baffling variety of ways in which the principle of legality may manifest itself. As a muddled terminology may be an impediment to clear thinking we should begin by abolishing the term of "customary law."

Notes

1. E. Sidney Hartland, *Primitive Law*, London 1924, p. 2, 5.
2. William Seagle, "Primitive Law and professor Malinowski," *American Anthropologist*, 1937, p. 280.
3. Seagle, op. cit. p. 283.
4. Van Vollenhoven, op. cit. 236, 400.
5. Diamond, op. cit. p. 187.
6. Thurnwald, op. cit. p. 1.
7. Thurnwald, op. cit. p. 2.
8. Thurnwald, op. cit. p. 3.
9. Thurnwald, op. cit. p. 4.
10. Thurnwald, op. cit. p. 5.
11. Thurnwald, op. cit. p. 13.
12. Mauss, op. cit. p. 110.
13, Mauss, op. cit. p. 111.
14. Mauss, op. cit. p. 112.
15. A.R. Radcliffe Brown, "Primitive Law," *Encyclopedia of the Social Sciences* IX (1933), p. 202.

A.W.B. SIMPSON

The Common Law and Legal Theory

In English legal parlance, the phrase of choice tends to be "common law" rather than "customary law," or "folk law." But no matter what idiom is employed, the theoretical issues remain more or less the same. One major issue which inevitably arises in attempts to delineate the nature of customary law is the question of "system." If law, usually written or codified law, is understood or defined in terms of belonging to a coherent system or pattern, then unwritten or customary law is very often dismissed. Unwritten or customary law seems to those trained in Western law to lack coherency or pattern. Instead, customary law appears to be a hodge-podge of unrelated normative rules. This is why so many colonial administrators were and are so exceedingly anxious to "write down" unwritten law, to codify it, so as to give it the appearance of system or pattern.

In the following essay, the issue is thrashed out, not in Africa, but in England, which should serve as a reminder that folk law exists in all *human societies. The author is a Professor of Law at the University of Michigan Law School and has written numerous studies of the law. See, for example,* Cannibalism and the Common Law *(Chicago: University of Chicago Press, 1984).*

For earlier discussions of the role of folk law in England, see F.A. Greer, "Custom in the Common Law," Law Quarterly Review, 9 (1893), 153–170; W. Jethro Brown, Customary Law in Modern England," Columbia Law Review, 5 (1905), 561–583; F.L. Schlechter, "Popular Law and Common Law in Medieval England," Columbia Law Review, 28 (1928), 269–299; E.K. Braybrooke, "Custom as a Source of English Law," Michigan Law Review, 50 (1951), 71–94.

It should perhaps be noted that much of the detailed research on folk law has been carried out on the local county or province level. For an example, see N. Neilson, "Custom and the Common Law in Kent," Harvard Law Review, 38 (1924–1925), 482–498.

© Oxford University Press, 1973. Reprinted from *Oxford Essays in Jurisprudence* (Second Series), edited by A.W.B. Simpson (1973) with permission of Oxford University Press.

I. Introduction

In England and in those parts of the world where the English legal tradition has been received the characteristic type of law is common law, as contrasted with statute law. Common law in this sense has of course been modified by equity, but then equity is just another form of common law. The common law has in its time been given a variety of classifying titles which reflect different views as to its distinguishing or characteristic feature—for example "case law," "judiciary law," "judge-made law," "customary law," and "unwritten law." Names such as these reflect theories as to the nature of the common law, and it would be easy enough to cull from legal writings the expression of very divergent views of the institution. It seems to me however that to date no very satisfactory analysis of the nature of the common law has been provided by legal theory; indeed the matter has received remarkably little sustained attention by theoretical writers. What has been the subject of much writing is the doctrine of precedent or *stare decisis*; indeed a search of the literature for discussions of the nature of the common law tends to locate only accounts of the working of this doctrine, which is itself I suppose "part of" the common law. To a historian at least any identification between the common law system and the doctrine of precedent, any attempt to explain the nature of the common law in terms of *stare decisis*, is bound to seem unsatisfactory, for the elaboration of rules and principles governing the use of precedents and their status as authorities is relatively modern, and the idea that there could be binding precedents more recent still. The common law had been in existence for centuries before anybody was very excited about these matters, and yet it functioned as a system of law without such props as the concept of the *ratio decidendi*, and functioned well enough.

Nor does the common law appear to have wholly altered its character over the years, and a theory of the common law, if it is to seem satisfactory, must cater for this continuity. It must accommodate the common law of the seventeeth century as well as the common law of the twentieth, or at least provide a view of the common law which will serve to explain whatever changes have occurred in the general character of the institution. One such change is indeed the increased importance attached to authority, in particular quoted judicial opinions, in the working of the system.

In the sense used here a theory or general view of the common law represents an attempt to provide an answer to the question whether the common law can be said to exist at all—and this has been seriously doubted—and if so in what sense. Put rather differently, such a theory will seek to explain how, if at all, statements in the form "It is the law that . . .," such as "It is the law that contracts require consideration," can meaningfully be made, when such statements are conceived to be statements of the common law. Such an explanation is essential to the understanding of the workings of the judicial process, which is conducted upon the assumption that the common law (we are not concerned with statute) always provides an answer to the matter in issue, and one which is independent of the will of the court. What may be called general theoretical propositions of the common law, which are the stuff of legal argument and justification, take a variety of forms. Sometimes they are said to state *doctrines* of the common law (the doctrine of offer and acceptance), sometimes *principles* or *general principles* (the principle of "volenti non fit iniuria") sometimes *rules* (the rule in *Rylands v. Fletcher*), sometimes *definitions* (the definition of conversion), and this is by no means an exclusive list of a diversity which is recognized more generously in the language of lawyers than in the writings of legal philosophers. Some attempts have been made to differentiate these concepts; thus Bingham,[1] and more recently Dworkin,[2] have sought to distinguish *rules* from *principles*. For present purposes these distinctions are not important, and all legal propositions may be considered together, and merely distinguished from propositions which purport only to be *about* the common law. An example would be such a statement as "The common law does not favour self-help." Put forward in a different form, for example like this, "It is a principle of the common law that self help is to be discouraged," this would in my scheme rank as a general theoretical proposition of the common law; it would then purport to state the law rather than pass an observation about the law. It is primarily with propositions of law that I am here concerned.

In passing it is however important to notice that in legal reasoning propositions which are neither propositions *of* law nor propositions *about* law feature prominently. For example, when Lord Devlin said in the course of his judgment in *Behrens* v. *Bertram Mills*,[3] "If a person wakes up in the middle of the night and finds an escaping tiger on top of his bed and suffers a heart attack, it would be nothing to the point that the intentions of the tiger were quite amiable," he was not making a legal observation, but justifying a decision on the law governing liability for dangerous animals by an appeal to common-sense. No doubt these non-legal justificatory propositions could be further divided—some for example refer to moral considerations, others to expediency—and they are used to claim for a decision a rationality which is not based upon the artificial reason of the law; though not themselves legal propositions they may be used to support the contention that this or that is the law. In the common law system no very clear distinction exists between saying that a particular solution to a problem is in accordance with the law, and saying that it is the rational, or fair, or just solution.

If, however, we confine attention to specifically legal propositions, how are they to be explained? The type of answer given to this question will depend upon the particular theoretical viewpoint adopted, for there appear to me to be a number of different possible conceptions of the nature of the common law. The predominant conception today is that the common law consists of a system of rules; in terms of this legal propositions (if correct) state what is contained in these rules. I wish to consider the utility of this conception, and to contrast it with an alternative idea—the idea that the common law is best understood as a system of customary law, that is, as a body of traditional ideas received within a caste of experts.

II. Positivism and the Common Law as a System of Rules

The idea that the common law is a set of rules, in some unusual sense forming a system, is intimately associated with the movement known as legal positivism. Though purporting to be an observation, it is best viewed as a dogma, which derives basically from viewing all law in terms of a model of statute law. In its purest form legal positivism involves two basic assumptions, which will be found, variously elaborated, or sometimes merely covertly adopted, in very many theoretical writings. The first is that all law is positive law, and what this means at its simplest is that all laws owe their status as such to the fact that they have been laid down. In the curious and archaic language of Austin, laws properly so called are laws *by position*;[4] they are set, or prescribed, and human law at least is laid down by humans to humans. Blackstone, though inconsistent in his positivism, thought that municipal law was prescribed by what he called the supreme power in the State,[5] whilst Gray thought that laws were rules of conduct laid down by the courts.[6] Both assumed that laws must have been laid down by somebody or other to rank as laws, and to this extent were positivists. When in a modern book on the doctrine of precedent Professor Cross[7] writes, "Such a rule (one derived from a precedent or series of precedents) is law 'properly so called' and law *because it was made by the judges*, [my italics] and not because it originated in common usage, or the judges' idea of justice and public convenience," he is expressing the first basic assumption of positivism. In an uneasily modified form the same assumption is writ large in Kelsen:[8] "Law is always positive law, and its positivity lies in the fact that it is created and annulled by acts of human beings, thus being independent of morality and other norm systems." The insistence that all law is positive law originally stood in opposition to the claim that some laws, or all laws, owed their status as such to the fact that they were in accordance with or sanctioned by nature. Pure positivism thus involves the notion that there is only one possible alternative basis for law to that provided by natural law theories. The most obvious point at which difficulty is encountered in maintaining the thesis that all law is posited is when dealing with custom, which common sense would suggest is not laid down; customs, we know, grow up. Kelsen runs into difficulty over this; though admitting custom as a possible type of law (to be contrasted with statute law) he is at pains to insist that even the norms of customary law, in a system which admits custom as "a law-creating act," are *positive*. To preserve the dogma the notion of laying down or prescribing law has to be emasculated until it means only that the norms of customary law are the products of acts of will, even though these acts of will are not directed to the making of law at all. "Since custom is constituted by human acts, even norms created by custom are created by acts of human behaviour, and are therefore like the norms which are the subjective meaning of legislative acts—'posited' or 'positive' norms."[9] This is hardly convincing, but my point is only to illustrate the basic *credo*.

The second basic assumption is less easy to state with precision. It involves conceiving of law as a sort of code. The law including the common law, is identified with a notional set of propositions which embody the corpus of rules, principles, commands, norms, maxims, or whatever, which have, at any given time, been laid down. For present purposes nothing turns upon distinctions between rules, principles, maxims, et cetera, so this second assumption can be put thus: the law exists as a set of rules, the rules being identical with and constituting the law. Combining these two assumptions of positivism the common law must be conceived of as existing as a set or code of rules which have been laid down by somebody or other, and which owe their status as law to the fact that they have been so laid down. We are to conceive of the common law, somewhat perversely, as if it had already been codified, when we all know it has not. And if communication by words is the manner in which the action of laying down the law takes place, then the words used will constitute the law. In terms of such a model the general theoretical propositions of the common law can be thought of as stating rules of the common law, if "correct," or as putative statements which may or may not be correct.

Around these two basic assumptions cluster various ideas either derived from them or at least intimately associated with them. Thus if all laws are laid down, all laws must have an author, for someone must have performed the act of positing the law. Secondly, there must be some test or criterion for identifying the lawmaker or lawmakers who have authority to lay down the law, or entitlement to do so, for it would be absurd if anyone who cared to do so could lay down law; the primary ground for saying that this or that is the law will be the fact that the right person or group laid it down. Thirdly, if law is by definition laid down, all law must originate in legislation, or in some law-creating act. Fourthly, law so conceived will appear as the product of acts of will, and the law which results as the will of the lawmaker. Fifthly, if laws owe their status to their having been laid down by the right author, it cannot be a necessary characteristic of law that it should have a particular content, for its content will depend upon the will of the lawmaker, who may be devil or angel or something in between—hence the separation of law and morals. And sixthly, if law consists of what has been laid down, then what has been laid down, conceived as a code, is exhaustive of the law at any given moment, so that where nothing has been laid down, there is no law; the law is conceived of as in principle a finite system. And unless one admits the possibility of the existence of a number of co-existing common laws, which seems absurd, there must at one moment be one unique set of rules constituting the common law.

This may be called the "school-rules concept" of law, and it more or less assimilates all law to statute law. In recent times there have been advanced what may be called weaker versions of positivism, which have gone some way towards abandoning the first assumption whilst retaining the second: law continues to be conceived of as a set of rules, but their status as law does not necessarily depend upon their having been laid down. Examples are to be found in the legal theories of Kelsen (who, as we have seen, still maintains that all law is positive in a peculiar sense) and Hart.[10] Such theories[11] are committed to giving some explanation of how one is to tell whether a putative rule belongs to the club or not. The answer given is that membership depends upon the satisfaction of tests provided by some other higher or basic rule or rules, sometimes called power-conferring rules or rules of competence, in absent-minded conformity to the idea that all law originates in legislation. Those which qualify are characterized as valid—valid meaning "binding" or "existing as a rule of the system"—and the corpus of rules possessing the quality of validity, together with the basic rule or rules (grundnorm, constitution, rule of recognition) constitute the legal system. A legal system is conceived not as an institution, but as a code of rules, systematic only in the peculiar sense that the contents of the code satisfies the tests. Although it might seem consistent with such an approach to admit the possibility that some rules might qualify because of their content (the rule possessing some supposed quality, such as being in accordance with the will of God or the principle of utility) both Kelsen and, less clearly, Hart seem to have in mind criteria dealing with the mode of origin of the rule, or, as Dworkin has put it, with the "pedigree"[12] of the rule, rather than content. All law is like statute law in that its authority is independent of its content.

As applied to the common law such weak versions of positivism could in principle no doubt cater for the possibility that it consists of rules which are not necessarily of legislative origin, nobody having ever laid them down. Kelsen does not really develop the application of his theory to the common law. In his *General Theory of Law and the State*[13] he conceives of law, in the form of general norms, as originating either in custom or legislation, statutory law and customary law being the two fundamental types of law. Insofar as the common law derives from judicial precedents he apparently conceives of it as statutory; insofar as it is based upon the long practice of the courts it is customary law. Hart too does not devote more than a small part of *The Concept of Law* to the detailed application of his theory to the common law. But he envisages the possibility that in a complex legal system the criteria for the validity of rules may include reference to "customary practice," "general declarations of specified persons," and "past judicial decisions" in addition to reference to an "authoritative text" or "legislative enactment;"[14] such criteria no doubt are included to cater for the common law. Elsewhere he seems to regard the activities of courts as sometimes legislative in character; like Kelsen, Hart perhaps conceives of the common law as a medley of rules of different character. But in the absence of a rather more full treatment of the subject it is not at all easy to see quite how the common law fits into the scheme of things.

III. Defects of Positivism

But both in its strong and weak forms positivism seems to me to present a defective scheme for understanding the nature of the common law. In its strong form, as presented by Austin, it claims that the common law consists of rules which owe their status as law to the fact that they have been laid down. Now the plausibility of claiming that the common law has been posited—presumably by the judges, there being no other obvious candidates for the honour—turns largely upon the offering of a choice between the devil and the deep blue sea. Austin presented his hearers with the alternative of either agreeing that the common law was laid down by the judges, or believing in the childish fiction (as he called it) that the common law was "a miraculous something made by nobody, existing, I suppose, from eternity and merely declared from time to time by the judges."[15] Confronted with this crude choice it is natural to prefer the former view. But difficulties arise if an attempt is made to apply Austin's view to a specific instance. Consider, for example, the rule that parole contracts require consideration (I choose this example because nobody would, I think, deny that this is a rule of the common law). Austin tells us "there can be no law without a legislative act"[16] and the legislative act here must be a judicial decision, if one is to be found. Now it is well known that this rule has been on the common law scene since the sixteenth century, and some hundreds of reported cases would seem to a historian to be relevant to the understanding of the history and evolution of the rule. There would be no difficulty whatever in citing *authority* for the existence of the rule—that is to say acceptable warrants for the contention that there is such a rule. One might for example cite *Eastwood v. Kenyon*,[17] decided some three centuries after the rule had, as we say, emerged, or perhaps *Rann v. Hughes*,[18] a little earlier, or perhaps a statement by a modern text-writer. No doubt the best possible authority would be a recent case in the Lords applying the rule. No such case in fact exists, but let us suppose there is a decision, reported in the Appeal Cases for 1970. It would seem to me to be absurd to identify such a case with an act of legislation, conferring the status of law on the rule. For we know that in some meaningful sense the rule has been law for centuries before this. The point is that the production of authority that this or that is the law is not the same as the identification of acts of legislation. Conversely what might plausibly rank as an act of judicial legislation will not necessarily rank as good authority. Suppose that one was able to find a case, decided say in 1540, where the assembled judges ruled that consideration was necessary in parole contracts, and there was every reason to suppose that this was the first case in which this ruling was given. Not only would it seem wrong to say that the rule derived its status as law today from this antique decision, but the decision would not even rank as particularly good authority for the rule. We may contrast the case of a rule which is of legislative origin—by way of example take that jurisprudential old chestnut, the rule that a will requires two witnesses. Here we can identify the act of legislation which conferred the status of law on the rule as the Wills Act of 1837, and this enactment (granted certain presuppositions) is the reason why today wills do require two witnesses for effective attestation. The statute is both the only reason and a conclusive reason for saying that this is the law. The notion that the common law consists of rules which are the product of a series of acts of legislation (mostly untraceable) by judges (most of whose names are forgotten) cannot be made to work, if taken seriously, because common law rules enjoy whatever status they possess not because of the circumstances of their origin, but because of their continued reception. Of course it is true that judges are voluntary agents, and the way in which they decide cases and the views they express in their opinions are what they choose to express. Their actions create precedents, but creating a precedent is not the same thing as laying down the law. The opinions they express possess in varying and uncertain degree authority, as do opinions expressed by learned writers, but to express an authoritative opinion is not the same thing as to legislate. There exists no context in which a judicial statement to the effect that this or that is the law confers the status of law on the words uttered, and it is merely misleading to speak of judicial legislation.

Weaker versions of positivism escape the difficulty involved in the claim that all the rules of the common law are the product of judicial legislative acts. They share however with pure positivism the claim that the law—and this includes the common law—consists of a set of rules, a sort of code, which satisfies tests of validity prescribed by other rules. Such theories suffer from defects which have their source in the confusion of ideals with reality. Put simply, life might be much simpler if the common law consisted of a code of rules, identifiable by reference to source rules, but the reality of the matter is that it is all much more chaotic than that, and the only way to make the common law conform to the ideal would be to codify the system, which would then cease to be common law at all.

It is firstly central to such theories that there exist rules setting out the criteria which must be satisfied by other rules for them to belong to the system. These rules exist either in the sense that they are used and accepted by those concerned—roughly by the caste of lawyers—as the proper way of identifying other rules, or in the sense that they are the necessary presuppositions which make the identification of other rules possible. Either way it seems we must locate these supposed rules by considering the way in which legal propositions are justified, and legal argument conducted. Now it is quite true that in relatively recent times in the long history of the common law growing attention has been devoted, both by the judiciary and by legal commentators, to the formulation of rules governing the use of authorities in legal argument. Such rules constitute attempts to state the proper practice over such questions as what courts are bound by what decisions, how one is to distinguish authoritative statements of law from statements of no authority, what law reports should be used and what difference, if any, it makes if a writer is dead or alive. It is all a very theological world, with mysteries similar to those which surround the doctrine of papal infallibility. These rules governing the proper use of authority and the reverence due to it are notoriously controversial, and we all know both that the practice of the courts is not at all consistent in these matters, and that judicial views as to the proper thing to do both differ and change. One moment the House of Lords or the Court of Criminal Appeal is absolutely bound by its own decisions, the next moment it is not. All is reminiscent of the smile on the face of the Cheshire cat. Such rules as are advanced are commonly vague or qualified by escape clauses (the *per incuriam* doctrine, for example), and on very many matters no rules can be said to exist at all. For example, what is one supposed to do with a House of Lords decision where they all say different things? And what is the authoritarian pecking order between a decision of the American Supreme Court, dicta by the late Scrutton L.J., and an article by Pollock? There are no rules to deal with conundrums of this sort. Furthermore arguments to the effect that this or that is the law are commonly supported by reference to ideas which are not specifically legal—expediency, commonsense, morality, and so forth—as in the example of Lord Devlin and the errant tiger; they are supported by reference to reason and not authority. And nobody, I think, would claim that rationality in the common law can be reduced to rules. These familiar facts form the background to the notion of tests of validity, which involves a claim that legal reasoning and justification is governed by rules to an extent which it is not; legal life is far too untidy. Only if it were the case both that the use of authority in the law was wholly rule-governed, and all legal argument based upon authority, would such a theory correspond with reality.

A second objection to the notion of the common law as a system of rules turns upon the contrast between the essentially shadowy character of the common law and the crisp picture of a set of identifiable rules. Consider for example contexts in which a common lawyer might well talk of rules—the rule in *Rylands* v. *Fletcher*,[19] the rule in *Shelley's Case*,[20] or the rule in *Hadley* v. *Baxendale*.[21] These I take to be paradigm cases of rules of the common law, and to say that the common law consists of rules suggests a system of law in which such rules are the norm rather than the exception. Now one obvious characteristic of these rules is that their text is fairly well settled, though even in the cases where this is so the text is not utterly sacrosanct; the rule in *Rylands* v. *Fletcher* might for example be reformulated or more elegantly stated without the heavens falling; furthermore there may exist exceptions to these rules which are not included in a statement of the rule. But the general position in the common law is that it lacks an authoritative authentic text; as Pollock put it, the common law " ... professes ... to develop and apply principles that have never been committed to any authentic form of words."[22] It consequently distorts the nature of the system to conceive of the common law as a set of rules, an essentially precise and finite notion, as if one could in principle both state the rules of the common law and count them like so many sheep, or engrave them on tablets of stone.

IV. Is the Common Law a Fiction?

Indeed in an important sense it is in general the case that one cannot say what the common law is, if its existence is conceived of as consisting of a set of rules, and if saying what the law is means reporting what rules are to be found in the catalogue. The realization that this was so led Jeremy Bentham into the most powerful attack ever made upon the idea that the common law could be meaningfully said to exist at all, and it is no accident that this attack was made by a positivist. Although his view of the matter wavered, his extreme and characteristic opinion was that the existence of the common law was "a fiction from beginning to end," and belief in its existence no more than "a mischievous delusion."[23] Of the expression "common law" he wrote: "In these two words you have a name pretended to be the name of a really existent object:—look for any such existing object—look for it till doomsday, no such object will you find."[24] The common law was "mock law," "sham law," "quasi-law," and in consequence the exercise of the judicial function an example of "power everywhere arbitrary."[25] It is instructive to see what drove Bentham into this scepticism. What he perceived very clearly was the existence of an incompatibility between the "school-rules concept" of law and the thesis that the common law could be regarded as existing in any real sense. His thesis is perhaps most clearly stated in the *Comment on the Commentaries*: "*As a system of general rules*, the common law is a thing merely imaginary."[26] The italics are mine, the point being that Bentham's scepticism leaves open the possibility that in some other sense the predication of existence of the common law might be meaningful. Bentham's scepticism depends mainly upon the fact that rules can only be stated in a language—if somebody asks me to tell him one of the rules of chess I have to *say* something or *write* something in reply. But it is a feature of the common law system that there is no way of settling the correct text or formulation of the rules, so that it is inherently impossible to state so much as a single rule in what Pollock called "any authentic form of words." How can it be said that the common law exists as a system of general rules, when it is impossible to say what they are?

Bentham's point depends upon the familiar fact that if six pundits of the profession, however sound and distinguished, are asked to write down what they conceive to be the rule or rules governing the doctrine of *res ipsa loquitur*, the definition of murder or manslaughter, the principles governing frustration of contract or mistake as to the person, it is in the highest degree unlikely that they will fail to write down six different rules or sets of rules. And if by some happy chance they all write down (for example) "killing with malice aforethought" an invitation to explain what *that* means will inevitably produce *tot jurisprudentes quot leges*. Again we all know that no two legal treatises state the law in the same terms, there being a law of torts according to Street, and Heuston, and Jolowich and James and the contributors to Clerk and Lindsell, and we buy them all because they are all different. And what is true of the academics is true perhaps even more dramatically of the judges, who are forever disagreeing, often at inordinate length. When, after long and expensive argument the Law Lords deliver themselves *ex cathedra* of their opinions— and this is the best we can do—they either confine themselves to laconic agreement or *all say different things, and this even when they claim to be in complete agreement.* It would hardly be worth their while to deliver separate opinions if this were not so. Nor does the common law system admit the possibility of a court, however elevated, reaching a final, authoritative statement of what the law is in a general abstract sense. It is as if the system placed particular value upon dissension, obscurity, and the tentative character of judicial utterances. As a system of legal thought the common law then is inherently vague; it is a feature of the system that uniquely authentic statements of the rules which, so positivists tell us, comprise the common law, cannot be made.

Such extreme scepticism as Bentham's seems to me to carry us too far, for at any given moment in time there appear to me to be many propositions of law which would secure general agreement amongst expert lawyers as being correct, and if there are wide differences in the way in which propositions of law are formulated there is at the same time a very considerable measure of agreement as to the practical application of the law in actual cases. If the common law is a fiction from beginning to end, and the exercise of judicial power everywhere arbitrary, it is difficult to see what explanation can be given of this. Now one way of explaining this cohesion of thought is to say that in spite of a certain degree of vagueness and uncertainty the source rules of the common law do not work at all badly. Hart, for example, says: "The result of the English system of precedent has been to produce, by its use, a body of rules of which a vast number of both major and minor importance, are as determinate as any statutory rule. They can only be altered by statute."[27] I doubt this explanation. If we look back into the history of the common law before there were doctrines of precedent and articles on the *ratio decidendi* of a case the same phenomenon—a cohesion of ideas—is to be found; indeed I suspect (though this is not capable of strict proof) that there was a much greater degree of cohesion in say the fifteenth century than there is today. The explanation for this cannot be the use of tests of valid law. Furthermore it seems to me that the contemporary rules for the use of authority in the common law are as we have seen vague, uncertain, changing, and in any event incapable of settling the correct formulation of legal rules. Nor does it seem to me to be true, as positivists must have us believe, that once a rule satisfies the tests it can only be altered by legislation. The reality of the matter is that well settled propositions of law—propositions with which very few would disagree—do suffer rejection. The point about the common law is not that everything is always in the melting-pot, but that you never quite know what will go in next. Few in 1920 would have doubted that manufacturers of products were immune from the liability soon to be imposed upon them, or in 1950 that the House of Lords was bound by its own decisions. Who ever heard of family assets in 1900?

V. The Common Law as Customary Law

If however we abandon the positivist conception of the common law, in terms of what other conception can the institution be more realistically depicted and its peculiar characteristic explained? Positivists take as their basic model of law an enacted code, but a better starting-point, if we are concerned with the common law, is the traditional notion of the common law as custom, which was standard form in the older writers. Hale[28] for example divided the law of England into the *lex scripta* and the *lex non scripta*. The former comprised statutes "which in their original formation are reduced into writing, and are so preserved in their original form, and in the same stile and words wherein they were first made." In contrast the *lex non scripta* comprised "not only general customs, or the common law properly so called, but even those particular laws and customs applicable to certain courts and persons." Blackstone[29] too adopted much the same view:

> The unwritten or common law is properly distinguishable into three kinds: I. General Customs, which are the universal rule of the whole kingdom and form the common law, in its stricter and more usual signification. 2. Particular customs which for the most part affect only the inhabitants of particular districts. 3. Certain particular laws; which by custom are adopted and used by some particular courts, of pretty general and extensive jurisdiction.

This view of the common law has today fallen almost wholly out of favour, and the reason for this, or at least one predominant reason, is not far to seek. By a custom we commonly mean some practice, such as drinking the health of the Queen after dinner, which is regularly observed and has been regularly observed for some time in a group, and which is regarded within the group as the normal and proper practice. It is also integral to the idea of a custom that the past practice of conformity is conceived of as providing at least part of the reason why the practice is thought to be proper and the right thing to do. Clearly the common law as an institution is in part customary in this sense. If however one considers general theoretical propositions of the common law—for example the rule against perpetuities, or the doctrine of anticipatory breach, it is perfectly absurd to regard propositions stating such rules and doctrines as putative descriptions of the customary practices of Englishmen. It may be true that such parts of the common law reflect, or are based upon, or consistent with, ideas and values which either are or once were current in the upper ranks of English society, or in society generally, but this does not make them into customs.

Writers such as Hale and Blackstone were perfectly well aware of this point. Thus Blackstone[30] points out that there are some (I suspect he had in mind Sir John Fortescue and Christopher St. Germain)[31] who have

> divided the common law into two principal grounds or foundations;
> 1. Established customs; such as that, where there are brothers, the eldest brother shall be heir to the second, in exclusion of the youngest; and,
> 2. Established rules and maxims: as, "that the king can do no wrong," "that no man shall be bound to accuse himself," and the like.

Fortescue, for example, conceived of the law as being derived from principles (*principia*), these being certain universals called maxims, which are not demonstrable by reason; a similar Aristotelian doctrine is found in St. Germain, and both writers distinguish these maxims or principles from other grounds of law. Blackstone rejects this distinction as irrelevant to his theme, "For I take these to be one and the same thing. For the authority of these maxims rests entirely upon general reception and usage; and the only method of proving, that this or that maxim is a rule of the common law, is by showing that it hath been always the custom to observe it." Hale[32] makes a similar point:

> But I therefore stile those parts of the law, *leges non scriptae* because their authoritative and original institutions are not set down in writing in that manner, or with that authority that Acts of Parliament are; but they are grown into use, and have acquired their binding power and force of laws

by a long and immemorial usage, and by the strength of custom and reception in the Kingdom.

Thus in characterizing the common law as custom these writers were primarily concerned to make a point about the contrast between the basis for the authority of statute law and common law. A proposition derived from statute counts as law because Parliament in the exercise of its law-making power has so prescribed—wills require two witnesses because Parliament so provided in 1837. Contracts on the other hand require consideration because as far back as anyone can remember this has been accepted as necessary. As Blackstone[33] puts it,

> . . . in our law the goodness of a custom depends upon its having been used time out of mind, or, in the solemnity of our legal phrase, time whereof the memory of man runneth not to the contrary. This it is that gives it its weight and authority; and of this nature are the maxims and customs which compose the common law, or *lex non scripta*, of the kingdom.

Nobody today would, I think, wish to express himself in quite this way. In the first place for the reasons given custom seems an inappropriate term for abstract propositions of law; laws are not customs simply. We need rather to conceive of the common law as a system of customary law, and recognize that such systems may embrace complex theoretical notions which both serve to explain and justify past practice in the settlement of disputes and the punishment of offences, and provide a guide to future conduct in these matters. In the second place we are rather more conscious of change in the law—we know for example that although the doctrine of consideration is old, it is not of immemorial antiquity, and that there are recently evolved doctrines too; some come and go, like the deserted wife's equity, and others survive. With these modifications however it seems to me that the common law system is properly located as a customary system of law in this sense, that it consists of a body of practices observed and ideas received by a caste of lawyers, these ideas being used by them as providing guidance in what is conceived to be the rational determination of disputes litigated before them, or by them on behalf of clients, and in other contexts. These ideas and practices exist only in the sense that they are accepted and acted upon within the legal profession, just as customary practices may be said to exist within a group in the sense that they are observed, accepted as appropriate forms of behaviour, and transmitted both by example and precept as membership of the group changes. The ideas and practices which comprise the common law are customary in that their status is thought to be dependent upon conformity with the past, and they are traditional in the sense that they are transmitted through time as a received body of knowledge and learning. Now such a view of the common law does not require us to *identify* theoretical propositions of the common law—putative formulations of these ideas and practices—with the common law, any more than we would identify statements of the customs observed within a group with the practices which constitute the customs. And this, as it seems to me, disposes of Bentham's main difficulty in admitting the existence of the common law. Formulations of the common law are to be conceived of as similar to grammarians' rules, which both describe linguistic practices and attempt to systematize and order them; such rules serve as guides to proper practice since the proper practice is in part the normal practice; such formulations are inherently corrigible, for it is always possible that they may be improved upon, or require modification as what they describe changes.

VI. The Achievement of Cohesion in a Customary System

It is no doubt impossible in principle to attach precision to such notions as acceptance and reception within the caste of lawyers, and the definition of membership of this group is essentially imprecise. Nevertheless it seems to me that the point made by Hale and Blackstone is correct—that the relative value of formulated propositions of the common law depends upon the degree to which such propositions are accepted as accurate statements of received ideas or practice, and one must add the degree to which practice is consistent with them. Now a customary system of law can function only if it can preserve a considerable measure of continuity and cohesion, and it can do this only if mechanisms exist for the transmission of traditional ideas and encouragement of orthodoxy. There must exist within the group—particularly amongst its most powerful members—strong pressures against innovation; young members of the group must be thoroughly indoctrinated before they achieve any position of influence, and anything more than the most modest originality of thought treated as heresy. In past centuries in the common law these conditions were almost ideally satisfied. The law was the peculiar possession of a small, tightly organized group comprising those who were concerned in the operation of the Royal courts, and within this group the serjeants and judges were dominant. Orthodox ideas were transmitted largely orally, and even the available literary sources were written in a private language as late as the seventeenth century. A wide variety of institutional arrangements tended to produce cohesion of thought. The organization of the profession was gerontocratic, as indeed it still is, and promotion depended upon approval by the senior members of the profession. The system of education and apprenticeship, the residential arrangements, the organization of dispute and argument—for example the sitting of judges *in banc* and the existence of institutions such as the old informal Exchequer Chamber—all assisted in producing cohesion in orthodoxy and continuity. So too did such beliefs as the belief that the common law was of immemorial antiquity, and the belief that if only the matter was considered long enough and with sufficient care a uniquely correct answer could be distilled for every problem. The combination between institutional arrangements and conservative dogma is well illustrated in Blackstone's description of "the chief cornerstone" of the laws of England:[34] " . . . which is general immemorial custom or common law, from time to time declared in the decisions of the courts of justice; which decisions are preserved amongst our public records, explained in our reports, and digested for general use in the authoritative writings of the venerable sages of the law."

Even more striking is this passage from Hale.[35] The context is that Hale is explaining the wisdom of holding jury trials mainly before justices who are selected from the twelve men in scarlet who sit in Westminster Hall. He says:

> It keeps both the Rule and Administration of the law of the kingdom uniform; for those men are employed as justices, who as they have had a common education in the study of the law, so they daily in term-time converse and consult with one another; acquaint one another with their judgements, sit near one another in Westminster Hall, whereby their judgements are necessarily communicated to one another, and by this means their judgements and their administrations of common justice carry a consonancy, congruity and uniformity one to another, whereby both the laws and the administrations thereof are preserved from the confusion and disparity that would unavoidably ensue, if the administration was by several uncommunicating hands, or by provincial establishments.

In such a system of law as the common law the explanation for the degree of consensus which exists at any one time will be very complex, and no *general* explanation will be possible, and this remains true today. For example, it is very generally agreed today that there are no legal limitations upon the legislative competence of Parliament. The explanation for this is very largely connected with the fact that the basic book and the best written book, is Dicey, and it is around Dicey that nearly all lawyers study constitutional law. This has been so for a long time now. Dicey announced that it was the law that Parliament was omnicompetent, explained what this meant, and never devoted so much as a line to fulfilling the promise he made to demonstrate that this was so. The oracle spoke, and came to be accepted. Again, a wide measure of consensus is apparent in magistrates' courts on very many points of law. Part of the explanation of this is that all clerks rely on Stone as a sort of holy writ. Settled doctrines, principles, and rules of the common law are settled because, for complex reasons, they happen to be matters upon which agreement exists, not, I suspect, because they satisfy tests. The tests are attempts to explain the consensus, not the reason for it.

To study such a system, whether one is concerned with it at present, or in the past, involves, amongst other things, an attempt to identify what ideas are or were current at any particular period, and what ideas received or acted upon. What is involved is basically an oral tradition, still only imperfectly reduced to published writing. No clearer modern illustration is provided than D. A. Thomas's *Principles of Sentencing*, which publishes in comprehensive literary form the customary laws of the criminal appeal in England for the first time; as Mr. Thomas says with a slight air of puzzlement, "It is almost true to say that the policies and principles of the Court [of Criminal Appeal and its successor] have developed as an oral tradition amongst the judges who sit as the Court, and the high level of consistency achieved is all the more remarkable for this reason."[36] A historian is confined to the use of written sources—records, note books, legal writings, and indeed any document which throws light on the matter; his interest is not limited to a search for authorities. From such sources it is within limits possible to show that the doctrine of offer and acceptance was not a going idea in 1800, though by 1879 when Anson published his book on contract law it had come to be orthodoxy. Opinions as to what ideas were current, and what ideas generally accepted, are necessarily imprecise; there cannot in principle be a catalogue of such ideas, and in any event different and incompatible doctrines and views can co-exist. This seems to me to be just as true today as it was in the past. To argue that this or that is the correct view, as academics, judges, and counsel do, is to *participate* in the system, not simply to study it scientifically. For the purposes of action the judge or legal adviser must of course choose between incompatible views, selecting one or other as the law, and the fiction that the common law provides a unique solution is only a way of expressing this necessity.

When there is disagreement within a customary system there must, if the system is to function, be some way of settling at a practical level which view should be acted upon—for example for the purpose of directing a jury or determining an appeal. This problem is solved by procedures, and these may take a wide variety of forms, though all will involve vesting a power of decision in some person or persons. In a system which lays claim to rationality—and the common law did—it will be supposed that differences can be resolved rationally by argument and discussion, and that the method adopted to solve disputes at a practical level is in principle capable of producing in general a correct solution to the general question—What is the law? In a tightly cohesive group there will exist a wide measure of consensus upon basic ideas and values as well as upon what views are tenable. Argument and discussion will commonly produce agreement in the end, and so long as this is the case there will be little interest in how or why this consensus is achieved. There is no *a priori* reason for supposing that just because agreement is commonly reached this is because there in fact is a rational way of deciding disputes. When however cohesion has begun to break down, and a failure to achieve consensus becomes a commoner phenomenon, interest will begin to develop in the formulation of tests as to how the correctness of legal propositions can be demonstrated, and in the formulation of rules as to the use of authorities—that is to say warrants or proofs that this or that is the law. This is the phenomenon of laws of citation, and it has really struck the common law only in the last century. It seems to me to be a symptom of the breakdown of a system of customary or traditional law. For the only function served by rules telling lawyers how to identify correct propositions of law is to secure acceptance of a corpus of ideas as constituting the law. If agreement and consensus actually exist, no such rules are needed, and if it is lacking to any marked degree it seems highly unlikely that such rules, which are basically anti-rational, will be capable of producing it. It is therefore not surprising to find that today, when there is great interest in the formulation of source rules in the common law world, the law is less settled and predictable than it was in the past when nobody troubled about such matters. In a sense this is obvious. There is only a felt need for authority for a legal proposition when there is some doubt as to whether it is correct or not; in a world in which all propositions require support from authority, there must be widespread doubt. The explanation for the breakdown in the cohesion of the common law is complex, but it is easy to see that the institutional changes of the nineteenth century, and the progressive increase in the scale of operations, had much to do with the process. In place of the twelve men in scarlet there are now (according to my most recent count) ninety-eight. How far it has proceeded may perhaps be brought home by comparing the current state of affairs with the fact that during the thirty years during which Lord Mansfield presided over the Court of King's Bench it is said that there were only twenty dissenting opinions recorded. In the period 1756–65 not a single decision was given which was not unanimous.[37]

How then are we to view the positivists' notion of the common law as a body of rules, forming a system in that the rules satisfy tests of validity? We must start by recognizing what common sense suggests, which is that the common law is more like a muddle than a system, and that it would be difficult to conceive of a less systematic body of law. The systematization of the common law—its reduction to a code of rules which satisfy accepted tests provided by other rules—is surely a programme, or an ideal, and not a description of the *status quo*. (Indeed even in the case of law of statutory origin common law judges shrink from identifying the law with the text of the statute, which they rapidly encrust with interpretation—consider the fate of the definition of diminished responsibility, no longer to be simply read out to the jury as "the law.") It is the ideal of an expositor of the law, grappling with the untidy shambles of the law reports, the product of the common law mind which is repelled by brevity, lucidity and system, and it is no accident that its attraction as a model grows as the reality departs further and further from it. It is, I suspect, a rather futile ideal; the only effective technique for reducing the common law to a set of rules is codification, coupled of course with a deliberate reduction in the status of the judiciary and some sort of ban on law reporting. But to portray the common law as actually conforming to this ideal is to confuse the aspirations of those who are attempting to arrest the collapse of a degenerate system of customary law with the reality.

Notes

1. J. W. Bingham, "What is the Law?" (1912), 11 *Mich. L.R.* 1 and 109 at p.22.
2. R. M. Dworkin. "Is Law a System of Rules?" *Essays in Legal Philosophy* (1968), ed. Summers, p. 25 at p. 34 ff.
3. [1957] 2 Q. B. 1 at p. 17.
4. J. Austin, *The Province of Jurisprudence Determined*, ed. Hart (1954), xliii.
5. W. Blackstone, *Commentaries on the Laws of England* (1809 ed.), p.44.
6. J. C. Gray, *The Nature and Sources of the Law*, 2nd ed. (1948), p.84.
7. Rupert Cross, *Precedent in English Law*, 1st ed., p. 23.
8. H. Kelsen, *General Theory of Law and the State* (1961), p. 114.
9. H. Kelsen, *The Pure Theory of Law* (1967), p.9.
10. H. L. A. Hart, *The Concept of Law* (1961).
11. There are of course very considerable differences between Kelsen's theory and Hart's.
12. Dworkin, op. cit., p. 28.
13. See pp. 114 and 149–50.
14. Hart, op. cit., p. 97.
15. Austin, *Lectures*, 5th ed. (1855), ii, 655.
16. Austin, *Lectures*, ii, 216.
17. (1840) II A. & E. 438.

18. (1778) 7 T. R. 350, 4 Brown P. C. 27.
19. 1866 L.R. I Ex. 265, L.R. 3 H.L. 330.
20. (1581) I Co. Rep. 936.
21. (1854) 9 Exch. 341.
22. F. Pollock, *A First Book of Jurisprudence*, 3rd ed. (1911), p.249.
23. J. Bentham, *Collected Works*, IV, 483.
24. Ibid., p. 483.
25. Ibid., p. 460.
26. J. Bentham, *A Comment on the Commentaries*, ed. Everett (1928), p. 125.
27. Hart, op. cit., p. 132.
28. Sir Mathew Hale, *The History of the Common Law*, 2nd ed. (1716), p.22.
29. Sir William Blackstone, *Commentaries on the Laws of England*, pp. 66 ff.
30. Blackstone, p. 68.
31. Christopher St. Germain, "*Doctor and Student,*" Dialogue I c.8, Fortescue, *de Laudibus Legum Anglie* (ed. Chrimes) (1942), p. 21.
32. Hale, p. 23.
33. Blackstone, p. 66.
34. Blackstone, p. 73.
35. Hale, op. cit.
36. p. xlvi.
37. See C. H. S. Fifoot, *Lord Mansfield* (1936), p. 46.

ALAN WATSON

An Approach to Customary Law

We conclude the initial section of this volume with an essay which once again tries to come to grips with the essence of customary (as opposed to legislated) law. In this instance, the author, Professor of Law at the University of Georgia, champions one of the principal views of customary law, namely, that it cannot be considered "law" unless or until it is ratified, accepted, or "re" enacted by a sovereign power of some kind. This view runs counter to the position that de facto *usage constitutes bona fide law regardless of whether or not it is officially recognized or sanctioned by duly constituted extra-legal geo-political entities. The reader may or may not choose to agree with the author's position, but the essay does raise most of the crucial issues involved in advocacy of that position.*

For an interesting discussion of whether custom's official institutionalization should be the result of judicial as opposed to legislative action, see G. Tedeschi, "Custom and Modern Law," University of Western Ontario Law Review, *15 (1977), 1–20.*

I. Introduction

A proper understanding of the nature of customary law is important for legal historians.* For students of European legal history, customary law is particularly important; from post-Roman times to the beginning of the modern legal age in the eighteenth century, the two main elements in European law have been Roman law and legal custom. In large measure, the main task of lawyers of that interim time period was to unify or harmonize the two strands of Roman law and custom.

Reprinted from the *University of Illinois Law Review* (1984), pp. 561–576, with permission. Copyright © 1984, Board of Trustees, University of Illinois.

*I wish to dedicate this paper to the Molt Illustre Govern de les Valls d'Andorra and to Antoni Morell, Secretari d'Estat. I am grateful to my friends Stephen B. Burbank, Michael H. Hoeflich, Neil MacCormick, and Ann E. Mayer, who read a draft of this paper and gave much helpful criticism. An invitation to deliver a lecture in Andorra gave me a much-valued opportunity to deepen my understanding of customary law.

Customary law flourishes in circumstances where law is likely to be the least theoretical.[1] Yet, the nature of any source of law requires theoretical underpinnings regardless of whether these underpinnings are always implicit and never expressed. Accordingly, for custom to be regarded as law in Western private law, more than simple usage must be and is required, even if the usage is general and has long flourished. The principal issue is that one cannot derive an *ought* from an *is*. Consistent behavior in accordance with particular implicit rules does not indicate that people should so behave, or conversely should be subject to some sanction if they do not.

The main problem for any theory of customary law seems to be determining the nature of the additional factor required to transform custom into law. The Roman sources clearly indicate that some additional factor is needed to recognize custom as law, even if the nature of this factor is not apparent. For example, the *Epitome Ulpiani* states that "[c]ustom is the tacit consent of the people, deeply rooted through long usage."[2] The additional factor is expressed by the otherwise tautological "tacit consent" or "tacit agreement" (*tacitus consensus*). But, this approach raises the question as to *what* has tacit consent been given? Certainly, tacit consent is not given to the long usage itself, although the tacit consent is rooted in the long usage. Another Roman source, the *Justiniani Institutiones*, states that "[u]nwritten law is that which usage has approved. For long-practiced customs, endorsed by the consent of the users, take on the appearance of statute."[3] In this instance, the additional factor is expressed by "endorsed by the consent of the users" (*consensu utentium comprobati*).

Nevertheless, the vagueness of Ulpian is not dissipated as a result of this other explanation. The *Justiniani Digesta*, however, clarifies the nature of the additional factor by stating that

> [d]eeply rooted custom is observed as a statute, not undeservedly; and this is what is called law established by usage. For since statutes themselves bind us for no other reason than because they have been accepted by the judgment of the people, then deservedly those things which the people have approved without writing will bind all. For what does it matter that the people declare its wish by vote or by positive acts and conduct? Therefore, it is very rightly accepted that laws are abrogated not only by the vote of him who proposes law, but also through desuetude, by the tacit consent of all.[4]

For Julian, the nature of the additional factor seems to be clearer: apparently the custom is law because the people accept it as law.

This article discusses the dominant theory which legal historians have adopted to explain how custom is transformed into law: *opinio necessitatis*. Although legal historians generally accept the doctrine, it has a number of theoretical failings which hamper its usefulness as an explanatory tool. Accordingly, this article analyzes those failings and an alternate theory that custom becomes law only when it is the subject of statute or judicial decision. Finally, the article proposes nine propositions related to the role of judgments in creating customary law.

II. Opinio Necessitatis

For a long time after Justinian, scholars made little progress in defining the nature of the additional factor.[5] Eventually, the idea of *opinio necessitatis*, which by implication may have its roots in Julian's text, appeared[6] and, despite some opposition, still appears to be the dominant theoretical explanation. The thrust of *opinio necessitatis* is that individuals purposely follow a certain rule simply because they believe it to be a rule of law. Modern theorists like Larenz have explained the concept in some detail:

> One can say the practice must be the expression of an "intention of legal validity" of the community or of a "general conviction of law," provided only that one is clear that this "intention of legal validity" or the "general conviction of law" is not solely a *"psychological fact,"* but the *"sense of fulfilling a norm"* (of a legally commanded behavior) developing or dwelling in the individual acts of conduct according to the judgment of those sharing the same law.[7]

Under this view, custom becomes law when it is known to be law, is accepted as law, and is practiced as law by persons who share the same legal system. But suppose that once the custom is known to be law and is accepted as law, the practice changes. Does the old law cease to be law, and the new practice become law? If this does happen, at what moment does it happen? And, what is the machinery for change?

In analyzing these questions, the legal historian will note two different responses to the change in custom. In the first situation, those subject to the law remember the past custom. In the second, they forget the past custom. In the first situation, which is of greater importance both in theory and in practice, a contrary practice cannot change the law. So long as people remember the past custom as being law, there can be no point on the custom-law continuum at which the new practice usurps what in consciousness has been the law. Accordingly, the outmoded practice must cease to be law before a different law can begin to emerge from customary usage. Unfortunately, the theory of *opinio necessitatis* contains no mechanism for deleting law that no longer commands approval.

Opinio necessitatis contains a number of theoretical flaws which limit its usefulness in explaining the transition from custom to law. A principal failing is that *opinio necessitatis* provides no mechanism to incorporate changing customs or to delete law which ceases to mirror common practice. One might try to resolve this inadequacy by postulating that the doctrine of desuetude is inherent in customary law. The doctrine of desuetude states that when a practice that is recognized as law ceases to be followed or to be regarded as law, it ceases to be law. At that stage, but not before, the road becomes clear for the creation of new customary law. Adherence to the new custom before the old customary legal rule becomes obsolete is a factor in making the old legal rule obsolete. However, under the doctrine of *opinio necessitatis*, overlapping practice does not create a new legal rule because the new practice was not followed in "the general conviction of law."[8] Thus, at the precise moment of desuetude, there is no law on the point at all.

Against this proposed resolution, however, stands Savigny's objection to *opinio necessitatis*. Savigny points out that within the framework that legal historians usually attribute to custom,[9] custom should not rest on error. Roman sources expressly make the same point.[10] According to Savigny, this principle nevertheless leads to a contradiction without solution. Under Savigny's reasoning, a rule of law should arise first through custom; but, at the time of the first behavior the law was, of course, not in existence. In order to create law through conformity to custom, however, *opinio necessitatis* should accompany this first relevant behavior. Consequently, the first behavior rested on an error because the behavior was not accompanied by *opinio necessitatis* and should not be counted towards the creation of the customary law. This analytic approach also applies to the second act of behavior, which then replaces and becomes the first, and so on for all subsequent acts.

Accepting this reasoning makes it logically impossible, under the current doctrine of *opinio necessitatis* and custom, for customary behavior to create law. *A fortiori*, when the new customary behavior was being adopted, a different rule of customary law already existed; therefore, any belief that the new behavior conformed to existing law was clearly erroneous. If custom cannot create a legal rule, custom certainly cannot both create and substitute a new legal rule for the established rule which custom abolished.

Thus, if *opinio necessitatis* is at the root customary law, the doctrine does not allow the desuetude of a customary legal rule when that legal rule is remembered. Customary law is a "general conviction of law"; hence, it corresponds to what people generally do. People conform to customary law because it is the law. Failure to conform would be an unacceptable deviant act contrary to law.[11] The point is not that customary behavior does not change; rather, under the doctrine of *opinio necessitatis*, when a rule of customary law exists and is remembered, the rule cannot become obsolete by desuetude. In other words, acts which are known to be contrary to the rule cannot affect the rule's efficacy.

The doctrine of *opinio necessitatis* presents a further and more important logical difficulty in accepting the doctrine of desuetude of customary law. A legal rule can only fall into desuetude if another legal rule replaces the existing rule regardless of whether this later rule merely states that the first rule no longer applies. But under a theory of *opinio necessitatis*, the new rule can only come into existence after the old known rule is recognized as extinct. Otherwise, those subject to the law would not be convinced that the new behavior corresponds to the law. Accordingly, no framework exists within which desuetude can operate in compliance with the doctrine of *opinio necessitatis*.

When those subject to the laws forget the past custom, the prior law effectively is not changed by a contrary practice. If the people completely forget customary law, then as a practical matter, the law does not and did not exist. In analyzing this issue, a theory of obsolescence is unimportant because creating law where none existed before is the only relevant matter. In this regard, historians should note that total amnesia of the customary law can occur only in two particular circumstances.[12] First, the past behavior may have occurred very infrequently. As a result, historians must question whether the behavior ever achieved the common consciousness necessary to become law. Alternatively, the people may have gradually adopted a very different lifestyle with respect to the past custom, e.g., perhaps as a result of migration. In that case, historians should regard the new practice as law, not simply because new law has replaced old law, but because law has been created for circumstances where no law previously existed. In either event, when the people completely forget a rule of supposed rule of customary law, the doctrine of *opinio necessitatis* unfortunately does not explain how a subsequent contrary practice has, as law, replaced previously existing customary law.

Thus, the doctrine of *opinio necessitatis* excludes the possibility of changing customary law by subsequent practice, both when the customary law is remembered and when it is forgotten. If, as theorists likely would agree, customary law should correspond with people's actions, then any theory of customary law must provide a means of changing the law through contrary practice. Therefore, *opinio necessitatis* must be dismissed on the basis of this failing.

Savigny, despite his powerful argument that *opinio necessitatis* does not fit within the framework which historians usually attribute to customary law, retains the notion. Savigny's solution rests on his general view of law as the "spirit of the people."[13] Under this view, law arises not from individual acts of behavior but from common consciousness. Individual acts of behavior do not create customary law but are merely appearances or indications of a preexisting common conviction about the law.[14] Under Savigny's approach, therefore, the *opinio necessitatis* exists before the first relevant act of behavior. Consequently, the first act does not rest on an error of law.[15] *Opinio necessitatis* is thereby saved, but only as a very different doctrine of the nature of customary law. The validity of Savigny's view of custom and *opinio necessitatis*, however, depends on the plausibility of his general theory of law which current legal philosophers universally reject.[16] Therefore, this article does not further discuss Savigny's doctrine.

III. A Proposed Theory to Replace *Opinio Necessitatis*

Under the preceding analysis, if the theory of customary law is to retain the power to reflect changing practices or to explain the power of customary behavior to create law, theorists must abandon the doctrine of *opinio necessitatis*. In addition to the prior criticisms, this article raises further objections to the doctrine of *opinio necessitatis*. The objections and proposed resolution reflect the reality that *opinio necessitatis* simply cannot explain what actually happens in practice.

John Austin suggests a different theory which legal historians may find more acceptable than *opinio necessitatis*. According to Austin, customary laws originate as rules of positive morality which arise from the consent of the governed. However, for moral rules to be transformed into positive laws, the state must establish these customary laws. The state may establish customary laws either directly by statute, or indirectly by judicial decree.[17] Thus, under Austin's approach, customary behavior does not make law; custom becomes law only when it is the subject of statute or judicial decision.

Austin's theory is consistent only with his position that law is the command of the sovereign. Under this view, a statute becomes law even before it is enforced by a court decision.[18] Scholars who do not accept Austin's reductionist theory of law will find Austin's theory of custom unacceptable. If one believes that other sources of law, such as custom, exist in theory, then law may also potentially exist without benefit of a court decision. One may argue convincingly that "it is precisely the binding force of custom which challenges [Austin's] initial assumption itself," and that "he failed to explain satisfactorily why the body of rules which he classified as 'positive morality' . . . lacked the true character of law."[19]

A second objection to Austin's theory concerns societal treatment of judicial decisions. Societies that do not treat judicial decisions, even a consistent line of decisions, as binding legal precedents may nevertheless treat decisions establishing a custom as binding. From this viewpoint, a legal historian might claim that custom rather than judicial precedent is law. In this system, when a court finds that a custom exists, the subsequent decision based on that custom is not binding as a decision. Accordingly, the court establishes the preexisting custom as a matter of fact, and the decision, which is now law, merely confirms the preexisting law.

Although these two points detract from Austin's theory, other arguments support his position. First, customary law often does not develop from a "general conviction of law" held by a community. When a general conviction that a practice constitutes law is missing, legal decisions play a fundamental role in determining the rule of customary law. Thus, those living under customary law who wish to reduce the custom to writing complain that the law is difficult to find, know, or remember. For example, the famous thirteenth century Philippe de Beaumanoir justified his *Coutumes de Beauvaisis* by stating: "it is my opinion and [that] of others also that all customs that are now used [should] be written down and recorded so that they be maintained without change from now on, because through memories that are liable to fade and human life that is short what is not written is soon forgotten."[20] Moreover, in his *Conseil*, written about 1260, Pierre de Fontaines recorded the customs of Vermondais and claimed that the old customs were much destroyed and that almost all customs were defective. He attributes this disintegration in part to judges who preferred their own wishes to the dictates of custom, in part to those who were more attached to their own opinions than to the practices of earlier generations, and primarily to the rich despoiling the poor and then the poor despoiling the rich. The country, de Fontaines said, was almost without custom.[21]

J.A. Brutails, in his celebrated work on the customs of Andorra,[22] also demonstrates the difficulty of knowing the coutours of customary law. He stresses that in a small geographic area the number of lawsuits is limited, and that in the absence of any methodical collection of decisions, the law announced in the cases fluctuates. He also emphasizes that there often is disconcerting uncertainty regarding contemporary and important matters. For instance, when Brutails asked prominent people, magistrates, former magistrates, and judges to ennunciate a widow's rights in the property of her deceased husband, he received five different answers.[23] Indeed, Brutails claims to have often heard that Andorra had no custom, but he insists that Andorra seems no different than other customary systems. Despite numerous and significant gaps in Andorran law, scholars have been uncertain whether the legal system intended that these gaps be filled by reference to Roman, canon, or Catalan law. The common view favored Roman law, but Brutails sought to demonstrate that Catalan law usually prevailed.[24] A much earlier work, King Charles VII of France's *Ordonnance de Montil-les-Tours*, dated April 1453, records a similar condition: "[I]t often happens that in one single region, the parties rely on contrary customs and sometimes the customs are silent and vary at will, from which great hardships and loss affect our subjects."[25]

In the absence of official redactions of the customs which then govern as statutes, court decisions embody the rules. As Philippe de Beaumanoir says in his unofficial redaction: "[W]e intend to confirm a great part of this book by the judgments that have been made in our time in the said country of Clermont."[26] The Maître Echevin's preface to the 1613 official redaction of the customs of Metz, which required forty-four years to compile, reflects both the difficulty of determining customary law and the necessary reliance upon judicial decisions in doing so:

> At last, gentle people, here is the methodical disposition, so passionately wanted, so impatiently awaited, the hardwon redaction of the customs according to which our ancestors so happily administered public business. The customs here, of course, cost much time to lift them from the dust; if so many thorns (that you know about) had not been met with, you would be right to be less pleased with your official, because truth to tell, one is not at all indebted for what one has rather dragged out than received. But apart from the incredible work employed simply to set out various opinions so that they agree on the same matter, there was need of several Hercules to overcome the difficulties, common and frequent, as much in seeking out the articles in each chapter, as in verifying them. This was not done by giving way to the opinions of individuals, but by a precise and painful reading through of the judgments, memorials and instructions which mossy antiquity left in the strong boxes of the town. Despite all this, the customs are dear to us for the utility the public will receive from them.[27]

Brutails claimed,[28] and Ourliac recently has agreed,[29] that the idea of legality is very obscure in Andorra. Brutails and Ourliac apparently believe both that great doubt often exists in Andorra as to which legal rules are appropriate in a given situation, and that ascertaining the precise legal rule to apply does not rank as a high priority in general Andorran thinking. If this is a correct reading of the Brutails-Ourliac position, their belief can be generalized. In customary systems, the nature and application of legal rules are often uncertain, but this uncertainty is not treated as a matter of great concern.

An Approach to Customary Law

Customary law most often flourishes in small communities with a high degree of kinship, where the law is not based on an academic tradition. Hence, there is a relatively small number of disputes and, in a customary system, disputes delimit the scope of legal rules. In the absence of a strong academic tradition, officials will be reluctant to generalize from specific instances and to extract principles which can be used in different situations. Moreover, those few important decisions that exist may not be adequately recorded or easily accessible.

The example of Andorra as a living customary law system illustrates the relatively minor role of legal principles in a customary law system. The first published Andorran decisions started appearing in a journal, *Revista juridica de Cataluña*, only in 1963;[30] only two collections exist in book form. Although the collection of Carles Obiols i Taberner covers a twenty-one year period from 1945 to 1966, it contains only ninety-six appellate decisions.[31] Ourliac's collection and commentary cover decisions on appeal to Perpignan from 1947 through 1970. Significantly, both sets of reports each occupy only one slim volume.

Most importantly, there is relatively little demand for a precise knowledge of the legal rules of a customary system. Many disputes in a small community are among relatives, friends, or neighbors. These disputants must live on close terms with one another afterwards, and they often have recourse to less formal means of dispute resolution. Respected friends or relatives may be invited to adjudicate or a recognized approach to adjudication may arise in a particular village. As a result, the appointed adjudicators often reach a decision based on personal perceptions of fairness and reason rather than by searching for a definitive legal rule. Furthermore, in a small community where great flexibility is required, formal legal rules do not necessarily give the most acceptable solution. If a problem situation occurs often enough, however, and if the same decision-makers usually reach the solution, a custom may emerge.

In addition to the difficulty of ascertaining common practices, scholars must cope with the tendency of customary law to originate not from what the people do, but from what the people borrow from other localities. The standard practice, particularly common in medieval France, in which one jurisdiction accepts the law of another system as its residual custom, gives striking testimony to the importance of nonlocal custom. Nonlocal custom plays an important role regardless of whether the outside customary system is the *Coutume de Paris*, is a neighboring custom as in the *pays de droit coutumier*, or is Roman law as in the *pays de droit écrit*. This wholesale reception of outside custom, though residual, is important for two reasons. First, reliance upon nonlocal custom reduces the adjudicator's discretionary choices in an individual situation. Second, the outside custom may have originated in a society based upon very different economic and political characteristics, such as ancient Rome, or for a much larger, more commercial, and more anonymous center, such as Paris.

Reliance upon nonlocal custom occurs even when a local patriot prepares an unofficial collection of customs. For instance, modern scholars agree that by far the greatest part of the *Conseil* of Pierre de Fontaines comes from Justinian's *Digest* and *Code*,[32] even though the *Conseil* was intended to be a practical work to use in training a friend's son in the local customs.[33] The same observations apply to the contemporary *Livre de Jostice et de Plet*, a product of the Orleans area, where the Roman and canon law origins of the rules are hidden and ascribed falsely to French notables.[34]

Moreover, unofficial collections incorporating both local and foreign customs may indirectly create customary law. Of course, unofficial works would not themselves create customary law, but the courts frequently treated the unofficial works as evidence of the custom. In those instances, court decisions had a particular relevance: by adopting the rules in the compilations, whatever the origin of the rules, courts expressed the rules as custom.

In perplexing cases, the courts frequently based their decisions upon foreign customs. Thus, Philippe de Beaumanoir also intended that decision-makers use his compilation of custom "for doubtful cases in the said county, by judgments of neighboring lordships."[35] Not only was a *foreign* source of law borrowed, and treated as the custom of the borrowing jurisdiction,[36] but the borrowed *foreign* rule was actually that embedded in the *foreign judgment*. The borrowed rule, however, would have the force of law only when a decision-maker incorporated it in a judgment of the borrowing jurisdiction.

IV. Role of Judgments in Creating Customary Law

The basis of local customary law is frequently treated as custom rather than judicial precedent even though acceptance of the rule actually stems from local judgments rather than from antecedent local behavior.[37] This treatment raises a question about the role of judgments in creating customary law. The following series of propositions, beginning with those already established, both clarify the question and suggest a resolution.

1. To become law, custom requires something more than behavior.
2. *Opinio necessitatis* fails to provide the extra factor required.
3. Court decisions declare customary law even when (a) custom is

uncertain (and there is no *opinio necessitatis*) and (b) there is no custom.
4. Proposition three is still accurate when, as in many systems, court decisions do not make law; hence, we cannot simply say the court decision is the entire basis of customary law.
5. Custom officially written down as law is equal to law in the form of a statute; the writing, however, is not proof that the custom was not previously law.

Propositions one through four were established earlier in this article. Proposition five is self-evident. To these propositions we can add:

6. Court decisions are not law, and therefore cannot be the basis of custom becoming law. But, if the decisions declare custom as law even without requiring preceding practice (i.e., combining propositions three and four), then the official declaration of a rule as customary law makes it law regardless of whether the behavior was customary.

Official recognition that particular normative behavior is customary makes such behavior law. But official recognition also entails official acceptance. Hence, the validity of this custom as law depends on its official recognition and acceptance.[38]

7. It follows that in societies where decision-makers treat customary behavior as law, there is also an attribution to the people of the power to make law by their tacit behavior.
8. But, this law is created only when decision-makers officially recognize or accept it. Just as the opinion of a sovereign is not law until it is institutionalized by statute, so behavior of the people is not law until institutionalized by an official court decision which recognizes and accepts it.[39]
9. As a corollary, if custom has not been expressed in a judicial decision, and hence is not law, but is set out in an official redaction, the custom becomes law but as statute rather than a custom.

This interpretation of the nature of customary law incorporates a theory for the creation or alteration of customary law. Normative customary behavior becomes customary law when it is recognized by the courts as law. Accordingly, the actors need not believe that they are already acting in accordance with an existing rule of law. So long as the courts treat the custom as law, the custom is the accepted customary law. Should the courts hold that the custom has changed, however, then the new ruling becomes the customary law.

These findings on the nature of customary law might support Austin's theory that law consists of the commands of a sovereign that are backed by sanctions. In this instance, a sovereign is defined as someone whose commands are habitually obeyed and who does not habitually obey anyone else. At this preliminary state, however, this article is not concerned with the validity of Austin's theory as a whole. Rather, this article, for the sake of argument, will for the moment accept his proposition that when judges made a legal rule, that rule is established by the sovereign legislature.[40] If there can be no customary law without a court decision, the concern at this point is whether customary law is at least as much a command of the sovereign as is binding precedent.

Only three factual situations need be considered in assessing the nature of the sovereign's command. First, some writers, notably Vinnius,[41] argue that there can be no customary law under an emperor. In situations where an empire exists, acceptance of this doctrine creates no problem for Austin with regard to custom.[42] Second, in some circumstances customary law is accepted and judicial precedent is binding. This situation also does not create a problem for Austin because decision-makers may resolve any conflict by recognizing that custom forms a rule of law when incorporated in a binding precedent. Third, occasionally customary law is accepted and judicial precedent is not otherwise binding. In this instance, the people as a whole are not the sovereign in Austin's sense. Their behavior creates law, but only at the moment when it is recognized and accepted by the court; judicial acceptance is a necessary precondition to creation of law. Hence, insofar as Austin is correct in arguing that the sovereign's acceptance of a court decision as creating law is thereby a command of the sovereign, a court decision accepting custom as law is equally a command of the sovereign. This point is significant because critics frequently argue that one of Austin's major weaknesses is precisely the difficulty of fitting customary law into his theory.[43]

Austin's theory implicitly assumes that all law is legislation and that judges, insofar as they create law, are legislators. My position is different. I agree that binding judicial precedent is both law-making in its own right and a source of law distinct from legislation. Judicial law-making, however, requires that the process be accepted by the sovereign as an appropriate method of creating law. Similarly, custom is a separate source of law distinct from both legislation and judicial precedent. But like judicial precedent, custom must be accepted by the sovereign in order to constitute law. To become law, custom, like legislation and binding precedent, must be clothed with the requisite form which marks its official acceptance by the sovereign. This requisite form requires that adjudicators incorporate custom in a judicial decision. A society may accept custom as law when incorporated in a judicial decision but deny law-making effect to precedent, thereby demonstrating that custom as a means of making law is not simply subsumed into binding precedent.

The conclusions that customary law does not necessarily derive from what people do and that official judicial decisions declare the law illuminate other problems with customary law. To begin with, the legal difficulties described by F. Pollock and F.W. Maitland[44] become understandable in light of these conclusions. Pollack and Maitland report that in the Middle Ages, neighboring villages were frequently inhabited by persons of the same race, religion, and language, who were subject for centuries to the same economic conditions. Yet, neighboring villages often had very different rules; for example, for the central institution of matrimonial property. The villages initially may have shared common means of arranging family property holding, but in each village one approach eventually became fixed as law through the process of judicial decision-making.[45] The final result in any one place, therefore, will contain some element of the arbitrary.

Secondly, the theory of judicially institutionalized customary law sheds new light on a common German medieval practice of resolving legal disputes. Independent towns governed by customary law selected a *mother* town to whose Schöffen, or adjudicatory body, the *daughter* town submitted unresolved legal issues.[46] The daughter town may have preferred, for various reasons, that the mother town provide a ruling. For example, the daughter town may not have had a dominant custom or the custom may have been unsettled or unknown. Further, the mother town's Schöffen may have had high prestige or the local Schöffen may have preferred to distance themselves from local disputes. Yet regardless of how the question to the Schöffen might be framed, the daughter town is not seeking to know its own customary practice.

The practice of submitting disputes to a neighboring town is a particular example of a more general phenomenon: local areas often display lack of interest in establishing local custom. The frequency of borrowing another's custom is itself an example of this lack of interest. A further illustration is provided by the popularity of the *Sachsenspiegel*. This unofficial statement of early thirteenth century practice in the bishoprics of Magdeburg and Halberstadt was widely used in northern Germany, Poland, the Low Countries, and elsewhere.[47]

Yet another example of lack of interest in establishing local custom is the enormous length of time that elapsed between the French royal command to reduce customs to writing and the completion of that effort. In 1453, Charles VII's *Ordonnance of Montil-les-Tours* required the redaction of the customs in each district, but a century passed before most of the work was completed.[48] The delay is attributable not only to the magnitude and difficulty of the task but also to a frequent lack of interest in establishing the custom.[49]

Although a doctrine of judicially institutionalized customary law resolves a number of issues in customary law theory, the doctrine raises other questions. For instance, the traditional explanation for the scarcity of legislation on private law during the Middle Ages may need to be reexamined. The traditional explanation is that great foci of centralized power were lacking, and that kings and other magnates were weak.[50] In some instances this may be a complete explanation, but in other instances the traditional view is clearly inadequate. For instance, magnates frequently granted charters to towns and issued statutes on matters relating to public law. And, as we have seen, it is unlikely that townspeople were so fiercely attached to their customs that they would have bitterly resented magnates' power to legislate on private law. In fact, as the doctrine of judicially institutionalized customary law teaches, people often displayed no great attachment to local customs.[51] The simplest explanation is that magnates frequently had more interesting, more exciting, and perhaps more important things to occupy their time than legislating private law for their subjects.

V. Conclusion

A major problem for any theory of customary law is determining the nature of the additional factor required to transform custom into law. The doctrine of *opinio necessitatis* generally has replaced earlier consent theories, but a major flaw of the *opinio necessitatis* doctrine remains. The doctrine fails adequately to incorporate the creation of new customary law or the deletion of obsolete customary law. Neither desuetude nor Savigny's theory of common consciousness sufficiently resolve the logical failings of *opinio necessitatis*.

Austin's work suggests that custom becomes law only by the additional factor of state confirmation. Redactions of customary law show that, although the basis of customary law is treated as custom rather than judicial precedent, acceptance of the rule often arises from official judgments rather than from antecedent local practices. Court decisions, not law themselves, function as official sovereign recognition and acceptance of rules of custom as law. Court decisions transform rules of custom into law, regardless of whether the antecedent custom was actually recognized as law. Customs do not become law until institutionalized by inclusion in an official court decision. This theory of customary law may help to explain several otherwise problematic aspects of medieval customary law and practice.

Notes

1. In view of the theoretical difficulties encountered in determining when a society has law, the nature of custom in modern "tribal societies" is not discussed here. For the development of a theory of custom in Roman law, insofar as there is one, see Nött, "Zur Entstehung der Gewohnheits-rechtlichen Theorie," in *Festschrift Für W. Felgentraeger* 353 (1969). For a very different view of the formation of customary rules, particularly in international law, see J. Finnis, *Natural Law and Natural Rights* 238 (1980). This paper also does not discuss custom as a source of international law.

2. *Epitome Ulpiani* 4.

3. See, e.g., *Inst. Just.* 1.2.9.

4. See, e.g., *Dig. Just.* 1.3.32.1 (JULIAN DIG. 84). The accuracy of Julian's account of the people's role in statute-making, or of custom bringing about the desuetude of statute, need not be discussed.

5. Because this is not directly an article on the history of legal theory, I have done little more than read the appropriate pages in the GLOSS and typical authors such as Oinotomus, Wesembecius, J. Voet, Vinnius, and Heineccius.

6. See, e.g., K.C.W. Klötzer, *Versuch eines Beytrags zur Revision der Theorie von Gewohnheitsrecht* 189 passim (Jena 1813); S. Brie, *Die Lehre von Gewohnheitsrecht* 1 (1899). Rudolf von Jhering described custom as the "pet" of the German Historical School. See R. von Jhering, *Geist des Römischen Rechts* ¶ 2.1 (5th ed. 1894).

7. I translated this quotation from K. Larenz, *Methodenlehre der Rechtswissenschaft* 338 (2d ed. 1969) (emphasis in original) [hereinafter cited as K. Larenz, *Methodenlehre*]. See also K. Larenz, *Allgemeiner Teil des Deutschen Bürgerlichen rechts* 10 (5th ed. 1980). In later editions Larenz is much less explicit, although he seems to hold basically the same opinion. See, e.g., K. Larenz, *Methodenlehre, supra,* at 345 passim (4th ed. 1979). Larenz expressly adopts Nörr's view that the theory of customary law, as such, is unsatisfactory.

8. K. Larenz, *Methodenlehre, supra* note 7, at 338. See *supra* text accompanying note 7.

9. 1 F. Savigny, *System des heutigen römischen Rechts* 174 (Berlin 1840).

10. See, e.g., *Dig Just.* 1.3.39. This view is generally accepted within the tradition.

11. No comparison can be drawn between desuetude of customary law and that of statutes. With statutes, there is no need for a belief that the contrary action accords with the law.

12. See, e.g., C. K. Allen, *Law in the Making* 136 (7th ed. 1964).

13. 1 F. Savigny, *supra* note 9, at 171.

14. *Id.*

15. *Id.* at 175.

16. See, e.g., C. K. Allen, *supra* note 12, at 87. Yet oddly, Austin's theory survives indirectly, without the theoretical trappings, in a number of writers. For instance, see the authors quoted in A. Watson, *Society and Legal Change* 1 (1977); L. Friedman, *A History of American Law* 595 (1973). In a curious way, Calabresi seems a modern distorting mirror of Savigny. For Calabresi, the

judges—like jurists—"represent" the people at one level, the current "legal landscape" generally reflects popular desires, and legislation inhibits law from giving the people what they want and need. *See* G. Calabresi, *A Common Law for the Age of Statutes* (1982).

17. J. Austin, *The Province of Jurisprudence Determined* 30, 163 (1954); 2 *Lectures on Jurisprudence* 222 (London 1863).

18. Gray argues that statutes are not law but only sources of law, because their meaning is declared by the courts and "*it is with the meaning declared by the courts, and with no other meaning, that they are imposed upon the community as Law.*" R. Gray, *The Nature and Sources of Law* 170 (2d ed. 1921) (emphasis in original).

19. C.K. Allen, *supra* note 12, at 70.

20. P. de Beaumanoir, *Coutumes de Beauvaisis* § 71 (n.d.).

21. P. de Fontaines, *Conseil* ch. 1, § 3 (n.d.).

22. J. Brutails, *La Coutume d'Andorre* (1904)

23. *Id.* at 55.

24. *Id.* at 47 *passim*.

25. King Charles VII, *Ordonnance de Montil-les-Tours* 125 (France 1453).

26. P. de Beaumanoir, *supra* note 20, at 6.

27. The Preface is not paginated.

28. J. Brutails, *supra* note 22, at 342.

29. P. Ourliac, *La Jurisprudence Civile d'Andorre—Arrêts du Tribunal Supérieur de Perpignan: 1947–1970*, at 12 n.7 (1972).

30. Further reports appear in subsequent volumes.

31. C. Taberner, *Jurisprudéncia Civil Andorrana—Jutjat d'Appellacions: 1945–1966* (1969).

32. *See* A. Watson, *Sources of Law: Legal Change and Ambiguity* 45 (1984).

33. P. de Fontaines, *supra* note 21, ch. 1, § 2.

34. *See* A. Watson, *supra* note 32, at 46.

35. *Preface* to P. de Beaumanoir, *supra* note 20.

36. Not all contemporaries saw borrowing of a neighbor's custom as borrowing it for the purpose of adopting it as the custom of the borrower. *See* G. Coquille, *Coutume de Nivernais* (n.d.) (preface).

37. Of course, one should not take this analysis as meaning that customary law never derives from local behavior. But where it does, there are nevertheless great difficulties in regarding *opinio necessitatis* as the key factor that turns behavior into law. The elaborate devices designed to discover what the nature of the custom was, such as the "*enquête par tourbes*" in France or the "*Weistümer*" in Germany, amply demonstrate that a behavior was not necessarily known to be law, or accepted and practiced as law by persons sharing the same law.

38. Critics may object that although official recognition transforms into customary law practices that were not previously customary, habitual normative behavior may nonetheless be law as custom prior to official recognition. This objection is especially powerful if the practice was universally regarded as the custom. The objection, though prima facie plausible, is ultimately untenable. Suppose a case involving a practice universally regarded as custom comes before a court and the court rejects the behavior as incorporating customary law. In

that case, one must conclude that the custom cannot be law. Yet, if the decision does not create law then the decision cannot change the law; hence, the normative behavior was not customary law before the decision. The official recognition of normative behavior as customary law makes such behavior law.

39. The text of Justinian's *Institutes* explains that the statement "[t]he will of the Emperor has the force of statute" means that the emperor's will comes to have the force of law when it is couched in the proper institutionalized form. *Inst. Just.* 1.2.6. Thus, "[d]eeply rooted custom is observed as a statute," similarly means, as we have seen, that custom comes to have legal effect when it is expressed in the proper institutionalized form, namely, in judicial decision. *Dig. Just.* 1.3.32.1. If the statute incorrectly specifies the will of the Emperor, however, the accepted statutory meaning prevails; likewise, if there is no custom, the accepted judicial interpretation prevails.

40. J. Austin, *supra* note 17, at 31.

41. Vinnius, *In Quattuor Libros Institutionum Imperialium Commentarius* ad 1.2.7.

42. The Bavarian civil code of 1756 expressly requires both the will of the people and the consent of the ruler for customary law. *See Codex Maximilianus Bavaricus* 1.2, Section 15 (n.p. 1756).

43. *See, e.g.*, A. Watson, *The Nature of Law* 3 (1977). One difficulty remains in accepting Austin's theory as a whole. Austin views binding judicial precedent and customary law as equivalent forms of law-making in the sense that both require the consent, acceptance, and tolerance of the sovereign to be law. Of course, that consent, acceptance, and tolerance might be withheld. Nonetheless, consent, acceptance, and tolerance are not equivalent to a command.

44. 2 S. Milsom, *History of English Law* 399 (2d ed. 1968).

45. *Id.*

46. For a description of this practice, see A. Watson, *supra note* 32, at 31.

47. Of the two parts of the *Sachsenspiegel*, one part survives in over 200 manuscripts, and the other in almost 150. The *Sachsenspiegel* has been translated numerous times. *See id.* at ch. 2.

48. *Id.* at 47.

49. All this alerts us to the danger of misconstruing similarity of customary law with societal similarity. Although scholars refer to "families" of customary law, one should not deduce that the members of one legal family group are closer to each other in economic, social, and political structure than they are as a group to the members of other legal families. The legal family may result more from the choice of legal approaches than from similarities of customs.

50. *See* F. Tomás y Valiente, Manual de Historia del Derecho Español 133 (3d ed. 1981).

51. Certainly the compilers of unofficial collections of customary law frequently praise the quality and the descent from their forefathers. But we cannot generalize from these writers. They wrote these works because they were attached to the customs, but this does not imply that the same feeling existed in other members of the community. Indeed, the authors often lament that the customs are not being kept.

Pioneers in the Study of Folk Law

All fields of academic endeavor have their founders and folk law scholarship is no exception. In the early nineteenth century when the scientific study of folklore, folkloristics, may be said to have begun, so also did the serious investigation of folk law commence. Many of the earliest researchers utilized questionnaires to gather data on folk law, while others carried out extensive fieldwork inquiries.

It is not possible, unfortunately, to pay homage to all the many workers worldwide who have gathered important data for the study of folk law. We have therefore selected a number of representative essays which seek to survey various pioneering efforts or schools. After an initial bibliographical survey of general European folk law studies, we have included discussions of Russian, German, and Dutch scholarship on the subject. The section ends with a review of nineteenth-century research on customary law in India and an essay on the more recent study of folk law in Africa by African scholars.

ERNŐ TÁRKÁNY-SZÜCS

Results and Task of Legal Ethnology in Europe

Because of the great influence of anthropologists and Africanists in folk law research, there has been a tendency to overlook the enormous amount of work that has been carried out in both Western and Eastern Europe. In the following magisterial survey of European research on folk law, we can get some idea of the wealth of data already in print on the subject. The polyglot talents of Ernő Tárkány-Szücs, a Hungarian scholar who has devoted much of his life to the study of the folk law of his native land, provide a running commentary on a multitude of sources not accessible to most readers. Perhaps his magnum opus is a 903-page monograph, Magyar jogi nepszokasok *[Hungarian Legal Folkways] (Budapest: Gondolat, 1981), which details folk law in Hungary from 1700 to 1945.*

For other considerations of "legal ethnology," see Jean Poirier, "The Current State of Legal Ethnology and Its Future Tasks," International Social Science Journal, 22 (1970), 476–494. For Hungarian folk law, in particular, see Tárkány-Szücs, "Collecting Legal Folk Customs in Hungary," Acta Ethnographica, 29 (1980), 194–205; Csaba Varga, "From Legal Customs to Legal Folkways," Acta Juridica, 25 (1983), 454–459; and Andor Csizmadia, "Hungarian Customary Law Before the Bourgeois Rebellion of 1848," Journal of Legal History, 4(2) (1983), 3–37.

There are, of course, surveys of folk law for almost every European country, many of which are cited in the following essay. One such national overview is Carmelo Grassi, Il Folklore giuridico dell'Italia. *(Catania: Tip. Sorace e Siracusa, 1932).*

The problems of legal ethnology have engaged the attention of European scientific life for more than a hundred years, especially ethnology, history of law and lately sociology. Even this period did not prove sufficient for working out satisfactorily the subject, the proper place, the

---

Reprinted from *Ethnologia Europaea*, 1 (1967), 195–217.

methodology and applicable results of legal ethnology though many important publications enriched its literature.

A circumstance which renders the clearing up of the problem more difficult is the fact that the operational sphere of legal ethnology has extended to the three aforementioned sciences, each of which has its own well-defined field and methodology. Not one of these sciences laid stress on the development of this new branch of science. The ethnologists did not consider it necessary to differenticate between legal and non-legal phenomena. The jurists were averse to acknowledging that, besides state norms, there existed a second legal sphere which it should be necessary to explore with scientific methods. Sociology also considers it infra dig to have any connections with a newly developing historical science.

Naturally this situation should be changed and every possibility is given for the elimination of formal artificial boundaries and for intensive coordination of common themes and methods. No solution will be given in this treatise; the author wishes to summarize the results of European legal ethnology and makes an attempt to define its task, that is we should like to promote the independence and common improvement of legal ethnology amid European social and economic conditions, where the historical existence of the states and the higher level of social evolution lay down other conditions than in the former colonial territories.

The specialists in legal ethnology in Europe are working under completely different conditions to those among primitive peoples and we must emphasize the importance of this fact. The great classical scholars, who had established legal ethnology, either under the name of ethnological law science or under the name of cultural anthropology, had used, for the interpretation of the development of modern law institutions, partly the law customs of primitive peoples, and partly they worked out the materials of the ancient world and of the Eastern high cultures with a comparative method (for example H.S. Maine, A.H. Post, J. Kohler, L.H. Morgan, J.F. MacLennan, J.J. Bachofen). Today an important branch of legal ethnology explores the societies lying outside the spheres of European and Asian high cultures (for example L. Adam, H. Trimborn, J. Gilissen), but rather as a constituent part of the national states, or in connection with them (for example R. Redfield).

What are these diverse conditions and specifications? We can summarize the chief characteristics, as follows:

1. There is no people or territory in Europe that does not belong to a state sovereignty. In Europe the consequence is that the law of their own state is predominant for every social class, stratum (social order) and group. Contrariwise in "primitive" (exotic, non-European) societies, even if living in an independent statehood, the state has

far diverse functions to the European. These primitive states very rarely give their inhabitants law codexes.
2. In Europe generally the territorial factor is the first determinant; in the case of "primitive" peoples the principle of the personality is the primary factor, that is the same legal rights are due to all consanguineous persons. We can notice some features of this consanguineity in European subgroups (family, the solidarity of kinship, vendetta, etc.).
3. The European legal systems are divided into so-called differentiated branches (private law, law of property, or law of domestic relations, hereditary law). The same diversification is artificial in the case of "primitive" societies. The specialists in "primitive" peoples use it in their publications, but in practice no primitive society differentiates between custom and legal custom, or between the custom of private rights and penal customs. The legally defended interests are also quite different to those of Europe.
4. Europe has a well specified law system for the defence of immaterial rights; in the "primitive" societies it has none at all, or only rarely (for example, authorship).
5. In place of the principle of causality, based on natural science, the "primitive" peoples take a magical view of life.
6. In Europe legal disputes are solved by special organs, that is by courts of justice. In organizations outside state life we do not find a similar establishment.
7. In Europe economic circumstances quickly cause changes in the law. In the milieu of "primitive" peoples these changes are relatively very slow.

This enumeration does not give a full picture, nor are all the conditions valid simultaneously, but it denotes that European juridicial ethnology has different objectives and methods from similar investigations among "primitive" peoples.

Legal Ethnology in Different European Countries

The conditions of the existing researches are more difficult in Europe than among the peoples living outside state relations. Notwithstanding these difficulties, the summation of the results of one century of scientific research is opportune and useful, though we can deal with only the most important studies.

We begin our conspectus of European legal ethnology with the *French*. Until World War II, French scholars had dealt with legal ethnology under the name of "folklore juridique." But in the present investigations this term has practically disappeared (as well as all other compounds of the word "folklore"), and the expression "ethnologie juridique" is of most current use in modern French academic language. The intensity of French researches is far more concentrated in the colonial or formerly dependent territories than in France.

On the development of European legal ethnology R. Maunier had a great influence with his famous book, "Introduction au folklore juridique"[1], published in 1938. Maunier wanted to define the activity of legal ethnology, so he compiled detailed questionnaires and bibliography[2]. According to his interpretation those parts of applied law belong to the sphere of legal ethnology which are oral, local and private ("privé"). According to Maunier there are two basic situations of the law : the law laid down by the legislature and the custom acknowledged by the people. The latter has four applicable possibilities: anonymity, condemnation by administrative organs, toleration and official recognition. Its observation is enforced either by the state or a moral obligation or both. In Maunier's opinion there are four basic sources of customs: the law of the family, the law of property, the contractual law and the penal law[3]. Besides Maunier, the studies of E. Jobbé-Duval[4], R. Nelli[5] and lastly R. Honin are worthy of attention. The last mentioned has dealt with commercial customs, pointing out that one part of them are "de droit" law customs, that is besides civil law there exists an autonomous living law which has its own sources in the customs.[6]

P. Saintyves[7] had an initiative rôle. In the French Ethnological Atlas some legal themes are also to be found which were widely investigated throughout the country[8].

We must deal yet with two French sociologists of law, G. Gurvitch[9] and H. Lévy-Bruhl[10], whose activities had a great influence on the legal ethnology of some Southern European countries. Their studies are respected in France as the foundation stones of legal ethnology. This can be accepted from one important point of view; they have done the same as E. Ehrlich in Germany; both French scholars declared jurisprudence to be essentially a social science, they observed the separating of law and life and gave essential part to folkloristic customs in their researches.

On the Iberian peninsula the *Spanish* people are divided into several ethnical units. In the last decades of the 19th century the unification of private law had created such great problems that from 1883 onwards they had to collect customary laws in preparation for legal codification. In the Ethnological Society of Castillia they organized a separate special group for this task.

The earliest research worker to collect living customary laws was I. Costa, who began in the surroundings of the river Aragon[11] and later expanded his interest to the whole territory of Spain[12]. In Alicante Altamira y Crevea[13], and in Catalonia J. Karreras i Artau[14] collected the living legal customs. A scientist worked out the rôle of common house ownership in living Spanish customary law[15]. E. Wohlhaupter also investigated the relation between the Spanish people and legal traditions[16].

In *Portugal*, it is chiefly P. Mereâ's intensive work which is noteworthy, as he made a study not only of legal history, but worked out many questions on legal ethnology[17].

G. Mazzarella was the first, but in many senses, an isolated representative of *Italian* legal ethnology. He laid great stress on the comparative method of legal ethnology, seeking the defining causes and rules which influenced the living legal customs. He differentiated three forms of living legal ethnology: (1) a descriptive, (2) an analytical, (3) a comparative ethnology. His outstanding merit is the investigation of correlative factors. Legal institutions can exist only in well definable social organizations. No legal institution may connect itself with other institutions at will[18].

In the research of living law, first F. Maroi's studies can be mentioned. With his program-giving treatise "Costumanze giuridiche popolari"[19], he gave a sound basis for understanding the problems of legal ethnology. In the following years he made a project for starting a systematic collection of all customs connected with legal ethnology[20]. In 1929–1930 he worked for a special committee of the Department of Justice on the collection of living customary law in agrarian life[21]. In his account he treated at length the problems of the inner organization of Italian peasant families, the types of peasant ownership, based on the recently collected material.

Many special studies originated from the material of the collection of 1930, of which the most important was the treatise of a lawyer named R. Trinchieri. Relating to the matters of principles he showed the important symbolism of contracts at markets in villages, such as, words, gestures, clauses, acts, but declared that he did not consider the collected material a sound basis for the purpose of codification[22].

Research work on legal ethnology was carried by E.N. Rocca[23], who, in 1962, at the Ethnological Congress in Modena, proposed that a questionnaire should be circulated in the valley of the river Po[24]. Legal ethnology did not escape the attention of R. Corso; he collected legal customs in many parts of Italy[25] and was especially absorbed in the collection and writing up of juridical proverbs[26]. E. Carusi[27] threw light on the connections with legal history, G. Perusini touched on legal agrarian relations[28].

In Italy there are excellent collections of legal agrarian essays and bibliographies[29]. The legal profession evinces great interest in these collections and the specialists in customary law use their material in their treatises[30].

The *Germans* have an extensive and manifold literature in legal ethnology, based chiefly on historical data and research in the archives. It is hard to say when and by whom these researches were initiated. The so-called German school of historical law, chiefly F.K. Savigny and G.F. Puchta, attributed great importance to customary law, and its issue, the people's ancient right. In their opinion the law of the people is a living reality in the legal customs, in the different manifestations of the cultural life of the people: in proverbs, in songs, in parables, in folk-tales, in countless ritual forms. They are in close touch with family law, the law of property, hereditary law, contract law and the penal law of the people. In their opinion the material of the law must be explained by the integral historical past of the nation. It means, the law is always a part history, from which may be deduced the fact that with the evolution of life, it changes with the alteration of customs, which are the direct expressions of the legal awareness of the people.

Savigny expressed it as follows: "gemeinsames Bewusstsein als gemeinsame Überzeugung des Volkes." He affirmed that a law which does not take into account the life of popular legal customs has not much value[31].

The research workers in German legal ethnology adhered firmly to the ideas and theories of the historical-law school, and this attitude remained the dominant characteristic in their later treatises, too. The influence of this school was felt to a greater or lesser effect all over Europe.

How was German legal ethnology developed on this basis?

It is not accidental that legal ethnology was derived from the history of law and through the decades the historians of law have been its promoters. J. Grimm[32] was the first to take note of the "antiquitates iuris," under which name they accumulated everything from the relics of former ages and indeed the Germans collected enormous material from such sources of the law. J. Kohler[33] directed his interest to comparative investigations, and by his method of comparing the legal materials of the different European peoples, both separately and in connection with each other, he became the protagonist of ethnological law studies. He expounded his theories for nearly 40 years in the *Zeitschrift für vergleichende Rechtswissenschaft*, which he founded in 1878; the supplement of which was devoted to legal ethnology. Kohler considered legal ethnology as a part of comparative jurisprudence.

Later, German scientists looked upon "Rechtliche Volkskunde" as adjacent territory between legal history and ethnology, but they emphasized that this new concept and science was the product of the history of law[34]. It became even more evident in so-called "legal archeology"[35], which among other things, dealt with the legal symbols, the instruments of penal law and torture, customs and such objects of art which portrayed the manifestations of legal things and activities. It was not till 1925 that living customs were admitted to be as important as the material and archival sources, though a systematic collection of living customary laws was not effected.

Among the more important scholars of legal ethnology we must mention the names of E. von Künssberg[36], C. von Schwerin[37], H. Meyer[38], K. Fröhlich[39] E. Wohlhaupter[40], K.S. Bader[41], and from among the generation after the Second World War, F. Merzbacher[42], K.S. Kramer[43], A. Gabler[44], and G. Lutz[45]. The works of Künssberg had an influence on the legal ethnologists of the neighbouring peoples (Poles, Czechs, Hungarians, etc.). Fröhlich drew up plans for an Atlas to illustrate the territorial extension of the results of legal ethnology.

In *Switzerland* and in *Austria* the development of legal ethnology was influenced by the German example. In Switzerland H. Fehr[46] was its most important representative who had worked together with Künssberg for seven years. The researches of F. Speiser[47] and H. Bächtold[48] were inspired by a purely ethnological interest, while those of H.F. Pfenninger[49] and E. Höhn[50] were motivated by the aims of the jurist or legal historian. In 1951 the Swiss Ethnological Society held a meeting at Brugg which was devoted to the field of legal ethnology[51].

In Austria H. Baltl published some excellent studies under the name of "Rechtsarchäologie"[52]. His theoretical foundations are also worthy of mention[53].

In *Hungary* at the end of the 19th century justiciary organs took the initiative for commencing research on law customs in connection with the proposition of the Civil Law Code, when a claim arose for creating a special hereditary law for agrarian people. With the help of questionnaires these repeated researches gave a comprehensive view of the preparation for the legislation. In 1922 K. Tagányi published a request for the collection of living law customs and, as an example, he communicated comparative material for domestic and hereditary law[54]. A. Szendrey applied himself to the research of both administrative[55] and penal customs[56].

In 1939, at the initiative of G. Bónis and L. Papp, a systematic work for collecting legal customs and law traditions was started again. More questionnaires were made, the intention of which was to ensure the common delimitations of the themes. It had to take into consideration the fact that, at the request of the Ministry of Justice, and under the direction of M. Hofer, collections were being carried on simultaneously in nearly one hundred places. They were headed under the name of "Research of the legal life of the people." In substance they followed ethnological methods with more or less sociological valuation. All this was mentioned in a detailed scientifical-historical summary[57].

One of the Hungarian scholars L. Papp[58] and the author[59] each completed the full legal monography of a village. G. Bónis treated the one-child system as a central problem around which revolved many customs and their sociological valuation[60]. E. Fél[61] wrote an ethnological synthesis on the law customs of the joint family organization in the village of Martos. Z. Tóth[62] elaborated the hereditary customs of a closed ethnical unity.

From 1942 till 1944 under the leadership of G. Bónis team collective work was instituted in about 35 villages of the district of Kalotaszeg[63] (now in Rumania) and at Bálványosváralja[64], (now also in Rumania). J. Morvay[65] has thrown a new light on the problems of the joint families. I. Katona dealt with the legal customs of pick-and-shovel men, with their organization of labour and the dividing of the wages which were paid to them in one common lump.[66] K. Kulcsár protested against the mis-use of the results of legal ethnology for legal-political purposes[67].

When turning our attention to the Balkan peninsula, we see that the *Albanians* are rather subjects more than workers in legal ethnology. In this country there still exists in abundance wide-spread traditions, and survivals of old tribal laws live in the memory of the older generation even today. In 1895 at the request of the Hungarian L. Thallóczy[68], a priest compiled a list of the living customary laws of the Dukadjin and Mi-Skodrak tribes as told to him by the old people. This compilation together with other collections produced a very rich literature on tribal customs[69]. In 1939 M. Hasluck collected a great variety of material on the mountain of Gheg[70]. Some questions on the Albanian customary law system were worked up separately in similar monographies, for example by D.E. Cozzi, who had written on the legal status of females, on marital customs[71] and on vendetta[72].

Under the heading of Southern-Slavs we deal with three different ethnical unities: the Serbo-Croatians, the Slovenes and the Bulgarians.

The *Serbs* took the first steps towards having their customary law recognized. In 1866 the Scientific Academy of Beograd gave orders that collections should be made, and in 1874 B. Bogišić the eminent statesman published them in a very considerable collection[73]. They were used for the preparation of the Civil Law Code of Montenegro in 1888[74]. Important summaries are to be found on this theme in the books of T. Saturnik[75] and J. Belović.[76] Among the *Croats* J. Strohal had developed intense activity in the collecting of living law customs, in fact the Ethnological Journal of Croatia published in 1909 a questionnaire touching on customary law.[77] On the family legal traditions of the Croat-speaking inhabitants of Alsómuraköz (zadruga, engagement, dowry, etc.), the work of J. Csányi[78] is exemplary. In the case of the *Slovenians* the draft of S. Vilfan sums up Slovenian legal ethnology; the study of B. Orel treats of everyday life and employments.[79] So does the minor study by M. Kostrenčić,[80] and M.S. Filipović's treatise on Bosnia follows the same trend.[81]

The example of Bogišić had a productive influence on the *Bulgarians*. The living legal customs awakened the interest of E. Bobčev, chiefly those connected with family law, hereditary law[82] and the zadruga.[83] The later writers L. Barbar[84] and J. Kohler[85] give a full portrayal of the living Bulgarian folk legal customs. The connections between the customs and the law were analyzed by I.V. Comov.[86]

Let us now turn to the Western-Slavs, to whom the Poles, the Czechs and the Slovaks belong. Each of them represents many ethnical unities.

In 1889 among the *Poles* Baron Grabowsky elaborated a voluminous questionnaire for the collection of legal customs both of the village and town people.[87] Concerning its results we have no information. In his younger years the law historian K. Koranyi evinced an interest in legal ethnology in his studies. He deals with law history using legal customs as demonstrative material, in fact, even in his independent shorter studies[88] he made use of living legal customs. In 1952, L. Halban's attention was turned to legal customs but founded on scientific-history and chiefly on the philosophy of law[89].

Among the *Czechs*, according to R. Horna, nobody dealt systematically with the problems of legal ethnology, and therefore in 1952 he took upon himself the prime task of giving a program[90]. Among the *Slovak* people Rath had worked out in 1907 a 27-page-long questionnaire for the purpose of collecting legal customs[91], but without any result. S. Luby elaborated many questions on customary laws[92] and S. Svecová did the same in respect to the systematization of Slovak family forms[93].

Among the Eastern Slavs the *Russians* had in earlier times (that is in the 18th century) made it possible for the conquered peoples to use their own laws. These special laws were treated as a supplementary law to the Russian state law and their compilation became necessary. This was completed on the scene, in the presence of the nobles and leaders. Some collections were extended to a number of peoples living in the European parts of Russia (for example the so-called Speransky-collection of the year 1822). We can find the scientific historical summary of the question in K. Tagányi's work[94]. M. Kovalevsky[95] completed the working out of a fragmentary part of living law customs.

In the U.S.S.R. since 1950 they treated of the legal phenomena of social life using the so-called examination of change. It was important for the Soviet State to take into consideration social structures and popular legal culture as in their territory there existed several nationalities of varying cultural levels and with different religious beliefs. A great part of these people still lived in feudal conditions. For example, the original source of the customary law of some peoples of the Caucasus was the scheria, the law of Islam, accepting polygamy, the agnate connection of the family, the almost outlawed state of women. Penal law had a strongly private law character (family revenge, etc.). For some time there were daily conflicts between the law and customary law[96]. Many of the peasants adhered firmly to the old traditions.

At first the collections and treatises on social transformations were schematical sketches, but later they treated the problems more dialectically, enlarging the scope of their researches to include more profound examinations of legal problems: thus many useful publications appeared. In 1953 G.M. Sverdlov's directory had a stimulating effect on the researches of the ethnologists. He drew their attention to the state-law side of the problems examined, that is to notice how the laws were merging into the everyday life[97].

A collection of legal-historical relics found in customs is in progress, its examples being the studies of E. Kagarow[98], M.O. Kosven[99], A. Ladyzenskij[100], R. Kharadze[101] and A.C. Omarov[102].

The *Rumanians* having many ethnological unities, possess a very rich customary law. The first Rumanian study in the field of legal ethnology was written by G. Draganescu, who has elaborated the marriage legal customs[103]. G. Fotino is supposed to have discovered many Rumanian folk peculiarities chiefly among the hereditary legal customs relating to real estate[104]. Much valuable material has been obtained from D.D. Mototolescu's history of law[105]; from S. Radivici's work[106] on the common ownership (razes and mosnen) of Rumanian peasants extant at the turn of the century; and from I. Radu's treatise on the living customs of family rights[107].

From the theoretical standpoint T. Herseni's study on the rôle played by custom in relation to the individual and to society is very important[108]. X.C. Costa-Foru and H.H. Stahl[109] in their treatise on family common property in the village of Nerej (Oltenia) show how the organized forms of the old life are dissolved by the new and modern state-issued conditions (for example the influence of the Code Civil). H.H. Stahl acquaints us with the rules of customary law relating to the landed estate beyond the village[110].

In old *Lettonia*, V. Sinalski, in a book of several hundred pages, dealt with the problems of legal ethnology based chiefly on history[111].

In *Turkey* there is only one short study that has any bearing on our subject and that is K. Yund's treatise on traditional family rights in Içel[112].

In *Greece*, G.L. Maurer was the first historian of law[113] in the beginning of the 19th century, who with the help of a questionnaire collected the customs of laws. From the material collected, it may be deduced that the living law customs can be traced back to Byzantine, Hellenic and Old Greek sources.

From among the Teutonic peoples of Scandinavia we shall deal first with the *Swedes*. To our best knowledge, no separate space has been devoted to legal ethnology in their vast ethnological literature. A. Eskeröd in one of his articles dealing with social problems, begins his study by mentioning that in the field of Swedish folk culture the structure and dynamics of social organization have not yet been touched upon[114]. We can deduce from the comprehensive ethnological studies that extensive basic works relating to legal ethnology have already commenced[115]. S. Erixon and S. Ljung collaborated in writing a treatise on the selfgovernment of peasant villages, which, though only a detail of legal ethnology, convinces us of the afore-mentioned fact[116]. C.H. Tillhagen studied some customary legal problems of the Gypsies living in Sweden[117].

In *Norway* K. Ostberg produced the most excellent study on European legal ethnology, the "Norsk Bonderet"[118]. It is a colossal collection and elaboration of Norwegian peasant rights. In a work of several volumes he treats of peasant rights in their entirety (bonderet), from the contracts of servants to proprietary marks. He mentions also the customs appertaining to the neighbourhood, to lumbering and an especially valuable ancient Old-Norwegian custom concerning communal whalefishing [119]. Ostberg's theoretical and comparative reflections are of less value[120]. In the first third of our century he had great influence on the formation of European legal ethnology. We have yet to mention E. Solem's book on the customary law of the Lapps[121] and a short article by G. Anohin[122].

The extensive ethnological interest of the *Finns* discourses on legal problems without its coming under the name of legal ethnology, nor is any endeavour made to use any legal systematic methods in their studies. Their scholars deal first of all with the Finno-Ugric age and the legal traditions of later-period primitive societies. E.A. Virtanen has written on the law of hunting[123] and fishing[124], on the occupation marks[125], on the private and common ownership of the primitive Finnish communities[126]. U. Harva[127] dealt with the systems of kinship and U.T. Sirelius with the legal questions concerning hunting[128].

In *Denmark* two studies attract our attention. P. Meyer occupied himself with rural autonomy, local communal customs, and freegrazing-systems[129].

A.F. Schmidt published important material on the customs of local administration[130].

In *Belgium* P. Heupgen[131], in *Luxemburg* J. Hess[132] and J. Engling[133], and in *Holland* the studies of G.A. Wilken[134] have some bearing on legal ethnology.

In *England* as in Sweden, the research work on the legal customs and conflicts, which arise in an organized society, do not come under the heading of "legal ethnology," but of "legal anthropology." This branch of science treats of the structure of law systems and examines the manner in which society reacts to legal regulations[135]. Legal anthropology differs from the characteristics of European research insofar as it looks upon the undeveloped communities as integral parts of the national state and does not perceive the influence of historical traditions on the inner pulsation of society; still less does it attach any importance to it[136].

In this country the importance of the customary law is traditional and besides customary law there is no such "folk customary law," as in Europe where it is the chief source of legal ethnology. The consequence is that what we treat of under the name of legal ethnology is in England an organic part of the history of law, and for example under the name of "juridical folklore" ancient historical systems of punishment may be included[137]. Researches among the documents of the law-courts give no greater results[138].

An exception being perhaps the English rural communities[139] or the grazing communities of Irish villages[140], of whose customary rights we have a rich collection. P. Vinogradoff made very fundamental statements relating to the connection between custom and right, especially on the manner of acquiring these rights. For this he took his examples from the life of medieval and modern peasantry[141].

Evaluation of Results

From the varied material listed we gain a wide survey of the situation of legal ethnology in Europe and this, more or less, determines its task. We can see that in nearly all European countries and among all peoples, initiatives were taken and with success. But it is equally perceptible, from the above outlined literary material, that the themes and their treatment are extremely varied. If we take into consideration the fact that we have dealt only with those works which contributed directly to the process of developing legal ethnology, on a European level, we may conclude the foundation was widely spread.

The works mentioned in the scientific-historical survey disclose the fact, that among the peoples of Europe, even in our times, there exist legal customs derived from different stages of social history. E.A. Virtanen has discovered among the Finno-Ugric peoples of today, surviving traces of primitive man's pursuits, such as the gathering of food-stuffs, in the occupation-marks and the legal rights relating to them. In the region of Vrancea, the Rumanians have a form of legal magic, called "sânger." This consists of a bloody stake being placed in each of the four corners of the field. In H.H. Stahl's opinion this is to protect it from strangers. K. Ostberg describes Old-Norwegian fishing, the distribution of the various parts of the caught whale's carcass and the customs derived from this which had their origins thousands of years ago. Let us look at Albania, where survivals of customs based on the internal functions of the ancient clan-organizations still exist in the family life of today. Seeing these customs, we can scarcely consider ourselves as independent of the pre-feudal age. In the case of the migrant gypsies and some transhumance shepherds in the Balkans, it is as if the wheel of time had stopped several centuries ago.

Remains of early and late feudalism are still to be found in the material of European legal ethnology. These are chiefly connected with the soil, its use, its concept, its heritage, and the family. It would be rather difficult to associate the joint family, house-community (zadruga) with any single given historical age, but the seed of its diverse forms, as might be studied from the end of the 19th century till our days, was sown by feudalism. Various elements of feudalism are embodied in the internal organization of the village, the countless economic, cultural and social institutions (for example law-courts, common pasture for animals, common defense against fire etc.), which were brought into being for the purpose of carrying out common tasks. These were examined chiefly by German and Swiss scholars. From the age of Capitalism, commercial customs (market-practices, "usance," etc.) came into the field of legal ethnology. In this respect we cannot as yet form any idea of the relation of Socialism to legal ethnology, but it would appear that the internal collaboration of the state organs has a tendency to follow stereotyped practices (as customs), while trade follows the usual commercial customs.

We can appreciate our material not only from the standpoint of social-historical development, but from the different branches of law as well. The customs disclosed can be classified chiefly under private law, that is it touches on personal law, proprietary law, (comprising commercial law), inheritance law, family law and marriage-property law. The customary material in the field of administrative law and penal law is not so rich.

The enormous diversity of legal customs and legal traditions, discounting ethnical and religious factors, is the direct consequence of the unequal economic and social evolution in Europe and within the various nations and peoples, as well. Thus, we draw the conclusion that no people exist who do not possess legal customs. This circumstance ensures research a wide field of variety in the future, even in those countries whose legal culture stands on a relatively high level. There are still many possibilities for research work on legal ethnology in Europe, whatever type of ruling system governs.

The material based on the national results of research certainly facilitates the comparison of parallel work done by the neighbouring countries who have identical or similar economic and social institutions. Further, it makes possible the appraisal of the attitude of some concrete legal forms (legal customs, motives or models of behavior) on the basis of codified laws and how they are put into practice by the people. It often happens that what is a law in one country is merely a legal custom in another. On the other hand, the revealed material based on common and united concepts and on developed methods may have a certain advantageous reaction on national researches.

In the literary material we find several solutions for the name of this research, according to what other science it was brought into contact with. In France, today, both ethnological and sociological investigators most frequently use the expression "ethnologie juridique" instead of the obsolete "folklore juridique." The Italians use several names: "folclore giuridico," "folcloristica giuridica," "etnologia giuridica" (chiefly used by jurists). In accordance with the historical interest of the Germans some call it "rechtsgeschichtliche Volkskunde" or "Rechtsarchäologie," some use A.H. Post's expression "ethnographische Jurisprudenz," others J. Kohler's term "ethnologische Rechtsforschung." But the term "rechtliche Volkskunde" is becoming more and more current in ethnologists' terminology. The Dutch use "juridicke folclore," Lettish researchers "juridiska folklora," the Poles "etnografia prawna," the Czechs "právni lidoveda." In Hungary they generally use "jogi néprajz" (legal ethnology), "jogi népszokáskutatás" (research of legal folk customs), "népi jogkutatás" (folk legal research), "népi jogéletkutatás" (research of legal life of the people). In Sweden and in England we find the term, "legal anthropology."

One part of the European researchers deals with legal ethnology, and all activities which come under the name, as a branch of ethnology; others look upon it as an auxiliary science to the history of law; and again there are researchers who consider it part of comparative jurisprudence or of sociology.

Concerning the results, we must mention that steps have already been taken towards a common cultivation of legal ethnology. Among them, we can consider as such the decision of the *Academie Internationale de Droit Comparé* (in 1932 at the Hague Congress) to take upon themselves the task of studying not only the written and unwritten legal customs of primitive peoples, but also the folk legal customs and legal folklore of all Europe. The Czechoslovakian R. Horna, with this aim in view, proposed in 1952, a congress of Polish, Czech, and Slovak jurists[142]. In 1964, at the 7th "International Congress of Anthropological and Ethnological Sciences" in Moscow, customary law appeared as the central theme for the common study of the source of legislation.

Legal Ethnology and Its Tasks

In connection with the concept of legal ethnology we shall find many obscure and much-debated problems. The themes of these topics can, in general, be divided into three greater parts: legal customs, legal traditions and their (real) material. Most discussions are about legal customs. Many persons doubt whether legal customs come into being at all, and if so, how do they stand in relation to the law, and why does one branch of ethnology deal with it, etc. Later we shall give detailed answers to these questions, but first we consider it necessary to elucidate the concept of legal ethnology with regard to other aspects.

For delimiting it from other sciences, the term "legal ethnology" gives us a certain starting-point, inasmuch as it conjures up for us a picture of the people, the law and the various forms of human behavior, that is the real object of research. Considering its diverse relations we must avoid rigid ideation.

According to our literary material, the greatest part of the researchers were interested chiefly in the agrarian strata, including the gathering economics (for example, the Gypsies). The power or the helplessness of the customs, the endeavour to stabilize the relations is most significant among the peasantry. From urban life legal ethnology picked up something from the customs of the traders (chiefly market-dealers, etc.) In addition to the living conditions of peasants and traders, our future task is to extend our researches to the workers (for example the industrial proletariat, the pick-and-shovel men, miners, etc.). We must first investigate the legal customs and only afterwards enquire who avails himself of them. We can say briefly: legal ethnology embraces all those who marry, inherit, make wills, transact business, or those who work in agricultural co-operatives, etc., and do but keep the state legal regulations in so far as is compulsory, in other respects living according to the customs of their smaller communities (micro-societies).

In the term "legal ethnology" with its reference to law, we find a certain conceptual constraint, as even the philosophy of law was unable in 2,000 years to define unanimously the exact meaning of law. As every country, people and scientist gave a different interpretation to the concept "law," it cannot serve us as a starting point. We can proceed only if we look upon law as a social product and approach it not from the theoretical but the practical aspect of human conduct.

The source of human conduct is consciousness: what is just and what is unjust, what we may do and what we may not: this, we say, is reprehended by man's consciousness of right, which decides whether to act or abstain. Now we will not touch on the very complicated dialectical question of decision and performance, for example expediency (as innovation) and powerlessness (as compliance), etc., which motivate the intention, we might say, man is influenced by his consciousness of right.

But what are the more important factors that influence the individual's consciousness of right and at the same time the existing so-called moral integration of the micro-communities?

They may be the following:

1. Inherited tradition (passed down by one generation to another);
2. the practices which are followed by other persons (for example the influence of higher classes, or of neighbours, or neighbouring communities);
3 religious beliefs (for example sects, scheria, etc.);
4. the law of the state and its coercive force;
5. individual experiences (which make social legal customs individual).

In a word, the consciousness of right is bound by historic, social, religious and state elements, and individual experience motivates all these. The influence of these factors may be occasional, tendential and exclusively from the point of view of individual conduct. If the influence of any one factor, from having once been conviction, now becomes a tendency or becomes exclusive[143], and repeatedly results in similar conduct on part of the major part of the community, in definite situations, if this influence is accepted socially, we then speak of custom, provided it is not identical with the state law. Basically one custom is similar to another: it is followed instinctively or consciously by the people, for if it were not, the inner mechanism of society, the intrastructural forces would enforce it[144].

From the mass of various customs, we can separate legal customs with the help of fiction. We say there are human relations which are generally reflected in the law, or relations, which have rules imposed upon them by the law. We may presume, that at the same time and in larger territories, they are relatively permanent and immutable, or at the most, change very slowly. To this group belong the relations of proprietorship, of distribution, of persons, and common procedures, etc. For example, for the distribution of the common property the civil law established rules, but the aforementioned examples of the Old-Norwegian distribution of whale fishing, or the distribution of benefits derived from communal sheep breeding in Transylvania, for the most part escape the attention of the legislation. In these cases larger or smaller groups constitute for themselves a "law," structurally identical with that of the state to which they subject themselves.

We have an example of a legal institution being established by state law, and custom applying it to different relations; among the Croats, the female brought a dowry to her husband's house, and this was based on state law, but (according to J. Csányi) custom compelled the man to do the same in the case of his going to live on the farm of his wife's parents. Whether the latter is to be considered a law or a legal custom is a moot question.

Our subsequent problem is, what is the state's attitude to legal custom? We must touch on this question as many scientists do not consider as an integral part of legal ethnology the legal customs which are acknowledged by the state, only those are so considered which are independent of the state or degrade it, or have a derogatory effect on it. We accept the former opinion, because the legal customs acknowledged by the state have their source in the community which established them.

From all this we have the means for delimiting the topics of legal ethnology from other sciences and defining its tasks. Jurisprudence deals with the establishment and employment of the state laws (including administrative organs and law-court practices); the examination of the concrete rôle they play in society is the occupation of legal sociology[145], and the task of legal history is the research of their relation to history. The task of legal ethnology is the examination of human behaviour (derived from all other sources) which is accepted and applied customarily by any socially defined community, even if with the aid of fiction it enters the field of law. Legal ethnology must deal also with the extant creations of man's consciousness of right, but which are not put into practice any more and live only in the products of folklore (tales, songs, legends, and fables) and appear in legal customs which are still remembered by the people of today. We will not occupy ourselves with these, the objective (real) mementos of legal customs and legal traditions as they indubitably belong to the field of legal ethnology.

Some Methodological Aspects

For the purpose of examining the themes belonging to the field of legal ethnology, experience has formed an adequate method, which takes into consideration the circumstance that customs are parts of some legal institution and the parts must be investigated in conjunction with the whole. Besides these customs stand in the closest relation to socio-economical realities, and legal traditions have inherited the criteria and relics from former legal systems. We must develop the existing methods further and make them suitable for the realization of common results. Attention must be paid to some points of view.

Customs and traditions must not be separated from the mode of living, as may be seen from the aforementioned. Examinations must be carried out showing that they have a bearing upon one another. Every phenomenon, which can be appreciated from a legal point of view, has forms, meaning, use and function, as well as development, change and migration. Today legal ethnology can be studied successfully only by using complex methods for revealing connections and certain phenomena. In the following we wish to give a rough outline.

The exact time and place must be ascertained concerning the forms of the phenomena of legal ethnology, such as, the connection with the culture (meaning) of a given community (group); the relation to state law (use); lastly the connection with the socio-economic basic structure of the community (function). This basic operation is our most important task and must be dealt with according to the generally accepted and known methods proper to legal ethnology. Only those phenomena may be taken into account which occur repeatedly in the collective mentality and actions of the majority of the community. In contrast with this, legal traditions as well as folk tales and folksongs may consider the perpetuation of single occurrences as indispensable. The reason we declare our science to belong to ethnology is because the most important basic work is done with the aims and methods pertinent to the science of ethnology, deviating only insofar as we look at it from the legal point of view.

Concerning technical questions, we wish to mention only questionnaires and atlases whose rôle in the preparation for common European research must be made clear without delay.

The questionnaires were of great help to national collections, but as experience has shown, they proved useful only for a general collection of experiences in the internal affairs of some community. For the purpose of obtaining a thorough and varied knowledge concerning certain communities or still more, of certain legal institutions (for example dowry), special questionnaires should be devised. Placing the problems on a European level, the initial aims should be the compilation of a thematic catalogue; and the publication of questionnaires relevant to the most important topics would be of great help.

All over Europe collections are being instituted towards the charting of ethnographical maps and in nearly every country some questions of interest to us have appeared in the questionnaires. It would have been better if everywhere identical questions had been agreed upon. The atlases have illustrated well the wide diffusion of customs, but for us they are useful chiefly because they show the points (villages) where it would be worthwhile later to commence deeper examinations.

There is another important question that must be mentioned if we wish to co-operate or find a base for comparison. That is a uniform terminology. But we must go not too far and create immoderately narrow conceptions, as such attempts would prevent us from understanding properly the many various ethnical characteristics (peculiarities) existing in Europe. Further, it would deprive us of the possibility of discoursing in a common language with those branches of science whose data we use or to whom we could give data. A common periodical for that purpose would be of great use.

The next phase of our work after having collected our data is its elaboration. The examined legal phenomena are integral parts of a nation's culture, the results of historical evolution. That is the reason why we must expose the historical sources, in which work we are helped both by national legal history and by universal legal history. The latter furnishes us with a base for understanding the adoption and migration of the phenomena, concerning which S. Svensson has given us countless useful observations on these problems as seen from the ethnological point of view. To find one's bearings among legal traditions without the aid of the ready data of the history of law is impossible. For the examination of the social aims of customs, we may employ the results and even the methods of sociology. The regular comparison of national and international results is also a phase of elaboration. We can find some very fine examples of this in the aforementioned work by K. Tagányi.

A gigantic task awaits the exponents of legal ethnology, whether we look at national results or the perspective of international collaboration in Europe. These prospects cannot be viewed simultaneously. Our only aim here was to give a survey of the existing and immediate tasks. Should we find co-workers in Europe willing to collaborate in this estimable endeavour, we feel we have not laboured in vain.

Notes

1. Paris, 1938
2. *Revue de folklore français et de folklore colonial* (Paris), 8 (1937), pp. 8–9.
3. Le Folklore Juridique. In : *Travaux du 1er Congrès International de Folklore.* Tours, 1938. pp. 185–190.

4. Les idées primitives dans la Bretagne contemporaine. Essai de folklore juridique et d'histoire générale du droit. *Revue historique de droit français et étranger*, (Paris), série 4, 8 (1929), pp. 431–472, 669–711.

5. Le folklore juridique du Languedoc. *Folklore* (Carcassonne), n° 69 (1952), pp. 63–77.

6. *Usages commerciaux et loi en droit français.* Paris-Rennes, 1958.

7. Le folklore juridique. In : *Chronique du mouvement scientifique.* Paris, 1933.

8. *Atlas folklorique de la France.* Paris, s.d. See p. 61 (on marriage), p. 69 (on common possession), p. 70 (on boundary-mark stones), p. 71 (on hire of servants).

9. *Eléments de sociologie juridique.* Paris, 1940.

10. *Initiation aux recherches de sociologie juridique.* Paris, 1949.

11. *Derecho consuetudinario de alto Aragón.* Madrid, 1886.

12. *Derecho consuetudinario y economía popular de España.* Barcelona, 1909.

13. *Derecho consuetudinario y economía popular de la provincia de Alicante.* Madrid, 1905.

14. *Indicacions bibliográfiques sobre costums jurédics d'Espanya i especialment de Catalunya.* Estudis universitaris catalans, 2. Barcelona, 1908.

15. Duarte-Ruben, Die Hausgemeinschaft im heutigen spanischen Gewohnheitsrecht. *Zeitschrift für vergleichende Rechtswissenschaft* [abbr. : *ZfVR.*] (Stuttgart), 28 (1905) pp. 110–165.

16. Beziehungen von Recht und spanischem Volkstum in Geschichte und Gegenwart. In : H. Konen und J.P. Steffes (Hsgg.), *Volkstum and Kulturpolitik.* Köln, 1932.

17. *Consideracões sobre a necessidade do estudo do direito consuetudinario portugues.* Coïmbra, 1923; Die Erforschung der nationalen Rechtsgeschichte in Portugal. *ZfVR*, 46 (1923), pp. 339–354.

18. E. Panetta, L'etnologia giuridica e il suo metodo secondo il Mazzarella. *Lares* (Roma-Firenze), 20 (1954), pp. I–XIX. He published his studies from 1902 till 1909 in a series *Studi di Etnologia Giuridica* under his own editorship.

19. Roma, 1925. We must note about A. Scialoja, that he proposed, in 1886, the investigation of the legal practices among the common people. (*Antologia giuridica*, 1886, p. 441.)

20. *Per una raccolta di usi giuridici popolari.* Roma, 1926.

21. *Rivista di diritto agrario* (Firenze), 7 (1930), pp. 17–40; Le costumanze giuridiche e la riforma del diritto privato in Italia. In : *Atti del I Congresso Nazionale delle Tradizioni Popolari.* Firenze, 1930. pp. 122–149. In their country-wide collecting work they collaborated with some courts of justice and a number of administrative organizations.

22. Risultato della raccolta degli usi e delle consuetudini giuridiche nei « contratti in fiera » effettuata nel 1930 dalle Procure generali delle Corti d'appello. *Lares* (Roma-Firenze), 20 (1954), pp. 135.

23. *Trenta anni di storia giuridica agraria.* Modena, 1954. *Il mondo agrario tradizionale nella valle padana.* Modena, 1963.

24. *Atti convegno studi sul folklore padano.* Firenze, 1963.

25. Ländliche Gewohnheitsrechte einiger Gebiete Kalabriens. *ZfVR.*, 22 (1909), pp. 430–456; Die Kleiderabgabe bei den Hochzeitsgebräuchen. *ZfVR.*, 31 (1914), pp. 321–339.

26. *Lo studio di proverbi giuridici italiani.* Roma, 1957.

27. Folkloristica giuridica e storia del diritto. *Rivista di storia del diritto italiano* (Roma), 2 (1929), pp. 129–159.

28. *Consuetudini giuridico-agrarie della provincia di Udine.* Firenze, 1944; *Vita di popolo nel Friuli. Patti agrari e consuetudini tradizionali.* Firenze, 1961.

29. *Archivio Scialoja per le consuetudini giuridiche agrarie.* Firenze, 1931–1942; *Bibliografia di diritto agrario.* Milano, 1959, 1962.

30. M.-Bareris Ricca, *Consuetudine e diritto.* Torino, 1955; C.E. Balossini, *L'accertamento del diritto consuetudinario compito del giurista e del sociologo.* Milano, 1963.

31. *Vom Beruf unserer Zeit für Gesetzgebung und Rechtswissenschaft.* Heidelberg, 1814. (Cf. G. Cocchiara, *Storia del folklore in Europa.* Seconda edizione. Torino, 1954. p. 242.)

32. *Deutsche Rechtsalterthümer.* Göttingen, 1828.

33. Der Mädchenmarkt auf dem Gainaberg. *ZfVR.*, 9 (1886), pp. 398–400; Studien über die künstliche Verwandschaft. *ZfVR.*, 7 (1884), pp. 415–440; Zur ethnologischen Jurisprudenz. *ZfVR.*, 9 (1886), pp. 407–429; Lebens- und Rechtsbräuche der Bulgaren. *ZfVR.*, 39 (1916), pp. 433–460.

34. K.S. Kramer, Problematik der Rechtlichen Volkskunde. *Bayerisches Jahrbuch für Volkskunde* (München), 13 (1962), pp. 50–66.

35. K. von Amira, *Rechtsarchäologie.* Strassburg, 1913.

36. *Rechtliche Volkskunde.* Halle, 1936; Rechtsgeschichte und Volkskunde. *Jahrbuch für historische Volkskunde* (Berlin), 1 (1925), pp. 67–125; Vergleichende Rechtsarchäologie. In : *Kunst und Recht. Festgabe für Hans Fehr.* Karlsruhe, 1948.

37. *Rechtsarchäologie.* Berlin, 1943; Volkskunde und Recht. In : *Die Volkskunde und ihre Beziehungen zu Recht, Medizin, Vorgeschichte.* Berlin, 1928; Volksrechtskunde und rechtliche Volkskunde. *Studi di storia e diritto in onore di Enrico Besta.* Milano, 1939. Vol. 2, pp. 518–535.

38. *Recht und Volkstum.* Weimar, 1933.

39. Begriff und Aufgabenkreis der rechtlichen Volkskunde. *Giessener Beiträge zur deutschen Philologie* (Giessen), 60 (1938), pp. 49–59.

40. Beiträgen zur rechtlichen Volkskunde Schleswig-Holsteins. *Nordelbingen* (Flensburg u. Kiel), 16 (1940), pp. 74–160; 18 (1942), pp. 51–88; Neue Beiträge zur rechtlichen Volkskunde Schleswig-Holsteins. *Kieler Blätter* (Kiel), 1943, pp. 67–92.

41. Gesunkenes Rechtsgut. In : *Kunst und Recht. Festgabe für Hans Fehr.* Karlsruhe, 1948; *Grenzrecht und Grenzzeichen.* Freiburg, 1940.

42. Rechtswissenschaft und Volkskunde. In : *Jahres- und Tagungsbericht der Görres-Gesellschaft 1960.* Köln, 1961. pp. 13–24.

43. *Haus und Flur im bäuerlichen Recht. Ein Beitrag zur rechtlichen Volkskunde.* München, 1950; Brauchtum und Recht. In : A. Erler und E. Kaufmann (Hgg.), *Handwörterbuch zur deutschen Rechtsgeschichte.* Vol. 2. Berlin, 1965. pp. 506–511.

44. Rechtsbräuche und Rechtsgewohnheiten im Hesselberggebiet. *Bayerisches Jahrbuch für Volkskunde* (München), 10 (1959), pp. 120–123.

45. Sitte, Recht und Brauch. Zur Eselshochzeit von Hütten in der Eifel. *Zeitschrift für Volkskunde* (Stuttgart), 56 (1960), pp. 74–88.

46. Volk und Recht, Volkskunde und Rechtsgeschichte. *Schweizer Volkskunde* (Basel), 41 (1951), pp. 2–6; Das Recht im Bündnermärchen. *Zeitschrift für schweizerisches Recht* (Basel), 84 (1935), pp. 219; Altes Strafrecht im Glauben des Volkes. *Deutsches Jahrbuch für Volkskunde* (Berlin), 1 (1955), pp. 147–156.

47. Sitte, Brauch und Recht. *Schweizerisches Archiv für Volkskunde* (Basel), 43 (1946), pp. 73–90.

48. *Die Verlobung im Volks- und Rechtsbrauch.* Basel, 1913.

49. *Übung und Ortsgebrauch im Schweizerischen Zivilgesetzbuch.* Zürich, 1911.

50. *Gewohnheitsrecht im Verwaltungsrecht.* Bern, 1960.

51. *Schweizer Volkskunde* (Basel), 41 (1951), p. 44.

52. Rechtsarchäologie in Österreich. *Die österreichische Furche* (Wien), 5 (1949), p. 8; *Rechtsarchäologie des Landes Steiermark.* Graz-Köln, 1957,

53. Rechtliche Volkskunde und Rechtsarchäologie als wissenschaftliche Begriffe und Aufgaben. *Schweizerisches Archiv für Volkskunde* (Basel), 48 (1952), pp. 65–82.

54. *Lebende Rechtsgewohnheiten und ihre Sammlung in Ungarn.* Budapest, 1922.

55. A közigazgatás népi szervei [Self-administrating organizations of the common people]. *Népünk és Nyelvünk* (Szeged), 1 (1929), pp. 23–38, 92–101.

56. Népi büntetőszokások [Penal customs of the common people]. *Ethnographia* (Budapest), 47 (1936), pp. 65–72.

57. László Papp, *A magyar népi jogélet kutatása* [The investigation of the everyday legal customs of the Hungarian common people]. Budapest, 1948; György Bónis, Magyar jogi néphagyományok [Customary legal traditions of the Hungarian common people]. *Magyar Szemle* (Budapest), 36 (1939); E. Tárkány-Szücs, A népi jogéletkutatás problémái a Nagy-Alföldön [The problems of the investigation of customary law in the Great Hungarian Plain]. *Alföldi Tudományos Gyüjtemény* (Szeged), 2 (1948), pp. 303–311; K. Kulcsár, *A jogszociológia problémái* [The problems of the sociology of law]. Budapest, 1960. pp. 109–125.

58. *Kiskunhalas népi jogélete* [The living customary law of the common people in Kiskunhalas]. Budapest, 1941.

59. *Mártély népi jogélete* [Living customary law of the common people in Mártély]. Kolozsvár, 1944.

60. Egyke és jogszokás a Garamvölgyén [One-child system and customary law of the common people in the valley of the river Garam]. *Társadalomtudomány* (Budapest), 21 (1941); Népi szemlélet és jogalkotás [The people's opinion and legislation]. *Puszták Népe* (Budapest), 3 (1948), pp. 15–23.

61. A nagycsalád és jogszokásai a komárommegyei Martoson [The joint family and its customary law in Martos]. *Társadalomtudomány* (Budapest), 23 (1943), pp. 408–437; 24 (1944), pp. 1–35.

62. *A barkók öröklési jogszokásai* [The hereditary customary laws of the Barko (ethnic group in the vacinity of Eger)]. Eger, 1947.

63. E. Tárkány-Szücs, Jogszokás-gyüjtés Kalotaszegen [The collection of customary laws in Kalotaszeg]. *Kolozsvári Szemle* (Kolozsvár), 12 (1943), pp. 64–70; Erdély öröklési jogszokásai [The hereditary customary law of Transylvania]. *Hitel* (Kolozsvár), 9 (1944), pp. 378–400; Jogi elemek a kalotaszegi népmesékben

[Juridical elements and relations in the folktales of Kalotaszeg]. *Kolozsvári Szemle* (Kolozsvár), 13 (1944), pp. 137–145.

64. E. Tárkány-Szücs, A juhtartás népi jogszabályai Bálványosváralján [Statutory provisions of the common people in the affairs concerning sheep-breeding in Bálványosváralja]. *Erdélyi Múzeum* (Kolozsvár), 49 (1944). These investigations were headed by J. Venczel, under the sponsorship of the so-called Transylvanian village exploring teams.

65. *Asszonyok a nagycsaládban* [The rôle of women in the joint family]. Budapest, 1956.

66. Types of Workgroups and Temporary Associations of Seasonal Labour in the Age of Capitalism. *Acta Ethnographica* (Budapest), 11 (1962), pp. 31–84.

67. A népi jog és a nemzeti jog [The customary law of the people and the common law of the State]. *Az Allam- és Jogtudományi Intézet Ertesitöje* (Budapest), 1961, pp. 153–193.

68. *Illyrisch-Albanische Forschungen*. München-Leipzig, 1916. Bd. 1, pp. 409–462.

69. F. Nopcsa, Die Herkunft des nordalbanischen Gewohnheitsrechtes, des Kanun Lek Dukadžinit. ZfVR., 66 (1923), pp. 371–376; J. V. Ivanova, Obyč]noe pravo severnoj Albanii kak etnografičeskij istočnik [The customary law of Northern Albania as an ethnographical source]. *Sovetskaja Etnografija* (Moskva-Leningrad), 1961, n° 3, pp. 53–65; s. Isljami, Semejnaja obščina albancev v period ee raspada [Community of family among the Albanians in the age of their dissolution]. *Sovetskaja Etnografija*, 1952, n° 3, pp. 119–132; Qu. Kastrati, Some Sources of the Unwritten Law in Albania. *Man* (London), 55 (1955), pp. 124–127.

70. *The Unwritten Law in Albania*. Cambridge, 1954.

71. La donna albanese con speciale riguardo al diretto consuitudinario delle Montagne di Scutari. *Anthropos* (St. Gabriel-Mödling b. Wien), 7 (1912), pp. 309–335, 617–626.

72. La vendetta del sangue nelle Montagne dell'Alta Albania. *Anthropos*, 5 (1910), pp. 654–687.

73. *Zbornik sadačnjih pravnih običaja u Južnih Slovena*. Zagreb, *1874*; F.S. Krauss *Sitte und Brauch der Südslaven*. Wien, 1885.

74. ZfVR., 31 (1908), pp. 122.

75. *Jihoslovanské právo soukromé ve světle právnich obyčejů* [The South-Slav private law as reflected in customary laws]. Praha 1926.

76. *Die Sitten der Südslawen*. Drezden, 1927.

77. K. Tagányi, *op. cit.*, p. 10.

78. *Alsómuraközi családi jogi néphagyományok* [The customary law traditions of Alsómuraköz (Northern Croatia)]. Perlak, 1943.

79. *Narodopisje Slovencev*. Ljubljana, 1952. Vol. 2, pp. 217–262, 263–350.

80. *Običajno Pravo* [Customary law]. Zagreb, 1948.

81. Društvene i ovičajno-pravne ustanove u Rami (Notes on social institutions and customary law in Rama (Bosnia)]. *Glasnik Zemaljskog Muzeja u Sarajevu. Istorija i etnografija* (Sarajevo), Nova serija 9 (1954), pp. 169–180.

82. *Sbornik na B'lgarskitje juridičesaki običai. Vol. 1.* Plovdif, 1897; Vol. 2. Sofija, 1902.

83. B'lgarskata čeljadna zadruga. Istorikopravni studii. Sofija, 1907.
84. Gewohnheitsrechtliches aus Bulgarien. ZfVR., 35 (1912), 37 (1914), 39 (1916), 40 (1917).
85. Lebens- und Rechtsbräuche der Bulgaren. ZfVR., 41 (1918), pp. 433–460.
86. Obyčej i zákon v Bulharsku. Sborník vêd právnich a státnich [Customary law and state law in Bulgaria]. Praha, 1926.
87. L. Halban, Znaczenie zwyczajów prawnych i ich badanie [The importance of customary law and its research]. Lud (Kraków-Lublin), 39 (1948–1951), pp. 148–180.
88. Lud (Lwów), 26 (1927), pp. 7–18, 96–97, 113–114; 27 (1928), pp. 1–25.
89. L. Halban, op. cit.
90. Folklore juridique. Lud, 39 (1948–1951), pp. 133–147.
91. Slovenské Pohlady. Turócszentmárton, 1907. p. 225.
92. Obyčajové právo a súdna prax [The rôle of the juridical custom in legal practice] Bratislava, 1939.
93. Klasifikácia rodinných foriem v Slovenskom materiáli [The classifications of the diverse family types based on Slovak ethnological material]. Český lid (Praha), 21 (1966), pp. 85–89.
94. K. Tagányi, op. cit., pp. 3–9.
95. Modern Customs and Ancient Laws of Russia, 1891; Zakon i obyčai na Kavkazie. Moskva, 1890.
96. H. Günther, Zusammenstösse zwischen Gesetz und Gewohnheitsrecht im nördlichen Kaukazus. ZfVR. 54 (1931), pp. 317–359.
97. Sovetskaja Etnografija, 1953, n° 2, pp. 202–211.
98. Reste primitiver Rechtsgewohnheiten in den ostslawischen Volksgebräuchen. ZfVR.,53 (1930), pp. 209–218.
99. Semejnaja obščina. Opyt istorišeskoj kharakteristiki. [The joint family. Attempt at a historical characteristic.] Sovetskaja Ethnografija, 1948, n° 3, pp. 3–32; Matriarkhat. Moskva, 1948.
100. Das Familiengewohnheitsrecht der Tscherkessen. ZfVR., 51 (1928), pp. 178–208.
101. Gruzinskaja semejnaja obščina [The Georgian joint family]. Tbilisi, 1960.
102. Pamjatniki obyčnaja prava Dagestana XVI–XVII vv. [Monuments of the Daghestanian customary law of the 16th and 17th centuries]. Moskva, 1964.
103. Rumänische Hochzeitsgebräuche. ZfVR., 31 (1908), pp. 68–105.
104. Contribution à l'étude des origines de l'ancien droit coutumier roumain. Paris, 1925. pp. 61–84, 134, 205, 238, 271; What is the Old Rumanian Law? Rumanian Quarterly (Bucureşti), 1939, pp. 31, 38–40.
105. Der Grenzeid mit der Erdscholle auf der Kopfe im alten rumänischen Recht. ZfVR., 60 (1937), pp. 269–305.
106. Mosnenii şi razesii. Bucureşti, 1909.
107. Raport asupra manifestărilor juridice din sânul familiei. Timişoara, 1938.
108. Individ şi societate în satul Fundul Moldovei. Arhíva pentru ştiinţa şi reform socială (Bucureşti), 10 (1932), pp. 135–158.
109. Caracterul devălmaş familiei nerejene. Ibidem, pp. 447–462.

110. Bornes, limites et signes de propriété champêtres. Notes de folklore juridique roumain. *Travaux du 1ᵉʳ Congrès International de Folklore*. Tours, 1938. pp. 201–205.

111. *Folklore juridique*. Riga, 1931.

112. Geleneklere göre Içel'de aile hukuku [Traditional familiary law in Içel]. *Türk Düşüncesi*, (Istanbul), 1 (1954), pp. 281–283.

113. E. von Künssberg, *Rechtliche Volkskunde*. Halle, 1936, pp. 3–4.

114. *Schwedische Volkskunde*. Festschrift für S. Svensson. Stockholm, 1961. p. 153.

115. See the studies by A. Eskeröd, (pp. 153–179), O. Hasslöf, (pp. 244–272) and N.A. Bringéus (pp. 424–429) in : *Schwedische Volkskunde*.

116. Svenska byordningar [Swedish village arrangements]. *Folk-liv* (Stockholm), 17–18 (1953–1954), pp. 81–124.

117. The Concept of Justice among the Swedish Gypsies. *Journal of the Gypsy Lore Society* (Edinburgh), 37 (1958), pp. 82–96.

118. 11 vol. Oslo, 1914–1936.

119. *Op. cit.*, vol. 9. Oslo, 1934. pp. 77–103.

120. *Op. cit.*, vol. 3. Hamar, 1922. pp. 1–17.

121. *Lappiske rettsstudier*. Oslo and Cambridge, 1933.

122. Izučenie perežitkov obščinnogo prava v Norvegii [The study of survivals of communal law in Norway]. *Sovetskaja Etnografija*, 1961, n° 1, pp. 198–200.

123. Über das Jagdrecht der Karelier. *Studia Fennica* (Helsinki), 4 (1940); *Suomalaista tapaoikeutta* [Finnish customary law]. Helsinki, 1949.

124. *Itäkarjalaisten kalastusoikeudesta ja -yhtiöistä* [On fishing rights and fishing companies in Eastern Karelia]. Helsinki, 1950.

125. Okkupaatiomerkeistä [Upon occupation-marks]. *Suomen Museo* (Helsinki), 58 (1951), pp. 49–55.

126. Über Privat- und Gesellschaftswirtschaft in der primitiven Gemeinschaft. *Sitzungsberichte der Finnischen Akademie der Wissenschaften* (Helsinki), 1960, pp. 115–131.

127. The Finno-Ugric System of Relationship. *Transactions of the Westermarck Society* (Göteborg), 1 (1947), pp. 47–52.

128. Über das Jagdrecht bei einigen finnisch-ugrischen Völkern. *Mémoires de la Société Finno-ougrienne* (Helsinki), 35 (1914), pp. 4–9.

129. *Danske Bylag* [*Danish villages*]. København, 1949.

130. *Studier over vider og vedtægter* [Studies on village organizations]. Brabrand, 1951.

131. Menus faits. Folklore judiciaire. *Le Folklore brabançon* (Bruxelles), 16 (1936–1937), pp. 93–94, 282–285.

132. *Luxemburger Volksleben in Vergangenheit und Gegenwart*. Grevenmacher, 1939. ("Rechtsüberreste," pp. 68–75).

133. In : *op. cit.*: "Alte Volkssitten und Gebräuche im Luxemburger Land," pp. 132–146.

134. *De vrucht van de bevefening der ethnologie voor de vergelykende rechtswetenschap*. Leiden, 1885.

135. See P. J. Bohannan's study "Anthropology and the Law" In : *Horizons of Anthropology*. London, 1965. pp. 205–211.

136. R. Redfield, *Peasant Society and Culture*. Chicago, 1956. p. 10.
137. I. W. Spargo, *Juridical Folklore in England*. Durham, 1944.
138. C. F. Tebbutt, Folklore from Court Records. *Folk-Lore* (London), 67 (1956), pp. 228–230.
139. Example : G. L. Gomme, *The Village Community with Special Reference to the Origin and Form of Its Survivals in Britain*. London, 1890.
140. *Ulster Folklife* (Belfast), 2 (1956); C. Arensberg and S. T. Kimball, *Family and Community in Ireland*. Cambridge, 1940.
141. *Custom and Right*. Oslo, 1925.
142. R. Horna, *op. cit.*, p. 147.
143. Legal ethnology—derived from branches both of ethnology and sociology—evaluates only the rules of behaviour, which had become general, but not its deviations.
144. Modern legal sociology also "steps beyond" the traditional concept of law. For example, H. Lévy-Bruhl referred to the fact that the research of rights must go beyond the rules of law, legal regulations and the legal written material in general. (*Initiation aux recherches de sociologie juridique*. Paris, 1949.) G. Gurvitch considers the most diverse mass of rules of behaviour as a law symbolic activities, suppositions, customs, and whose value may be discovered in the spontaneous normative facts. (*Sociology of Law*. London, 1947 p. 48.).
145. J. P. Poisson, Le concret en sociologie juridique. *Revue de l'Institut de Sociologie* (Bruxelles), 39 (1958), pp 505–511

SAMUEL KUCHEROV

Indigenous and Foreign Influences on the Early Russian Legal Heritage

Each country in Europe and for that matter, the world, has its own special history of folk law and research devoted to folk law. The Soviet Union is no exception. The following essay gives us a glimpse into early Russian folk law, some of which continues up until the twentieth century.

For additional data on Russian folk law, see the excellent article "The Law of the Russian Peasant Household," by William T. Shinn, Jr., Slavic Review, *20 (1961), 601–621. See also Rene Beermann, "Prerevolutionary Russian Peasant Laws," in William E. Butler, ed.,* Russian Law: Historical and Political Perspectives *(Leyden: A.W. Sijthoff, 1977), pp. 179–192; Moshe Lewin, "Customary Law and Russian Rural Society in the Post-Reform Era,"* The Russian Review, *44 (1985), 1–19; Christine D. Worobec, "Reflections on Customary Law and Post-Reform Peasant Russia,"* The Russian Review, *44 (1985), 21–25; and Cathy Frierson, "Crime and Punishment in the Russian Village: Rural Concepts of Criminality at the End of the Nineteenth Century,"* Slavic Review, *46 (1987), 55–69.*

For further discussion of Russian law by Samuel Kucherov, see his book Courts, Lawyers and Trials under the Last Three Tsars *(New York: Praeger, 1953).*

For long years Russia's legal history has intrigued the scholars of Eastern Europe, and some in the West, but little attention has been devoted in English to the most ancient sources, those to be found in the chronicles and the *Russkaia Pravda*. Although Russian legal history offers little of the continuity of institutions to be found in Anglo-Saxon law, its earliest documents are matters of concern even to Soviet legal historians in an effort to understand a heritage that has left its impact upon contemporary developments. In order to sketch a part of that heritage conveniently for English-language readers, this brief article has been prepared.

Reprinted from *Slavic Review* 31 (1972), 257–282, with permission. Only the first portion of the essay, pp. 257–268, has been reprinted here.

Historians generally divide prerevolutionary Russian history into three periods: Independent Principalities, Muscovite, and Imperial. Legal history may be similarly partitioned. After the foundation of the Russian state in 862, its supreme power in the person of the prince of Kiev brought into union under his sovereignty several Slavic and foreign tribes living in the middle flow of the Volga, Dnieper, Pripet, Western Dvina rivers and the Chudskoe and Ilmen lakes. Yet, soon after this foundation the unity was destroyed, as princes divided their principalities among their sons at death. The supreme power thus became decentralized, for the Russian land was broken up into a system of independent principalities which engaged in constant rivalry and open hostilities.

Parallel to the princely power there emerged another force, that of the people. This will of the people came to be expressed in the decisions of the *veche* (popular assembly). Although the prince was able to maintain a balance of power, it swung sharply in favor of the *veche* in the two "republics,"[1] as they are often called, of Novgorod and Pskov.

Contractual relations permeated the political, public, and social life in the first period of Russian history. Indeed, the contractual principle was the basis of relations not only between the prince and the people, and among the princes themselves, but it regulated also class and social relations.

The primary source of law in the first period was custom. A custom that is used in a society for a long time becomes customary law—that is, obligatory for everyone. Customs are observed in individual cases "because of the concordant conviction of the actors of the necessity to submit to them" writes V. I. Sergeevich, "or because custom has been promoted to customary law, and its violation or nonobservance is punishable. Since custom has no distinct beginning—that is, is not related to a publication date—we become aware of it when it is already functioning in definite form for certain actions. These forms are provided by customary law and are obligatory for these actions."[2]

René A. Wormser asserts that "customs . . . came into being very late in man's career. Customs were then followed consciously, even though men might have no idea why a custom had originated or what purpose it served. . . . Great numbers were merely accidental in their origin, and customs have a way of persisting long after their origin has been lost and even after their usefulness has completely disappeared. . . . Each people built up its set of customs, and many of these customs developed into law. I might put it that the customs turned into 'customary law,' and from that into 'law.'"[3] Consequently, customary law has no personal source, such as a law provided by a legislator. Its source is the people.

Sergeevich, however, explains the origin of customary law as follows: "Common norms are generated by actions of individual persons, not certainly and not always, but only under favorable conditions. Various persons with common interests and similarity in their way of life can, in similar circumstances, act identically. Similar actions are generated by the similarity of characters, needs, and the entire conditions of life. If the conditions in which these persons act remain the same during a certain time, a consecutive series of similar actions in similar cases is created" (p. 5). The oncoming generations observe the actions of their parents before taking action themselves. Thus, according to Sergeevich, customary law is generated by a person's individual consciousness of the vital interests influencing this or that action. This autonomy is based on personal interest and individual judgment about what must happen under given conditions, and not on the abstract idea of truth and justice. This does not yet create customary law, but only individual actions—a certain practice. However, with the realization that the individual wills of various persons have become identical in similar cases and in substantial quantity, a second force—which inspires subsequent practice through the knowledge that there exists a definite practice to act similarly—is created. "This is the inert force of habit," writes Sergeevich (p. 11). The way of action chosen by some (always more energetic) persons becomes a common norm—a custom—because other persons (more or less passively) become accustomed to act similarly. A certain practice becomes transformed into a general custom as a consequence of the passive imitation of the action of leading personalities, and establishes a conviction that all persons must act in a certain way and not in any other.

It must be noted that it is not necessary for everyone to be convinced of the adequacy and justice of a customary law for it to be applied. Like a regular law, customary law can be enforced anyway (for example, the ancient custom of burying the living widow with her dead husband). However, a simple custom, having acquired no obligatory character, can be violated without penal consequences.[4]

Sergeevich's explanation of the origin of customary law was opposed by M. F. Vladimirsky-Budanov.[5] He was of the opinion that "autonomy—the arbitrary actions of energetic persons, followed by passive imitators and establishing a certain practice—could not be the source of customary law. Arbitrariness (that is, the negation of law) is not able to create law. Another argument against the scheme put forward by Sergeevich is, according to Vladimirsky-Budanov, the fact that customs of different people, separated by space and time, are similar and frequently even identical. In his opinion, the principal source of law is human nature—physical and moral—subjected to the same laws as organic and inorganic nature. Law on the first level of development is a feeling, an instinct—

such as vengeance, the protection of children by parents and vice versa, and the primary right of possession. In general, such a character is retained by law in familial and tribal unions. Everyone acts identically not because of imitation of someone, but under the influence of an identical feeling everywhere and at the same time. On the second level, law is penetrated by consciousness (in communal and state unions) transforming itself from natural phenomena into volitional acts; that is, what *is* (fact) is transformed into what *must be* (law): "Laws governing consciousness and will are identical with regard to all human beings in the same way as physical laws of nature. Consciousness sanctifies the same norms established by nature. Thus, personal and public activities in law are completely merged. Custom only fortifies the action of similar norms, but does not create them. The diversity of customs in various tribes and nations is explained by the different levels of culture and the conditions of economic and social life."[6]

In resolving the question of the origin of custom and customary law, it seems to the present author that preference must be given to Sergeevich's explanations. Customs were formed in ancient human society to meet the need to bring some order into the development of social life. Aristotle's *zoon politikon* from the very beginning of his existence must be directed by rules of behavior. The initiative in creating such rules has to be taken in a certain sphere by an individual. The "people" cannot act as initiator. It is always an individual, or a group of them, who starts the action which is accepted by the people and becomes popular. When a certain way of action is accepted by a considerable number of persons behaving in the same way under similar conditions, a custom is created. This custom gains the character of law if it is applied by the overwhelming majority of the people: it becomes obligatory and its violation is punishable.

Indeed, Vladimirsky-Budanov's assertion that the primary source of law is *human nature* (physical and moral) which is subjected to the same laws as organic and inorganic nature seems to be unwarranted. To what laws of organic and inorganic nature is human nature subjected to provide the sources of mankind's law? Is it the protection of children by parents, and vice versa, and the primary feeling of passion? Is vengeance a "natural" feeling? Is protection of children, not to mention protection of parents, common to all beings created by nature? We know that this is not the case. Indeed, the greatest moral law of human beings—not to kill—does not correspond to a law of nature in which the survival of larger species of animals and fishes is based on the killing (eating) of smaller species. By the same token, one cannot agree that "laws of consciousness and will are identical to those established by nature" and that "the same norms are sanctified which were established by nature." Man's morality and law are not identical with laws of nature, and are often created in order to restrain the influence of natural law (for instance, the unlimited sexual urge).

Finally, Vladimirsky-Budanov's conclusion that "the diversity of customs in various tribes and nations is explained by the different levels of culture and the conditions of economic and social life" is in contradiction to his assertion that "the laws governing consciousness and will are identical with regard to all human beings in the same way as physical laws of nature." If the variety of customs is to be explained by the diversity of cultures and economic conditions, what does human nature have to do with it, since human nature is identical everywhere? If human nature is the primary source of custom, then custom must be identical in all countries; and if cultural and economic conditions are the source of different customs, how can it be explained that people living under the same cultural and economic circumstances have different customs?

Ancient Chronicles

The ancient chronicles were written by hand in the old Slavic-Russian language. There are three kinds of orthography in old Slavic: (1) The *ustav* letters are written straight, perpendicular to the line, with every letter at the same distance from the next one, but the words are not especially separated from each other. A particularity of the *ustav* is the square form of the letters, equally high and overly wide. (2) The *poluustav* (created in the fourteenth century) is characterized by numerous abbreviations of words, by omission of vowels (*tsr* for *tsar*, *knz* for *kniaz'*), and even use of a single letter (*d* for *dvor* 'court' and *m* for *monastyr'* 'monastery'). As its name implies, it was adapted to a more fluent form of handwriting—with frequent abbreviations and less rigid formation of letters. (3) The third is *skoropis'* (cursive), which originated in the fifteenth century, was much used in the sixteenth, and predominated in the seventeenth.

Figures were represented by alphabetic symbols (as in old Hebrew) up to the eighteenth century, with the exception of zero, which was not used at that time (hundreds and thousands were indicated by special symbols). Thus *a* (*az*) symbolizes also the figure one, when it has a particular sign (*titlo*) on its head; *v* (*vedu*) means two; *g* (*glagol'*) three; *d* (*dobro*) four; *e* (*est'*) five; *s* (*zelo*) six; *z* (*zeulia*) seven; *u* (*izhe*) eight; *o* (*fita*) nine; *i* (*i deseterichnoe*) ten. To symbolize eleven to nineteen two letters were necessary, and the units were put before the tens according to the Russian pronunciation—*odinnadtsat'* (one/ten), *dvenadtsat'* (two/

ten), and so forth—whereas figures between twenty and ninety were formed again according to the Russian pronunciation by putting tens in the first and units in the second place.

The oldest chronicles (as of the fourteenth century) used parchment, at first imported from Byzantium and Western Europe and later produced also in Russia. The chronicles of the fourteenth through seventeenth centuries were written no longer on parchment but exclusively on paper imported from Western Europe (paper production did not begin in Russia until the eighteenth century). Most of the Old Russian manuscripts are on single pages pasted together and rolled in the form of tubes (similar to the Hebrew Torah, which is written by hand on parchment up to the present time) or sewn together in the form of a book. The roll form was much used for documents in *prikaz* (department) offices of the sixteenth and seventeenth centuries, and the rolls were collected there—*stolbtsy, stolpy,* or *stolbiki* (columns, pillars, small columns). I. L. Sherman relates that the ancient Russian writings were formed by a great number of such tubes, some of them very long.[7] For instance, the text of *Sobornoe ulozhenie* (Assembly's Code) of 1649 occupies 959 sheets, and unrolled is 309 meters long.

The chronology of the old chronicles was taken over from Byzantium, where, beginning with the seventh century, time was calculated from the creation of the world. The period from the creation of the world until the birth of Christ was established as 5,508 years. The beginning of the year was the first of September. In Russia, however, the year started with the first of March (until the fourteenth century). The contemporary system of chronology, introduced by Peter the Great in 1700, is not the Gregorian calendar of 1582 that is accepted in the West but the Julian calendar of 46 B.C. The Julian calendar was eleven days behind the Gregorian calendar at that time, and thirteen days behind in the twentieth century. The new style calendar was established in the Soviet Union simply by declaring the first of February 1918 to be the fourteenth of February.

More than two hundred chronicles have been found, and their originals are kept in the Central State Archives of Ancient Documents in the Central State Historical Archives in Leningrad and the major libraries of Moscow and Leningrad. Using these most precious historical memorials, Russian scholars have reproduced the ancient history of Russia and its old customs from the tenth through the fifteenth century. The chronicles by monks of various monasteries were written as continuations of preceding chronicles and were arranged chronologically by separate years. Several chronicles have been put together in the form of collections (*svody*) named after various chroniclers. The study of the chronicles started in Russia in the eighteenth century and was intensified in the nineteenth and twentieth centuries, also by Soviet scholars.

The most prominent student and interpreter of the chronicles is A. A. Shakhmatov (1864–1920).[8] It was he who proved that the oldest chronicle known to us, the *Povest' vremennykh let* (*Chronicle of Times Past*) of the Laurentian Collection,[9] contained quotations from even older chronicles (not discovered yet) by analyzing the text and comparing it with other chronicles. According to him the chronicles of 1037, 1050, 1073, and 1093 preceded *Povest' vremennykh let*, which was written by the monk Nestor in 1113.[10]

Let us take a look into *Povest' vremennykh let* for some customs and customary laws of that time. The Chronicle starts with the words in ancient Russian: "Se povesti vremian'ykh let otkudu est' poshla Russkaia zemlia, kto v Kieve nacha pervee kniazhiti, i otkudu Russkaia zemlia stala est'" ("This is the narration of the past years, from where the Russian land started, who was the first ruler in Kiev, and how the Russian state came into being").[11]

Custom's Particularism

Although basic customs are common to all Slavic tribes of the epoch, still the particularism of custom and customary law is evident in many aspects.

The chronicler of the *Povest' vremennykh let* narrates: "Slavic tribes, all of them had their customs and laws of their fathers and traditions— each of them their own usages. Polianye had gentle and quiet customs, respectful with regard to their daughters-in-law, sisters, mothers, and parents; outwardly very restrained toward their mothers-in-law and brothers-in-law [*dever'*, groom's brother]; they have also matrimonial customs of their own; the bridegroom [*ziat'*] does not fetch the bride, but she is brought in the evening, and what is given with her [dowry] is given the next day. But Drevliane following bestial customs lived like animals, killed one another, ate impure food, and did not conclude marriages, but abducted girls at the spring [or where they went for water]. However, Radimichi, Viatichi, and Severiane had common customs: lived in the forest like animals, ate impure food. They used foul language in the presence of their fathers and daughters-in-law. Nor did they conclude marriages, but instead plays between villages were arranged. People gathered for games, dances, and any kind of devilish songs, and there they abducted girls on agreement with them; each man agreed to take two or three wives" (pp. xiii–xiv).

But all these tribes, which displayed different behavior with regard to family relations, had at the time of idolatry a common horrible custom described by the chronicler of *Povest' vremennykh let* as follows: "If someone died, a funeral feast [*trizna*][12] was arranged and afterward the corpse was laid on a big log and burned; the ashes were collected and put into a small container and put on a pole at the roadsides exactly as the Viatichi do it up to the present time. This custom was observed by Viatichi, and other pagans, unaware of God's law, but making laws for themselves" (p. xiv). A wife or a girl from the household of the defunct was burned and buried with him.

Arab writers of the epoch relate that the killing and cremation of one of the defunct's wives and of a girl of his household belonged to the burial customary law. Abul'-Khasan Ali ibn-Khusein (known under the name Al'-Masudi) related: "When a man dies [in Slavic and Russian pagan tribes] also his wife is buried alive with him; but if a woman passes away, the husband is not burned. If a single man dies, he is married after his death. There was a desire among wives to be burned in order to enter Paradise together with their husbands." This custom of burning the wife has the form of law and according to Masudi cannot be avoided by the wife. He asserts that an identical law exists in India, but there the burning depends upon the consent of the wife.[13] Abu-Ali Akhmed ibn-Omar ibn-Dasta relates that one of the wives of the defunct who loved him the most "brings to the corpse two pillars and they are driven through the ground. Then a third pillar is put over the other two and a rope is tied to the crossbeam; the wife mounts on a bench, and the rope is tightened around her neck. After this is done the bench is taken from under her feet and she remains hanging until she chokes and dies, and then she is thrown into the fire and burned."[14] From another Arabian writer, Akhmed-ibn-Abbas ibn-Rashid ibn-Khammad (tenth century A.D.), we know that a girl from the household of the dead person had to die with him. The writer witnessed a funeral ceremony and related in great detail how all the girls were asked which one wanted to be burned with the defunct. The girl who volunteered was choked to death and burned in the same fire.

Besides the great diversity of customs and customary laws, as reported by the chronicler, they were very stable. The people were conservative and observed the customs through centuries. Certainly some of them were changed or abrogated in the process of cultural development. Wives and servants ceased to be cremated with their husbands and masters. But other customs proved amazingly durable and became common among the whole people. An example is the *bania*.

What Saint Andrew saw of the *bania* during his travels through the Slavic lands to Rome is told in *Povest' vremennykh let*: "I saw wooden *bani*, heated red hot, in which people undress and naked, after having drenched in *kvas*,[15] use young twigs for flogging themselves and are half dead when they come down [from the upper shelves]. They are revived by cold water spilled over them, and repeat this self-torture every day, but it is not a torture but a cleaning process. Those who heard it were amazed" (pp. vii–viii). Indeed, the habit of using a *bania* for cleaning the body has lasted through centuries of Russian history to the present time. As a rule, every peasant household has a shed in the yard equipped with a hearth surrounded by stones. Steam is produced by pouring cold water on the burning hot stones. The room is divided by horizontal shelves. Since steam concentrates in the upper levels of the room, the air nearest the ceiling is the hottest. The bathing person increases the temperature to which he is submitted by ascending the shelves. Flogging is still used in order to stimulate blood circulation. *Bani* existed and still exist in all small and large cities, and they were and are visited regularly by all classes of the urban population. They have survived even the building of modern apartment houses with a bathroom in every apartment. Even though they can bathe at home, citizens of the Soviet Union still also go to the *bania* in order to enjoy this peculiar but very pleasant sensation that their forefathers enjoyed for centuries.

Customs in Family Relations

The power of the *pater familias* over his wife and children was unlimited at the time of the *Povest'*. There is, however, a curious description of how Prince Vladimir, the future Saint and Baptizer of the Russian People, proceeded in order to get Rogneda, the daughter of Prince Ragvold in Polotsk, for his wife. "And he sent [envoys] to Ragvold, to declare 'I wish your daughter to be my wife,'" relates the chronicler. Surprisingly enough, Ragvold demanded the consent of his daughter for the marriage: "Do you want Vladimir for a husband?" he asked.[16] She answered, "I do not want to take the shoe off the son of a slave, but I want Iaropolk for a husband."[17] Her answer was made known to Vladimir, who "went to war against Polotsk, killed Ragvold and his two sons, and took Rogneda for his wife" (p.75).

A remnant of polyandry, *snokhachestvo*,[18] which existed at a low level of cultural development, was known to the Slavic tribes in the earliest period of Russian history, and it lasted for centuries. We have seen that *Povest' vremennykh let* describes the Radimichi, Viatichi, and Severiane as living in forests like beasts and having no restraint toward their daughters-in-law. "*Snokhachestvo*," writes Kovalevsky, "is not something new in our legal life. Its existence since the ancient times of our society is proved by many customs, and it is retained in some places up to our time."[19] One of the circumstances favorable to these relations was the marriage of the son at a tender age to a much older girl. Kovalevsky relates that such marriages, allegedly to gain a worker for the family, were very frequent in Siberia. In 1749 a peasant in Yeniseisk Province complained that his father had married him when he was seven years old to a girl of forty. "Some facts testify to the substantial spreading of *snokhachestvo*, also in our time," remarks Kovalevsky. If the daughter-in-law did not agree to sexual relations, she was persecuted by the father-in-law, in whose house she usually lived, and the entire family joined in the persecution. The situation was often the cause of scuffles in the family and fights between father and son. The church fought *snokhachestvo* from ancient times. Accordingly to the Church Statute of Iaroslav (art. 17) in cases of sexual intercourse between the father-in-law and his daughter-in-law, the father-in-law had to pay a fine of one hundred grovers to the bishop and he had to undergo public penance.

Marriage

Legally marriage and divorce were regulated by canon law in Russia prior to 1917. Civil marriage or divorce did not exist there before the Revolution. Marriage—a sacrament—had to be performed by a priest. But "for many centuries," Kovalevsky narrates, "the Russian clergy had to fight against the inveterate custom of our lower classes to contract unions without the sanction of the Church.... No later than the end of the sixteenth century an assembly of Divines convened by Ivan the Cruel entered a strong protest against the custom which everywhere prevailed of omitting the religious consecration of the marriage tie, and strong measures were in consequence taken against those who did not comply with the requirements of the clergy. All [measures], however, failed and marriage remained in the eyes of the common people nothing more than a sort of civil contract, entered into in the presence of the community as a sign of its recognition and sanction."[20]

Charusin wrote, no more than a century ago, that the following method of concluding marriage was the general rule among the Don Cossacks: The young couple appeared before the popular assembly of the village and declared their intention to be husband and wife. "Be my wife," said the bridegroom; "Be my husband," replied the bride. "So be it," proclaimed the assembly, and that was all.[21] Also, in some places in the Ukraine the religious consecration of marriage was even in modern times considered a superfluous ceremony, according to Kovalevsky (p.

39). Thus through hundreds of years the custom of concluding marriages without civil or clerical sanction was retained.

When after the October Revolution the clerical marriage lost its mandatory character and civil marriage was introduced, the "factual marriage" (the common-law marriage of Anglo-Saxon countries), with all its legal consequences, was recognized by Soviet law (until the Ukase of July 1944, when registration of the marriage was made obligatory for it to be valid). Thus the old Russian custom of factual marriage enjoyed legal sanction in the Soviet Union for twenty-four years.

Conservatism of Custom

Since customary law functioned in place of written law, it acquired the stability usually reserved to written law. Its observance remained mandatory even after laws issued by legislators began to be the usual form of social norm. It was held in such respect by the people that as late as the fifteenth century even such autocrats as Ivan III considered it necessary to have the support of custom for actions which under written law required no support from any side. For instance, when Ivan decided, after the death of his son Ivan, to establish as his heir apparent Dmitrii, the son of his late son, he referred to the "custom of our fathers who used to give the Grand Princely Throne to the oldest son,"[22] and asked the metropolitan to bless his grandson, Dmitrii, in this position, by virtue of old traditions. Furthermore, in his correspondence with Prince Kurbsky, Ivan the Terrible based his autocracy on custom. He wrote that "up to the present time, Russian rulers never gave account to anyone, but were free to reward or punish their subjects, and did not go to court with them."

When the same monarch was to be crowned, he ordered research to be undertaken to establish the procedure "applied by our forefathers, Tsars, and Grand Princes, and our relative, the Grand Prince Vladimir Vsevolodovich Monomakh, when he took over sovereign power." "This indicates," wrote Sergeevich, "that according to the feelings of the Muscovite people of the Muscovite state, the notion of what is right corresponds to what was done in olden times" (p. 23). Even a religious character was given to customary law: its origin was attributed to God himself. So the Russians swore to fulfill the treaty with the Greeks according to the customs (*zakon i pokon*) of their country, "as God's creation."[23] V. N. Latkin wrote, "Ancient Russians valued custom as a norm of divine origin, a Sacred rule."[24]

But how did a custom change or disappear completely? If a time arrived when an ancient custom did not correspond any longer to the culture or moral level of the society in which it was applied, and was rejected by individual persons, then when it was a secular custom, not a customary law, it was gradually abandoned by an increasing number of people and was finally dropped by the great majority, and ceased to be a general custom. Only individual persons still followed it in some places. But a customary law, the violation of which was punishable, could be abrogated only by written law.

The status of "law," in the sense of a general rule obligatory for everyone, was found first of all in custom as late as the sixteenth century. "Law is that which is sanctified by observation," as Sergeevich said.[25] The whole life of the ancient principalities, private and state rights, was, therefore, regulated chiefly by custom.

Legal Symbols

Customary law was also expressed in legal symbols. These were actions, testifying to the legality of a certain relationship: for instance, the exchange of rings and confarreation (the eating and drinking from the same plate and cup by spouses to symbolize their community of life). To shake hands as a symbol of a completed bargain has remained a custom throughout the centuries in Russia even to the present time. As Chislov put it, "By symbols people on the first steps of culture express their notion of rights, striving to give them a comprehensive form for everyone. Serving as a means for the knowledge of origin of ancient law, they disclose to us features of the life of ancient people, not to become known in another way."[26]

Notes

1. They are called "republics" not because the two principalities had a political structure different from other principalities but because of the predominant power of the *veche*.

2. V. I. Sergeevich, *Lektsii i izsledovaniia po drevnei istorii russkago prava* (St. Petersburg, 1910), p. 5.

3. René A. Wormser, *The Law* (New York, 1949), pp. 3–4.

4. For example, no one was obliged to use the *bani* for bathing.

5. Sergeevich and Vladimirsky-Budanov are the foremost historians of Russian law for the tsarist period. They diverge in their opinions on almost all important questions.

6. M. F. Vladimirsky-Budanov, *Obzor istorii russkago prava* (St. Petersburg and Kiev, 1905), pp. 88–89.

7. I. L. Sherman, *Russkie istoricheskie istochniki* (Kharkov, 1959), pp. 12 ff.

8. His best-known work is *Razyskaniia o drevneishikh russkikh letopisnykh svodakh* (St. Petersburg, 1908; reprint, The Hague, 1967).

9. The *Lavrentievskii svod*, the oldest collection known, was composed by the monk Lavrentii for the Suzdal Prince Dmitrii Konstantinovich in 1377. The major part of the collection is written in *poluustav* letters and the rest is in *ustav* handwriting. See *Polnoe sobranie russkikh letopisei* (Leningrad, 1926), 1:1 ff.

10. Nestor's authorship is contested; but it is not possible to have a full discussion of the question in this article. The *Povest'* has been translated into English by Samuel H. Cross and O. P. Sherbowitz-Wetzor, *The Russian Primary Chronicle: Laurentian Text* (Cambridge, Mass., 1953). As in the case of other texts in this article, the translations are by the present author.

11. *Polnoe sobranie russkikh letopisei*, 1:1.

12. See Pushkin's *Pesn' o veshchem Olege*. A *trizna* also takes place in memory of the deceased one year after his death.

13 A. E. Harkavy [A. Ia. Garkavi], *Shazaniia musul'manskikh pisatelei o slavianakh i russkikh* (St. Petersburg, 1879; reprint, The Hague and Paris, 1969), p. 129.

14. Ibid., p. 265.

15. *Kvas*, an acid beverage, is no longer used for bathing, but as a beverage and soft drink it is no less popular with the Russian people than vodka is as a liquor.

16. He certainly must have only been seeking a pretext to reject Vladimir's bid.

17. For a wife to take off her husband's footwear is a symbol of her submission to him. Vladimir's mother was a slave (this is an interesting example of the social prejudice of the time). Iaropolk was an older brother of Vladimir's, and his bitter foe.

18. *Snokhachestvo* is sexual relations between the father of the groom and the daughter-in-law (*snokha*).

19. M. M. Kovalevsky, *Pervobytnoe pravo*, 2 vols. (Moscow, 1886), 2:58.

20. Maxime Kovalevsky, *Modern Customs and Ancient Laws of Russia* (London, 1891), pp. 37–38. Russians just persisted in concluding marriages unofficially, as they did at the time of the *Povest'*.

21. Ibid., p. 38.

22. See Sergeevich, *Lektsii*, p. 22.

23. The chronicles do not differentiate between written law (*zakon*) and unwritten law or custom (*obychai*). Both customs and customary laws are designated by the following words: *pravda, norov, obychai, predanie, poshlina, starina, pokon*, and *zakon*.

24. V. N. Latkin, *Lektsii po istorii russkago prava* (St. Petersburg, 1912), p. 6.

25. Sergeevich, *Lektsii*, p. 23.

26. P. I. Chislov, *Kurs istorii russkago prava* (Moscow, 1914), p. 21.

RÜDIGER SCHOTT

Main Trends in German Ethnological Jurisprudence and Legal Ethnology

There is a distinctive disciplinary difference between anthropology and folklore. Generally speaking, anthropologists study "other" cultures while folklorists tend to study their own culture or a segment of their own culture. In Germany, the key terms are Völkerkunde *versus* Volkskunde, *the first meaning the study of peoples, that is, anthropology, while the second refers to the study of the folk, that is, folklore.*

As we shall see later in this volume, the German folklorists have a tradition of studying folk law that goes back to Savigny and Jacob Grimm. However, German anthropologists or ethnologists have a different tradition, which arises from research carried out in what were formerly German colonies, e.g., in Africa. This German ethnological research tradition goes back to Albert H. Post (1839–1895) and to Josef Kohler (1849–1919) rather than to Savigny and Grimm. Because the important work of German ethnologists seems to be so little known among students who cannot read German, we have elected to include a fine survey essay by Rüdiger Schott, Professor at the University of Munster/Westphalia. For a useful summary of German ethnology in general, see Robert Heine-Geldern, "One Hundred Years of Ethnological Theory in the German-Speaking Countries: Some Milestones," Current Anthropology, *5 (1964), 407–418.*

For those who would like to sample some of Post's thoughts on folk law, see his essay "Ethnological Jurisprudence," The Monist, *2 (1891–1892), 31–40, or "An Introduction to the Study of Ethnological Jurisprudence,"* The Open Court, *11 (1897), 641–653; 719–732.*

Reprinted from the *Journal of Legal Pluralism*, 20 (1982), 37–67, with permission.

1. The Influence of Jurists on German Ethnological Jurisprudence

1.1. Introduction

German ethnological jurisprudence (*ethnologische Jurisprudenz* or *ethnologische Rechtsforschung*: for a discussion and definition of both terms see Adam, 1919:17–20) began its work under the assumption that law manifests itself among all the peoples of the world in the form of legal rules. It consequently behoved the comparative jurist who was interested in the laws of foreign, "exotic" peoples, to elucidate these rules and to write them down in a systematically ordered code.

The theoretical system and the terminology for performing this task were, for the greater part, derived from European legal systems. Ethnological jurisprudence in Germany was at first and for a long time solely the work of lawyers or jurists and not of ethnologists or anthropologists. It is therefore somewhat anachronistic to take the founders of ethnological jurisprudence in Germany to task from a present-day anthropological point of view for their "inadequate methodology" and for "serious theoretical faults," as Nader, Koch, and Cox (1966:268) have done, apparently in ignorance of the particular aims and methods of the pioneers of ethnological jurisprudence. The basic assumptions of the founders of ethnological jurisprudence concerning "primitive law" may have proved to be wrong, but their mistakes as well as their merits must first of all be weighed in the context of the historical situation in which they developed this new academic discipline. Before their time, there had appeared the works of J.J. Bachofen (*Das Mutterrecht*, 1861), Sir Henry Maine (*Ancient Law*, 1861), J. F. McLennan (*Primitive Marriage*, 1865), and L. H. Morgan (*Systems of Consanguinity and Affinity*, 1871; *Ancient Society*, 1877). These books—all of them by learned jurists— had laid the foundations of modern ethnology and social and cultural anthropology. But they had not created an "ethnological jurisprudence," i.e. the scientific treatment of "exotic," non-European law on its own merits *with the methods of jurisprudence*.

1.2 The Evolutionist Method of Albert H. Post

The first stepping stones in the direction of such an endeavour were laid by Albert Hermann Post (1839–1895), who was a judge at a regional court in Bremen. In 1872 he published his first book on comparative law: *Einleitung in eine Naturwissenschaft des Rechts* [Introduction to a

Science of Law). The title of this book proclaimed a program: Post wanted to get away from the speculative approach of philosophy of law in order to establish an inductive, scientific method capable of reconstructing the development and evolution of law from its very beginnings up to the present time.

In his second book, entitled *Die Geschlechtsgenossenschaft der Urzeit und die Entstehung der Ehe. Ein Beitrag zu einer allgemeinen vergleichenden Staats- und Rechtswissenschaft* [The Lineage Community of Ancient Times and the Origin of Marriage. A Contribution toward a General Comparative Science of State and Law] (1875), Post set forth his belief that a comparative method entitles the researcher "to pull together the analogous [*gleichartigen*] facts taken out of the most diverse times and from the most diverse peoples" because "unchangeable natural laws govern the lives of all peoples, especially the life of the body politic and the law. These laws may be established by comparing the corresponding periods of the different peoples." This method presupposes:

> that all steps of civil and legal organisation exist side by side on earth—from the most primitive community of peace [*Friedensgenossenschaft*] up to the most developed political system [*Staatswesen*], and that every higher organism has developed previously from most primitive stages up to its later stage in conformity with the sequence of natural law, and that every higher organism still embodies the rudiments of the whole sequence of stages, recognizable to the trained eye (Post, 1875:IV–V).

Post was thus an "evolutionist" in the purest sense. He thought, for instance, that the *Geschlechtsgenossenschaft* [lineage or sib community] was the original form of human society, characterized by a community of wives, children, and chattel, "and there was no individual property at all" (Post, 1875:16). From this stage monogamous marriage developed through intermediate steps of a "restricted community of wives," polyandrous, and polygynous marriage. Post brought together examples of customs from the most diverse populations of the world as "proofs" for this general evolutionary pattern. Yet Post refuted Bachofen's idea of a gynaicocracy or matriarchy as a "normal stage of development in the history of peoples" (Post, 1875:94) since women are, even in matrilineal societies, excluded from succession to property and to positions of authority; they only function as intermediate social links.

Post expounded these ideas in many further publications such as *Der Ursprung des Rechts* [The Origin of Law], 1876; *Die Anfänge des Staats- und Rechtslebens* [The Beginnings of Political and Legal Life], 1878; *Bausteine für eine allgemeine Rechtswissenschaft auf vergleichend-ethnologischer Basis* [Elements of a General Jurisprudence on a Comparative-

Ethnological Basis], 1880/81; *Die Grundlagen des Rechts und die Grundzüge seiner Entwicklungsgeschichte* [The Foundations of Law and the Fundamental Traits of Its Historical Development], 1884; *Einleitung in das Studium der ethnologischen Jurisprudenz* [Introduction to the Study of Ethnological Jurisprudence], 1886. (For a thorough critique of Post's work see Trimborn, 1928:429–447.)

1.3 The Universalistic Comparative Approach of A. H. Post and Josef Kohler

Post's *magnum opus*, which appeared in two volumes one year before his death, was entitled: *Grundriss der ethnologischen Jurisprudenz* [Outline of Ethnological Jurisprudence], 1894. In this work, Post attempted to assemble in a systematic manner the knowledge of his time with regard to the laws of all ethnic groups, organized according to the different fields of law. "There are . . . certain fundamental forms in the law of the peoples, which recur in essentially the same form at all times and at all places in innumerable local variations" (Post, 1894, I:IV).

In the first volume of his *Grundriss* he describes the *Universalrecht der Menschheit* [the universal law of mankind] in terms of different forms of social organisation, since "the law is a function of social formations" ["Das Recht ist eine Funktion der sozialen Verbände"] (Post, 1894, I:1), created by the *Volksgeist* [the 'spirit' or 'mentality' of a people]. The study of comparative law by the "Historische Rechtsschule," founded by Gustav Hugo and Carl von Savigny, had, according to Post, received "a considerable enlargement and deepening through ethnology—that new science which deals with the life of all nations according to a method arising purely from the natural sciences and which has taken into its realm all peoples on earth" (Post, 1894, I:2ff.).

The comparative ethnological method had, according to Post, led jurisprudence to the discovery "of far-reaching parallels in the laws of all peoples on earth which could not be reduced to accidental correspondence, but which could only be regarded as emanations of the common nature of mankind" (Post, 1894, I:4). The genuine field of ethnological jurisprudence, therefore, consists in those legal norms and legal institutions which recur among all peoples on earth (Post, 1894, I:7). Law is a universal phenomenon: "There is no people on earth without the beginnings of some law. Social life belongs to human nature and with every social life goes a law" (Post, 1894, I:8). Even the "least cultivated" [*die allerunkultiviertesten*] peoples possess some form of customary law [*Gewohnheitsrecht*], "an inherited treasure of legal rules" (Post, 1894, I:11).

In the *Grundriss* Post is less concerned with the evolution or development of law than with the systematic ordering of the bewildering multitude of legal customs. Although especially the second part of his *Grundriss* resembles a modern code or statute book, divided into chapters and paragraphs such as "Das Personenrecht" [the law of persons], "Das Familienrecht" [family law], "Das Erbrecht" [the law of inheritance], etc., Post takes a functional view of law: it is, in his view, an emanation of the respective social order and of psychological factors. However, he never questions the fundamental idea of a continental lawyer, that law is everywhere expressed in codifiable rules.

Another cornerstone of ethnological jurisprudence was laid by Franz Bernhöft and Georg Cohn who in 1878 edited the first volume of the *Zeitschrift für vergleichende Rechtswissenschaft* [Journal of Comparative Jurisprudence]. In his introductory essay "Über Zweck und Mittel der vergleichenden Rechtswissenschaft" [On the purpose and methods of comparative jurisprudence], Bernhöft (1878:2) welcomed efforts "to expand the limits of jurisprudence." Legal philosophy and the theory of natural law had been founded upon the empirical evidence and the epistemology of only two legal systems: the Roman and the Germanic. These efforts were just as inadequate as if someone wanted to found comparative linguistics on the study of only two languages. Also, with a practical view to producing new general German legal codes on a national level, Bernhöft hoped to obtain helpful suggestions from the comparative study of foreign laws "so as to learn to imitate foreign virtues and to avoid foreign faults" (Bernhöft, 1878:4). However, the final aim of comparative jurisprudence was "to find general laws of the development of law and to apply them to the history of particular nations" (id.). Bernhöft restricted himself to a consideration of the law of peoples of Indo-Germanic languages, assuming corresponding analogies in the field of law itself (Bernhöft, 1878:12). Yet he also voiced a word of warning that, in expanding its limits, comparative jurisprudence should "not transcend law in the strict sense of the word." Customs, being merely a preliminary phase of law, should only be considered insofar "as they had contributed to the formation of law." Jurisprudence "must exclude completely those people who had not yet reached this phase" (Bernhöft, 1878:37).

This ill-defined borderline between peoples with and without law was boldly transgressed by Josef Kohler (1849–1919) who joined the above-mentioned editors of the *Zeitschrift für vergleichende Rechtswissenschaft* from its third volume onwards in 1882. Kohler, being himself a practical jurist who had demonstrated exceptional merit in the fields of incorporeal law and commercial law (see Adam, 1919:5–8), was convinced that jurisprudence, although a practical science, did not exhaust itself in practical aims and purposes, but had to aspire to a history, a science, and a philosophy of law (see Adam, 1919:9). Kohler was averse to a purely formalistic jurisprudence. Law, for him, was a social phenomenon of political life (Adam, 1920:4). Kohler understood law as a *"Kulturgut* [cultural heritage] of the highest order" that had to be studied "in connection with the total cultural organism" of a people (Kohler, 1884, quoted from Adam, 1919:21). He saw law not as an isolated phenomenon, but as an interdependent "factor" of the mental and material culture of a people and he paid special regard to the religious foundations of law (see Adam, 1919:21; 1920:3, 6).

Kohler's approach to comparative jurisprudence was strictly empirical. Starting his publications on *Rechtshistorische und rechtsvergleichende Forschungen* [research on legal history and comparative law] in 1882 with articles on the law of bonds and pledges and on marriage and family law in India, Kohler explored and exposed to the readers of the *Zeitschrift* the laws of the peoples in all corners of the earth. Some of these numerous articles had the size of full-blown books (cf., for instance, his famous "Recht der Azteken" [The law of the Aztecs], Kohler, 1895a). Out of a total of more than 2,300 scientific publications—books, articles, and reviews—written by Kohler (see the bibliography composed by his son: Kohler, 1931:12–30) no less than 106 dealt with general problems of a universal history of law, with the laws of indigenous peoples, and with the "development" of certain legal institutions on a comparative basis. Another 210 dealt with the laws of particular non-European peoples.

As early as 1887 Kohler published an article "Uber das Recht der Australneger" [On the law of the Australian aborigines] and another "Uber das Recht der Papuas auf Neu-Guinea" [On the law of the Papuas in New Guinea]. Basing his views on Howitt, Fison, Smyth, Eyre, and other travellers and field researchers, Kohler came to the conclusion that the Australian aborigines, however "primitive" their economic life:

> possess law. They possess legal institutions which are put under the sanction of the general public, for law exists before any organisation of the state, before any court or any executory performance exists: it exists in the hearts of the people as a feeling of what should be and what should not be.... Although it may be left to the single individual to obtain justice for himself, and although there may be no possibility to obtain a formal decision on the question of right or wrong—law shows itself in that the community as a whole not only approves or disapproves of the act of the individual, but also supports the one who is believed to have justice on his side in his pursuance and exercise of law (Kohler, 1887:323).

Compare this wide and yet precise concept of law with later attempts to define law as Radcliffe-Brown did, as:

> "Social control through the systematic application of the force of politically organised society" (Pound) . . . ; the field of law will therefore be regarded as coterminous with that of organised legal sanction . . . in this sense some simple societies have no law, although all have customs which are supported by sanctions (Radcliffe-Brown, 1952 [1933]:212).

Another "modern" anthropologist tells us that "the really fundamental *sine qua non* of law in any society—primitive or civilized—is the legitimate use of physical coercion by a socially authorized agent" (Hoebel, 1954:26). Neither of these two renowned authors tells us what they mean by the terms "legal" and "legitimate" on which their tautological definitions of "law" hinge!

Kohler as a jurist was far more broad-minded and less ethnocentric than many modern anthropologists in attributing law to peoples in a colonial situation of European domination that had left them virtually without rights and "law-less" in every sense of the word. Kohler's important contribution to ethnological jurisprudence may have suffered "from inadequate methodology" and "serious theoretical faults" as Nader, Koch, and Cox (1966: 268) proclaim without taking the trouble to substantiate their charges—and yet his fundamental insight into the law at work in societies that were (and are) disdained as being "primitive" or "savage" certainly surpassed that of many of his later critics. Kohler thought that there is a *Rechtsgefühl* [feeling for law] recognised by the public in each and every human society:

> Therefore there is no people without law: there are people without courts, there are peoples that lack a state organisation or that possess one which is developed only in merest rudiments—but there is no people without law: Man cannot be Non-Man (Kohler, 1887:324).

With great acumen and assiduity Kohler utilized the ethnographic sources at his disposal long before the times of any systematic ethnographic fieldwork. In view of these severe limitations it is amazing what he achieved. He gives, for instance, a succinct description of the Australian exogamous "class" system, especially in respect of its legal aspects (Kohler, 1887: 329–337). His exposition may be marred by evolutionist assumptions that held sway over most minds of his day, yet he knew how to differentiate where others thought in gross categories.

Kohler, in his grand effort to assemble materials for a truly comparative jurisprudence, in principle excluded no society from his investigations, however "primitive" or "developed" it may have been. These ethnocentric categories, in fact, had no meaning for him: every people had its own laws which were worth being recorded. The results of these efforts were to serve as a base for a universal science and history of law. (For an assessment of Kohler's life and work see Adam, 1919 and 1920).

2. Applied Ethnological Jurisprudence in German Colonial Administration: The Fragebogen Projects

Kohler's efforts toward founding a universal comparative jurisprudence soon came up against limits resulting from the relative paucity of published materials pertaining to the laws of non-European, especially non-literate peoples at the turn of the last century. Yet Kohler was not discouraged by this circumstance. After he had exhausted the relevant legal material in the existing literature with his astounding assiduity, an impressive example of German *Gründlichkeit*, he searched further for original material, based on observations and information on legal norms from other societies. His academic interest was combined with the conviction that the knowledge of legal norms among overseas peoples could be usefully applied in the administration of the newly acquired German colonies. From the nineties of the last century onwards, Kohler had succeeded in gaining the support of the German Imperial Government, especially the Foreign Office, for his project of registering the laws (or what he and his collaborators thought to be "laws") of the *Eingeborenen* (indigenes) in all German overseas territories.

As there were no trained ethnologists to perform this tremendous task, Kohler fell back on the *Fragebogen* (questionnaire) method. This method, developed and applied before by Lewis Henry Morgan in the United States, had been first worked out in Germany for field research in ethnological jurisprudence by Albert Hermann Post (see Post, 1903) who, together with Felix Meyer, had drafted a questionnaire on the legal customs of the *Natur- and Halbkulturvölker* [primitive and half-civilized peoples] in 1893. This *Fragebogen* was sent by the two scholars privately through the German Foreign Office, the Union Coloniale Française, and various missionary societies to officials, missionaries, and other persons in various European colonies of Africa and Oceania. The replies to these *Fragebogen* were published by the eminent Dutch scholar S. R. Steinmetz (1903), at that time *Privatdozent* (unsalaried lecturer) at the University of Leiden, who closely collaborated with his German colleagues. He, together with Richard Thurnwald, afterwards worked out another, very detailed *Fragebogen* which was published in 1906, but was never put to any practical use.

In the same year (1893) that Post and Meyer started their *Fragebogen* project, Josef Kohler addressed to the Deutsche Kolonial-gesellschaft

[German Colonial Society] a number of questions pertaining to the laws of indigenous peoples. According to Schultz-Ewerth and Adam (1929:VI; cf. also Kohler, 1931:14), whose report I follow here, Kohler had received a considerable amount of ethnographic information on African laws through the Colonial Department of the German Foreign Office. He used these materials in some of his publications (see, e.g., Kohler, 1895b). In 1897 Kohler published his own *Fragebogen* which the German colonial administration sent out to all the German colonies. Kohler published the incoming material, which was collected by numerous officials and missionaries, in the *Zeitschrift für vergleichende Rechtswissenschaft* from 1900 (vol. 14ff.) onwards.

In March 1907, Felix Meyer suggested in a letter to the Colonial Department of the Foreign Office that for the practical purposes of jurisdiction over the "natives" in the German colonies a systematic collection of "the authentically established law of the natives . . . was urgently required." A corresponding petition to the German Reichstag [Imperial Diet] was submitted and adopted on 3 May 1907. An official commission in charge of the undertaking was formed. This commission consisted, among others, of Father Wilhelm Schmidt as ethnologist. Its chairman, however, was Josef Kohler, who in the same year (1907) sent out a somewhat enlarged version of his *Fragebogen* of 1897 with questions pertaining to all fields of law. Administrators, judges, and missionaries were required by the German colonial administration to use this *Fragebogen* in order to elicit information from their native informants concerning what legal norms they allegedly possessed.

The *Fragebogen* method appeared at that time as the only practicable ethnographic method available: it ensured quick returns and covered, if not all "tribes" in the colonies, at least a fairly wide area and a considerable part of the population. Seen from the vantage point of our time, it had, of course, serious defects—the worst being that the *Fragebogen* was worked out at the desk of European jurists according to the categories of European law which bore little or no affinity to the legal concepts and practices of the "natives" who were more or less summarily interrogated by local German officials or missionaries. Clearly the answers, apart from thorny linguistic problems of understanding and translation, often bore little or no relation to the "living law" of the people concerned. What the questions elicited were threads and patches of concepts and practices torn out of their living context. Moreover, the whole procedure was, according to the bias of continental law, directed towards eliciting legal norms, which, if they existed at all, often had little relevance to legal practice in settling disputes and other aspects of the actual functioning of law.

Kohler himself seems to have perceived some of the severe limitations of the *Fragebogen* method, for in the introduction to his 'Questionnaire on the laws of the native in the German colonies' (Kohler, 1897:427) he insisted that a "general description of the country and people in their ethnological and economic aspects," especially with regard to their "religion, language, history, tales and stories" should precede the answers to the juridical questions. Although Kohler was well aware of the functional interdependencies of legal norms with all other aspects of culture, he failed to follow his own methodological postulates to their logical conclusions.

Before the findings of the official *Fragebogen* project could be published, let alone be applied in colonial administration and jurisdiction, the First World War broke out. Josef Kohler died immediately after the war and with the demise of the German colonial system interest in the indigenous laws of the peoples of the former German colonies became negligible. It was ten years after Kohler's death before Leonhard Adam and Erich Schultz-Ewerth, the latter being the former governor of German Samoa, edited the combined results of the *Fragebogen* venture in two large volumes under the title *Das Eingeborenenrecht* (1929/30), which they presented as a "work with source material for ethnological jurisprudence." The articles in this collection covered the *Rechtsverhältnisse* [legal conditions] of the indigenous peoples of all former German colonies. Most of the articles were written by German scholars, ethnologists and/or jurists, such as Bernhard Ankermann (German East Africa), Julius Lips (Cameroons), Hermann Trimborn (Micronesia), and Richard Thurnwald (German New Guinea and the Bismarck-Archipelago).

3. The Post-Kohler Era in German Ethnological Jurisprudence and the Work of Leonhard Adam

There were a number of learned jurists who continued the work of Kohler, most of whom shared his truly universal comparative outlook, such as Richard Thurnwald, the founder of German legal ethnology, and Hermann Trimborn, who in 1928 wrote his *Method of Ethnological Jurisprudence*, aiming at a universal cultural-historical study of law. Their work will be dealt with further on.

After Kohler's death in 1919, the *Zeitschrift für vergleichende Rechtswissenschaft* was edited by Leonhard Adam (1891–1960), another eminent jurist who had published monographs on the law of various Northwest Coast Indians (see Adam, 1913; 1918). During the war he did original research on the law of the Nepalese by systematically questioning prisoners of war (Adam, 1934; 1936a). The results of similar research concerning prisoners of war from North Africa were published by Ubach and Rackow (1923). These were the last instances in which the *Fragebogen* method was applied.

Leonhard Adam contributed a methodological and terminological essay entitled "Recht im Werden" [Law in the making] to the Festschrift presented to R. R. Marett on his 70th birthday (Adam, 1936b). He also wrote the chapter on "Ethnologische Rechtsforschung" [ethnological jurisprudence] for the first edition of the *Lehrbuch für Völkerkunde* [Textbook of Ethnology] (1937), which immediately after its appearance had to be withdrawn by order of the Nazi authorities because Adam fell under the Nazi racist laws. In the second edition, which appeared in 1939, the article was rewritten by Richard Thurnwald who before had come under heavy attack by his colleagues W. Krickeberg (1937:466; 1938:122) and H. Baumann (1938:124) because of his Jewish collaborators and because he was supposedly a propagator of British functionalism. Adam himself left Germany in 1938 and went into exile in England and later on in Australia where he was first interned after the outbreak of the Second World War as an "enemy alien" but later occupied a post at the University of Melbourne. After his return to Germany towards the end of his life, he, together with Hermann Trimborn, edited the third edition of the *Lehrbuch für Völkerkunde* (1958) where his original article on "Ethnologische Rechtsforschung" appeared in a revised form.

In this article Adam tried to define the position and method of *ethnologische Rechtsforschung*. He said that it finds its subject, the legal system of non-literate peoples, "between the disciplines" of jurisprudence and ethnology; accordingly it had developed its aims and methods in an "interdisciplinary" manner since its beginnings in the last century. Adam remarked on this:

> One should imagine jurisprudence and ethnology as two intersecting circles; the segment belonging to both circles constitutes ethnological jurisprudence (*ethnologische Rechtsforschung*). However, ethnological jurisprudence has hardly anything to do with legal dogmatics or with "analytical jurisprudence" of the highly developed legal systems; therefore, it belongs predominantly to ethnology (Adam, 1958:190; cf. also Adam, 1936b:217; 1937:281).

Nevertheless, from its very beginnings, the laws of non-European peoples were considered to belong to the academic sphere of jurists rather than ethnologists or anthropologists in Germany. But since the jurists at German universities were hardly interested in "exotic" laws and since German ethnologists usually had little or no legal training and interests, *ethnologische Rechtsforschung* instead of finding a happy hunting ground between the two disciplines, fell by the wayside, especially after Germany lost her colonies in World War I. (On the relation of comparative jurisprudence and ethnology see also the article by M. Schmidt, 1920.)

4. Richard Thurnwald's Ethnographic Fieldwork and Comparative Functional Approach in Legal Ethnology

Richard Thurnwald (1869–1954) may be said to have founded not only German legal ethnology (*Rechtsethnologie*), in contrast to the older comparative ethnological jurisprudence, but to have given legal ethnology or, as it is usually called today, anthropology of law, some of its fundamental concepts and methodological precepts.

Thurnwald was born in Vienna where he later studied law and Oriental languages at the university and where he passed his state examinations and his doctorate as a jurist. (For an outline of his life and work cf. H. Thurnwald, 1950). He did his first ethnographic fieldwork in the service of the Austrian administration in Bosnia from 1896 onwards. In 1901 he went to Berlin where he was made assistant curator at the Berlin Ethnographic Museum. In this capacity he travelled from 1906–1909 in the then German colonies of Micronesia and Island Melanesia. In 1908 he lived for almost nine months amidst the inhabitants of Buin, the southernmost part of the island of Bougainville (Solomon Islands), doing—probably for the first time at least in German ethnology—stationary ethnographic fieldwork that was, for a considerable part, concerned with legal ethnography (see Thurnwald, 1910b:98ff.) The results of this fieldwork, as far as they concerned legal matters, were published in the *Zeitschrift für vergleichende Rechtswissenschaft* (Thurnwald, 1910a).

He undertook a second field trip, to German New Guinea (Kaiser-Wilhelms-Land), towards the end of 1912. The German Imperial Colonial Office asked him to penetrate into the interior of this island, following the Sepik to its up to then unknown middle and upper parts. After the outbreak of World War I Thurnwald stayed in New Guinea until autumn 1915 at which time he left for the United States; there he worked on some of the findings of his expedition until 1917. Part of the results of his ethnographic research in New Guinea was published in his famous studies on the *Gemeinde der Bánaro* [The Community of the Bánaro] (Thurnwald, 1916; 1920/1921). These studies were mainly concerned with kinship and social structure. They also bore on the legal aspects of the complicated two-class kinship system which Thurnwald had analysed.

By closely observing the economic and social life of the people among whom he lived and by noting down information on their religious concepts, he soon discovered the inadequacy of the *Fragebogen* method as it had been conceived by German jurists. Before World War I he had reached the insight that law, however defined, could only be studied and understood in connection with the totality of all the other manifestations of the life of a given people. The "comparison of norms, torn out from here and there, in the manner of the older 'comparative law,' is an interesting playing about with curiosities" (Thurnwald, 1934:8).

He regarded "law as a function of the conditions of life and of the mentality of a society, a regulative order for the behaviour of personalities in a community." He consequently put forth the methodological postulate that it is necessary "to conceive the law as the expression of a cultural attitude, i.e. to comprehend and to understand the legal order functionally in the context of a cultural system," especially since in the relatively small communities of "primitive peoples" (*Naturvölker*) the connection of law "with the rhythm of other cultural functions" is likely to be much closer than in complex societies with a highly differentiated division of labour (Thurnwald, 1934:2ff.).

Thurnwald stressed the importance of ethnographic fieldwork: in order to explore the "functional interdependencies" of law with all other aspects of life, the researcher had to observe the ways of acting and thinking of the people he studied himself; he could not rely on secondhand reports by amateur ethnographers. Thurnwald did not stay for as long a time amidst "his" people as did Bronislaw Malinowski (willynilly as an "enemy alien"), also in Melanesia, among the Trobriand Islanders during the long years of World War I. Yet Malinowski's method of "participant observation" was in fact preceded by Thurnwald's research on the spot in the Solomon Islands and in New Guinea.

As a fundamental insight of his field research, Thurnwald stressed the importance of "symmetrical" social relations that manifest themselves in a "chain of gifts and counter-gifts" and in other forms of reciprocity which he recognized as the fundamental principle of law in so-called primitive societies, or rather, in all human societies (see Thurnwald, 1920:378, 395, 406, 414; 1919:385). Malinowski, in *Crime and Custom in Savage Society*, explicitly recognized that Thurnwald was the first to have pointed out the far-reaching import of reciprocity for the functioning of the social order in "primitive" societies (Malinowski, 1926:24). Thurnwald himself described this principle of reciprocity as follows (translation mine; emphasis by Thurnwald):

> If one tries to get at the core of all regulations which govern the behaviour between human beings and which are entwined by religious and magic phantasies, one arrives at the insight that it is *reciprocity* which balances out the scales of law. This applies to *retaliation* (for instance, in the form of

blood-revenge or as symmetrical punishment) as well as to punishment in general, or—in the field of economics—to the *return of a gift*, to the adequate payment, or—in the realm of personal relations—to the *exchange of daughters* between communities, to the *marriage order* between groups, to *bridewealth* (return of distinguished objects), or—in the law of obligations—to the repayment of credits, to interest payments etc. . . . . . On the other hand, one-sided services are felt to be unjust: the tributes of bondmen, the economic services of slaves. . . . *Abuse is the violation of reciprocity* (Thurnwald, 1934:5).

From his own personal experience among tribes in the mountainous regions of central New Guinea, which had never seen a white man before, Thurnwald concluded that the fundamental principle of reciprocity is understood "spontaneously" in all human societies (Thurnwald, 1934:5–6).

Thurnwald was, to my knowledge, the last to write a comprehensive book covering systematically the whole field of legal anthropology on a comparative basis: *Werden, Wandel und Gestaltung des Rechts* [The Beginning, Change and Configuration of Law] (1934). This book grew out of numerous articles which he contributed as ethnologist to *Eberts Reallexikon der Vorgeschichte* [Ebert's Encyclopedia of Prehistory] during the twenties. The book forms the fifth volume of Thurnwald's *magnum opus*: *Die menschliche Gesellschaft in ihren ethno-soziologischen Grundlagen* [Human Society in Its Ethno-Sociological Foundations] (Vol. I–V, 1931–1934). It deals systematically with all major subjects of law without being confined to a narrow division according to ethnocentric categories of European law. With its wealth of ethnographic detail and its sober theoretical insights, it has not been matched or superseded by any other work.

In the introduction to this book, Thurnwald stressed the great diversity of laws in so-called primitive societies, a diversity which corresponds to the variability of the cultural context in all its aspects:

Primitive law cannot be opposed to the law of peoples with higher civilisations (*Kulturvölker*) as something uniform. . . . This follows from the mere fact that the political organisation [of 'primitive' societies] shows a great diversity: from the homogeneous democratic associations of hunting-and-gathering tribes, through the agglomeration of ethnic groups, to stratification according to descent and according to social and occupational characteristics, and from chieftainship without [official] authority up to the sacred sovereign and the rationalistic despot (Thurnwald, 1934:16).

To these extremely diverse political systems correspond legal concepts and practices which are just as varied.

Thurnwald saw another functional variable of law in the different degrees to which societies are equipped with technical knowledge, abilities, and appliances. The objects to which laws refer change with the process of "irreversible accumulation" that marks the universal increase in the number of goods available to mankind and which corresponds to the growth of civilisation. This process has its effects on numerous other aspects of life. A people that has at its disposal improved technical means can force other, less well-equipped ethnic groups into a state of economic and/or political dependency. This process is often accompanied by the extension of "areas in which peace was maintained under the rule of a more or less unified administration of justice" (Thurnwald, 1934:7). Interethnic relations and processes were one of the main fields of Thurnwald's interest in political and legal matters. He never saw "primitive" or "civilized" societies as isolated entities as some British "functionalists" working in insular communities were wont to do.

5. The Historical Trend in German Legal Ethnology and the "Kulturkreis" Theory of W. Schmidt, W. Koppers, and H. Trimborn

It would be completely wrong to label Thurnwald a "functionalist" pure and simple. He never developed the anti-historical or a-historical affect that was characteristic of British functionalism for a long time (cf. in opposition to this trend: Evans-Pritchard, 1962:46–65). The title of Thurnwald's book as well as the quotations above show that he was historically minded to a high degree.

True enough, he was opposed to the bare speculations of "evolutionists" as well as of "diffusionists," and he certainly did not agree with the schemes of the *Kulturkreis* theoreticians, which he severely criticised on account of their unrealistic assumptions and their lack of firsthand experience with so-called primitive peoples (see Thurnwald, 1931:12–19). But Thurnwald was not averse to the idea that civilisation had evolved in a slow process of "irreversible accumulation" of techniques and skills and a growing rationality that had its effects upon all aspects of social life. Nor was Thurnwald opposed to the idea that cultural traits had diffused from one people to others and that this process had great import for the development of specific cultures as well as for human culture in general. But he was more interested in the actual processes and interactions between concrete peoples. He was well versed in Oriental and in European history and this knowledge gave his treatment of law, whether "primitive" or "civilized," a highly realistic character.

The much-abused *Kulturkreis* method and theory has been caricatured by many Anglo-American anthropologists who have little or no firsthand knowledge of what Frobenius, Graebner, W. Schmidt, W. Koppers, and many others had actually thought and written (as a recent example see Voget, 1973:35ff.). Schmidt and Koppers, in their great work, *Völker und Kulturen* [Peoples and Culture], which was published only in 1924 but was, for the greater part, written before World War I, dedicated much space to law as it appeared in different *Kulturschichten* [cultural strata]. Schmidt even designated his various *Kulturkreise* ['culture circles' or 'culture spheres'] with purely sociological and legal terms—thereby promptly falling back into the schematic thinking in evolutionary "stages" (*Entwicklungsstufen*) that had characterized his sociological predecessors. Although Schmidt did not accept unilineal evolutionism, the idea of cultural evolution was a correlate of the ultimate aim which he shared with the "evolutionists": viz., to write a universal history of mankind in all its aspects. Schmidt, at least in *Völker und Kulturen*, was far removed from the pedantry of tracing innumerable *Kulturelemente* [cultural elements or traits] in their diffusion all over earth. Instead, he often all too boldly postulated functional interdependencies. He attributed the invention of agriculture to the work of women who subsequently laid claims of inheritance to the fields on which they grew their produce. These possessory rights, in the opinion of Schmidt, led to the matrilineal and uxorilocal social order of his *Mutterrechtlich-Exogamer Kulturkreis* [matriarchal-exogamous culture circle.] This, of course, is pure speculation and perhaps not even very original, but the example shows that Father Schmidt was less given to spiritual speculation on the mystic aspects of the *Mutterrecht* (as Bachofen and his epigones had been), than to a sound if somewhat flat materialism.

Admittedly, he saw all technologically developed cultures as degenerations from the purer state of his beloved *Wildbeuter-kulturen* [cultures of hunters-and-gatherers] which he thought represented, at least in their common traits, *Urkulturen* [original cultures]. This could be passed over with a smile as just another proof of the simplistic naiveté and the pious beliefs of Father Schmidt and his school were it not for the fact that in the course of a revived interest in evolution and in the most simple cultures still found on earth, innumerable American and other anthropologists and ethnologists have started to study the very same hunters-and-gatherers—Bushmen, African Pygmies, Australian aborigines, etc.—with the hope of gaining some insight into "original" human behaviour (see, e.g., Service, 1966).

The legal aspects of this behaviour, as it can be observed in the small bands of these hunters-and-gatherers, form one of the most important subjects of these more recent studies. The same can be said with regard to the studies of Schmidt, who unfortunately never performed ethnographic fieldwork himself but sent out many of his disciples who, like Father Schebesta and Father Gusinde, have done admirable fieldwork under difficult conditions and have contributed greatly to our knowledge of law among hunters-and-gatherers. This work, however, is not even known among our Anglo-American colleagues who seem to master the most exotic idioms for their ethnographic field work but are apparently unable to acquire a reading knowledge of German. "The *Kulturkreislehre* never developed any impulse for fieldwork...," writes Voget (1973:35), for example. He even quotes but apparently had never glanced at the volumes of Martin Gusinde on the Fuegians and of Paul Schebesta on the Bambuti-Pygmies, otherwise he would not have written the nonsense on the next page of his article (Voget, 1973:36).

Out of ignorance, the *Kulturkreishlehre* is usually lumped together with the "extreme diffusionism" of G. Elliot Smith and W. Perry (Voget, 1973:32, 36–38), both Englishmen, by the way, whose wild imaginations had nothing in common with the sober, if not pedantic work of a Fritz Graebner. He, being trained as a historian, tried to introduce the strict methodological principles of the traditional historical discipline into the rather anarchic field of ethnology. In his *Methode der Ethnologie* [Method of Ethnology] (1911), he demanded that each and every object or literary testimony pertaining to any people under study be subjected to the merciless scrutiny of "outer" and "inner" critique before being accepted as a valid source. Few of our standard ethnographies on which we happily build our lofty "theories" would stand up to the standards which Graebner set. His formal and quantitative criteria to be applied in the comparison and combination of "culture elements" are likewise worth being carefully considered in any comparative work (e.g. with the Human Relations Area Files), whatever its theoretical purpose. Graebner's *Kulturkreis* theory is obsolete today, but what other theory in anthropology is not obsolete after almost seventy years?

Graebner's historical method was taken over in a modified form by Hermann Trimborn, a student of economics and law, in his article on "Die Methode der ethnologischen Rechtsforschung" [The method of ethnological jurisprudence] (1928). Although his "method" was based on the theoretical assumptions of the *Kulturkreise*, which are no longer tenable, its lasting value lies, in my opinion, in that Trimborn introduced into the field of legal ethnology the stern demands which the professional historian places on his source materials, thereby expressly following the example which Graebner set for general ethnology (see Trimborn, 1928:422–429). Trimborn considered *ethnologische Rechtsforschung* to be part of a general legal history or a universal history of law (Trimborn, 1928:420ff.) an "exclusively historical science" (Trimborn, 1928:430). In his article on "Familien- und Erbrecht" im präkolumbischen Peru" [Family Law and the Law of Inheritance in Pre-Columbian Peru] Trimborn (1927) applied his "culture-historical" method of ethnological jurisprudence to a concrete example.

6. Punishment and Property as Major Subjects of German Legal Ethnology

6.1 Crime and Punishment

Trimborn thus not only established methodological principles, but he also produced a number of outstanding monographs in the field of legal ethnology, based on ethno-historical research. In 1925 he published an article on "Straftat und Sühne in Alt-Peru" [Crime and expiation in Old Peru] in which he worked out the contrast between the criminal law in the local clan communities (*ayllus*) and that of the central state of the Inca. Trimborn showed that concomitant with the historical expansion of the Inca empire, completely new criminal offences developed as a function of Inca rule, such as high treason and criminal offences committed by public officials in breach of duty.

In another article, "Der Rechtsbruch in den Hochkulturen Amerikas" [The breach of law in the high civilisations of America] (1936/1937), Trimborn compares the substantive criminal law as was practised in the Inca empire with that practised by the Chitcha in Columbia and by the Aztecs of the Triple Confederation in Mexico. Trimborn investigates in this article the "causal dependency of law on the total culture" as well as the "historical stratification" of different concepts of law according to the "lower" or "higher" levels of civilisation. These terms do not imply a value judgment, but Trimborn shows that in the "pure criminal law," as practised in the ancient civilisations of the New World, psychological considerations pertaining to the concept of guilt gained prevalence, although the older concept of objective liability according to the damage caused lingered on.

In two general contributions, Trimborn dealt with the evolution of the "modern" concept of offences and punishments: *Auffassung und Formen der Strafe auf den einzelnen Kulturstufen* [Concepts and Forms of Punishment at the Different Stages of Culture] (1931) and "Die Privatrache und der Eingriff des Staates" [Private vengeance and the intervention of the state] (1950). To each major phase in the development of cultures—hunters-and-gatherers, agriculturalists, cattle-herders—he attributes certain concepts and practices in the treatment of crime and punishment. The latest phase, marked by "the organisation of public authority according to the principles of the division of labour," is characterized by the separation of "private" claims for damages from "public" demands for punishment—the latter intended to work as a deterrent.

Thurnwald (1939) had expounded a similar culture-historical development of crime and punishment, stressing however the idea that contract and the breach of contract stood at the beginning of legal ideas. Much of this may be speculative, but Trimborn and Thurnwald at least made the attempt to correlate certain socio-economic and political structures with definite concepts and practices of crime and punishment. This they did on the basis of empirical facts, documented by ethnographic research, comparing the legal conditions existing among peoples with similar material equipment.

Julius Lips (1928; 1938) added to these general outlines a certain differentiation with his concept of *Erntevölker*, i.e. peoples specialised in gathering certain foodstuffs, among whom particular forms of punishable and non-punishable "offences" can be observed. Other monographs on crime and punishment, like those by König (1923–1925) on the Eskimo or by Harrasser (1936) on the Australian aborigines have also contributed to a differentiated picture of law among specialised hunting and gathering peoples. It is to be regretted that these studies of functional correlates have not been continued. (For a summary of ethnological researches on crime and punishment with special attention to German legal ethnology, see Schott, 1965).

6.2 Property

Another even more controversial subject which has engaged German legal ethnology since its inception is property. The discussion was opened by Lothar Dargun in 1883. After a careful study of the ethnographic sources at his disposal, he came to the conclusion that, contrary to the received conviction (Justinian, Pufendorf, Montesquieu, Laveleye, Bücher, etc.), "there existed among the savage natural peoples [*bei den wilden Naturvölkern*] only individual property and nothing else" (Dargun, 1883:76). *Gemeineigentum* [communal property], especially *Feldgemeinschaft* [communal land tenure] was, according to Dargun (1883:3, 13, 29, 32, 38, 43 *et passim*) nothing original or ancient, but a later development and merely a transitory phase on the way towards a renewed individualization of property rights. "The lowest and the highest developments of law on our earth resemble each other" (Dargun, 1883:28–29, 45, 49). Dargun was of the opinion that "individual property is, without exception, the more marked and pronounced, the more original and simpler the conditions are" (Dargun, 1883:59). Dargun (1883:24) recognized long before Pospisil (1963) that "among the Papuans of New Guinea the dominance of individual property is most marked among the rudest" tribes. Among *Jägerbauern* ['hunter-farmers'] in general, individual property prevails with regard to land (Dargun, 1883: 29, 43). "Equality and independence of all is a characteristic feature of lowest barbary and can be shown to have existed wherever men were still rude and without agriculture" (Dargun, 1883:44). Individual freedom and individual property were correlates, according to Dargun, and only with the institution of formal authorities such as chiefs could communal land tenure arise as a functional correlate of restraining the unhampered personal liberty (Dargun, 1883:40–42). Although Dargun shared the evolutionist convictions of his time (see Dargun, 1883:4–5), he voiced severe doubts on the validity of the so-called stages or phases which were thought to have marked the evolution of humanity in all its branches: "One has to cease propounding the three phases of hunting, herding, and farming life as a norm of human progress" (1883:60).

Dargun's views were in complete opposition to those held by most of his contemporaries, among them Friedrich Engels, who in 1884, only one year after the death of Karl Marx, published his famous book *Der Ursprung der Familie, des Privateigenthums und des Staats* [The Origin of the Family, Private Property and the State], based on the ethnographic material which the American lawyer and ethnologist Lewis Henry Morgan had gathered in his *Ancient Society* (1877). Marx himself had made extensive notes from Morgan's work (cf. Krader, 1972), which fitted admirably the materialistic concept of the development of human society before the formation of the class society and the state. According to Engels, the communal production and consumption of goods in primitive societies disappeared in the face of the amassing of private property— mainly in the form of herds of cattle—in the hands of privileged groups. With incipient division of labour and the alienation of the goods produced from their producers, communal property as well as the communal family or gens were destroyed (cf. Schott, 1968; 1976).

Wilhelm Koppers (1919; 1921), the collaborator of Wilhelm Schmidt, was the first ethnologist to criticize Engel's concept from the point of view of culture-historical ethnology in Germany. According to Koppers, there was no "unbounded primitive communism" among peoples which he and Schmidt thought to represent the *Urkultur*. Among these primitive hunting-and-gathering peoples there was only a "family communism" with regard to food, whereas weapons and other utensils were individual property of the producer. The land was the common property of the whole group. The fact that individuals exchanged goods (foodstuffs, minerals, utensils) even under these most primitive conditions was for

Koppers proof of a clear concept of individual property among these peoples.

Wilhelm Schmidt (1937–1942) carried these ideas further and based them on research on a large scale, reflecting the great ideological importance which both Marxists and Roman Catholics attach to the concept of property in their respective doctrines on society. Yet it would be wrong to charge either side a priori with prejudices which completely blind them to the reality of property among "primitive" peoples. As I have shown elsewhere, there are many points of agreement between Marxist and non-Marxist authors concerning this subject; at the same time, there are, of course, also fundamental differences in the evaluation of the ethnographic facts (see Schott, 1968:47–54).

In the first volume of his work on *Das Eigentum auf den ältesten Stufen der Menschheit* [Property in the Earliest Stages of Mankind], Schmidt (1937) pointed out that among the peoples of the so-called *Urkultur* (Pygmies, Bushmen, Andaman Islanders, Tasmanians, and others) there exists a clear concept of individual property. Moreover, this concept is subject to no restrictions according to sex, age, status, or class: "Taken in a relative sense, the *Urkultur* [original culture] shows the greatest and the greatest possible number of proprietors, and all further developments of mankind have not increased but reduced this number" (Scmidt, 1937:284). The openhandedness which people show, especially in sharing their food, should not be taken as the expression of an original communistic attitude, but rather as a primitive altruism which confirms the idea of individual property rights which are sanctioned and limited in their exercise by the religious commands of a High God.

In contrast, Richard Thurnwald voiced the opinion that the sharing of food among hunters-and-gatherers derives mainly from the necessity of mutual help and of reciprocity in a continuous process of give and take which leads to an equal sharing of the produce and to a distribution of the risk to which the single hunter is exposed (Thurnwald, 1934:39). Walter Nippold (1954; 1958) has stressed that one can understand the concepts and practices of property in the communities of hunters-and-gatherers only in the context of their whole culture and way of life.

One fundamental principle comes out clearly in all recent ethnological works on property: individual work provides a title to individual property in the sense that the individual may enjoy the fruits of his labour, subject to certain restrictions which proceed from the interests of the community. In my doctoral thesis on food distribution among hunters-and-gatherers I showed that this principle applies also to the sharing of prey after a communal hunt (Schott, 1955). The principles of communal sharing either according to certain fixed rules or according to the decision of a person in authority, on the one hand, and of private distribution of food on a reciprocal basis or in exchange for other goods, on the other hand, can both be observed in communities of hunting-and-gathering peoples: the incipient forms of a centrally planned and of a private economy are both present in these "primitive" cultures. In a report to the Sixth International Congress of Comparative Law, I described recent research on private and communal property among so-called primitive peoples (Schott, 1962).

Wilhelm Schmidt published "only" three volumes of his work on *Property in the Earliest Stages of Mankind*, in which he dealt with hunter-and-gatherers and with cattle-breeders in Asia and Africa. His work was, in a way, continued by an interdisciplinary undertaking which was started in 1954 under the direction of Hermann Trimborn. Under the general heading of *Frühgeschichte des Eigentums* [Early History of Property] more than forty collaborators, ethnologists, jurists, and orientalists, produced monographs on property rights, taken in the widest sense of the word, among peoples representing different economic, social, and political orders in all parts of the world. More than half of these monographs have been published in the meantime; a preliminary report on one aspect, the religious ties to which property is subject among various peoples, has been published by the present author (Schott, 1960) but a comprehensive summary of the results of this undertaking has yet to appear.

7. Recent Trends in German Legal Ethnology

Some of the monographs contributed to the project of the *Frühgeschichte des Eigentums* just mentioned were based on ethnographic fieldwork of the authors themselves, such as those of Ertle (1971b), E. W. Müller (1958) and Odermann (1957). Yet even these few articles, apart from Ertle's doctoral thesis on the property rights of the Cape Nguni, were mere by-products of ethnographic research that was mainly directed to other concerns. There has been, to my knowledge, no ethnographic fieldwork performed by any German student that has aimed exclusively or even primarily to elucidate legal phenomena. (My own ethnographic fieldwork among the Bulsa in Northern Ghana is still in the process of publication; it, also, deals only partly with legal matters.) The work of present-day German ethnographers shows very little concern with the legal aspects of society.

On the theoretical side as well German legal ethnology has produced almost nothing in recent years. Müller (1962:55–64), in his report to the Sixth International Congress of Comparative Law, discussed certain fundamental questions of the applicability of Euro-American legal terms, but he has, as far as I know, never further developed his short, yet important contribution to a seemingly interminable discussion. I myself have published a contribution to an interdisciplinary conference on legal sociology that was directed by Werner Maihofer (Saarbrücken) and Helmut Schelsky (Münster) in 1968. In this article I summarized certain aspects of the functions of law in primitive societies (Schott, 1970). I differentiated between primary and secondary functions of law and divided the former into functions of social order and of social control. In a final section I tried to say something on the institutionalisation of legal functions.

My own work is especially concerned with the legal relevance of the *Weltanschauung*, especially with the religious ideas that influence the legal concepts and practices of people past and present (see Schott, 1960). I also dealt with this topic in my paper on "The Trivial and the Transcendental: Some Aspects of African Traditional Law with Special Reference to the Bulsa in Northern Ghana" (Schott, 1980a). In other articles I have tried to show the connection between historical consciousness and legal concepts (see Schott, 1961; 1968a:184–186; 1970:151ff.) and the relations between vengeance, legal, and supernatural sanctions (see Schott, 1981) and between law and anarchy (Schott, 1979).

E. W. Müller (1961) has written about modern changes in African land law based partly on his own experiences during two years' fieldwork in Zäire (Müller, 1958). Ertle has treated a similar topic with respect to South Africa, and the present author has reported on conflicts between traditional and modern administration of justice among the Bulsa of northern Ghana (Schott, 1978; 1980c and d). In another article I have dealt with the connections between law and modern developments in Africa (Schott, 1980b). In this connection the important contributions of the German sociologist Gerd Spittler on modern developments in African law and administration should also be mentioned; Spittler has done intensive fieldwork on these topics, especially in Niger (see Spittler, 1973; 1980a; 1980b). Among recent trends in German legal ethnology and related disciplines there has, thus, been an interest in present-day problems of legal change.

Compared with the work done in other countries, such as the United Kingdom, France, the United States or even the Netherlands, the German efforts in the field of legal ethnology or anthropology of law are trifling. We can only repeat the deep regret which Trimborn expressed as far back as in 1951, that a field of research in which German scholars once enjoyed an international reputation had become almost completely barren and neglected even before the last war.

The present generation of German students of ethnology seems to be terrified of "law and order" and therefore shrinks back from a subject that smacks of it, such as legal anthropology or ethnology. Yet there is hardly any subject in the whole field of ethnology that has more connections with all other realms of culture, since law concerns all aspects of life. And, what is more, it is of immediate importance to the people in many developing countries today who are torn between "traditional" and "modern" laws and who are helpless in situations where their inherited rights to their lands are not recognized or are threatened, where their families are disrupted because of conflicts over inheritance laws that have become meaningless in a new economic and political situation, where governments are unsure whether to codify traditional ideas of law and justice—to name only a few of the problems that cry, in the interest of the people concerned, for thorough investigations in many countries of the world. Why do German ethnologists keep aloof from these urgent tasks?

References

ZfE. = Zeitschrift für Ethnologie
ZvglRw. = Zeitschrift für vergleichende Rechtswissenschaft

Adam, Leonhard.
1913	"Stammesorganisation und Häuptlingstum der Tlinkit-Indianer." *ZvglRw.* 29:86–120.
1918	"Stammesorganisation und Häuplingstum der Wakashstämme." *ZvglRw.* 35:105–430.
1919	"Josef Kohler und die vergleichende Rechtswissenschaft." *ZvglRw.* 37:1–31.
1920	"In Memoriam Josef Kohler." *ZvglRw.* 38:1–30.
1934	"Sitte und Recht in Nepal." *ZvglRw.* 49:1–269.
1936a	"The Social Organisation and Customary Law of the Nepalese Tribes." *American Anthropologist* 38:533–547.
1936b	"Recht im Werden." In *Custom is King. Essays Presented to R. R. Marett on His Seventieth Birthday*, pp. 217–236.
1937	"Ethnologische Rechtsforschung." In *Lehrbuch der Völkerkunde*, ed. Karl Theodor Preuss, 1st ed., pp. 280–306.
1958	"Ethnologische Rechtsforschung." In *Lehrbuch der Völkerkunde*, ed. Leonhard Adam and Hermann Trimborn, 3d ed., pp. 189–207.

Baumann, Hermann.
1938	"Richtigstellung." *ZfE.* 70:123–124.

Bernhöft, Franz.
1872	"Uber Zweck und Mittel der vergleichenden Rechtswissenschaft." *ZvglRw.* 1:1–38.

Dargun, Lothar.
1883 "Ursprung und Entwicklungs-Geschichte des Eigenthums." *ZvglRw*. 4:1–115. (Also published as a book in 1895.)

Engels, Friedrich.
1884 *Der Ursprung der Familie, des Privateigenthums und des Staats.*

Ertle, Dieter.
1970 "Erbrecht, Familienstruktur und moderne Wirtschaftsordnung in Afrika (Römisch-holländisch-rechtlicher Einflußbereich)." *ZvglRw.* 71:127–140.
1971a "Ethnologische Rechtsforschung." In *Lehrbuch der Völkerkunde*, edited by Hermann Trimborn, 4th ed., pp. 296–322.
1971b "Das traditionelle Eigentumsrecht der Kap-Nguni in Südafrika." *Arbeiten zur Rechtsvergleichung 52.*

Evans-Pritchard, E. E.
1962 *Essays in Social Anthropology.*

Harrasser, Albert.
1936 "Die Rechtsverletzung bei den australischen Eingeborenen." Suppl. to *ZvglRw.* 50.

Hoebel, E. Adamson.
1954 *The Law of Primitive Man.*

Kohler, Arthur.
1931 *Josef Kohler-Bibliographie.*

Kohler, Josef.
1887 "Uber das Recht der Australneger." *ZvglRw.* 7:321–368.
1895a "Das Recht der Azteken." *ZvglRw.* 11:1–111. (Also published as a book in Stuttgart.)
1895b "Uber das Negerrecht, namentlich in Kamerun." *ZvglRw.* 11:413–475. (Also published as a book.)
1897 "Fragenbogen zur Erforschung der Rechtsverhältnisse der sog. Naturvölker, namentlich in den deutschen Kolonialländern." *ZvglRw.* 12:427–440.

König, Herbert.
1923–1925 "Der Rechtsbruch und sein Ausgleich bei den Eskimo." *Anthropos* 18/19:484–515, 771–792; 20:276–315.

Koppers, Wilhelm.
1919 *Privat- und Kommunaleigentum auf den frühesten Stufen der Menschheit.*
1921 *Die Anfänge des menschlichen Gemeinschaftslebens im Spiegel der neuern Völkerkunde.*

Krader, Lawrence.
1972 *The Ethnological Notebooks of Karl Marx.*

Krickeberg, Walter.
1937   Review of *Lehrbuch der Völkerkunde*, ed. Karl Theodor Preuss. ZfE. 69:464–466.
1938   "Abwehr." *ZfE.* 70:119–123.

Lips, Julius E.
1928   "Die Anfänge des Rechts an Grund und Boden bei den Naturvölkern und der Begriff der Erntevölker." In *Festschrift für P. Wilhelm Schmidt.*
1938   "Government." In *General Anthropology*, edited by Franz Boas., pp. 487–534.

Malinowski, Bronislaw.
1926   *Crime and Custom in Savage Society.*

Müller, Ernst Wilhelm.
1958   *Le droit de propriété chez les Móngo-Bokóté.* Academie Royale des Sciences Coloniales, Classe des Sciences Morales et Politiques, Vol. 9, 3, Brussels.
1961   "Moderne Wandlungen im afrikanischen Bodenrecht." ZvglRw. 63:58–71.
1962   "Problematik des Gebrauchs juristischer Kategorien bei der Aufnahme und bei der Kodifizierung von Eingeborenenrecht." Deutsche Landesreferate zum VI. Intern. Kongress für Rechtsvergleichung. *Rabels Zeitschrift*, pp. 55–67.

Nader, Laura; Koch, Klaus F.; and Cox, Bruce.
1966   "The Ethnography of Law: A Bibliographical Survey." *Current Anthropology* 7:267–294.

Nippold, Walter.
1954   *Die Anfänge des Eigentums bei den Naturvölkern und die Entstehung des Privateigentums.*
1958   "Die Probleme des Privateigentums und des Gemeineigentums bei den Naturvölkern." In *Deutsche Landesreferate zum V. Intern. Kongress für Rechtsvergleichung*, edited by Murad Ferid, pp. 33–46.

Odermann, Gisela.
1957   *Das Eigentum in Nordwest-Australien.* Annali Lateranensi, Vol. 21.

Pospisil, Leopold.
1963   *Kapauku Papuan Economy.* Yale University Publications in Anthropology, No. 67

Post, Albert Hermann.
1875   *Die Geschlechtsgenossenschaft der Urzeit und die Entstehung der Ehe. Ein Beitrag zu einer allgemeinen vergleichenden Staats- und Rechtswissenschaft.*
1894   *Grundriss der ethnologischen Jurisprudenz.* 2 vols.

1903	"Fragebogen der internationalen Vereinigung für vergleichende Rechtswissenschaft und Volkswirtschaftslehre zu Berlin über die Rechtsgewohnheiten der afrikanischen Naturvölker." In *Rechtsverhältnisse von eingeborenen Volkern in Afrika und Ozeanien*, edited by S. R. Steinmetz, 1903, pp. 1–13. (Further works by Post are cited in the text.)

Radcliffe-Brown, A. R.
1952	*Structure and Function in Primitive Society*.

Schmidt, Max.
1919	"Die Bedeutung der vergleichenden Rechtswissenschaft für die Ethnologie." *ZvlgRw*. 37:348–375.

Schmidt, Wilhelm.
1937–1942	*Das Eigentum auf den ältesten Stufen der Menschheit*.
1937	Vol. 1: *Das Eigentum in den Urkulturen*.
1940	Vol. 2: *Das Eigentum im Primärkulturkreis der Herdenviehzüchter Asiens*.
1942	Vol. 3: *Das Eigentum im Primärkulturkreis der Herdenviehzüchter Afrikas*.

Schmidt, Wilhelm, and Koppers, Wilhelm.
1924	"Völker und Kulturen." In *Der Mensch aller Zeiten—Gesellschaft und Wirtschaft der Völker*.

Schott, Rüdiger.
1955	*Anfänge der Privat- und Planwirtschaft. Wirtschaftsordnung und Nahrungsverteilung bei Wildbeutervölkern*.
1960	"Religiöse and soziale Bindungen des Eigentums bei Naturvölkern." *Paideuma* 7:115–132.
1961	"Zur Geschichte des Bodenrechts bei mutterrechtlichen Stämmen in Nordrhodesien." In *Festschrift für Hermann Trimborn zum 60. Geburtstag*, pp. 134–168.
1962	Die Arten des Übergangs vom Gemeineigentum zum Privatbesitz." Deutsche Landesreferate zum VI. Intern. Kongress für Rechtsvergleichung. *Rabels Zeitschrift*, pp. 68–86.
1965	"Ethnologische Forschungen." *Handwörterbuch der Kriminologie*, 1:191–205, 2d ed.
1968a	"Das Geschichtsbewußtsein schriftloser Völker." *Archiv für Begriffsgeschichte* 12:166–205.
1968b	"Eigentum in ethnologischer Sicht." In *Sowjetsystem und demokratische Gesellschaft—Eine vergleichende Enzyklopädie* 2:41–55.
1970	"Die Funktionen des Rechts in primitiven Gesellschaften." In *Jahrbuch für Rechtssoziologie und Rechtstheorie* 1:108–174.
1976	"More on Marx and Morgan." *Current Anthropology* 17:731–734.
1977	"Sources for a History of the Bulsa in Northern Ghana." *Paideuma* 23:141–168.

1978	"Das Recht gegen das Gesetz: Traditionelle Vorstellungen und moderne Rechtsprechung bei den Bulsa in Nordghana." In *Festschrift für Helmut Schelsky,* pp. 605–636.
1979	"Anarchie und Tradition—Über Frühformen des Rechts in schriftlosen Gesellschaften." In *Begründungen des Rechts*, edited by U. Nembach, pp. 22–48.
1980a	"Triviales und Transzendentes: Einige Aspekte afrikanischer Rechtstraditionen unter besonderer Berücksichtigung der Bulsa in Nord-Ghana." In *Entstehung und Wandel rechtlicher Traditionen*, Histor. Anthropologie 2:265–301.
1980b	"Recht und Entwicklung in Afrika." In *Afrika zwischen Tradition und Fortschritt*, edited by H. D. Ortlieb and J. Zwernemann, pp. 69–88.
1980c	"Justice versus the Law: Traditional and Modern Jurisdiction among the Bulsa of Northern Ghana." In *Law and State—A Biannual Collection of Recent German Contributions to These Fields* 21:121–133.
1980d	"Le droit contre la loi: Conceptions traditionelles et juridiction actuelle chez les Bulsa au Ghana du Nord." In *Dynamiques et Finalités des Droits Africains*, edited by G. Conac, pp. 279–306.
1981	"Vengeance and Violence among the Bulsa of Northern Ghana." In *La Vengeance 1:Vengeance et Pouvoir dans quelques Societes Extra-occidentales*, edited by Raymond Verdier, pp. 167–199.

Schultz-Ewerth, Erich, and Adam, Leonhard.
1929	"Vorwort." In *Das Eingeborenenrecht*, edited by Erich Schultz-Ewerth and Leonhard Adam, 1:V–IX.

Spittler, Gerd.
1973	"Die Reichweite staatlicher Rechtsprechung auf dem Lande in frankophonen Westafrika." *Verfassung und Recht in Übersee* 6:203–217.
1980a	"Konfliktaustragung in akephalen Gesellschaften: Selbsthilfe und Verhandlung." In *Jahrbuch für Rechtssoziologie Rechtstheorie* 6:142–164.
1980b	"Streitregelung im Schatten des Leviathan—Eine Darstellung und Kritik rechtethnologischer Untersuchungen." *Zeitschrift für Rechtssoziologie* 1:4–32.

Steinmetz, S. R. (editor)
1903	*Rechtsverhältnisse von eingeborenen Völkern in Afrika und Ozeanien.*

Thurnwald, Hilde.
1950	"Richard Thurnwald—Lebensweg und Werk." In *Beiträge zur Gesellungs- und Völkerwissenschaft* (Festschrift for Richard Turnwald on his 80th birthday), pp. 9–19.

Thurnwald, Richard.
1910a	"Ermittlungen über Eingeborenenrechte der Südsee." *ZvglRw*.23:309–364.

1910b	"Im Bismarckarchipel und auf den Salomoninseln 1906–1909." *ZfE.* 10:98–147.
1916	"Banaro-Society, Social Organisation and Kinship System of a Tribe in the Interior of New Guinea." *Memoirs of the American Anthrop Association*, vol. 3.
1920–1921	"Die Gemeinde der Bánaro. Ehe, Verwandtschaft und Gesellschaftsaufbau eines Stammes im Innern von Neu-Guinea." *ZvglRw.* 38:362–474; 39:68–219 (Also published as a book.)
1931	*Repräsentative Lebensbilder von Naturvölkern.* (*Die menschliche Gesellschaft*, vol. 1.)
1934	*Werden, Wandel und Gestaltung des Rechts.* (*Die menschliche Gesellschaft*, vol. 5.)
1939	"Ethnologische Rechtsforschung." In *Lehrbuch der Völkerkunde* edited by Karl Theodor Preuss. 2d ed., pp. 280–306.

Trimborn, Hermann.

1925	"Straftat und Sühne in Altperú." *ZfE.* 57:194–240.
1927	"Familien—und Erbrecht im präkolumbischen Perú." *ZvglRw.* 42:352–392.
1928	"Die Methode der ethnologischen Rechtsforschung." *ZvglRw.* 43:416–464.
1931	*Auffassung und Formen der Strafe auf den einzelnen Kulturstufen.*
1937	"Der Rechtsbruch in den Hochkulturen Amerikas." *ZvglRw.* 51:7–129.
1950	"Die Privatrache und der Eingriff des Staates." In *Deutsche Landesreferate zum III. Intern. Kongress für Rechtsvergleichung*, pp. 133–148.
1951	"Ein Mittelpunkt für die ethnologische Rechtsforschung." *Anthropos* 46:995–996.

Ubach, Ernst, and Rackow, Ernst.

1923	"Sitte und Recht in Nordafrika." Suppl. to *ZvglRw.* 40.

Voget, Fred W.

1973	"The History of Cultural Anthropology." In *Handbook of Social and Cultural Anthropology*, edited by J. J. Honigman, pp. 1–88.

A.K.J.M. STRIJBOSCH

Methods and Theories of Dutch Juridical–Ethnological Research in the Period 1900 to 1977

Most colonial powers were forced to deal with folk law whether they wanted to or not. Among the colonial powers, Holland was one which became extremely active in encouraging the recording and study of folk law. The concern was governing the so-called East Indies. As a result, there have been a good many outstanding Dutch scholars specializing in folk law. One of the first was C. van Vollenhoven (1874–1933) who became famous for his attempts to record and study "adat law," the folk law to be found in what is now Indonesia and Malaysia. No account of the history of the study of folk law can afford to neglect the considerable contributions of van Vollenhoven and his followers. For further details of van Vollenhoven's life, see Henriette L.T. de Beaufort's biography, Cornelis van Vollenhoven *(Haarlem: H.D. Tjeenk Willink, 1954). For a brief account on van Vollenhoven's interesting suggestion that there were cognate families of law analogous to language families, see his essay, "Families of Language and Families of Law," Illinois Law Review, 15 (1921), 417–423.*

The following survey by A.K.J.M. Strijbosch, who is on the Law Faculty at the University of Nijmegen, provides an admirable sketch of some of the major contributions of Dutch scholars working in Southeast Asia. For other discussions, see C. van Vollenhoven, "The Study of Indonesian Customary Law," Illinois Law Review, 13 (1918–1919), 200–204; Amry Vandenbosch, "Customary Law in the Dutch East Indies," Journal of Comparative Legislation, 3rd series, 14 *(1932), 30–44; A. Arthur Schiller, "Native Customary Law in the Netherlands East Indies,* Pacific Affairs, 9 *(1936), 254–263: L. Adam, Méthodes et modalités d'investigation et de relevé du droit coutumier indigène aux Indes orientales Néerlandaises avant la guerre,* Kongo–Overzee, 14 *(1948), 280–304; and for one of the very best surveys, see Indonesian anthropologist Koentjaraningrat's superb essay, "The Study of Adat Law in Indonesia," in his* Anthropology in Indonesia: A Bibliographical Review *(The Hague: Martinus Nijhoff, 1975), pp. 86–113.*

Reprinted from the *Netherlands Reports to the Xth International Congress of Comparative Law, Budapest 1978* (Kluwer-Deventer, 1978), pp. 1–15, with permission.

For an overview of the history of Dutch anthropology in general, see Roy F. Ellen, "The Development of Anthropology and Colonial Policy in the Netherlands: 1800–1960," Journal of the History of the Behavioral Sciences, 12 (1976), 303–324.

1. Introduction

This paper will deal with juridical-ethnological methods and theories as applied by Dutch researchers in the period between 1900 and 1977. The matter is suited for division into two parts. In the first part I want to talk about the juridical-ethnological studies, which took place in the period from 1900 until World War II. In this period this study went through times of rapid development and prosperity. The field of study was almost exclusively formed by the Indonesian archipelago, and roughly coincided with the colonial boundaries of The Dutch East Indies at that time. The object of study was the indigenous 'ethnological' law of the Indonesian peoples which had come to be referred to as 'adat law'[1]. In this paper the term will be used with regard to the law, which was studied by Dutch scholars in The Dutch East Indies before 1945.

Around this object of study a school of thought was formed, the representatives of which were united by a similarity of their methodological conceptions. This school, of which the late professor Van Vollenhoven was the founder, never became known by a set name. In this paper it will be referred to by the term 'Adat Law School'.

After the independence of Indonesia in 1945 the activities of this school abruptly came to an end. The political relations between The Netherlands and the former colony worsened, and as a result of this one was barred—at least physically—from the field of study. The period after 1945, with which the latter part of this paper is concerned, is characterized by occasional activities in the area of juridical ethnology. The few researchers of the new generation are dispersed over the world; their forces were hardly gathered at all; A new school of thought has not as yet arisen.

For understandable reasons I shall give more attention in this paper to the Adat Law School than to postwar juridical-ethnological studies. In my discussion of its methods I shall try, however, to place them in a somewhat wider perspective, in which I shall incidentally indicate their relation to approaches applied in the present time.

2. The First Period, 1900-1945

2.1. Van Vollenhoven

In the prewar period, the Dutch study of the indigenous law of the Indonesian population was largely dominated by the ideas of one scholar, C. van Vollenhoven (1874-1933, professor in the faculty of law at Leiden from 1901 to 1933). With his descriptive and theoretical studies, especially in his chief work 'Het Adatrecht van Nederlandsch Indië[2], (which appeared in installments between 1906 and 1931) and in many other writings, van Vollenhoven laid the foundation of the Adat Law School. Van Vollenhoven's views not only influenced the work of many scholars in this field but they also had a considerable impact upon the government's legal policy with regard to the area of adat law.

If in the following a necessarily fragmentary consideration is attempted of the chief scientific and social currents which influenced van Vollenhoven's thinking as well as a further description of a number of his most important methodological insights, I wish to point out that, along with this, a large part of the theoretical frame of the entire Adat Law School is presented.

2.2. Van Vollenhoven's frame of reference

The 'Adatrecht van Nederlandsch Indië' made a great many Dutch and Indonesian researchers aware of the possibilities of scientifically studying adat law. It has been said that van Vollenhoven 'discovered' adat law as a field for systematic analytical study. This must be qualified. In other countries theories already existed, to which he could refer, and much preliminary work had already been carried out in Indonesia by earlier researchers. The whole work was made possible by a combination of factors, which, on the one hand, can be traced to van Vollenhoven's personal qualities, and on the other hand, to the intellectual and spiritual climate of his time.

In the first place, mention must be made of Savigny's 'Historical School' and of Post and Kohler's 'Ethnological Jurisprudence'. Van Vollenhoven borrowed from both the notion that law is an historical product—differing according to time and place—of a given culture, the development of which is determined by 'sociological' processes, which take place largely beyond the conscious human will (Vollenhoven 1918: 72).

He further underwent the influence of Linguistics and Theology (Sonius 1976: 8). At that time, the representatives of these sciences concerned themselves especially with the study of the contents and history of the various linguistic and religious systems. The aim of their study was the description of all systems in the world in order to classify these, subsequently, according to their own characteristics, sort by sort.

Van Vollenhoven saw a similar task laid aside for legal science. Imitating the other sciences mentioned above, he wanted to describe and systematize the legal order of the entire world. And as in the case of linguistics, jurisprudence had to be an 'exact' science, aimed at the description of concrete, observable, (normative) phenomena (1930: 30). The final arrangement at global level of the described systems would be the task of what he called the 'comparative history of law'. Towards the end of his life van Vollenhoven made a beginning with this gigantic task, but the work was not completed due to his death in 1933.

Van Vollenhoven, however, wanted as yet a work terrain suitable for profound studies. He criticized the 'Ethnological Jurisprudents' because of the tendency, as he put it, to spread their wings too soon and to offer slight theories, based on insufficient knowledge of the area[3]. Given the colonial situation his choice was—obviously—mainly the Dutch East Indies.

Also the insights of the then still young science of ethnology influenced van Vollenhoven's thinking. New methodological concepts were developed by Durkheim and Levy-Bruhl, by Vierkandt and Preusz. Among other things, these concepts were concerned with 'participatory thinking' and 'magical-religious mentality'. They were introduced into the study of adat law, in particular by Van Ossenbruggen (Koentjaraningrat 1975; 94). From ethnology van Vollenhoven learned, as he put it, to 'perceive that which is oriental through oriental eyes' (*het Oostersche Oostersch zien*)[4], as a consequence the distinctions and concepts, which he used in his own study, had to be consonant with the 'native' concepts and notions.

Finally, van Vollenhoven's works must be understood in the light of the spirit of his time. In Europe at the beginning of this century, van Vollenhoven thought he discerned a new spiritual current which turned itself away from the 'rationalism' and the 'materialism' of the 19th century, and instead became sensitive to 'eastern', 'medieval' and 'mythical' thought (1928: 125). Certainly characteristic of the spirit of that time is a new principle—the 'ethical appeal'—introduced into the colonial politics by the Dutch government in 1901. In its broadest sense this meant that the colonial policy should no longer be directed towards profitable exploitation, but rather to the emancipation of the indigenous population. According to van Vollenhoven, the translation of this principle in terms of legal policy involved the generous support of the adat law and that any plans for the unification of the law on a Western basis had to be abandoned.

This, then, is the background which determined van Vollenhoven's thinking. Finally, it must be mentioned that the Dutch East Indies as field of study was by no means virgin territory. At the end of the 19th century, a large quantity of data on adat law had been collected, mainly by administrative officers. The quality of these data ranged from partly unreliable to partly outstanding[5]. This was the basic material which van Vollenhoven analyzed and later arranged into an entirely new methodological system.

2.3. Van Vollenhoven's methods and concepts

2.3.1. LAW AREA (RECHTSKRING) AND AUTONOMOUS COMMUNITY (RECHTSGEMEENSCHAP)

Both the concepts of 'law area' and 'autonomous community' assume an important place in van Vollenhoven's conceptual frame. The origin of the first concept must be sought in linguistics. For the ordering and classifying of language systems concepts such as language family, language tribe, and language area were used. All these concepts referred to groups or areas with similar languages. Analogous to this, a terminology was developed by van Vollenhoven, which could serve him in ordering the law material. Thus, he distinguished law families, law tribes and—in descending order—law areas, law districts and law dialects, each of which comprised groupings of similar law-systems.

In tracing and delineating these units he made use of the criteria derived from linguistic sciences. Thus, 'language area is law area', but he emphasized that it was only a working hypothesis, which would have to be verified by further research.

An example of a law family could be an Indo-Germanic one, which in turn could be subdivided into a Germanic law tribe and again in a Dutch law area, etc. In the same way—according to the principle that language area is law area—van Vollenhoven could point to the hypothetical Austranesian or Melanesian-Polynesian law family, within which the law of the Indonesian archipelago functions as a distinctive law tribe. The law of this law tribe[6]—the adat law—he now further divided into 19 law areas, each of them again comprising distinctive law districts with different law dialects. The law areas mentioned here formed the geographical units, from within which van Vollenhoven described the law.

The concept of law area reminds one of that of culture area, and it is likely that both concepts are subject to the same methodological objections. For the danger exists that the researcher may define such areas somewhat arbitrarily to suit his own purposes; that he may address himself too much to the general culture traits and have too little eye for the details of the behavioural processes, which take place in reality. Van Vollenhoven worked cautiously, however, and used his units for an initial arrangement of the data, repeatedly warning that the definitive delimitation of the law areas in The Dutch East Indies could be done only after extensive field research.

(Incidentally, the concept has once again become active in juridical ethnology now that Allott has used it in researching the law in Africa—Allott 1960: 215—, for he directs his attention to 'homeonomic groups', by which he means ethnic groups with similar law.)

In the Adat Law School the concept of autonomous community has become just as well-known as law area. Van Vollenhoven understood by it: small autarchic groups with (sometimes without) their own territory, possessing their own authority and their own property. According to him these autonomous communities—village communities, family groups, clans, etc.—are present everywhere in the Dutch East Indies and form the basic units of the whole society (see van Vollenhoven 1918: 135–147).

The importance of the concept was considerable, for it referred to units with their own specific social-political structure, within which autonomy prevailed, i.e. within which autonomous law development could take place. Within each village the adat law has acquired its own expression and interpretation, since it was formed and enforced by village authorities, who had the power to do this in their own way. Thus on the level of the communities—in the Indonesian villages and clans—law is prospering in its variety.

The function of the concepts law area and autonomous community was different. The former offered a frame within which data of law, gathered from all parts of Indonesia, could be ordered. The latter referred to specific groups and their social-political structure. The law area represented a unit with law, that only existed 'in abstracto', as a product of analytical ethnological study, whereas the law of the communities functioned as a living system consisting of concrete binding rules.

Van Vollenhoven has stressed, however, that one did not need to expect that the differences of law between the communities would be considerable. He pointed out, that, on the contrary, these differences concerned details, and that it was easy to find their largest common denominator (1918: 146).

In doing so he reminds us again of his major premises concerning law as mainly a product of historical growth. According to this view the law of the communities—in spite of their 'beneficial autonomy'—could not develop otherwise than along lines conditioned by 'structural' principles. It is against this background understandable that van Vollenhoven could suggest that the law of the communities had to be considered as a 'dialect' from which by research a 'language' for the law area could be ascertained. (See van Vollenhoven 1918: 146).

2.3.2. CONCEPT OF LAW

As indicated above, van Vollenhoven's concept of law holds that all law is historically determined and that jurisprudence as an 'exact' science aims at abstracting the legal rule by observing the regularities of human behaviour. He did not, however, want to take all behaviour into account, but only such behaviour as was subject to the sanctioning influence of the recognized village authorities. Here van Vollenhoven argued for the distinction between legal and social control. His ideas on this point are somewhat ambiguous. In the beginning of his great work he seems to find the difference between legal and social rule in the application of sanction (1918: 8–9). Later he places the concept of adat law on a much broader basis. He no longer considers sanction to be only the reaction by authority, but also as the 'punishment by the gods', 'social reaction in the form of scorn and derision', etc. (1931: 236) and argues that also rules, which are so 'voluntarily' observed and need never to be enforced by the village authorities, should be considered as legal rules. By accepting the concept of such 'voluntary law observance,' the means of distinguishing law and custom seem done away with. Van Vollenhoven has never totally abandoned the sanction-criterion, however, he has only dropped the preliminary condition that a sanction should be *applied* to turn a social rule into a legal one (1931: 401).

As far as the concept of sanction in the sense of a reaction by authority is concerned, van Vollenhoven makes yet another important distinction. Not only does maintenance of the behavioural rule, through the intervention of the judge, count as sanction; of much greater importance is the kind of sanction which takes place *without dispute*, that is when community officials vouch for the validity of legal transactions and thus guide the course of law. In this respect van Vollenhoven points out that in the everyday practice of Indonesian life important transactions (e.g, the arrangement of a marriage, an inheritance, a transfer of land) usually take place before the village authority, in order to obtain its active or tacit approval. This concept of 'attested law observance' (gesteunde naleving) was prominent in van Vollenhoven's thinking about the maintenance of law, and it did much to direct the attention of field researchers to a most important source of adat law[7].

2.3.3 METHODS OF RESEARCH

Although van Vollenhoven kept in close contact with field workers, he never carried out field research himself. Nevertheless, he considered such research to be indispensable. At different points he accurately indicated on which conditions research on adat law should ideally be carried out[8].

I want to turn my attention briefly now to some of his methodological conceptions, arranged under the headings 'field research on law' and 'reporting legal data'.

a. field research on law   From the previous sections it has become clear that van Vollenhoven considered the autonomous communities the most important unit for research, and that within them attention must be directed toward the behaviour of the group members, especially where it is governed by the regulatory and controlling influence of the community heads. The first task of the researcher now was to become informed of 'examples', in van Vollenhoven's terminology, in order to understand the legal life in practice. This was the core of his theory of research. The material had to be collected by means of examples—case histories—which the informant knew from his own experience[9]. The cases had to be gathered during conversation with 'experts', and with 'common' people or by means of a debate in a meeting. The panel method was frequently used by administrative officers at that time for various kinds of 'official' research. Van Vollenhoven did not reject this but warned that the best material would be gathered in small meetings.

b. reporting legal data   In the adat law of the Dutch East Indies a classification system and a terminology was developed by van Vollenhoven, which could serve the researcher as an example in reporting his material. In order to be able to represent the Indonesian concepts and distinctions adequately, he abstained in many cases from using Western-Roman categories of law. When he saw for example, that the adat law did not know the distinction between public wrongs and private wrongs he dropped these categories and introduced others, which correspond better to the Indonesian legal practices. Thus, he created a new language of law for describing the most important indigenous legal institutions. He did this, knowing that the Dutch law language did not yet possess adequate terms to denote the specific institutions of adat law and that the existing Indonesian law language had not as yet attained the fully technical level necessary for a good description[10].

2.4. The Adat Law School

Almost without exception van Vollenhoven's theories found acceptance among a new generation of adat law researchers. All the concepts sketched above formed together the theoretical frame within which the Adat Law School operated during its short existence. Most people, who in one way or another—as judge, lawyer, administrative officer, (juridical) ethnologist or Indologist[11]—came into contact with adat law, adopted the new conceptual apparatus and terminology.

Soon after the beginning of van Vollenhoven's teachings one started to research adat law in a systematical way. Since 1910 the so-called 'Adat-recht-bundels' regularly appeared in which diverse data gathered from all parts of Indonesia were put together and ordered law area-wise. Legal dictionaries were written and records of case law were compiled, bibliographic and field studies were made, resulting in hundreds of publications[12]. In matters of legal policy the Adat Law School functioned at times as a kind of pressure-group. Many of the adat-lawyers felt attracted to the'Ethical Movement[13] and favoured the political recognition of the adat law.

It is true, that this law had been recognized in the 19th century already, yet since the beginning of this century government plans emerged from time to time aiming at unification of law on a western basis. In 1928 these plans were given up not in the last place under pressure of the Adat Law School, and policy was altered in favour of adat law. From now on the government started to stimulate and subsidize research on adat law. In this respect mention must be made of a most important officially subsidized project aimed at the systematic description of the entire adat law of all 19 law areas—in the form of handbooks for lawyers, judges and government. By the outbreak of The Second World War a total of five handbooks had been prepared[14]. I want to sketch briefly here their methodological setup.

The research in the field was carried out in all cases by experts, mostly judges and civil servants with a good scientific training and knowledge of the language and law of the area where they went to work. The field research usually lasted about two years. For the research mainly the panel method mentioned above was applied, in which short, prearranged visits to certain, selected villages took place, complemented by districtwise explorations of the area. Each district in the law area was essentially covered, and at one or more points meetings ('panels') were called, to which the 'experts'—but also 'commoners'—of the adjacent villages were invited. During this period, the data were gathered with the aid of checklists. For this they almost always made use of van Vollenhoven's case method; that is, they allowed those present to tell 'case-histories', which the latter had themselves experienced. For the elaborating and recording of the material two different methods were followed. One can distinguish the 'state and prove' method (*a*) from the 'descriptive' method (*b*).

a. This method, which was used by Supomo and Djojodigoeno/ Tirtawinata started from a statement which was made about each separate subject concerning a certain aspect of the legal reality. Each statement was verified by means of cases and sentences (the 'evidence'). Reference to a variation in the law is frequently made in the abstractions and sometimes in the 'statement'. The statements which were made had in no way the pretence of serving as binding rules or as codification. In the handbooks of this type a separate consideration of the social structure which was sufficiently known from other literature is absent.

b. The second method is applied by Korn, Vergouwen and Mallinckrodt. They all give a rule-directed description of the law of their law area, by which they delve deeply into the social and religious context in which the rules are imbedded. Variations in the law are often indicated in detail. All handbooks mentioned here contain mainly descriptions of normative processess within certain regions. In all cases it occurs now and then that the researcher assumes a value-judgment standpoint in his report. That is, one does not suffice only in describing how the law works in practice, but one indicates how it actually should work. These personal notes are posited in the form of a recommendation or an indication to the judge, and purport to offer a solution in the few instances in which the law of a certain area is very unclear, complicated or contradictory. 'Better,' uniform, rules are proposed as well, because one finds that the existing practices conflict with the principles of the 'civilization' or of 'humanity'.

2.5. *Ter Haar*

After my discussion of the Adat Law School I want to turn to some new methodological thoughts of Ter Haar. He was, after van Vollenhoven, one of the outstanding theorists of that school. Ter Haar has become known primarily through his 'Beginselen en Stelsel van het Adatrecht', (Principles and System of Adat Law) in which he presents a comparative typological treatise of the most important institutions of adat law. The study is directed toward finding the basic morphological characteristics of adat law and based on literary and court-records research.

In an academic oration of 1937 Ter Haar offered two refinements in the field of theory.

a. As regards the concept of law: he chose a clear criterion in order to distinguish law from custom. He recognized as legal rules only those rules which can be deduced from applied authorititive decisions, of e.g. village heads, village meetings and (government) judges. For van Vollenhoven the *possibility* of sanction was sufficient, whereas for Ter Haar the *applied decision* is a necessary condition for the recognition of a rule as adat law. However, he followed van Vollenhoven when he included in his concept decisions reached within and without conflict situations.

Finally Ter Haar did demand that the decision reached—here he thought especially of sentences of government courts—had been made consonant with the structural ties and the values in the community (Ter Haar 1950: 479).

To this strict concept—compared with that of van Vollenhoven—objection was raised by F.D. Holleman (1938: 431) and Van Dijk (1948: 100) both prominent exponents of the Adat Law School. F.D. Holleman stood by van Vollenhoven's broader premises that also those norms of conduct which are being generally observed as binding in a community, even without their having been formally tested and confirmed by such decisions, should be regarded as legal norms. In addition he pointed out that decisions are by no means always such as to make it possible to derive rules from them. The 'adat' judges are prone in their decision to restore peace between parties (and in the community), and thus they may well appear to deviate from otherwise generally observed rules (Holleman 1938: 434). Van Dijk generally supported Ter Haar's concept but he has widened it. He argued that legal rules could be derived not merely from decisions of authorities, but also from decisions of community-members (here he thought especially of decisions made by parties in the contractual relations). However, Ter Haar's new view won the support from the equally authoritative expert on adat law, Logemann (Logemann 1939: 27–37).

b. Ter Haar also claimed that as a science adat private law belonged to the field of positive jurisprudence, and not to juridical ethnology (1950: 472 ff). He argued that this study was directed toward establishing the 'law valid for here and now' and that it faces the same problem as the disciplines of positive law in other countries. He was aware for that matter, that there did exist an important methodological difference with other—e.g. English or Dutch—jurisprudence, since the latter has to reckon with rules, which are derived from respectively case law and statutes, whereas in adat law the rules must be won directly *from reality*.

Ter Haar's argument of 1937 implied that the science of adat law was (had become) a 'practical' or 'practitioners' science in that it concerned itself not only with describing, but also with evaluating rules and, in doing so, was concerned with 'establishing, in last instance, that which must be valid' (Ter Haar 1950: 486). With this conception Ter Haar implicitly opposed van Vollenhoven's view that law was an exact science of a theoretically descriptive science.

The importance of Ter Haar's statement is not so much couched in its deviation from van Vollenhoven's concept. (Nowadays few will consider jurisprudence as merely an exact science; more often law is referred to as a theoretical-practical complex dealing with specific kinds of norms. Theorists—e.g., in comparative and historical jurisprudence, also in ethnology of law—are directed at describing these norms; practitioners—e.g. legislators, judges and barristers—are concerned with making, applying or interpreting them). However, what was new was Ter Haar's belief that the *study of adat law* had been developed to a point at which one could speak of a practical legal science.

In my judgment, the new thought which Ter Haar launched is correct, because it contains nothing other than the description of a development which had indeed taken place. Adat Law had initially been studied primarily by administrative officers and ethnologists—among whom, Wilken, Snouck Hurgronje, Lieffrinck—who, together, had gathered a large quantity of data concerning rules of adat law and customs. But then van Vollenhoven arranged this unstructured material. He distinguished between legal and customary rules, recognized the system in adat law and described the law with the aid of a new, consistent conceptual apparatus. Thus 'despite his empirical science of law', van Vollenhoven wrought the practical science of adat law (1950: 490). Practitioners of this science soon were judges and administrators (in their decision making) and writers knowledgable of law (in commenting on decisions), who formed together the 'corps of adat law jurists'. In order to emphasize even more this practical character of the adat law science Ter Haar referred to the Dutch East Indies no longer of *field of study* but of *work terrain* (1950: 492).

The development in the study of ethnological law as referred to here has for that matter not only occurred in the Dutch East Indies, but is also present in various countries of Africa. There, too, African ethnological law, after having been the exclusive object of study of anthropologists for a long time, has also become 'domain' of jurists. This new generation of lawyers concerns itself with the practical arrangement of the law within a certain state (Allott 1967: 5).

Yet it is important to point out that within the Adat Law School the study of adat law was carried out not *only* in practical juridical fashion. On the contrary, many studies bore a theoretical ethnographical or theoretical-ethnological character. Nearly all works mentioned in Ter Haar's bibliography are primarily a product of empirical research, including the main works of van Vollenhoven and Ter Haar themselves. At most, one can say that the Part II volume of van Vollenhoven's Adat Law in which the relation between adat law and imported Dutch law is investigated bears a practical juridical strain, especially where the author critically examines the position of adat law in the overall legal system of the Colony. Also the handbooks discussed above in my judgment can be considered law ethnographies. The elements of evaluation which one comes across here and there in them concern only details.

Nevertheless, in conclusion, I must state, that in my eyes, the law-ethnographic studies of the Adat Law School bear the stamp of the practical goal which they served. Much as the researchers, in following van Vollenhoven, took the indigenous concepts into consideration when formulating their categories, one can find that in many studies—in seeking and selecting data—the juridical bias has influenced their work: in the descriptions incidentally use is made of inadequate western juridical concepts, and much attention is paid to those parts of reality, of which the researchers—often from their experience as a judge—knew, that knowledge of it was of importance to the administration of justice. One could object to this setup. Nader and Yngvesson (1973: 804) did recently, when they stated that the researchers of ethnological law allow themselves to be influenced too much by western juridical categories and concepts (see also v. Benda Beckmann 1975: 20). However, as regards the prewar Dutch law ethnographies, such objections could as I see it, only concern the method, but not the theoretical-empirical-orientation of that work.

3. The Period 1945–1977

The Dutch activities in the area of legal ethnography were relatively narrow in scope in the period from 1945 to 1977. The attention was pretty much scattered over all different fields of study in the world. I shall, nevertheless, try to sum up below the most important developments under three headings. The given classification is valid only for the aim of this study, because it cannot as yet refer to any homogeneous groups or currents, within which sharply marked theoretical conceptions have been formed.

3.1 The 'adat law' study in Indonesia after 1945

After the independence of Indonesia there was no longer room for the 'practical' approach by Dutch adat law researchers. The law machinery was soon attended only by Indonesian jurists and politicians. The law of the Indonesian population groups could only be approached theoretically/ethnologically by Dutchmen. As an example of the way in which the political changes at that time influenced the scientific practice, the work of Chabot can be considered (Chabot 1950).

When—after a period of forced nonactivity in 1948, resulting from changed political relations—in 1948 Chabot once again pursued his field study started in 1940, he no longer chose a practically directed study, which had to result in a new handbook on behalf of the administration of justice in South Celebes; but he shifted his aim in a purely ethnological direction. The result was a book devoted mainly to the 'structure' of the society where a few institutions of law were incidentally described.

Because the relations between The Netherlands and Indonesia worsened more and more, this possibility vanished as well. Finally the last part of the former large work terrain became lost in 1963, when New Guinea was added to the republic of Indonesia.

The Indonesian representatives of the Adat Law School have continued just as little the course. In post-colonial Indonesia means and possibilities for new law research were still absent. Just as in many other new states one showed more interest here in ideas concerning the unification of law. At the same time, with the translation of the Dutch term 'Adatrecht' into the Indonesian 'hukum Adat', the concept gained another broader content. Above all, one strove for a concept in which more attention was given to the common traits and the unity in the law; the 'variety', emphasized by the Adat Law School, became more remote. The aim was to make the new concept useful for the needs at the national level (Koesnoe 1977: 64).

3.2. Africa Study Centre, Leiden

Since the beginning of the sixties, studies in the area of ethnological law in Africa have been carried out by a small group of researchers, led by Professor J.F. Holleman. He was trained in law and ethnology in South Africa and did—among other things—lengthy fieldwork among 'Shona'-speaking tribes in Rhodesia. This research resulted in a book which was 'a systematic and up-to-date account of Shona customary law' (Holleman 1952: IX). According to himself, Holleman was influenced during his study, among others, by the ideas of the Adat Law School

Methods and Theories of Dutch Juridical-Ethnological Research

(Holleman 1973: 585) and showed interest in the norm-directed approach to law. In his book on Shona law, however, he offers not so much a digest of legal rules, but rather an analysis of legal concepts and principles, which he describes in close connection with the social structure.

In his field study Holleman made use of the 'common' anthropological methods. He observed, therefore, (among other things) the behaviour of individuals and groups in every day life as well as court disputes. He attested personal case histories and used these as topics for panel discussions (Holleman 1952: IX). Considering his working methods in retrospect Holleman found (1973: 585) that, without consciously theorizing about research methods, he had in fact combined all three of the methodological approaches (ideological, descriptive and case-oriented) as advocated by Hoebel (Hoebel 1954).

Holleman also observes that the 'case-method', which Hoebel considered to be the best, but not the only successful one, has almost invariably been identified with the analysis of *trouble-cases*. He concedes the great importance of these, but remarks that the other methodological means also yield valuable results. Ideally *all* methods mentioned by Hoebel should be applied in combination with each other. He who uses only the trouble-case will, according to Holleman, often not succeed in giving a complete picture of the law, for there are many legal transactions which do not or very rarely give rise to formal litigation. That is why, in addition to the trouble-case, the 'trouble-less' case of every day practice should serve as methodological instrument. In this connection Holleman refers to concepts developed by the Adat Law School, such as, for example, 'attested law observance', the practice of which offers a fruitful source of factual information on a wide variety of transactions sanctioned by competent legal authority (Holleman 1973: 585–604)[15]. Also other representatives of the Africa Study Center have tested this concept in their studies of African law and have found it suitable (Van Rouveroy van Nieuwaal 1976: 293).

3.3 Institute of Folk Law, Nijmegen

Since 1970 a small center operates in Nijmegen which a.o. is directed toward the study of 'ethnological' law. The director of this center, Professor van den Steenhoven, began his studies with an investigation of 'Eskimo law', in which he was influenced methodologically by Hoebel; see e.g. his concept of law and case method (Van den Steenhoven 1962). After 1968, he turned his attention to the former 'work-terrain' of the Dutch researchers in Indonesia. Cooperative projects arose, directed toward juridical field research in three regions of Indonesia (Bali, Lombok, Karo-Batakland)[16].

Currently at this institute it is also explored how to relate its field of interest to the study of legal life in the Netherlands beyond the realm of legislation and courts, probably chiefly in small functional groups (the so called 'folk law'). Here it is not only the intention to work descriptively but also to investigate the position which folk law could assume within the currently valid Dutch legal order.

Notes

1. The term adat law was used for the first time by Snouck Hurgronje (1893–1894: 16).

2. C. van Vollenhoven, 'Het Adatrecht van Nederlandsch-Indië' I–II, Leiden 1918–1931. In 1933, part III appeared (also at Leiden) with collected papers on adat law in the period 1901–1931.

3. See van Vollenhoven 1918: 75. On the same page he also rejects the evolutionistic character of those theories.

4. See van Vollenhoven 1928: 125. Compare also the opening sentence of 'Het Adatrecht van Nederlandsch-Indië': 'He who takes up the study of the law of the Dutch Indies after the law of The Netherlands, enters a new world'. (*Wie na het recht van Nederland het recht van Nederlandsch-Indië in studie neemt komt een nieuwe wereld binnen*).

5. In 'de Ontdekking van het Adatrecht', (The Discovery of Adat Law) p. 96–110, van Vollenhoven discusses, among other things, the methods and results of ethnological law researchers in the 19th century. In particular he praises the work of Snouck Hurgronje, Lieffrinck and Wilken. The first two gave law descriptions of the adat law within a certain region of The Dutch East Indies. The latter worked according to Post's method in the sense that he gathered adat law data—inside The Dutch East Indies—from all regions and ordered them according to theme.

6. For practical reasons—because of the connection between the adat law and the imported Dutch law—van Vollenhoven limited his research to the law of the Dutch East Indies. This implied that he excluded other parts of the same law tribe (in this connection he also often used the term 'law basin'), e.g. the Philippines, Malaysia, etc. (see van Vollenhoven 1918: 77, 78).

7. Van Vollenhoven borrowed this concept from F. D. Holleman, who had used it for the first time in 1920. See his 'Het Adatrecht van de Afdeling Toeloeng Agoeng' (1927: 17–35). Logemann (1924: 128) demonstrated that the idea behind this 'attested law observance' was not to procure evidence which at a later moment could be used *repressively*, in defence against infringement or denial of a right. On the contrary, its function is one of a guarantee that the transaction in question and its attestation is not against the law, thereby helping to *prevent* its being questioned in the future. In this connection he used the term 'preventive law care' (*preventieve rechtszorg*).

8. See van Vollenhoven 1918: 87, 88. Also of interest is the 'Adat Law Guide' ('*Adatrechtwijzer*') a listing of methodological guidelines written by van Vollenhoven, intended for the aspirant field worker, published in 'Adatrechtsbundels' no. I, 1919, p. 16–20.

9. It is therefore not entirely correct that Hoebel qualifies van Vollenhoven's method 'ideological'. See Hoebel 1954: ch. 3.

10. Compare as well the place, which this method is given in relation to other methods of law description, by Gluckman (1966: 16).

11. Indology was a study especially intended for civil servants, which was directed toward 'the Indonesian culture' in the broadest sense.

12. For a concise bibliographic survey of the most important works of the Adat Law School see Ter Haar 1939: 239–248 or Ter Haar 1948: ch. XV. N.B.: The collected papers of Ter Haar were published in 1950.

13. The 'Ethical Movement' was the name of a strong social current—to which especially scientists, artists and others felt akin—which aimed at truly expressing the idea of the 'ethical appeal', in all areas of society, politics and law.

14. The titles of these handbooks can be found in the bibliography of this paper under the names: Djojodigoeno/Tirtawinata, Korn, Malinckrodt, Supomo and Vergouwen.

15. Two (related) concepts from the Adat Law School are indicated by J.F. Holleman. Besides the concept of 'attested law observance' he discusses, too, the concept of 'preventive law care'. Holleman 1973: 594.

16. The final report concerning the research on Bali and Lombok written by the Indonesian project leader Moh. Koesnoe, was already completed in the Indonesian language (1975). An English translation has appeared in 1977.

References

Adam, L.	1948	'*Methods and Forms of Investigating and Recording of Native Customary Law in the Netherlands East Indies before the War*' (Leiden).
Adatrechtsbundels	1910	'*Adatrechtbundel I bezorgd door de Commissie voor het Adatrecht*' ('s-Gravenhage).
Allott, A.N.	1962	'The Recording of Customary Law in British Africa and the Restatement of African Law Project', in '*La Redaction des Coutumes dans le Passé et dans le présent*', ed. J. Gilissen (Bruxelles).
	1964	'Law and Social Anthropology, with Special Reference to African Laws', in: '*Sociologus, Zeitschrift für Empirische Soziologie, Sozialpsychologische und*

Benda Beckmann von K. and F.	1975	'Om de Taak van den Onderzoeker', in 'Herdenking van de 100ste Geboortedag van Cornelis van Vollenhoven (1874–1974)' Leiden.
Chabot, H.Th.	1950	'Verwantschap, Stand en Sexe in Zuid Celebes' Djakarta.
Dijk, R. van	1948	'Samenleving en Adatrechtsvorming' ("s Gravenhage)
Djojodigoeno, M.M., & Tirtawinata, R.C.	1940	'Het Adatprivaatrecht van Midden-Java' (Batavia)'Het Adatprivaatrecht van Midden-Java' (Batavia)
Ter Haar Bzn. B.	1937	'Het Adatrecht van Ned.-Indië in Wetenschap, Praktijk en Onderwijs' (Groningen-Batavia)
	1939	'Beginselen en Stelsel van het Adatrecht' (Groningen-Batavia).
	1948	'Adat Law in Indonesia' (with an introd. by A. Arthur Schiller & E.A. Hoebel) (New York) (English translation of Ter Haar 1939).
Ter Haar Bzn. B.	1950	'Verzamelde Geschriften van B. Ter Haar Bzn.' I–II (Djakarta)
Holleman, F.D.	1927	'Adatrecht van de Afdeling Toeloengagoeng' (Buitenzorg)
	1938	'Het Adatprivaatrecht van Nederlandsch Indië in Wetenschap, Praktijk en Onderwijs,' in: Indisch Tijdschrift van het Recht', Deel 147, 1938. (Batavia)
Holleman, J.F	1952	'Shona Customary Law' (Capetown)
	1973	'Trouble-cases and trouble-less cases in the Study of Customary Law and Legal Reform', in: 'Law & Society Review, Vol. 7, no. 4, Summer 1973.
Koentjaraningrat, R.M.	1975	'Anthropology in Indonesia, a Bibliographical Review'. ('s-Gravenhage).
Koesnoe, M.	1975	'Penelitian Hukum Adat di Bali dan Lombok 1971–1973, Laporan Pokok' (Surabaya).
Korn, V.E.	1932	'Het Adatrecht van Bali'. ('s-Gravenhage) 2e druk (Leiden)

Above the table, first entry:
Ethnologische Forschung'. Thurnwald, H.C. Ed. (Berlin) jahrgang 17, Vol. I.

Logemann, J.H.A.	1924	'De Beteekenis der Indonesische Getuigen', in 'Adatrechtsbundels XXIII' ('s-Gravenhage)
	1939	'Om de Taak van den Rechter' in: Indisch Tijdschrift van het Recht, deel 148, 1939. (Batavia).
Mallinckrodt, J.	1928	'Het Adatrecht van Borneo', I, II (Leiden)
Nader, L. & Yngvesson, B	1973	'On Studying the Ethnography of Law and its Consequences' in 'Handbook of Social and Cultural Anthropology', J.J. Honigmann (ed.) (Chicago)
Rouveroy van Nieuwaal E.A.B.	1976	'Vrouw, Vorst en Vrederechter'. (Leiden)
Van Snouck Hurgronje, C.	1893–1894	'De Atjehers I-II' (Batavia-Leiden).
Steenhoven, G. van den	1962	'Leadership and Law among the Eskimos of the Keewatin district' Northwest Territories' (Rijswijk).
Supomo, R.	1932	'Het Adatprivaatrecht van West-Java' (Soekamiskin).
Sonius, H.W.J.	1976	'Over Mr. Cornelis van Vollenhoven en het Adatrecht van Indonesië', Publikaties over Volksrecht deel I, (Nijmegen)
Vergouwen, J.C.	1933	'Het Rechtsleven der Toba-Bataks' ('s-Gravenhage). English version: 'The Social Organisation and Customary Law of the Toba Batak of Northern Sumatra' (The Hague, 1964).
Vollenhoven, C. van	1901	'Exakte Rechtswetenschap' (Leiden)
	1918, '31, '33	'Het Adatrecht van Nederlandsch Indië', I, II, III (Leiden)
	1928	'De Ontdekking van het Adatrecht' (Leiden)
	1934	'Staatsrecht overzee' (Leiden)

C. VAN VOLLENHOVEN

Aspects of the Controversy on Customary Law in India

As we learned in the previous essay, one of the pioneers in the study of folk law was Dutch scholar Cornelis van Vollenhoven. His lifelong devotion to the study of adat law resulted in a lasting monument of folk law scholarship. For a substantial selection of his writings on the subject in translation, see J.F. Holleman, ed., Van Vollenhoven on Indonesian Adat Law *(The Hague: Martinus Nijhoff, 1981) with its excellent biographical introduction (pp. xxiv–lxvii) by H.W.J. Sonius.*

In the following essay, van Vollenhoven discusses not adat law, but historical developments in the attitudes towards folk law in India. For additional consideration of some of the important figures mentioned, see John L. Clive, Macaulay: The Shaping of the Historian *(New York: Knopf, 1973); Margaret Cruikshank,* Thomas Babington Macaulay *(Boston: Twayne Publications, 1978); and Owen Dudley Edwards,* Macaulay *(New York: St. Martin's Press, 1988). See also William A. Robson, "Sir Henry Maine To-Day," in* Modern Theories of Law *(London: Oxford University Press, 1933), pp. 160–179; Robert Redfield, "Maine's* Ancient Law *in the Light of Primitive Societies,"* Western Political Quarterly, *3 (1950), 574–589; J. Duncan M. Derrett, "Sir Henry Maine and Law in India,"* The Juridical Review *(1959), 40–55; and Raymond Cocks,* Sir Henry Maine: A Study in Victorian Jurisprudence *(Cambridge: Cambridge University Press, 1988).*

I

In the Malay Archipelago three men of British nationality—Marsden, Raffles (with the help of the Netherlander Muntinghe), and Crawfurd—were the first to give serious attention to the study of customary law (1783, 1814, 1820). About the same time the native customary law of India began to excite the interest of Mountstuart Elphinstone (1779–

Reprinted from *The Asiatic Review*, 23 (1927), 113–128.

1859). This attractive personality was the fourth son of a Lord Elphinstone, related to a later Lord Elphinstone who was Governor of Bombay, but he himself was not a peer. It is hardly possible to understand the two distinct lines of policy in regard to customary law in the India of to-day, not only in the British India under direct government of the Crown, but probably in the Indian States as well, if we fail to go back to this Elphinstone and his work.

The great Warren Hastings had been Governor-General before Elphinstone commenced his Indian career, the career of the ideal administrator; for Elphinstone landed more than ten years after Hastings left (1796). This sequence has its importance. The two men, moreover, worked on an entirely different basis and in quite different territories. The work of Mountstuart Elphinstone was field work: he served as an official, not in Calcutta or elsewhere in Bengal, and not in an office of the central Government, but in Poona, and in Nâgpur, and Kabûl, and again in Poona, in fact in the States of Central India and in Afghânistân, where the life of the indigenous population was untouched by foreign influences; while he was in Afghânistân, he was the first man to turn his attention to the Karakoram (1808–1809). Coming to India very young (at the age of seventeen), without any academic training, he taught himself Latin and Greek, studied history (including Oriental history), collected legends and linguistic data; thus his eyes were opened to things Oriental, and he conceived love and appreciation for them. After a short stay in the Holy City on the Ganges, Benares, he next joined the British Resident (*i.e.*, the representative of the East India Company) at the court of the Pesvâ of Poona, the famous Maratha chieftain. Then he served for five years in what is now called the Central Provinces, at the court of the Râjâ of Nâgpur, the Bhonsla; then, for one year, he was Minister to Afghânistân; next Resident at Poona, where he remained for seven years; afterwards Commissioner for the affairs of the Dakhan, Central and South India; and finally, from 1819 till 1827—*i.e.*, from the age of forty to forty-eight—he was Governor of Bombay Presidency. All of them were spheres of activity far from the centres of British rule at that period, in the midst of real Indian life.

Work in these regions convinced Elphinstone of two things. First that the Occidental cannot be too careful to avoid forcing his own views upon existing conditions, which he cannot easily grasp and which he may not appreciate at their full value; next, that indigenous education was much needed, but education on indigenous lines: Eastern knowledge fructified not supplanted by Western knowledge—Eastern culture not destroyed but enriched by Western culture. Hasty and rough dealings, such as Clive and Warren Hastings had been forced to, filled him with anxiety; he disliked the system of land revenue, established in Bengal

Aspects of the Controversy on Customary Law

by Lord Cornwallis—the noble general who had been defeated in the American War of Independence—Hastings' successor; he was offended by the ruthless annexation policy of the Governors-General Lord Auckland (1836–1842) and Lord Dalhousie (1848–1856); he was shocked by Lord Dalhousie's land expropriations; a zealous defender of decentralization to the benefit of indigenous communities, he was mortally afraid of a system of indigenous education that aimed at converting the Indians to Christianity or at anglicizing them. His opinions were definite, and established on a broad basis, and never reckless. There was certainly good reason for the people of India to express their warm feeling for him, when he left that country in 1827; and there was good reason for the erection from indigenous funds of an Elphinstone College (Elphinstone Institution) on one of the squares of Bombay.

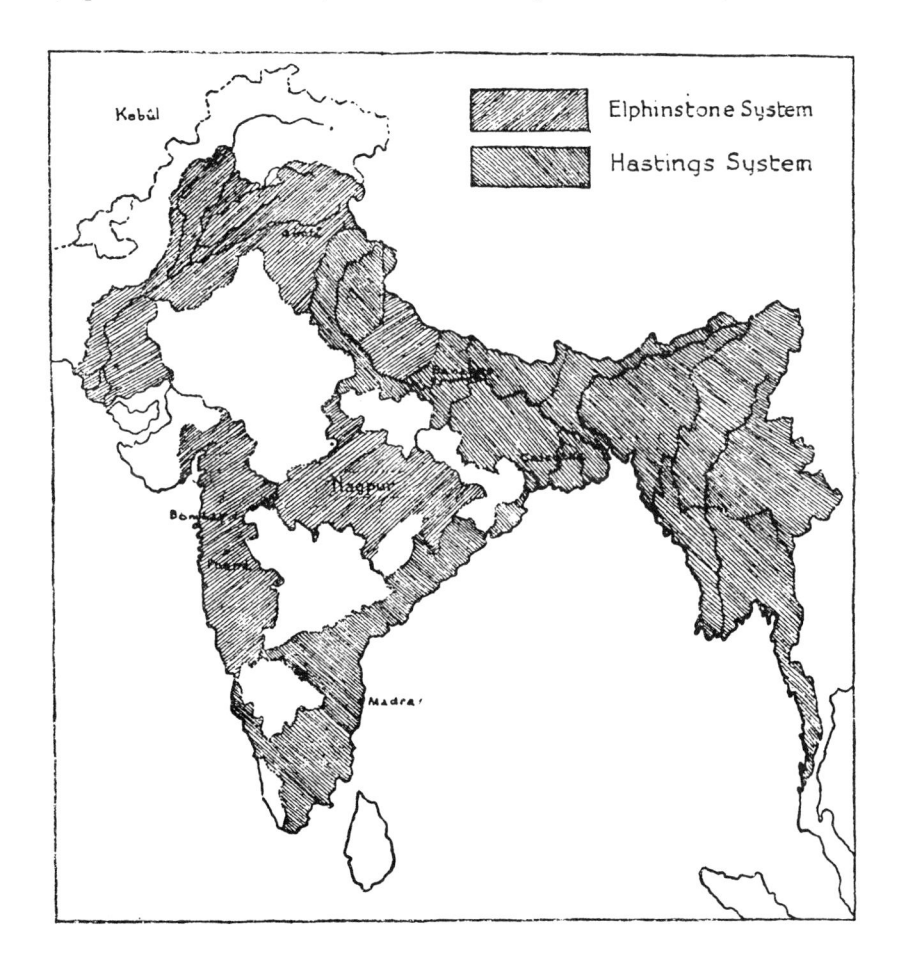

What significance had this experience and these opinions of Elphinstone for the development of customary law in India?

Towards the collection of facts he contributed less than Marsden, Raffles, and Crawfurd did for the customary law of the Malay Archipelago. His book of 1815 on Afghânistân contained some material concerning native law in this predominantly Muhammadan country; his book of 1841 about India acknowledged (II., p. 233) that, during the period of Muhammadan domination, the law of Islam had never wholly prevailed, but that the country's law had been "a sort of common law ... derived ... from the custom of the country and the discretion of the kings." When in 1819 he presented a report to the Governor-General on the former territories of the Pesvâ of Poona, he stated that "the knowledge of the common people in the customary law of this country ... is far beyond what could be expected"; that it was of "incalculable value" to have judges from the people themselves, who "could act on no principles that were not generally understood"; that the native judges consulted no books, and only sought enlightenment from a Hindû adviser in rare cases connected with the law of marriage or inheritance; that therefore the Government, while rooting out abuses—since law and judicial practice must accommodate themselves to the needs of society—ought "to cherish whatever is good in the existing system, and to attempt no innovation that can injure the principles now in force, since it is so uncertain whether we can introduce better in their room"; that the Government ought not to introduce a Governmental Judicature like that of Bengal (the adalats, etc.) nor rules "founded on European notions"; and that it should take care above all "(to) escape the evil of having a code unsuitable to the circumstances of the people, and beyond the reach of their understanding" (Forrest, "Selection from the Minutes ... of Mountstuart Elphinstone ... ," 1884, pp. 341, 347, 349, 355–359, 370).

When shortly afterwards Elphinstone was Governor of the Province of Bombay, he exerted himself to promote not only good government, education, and the welfare of the people, but customary law also.

His provincial administration at once envisaged two objects—namely, to investigate and record the contents of judicial usages in his Presidency, and, after that, to lay down a rule for its application. For this double task Elphinstone as early as 1820 appointed an advisory commission with which he actively co-operated.

The second half of its task succeeded, and produced what might have been expected. In an education report the author had earnestly recommended that "the fountains of native talent" should not be dried up, nor "the actual learning of the nation" be neglected, but that what already existed should be rejuvenated and inspired: "The future attainments of the natives will be increased in extent as well as in variety by being, as it were, engrafted on their own previous knowledge, and imbued with their own original and peculiar character" (Forrest, 1884, pp. 102, 110–111). In accordance with the wish of Elphinstone the fundamental principle of administrating justice ran that, where regulations were lacking, "the usage of the country" should prevail, supplemented, where necessary, by "justice, equity, and good conscience alone"; and this principle became part of that collection of twenty-six regulations, established by him in 1827, which dealt with judicial administration and procedure in his Presidency and is generally called the "Elphinstone Code." After having been in force for forty years, the greater part of that legislation of 1827, as can be easily understood, has been replaced by later enactments, "but Section XXVI. of Bombay Regulation No. IV. of 1827, from which the above quotations are taken, still holds good, and similar provisions are to be found in the Punjab Laws Act (1872), the Central Provinces Laws Act (1875), and the Oudh Laws Act (1876) which are still in force. In several parts of India, therefore, customary law occupies a prominent place in the decision of disputes, and the personal law of parties is only brought in to supplement it."

This second part of Elphinstone's plan for customary law met with a success that has lasted for nearly a hundred years. The first part, however, the recording of the legal usages themselves, failed. They failed for a strange reason. When, in 1815, Elphinstone wrote accurately about indigenous law in Afghânistân, he suddenly inserted an untenable remark on the relation of dowry and Islam (*ibidem*, p. 179); when, in 1819, he wrote an accurate report upon the judicial system in the former territory of the Pesvâ, he added to his account of the law of the people the unintelligible remark, "founded, no doubt, on the Hindu law, and modified by the custom of the country" (Forrest, 1884, p. 341); in his "History of India" (1841) he constantly derived the modern condition of law among the Hindûs from the laws of Manu (I., pp. 20, 21, 156–160, 315, 351). The theory of the problem of the relation of indigenous law to religious law he had evidently not clearly grasped. Now, Elphinstone's Commission of 1820—with his knowledge and co-operation—when recording the customary of law of Bombay, took the wrong path in deciding that first of all Hindû law should be determined, and only then attention be given to the divergencies from Hindû law in the Bombay Presidency. On this entirely superfluous task of determining Hindû law the work was miserably wrecked. Not till forty years later did the collection of the customary laws of Bombay, based upon Elphinstone's proposal, appear in the form of a book (Steele, 1868), supplemented since by land-revenue investigations into the actual law of the people. Though Elphinstone evidently failed in working out the first part of his plan, it is to him that we are indebted for the legal principle that the judge must put indigenous, not religious, law into application, and it is again to him that we are indebted for the wise idea of maintaining, with gradual emendations, that which has always existed among the Indian population.

Besides Elphinstone there appears the name of Sir Thomas Munro (1761–1827), who was eighteen years his senior. His field of activity lay in the interior of South India and in Madras. There is also Sir John Malcolm (1769–1833), his senior by ten years, son of a farmer, a soldier, civil servant, and author. Munro and Malcolm have more than one point in common with Elphinstone in their love of study and their careers; the three men form an illustrious triumvirate in the tradition of the Civil Service of India. But in the controversy on customary law we only meet Munro and Malcolm by chance.

After his departure from Bombay, Elphinstone lived on for thirty-two years—the last thirty years in England. He was destined to see an entirely different policy in regard to customary law shoot up like a rocket.

II

Indeed, even before Elphinstone landed in India, an entirely different policy in regard to customary law had prevailed in the older English territory, Bengal and the adjacent country: not after a struggle, nor after reflection and careful choice, but by overlooking the difficulty in the question. We must not, however, judge the author, Warren Hastings (1732–1818; Governor first, afterwards Governor-General, from 1772 to 1785), severely. The interest in the Oriental life of India, which in his day grew up and rapidly developed, was the work of scholars; it concerned itself with Sanskṛt as a language, Sanskṛt literature and Hindû religion, as well as Persian, Arabic, and Muslim learning. To establish order in the administration of justice for Hindû and Muslim subjects, Hastings laid down the well-known rule, that, in principle, Hindû law shall be applied to Hindûs, Muslim law to Muslims (August 15, 1772), and he ordered books on these two bodies of religious law to be compiled or translated into English. The indigenous law of the people did not come in at all.

This principle of Hastings was accepted, and is still operative for the greater part of India—namely, for the provinces of Bengal and Assam, for Agra in the North-Western Provinces (for these three it is laid down in an Act of 1887), for Madras, and Burma. In Burma Buddhist law is used instead of Hindû law; the religious law in these territories is, when necessary, supplemented—no more than that—by the indigenous law of the people and equity, or by the rules of equity alone.

In the India of to-day we find, therefore, two types of policy on customary law: the Elphinstone type (the younger, found in the smaller part of the country) and the Hastings type (the older, found in the greater part of the country). Writers on the Indian Empire as a whole generally give all their attention to the system of Hastings; which, in the opinion of an unprejudiced observer of a later generation, has broken down (Ilbert, "Government of India," third edition, 1915, pp. 368–369). In connection with the system of Elphinstone, collections of extant customary law of the people of Bombay and the Panjâb have been compiled (Steele, Tupper); in the majority of the remaining provinces such a procedure was never undertaken.

III

It is hardly possible to imagine a stronger contrast than between the work of Elphinstone on the one hand, and, on the other hand, that Indian reform which was to attract so much attention ever since 1833: the projects and the work of Macaulay (1800–1859). Love of study, especially of history, and a genuine desire to treat India well, these two men both possessed. But in other respects they were quite different. Elphinstone, who was a warm advocate of the admission of Indians to official posts (a hundred years ago) and who was on intimate terms with Indians (a hundred years ago), loved the land and the people, and had high hopes of them: "He is evidently attached to, and thinks well of the country and its inhabitants" (Heber, "Narrative," III., 1828, p. 134). Macaulay, on the contrary, he himself an exile during his four years in India: "I have no words to tell you how I pine for England, or how intensely bitter exile has been to me" (Trevelyan, "The Life and Letters of Lord Macaulay," I., 1876, p. 423). Elphinstone for thirty years closely observed the habits and customs, the aspirations, the motives, and the lot of the Indian population; Macaulay knew nothing of all this, was not prepared for his Indian work and did not prepare himself for it, had an intimate knowledge of the extension of British rule in India and its administration, would think India habitable only when it had all been anglicized. Elphinstone was deeply interested in the culture of Ancient India; to Macaulay it is a "history abounding with kings thirty feet high, and reigns thirty thousand years long, and geography made up of seas of treacle and seas of butter"; imagine that England had been content with "chronicles in Anglo-Saxon and romances in Norman-French" (Trevelyan, I., p. 402). Elphinstone would give Sanskṛt books as school prizes, Macaulay English books, and when he saw the "Merchant of Venice" acted by Indian students it vexed him that their skin was not fair (Trevelyan, I., p. 409). The educational reforms planned and promoted by Macaulay—English subject-matter, English methods, English as the medium of instruction—have broken down still more badly than Hastings' policy in regard to customary law.

Macaulay's legal reforms fit in with this manner of thinking. He rightly saw that judicial procedure and law ought not to be curiosities, but are meant to satisfy social needs. But just as, in his opinion, Indian literature and art and education must give away before the English, so, for the same end, Indian law should give way before Western law adapted for the purpose. This project of "enlightenment" found its application in section 53 of the Company's charter of 1833, and was defended in the House of Commons by Macaulay himself, who afterwards had to administer it in India. In his famous speech of Wednesday, July 10, 1833, he fabricated this witty but meaningless variation on an alleged saying by St. Augustine, which is not by St. Augustine: "Uniformity where you can have it, diversity where you must have it, but in all cases certainty." In the opinion of Macaulay, unification of the law for India on a British basis would prove to be a trifle: "I believe that no country ever stood so much in need of a code of laws as India; and I believe also that there never was a country in which the want might so easily be supplied" ("Works," VIII., p. 137: compare p. 139).

By an accidental coincidence we know fairly well what Elphinstone thought of all this. The Governor-General, Lord Bentinck, resigned in 1834, and Elphinstone in London was sounded as to whether he might perhaps be willing to become Governor-General. Reasons of health compelled him to decline; his age was then fifty-five. But in his diary he put down, among other things, for his own consolation, that the recently voted policy of customary law of 1833 would suit him very little: "With respect to the Code, I fear I should be more against sudden changes than would suit the Commissioners, and I should, therefore, probably have the talents of Macaulay, backed by public opinion at home, to contend with" (T. E. Colebrooke, "Elphinstone," II., 1884, p. 334).

Elphinstone and Macaulay both lived to see the Mutiny of 1857; Elphinstone died at the age of eighty in 1859, only one month before Macaulay, who was not yet sixty. The Mutiny changed Macaulay's disdain of the people of India into dislike; in Elphinstone, on the contrary, it confirmed the opinion that the policy of Lord Auckland and Lord Dalhousie had revenged itself now that it was too late.

IV

At the commencement of the new period (November 1, 1858), after the end of the Company, a twofold contrast was to be found in the controversy on customary law in India: that between Hastings and Elphinstone, and that between Elphinstone and Macaulay—the contrast between religious law as the normal or indigenous law, and the contrast between Oriental law as a basis for jurisdiction over Indians and a unified law on Western lines. Which solution of these antitheses do we find after seventy years of British authority over India?

The first man we now meet with is Sir Henry Sumner Maine, the well-known professor—Cambridge and London, Oxford, London—and author (1822–1888). His career had more than one marked feature in common with the career of Macaulay. He too, like Macaulay, had been Judicial Member of the Viceroy's Council in Calcutta (the former 1834–1838, the latter 1863–1869); he worked at Macaulay's legal reforms and promoted simple, uniform laws after good European models; he too had a fluent style and was an excellent writer. But in contrast to Macaulay he had the advantage of appreciating what was Oriental; like Elphinstone he thoroughly enjoyed his life in India and his contact with Indian ideas. His readership in London (since 1852), where for the first time in England he treated Roman law as history, and compared it to Greek and Hindû law; his famous book of 1861, with that well-chosen title "Ancient Law," which appeared shortly after the deaths of Elphinstone and Macaulay; his grief when in 1861 the doctor forbade his visit to India (in 1862 he went nevertheless)—all this was promising for his work in India.

The view he took of the Mutiny was nearer to that of Elphinstone than of Macaulay; his interest in Indian law was not diminished after his return; in a speech of 1875 at Cambridge he gave it as his opinion that the first thing necessary to approach and understand a strange world is to consider it as equal to, not less than, the world we know ("Village Communities," fourth edition, 1881, p. 224; compare pp. 13, 22, 24); he even thought that the study of Indian law could bear the same relation to the comparative history of law as the study of Sanskṛt about 1800 had borne to the comparative study of languages ("Village Communities," 1881, p. 224, as compared with p. 22). But just as his historical juridical work had occasionally been based on loose information, and on the whole more on imagination and flair than on sober facts, so his legal work for India neglected to seek out the right starting-point. To Sir Henry, Indian law was synonymous with Hindû law (he too had only taken notice of the system of Hastings, not of Elphinstone); when back in England with twofold material and tenfold interest, Hindû law was all he cared for when he spoke about legal conditions in India. The purpose was excellent; the achievement fell short.

Nevertheless, Sir Henry Maine gave a considerable impulse to the study of Indian customary law. It was he who discovered the truth and inculcated others with his views that we have to consider an Eastern system of law from a different point of view to a Western one, a mediaeval system from a different point of view to a modern one. Every study of customary law, also in the Malay Archipelago, entails three stages: the stage of contempt and neglect, the stage in which facts were collected, the stage of the study of these collected facts from an Eastern point of view. Sir Henry Maine represents this third and highest stage, though he applied it to the wrong facts; though he put on the same level the Hindû law of the schools and the practice of ancient Greek law, of Roman law, of Irish and ancient German law. To him and by him it was revealed—and here is his great virtue—that there a different world of ideas lies open before us, which we can only understand by means of patience and devotion; even Elphinstone had not realized this truth. All his life Sir Henry fought against the "insularity" of the English attitude towards jurisprudence. Whoever reads the four most important works by Sir Henry in order to gather therefrom the best available theoretical knowledge—late in the evening, in his study—runs a risk; but whoever reads them to gain inspiration, a widened view—on a lawn, or in a forest, or lying on his back in a boat—to him the reading of them is an enjoyment and a gain for his whole life.

Shortly after Maine's return to England, Macaulay's legal reforms were brought to a standstill (1882). Yet another student of the comparative history of law, the Celtic scholar Whitley Stokes (1830–1909), was to work at the unified code in India, 1877–1882. After him the project of 1833 proceeded no further.

The problem of customary law therefore still remains a problem in the policy of India. And here new names demand our attention.

In the years 1877, 1881, 1887, in India itself, a new voice was raised by a Civil Servant from the Madras Presidency, James Henry Nelson (died in 1898). The idea that such a unified code as that of Macaulay or Maine or Stokes could be put together in a few years—or decades— a code which would satisfy all, made him laugh. But he exploded with wrath at the idea that the customary law of the Madras population was Hindû law. The Madras Presidency has been conquered by the system of Hastings, which lays down religious law as the basis. After projecting an official manual on native conditions, the Madura Manual, and acting as an administrator and a judge in the lower courts, Nelson reached an altogether different view. His "View of the Hindû Law" of 1877, his "Prospectus of the Scientific Study of the Hindû Law" of 1881, his

"Indian Usage and Judge-Made Law in Madras" of 1887, often went too far in their denial; but the system of Hastings after a life of a hundred years really needed a strong denial. It is a noteworthy fact that Nelson, who followed the fresh suggestion of that Sanskṛt student, Arthur Coke Burnell (1840–1882), never appealed on behalf of his thesis to the views of Mountstuart Elphinstone, probably because Madras lies too far away from Bombay.

The next name in this controversy on customary law is that of John Dawson Mayne (1828–1917); he, too, was not from Bengal, but from Madras, where for fifteen years he practised as a lawyer and was a member of the judicial service and Attorney-General. In 1878, six years after his return home, his book on "Hindû Law and Usage" (ninth edition, 1922) appeared. Its contents did justice to native usage, but the title and design gave precedence to Hindû law. It can easily be understood that when Nelson, in his book of 1881, went for this fresh and unbiassed work, Mayne, in the preface of his third edition (1883) smiled a little over the "volcanic" attack. To Mayne also this codification, "satisfying all," of which Macaulay and Maine and Stokes had dreamed, was a chimera: "the age of miracles has passed."

Baden Henry Baden-Powell (1841–1901), for almost thirty years a Civil Servant in the Panjâb, as well as a judge in the chief court of that province, also deserves mention. The experience of this son of a professor and descendant of a well-known military family brought him into constant collision with the Hindû law of Sir Henry Maine; his works of 1892, especially that in three volumes on agrarian law (besides village organization and land revenue), contained valuable material upon indigenous law. A coherent system of native customary law, however, was no more given by Baden-Powell than by any of his predecessors.

After British students, Indian students began to assert themselves; witness the study of Malabar law by P. R. Sundara Aiyar (1862–1913), which appeared in 1922, or the books by Rādhākumud Mookerji (born in 1881), on "Local Government in Ancient India," 1919, and by Benoy Kumar Sarkar on "The Political Institutions and Theories of the Hindûs," 1922, which drew extensively on living material for the ancient law of India. However, they so far have not succeeded in laying new foundations.

Finally, a Government conference on the policy of customary law in the Panjâb, held at Simla, in August and September 1915, though it arrived at no positive result, proved in a negative manner that the days of Hastings' error and Macaulay's work of demolition were numbered.

Nevertheless, the controversy on customary law has not yet been decided: it remains unsettled.

V

What is narrated here could only be nicely rounded off if it were possible to conclude with the name of a statesman or writer in whose work the virtues of Elphinstone, Maine, Nelson, and those coming after them were united: reverence for the indigenous element in customary law, a vigilant eye for the legal needs of the Indians, understanding of an altogether different system of law, and all this applied to living Indian law. Such a name is wanting; the story, therefore, has no ending.

But, in a more general sense, India, especially that of a hundred years ago, can give a lesson to other colonial powers of the present day. In the triumvirate Munro—Malcolm—Elphinstone, esteem for customary law as only one of the expressions of their esteem for the Oriental; they could not imagine anyone to be a good civil servant without that esteem. This same Sir Thomas Munro, who had written in a note of 1822: "It is not necessary to go to Arabia, or even to Hindostan, to discover the usage of the Carnatic; we ought to search for it on the spot" (Gleig, "The Life of Sir Thomas Munro," 1830, II., pp. 339–340); who, in a report of 1824, dared to mock at "our anxiety to make everything as English as possible in a country which resembles England in nothing," which was preceded by: "What we do wrong is not noticed, or but seldom and slightly; what they (the Indians) do wrong meets with no indulgence" (Gleig, III., pp. 358–359, 381); and from whom Nelson, in 1887, borrowed a telling motto against code law and religious law—this same civil servant wrote, on December 31, 1824 (Gleig, III., p. 389): "The higher the opinion we have of the natives the more likely we shall be to govern them well.... I therefore consider it as a point of the utmost importance to our national character and the future good government of the country, that all our young servants who are destined to have a share in it should be early impressed with favourable sentiments of the natives."

IRINA SINITSINA

African Legal Tradition: J.M. Sarbah, J.B. Danquah, N.A. Ollennu

It was only a question of time before educated members of the native societies controlled by colonialist powers began to make their own studies of their indigenous folk law. Obviously, members of the society have the unquestionable advantage of being de facto insiders as opposed to the outsider status of intrusive missionaries or colonial government administrators. In theory, then, the research in folk law carried out by members of the society being studied ought to be infinitely superior to the sometimes superficial and partial knowledge obtained by colonialist investigators. In practice, however, this was not always the case. Sometimes, the native scholar would became unduly defensive about his or her own culture. This was caused often by the fact that the education the scholar had received came from the colonialist governing country. African scholars-to-be might go to England, for example, to be educated. In an attempt to be "more English than the English," such scholars might unfortunately be patronizing and condescending towards their own folk law, even more so than English colonial administrators.

In the following interesting essay by a Russian scholar from the Institute of African Studies of the Academy of Sciences of the USSR, we learn how native scholars in Ghana contributed to the study of folk law among the peoples of that country. For another general discussion of African folk law scholarship, see Yash Ghai, "Law, Development and African Scholarship," Modern Law Review, 50 (1987), 750–776.

The systematic study of African customary law and of the establishment of its role in the legal systems of African states was initiated, above all, by works of A. N. Allott.[1] The scholar gives unflagging attention to the local legal schools which laid a serious basis for the present-day comparative study both of customary law and of national legal systems, for clarifying the possible ways of their development, and for a search for optimal legal forms which would take due account of the interests

---

Reprinted from the *Journal of African Law*, 31 (1987), 44–57, with permission.

of small ethnic groups. The formation of national legal systems of African states has aroused a major interest in the customary law of ethnic groups. A. N. Allott correctly observed that it was necessary to pay heed, in particular, to the historical aspect of customary law.[2]

The most vivid example of the high level of development of autochthonous legal institutions and of their study of local legal scholars is furnished by the legal school of the ethnolinguistic group known as Akan (the Gold Coast, later Ghana).[3]

Present day Ghana in the pre-colonial period formed the states of the Akan peoples—Fanti and Ashanti—and of the inhabitants of the Birim-Volta river region—Akim and Akuapem. Screened by a tropical forest from the north and facing the Gulf of Guinea, the region remained isolated from external influences for many long epochs, creating specific systems of state law. The types and forms of their customary law mechanism characterise the level of development and specific features of appropriate societies. The norms preserved to this day in the field of private law register the status of an individual, the structure of a large family, the specific features of marriage, divorce, the law of property, possession and use, the norms of succession, guardianship, etc.[4] In common with the European societies of the early Middle Ages, the Akan societies had a number of stable constitutive indicators. They exhibited traditionalism and stability more than changeability. In the colonial period the official recognition of "archaic native law" furthered the strengthening of local legal culture. Formally, the Gold Coast colony was recognized by the British Crown following the conclusion with the local rulers of the Bond of 1844. However, the influence of British law and the enforcement of the legislation began earlier. Subsequently common law, doctrines of equity and statutes of general application in force in England in 1874 were officially introduced in the Gold Coast.

In the Gold Coast, one of the early British colonies in Africa, the combination in the local courts of the oral African customary law tradition with the newly introduced system of common law, largely based on precedent, antedated the similar process in other British possessions.[5] The use of local customary law alongside British common law in the colony was recognized by the British authorities in the Supreme Court Ordinance, 1876.[6] In 1883, the Native Jurisdiction Ordinance confirmed the customary law jurisdiction of the local chiefs and their courts, which was supported by the British Crown afterwards as well. Thus, the Native Courts (Ashanti) Ordinance, 1935, confirmed the full jurisdiction of chiefs' courts over all civil and criminal cases in which the parties were natives.[7]

The involvement of the European administration and courts in the solution of local lawsuits and the conflict between the laws of Britain and the local custom required, on the one hand, the exact restatement and recording of customary law and, on the other hand, the drawing of local legal experts into cooperation in the administration of justice. As a result, the first legal scholars—scholars of customary law—made their appearance. The researches of the three leading exponents of the Akan legal tradition—J. M. Sarbah and J. B. Danquah, jurists of the colonial period, and N. A. Ollennu, our contemporary, cover almost a hundred years' period of legal history—from the mid-nineteenth century to the present. Recording existing laws, the legal experts compared them with those of the late seventeenth century. Therefore their researches embraced customary law provisions over an almost 300-year period. Works by scholars of the Gold Coast became the first fundamental legal studies pertaining to African customary law. They are not only of historical and sociological relevance, but have become recognized guidelines for courts.

The Gold Coast legal scholars traced the ancient roots of local statehood and culture and developed an independent and, considering the times, progressive approach to the assessment of the autochthonous social, political and legal traditions. Their works have added value in that they reflect the legal views of practically the entire African intelligentsia of their time.

A distinguished place in the history of the legal science of the whole of Africa is occupied by John Mensah Sarbah, an outstanding political leader of the Gold Coast.[8] A Fanti by origin, Sarbah was born in Cape Coast, one of the lively seaport cities of the coast. He was educated at a missionary school at Mfantsipim (A Thousand Fanti)[9] and then received legal training in Britain. Sarbah was one of the first legal experts of Western Africa, a well-known journalist and then one of the few African people with a European education to his credit. He took part in the activity of the National Political Society of the Fanti, established for the protection and revival of national traditions, and founded the newspaper *The People of Gold Coast*, to which he contributed articles. In 1897 Sarbah became one of the leading members of the Gold Coast Aborigines' Rights Protection Society. For a number of years he was a member of the Legislative Council. Sarbah was a scholar not only of customary law, which he upheld by practical actions, but also of the common law of the British Empire.

Sarbah examined the system of government and jurisdiction historically found among the Akan peoples. His works were based on a meticulous study of the oral tradition of the Fanti. He questioned scholars of customary law, including local kings—Aminu, the king of Anamabo, and Otoo, the king of Abura. Shortly before the publication of his first book, the colony's administration circulated among the African legal practitioners a questionnaire pertaining to the local legal customs. The questions were concerned primarily with the rules and methods of property conveyance. Sarbah studied and generalised these materials. He also relied on the work by William de Graft Johnson and *Description of the Coast of Guinea* by W. Bosman.[10] Before the publication of his research there were no serious books on the history of the Gold Coast, still less so, on its legal systems. The work of another native of the Gold Coast, the Reverend Carl Reindorf, born of a Ga mother, a pastor of the Basel mission in Christiansborg, was published[11] only eight years after Sarbah's first book.

In 1887 in London Sarbah published a major enquiry, *Fanti Customary Law: A Brief Introduction to the Principles of the Native Laws and Customs of the Fanti and Akan Districts of the Gold Coast with a Report of Some Cases Thereon Decided in the Law Courts.*[12] It was an outstanding work for those times. Sarbah concluded that customary law lent itself to accurate clarification and that its provisions recorded before 1705 had not exhibited considerable changes in the following two centuries.

Following the example of Sir Henry Maine, the founder of the English historical school of legal studies, Sarbah traced the similarity of certain Fanti norms with the provisions of the Twelve Tables and to early European and Indian law and analysed numerous precedents, thus introducing African material into comparative jurisprudence. After nineteen years Sarbah published another book.[13] Alongside an outline of Akan history and the Akan social structure, this work explained the legal status of various strata of the Akan population. It also traced the genesis of the conflict between common law and local customary law.

Another legal scholar of the Gold Coast, Joseph Buaki Danquah, continued the efforts of his renowned predecessor. Danquah was born in 1895, in the period of the flourishing of Sarbah's work, in Bipong. He began his career as secretary of the court registry of the Omanhene of Akim Abuakwa. Danquah was a brother of Nana Ofori Atta and used the court archives for the study of cases. On completing his course of study in Britain, Danquah published a book dealing with Akan customary law, primarily, with that of the oldtime state of Akim Abuakwa.[14]

Danquah surveyed a wide spectrum of customary laws relating to the status of the extended family, the rights of individuals, regulation of marriage and divorce, types of lawsuit related to the infringement of the rights of a husband, and succession. He gave considerable attention to the law of property. The undiminished significance of his book consists in the fact that it is concerned with state and legal institutions vital in the eyes of a representative of the aristocracy and of an official of the peripheral state apparatus. His books, especially those treating of the legal system, reflect the positions of the elder, to whom the old principles seem to be the only correct ones in line with the people's way of life. Danquah was a lifelong exponent of the conservative views of the late nineteenth century. Nevertheless, the wide scope of his interests is illustrated, for instance, by the fact that his next book, which he worked on during the Second World War, was devoted to the Russian philosopher Vladimir Solovyov (1853–1900). Danquah witnessed the declaration of his country's independence and for a long period was one of the notable figures in Ghana's political life. However, the realities of new Ghana proved to be at variance with his views. His world view, which was of interest to historians, seemed outdated to the builders of this new country. This explains why Kwesi A. Dickson said that Danquah had died in isolation.

Just as the works by Sarbah, Danquah's books, devoted to the traditional state and law system of Akim Abuakwa and of the religious-philosophical views of the Akan, are a monument to a conflict between European laws of the capitalist era and the world of unwritten ancient African traditions.[15]

In the Gold Coast's interior the traditions were, naturally more stable than on the coast, and there were differences in family organisation, forms of marriage, and succession. Nevertheless, Sarbah correctly noted that all Akan maintained a unified basis for personal legal systems. This justifies the parallel legal survey of the law of the Fanti, Ashanti and Akim as made by Sarbah and Danquah.

Family law as outlined by Sarbah and Danquah to this day regulates the broad complex of relations of a traditional community, i.e., virtually bears the character of civil law.

According to Sarbah and Danquah, the extended family community—*abusuapon* or *abusua*—constitutes the basic primary social unit. Although the authors did not see any particular difference between *abusuapon* and *abusua*, in effect, *abusua* is a clan association of a closer circle of kinsmen (three or four generations). Sarbah and Danquah referred to the legal practice which assumes that an individual is a member of the family (*abusua*) of his mother with her sisters and brothers and of that of his grandmother with her sisters and brothers. The large family association assumed joint life and a combination of the common property of the entire family community with the separated property of its constituent hearths.

Abusuapan was apparently a territorial-clan group which presupposed a more distant common origin. By the beginning of the nineteenth century *abusuapon* had already been taken as divisions based on the formal establishment of the common origin fixed through symbolism and customs.

The status of each individual is determined, above all, by his membership of *abusua*. The majority of the Akan trace their origin along the maternal line from the common real (or mythical) progenitress down the straight female line. But in some groups the patrilineal counting of kinship is adopted.

The father of the family (in reality, the head of the clan group)—*penin* among the Fanti and *abusuapanin* among the Ashanti—is elected by the elder blood relatives. He disposes of the family property, performs court functions as the first instance and exercises power over legal minors.

The members of the family share a common responsibility for the repayment of debts, frequently share a common place of residence and are buried in a common cemetery with the performance of unified funeral rites. A family can live with outsiders adopted into its midst due to property or debt dependence; such individuals place themselves under the protection of a more powerful family, etc. Their rights bear a secondary character.

From the large family organisation stemmed the principle of collective possession of property. Sarbah noted that common property was a rule everywhere. However, in his time communal property was no longer recognized as a single type of property. Sarbah and Danquah pointed to the existence of three categories of property—both movable and immovable.[16]

Sarbah:	*Danquah*:
1. Family property.	1. Family or patriarchal property.
2. Ancestral property, including Stool property.	2. Stool property.
3. Self-acquired property or private property.	3. Private or individual property.

The types of property are divided by owner and by the mode of acquisition. In the next generation individual or private property becomes family property. The separation of "ancestral property" and the Stool property into a specific category was uncritically adopted by a number of authors. Subsequently, this led to confusion regarding the definition of the types of property in land.

Family property includes the property created by the work of two or more family members or acquired by them during their lifetime. The head of the family may dispose only of the movable property. The alienation of the immovable property necessitates the sanction of the senior family members—*abusuafu* ("people of the family"), who have shares in the property. Family and inherited property may be alienated only in certain cases, for instance, in the case of a gift to any of the kinsmen. This has the aims of enabling them to receive an education, of assisting them when they are in need, of founding a trading enterprise, or of making marriage payments. The law limits the number of cases when alienation is regarded as possible.

Although both Sarbah and Danquah witnessed the change whereby plots of land became an object of monetary transactions and categories of property borrowed from Roman law, their works revealed older rules of communal land tenure, based on the dominance of a self-sustained economy and extra-economic coercion.

In the system of intersecting rights and duties were distinguished acquired (family or individual) rights and "natural", hereditary, or "eternal" rights, connected with the individual's affiliation to his native clan. However, in specific cases this ancient presumption could diverge from reality.

Sarbah included in "ancestral property" any type of inherited property. It is not quite clear why he should have made "ancestral property" into a separate category. Just as family property, it forms part of the indivisible property of the family, only it is inherited. Perhaps Sarbah simply followed tradition? At the same time, he placed "ancestral property" into the same category as Stool property. In the cases in which the head of the family is a ruler, both types—family property and "ancestral property"—are regarded as Stool property. Danquah identified extensive family property with patriarchal property, but he classed Stool property, i.e., the property of the ruling family, as a separate category. In Danquah's times the functions of many rulers who disposed of property indeed became hereditary along the descending male line, from father to son. Consequently, their property regime had undergone changes.

Sarbah's writings demonstrate a basic discrepancy between the Stool property and the categories of European (and Roman) law. The conception of the head of the traditional ethnic group as the father of the people (or "guardian") developed in pre-state times and was adopted by early class ideology. From the explanations furnished by Sarbah and Danquah it can be inferred that Stool property was simultaneously the property of an ethnic group and of the ruling family. Lands could be transferred from one family to another and from one Stool to another. Land transactions such as rent, pledge, mortgage, and sale were permitted. But the head of the Stool, just as the head of the family, had no right to transfer the Stool (family) property to outsiders by lifetime instructions.

Sarbah and Danquah identify self-acquired individual or private property as a cohesive category. Both authors present the limitation of the types of private property as dependent on the personal activity of an individual—added evidence of the influence of traditional legal views.

The precedents cited in Sarbah's work reveal that, in spite of the traditional principles, the land (especially on the coast) acquired market value. In the case of the alienation of immovable property by private individuals it was assumed that the estate, and not the land was subject to alienation. In such cases one-third of the sale price was to be repaid to the Stool. An infraction of the order was made punishable by the confiscation of property sold. Both legal scholars points out the property inequality between families and within the family. According to Danquah, after the death of the rich head of a large family his wealth—the lands, slaves, wives, houses, and personal property—become property of the family. Consequently, those types of value could be regarded as individual or private property. After their owner's death his personal belongings also became property of the kinsmen or were distributed among them. The property which was not alienated during the owner's lifetime was regarded after his death as "ancestral property", or the hereditary property of the family. The termination of the individual's property right by death explains why the Akan have not established the institution of the will or testament.

Special types of agricultural features were not subject to sale. This applied to lakes, rivers, streams, sacred groves, and deity images. Thus, the legal tradition recognized various types of property. The definition of the type and of the scope of rights is difficult to establish in the absence of written documents. Therefore the study of property alienation necessitates meticulous collection of information and of a great number of witness statements. The works of Sarbah and Danquah (just as evidence furnished by other African authors of the late nineteenth and early twentieth centuries as well as by local chiefs) do not yield a clear picture of the character of possessory and usufructuary titles to land in keeping with the criteria of modern legal science. Experts strive to solve this question in the context of the theoretical development of the problems of social formations among the African peoples.

In the early 1960s the distinguished Soviet scholar I. I. Potekhin, basing himself, among other works, on those of Sarbah and Danquah, put forward the thesis that the Akan had developed patriarchal-feudal and early feudal forms of land tenure. Another Soviet scholar, I. V. Sledzevsky, noted the existence of divided property rights to land. A major contribution to the study of this question was made also by Allott.[17] Nevertheless, its final solution lies ahead.

The tangled character of property rights, the instability of the types of property, the oral form of proofs, the numbers of possible claimants to inheritable property all increased the role and significance of the traditional judges, the heads of the ruling families, and the *Ohene*. Customary law integrated heterogeneous rules, and the body of its provisions was fairly flexible. The interpretation of the rules could be different, and the same provision could be applied differently. Therefore even such major scholars of African reality as Sarbah and Danquah, who had a thorough schooling in bourgeois law, could not always accurately classify the different types of property rights. Precedents show that the parties also not infrequently erred as to the scope of their rights. Such a complex picture is explained by the fact that among the Akan coexisted the standards of different social epochs—prehistoric communal, early class, and capitalist. Moreover, a hundred years ago domestic slavery was still in existence.

In the works of Sarbah and Danquah kinship relations are included among the basic social factors. However, their increasing change under the influence of property development is apparent. A major role in the organization and functioning of the large family as a social institution is played by the system of marriage contract. A tangled web of intergroup and interpersonal relations is associated with marriage. Above all, it is an inter-family "collective" contract. In the case of polygamy (polygyny), it assumes an alliance of several families through kinship by blood or marriage. Each of the spouses remains a member of his large family. The most widespread form of this agreement is marriage with bridewealth, which presupposes a marriage payment to the wife's family. There are also marriages where payment takes the form of work performed by the prospective husband for his wife's family. The poor sections of the population also practise concubinage—marriage without the marriage payment. Until recently wide dissemination was registered by levirate marriage—marriage to the widow of a relative. In the past, there also existed what is known as "infant betrothal" (*asiwa*). According to Danquah infant betrothal was the most common type of marriage before its abolition in 1918. Bridal consent to marriage was not required. In the ruling families were widespread matrilineal cross-cousin marriages, since the rulers' daughters were not supposed to be given in marriage to unaristocratic men.

Danquah wrote that it was useless to take a woman away in the event of her family's refusal, and there were no marriages involving elopement from families. Fanti Law, however, already protected the interest of individuals who wished to marry. In the case of the "unreasoned" refusal of the woman's family to give permission for her marriage, the bride and groom could marry in the presence of the chief or the elder and witnesses without family permission. Marriages between individuals tied by close kinship (incest) were banned. According to Sarbah's evidence, in 1625 among the Fanti the head-money (*aseda*) in the bride-price reached two ounces of gold dust (over 1.5 ounces were contributed by the father and 0.5 ounces by the mother or her family). Consequently, the woman had enough property to pay for her son's marriages in gold. The size of the bride-price and fine for seduction depended on the woman's social status and the circumstances surrounding the marriage. These marriage customs, including large-sum marriage payments in the privileged stratum, point to social stratification and a close connection between the property qualification and the social status of individuals.

The Akan tradition regards the marriage of the heir to the relative's widow as morally binding. Allott correctly observes:

> "It's not a true "levirate' marriage, since children born to the new marriage belong to the successor, and not the dead husband."[18]

This "incomplete" form apparently shows the adaptation of the ancient blood kinship principles to the conditions of statehood in formation. Tradition prohibits forcing the widow into a marriage. But a childless widow must receive a divorce. In the case of a divorce both the marriage payments and everything else received from the husband are subject to return to his family. Danquah pointed out that cases when widows chose divorce were rare. This has a simple explanation: levirate preserves the woman's right to cultivate the fields of her deceased husband.

The heir renounced the levirate marriage if he had already entered into a cross-cousin marriage with the daughter of an uncle. The levirate custom here was at variance with more ancient marriage bans with respect to the wife's female relatives along the descending or ascending line.

When money-commodity relations were introduced and subsequently capitalist relations developed, the extended family ties weakened in a number of places; provisions for the separation of the property of husband and wife began to be used not for the protection of commodities, but in the interests of private individuals.

The families had a right to solve questions pertaining to the dissolution of marriages. The courts of arbitration usually included the head of the wife's family, the elder members of the relevant families and several respected individuals. Customary law protected the interests of the large family, whose basic aim was the reproduction of its members and of the material necessities of life. Its standards were directed at keeping the woman in marriage. With the development of commodity-oriented estates and the strengthening of social differentiation these standards began to further the enslavement and exploitation of women.

Before the husband's suit is satisfied the wife cannot enter into a new marriage or concubinage since the husband would then receive a right to compensation for adultery. Customary law regarded the seduction of another man's wife (*asommo*) as the gravest of the marriage offences, carrying the penalty of a fine in favour of the Ashantihene. The fine was double the marriage payment. Furthermore, the woman's family returned to the husband all marriage expenses. Liaison with an unmarried girl was made punishable by marriage payments and compensation: the marriage of female members was for the families a financial matter, and such a liaison therefore was the basis for an action for damages. The bigger the marriage payment, the higher was the prestige of the marriage. The higher the social status of a spouse, the bigger the fine was to be paid for adultery with his wife. The woman's relatives, in their turn, had a right to file an action for exoneration against the "adulterer". The protection of the morality and property interests of families was included in the jurisdiction of the state bodies. Major fines constituted a substantial source of the replenishment of the treasury, and the difference between them points to the development of a hierarchy of social estates.

In the opinion of Danquah, divorce among the Akan was a simple procedure. In reality, it was within the reach of only the chiefs and rich tradesmen, individuals who could pay judicial expenses, renounce the return of the marriage payment or force the wife's family to pay it back. The wife appeared to be a valuable family asset, and divorce among the ordinary people was a rare occurrence. The woman's family found it particularly unprofitable to return the bride price and to repay the marriage expenses to the husband. The existence of separate property of the spouses assumes that the wife has no rights on her husband's property. She uses her land as usufruct. According to Danquah, a man's property rights are much broader: "a husband is entitled to one-half portion of his wife's property."[19]

In an effort to convey the essence of the Akan marriage traditions Danquah observed that the very notion of "marriage" in the European sense was out of harmony with the spirit of the African marriage-family relations. In the colonial period it was widely contended that marriage did not exist in Africa at all. Prejudices received indirect reflection in the legislation: local marriage was defined as a "customary union". This presupposed a simple association. The relevant stereotyped view was assimilated, among others, by Danquah, who to a certain extent idealised the bourgeois form of marriage. Danquah is right only in saying that customary law marriage is above all a contract concluded between families which connected many people.

The materials of Sarbah and Danquah confirm the connection of kinship systems and types and forms of marriage with the right of succession. In keeping with the tradition of the majority of the Akan, the founder of the family is a woman—mother, grandmother or a more distant progenitress. There is a presumption that she has a right to dispose of the inheritance. However, the woman has limited legal capacity: in litigation she is usually represented by her husband or guardian. Sarbah emphasised that in the event of succession a man is always given preference to a woman. In reality, the mother, as it were, delegates her original right to dispose of the property to one of her sons (the brother of the deceased) or to one of her grandsons (the children of her daughters—sisters of the deceased). However, there is no clear pattern of succession. The succession is elective. The heir is chosen by the maternal relatives of the deceased in the family council. Thus, the household left by the deceased does not pass automatically to a successor known in advance. The claim of any of the relatives to his personal share of the property is regarded as contradicting the law since only the body of kinsmen is regarded as the property owner. The mother's opinion is held to be the most important in choosing one of the aforementioned categories of relatives. However, there must be serious grounds for the removal of individuals enjoying preferential rights.

If there are no relatives or if they are unsuited for the acceptance of the inheritance, in the order of seniority are chosen those members of the household who are related with the deceased by ties of blood kinship. In the absence of blood relatives the successor is the head of the household and its members in the order of seniority. Danquah's sequence of individuals entitled to succession is slightly from that of Sarbah.[20]

The data left by Sarbah and Danquah have been amplified by other authors. Their combined data make the picture of succession among the Akan clearer. In the opinion of R. S. Rattray, the mother's brother theoretically has the absolute right of succession. In reality, however, the maternal uncle delegates his right to other potential claimants—the senior and junior brothers of the deceased, the son of the mother's sister (cousin), the sister's son (nephew), etc.[21] Allott (basing himself on Ashanti material) concludes that there is the presumption of succession by the nephew but the brothers have precedence over the nephews. The ultimate solution in any case rests with the family.[22] The differences between the various data pertaining to property devolution shows the instability of the right of succession and the coexistence of the early, avuncular forms and the later system of patriarchate—succession by the male siblings of the group. The brothers' usual 'concession' "on ethical grounds" in favour of the sister's children demonstrates the stability of traditional standards and the traditional character of the rules of succession. Apparently, which prevailed depended on the changing situations in the families. Thus, the Akan succession system shows extremely ancient roots and an interweaving of maternal-clan and paternal-clan principles and succession. As shown by Sarbah and Danquah, a changeover to the succession of individual property along the paternal line on a testamentary basis began to gain ground. Simultaneously, within the traditional succession systems, beginning with the rulers, a patrilineal order of succession in the form of a changeover of functions developed along the descending male line—from father to son.

The mother's personal property is not inheritable by the sons. As a rule, one of her sisters, daughters of some other woman relative on the female line becomes the successor. The son receives the inheritance only in the complete absence of close female relatives. Danquah pointed out the extreme infrequency of the cases in which a woman is succeeded by a man. However, when a woman occupies the Stool the man is the proper successor. A substantial contribution to the interpretation of the law of succession with regard to the property of women was made by Allott. The individually acquired property of a woman—other than personal property—is inherited by the elected head of her family.[23]

The information provided by the Akan scholars points to the stability of local traditions, although the gradual introduction into their body of changes made by capitalist society becomes clear. The centres of amalgamation of the legal standards were towns.

Of particular interest is the study of the operation of the provision of modern customary law by the outstanding Ghanaian legal scholar Nee Amaa Ollennu, widely known in other African countries. A scholar of the legal traditions of various ethnic groups of Ghana and a member of the National Assembly of Ghana for a number of years, in the 1960s and the 1970s Ollennu was Justice of the Supreme Court of Ghana and president of the International African Law Association.

Ollennu wrote a number of works on customary law, above all, *Principles of Customary Land Law in Ghana*, based on extensive factual material.[24] The book grew from lectures given to the Council of Legal Education, shortly after independence. Ollennu's next work was devoted to the passing of title—traditional and testate succession. In other words, it took due account of the changes which had taken place under the influence of English law.[25] Ollennu analysed the exceedingly tangled practice based on the precedents of several centuries. It was a truly titanic effort.

Ollennu researches the synthesis of traditional custom with newly introduced legal provisions and the formation of legal norms and institutions at a new level with an eye to existing traditions. The scholar bases himself on a decision of the Supreme Court made in 1961, which said that customary law represented a progressive system and that its principles were so elastic that they could be used at any stage of the cultural, social and economic progress of a state and tribe.[26]

Following his predecessors, Ollennu stated that "among the things which a Ghanaian treasures most is his belonging to a family."[27] The community remains a source and custodian of customary law. In various ethnic groups there coexist different types of family: matrilineal, which includes all descendants (men and women) of one progenitress along the straight female line; patrilineal, which includes all descendants along a straight male line; "a mixture of the matrilineal and patrilineal constituted by all descendants, male and female, of a remote ancestor or ancestors in either direct or broken male and female line of descent.[28]

The notion of "family" virtually implies a clan structure. Both types of family—maternal and paternal—are preserved all over Ghana. Sometimes families of different kinship systems are neighbours in one town. Each Ghanaian belongs to one of the two types of family. Membership of one family offers a certain social or legal advantage. Membership of the other family, according to Ollennu, offers advantages in other fields. The preservation of an extended family creates conditions for the resumption of the principle of communal property, according to Ollennu, even when it exists rather as a presumption than *de facto*.[29] The family has a title to inherited movable property and to property created by the work of its members as well as to the possession of land. The family bears responsibility for aid to relatives in need and illness. It is responsible for funerals, etc.

The establishment of affiliation to a certain family type and of the scope of the rights of individuals is made complex by the interweaving of archaic norms, innovations and a combination of common law and legislation. In litigation on property rights the courts strove, above all, to establish the litigants' family affiliation.

Ollennu's propositions concerned with the status of the head of the family and with the grounds for preventing him from disposing of the family property have been specified by Allot. In particular, by one of the grounds, namely, "extravagance", Allott understands an attempt to carry out the arbitrary alienation of property without family consent. Refusal to help widows and children is also understood in quite precise terms as is refusal to grant trusted persons land for cultivation where there are free lands.[30] It is a very important specification, which sets the limit to family commitments under customary law.

Considerable complexities in the establishment of the status of individuals and the scope of their rights stem not only from the definition of the type of the individual's family, but also from the identification of the individual's real place in the intrafamily hierarchy. Ollennu points out that the Ghanaian notions of "son", "daughter", "father", and "mother" do not correspond to their European analogues. All over Ghana they are used broadly with respect to close relatives of the younger and older generations. "Father" also stands for "heir to the father" and by "children" are meant the children of the heir as well. The differences in the interpretations of the terms both in the colonial period and in modern Ghana has resulted frequently in conflicting court decisions.

As said earlier, for several decades legal scholars have been holding different views with regard to the type of social relations among the

Ghanaian peoples, primarily the most developed people, the Akan. Above all, the character of property in land is debated. In the opinion of Ollennu,

> "the first concept of land tenure ... is that absolute and unqualified ownership of land is vested in a community."[31]

With "real" property, that which has the status of immovable, Ollennu classes not only land, households, plantations, and buildings, but also horned cattle. The principle of family property in land has also been confirmed by precedent and by practice.

Ollennu assumes that the Stool possession is reduced to the collective acquisition by subjects of a right to use and occupy land. It exists alongside the power of the community to distribute the land among individuals. But it is the Stool which can turn over a derelict plot of land to another individual.

Ollennu denies the presence of feudal features in the social structure and land tenure of Ghana. But the data cited—innumerable landed property suits—refute the conception of patriarchal land tenure. The fact that the possessor can alienate his right to use land on condition of the recognition of the supreme rights of the Stool and of the discharge of the traditional duties by the purchaser amounts to the legal recognition of the existence of the ruling family's supreme ownership of lands. Ollennu writes that

> "the Stool or Skin constitutes a corporation; and the occupant of the Stool or Skin, or the head of the tribe, together with his elders, and councillors, are trustees holding the lands for the use of the community, the tribe and the family. The Stool or Skin means the community or tribe as a whole ..."[32]

It is a doubtful proposition: after all, he thus brackets as cohesive communal property a set of different lands, including the lands under the control of the ruling families, which are not equivalent to communal. It turns out that the historically formed divided right of landed property is regarded by Ollennu as a cohesive type of public property. In a remote historical period the Stool property could represent a collective possession. Apparently, this explains why Sarbah classed Stool property and ancestral property as one category. Subsequently, with the growth of population and the emergence of different categories of dependent people, the Stool no longer had anything to do with the entire population. Sarbah and Danquah themselves unambiguously identified stools exclusively with the ruling families, which held in their hands the functions of control of society, having monopolised the right to authority. In reality, the Stool had ceased to be a patriarchal, corporate proprietor. The historical relations of property development among the Akan were the same as in the early states of Europe. But in African societies, closed by virtue of geographical conditions, the new relations grew into the old forms and were interwoven with archaic traditions, and it was difficult to identify the new element. The growth of absolute communal power over the land also manifested itself in the fact that, in contrast to Sarbah and Danquah, Ollennu in general denies the existence among the Ghanaian people of private (or individual) property in land and recognises only the right of usufruct.

The study of Ollennu's work concerned with the traditional property regime suggests two conclusions: 1) the traditional norms in Ghana, just as in other African countries, have acquired a wider interpretation; they now extend to previously unknown property types (libraries, collections, personal archives, technical equipment, etc.); 2) due to the flexibility of customary law, the complexity of the norms and the lack of clear general principles, the state can maintain its communal principles, protecting collective types of property.

In common with previous authors, Ollennu emphasizes the differentiation or property by the mode of its emergence—a differentiation characteristic of West Africa. Among the objects of research he includes: 1) the incomes from the land, 2) the incomes from movable property, 3) the rights and responsibilities with regard to dependents, 4) money, 5) personal actions, 6) the debts due to the deceased. In the event of the death intestate, self-acquired private property of the deceased again passes to the family.

The Wills Act, 1971, strengthened the trend towards the devolution of property upon the nuclear family. The Act replaced the English Wills Act, 1837, (previously applied in Ghana). However, the provisions of the 1971 Act closely followed the old law, thus confirming a gradual departure from the traditional family property structure. In fact, they shake the foundations of "the things which a Ghanaian treasures most". The change of the law of succession was also influenced by new economic conditions of life in towns, by rapid urbanisation, and by changes in the position of women.[33] An inevitable influence was exercised by the "neighbourhood" of British common law. Nevertheless, as was pointed out by Allott, customary law embraces institutions parallel to those of common law, and in a wide range of cases individuals, depending on their social orientation, can use either autochthonous standards or those introduced from the outside. Ollennu holds that changes penetrate into traditional family succession rules slowly and that the adoption of new legislative provision by society (except the higher town strata) will take decades. The extended family and the customs related to it will survive for a long time yet. Consciousness, in particular, ideology, lags behind the rapid pace of modern life. Therefore the works of legal scholars of the past are not merely a document of past history.

The tasks connected with the creation of national legal systems facing the independent African states have intensified interest in traditional institutions. A search for principles that would be in line with those of the development of states and simultaneously reflect local economic forms clear to the population is impossible without the study of the scope of continued operation of customary law.

In the last thirty years traditional norms are studied not only by ethnographers, but also by sociologists, psychologists, historians, and legal practitioners. A fertile new element can be expected to emerge from the symbiosis of legal expert and economist, and although the works of Sarbah, Danquah and Ollennu vividly show the "image" of African scholarship, they should not be regarded on the exclusively historiographic plane. Their work contains valuable material from field studies recorded by observers from within society. A comparison of these works makes it possible to trace the development of local traditions as exemplified by one country. This is of importance for the understanding of the processes at work in other countries of modern Africa and for the forecasting of the future of traditional structures under the influence of modern conditions.

Notes

1. A. N. Allott, *Essays in African Law with special reference to the law of Ghana*, London, 1960. A. N. Allott, *New Essays in African Law*, London, 1970; A. N. Allott (cd.), *Judicial and Legal Systems in Africa*, London, 1970; A. N. Allott, "The Recording of Customary Law in British Africa and the Restatement of African Law Project", *La rédaction des coutumes dans le passé et dans le présent*, (ed. J. Gilissen) Brussels, 1960; A. N. Allott (ed.). The Future of Law in Africa (record of Proceedings of the London Conference), 1960, etc.

2. A. N. Allott, "The Evolution of African Law," Summary Paper presented to XXVth International Congress of Orientalists, Moscow, 1960.

3. For a detailed discussion see I. Ye. Sinitsina, *Traditional Institutions in Works by African Scientists J. M. Sarbah, J. Danquah, and N. A. Ollennu; A Study of African History, Problems and Achievements*, Moscow, 1985 (in Russian).

4. Allott, *Essays in African Law* ..., p. 206.

5. For a detailed discussion of the legal system adopted in the countries of West Africa see T. L. Roberts, *Judicial Organization and Institutions of Contemporary West Africa: a Profile*, New York, 1966.

6. *Judicial and Legal System in Africa*, 25.

7. *Handbook for Native Courts in Ashanti, Gold Coast*, Accra, 2.

8. For data about Sarbah see I. I. Potekhin, *The Formation of New Ghana*, Moscow, 1965 (in Russian).

9. See F. L. Bartels, *A Record of the Beginnings and Development of Mfantisipim*.

10. W. Bosman, *Voyage de Guinée, contenant une description nouvelle et très exacte de cette côte òu l'on trouve et òu l'on trafique l'or, les dents d'elephant et les esclaves; de ses pays, royaumes, républiques, des moeurs des habitants, de leur religion, gouvernement, administration de la justice, de leurs guerres, marriages, sepultures, etc.*, Utrecht, 1705.

11. See C. Ch. Reindorf, *The History of the Gold Coast and Asante, based on Traditions and Historical Facts, comprising a Period of More than Three Centuries from about 1500 to 1860*, Basel, 1895.

12. London, 1887.

13. J. M. Sarbah, *Fanti National Constitution. A Short Treatise on the Constitution and Government of the Fanti, Ashanti and Other Akan Tribes of West Africa*, London, 1906.

14. J. B. Danquah, *Gold Coast: Akan Laws and Customs and the Akim Abuakwa Constitution*, London, 1928.

15. J. B. Danquah, *The Akan Doctrine of God. A Fragment of Gold Coast Ethics and Religion*, London and Edinburgh, 1968.

16. Sarbah, *Fanti Customary Law* . . . , 57; Danquah, *Gold Coast: Akan Laws* . . . 198.

17. Sledzevsky, *Community in Africa: Problems of Typology*. Moscow, 1978, p. 80 (in Russian); Allott, 'Legal Personality in African Law", [in] *Ideas and Procedures in African Customary Law*, (ed. Gluckman), London, 1969, 179, 189.

18. Allott, *Essays in African Law*, 234.

19. Danquah, *Gold Coast: Akan Laws* . . . , 209. Allott points out that a woman bears no responsibility for the debts of her husband but the authorities are agreed that a husband bears responsibility for the debts of his wife.

20. Sarbah, *Fanti Customary Law* . . . , 101–102; Danquah, *Gold Coast: Akan Laws* . . . 184.

21. R. S. Rattray, *Religion and Art in Ashanti*, Oxford, 1927, 41.

22. Allott, "The Ashanti Law of Property", (1966) *Zeitschrift für vergleichende Rechtswissenschaft*, 129.

23. Ibid.

24. Ollennu, *The Principles of Customary Land Law in Ghana*, London, 1962.

25. Ollennu, *The Law of Testate and Intestate Succession in Ghana*, London, 1966.

26. See Ollennu, "The Family Law in Ghana," [in] *Le droit de la famille en Afrique Noire et à Madagascar, Etudes Preparées a la requête de l'UNESCO*, Paris, 1968, 177.

27. "The Changing Law and Law Reform in Ghana", [1971] J.A.L. 150.

28. For a detailed discussions see *Lee droit de la famille* . . . , 159.

29. Ibid.

30. Allot, *The Ashanti Law of Property*, 181.

31. Ollennu, "The Changing Law", *loc. cit.*, 130.

32. Ollennu, *"The Principles . . ."* 9.

33. See in this connection A. St. J.J. Hannigan, "The Present System of Succession amongst the Akan People of the Gold Coast", (1954) *J. African*

Administration, vol. VI, no. 4, 166; P. Roberts, "Feminism *in* Africa; Feminism *and* Africa," *Review of African Political Economy* (1983), nos 27–28, 175.

The Ascertainment of Folk Law

Having considered the definition of folk law and some of the pioneers in historical development of studies of folk law, we may now turn to the sometimes vexing question of what is normally termed the ascertainment or identification of folk law. Inasmuch as folk law is typically transmitted orally, there are not always convenient written records to consult to document the existence of a particular folk law at a given place and time.

In part, questions concerning the ascertainment of folk law involve what social scientists refer to under the rubric of fieldwork. An investigator, e.g., an anthropologist or folklorist, goes into the field to elicit data from informants. In this instance, the task is to record principles of folk law in a specific society. We therefore have begun this section with several essays explaining how to record folk law, how to transform something oral into something written—without losing oral style and cultural context. There is also the critical question of authenticity. Just because an informant says something does not necessarily mean that his or her statement is true. As most anthropologists and folklorists know, informants sometimes try too hard to please their questioners—by telling them what they think these questioners want to hear. In other instances, informants simply mistrust the investigators or their motives and they elect to deliberately prevaricate.

One convenient rule of thumb in folkloristics is that one must collect *at least* two versions of any item of folklore. Since all folklore—in order to qualify as folklore—must demonstrate multiple existence and variation, one would normally expect to find multiple versions of a folk law and to find some variation existing between different versions of the same law.

We have included several essays which concentrate on the problems of eliciting folk law in the field. Unreliable informants and unreliable documents are examples of the kinds of problems encountered. Such problems notwithstanding, there are established techniques that have been developed to assist in the so-called judicial ascertainment of folk law. While native peoples around the world may rightfully question why colonial administrators required these peoples' laws to be "ascertained" or "validated"—whereas the British, French, German, etc., law of these same administrators required no such "ascertainment" to be in force—even in a "foreign" colonial context, the impact of literacy on a hitherto oral culture did inevitably entail procedures aimed at transforming unwritten into written law.

The final essays in this section are concerned with precisely the changes that are to be expected in the transformation of folk law into written or legislated law. The extreme position, as has already been discussed in this volume, is that oral law has no legal status unless or until it has been "ascertained" or "recognized" as law, namely, by putting it in written form.

A.N. ALLOTT

Methods of Legal Research into Customary Law

Some of the most thoughtful considerations of the "ascertainment" issue have been written by Africanists who have been particularly active in what is sometimes referred to as the "restatement" of African folk law. The "restatement," of course, is in writing! Of those Africanists who have been concerned with the study of folk law, none has been more influential and prolific than Professor Antony Allott. For a detailed intellectual and personal appreciation of Allott, Professor of African Law, who taught at the School of African and Oriental Studies, University of London, for more than thirty-eight years, see James C. Read, "Tony Allott: A Colleague's Tribute," Journal of African Law, *31 (1987), 3–14. For Allott's writings, see the "Bibliography of the Works of Antony Allott 1948–1988,"* Journal of African Law, *31 (1987), 226–231.*

The following brief essay, the first of two by Allott, succinctly introduces the whole question of recording folk law, especially in an African context. For other discussions of ascertainment, see Lindsay J. Robertson, "The Judicial Recognition of Custom in India," Journal of Comparative Legislation, *3rd series, 4 (1922), 218–228; Paul Vinogradoff, "Some Considerations on the Methods of Ascertaining Legal Customs,"* The Collected Papers of Paul Vinogradoff, *Vol. II (Oxford: Clarendon, 1928), pp. 402–409; A.L. Epstein, "Procedure in the Study of Customary Law,"* Melanesian Law Journal, *1 (1970), 51–57; and Campbell McLachlan, "The Recognition of Aboriginal Customary Law: Pluralism beyond the Colonial Paradigm—A Review Article,"* International and Comparative Law Quarterly, *38 (1988), 368–386. See also the Australian Law Reform Commission's Report No. 31,* The Recognition of Aboriginal Customary Laws: Summary Report *(Canberra: Australian Government Publishing Service, 1980).*

Sometimes guides or questionnaires were issued to help beginners record folk law. See, for example, the English translation of the brief "Adat Guide" first distributed in 1910 in J.F. Holleman, ed., Van Vollenhoven on Indonesian Adat Law *(The Hague: Martinus Nijhoff, 1981), pp. 262–265, or the English translation of Joseph Kohler's elaborate questionnaire of more than 100 queries, which was*

Reprinted from the *Journal of African Administration*, 5 (1953), 172–177, with permission of John Wiley & Sons Ltd. Copyright © 1953.

first published as Kohler's "Fragebogen zur Erforschung der Rechtsverhältnisse der sogenannten Naturvölker, namentlich in den deutschen Kolonialländern," Zeitschrift für Vergleichende Rechtswissenschaft, *12 (1897), 427–440. The English translation appears as Appendix A, Questionnaire Concerning the Laws of the Natives in the German Colonies, in Alison Redmayne and Christine Rogers, "Research on Customary Law in German East Africa,"* Journal of African Law, *27 (1983), 22–41 (the Appendix runs from pp. 28–36). For another valuable folk law questionnaire, see Jean Poirier,* Questionnaire d'ethnologie juridique appliqué à l'enquête de droit coutumier *(Bruxelles: Editions de l'Institut de sociologie, Université libre de Bruxelles, 1963), which contains some 316 queries. This questionnaire is more ethnographic than an earlier 32-page folkloristic one issued in 1938. See René Maunier,* Questionnaire de folklore juridique *(Paris: Éditions d'art et d'histoire, 1938).*

Most existing research into customary law in Africa has been carried out from a non-legal angle; research from the legal point of view is at present only in its beginnings. It therefore seemed likely that it might be helpful to set down some of the aims and methods of such research, as gathered from my own experience.[1]

Although anthropologists and lawyers investigating customary law may make use of the same material, they do so with very different aims. The aim of anthropology is wide, to record custom as one of the various phenomena of social life in the tribe or people under investigation. The anthropologist seeks to show the social purpose of customary rules, and how they fit into the structure of behaviour. The aim of legal research is narrow, to record those rules of custom or usage which are either enforced in the courts, or are of a kind which the courts would enforce. Appreciation of the part which these rules play in the social structure is therefore irrelevant, or at most only needed as background-knowledge, or for the better elucidation of the meaning of these rules. It is fundamental that a clear distinction should be made where possible between rules having legal force, and those lacking the force of law, being backed merely by a social or moral sanction.

This raises the difficult problem of the binding character of customary law, a problem which need not worry the anthropologist. It would be inappropriate to discuss the matter here, though the reader may refer with benefit to such authorities as Maine[2], Allen[3], and Seagle[4], for a full canvass of the question.

Although the aims of the anthropologist and lawyer differ, the work of the former is important for the customary lawyer. Much of our existing knowledge of customary law is derived solely from the researches of anthropologists, and will continue to be so derived, until a considerable amount of legal research has been carried out. One can treat such work as secondary source-material, provided it is used with caution. After all, the anthropologist does not attempt to produce a legal text-book, which could be cited in the courts; and this must be the eventual aim of the lawyer. Again, from existing non-legal writings one gathers a wealth of background information, invaluable for one who wishes to appreciate the manners, way of life, and history of the people under investigation.

Legal research is usually carried on through documentary sources: when one has to deal with unwritten customary law, to be elicited by oral enquiry, anthropological methods in the field may suggest the most profitable procedure to adopt.

Survey of Available Sources

Before beginning a programme of research one should examine the existing sources of information on the customary law concerned. The sources may be either written or unwritten. The following nine types of *written* sources are for consideration.

Legal text-books: if there were more of these, the task of the investigator would dwindle. They are unfortunately rare or non-existent in Africa. South Africa, the Belgian Congo, and the Gold Coast appear the best equipped. Even where such books exist caution must be exercised in using them; many suffer from being out of date, which follows from the fact that they record mutable custom and not unchanging law. The statements they contain should therefore be tested where possible by subsequent oral enquiry. The works of Sarbah[5] and Whitfield[6] may be taken as examples of this category.

"Para-legal" works: by "para-legal" is meant here those works which, although not written as legal text-books, may be of use to those who have to administer or investigate customary law. Some invaluable treatises have been written by those with anthropological training: as examples, there are the works of Rattray[7], Schapera[8], Meek[9], Cory and Hartnoll[10], etc.

Anthropological works: the previous category shades off into the present one. From the lawyer's point of view descriptive works are more useful than those concerned with the analytical or theoretical side of anthropology.

"English" court reports: i.e. the reports of courts primarily administering law based on English law—courts of appeal, supreme or high courts, magistrates' courts, etc. These courts are not primarily concerned with customary law; but necessarily many questions involving customary law reach them and may be reported. Since the decisions of such courts

make or recognize law, no lawyer can neglect them. They should be studied, however, bearing in mind that:

(i) a custom as recognised may be out-of-date;
(ii) a custom may be recognised without qualifications to which it is subject, or a different complexion put on it from that which it bears in the customary legal system;
(iii) the customs of different tribes may be confused or insufficiently differentiated;
(iv) since native custom must usually be proved as a fact in such courts until judicial notice is taken of it, the fact that a custom has not been recognised by a court does not necessarily imply that that custom does not exist.

Native court records: the proceedings of native courts, primarily concerned with administering customary law, are an essential source of information on the law as it is practised. And, since modifications of the customary law are often introduced by native courts today, they also tell us the how the law is evolving. The potential investigator should be warned that:

(i) records of proceedings are frequently imperfect (perhaps containing little more than the claim and the decision without any reasons therefor), or unintelligible, or not in English;
(ii) native court records are often disappointing for one seeking statement of the rules of customary law (it may be necessary to read the whole case, including the evidence as recorded, to get an idea of the point at issue);
(iii) bias or perversion of justice may intrude into a decision;
(iv) court-members may state the law, not as it is, but as they would like it to be.

Not many reports of cases in native courts have been recorded for a wider public, so that in most cases the investigator must read and edit them for himself in the original. There are arguments against the uncritical diffusion of native court judgments (such as that it might lead to the application of the English doctrine of precedents to material on an unscientific nature); but the pros and cons cannot be considered here.

Documents of transfer, etc.: writing is coming to play an increasingly important part in transactions between Africans, many of which are now made or recorded by some sort of document. Study of such documents—where they are used for creating or transferring interests—is valuable; though they should not always be taken at their face-value (e.g. where an English form has been unthinkingly adopted).

Reports of commissions of enquiry, etc.: at various times government enquiries have been carried on relating directly or indirectly to customary law. The accuracy of the evidence submitted, and the value of the conclusions formed, vary considerably.

Other official papers: these are of numerous kinds, varying from territory to territory. Some examples are complaint files in the offices of the administration, boundary-books, district note-books, notes on local customs and history, maintained by district officers, native affairs department files, and forestry, agriculture, and other departmental files.

Legislation: account must be taken of the effect of legislation, both in prescribing the law applicable, and in affecting customary law indirectly through adjectival provisions. Central legislation, for instance, establishes, or recognises native courts, lays down the law to be administered (e.g. restricting the application of customary criminal law), and increasingly interferes with the working of the customary law itself.

Local legislation, by means of rules, orders and by-laws made by local or native authorities, may also restrict or vary the application of customary law. Native authorities may be permitted by statute to declare or modify the customary law applicable in their areas.

The three main categories of *unwritten* sources are:

Oral information, which is now—and will be for some time to come—a prime source of knowledge about customary law. A large part of an investigator's time will be taken up in eliciting the rules of law by oral question-and-answer from those expert in the law. This means that one must discover who are the customary experts: in many areas the elders and councillors of a chief have judicial functions and superior knowledge. There may be individuals with special qualifications, like the so-called "linguists"[11] in the Gold Coast. There should be no need to stress here that the time during which this expert, unwritten knowledge will be available is fast running out.

It is recommended that enquiry should not be restricted to experts; it is valuable to discover the opinions and practice of the ordinary man as well. This will sometimes show that the expert's answer is theoretical or out-of-date.

Observation: carried out by the investigators. This is necessary for confirming the results of oral enquiry, and should go hand-in-hand with it. Facts not easily elicited by questioning may be discovered by observation. The method of observation is a *sine qua non* for anthropologists (but not to be rejected on that account.) It may be applied to such questions as how boundaries are defined, the size of farms and their use and method of working, farming and market-days, working units on farms, types of houses and the number and type of occupants, types of councils and customary courts and their procedure, marriage ceremonies, etc.

Non-native unofficial sources: missions and commercial enterprises not only acquire a great store of knowledge about the customary law, but also modify it in various ways.

Initiating Research

The investigator should have a plan of campaign (which will probably need extensive modification in the course of research). His first task is to survey the available sources and evaluate them. His evaluation will determine possible fruitful lines of research, and the end at which he should aim. If there are no books of a high calibre already in existence, the investigator may have to be satisfied with producing a preliminary statement of the customary law, and not a definitive legal textbook. He should soak himself in the social background; the fact of having been on the spot for some time is obviously of great assistance.

From a survey of the sources the investigator should be able to determine profitable lines of research. As a general rule, the more restricted the enquiry, the greater the chance of success, of achieving an accurate statement of the law. He should also determine his areas of research: should he investigate over a wide area, or within a small area? The intensive method of research is typically anthropological; by restricting the geographical scope of the research, an exact description of all facts and events within this small compass (e.g. a village, or even a household) is achieved. But the lawyer primarily aims at stating the law for wider areas; and his method is thus typically extensive. This facilitates cross-checking (as by revealing local bias), and increases the possibility of finding a particular rule in action (e.g. in a native court case). The best answer is perhaps to combine the two methods, confirming the results of extensive enquiry by intensive investigation in one or more selected areas.

It is invaluable for the investigator to have a knowledge of one or more African languages. For instance it enables him to dispense with interpreters, who are a notorious source of error, and also slow up the enquiry. It allows him to sit in on court cases, and understand what the parties and witnesses are saying (perhaps to be elucidated later by talks with them). Further, a knowledge of the vernacular enables him to go to remoter areas at will. Sometimes, however, the prestige of the investigator, or local custom, demands that he use an intermediary.

Non-official investigators should notify the administrative officers in the areas where they wish to work; and obtain introductions, where possible, to African authorities from a responsible person. The African, especially when he is going to be examined on a subject very close to him, dislikes being taken by surprise. I found it helpful to make appointments for a serious discussion after making a preliminary semi-social visit. This may cut down time-wasting, and enable the necessary experts to be gathered.

Although it is helpful to draw up a plan of action and itinerary, this must be flexible. It is sometimes useful to draw up questionnaires, designed to bring out the main points which the investigator wishes to elucidate. These should generally be kept for his own use only.

Techniques in the Field

Oral investigation: this is the main method of research, but not the only one. A great deal will depend on how the questioning is handled. The following points may be of use.

Have a clear idea of the points that you wish to investigate. The questionnaire already suggested can make sure that you miss no important point, and that you do not waste too much time. It may also be used as a framework in writing-up the results. The questions as they appear in this *aide-memoire* should not be put to the informants as a rule.

Questions asked should be specific, rather than general. That is, they should be tied to particular, easily-appreciated facts. This principle has many advantages: it lessens the chance of bias, misconception, or theorising; it minimises the disadvantage of working through an interpreter.

It is often a good idea to start off with an easy question, to which the investigator already knows (or thinks he knows) the answer. Firstly, it puts the informants at their ease, and gets them talking fluently. Secondly, it tests their knowledge, and checks the value of what they may have to say.

Perhaps the quality needed above all else by the investigator is that of patience. Informants may often wander off into history or other unrelated topics. It may be necessary to permit this for a time; useful material may thus appear, or else hints of other points requiring investigation.

If one uses an interpreter, it helps in some ways to have one who knows no English law, as otherwise the answers may be distorted by the introduction of English legal concepts. Alternatively—with a competent interpreter—previous agreement can be reached on how stock vernacular phrases and ideas are to be rendered.

In the recording of information given orally I found it useful to make rough notes during the course of the enquiry (certain informants may be put off by too much notetaking). Immediately the interview was finished, a full account was written up in a note-book. Every entry in a note-book should be identified with the date, place, names (rank, quality or position) of the informants, their tribal affiliations, the subjects of enquiry in bold cross-heads. Note-books can be numbered and paged for cross-reference. Further files can be kept for cases (arranged by subjects if possible, with the main points involved), documents of various kinds, miscellaneous written matter (extracts from complaint files, etc.).

With more intelligent informants statements recorded in the note-book—including one's own general conclusions—should be checked back. This may often disclose further points, or misconceptions.

In some tribes there are awkward questions which informants dislike answering, e.g., in regard to their history, family relationships, religious observances, domestic arrangements, and so on.

If there are already decided cases, or statements in books, enquiries, etc., they should be tested by oral enquiry if possible.

Native court records: discovering cases involving points of importance usually involves reading through the court records and abstracting matters of interest. It helps to have an assistant who will copy out passages marked by the investigator. Passages of evidence may need abstraction.

The investigator's record of a case should include the names of the parties, the court, the date, the page of the record book or other reference, if possible the points at issue, and the history of the case (did it go on to appeal?). In more complicated cases I drew up block diagrams showing the relationships of the leading persons involved, and the history of the subject-matter in dispute.

With some court registrars or clerks progress is quicker by asking them if any interesting cases, or cases involving certain points, have been decided in their court, and by consulting the references they give. Nevertheless, it is usually essential for the investigator to make his own search through the records as well.

Native court cases may be explosive; further investigation of decided cases (by examining the parties), or investigation of undecided cases, may be misunderstood. The investigator must not try the case again.

Observation: when writing up his results the investigator should remember that not all his readers may be familiar with the background; it may thus be necessary to introduce explanations which are not strictly legal.

Taking some defined subject-matter—a farm, house or other property—and investigating its devolution is a technique close to anthropology; but it is often illuminating, though by itself no substitute for oral enquiry.

Writing-up

In writing-up his material the investigator must determine what he wishes to produce—a legal text-book which may be quoted in the courts, a brief manual suitable for consultation by the administration and others, a preliminary survey, the basis of a code, an anthropological or sociological work, etc. The decision affects the material sources which should be brought into the finished product.

Although there is no absolute, logical arrangement of the material, it will usually be found that the rules of customary law discovered suggest only one framework which coincides with the social facts and customary thought-processes. It is unusual for this framework to resemble either the theoretical perfection of Roman law, or the more haphazard arrangement of English Law. One must regret the frequent attempts to force customary legal systems into alien frameworks.

Where possible, the writer should give not merely his conclusions, but the facts upon which they are based; so that other workers can test the conclusions. Sometimes the nature of the sources drawn on will preclude this; and in any case the authority for statements of customary law will often not be such as English-trained lawyers are accustomed to. The recording of customary law in the Punjab, and Natal Native Code, may serve as examples, or as a warning of the traps to be avoided.

Notes

1. In research into Akan customary law in the Gold Coast during the period 1949–51. I would not be so presumptuous as to claim that my own discoveries and methods are of universal validity; but they may be helpful to those working in other areas.
2. In his *Ancient Law*, etc.
3. In his *Law in the Making*.
4. In his *The Quest for Law*.
5. *Fanti Customary Laws*.
6. *South African Native Law*.
7. In his series of books of varying value on Ashanti.
8. In his *Tswana Law and Custom*, and many others.
9. In his *Law and Authority in a Nigerian Tribe*, etc.
10. In their *Customary Law of the Haya Tribe*.
11. In Twi *okyeame*, or "spokesman" of a chief.

A.N. ALLOTT

The Judicial Ascertainment of Customary Law in British Africa

It is one thing for anthropologists, folklorists, lawyers, colonial administrators to record folk law; it is another for courts or governments to take official notice of such law. One of the best surveys of the question in an African context is the following essay by Allott.

As will be immediately obvious from this entire section of the volume the bulk of ascertainment research with respect to theory and method has been carried out in Africa. See, for example, Julius Lewin, "The Recording of Native Law and Custom," Journal of the Royal African Society, *37 (1938), 483–493; Lewin, "The Recognition of Native Law and Custom in British Africa,"* Journal of Comparative Legislation, *3rd series 20 (1938), 16–23. Sebastian Poulter, "An Essay on African Customary Law Research Techniques: Some Experiences from Lesotho,"* Journal of Southern African Studies, *1 (1975), 181–193.*

One of the most blatant ethnocentric factors in the colonialist assessment of folk law was the so-called "repugnancy rule." According to this rule, any folk law that was deemed "repugnant" to "natural justice, equity or good conscience" was to be put aside. This, of course, assumed that what constituted "natural justice" or "good conscience" was already known. In fact, such abstractions turned out to be part of the moral code of the colonialist regime. In other words, if a given customary practice was considered "repugnant" to a proper Englishman (Frenchman, German, Belgian, etc.), then it was to be adjudged null and void. For representative discussions of the repugnancy rule, see Abiola Ojo, "Judicial Approach to Customary Law," Journal of Islamic and Comparative Law, *3 (1969), 44–53; and R.D. Leslie, "The Repugnancy Rule in African Law and The Public Policy Rule in Conflict of Laws,"* Acta Juridica, *1977 [1979], 117–127.*

Reprinted from *Modern Law Review*, 20 (1957), 244–263, with permission of Basil Blackwell Ltd.

Introductory

The ascertainment of usage or custom which is to be administered by the courts presents problems in England; how much greater is the problem when the way of life, and even the language, of the people concerned are entirely alien to the judges and magistrates administering the customary law! This is the case in British Africa, where still—to a large extent—the personnel both of the superior courts[1] and of the subordinate courts other than native courts[2] is British. It is natural that in the course of time the individual judge, magistrate, or administrative officer should acquire a certain knowledge of the political and social systems, and the customary law which expresses those systems, of the indigenous African population; but this knowledge is unlikely to be deep (through transfers of the officers between territories or postings within them); and the officer is often legally debarred from expressly drawing on his own knowledge in the decision of cases involving customary law. It is necessary to fall back on other means of discovering what are the rules of customary law on any particular topic. A consideration of what means are open to parties or courts is therefore of central importance to the present-day administration of justice in Africa; there appears to have been no previous attempt, other than a valuable paper by Mr. J. Lewin, to collate the available statute and case law on the subject.[3] This paper endeavours to remedy the omission.

The difficulty experienced by a court in finding out, and then applying, the customary law applicable to a case before it flows partly from the multiplicity of different tribal laws (varying widely from tribe to tribe), partly from the uncertainty regarding the limits of the operation of customary law in competition or conflict with English or, where prevalent, Islamic law, and partly from the fluid nature of customary law itself. The rules of customary law were, in the past, generally not as certain as the courts would now like them to be; the object of many customary legal proceedings was negotiation leading to compromise and reconciliation of the parties, rather than the rigid application of rules to facts. The "rules" of customary law—*e.g.*, that a wound should be compensated by the payment of so many cattle—often only set a standard or provided a talking point. The modern customary law is generally more rigid, through its administration by British courts or by native courts influenced by English legal ideas; but the rapid change in social and economic life—cash crops, labour at a wage, education—induces a corresponding fluctuation in customary law, which renders out of date many past findings on its rules. A study of judicial decisions shows that the diversity and flexibility of customary law have sometimes been overlooked by the British courts.

The primary law of the British courts is "English law."[4] This inexact phrase covers two types of law: the law of England as at the date of the constitution of the territory in question (*i.e.*, the rules of common law, the doctrines of equity, and statutes of general application), and colonial legislation, whether by ordinance, proclamation, order, or otherwise, made after that date. But exceptionally, in cases to which the parties are "natives" or "Africans," the courts are to "observe" or "be guided by" the rules of native customary law. Native customary law, however, is only applied subject to certain conditions:—

(1) It must be applicable; *i.e.*, the transaction must be one known to customary law, and there must be rules of the particular customary law available for the decision of the dispute.
(2) It must not be repugnant to natural justice, equity, or good conscience. This requirement extends as much to the adjectival as to the substantive law, but in practice it is interpreted liberally.
(3) It must not be incompatible with any legislation for the time being in force in the territory. Customary law may be expressly overridden by statute law (as where customary criminal law is replaced by a penal code); or it may be in principle in conflict with it, and thus impliedly inapplicable.[5]

In many of the British African territories Islamic law is also applied to a greater or less degree, either expressly by statute, or in the guise of native customary law.[6]

A further general difficulty faced by the courts is that of discriminating between custom having the force of law, and that which lacks that force though perhaps having a moral or religious sanction. Although some of the ordinances provide for the administration of "native law and custom," others for "native law," and yet others for "native customary law," it is submitted that the verbal variations are legally insignificant,[7] that a court may only administer customary law, though it may incidentally have regard to custom not having the force of law, *e.g.*, for weighing evidence, for deciding what constitutes provocation, and in assessing what punishment is suitable.

Native Customary Law as a Question of Fact

That, in England, any local custom at variance with the law of the land should be proved by the party alleging it is fair and reasonable; and similar considerations might seem relevant in Africa, since customary law derogates from the general law as applied by the courts. It is true that customary law is in a sense local or personal, since it attaches to a given tribe or the members of that tribe, or to the area within which they are dominant. Nevertheless, as far as the Africans who are members of that tribe are concerned, their customary law is not an occasional variant from the general law applicable to them; it is their general law prima facie applicable in civil and criminal matters. The tests for its application, and the method by which its rules are ascertained, should not be blindly borrowed from the English law relating to local custom. After a period of uncertainty, colonial courts have recognised as much; *e.g.*, the English test of antiquity (that a custom should date from A.D. 1189), which was applied to African customary law in the early Gold Coast case of *Welbeck* v. *Brown*,[8] have since been impliedly abandoned.[9]

If the analogy is not to be made with local custom in England, with what is it to be made? The answer given by some colonial courts is, with foreign law: "As native law is foreign law, it must be proved as any other fact."[10] This dictum of Francis Smith J. overstates the case; customary law is not foreign law, though its rules may be unknown to the judges who have to apply them; nor is the proof of customary law identical with that of other facts. The analogy has, however, a certain force; one may compare the rules that customary law must be specially pleaded by the party alleging or relying on it; that it must be proved by witnesses; that the effect of their evidence is for the judge and not the jury. But the analogy is not complete: there are other methods of ascertaining customary law; and the operation of the second branch of the rule in *Angu* v. *Atta*[11] may take a particular rule of customary law out of the realm of fact, and into the realm of law, of which judicial notice will be taken.

Native Customary Law to be Specially Pleaded

Whilst there does not appear to be express legislation on the point in every territory, customary law, if relied on by a party to a civil case, must usually be specially pleaded. This was laid down in the Gold Coast case (in the West African Court of Appeal) of *Bonsi* v. *Adjena*[12]; but the practice has been specifically provided for in the new Gold Coast[12a] Supreme Court Rules, modelled on the English Supreme Court Rules, which say[13]:

> "In all cases in which the party pleading relies upon a native law or custom, the native law or custom relied upon shall be stated in the pleading with sufficient particulars to show the nature and effect of the native law or custom in question and the geographical area and the tribe or tribes to which it relates."

This admirable provision[14]—which might be copied elsewhere with advantage—may go far to rectify the rather loose way in which, in the past, customary law has been applied, without a sufficient realisation that it may radically vary from tribe to tribe, and that a book or dictum on, say, Fante law is of little or no value for the decision of a case on Ewe law.

Native Customary Law to be Proved by Witnesses; the Rule in Angu v. Atta[15]

Their Lordships of the Privy Council laid it down in this Gold Coast case that—

> "As is the case with all customary law, it has to be proved in the first instance by calling witnesses acquainted with the native customs until the particular customs have, by frequent proof in the courts, become so notorious that the courts will take judicial notice of them."[16]

This dictum was approved in the later Gold Coast case of *Amissah* v. *Krabah*[17]; it has, in addition, been widely followed in other territories.[18]

Who are eligible witnesses to native law and custom? It is generally assumed that the witnesses must be "expert"; and that they should be native Africans. Neither of these requirements are, it is submitted, essential (except where required by ordinance).[19] There are two ways in which the existence of a custom may be proved; by the testimony of witnesses able to testify to actual occasions in the past when such-and-such was done (*i.e.*, they are witnesses of fact); and by the opinions of those with peculiar or special knowledge of the customary law, who state what, in their opinion, the customary law on such-and-such a topic is (they may, of course, at the same time give specific instances of occasions when the custom they allege has been followed). The former course is normally unduly laborious, so that the production of expert witnesses is preferred; but there are occasions when actual events must be investigated (as where there is a dispute about the procedure for the deposition of a chief).

Once one has discarded possible misrepresentation of the law due to the ignorance, bias, or corruption of witnesses, there may be other causes for a variation between the actual customary law and the law as presented by expert witnesses. Two of these are a tendency to idealise the law, to present what it ought to be instead of what it is; and a failure to appreciate that the ancient, traditional law has been modified by subsequent practice, by native court decisions, or by the influence of English ideas.

Although there does not appear to be express provision on the point in most territories, it is submitted, as a matter of principle, that the effect of evidence given as to the existence of a custom is for the judge, and not for a jury or for assessors when sitting with him (though assessors may be required to give their opinion on the testimony).[20] This is by way of analogy with the proof of foreign law in English courts, though not with that of local custom.

The second branch of the rule in *Angu* v. *Atta* lays down that a particular custom may become so notorious by frequent proof in the courts that the courts will take judicial notice of it; this aspect of the law is considered later under the heading of "Judicial Notice."[21]

The Function of Assessors

The law of most territories[22] provides that British courts may summon to their aid chiefs or other persons expert in the customary law to advise them as assessors, *inter alia*, on customary law. This power may extend to civil matters, to criminal proceedings, or to both. Almost universally a judge is empowered to sit with assessors in criminal matters.

The idea of appointing assessors, by whatever name called, to sit with a judge and advise him on questions of fact and custom, was taken from the law of British India.[23] An Indian judge, Bhashyam Ayyangar J., in a Madras case, *King Emperor* v. *Tirumal Reddi*,[24] stated what in his view the functions of an assessor are. He said—

> "... assessors are analogous to expert witnesses and in principle the opinion of an assessor is substantially on the same footing as the opinion evidence of expert witnesses.... Thus it will be seen that provision was made by the legislature for Europeans administering justice in a foreign land and therefore deficient in their knowledge of the customs and habits of the parties and witnesses appearing before them, and also deficient in judging of their demeanour in the witness-box, having the benefit of the opinion of two or more respectable natives of the land as assessors possessing such knowledge and judgment ... the opinion of an assessor given upon the whole case tried before a Court of Session or any portion of such case is, in principle, on the same footing as the opinion evidence of a person specially skilled in foreign law, science or art."

These observations were cited and approved by the Court of Appeal for Eastern Africa in a criminal appeal from Kenya, *R* v. *Mutwiwa*.[25] The question for decision was whether a judge was entitled to take into consideration the opinion, unsupported by evidence, of one of the assessors in regard to the existence of a certain type of native oath. The court answered in the affirmative; but this finding is suspect in the light of the later decision of the Court of Appeal for Eastern Africa in a criminal appeal from Tanganyika, *Ndembera* v. *R.*[26] Accused had killed deceased whilst the latter was arresting him; and the question at issue was whether this arrest was justified by native law and custom (and thus the killing murder), or not. The trial judge held that the arrest was lawful by native law and custom. On this the Appeal Court commented—

"This statement of the law by the learned judge would be unimpeachable if there was evidence on record from which the existence of the custom could be inferred."

But there was no evidence, except the opinions of the assessors.

"Had such evidence been forthcoming, either *pro* or *contra*, or both, the opinions of the assessors would then have been pertinent and could rightly have been acted upon by the learned trial judge."[27]

The court further observed in *R.* v. *Mutwiwa*[28] that the function of assessors in Kenya was essentially the same in criminal and in civil cases. It is submitted, however, that the roles of assessors in criminal and in civil proceedings are not the same, though there is a considerable overlap. The functions of assessors can be collected under two heads—their duty to assess, and their duty to advise. First, assessors may assess or weigh the evidence and whether an accused is guilty or not, in the light of their special knowledge of African habits, customs, modes of thought, and language; they are peculiarly qualified to judge the probability of the story told by a witness, and may detect in his demeanour what may escape the presiding judge. In this role the assessor's task is similar to that of the juror's, though he gives no verdict, but only his opinion, on the evidence. Secondly, the assessors' duty is to advise the judge or magistrates on the matters of which they have special knowledge, and to give their view, in the abstract, of what the custom or law is in the circumstances postulated. The former function is of special importance in criminal, the latter in civil, proceedings. When they act as advisers on African life and customs, the opinion of assessors is not, by itself, admissible evidence of those matters upon which a judge is entitled to rely in reaching a decision.[29] This is a salutary rule, as the party to whom such an opinion is unfavourable has no chance to contest the opinion, or introduce rebutting evidence, or cross-examine the assessors. The assessor is not, therefore, an expert witness in the ordinary sense. It would seem sound practice for the opinion of assessors, on matters of customary law pertinent to the case, to be given publicly, and to be recorded in writing.[30]

Whether the rules suggested here for the use of assessors are, or indeed should be, followed by administrative officers when exercising their appellate or revisionary powers in cases from native courts it is difficult to say. The system of assessors is open to abuse, as where the assessors sitting with a District Commissioner hearing an appeal from a native court are members of the native court which originally tried the case. It is noteworthy that the institution has been criticised in its country of origin, India, and that legislation has been recently introduced abolishing it.

Referees

Provision is made in a few territories for the reference of points of customary law to referees, who will be chiefs or other persons with special knowledge of customary law, or bodies with similar knowledge.[31] The referees have similar functions to the "assessors" we have been considering above, but their opinion on customary law is evidence thereof (unlike that of assessors), and that evidence is presumed correct, though the presumption can presumably be displaced by evidence to the contrary. If the presumption is irrebuttable, then the referees' statements of customary law are statements of law, and not evidence of fact at all. The latter interpretation of the similar provision in the Gold Coast Colony Supreme Court Ordinance, 1876, seems to have been assumed as the right one by Gold Coast judges; *e.g.*, in the old case of *Toku* v. *Ama*.[32]

The Gold Coast Colony courts used to, at an early period, ascertain the relevant customary law by writing a letter to a local "king" or chief, in which they requested the chief to give his opinion on the case stated (the identity of the parties being theoretically concealed). We find the Supreme Court at a later date referring a question of customary law to a native authority (*e.g.*, to the Ga State Council in the case of *Sackeyfio* v. *Tagoe*[33]).

By section 89 of the present Gold Coast Courts Ordinance,[34] the Supreme Court or a magistrate's court may, in a civil cause or matter, refer a question as to the rights of any native under native law and custom to a competent Native Court for determination. No appeal lies from the Native Court's decision on the issue; but the court seised of the case may adopt the Native Court's finding in whole or in part, or reject it *in toto*.[35,36]

Textbooks

Customary law may be proved as a fact by documentary, as well as by oral, evidence, where books or manuscripts purporting to describe native law and custom are admissible in evidence.[37] If the statements of customary law are treated as binding or conclusive, then the book is an authority, and the customary law is administered as law (*e.g.*, in the Gold Coast); whilst if the statements are only evidence of what the customary law is (as in Uganda and elsewhere), then that law is ascertained as fact.

The first point is that it is possible to have a legal textbook dealing with customary law, despite the fact that customary law must generally be proved by witnesses, and despite the observation of Verity C.J. in the Nigerian case of *Adedibu* v. *Adewoyin*,[38] where he said, in regard to a work dealing with native land tenure which was relied on by the trial judge:

> "The learned judge appears to have referred to it as though it were a legal textbook of such authority as would warrant its citation to the court, which it certainly is not, for native law and custom is a matter of evidence and not of law."

In the Gold Coast the British courts are specifically empowered to "give effect to any book or manuscript recognised in the Gold Coast as a legal authority"[39]; in fact Sarbah's *Fanti Customary Laws* has been very frequently cited to the Gold Coast courts (even as an authority for non-Fante custom). In the courts of the Union of South Africa and the High Commission Territories such legal textbooks as that by Whitfield on *South African Native Law* are constantly referred to. To be a work of legal authority it would seem, at first sight, that the author should possess professional legal qualifications, and that the approach, arrangement and scholarship should be those of standard English legal textbooks. A treatise by an anthropologist or administrator would thus, prima facie, not come within this category. It is all the more remarkable that a work by a well-known anthropologist, I. Schapera, *viz.* his *Handbook of Tswana Law and Custom* (the Tswana being the eponymous people of Bechuanaland), should be frequently cited and followed in the courts of the Union. In the Uganda case of *Njirwa* v. *Kagang'ama*[40] a similar compliment was paid to a work by a deceased anthropologist, Roscoe, on *The Banyankole*. The question was whether, by the customary law of Ankole, an African was entitled to make a will. The learned judge referred to Roscoe's old treatise, which says (at p. 144) that a man may nominate the successor to his estate, and applied this statement of the law to the present case (which in fact dealt with a rather different question, whether a man might bequeath *part* of his property away from his general heir).

In the already cited Nigerian case of *Adedibu* v. *Adewoyin*[41] the court came down on the other side. The dispute concerned the appointment by Yoruba customary law of the *Mogaji* of a House (*i.e.*, the head of a lineage or family). Conflicting evidence on the traditional custom in the matter had been adduced by each side in support of rival claimants to the position. The learned trial judge, in his judgment, had also referred to a published work by Ward Price, *Memorandum on Land Tenure in the Yoruba Provinces*, the author being an administrative officer who had carried out an intensive investigation of the customary law. On appeal to the West African Court of Appeal, one ground of appeal was that the court of first instance had erred in basing its judgment on this *Memorandum*.

Verity C.J., delivering the judgment of the W.A.C.A., said[42]—

". . . It is well established that native law and custom is a question of evidence. It is only in so far as this case is based upon such law and custom that Mr. Ward Price's Memorandum is relevant. By section 38 of the Evidence Ordinance, c. 63, it is provided that:

'In deciding questions of native law and custom the opinions of native chiefs or other persons having special knowledge of native law and custom and any book or manuscript recognised by natives as a legal authority are relevant.'

In my view this involves two postulates, firstly that the Memorandum must form part of the evidence in the case, and secondly that it must be shown that it is a book or manuscript recognised by natives as a legal authority. In the present case it does not appear to have been tendered in evidence. The learned judge appears to have referred to it as though it were a legal textbook of such authority as would warrant its citation to the court, which it certainly is not, for native law and custom is a matter of evidence and not of law. Moreover, whatever may be the respect due to the result of the writer's researches, they are only relevant as evidence if shown to be recognised by natives as a legal authority, which again was not done in the present case. The learned judge makes reference to an earlier case in which he states that this Memorandum was relied on by both parties, from which he assumes that it is regarded as a legal authority. I do not think this necessarily follows, but in any event, the question is, as I have said, a matter of evidence and therefore a matter of legal proof and not a matter to be assumed. In my view, therefore, the learned judge erred in so far as he based his conclusions upon this document, which was not properly before him as part of the evidence in this case."

Judicial Decisions

How far are judicial decisions evidence of African customary law, as opposed to precedents which establish customary law as law?

Cases involving customary law rarely reach the British courts originally, but only by way of appeal or revision,[43] since Africans are normally required to commence proceedings in the lowest competent court, to wit, a native court. It follows that disputes between Africans have already been adjudicated on by a court which treats customary law as a matter of law, not of fact or evidence, before they reach a British court. How is the appellate court to classify a finding of customary law by a native court of first instance or a native appeal court? On the theory that customary law is a question of fact in a British court, the native court's finding of customary law should be treated by the appellate court as if it were a finding of fact. An appeal court can freely consider and reject a finding of law in the court below; but there is a presumption that a finding of fact by a court which has heard the witnesses or which is peculiarly qualified to judge of the existence or nature of facts is correct. On this argument we should expect to find that appeal courts were reluctant to contest statements of customary law in the native court of first instance. Such indeed is the case: the principle was vigorously asserted in the Uganda case of *Kigizi* v. *Lukiko of Buganda*,[44] where the defendant had been prosecuted before the Principal Native Court of Buganda by the Buganda native government for an alleged offence against Buganda customary law, *viz*., marrying the mother of the Kabaka (or ruler) of Buganda. The learned judge of the High Court (to which the case had come on appeal, by way of the Judicial Adviser, from the Buganda court), after remarking that proof of custom is different in native courts and British courts, went on to hold[45]—

". . . generally speaking, where a Native Court has held that a certain act is contrary to custom an appellate court should I think be reluctant to hold otherwise except upon very substantial grounds and should, unless it be repugnant to natural justice, give effect to the custom in its judgment, provided of course that it agrees with the Native Court's finding as to custom."

The learned judge, on the point whether the native court's finding that the act was contrary to customary penal law was justified, held in effect that this must be left in the hands of the native court, which was the best judge of whether it was a crime against the State and the whole community meriting criminal punishment.

With all respect, this is hardly a satisfactory position; it is vital that criminal law should be certain, and this applies to customary criminal law as much as to any other. Where the question before a native court is not whether the defendant committed the offence alleged, but rather whether the act or omission constitutes an offence by customary law at all, an appeal court should be specially vigilant on behalf of accused, and should not lightly surrender the decision to the court of first instance. A Nyasaland case, *Limbani* v. *R.*[46] is relevant here. This was a criminal appeal before Jenkins C.J., the accused having been found guilty of adultery by a native court, the native court holding adultery to be a criminal offence by customary law. The learned judge refused to accept this finding (despite previous decisions of the native court the same way) on the ground that inquiry showed that the native law and custom prevalent in the district in question did not recognise adultery as an offence, and that native court decisions alone could not make it so.

The principle under discussion applies to civil, as well as to criminal, law; and to modified, as well as to ancient or original, native custom. That is the effect of the Uganda case of *Kajubi* v. *Kabali*,[47] before the Court of Appeal for Eastern Africa, which involved the Buganda customary law of succession. The Lukiko court of Buganda had applied a modified customary law; Gray C.J., delivering the judgment of the E.A.C.A., accepted the Lukiko court's statement of customary law, and said that there would have to be "very strong and cogent reasons" before the statement could be held wrong in an appeal court. But the presumption in favour of a native court's finding of customary law is not so strong where it is a question of modified, and not original, native custom; as the Judicial Committee observed in the Nigerian appeal of *Eleko* v. *Government of Nigeria*[48]:

". . . the more barbarous customs of earlier days [*e.g.*, to kill, and not to banish a deposed chief] may under the influence of civilisation become milder without losing their essential character of custom. It would, however, appear to be necessary to show that in their milder form they are still recognised in the native community as custom, so as in that form to regulate the relations of the native community *inter se*. In other words, *the court cannot itself transform a barbarous custom into a milder one.*[49] If it still stands in its barbarous character it must be rejected as repugnant to "natural justice, equity and good conscience." It is the assent of the native community that gives a custom its validity, and, therefore, barbarous or mild, it must be shown to be recognised by the native community whose conduct it is supposed to regulate."

Gray C.J., in *Kajubi* v. *Kabali*,[47] held that the principle expressed in *Eleko* v. *Government of Nigeria*[48] applied equally to customs in Buganda, if for "barbarous" we substitute "original," and for "milder,' "modified." He said[50]:

> "The native community may assent to some modification of an original custom, but the modification must be made with the assent of the native community. It cannot be made by an individual or a number of individuals. Least of all can it be made by a court of law."

The reluctance of the appeal courts to disturb a native court's finding of customary law, and the fact that they treat such a finding as one of fact, may, when taken with the Privy Council's settled practice regarding concurrent findings of fact, lead to an unsatisfactory situation where the customary law is not fully canvassed and examined except in the original court. The attitude of the Judicial Committee is clearly brought out in the Nigerian appeal of *Ometa* v. *Numa*,[51] where their Lordships observed—

> "The question was ... entirely a question of fact and a question depending upon the knowledge of tribal tenures and of the habits and customs of native people in relation to dealings with land. It was decided by both courts in favour of the defendants, and it appears to be a case peculiarly within the principle of the rule that their Lordships have laid down themselves, that as a general rule they will not interfere with concurrent finding of fact in cases of this description."[52]

The Privy Council rule about concurrent findings of fact may have very good reasons behind it; but it also has a certain attraction to courts below the Judicial Committee, and there is a risk that some appeal courts (especially territorial Supreme Courts and regional Courts of Appeal) may adopt a similar rule in cases which may already have been before two or three courts successively. In this way the development of customary law as law might be seriously impeded.

What is the effect of a previous final judgment *inter partes* on the same or similar cause of action, or where a rule of customary law was proved in evidence, or was relied on by the court in arriving at its decision? First, as between the parties and their privies, the decision operates as an estoppel *per rem judicatam* (if so pleaded) and debars the parties from re-litigating, in later proceedings, the same cause of action, and from contesting the rules of customary law which formed the ground or part of the ground for the earlier decision.[53] Where a rule of customary law was proved or asserted by a party in the earlier proceedings, but it did not form part of the *ratio decidendi*, then that rule does not bind him in subsequent proceedings as law, though he may be estopped from later denying it. To summarise, previous decisions *inter partes* may either conclusively declare the law binding between the parties or may be admissible as evidence of that law.

Decisions Between Strangers

These, by virtue of being *res inter alios acta*, cannot be conclusive of the law binding on persons not party to the decision, unless they are judgments *in rem*, or enable later courts to take judicial notice of the customary law as found.[54] But such decisions are admissible as evidence of custom in the terms of the Indian Evidence Act, 1872, s. 13, and by the English law relating to local custom, it being a matter of public and general interest what the rules of customary law are.

Native Customary Law as a Question of Law

The ascertainment of customary law as if it were a matter of fact or of foreign law, to be proved by evidence, has many practical disadvantages; it may work injustice between the parties, and it is juristically inelegant. In the early, formative stage of customary law as applied by the courts, the proof of customary law as fact may be an inescapable necessity; but the goal must be to place customary law on an equality with the rest of the body of law that the courts are empowered to administer, *i.e.*, apt to be judicially noticed as part of the law of the land. The doctrine of judicial notice as expounded in the second branch of the rule in *Angu v. Atta*[55] serves progressively to incorporate the rules of customary law in the fabric of the law of the land; but the progress is slow. This has led legislators, administrators and others concerned with the development of African law to examine other means. Codification has a superficial attraction as the ready answer to the problem; but the modern view, in the light of experience with the Natal Code, shies away from codes in favour of manuals or records which shall be guides rather than authorities. A similar method of making the law accessible is through declarations by native authorities; but where the power has been given by statute it has rarely been used. If customary law is truly law, a single decision of a court would be a precedent of binding or persuasive authority for the future; but the method of case-law has been little used, except in the native courts. Legal textbooks, too, might be accepted as works of authority; but these are generally still to be written. A further complication is this, that when customary law is administered as law by virtue of its having been judicially noticed, laid down in a binding precedent, codified, declared, or stated in a work of authority, the basis of its application alters. The binding force of custom ultimately rests on the fact that it is habitually obeyed by those subject to it; if not fortified by established usage it is not law. But once custom has been codified or settled by judicial decision, its binding force depends on the statute or the doctrine of precedent; in short, it ceases to be customary law. A divergence is therefore not merely possible but likely between the law as administered by the courts and that followed by the public. The doctrine of judicial notice and the doctrine of precedent do not appear to be flexible enough to meet this divergence, in the absence of statutory provision or other direction to the contrary. Africa social, political and economic life are altering rapidly and radically, which makes the question of modification in customary law one of great importance. Old customs disappear or are modified; new ones appear to deal with new situations. The Gold Coast Native Courts (Colony) Ordinance,[56] s.2, defines "native customary law" as "a rule or a body of rules ... which obtains and is fortified by established native usage ... ," so that, in the Southern Gold Coast at any rate, usage triumphs over judicial recognition; and it is submitted that, even where a custom has been judicially recognized, it is open to a party to show that it is no longer supported by established usage. But this Gold Coast provision is not found elsewhere.[57] The dictum of the Privy Council in *Eleko* v. *Government of Nigeria*[58]—"It is the assent of the native community that gives a custom its validity"—means (1) that when an "original" or "barbarous" custom ceases to be recognised by the native community it loses the force of law; (2) that a court, whether British or native, cannot itself modify a custom; (3) that when a modified custom is alleged, then it must be shown to be recognised in its modified form by the native community whose conduct it is supposed to regulate. But the dictum does not cover the case where a custom has been judicially noticed, but it is alleged that the custom as observed has altered from the custom as noticed. If the possibility of varying by oral evidence a custom which has been judicially noticed is allowed, then there is an end to the certainty which the judicial recognition of a custom is designed to achieve.

Judicial Notice

The power of colonial courts to take judicial notice of customary law was expressly stated in the second branch of the rule in *Angu* v. *Atta*,[59] the first branch of which—requiring the proof of customary law as a fact—has already been considered.[60] The rule says that customary law must be proved in the first instance by calling witnesses "until the particular customs have, by frequent proof in the courts, become so notorious that the courts will take judicial notice of them."

The Judicial Committee, when approving this rule in the later case of *Amissah* v. *Krabah*,[61] observed—

"Their Lordships have not been informed of any customary law so established [by judicial notice]; and they may observe that it would be very convenient if the courts in West Africa in suitable cases would rule as to the native customs of which they think it proper to take judicial notice, specifying, of course, the tribes (or districts) concerned and taking steps to see that these rulings are reported in a readily accessible form."[62]

To what extent may a judge or magistrate in a court in Africa rely on his own actual or presumed knowledge of customary law, and dispense with proof by other means? It is submitted, first of all, that a judge is not entitled to rely on his own personal knowledge of a rule of customary law, if unsupported by oral testimony or other proof.[63] A judge, if he wishes to rely on his personal knowledge of custom, may follow the English practice and himself be sworn and give his information as evidence; but the better course is for him to call evidence himself, or suggest to the parties that they should do so, in support of his personal view. A judge may also rely on his own knowledge where his knowledge is generally shared (*i.e.*, the fact is notorious), and where the rule has been judicially recognised. These aspects are considered below.[64]

In the law of England the doctrine of judicial notice, that a court shall notice, without further evidence, things which are or are deemed to be notorious, covers, it is submitted, two main categories: matters of law and matters of fact. Facts which are matters of general or common knowledge—the usual course of nature, what animals are domesticated— are judicially noticed as a matter of convenience, because it would be absurd and time-consuming to have formal proof of them; the basis of this rule is the notoriety of the facts concerned. But when a court is required to take judicial notice of matters of law, which are deemed to be within the knowledge of the court, the doctrine rests on a different principle; the notoriety of the law is irrelevant. Now in taking judicial notice of African customary law the two aspects of the doctrine are sometimes confused, *i.e.*, it is not clear whether any given rule of customary law is noticed because it is a notorious fact, or because it has previously been recognised by a competent court and is now a rule of law. Both the dictum in *Angu* v. *Atta*[65] and the Nigerian Evidence Ordinance[66] appear to support the former interpretation. The analogy with foreign law breaks down at this point, since foreign law cannot be judicially noticed. It is submitted that the misleading principle that native law is foreign law, to be proved as a fact, is at fault here, since it is based on what Vaihinger[67] would call an "analogical fiction"; *i.e.*, customary law is treated *as though* it were foreign law for purposes of proof or ascertainment. Once so ascertained it applies as law. Hence if a rule of customary law is judicially noticed it should be noticed as law, and not as notorious fact, and the analogy with foreign law should be disregarded.

The rule in *Angu* v. *Atta*[68] appears to have been borrowed from the law of England relating to the proof of usage in trades and professions so as to vary the existing terms of, or annex implied terms to, a contract. Now the principle upon which usage is admitted is essentially that it is notorious, and that it is thereby to form an implied term in a contract of the type affected by it. But customary law is not an implied term or series of implied terms; it applies whether a particular person was aware of its existence, or had turned his attention to its existence, or not. If customary law need not be notorious amongst those subject to it, the rule in *Angu* v. *Atta*[68] must be differently interpreted from the similar English rule. "Notorious," in relation to African law, means—it is submitted—notorious to the judges or courts concerned with its administration. At the same time matters of common or general knowledge can be judicially noticed as notorious fact—judges have a wide discretion in what they thus admit; so the habits, manners or customs of the Africans can be judicially noticed. A distinction must thus be made between customs or habits, which can be noticed as notorious fact, and customary law, which can be noticed as law.

Case-law[69]

If native customary law were strictly a question of fact, then—as with foreign law—previous decisions on a point of customary law would be no precedent in subsequent cases. In practice, however, previous decisions are relied on as expository of the law; courts are encouraged in this practice by the dictum in *Angu* v. *Atta*.[70] Judicial decisions have, in England, been a major factor in legal development; their scope in Africa—at least for the development of African law—is much more limited, since the superior courts of several territories have no jurisdiction, original or appellate, in suits based on customary law, and the reporting of decided cases in those other territories where customary law is administered in the superior courts is generally inadequate. No clear doctrine has emerged regarding the effect of previous judicial decisions on customary law. Where these are treated as authority (binding where a custom has been previously judicially noticed in terms of the rule in *Angu v. Atta*,[70] otherwise persuasive), problems may arise over the relative status of decision and usage.[71]

It is in the magistrates' courts (usually constituted by administrative officers) hearing appeals from native courts that the question of precedent is most likely to arise. Such courts will tend to follow the rulings of superior courts on customary law, whether judicially noticed or not; and they will also tend to follow their own previous decisions, though perhaps they are not bound to do so.

Legislation

An apparently attractive solution to the problem of the ascertainment of customary law is that of a written code; after all, the customary law of the Punjab was successfully recorded in writing.[72] Such a code might be enacted by the central legislature, or it might be the result of local legislation.

The only attempt to codify customary law from the centre has been made in Natal. The Natal Code of Native Law, originally compiled and issued in 1875–1878 and 1891 respectively, was revised in 1932.[73] Although that was the intention, in the nature of things the Code could not be made comprehensive and exclusive; there remain parts of the customary law which have not been codified, and these are to be proved to the satisfaction of the court, in the usual way, by evidence. Parties can adduce evidence tending to supplement, but not to oust or contradict, the provisions of the Code. Modern opinion is against codification of customary law, in that it would freeze the law at one state of its development, and would tend to inhibit future change at the hands of the courts, native and British. Natal's initiative has thus not been imitated.[74]

Central legislation may also have an incidental effect on customary law, by abolishing, limiting, or modifying its rules. For example, Native Courts Ordinances prescribe how customary law is to be administered, and may expressly restrict its application through "repugnancy–clauses." In some territories much of the customary criminal law has thus ceased to apply.

Local legislation, *i.e.*, by native or local authorities, may also be a source of customary law; directly, where customary law is declared or modified; indirectly, where local rules, orders and by-laws restrict its operation. The law of many territories contains provisions which enable native authorities to declare, in prescribed form, any part of the customary law applicable in their areas.[75] The power has been sparingly used. The Basuto *Laws of Lerotholi*[76] are, in their 1946 form, mainly a collection of rules and orders unconnected with customary law; the first part, the Declaration of Basuto Law and Custom, is the product of the Basutoland National Council. The Council in fact lacks legal power to make an enforceable declaration of custom; nevertheless, the *Laws of Lerotholi* are reported to be unhesitatingly followed in the Basuto Native Courts, and even to be treated as of some authority in the High Court of Basutoland. This Declaration is not, however, a complete or ordered statement of Basuto customary law. H. Cory's statement of Sukuma Law[77] is in effect a declaration by the native authorities in Sukumaland of their customary law, although not made in pursuance of any statutory power.

Native authorities are also permitted in many territories to modify their customary law by declaration or resolution.[78] This power has also been sparingly used. Declarations and modifications of customary law generally have the force of law in the native courts of the area in question, and are admissible as evidence of that law. Some competent students of the law in Africa look to such declarations and modifications of customary law as the best way in which the present law can be made available, and in which it can be modified to suit future developments.

Again, local legislation by means of rules, orders and by-laws often has the effect of varying customary law. The Ashanti Confederacy Council, for instance, at various times made rules regulating the payment of adultery fees, the cultivation of cocoa farms, repayments on divorce, etc.[79]

Envoi

This paper seeks merely to describe the *machinery* for the ascertainment of customary law; space does not permit examination of how the machinery works in practice. Nor has anything been said about the ascertainment of customary law in the native courts, which was not, but which is and will be, a problem to be tackled. Since it is practice that breathes life into the law, a complementary paper that would deal with these aspects of the subject is urgently needed, if a full picture is to be given. Deficiencies in the ascertainment and administration of customary law revealed by reported cases emphasise the need for such an examination.

Notes

1. *Viz., the r*egional courts of appeal (for East and West Africa); the Supreme or High Courts of the different territories.

2. Constituted by professional magistrates (District or Resident Magistrates), or by administrative officers in their magisterial capacity.

3. See J. Lewin, "The Recognition of Native Law and Custom in British Africa," (1938) 20 J. Comp. Leg. (3rd ser.) 16; see also a note on "Methods of Recording Native Customary Law," (1950) I J. African Admin. 130; and (for the Punjab) Rattigan, *Digest of Civil Law for the Punjab, etc.* (13th ed.), 1953, 148 *et seq.*

4. Except in the High Commission Territories.

5. For which see my "The Extent of the Operation of Native Customary Law: Applicability and Repugnancy," (1950) 2 J. African Admin. 4, and references therein.

6. For which see J. N. D. Anderson, *Islamic Law in Africa*, 1954.

7. *Cf. Ayoola & ors.* v. *Foluwiya & ors.* (1942) 8 W.A.C.A. 39 (Nigeria), on the construction of "Mohammedan Law or Custom."

8. (1882) Sarbah F.C.L. 185 (Gold Coast).

9. See *Mensah* v. *Wiaboe* (1925) D. Ct. 1921–1925, 172 (Gold Coast).

10. *Hughes* v. *Davies* (1909) Renner 550, at 551 (Gold Coast).

11. (1916) Gold Coast Privy Council Judgments, 1874–1928, 43, 44 (P.C.): "particular customs" may "by frequent proof in the courts, become so notorious that the courts will take judicial notice of them."

12. (1940) 6 W.A.C.A. 241.

12a. To avoid confusion, "Gold Coast" is used throughout this paper to include "Ghana," where appropriate.

13. Supreme Court (Civil Procedure) Rules, Ord. 19, r. 31; made under s. 107 of the Courts Ordinance, c. 4, Laws of the Gold Coast, 1951 Revision.

14. But it is inapplicable to trials without written pleadings, as many civil proceedings by illiterate parties unassisted by counsel before the subordinate courts may be.

15. (1916) Gold Coast Privy Council Judgments, 1874–1928, 43.

16. At p. 44

17. (1936) 2 W.A.C.A. 30, at p. 31 (P.C.).

18. Uganda: see *Kigizi* v. *Lukiko of Buganda* (1943) 6 Ug.L.R. 113, at p. 117. and the Evidence Ordinance, c. 9 s. 46.

Sierra Leone: see *Macauley* v. *Bungay* (No. 1) (1930) 2 S.L. Law Recorder 28 (W.A.C.A.).

Nigeria: the Evidence Ordinance, c. 63, s. 14, adopts the principles of the rule in *Angu* v. *Atta*; and see also ss. 56 (1) and 58.

Nyasaland: see *Mwase and the Blackman's Church of God which is in Tongaland* v. *Church of Central Africa, Sanga Division* (1935) 4 Ny.L.R. 45, and *Mwale* v. *Kaliu* (1950) Ny.L.R. 169, at p. 171.

Northern Rhodesia: see *R. v Mporokoso* (1939) N.R.L.R. 1938–1942, 152, at p. 154.

For East Africa generally, *cf.* *Ndembera* v. *R.* (1947) 14 E.A.C.A. 85; and see also the Indian Evidence Act, 1872, ss. 45 and 48; the I.E.A. is in force in Kenya, Tanganyika and British Somaliland.

19. *Cf.* the mention, in *Angu* v. *Atta,* of "witnesses acquainted with native customs," and the wording, *e.g.,* of the Uganda Evidence Ordinance, s. 46, and of the Northern Rhodesia High Court Ordinance, s. 63.

20. *Cf.* the Nigerian Supreme Court Ordinance, s. 19, and Sierra Leone Courts Ordinance, s. 18.

21. See pp. 258 *et seq.*

22. *Cf.* Sierra Leone Courts Ordinance, s. 18; Gold Coast Courts Ordinance, s. 87 (2); Uganda Civil Procedure Code, s. 91 (1); Kenya Civil Procedure Code, s. 87 (1), Criminal Procedure Code, s. 258. Tanganyika and Northern Rhodesia have similar provisions, and see also Tanganyika Subordinate Courts Ordinance, s. 11, and Local Courts Ordinance, s. 38 (4) (*a*).

23. But India only had assessors in criminal cases.

24. (1901) I.L.R. 24 Mad. 523.

25. (1935) 2 E.A.C.A. 66.

26. (1947) 14 E.A.C.A. 85.

27. At p. 86.

28. (1935) 2 E.A.C.A. 66.

29. *Ndembera* v. *R.* (1947) 14 E.A.C.A. 85; *Mwale* v. *Kaliu* (1950) 6 Ny.L.R. 169; *R.* v. *Mporokoso* (1939) N.Rhod.L.R. 1938–1942, 152; Nigerian Evidence Ordinance, c. 63, s. 14.

30. See *Dhalamini* v. *R.* [1943] 1 All E.R. 463 (P.C., Swaziland); and also *Kwanin* v. *Ewuah* (1955) P.C. Appeal No. 6 of 1954 (Gold Coast).

31. *Cf.* the Nyasaland High Court Ordinance, s. 16.

32. (1890) Sarbah, Fanti L.R. 58; the dangers of this view are obvious.

33. (1945) 11 W.A.C.A. 73.

34. c. 4.

35. *Quaere* whether the power of the court (under Gold Coast R.S.C., Ord. 37A) to appoint an independent expert as "Court Expert" applies where the question for an expert witness is one of native law or custom.

36. And *cf.* Somaliland Indian Evidence Act (Modification) Ordinance, c. 14. s. 2.

37. *Cf.* Uganda Evidence Ordinance, s. 58, which is identical in wording with the Indian Evidence Act, 1872, s. 60 (in force in Kenya, Tanganyika and British Somaliland); Nigerian Evidence Ordinance, s. 38; Gold Coast Courts Ordinance, s. 87 (2). For the Indian Riwaji-i-am (or public record of village and tribal customs) see Mayne, *Hindu Law and Usage,* 11th ed., 62.

38. (1951) 13 W.A.C.A. 191, at p. 192.

39. Courts Ordinance, s. 87 (2).

40. (1935) 4 Ug.L.R. 146.

41. 13 W.A.C.A. 191, at p. 192.

42. At p. 192.

43. Except where the proceedings concern a claim or charge based on English law, or there is a "mixed transaction" (involving both English and African law), or where the dispute is between a native African and a non-native, or where

natural justice, the absence of a competent native court, or the difficulty of or the amount at stake in the case, require or indicate that trial should not be in a native court.

44. (1943) 6 Ug.L.R. 113.
45. At p. 116.
46. (1946) 6 Ny.L.R. 6.
47. (1944) 11 E.A.C.A. 34.
48. [1931] A.C. 662, at p. 673.
49. My italics.
50. At p. 37.
51. 11 N.L.R. 18 (P.C.).
52. See also the Gold Coast appeal, *Ameyaw III* v. *Safo* (1947) P.C. Appeal No. 66 of 1945 and the very recent Nigerian appeal. *Chief Joseph Wobo* v. *Att. Gen., Federation of Nigeria* (1956) P.C. Appeal No. 18 of 1953, unreported.
53. The earlier decision is also relevant by the terms of the Indian Evidence Act, 1872, s. 13.
54. See below at pp. 309 *et seq.*
55. (1916) Gold Coast Privy Council Judgments, 1874–1928, 43 (P.C.).
56. c. 98.
57. Commissions on native courts in Nigeria and Sierra Leone have recommended its adoption in those territories.
58. [1931] A.C. 662, at p. 673. The dictum applied in the cases of *Limbani* v. *R.* (1946) 6 Ny.L.R. 8 and *Kajubi* v. *Kabali* (1944) 11 E.A.C.A. 34 (Uganda).
59. (1916) Gold Coast Privy Council Judgments, 1874–1928, 43.
60. See above, at pp. 299 *et seq.*
61. (1936) 2 W.A.C.A. 30, at p. 31 (Gold Coast).
62. The Board's observation is an interesting one, which has not, however, been expressly acted upon. Presumably a court could only rule on a custom as worthy of judicial notice if that custom were material to the decision of a case before it.
63. *Cf. Ndembera* v. *R.* (1947) 14 E.A.C.A. 85, at p. 86 (Tanganyika); and see also *Mwale* v. *Kaliu* (1950) 6 Ny.L.R. 169.
64. A further point to be borne in mind is that frequently an administrative officer is called on to deal with a case involving customary law by way of revision of a native court's decision, and not by way of appeal. Normally revision takes place without any of the formal procedure appropriate to the hearing of an appeal, and the power to review may be exercised by the officer in his executive, and not in his magisterial, capacity. In these circumstances the officer will not be inhibited from relying on his personal knowledge of customary law.
65. (1916) Gold Coast Privy Council Judgments, 1874–1928, 43, 44; see especially the words" . . . until the particular customs have, by frequent proof in the courts, become so notorious that the courts will take judicial notice of them."
66. c. 63, s. 14 (2): "A custom may be judicially noticed by the court if it has been acted upon by a court of superior or co-ordinate jurisdiction in the same area to an extent which justifies the court asked to apply it in assuming

that the persons or the class of persons concerned in that area look upon the same as binding in relation to circumstances similar to those under consideration."

67. In his *The Philosophy of "As If."*

68. (1916) Gold Coast Privy Council Judgments, 1874–1928, 43, 44.

69. See T. O. Elias, "Colonial Courts and the Doctrine of Judicial Precedent (1955) 18 M.L.R. 356.

70. (1916) Gold Coast Privy Council Judgments, 1874–1928, 43, 44.

71. See above at pp. 308 *et seq.*

72. By Sir W. Rattigan, *op. cit.*; his work, though lacking the force of a code, has great authority.

73. See Stafford and Franklin, *Principles of Native Law and the Natal Code*, 1950.

74. But see R. J. H. Pogucki, "A Note on the Codification of Customary Land Law in the Gold Coast" (1956) 8 J. African Administration 192.

75. *e.g.*, Ashanti, Gold Coast: Native Law and Custom (Ashanti Confederacy Council) Ordinance, c. 102.

76. Originally compiled in 1903, published in 1922, and re-issued in revised form in 1946.

77. In his *Sukuma Law and Custom*, 1953, the materials for which were collected and formulated in close collaboration with the various native authorities in Sukumaland, Tanganyika.

78. *e.g.*, Sierra Leone Protectorate Ordinance, c. 185, s. 5 (7): ". . . it shall be lawful for a District Council, with the approval of the Governor in Council, to make rules altering or modifying native customary law in the District and all Native Courts in the said District shall take cognisance of all rules so made."

79. For which see J. N. Matson, *Digest of the Minutes of the Ashanti Confederacy Council*, etc., 1951.

T.O. ELIAS

The Problem of Reducing Customary Laws to Writing

Dr. Taslim Olawale Elias is a prime example of an African specialist in folk law who was trained in the British system. He received his doctorate from the University of London in 1949. His dissertation "Land Law and Custom in Nigeria" was published by Routledge and Kegan Paul in 1951. His important work, The Nature of African Customary Law, *was published in 1955 and in 1960, he accepted the invitation to become the first Attorney-General of an independent Federation of Nigeria. In 1966, he received a chair of law at the University of Lagos. He also served on the International Court of Justice from 1976 until his death in 1991. In the following essay, he shares his great expertise in African folk law with special reference to the task of recording such law accurately.*

There is a considerable literature devoted to the study of folk law in Nigeria. Representative are B.O. Achimu, "Wanted: A Valid Criterion of Validity for Customary Law," Nigerian Law Journal, *10 (1976), 35–55; Chukwuemeka Ebo, Indigenous Law and Justice: Some Major Concepts and Practices,"* Vierteljahresberichte *Nr. 76 (1979), 139–150; J. Olabosipo Ani Falaye, "Judicial Development of Customary Law in Nigeria,"* Journal of Legal History, *9 (1988), 40–49; and Derek Asiedu-Akrofi, "Judicial Recognition and Adoption of Customary Law in Nigeria,"* The American Journal of Comparative Law, *37 (1989), 571–593.*

For more of Elias's writings on folk law, see Oluremi Jegede, A Bibliography of the Writings of the Hon. Judge T.O. Elias *(Lagos: The Nigerian Institute of Advanced Legal Studies, 1979), 54 pp.*

The age-old problem of customary law has been one of ensuring its certainty. It was, for example, the demand for certainty that led to the Assyrian Code of Hammurabi in ancient times, to the Greek Codes of

---

Reprinted from *British Legal Papers presented to the Fifth International Congress of Comparative Law, Palace of Justice, Brussels, 4th–9th August, 1958* (London: Stevens & Sons, 1958), pp. 57–69. Permission granted on behalf of the Executors of the Estate of Judge T.O. Elias.

Draco and of Solon in the 7th century B.C., to the Roman Law of the Twelve Tables in the 5th century B.C., Justinian's Code in the 6th century A.D., and to the French Code Napoleon of the early 19th century. Whereas none of these except the last can truly be described as a code in the modern sense, each represents an imperfect attempt at, and a divergent approach to, the reduction of the respective customary laws to writing. We need not dilate here upon the peculiar historical circumstances that combined in each case to produce the particular form adopted in reducing the relevant customary law to writing.

If modern Continental European law is largely to be found in codes, English law remains in essence "the common custom of the realm," and this is as true, by and large, of the American as it is of the Scandinavian laws. In these "common law" systems, the residuary body of law is still customary, even though heavily eaten into by statute law adapting it to the ever-changing social and economic needs of the community. Codifying legislative enactments are as much a feature of the landscape as are the judges' decisions in which aspects of the customary law are from time to time enshrined. Which of these two major approaches should modern customary law follow?

Although it has been powerfully argued, as for example by Jerome Frank in "Law and the Modern Mind" and by Karl Llewellyn in "Bramble Bush," that uncertainty characterises all systems based on judge-made law, i.e., on the doctrine of Judicial Precedent, it has nevertheless yet to be shown that certainty is an outstanding virtue of the code system. Judicial interpretation of the necessarily often cryptic provisions of a code is probably more open to the judges' "hunches" than is judicial reasoning involved in the case-law method.

It has also been claimed that, besides certainty, codification promotes the unification of divergent bodies of customary law within the same territory, by laying down uniform provisions for all its inhabitants without regard to ethnic and other distinctions. That this claim is not well-founded will, it is hoped, be made abundantly clear in the account that follows.

Importance:

Because of the uncodified nature of customary law uncertainty and confusion are bound to arise, particularly as what used to be a compact and homogeneous community, with a largely subsistence economy, becomes increasingly diverse and heterogeneous. Formerly self-contained human groups based on the lineage or the family have often changed into highly complex aggregations whose unifying force is now *territorial*

The Problem of Reducing Customary Laws to Writing

rather than *ethnic*. The resulting conjunction of two or more bodies of customary law within the same political framework raises problems of conflicts of laws of a nature and character hardly covered as yet by existing Western doctrines and concepts. In such a situation, it is naturally the immigrant or minority groups that often initiate the demand for an express and clear statement of the unwritten law in some readily ascertainable form: fears about oppression (real as well as imaginary) by the host or majority group in the new polity are the usual cause of this agitation.

But another equally compelling reason is the fact of the growing complexity of modern life in many an African, Asian or Pacific community. The introduction of a money economy and of Western legal and political ideas and values has meant the partial, and in some cases total, dissolution of the traditional ways of life of the peoples. The old values and concepts, especially in the field of law and government, no longer seem valid in the new mixed society, which is neither entirely traditional nor entirely Western (even among the most sophisticated African or Asian societies). At such a point, there is clearly a need for a new set of canons of behaviour which shall ensure social order and political stability. In customary, no less than in non-customary, societies the regulation of individual conduct, so that security and liberty may be achieved, is as urgent as it is necessary. In England this is expressed by the rubric—maintenance of the Rule of Law; in Africa and Asia, the familiar phrase is—maintenance of the social equilibrium. In both cases, the exact ambit is sometimes difficult to delimit, but the central idea is clear and unambiguous. Judges of customary courts nowadays demand guides, especially written ones, to assist them in their daily task.

Whether the society subject to customary law is pure or mixed, the impact of alien ideas and exotic influences upon the traditional polity has generally the same effect. Certain customary law notions have perforce to be modified, others have to be dropped or suppressed altogether, while yet others must be kept, at least for some time. In the general state of uncertainty that normally prevails when a society is faced with the question of making a choice of one or more of these alternative courses, the desirability and even necessity of settling the precise limits of applicable rules of conduct become inevitable. This is not to say that writing is the only way of solving the problem. In the evolution of past empires and principalities in Asia and Africa we can indeed discover instances where complete assimilation of alien peoples by host communities had taken place; but this process required time as well as an unhurried pace of development. Both these essentials are absent in the conditions of present-day customary societies. The world of Asia and Africa is in a great hurry, and the West consciously or unconsciously will not let it tarry. The importance of charters or documents in semi-literate societies at a stage of rapid transition cannot be over-estimated, and it would accordingly be easy to conclude that a reduction to writing is the only solution to the problem of uncertainty about customary law. But before we do that, we would do well to point out another dynamic of legal change—the judicial process of the courts, which has been the principal mode by which the English common law has evolved since Anglo-Saxon times, though supplemented by amending legislation as and when necessary. However, the title set for the present report seems to exclude in terms any detailed consideration here of this absorbing theme.

Finally, the reduction of customary law to writing is an absolute necessity if it is to be properly studied and understood by (a) those who administer it in customary courts, (b) those whose contact with it is either through review or on appeal from the courts of first instance, (c) the members of the public at large, and (d) those who will teach it, as well as those who will learn it, as a subject of academic discipline. Probably, the greatest handicap to the earlier institution of courses in customary law in most metropolitan universities has been the lack of such suitable written records of it as would satisfy the high standard required of all courses at that level.

Problems:

If, then, we restrict ourselves to the issue of reducing customary law to writing, we are at once confronted by a whole set of problems. The immediate questions are:

(a) How is the work to be done?
(b) Who is to do it?
(c) What form should it take?

It has to be decided *in limine* whether and, if so, what preliminary investigation is needed before the writing stage is reached. If it is agreed that some kind of investigation is requisite, the next thing is to decide on the type: anthropological field work, distribution of questionnaires, study of case records of Native Courts, etc. It seems that a combination of two or more of these modes of approach would in varying degrees be inevitable if the result is to be worthwhile.

This at once brings up for consideration the issue as to whether the work in a given territory is best undertaken by a team of specialists in the various complementary disciplines, or by a single individual with the necessary versatility. The first alternative has, so far as the writer is aware, never been tried anywhere for this type of undertaking. It seems the cost would be prohibitive, even if the necessary personnel could be mustered and made to co-ordinate their research activities; the collation of the fruits of their investigation and the reconciliation of facts and inferences might prove well-nigh impossible. For this and other reasons, the best approach is to entrust the entire work to one or more (the fewer, the better) specialists with adequate background training in extensive legal and sociological research and writing. Where more than one person has to be thus employed, probably because of the vastness of the territory, the work should be so organised not only that their areas of investigation do not overlap but also that they adopt, as far as possible, identical techniques of investigation. To make the results as authentic and inter-dependent as practicable, each specialist could be made later to cover one or more of the other areas already covered by his colleague(s).

If we assume that only one person with the right qualifications can be found to undertake the work for a given territory, the following considerations apply:—

(i) The investigator must remember from the outset that there is a clear *distinction* to be made between *law* and *custom*, difficult through the operation often is. Where Native Court records exist, these might be consulted in cases of doubt or difficulty, always subject of course to a scrupulous observance of the law of averages. But where such records do not cover the points at issue, one useful but by no means conclusive test would be to ask whether the alleged practice is *law*, which the Native Courts would enforce, or *custom*, which they would not; perhaps it is better to say whether the particular practice is recognised by the majority of the local community as binding on all and sundry, or whether it is merely conventional or permissive.

(ii) Equally, the investigator will need to assure himself that some watered-down versions of English or a European law which Native Authorities have been permitted to administer are not passed off on him as customary law. It is not that the two should not finally fuse together; it is that they must first be distinguished in the stage of investigation.

(iii) In the process of collecting his data, the investigator will often come up against conflicting versions of the customary law of a given community, whether these are contained in court records or given by informants. In the latter case, the most noticeable divergence of view-points is as between the older and the younger members of even the same community, the former sometimes being conservative and the latter often impatient of immemorial usages. Another divergence also occurs between the illiterate and the literate elements among the older as well the younger groups. To whatever the divergence may be attributed, it is the investigator's duty to arbitrate between any two or more views of what the customary law on certain disputed issues may be.

(iv) Another pitfall that must be avoided is to assume that a community with an apparently homogeneous body of customary law has a uniform set of rules governing all its members without exception. While the ideal is to foster this objective as much as circumstances permit, it is of the first importance to realise that customary law may vary from place to place within the same territory and accordingly to watch and record the discernible "law regions." Such recognition of possible divergences might often help in the ultimate promotion of uniformity. The general as well as the particular principles of even a homogeneous body of customary law must be recorded if a true picture of the whole legal community is to be obtained.

(v) Again, the investigator might decide to obtain his information through the distribution of questionnaires among a large and miscellaneous body of people selected at random. The questions put must be short, simple and directed to the point requiring clarification; but, even so, a large element of arbitrariness remains, both about the questions themselves and about the answers received from those who will have co-operated. Not all the answers would be satisfactory; a good many might be blatant or downright silly. But even if the returns were sufficiently large and careful, it would still be unscientific to build up a coherent body of principles upon them alone. However good the answers to the questionnaires might be, there can be no doubt that they would still have to be supplemented by information gleaned from other sources.

(vi) Some colonies in British Africa, e.g., Nigeria and the former Gold Coast colony (now Ghana) gave statutory powers to the chiefs to declare, as and when necessary, what they considered to be the customary law within the areas of their jurisdiction. The trouble here is of a two-fold nature. The first is that, in far too many cases, these chiefs concurrently exercised executive and judicial functions and it may often be difficult to know whether the law they declare is *de lege lata* or *de lege ferenda*. The second is that, as chiefs, they may tend to be behind the current legal thought and practice of their community; it is notorious that, with but few important exceptions, they are the least competent to make an effectual synthesis of the old and the new rules of conduct in a fast-changing social and economic scene. Nor must it be forgotten that many Native or Local Authorities now comprise traditional or hereditary elements as well as a growing proportion of elected ones, and the general problem of welding together these two groups into a harmonious body of administrators has yet to be solved. The issue is not now nearly so acute in those few territories, like Northern and Western Nigeria and Uganda, where the judicial and the executive powers have become sufficiently differentiated to make possible the exercise of these powers by separate panels of the Native or Local Authorities.

But the very exercise by chiefs of their statutory powers to declare customary law carries the danger that too many divergencies in an otherwise homogeneous legal community could result after a few years. The arrangement would then defeat its own ends by making the ideal of uniformity ever more difficult to achieve.

It is accordingly feared that an investigator might not derive much real profit from using the declarations of Native Authorities as a source of customary law. A better body for this purpose would be one consisting of a fixed number of the more knowledgeable members of the Native Court panel and the Judicial Adviser—a kind of Customary Law Revision Committee to which difficult issues could be referred, from time to time, for study and the making of recommendations to the appropriate legal and legislative authorities. Where their views on a particular issue of customary law are unanimous or approved by an overwhelming majority, the investigator might accept them for what they are worth, since not all such points would or should be passed into law by the legislature. The investigator might for his own purposes adopt a kind of personal Law of Citations according to which he could decide, in cases of division of opinion, on whichever side certain expert members should happen to be; this is because a simple majority might not always yield the best results.

Methods:

Having described and analysed most of the main problems attending the reduction of customary law to writing, we may now turn to a consideration of the form in which the investigator should record the results of his labours. For this purpose various media have been suggested or adopted, but we will list the chief types as follows:—

(a) The Code is the most popular form to which those considering the question of reducing customary law to writing almost habitually turn. It seems important initially to decide whether the customary law of a territory should be wholly or only partially codified, although all too often the advocates of codification want it to be total. Many lawyers in Africa and Asia, trained as they are in Western legal systems which strike them as certain and therefore respectable, go all out in their demand for complete codification of their country's customary law where it is not recommended for wholesale abolition. They understandably have little sympathy for a body of law which they have never had to study as part of their course for membership of the profession, and which in any case they are not permitted to practise in the Native Courts, where they have no right of audience. One suspects that the reason underlying their agitation for codification of the customary law is not so much that it should be certain as that codification would inevitably involve problems of statutory interpretation and *recherches techniques* such as only professional Western-trained lawyers and judges could handle. The way would thus be open to the conversion of all Native Courts into magistracies administering technical and lawyers' law. It would be irrelevant to pursue further here the question of the future of Native Courts and of customary law, and so we must desist.

But two points emerge from what has been said so far. One is that codification, even if successfully accomplished, would render customary law less customary and more artificial, far removed from the experience and comprehension of the people: judges and litigants alike would hardly be disposed to acknowledge it as their own. The second is the serious risk that customary law or the version of it put into a code might become fossilised, as the processes of legislative amendment or adjustment to the changing needs of social and economic life are notoriously slow. To subject customary law to such premature crystallisation during a period of transition and rapid change would be a disservice to the cause of comparative law in general and customary law in particular. Besides, it would seriously irk the people who live under it, and whose interests and welfare should be the overriding consideration.

The Natal Code of Native Law, first promulgated in 1878 and later passed into law in 1891, should be sufficient warning to advocates of total codification of customary law. The questionnaire method was used, and the resulting code has so ossified the customary law of the African communities of Natal in the Union of South Africa that it proved to be a failure, even as early as 1901. Similarly, in the case of Indonesia, the States

General appointed Carpentier Alting to study and eventually to codify the *adat* law of the native Christians in the Minahasa. This attempt also came to nothing between 1901 and 1904. In spite of the Order in Council of 1917 which granted to Indonesians the right to opt for Dutch law if they wished, and in spite of the efforts of the Adat Law Foundation established in 1917, the question of codification of the customary law in these parts seems to have been shelved ever since.

If an attempt to codify were to be limited to certain spheres, such as the law of marriage and the family or the law of succession and inheritance, something could be said for it. But a good deal of study and cogitation must precede even such partial codification. At the time of the appointment of the first Law Commission for British India in 1833, it was freely mooted that the whole of Hindu law and of Mohammedan law there should be codified. But, in the event, that idea had to be abandoned in favour of piece-meal codification of sections of Indian law. Even then, it is significant that it was the criminal law that was first tackled, to be followed by yet more non-customary aspects of the local law.

(b) Apart from early legal writing on general customary law, such as Sir Henry Maine's "Ancient Law" and Sir Paul Vinogradoff's "Historical Jurisprudence," those who have in recent times been concerning themselves seriously with customary law have been certain anthropologists. The form normally adopted has been a *Handbook* or monograph in which the customary law rules, so far as ascertainable, are set down according to a pattern and under headings familiar in Western legal writings. Four main types may be distinguished: (i) The type popularised by Schapera's "Handbook of Tswana Law and Custom," first published in 1938, having been commissioned by the Bechuanaland Administration. P. P. Howell's "A Manual of Nuer Law" (1954) is in this genre. (ii) The type pioneered by Cory and Hartknoll's "Customary Law of the Haya Tribe, Tanganyika Territory," published in 1945. It has since been followed by Cory's "Sukuma Law and Custom" (1953). (iii) The type recently provided by J. F. Holleman's "Shona Customary Law" (1952), a descriptive account of the social, cultural and legal ways of the people, from which it is not always easy to extract the purely legal principles. Far less ambitious but probably more legal are a number of administrative monographs in more or less the same category, of which D. J. Penwill's "Kamba Customary Law" (1950) and G. S. Snell's "Nandi Customary Law" (1954) are perhaps fair samples. (iv) The type most recently introduced by Max Gluckman's "The Judicial Process among the Barotse of Northern Rhodesia" (1955). This illustrates an interesting use of the case-law method, whereby certain representative Native Court records of cases are reproduced and briefly commented upon. This type of book is more general than anthropological, and is not designed for use in Native Courts of the territory concerned. Only Schapera's and Cory and Hartknoll's are expressly written with such an aim; but while both combine the method of anthropological investigation with a study of Native Court cases, Schapera's appears the more valuable in supplying the sociological background to the customary law. Cory and Hartknoll's is, on the other hand, more useful to the Native Courts concerned in that it contains not only clear formulations of the rules of customary law but also brief references to decided cases. Its two main defects are that it tends to become too authoritative, being regarded as if it were a legislated code of the Government of the territory, while it is after all only a record of the customary law at a particular stage of development: possible ossification of the customary law, as in a code, is hard to avoid.

(c) But, for purposes of reducing customary law to writing, far and away the best form is the Legal Textbook. Nearly all the methods of investigation and research previously suggested should be pressed into the service of producing a legal textbook. The advantages of this form over those so far described are (1) that, if well done, it separates the wheat of legal principles from the chaff of cultural and economic irrelevancies, without however sacrificing that amount of sociological background of the rules that is essential to their appreciation; (2) that it is, or should be, more precise and definite in its formulation of the relevant principles than the average anthropological study on the same subject; (3) that it lacks official authority, and is therefore far more flexible and adaptable than a duly enacted code—e.g., the Courts and other users need not follow its statement of the law on any issue not *either* previously defined in the judgment of a competent court of law *or* legislated upon by the proper authority. Mis-statements and other errors as to the law can be and often are corrected in subsequent editions of law books, the intervals between two editions being largely though not exclusively determined by the quantity of changes necessitated by legal change. (4) That it is not a merely *descriptive* account of the particular customary law; it is also a critical statement and evaluation of both past and living principles of the law, as well as being a cautious prediction of the trends in general legal development and in particular aspects of it. All these it seeks to supply by the processes of historical, analytical and functional assessment of the total legal situation, in order to state existing law in terms of current social and economical life. Any suggestions for the reform of the law must, however, be clearly indicated as such, so that there is no confusion between the law as it is and the law as it ought to be; (5) That a legal textbook, if properly compiled, can promote the unification of diverse bodies of customary law better than a code; it is also the best method of relating customary law to the enacted law of the country concerned, and so helps in producing the synthesis and harmonious relationship between the two, which is so vital to African and Asian societies today. English law introduced into the colonies in suitable form must be made to look like the customary law in the minds of the local judges as well as in the eyes of the ordinary people there.

When, for instance, the Natal Code of Native Law proved such a failure, textbooks began, and have continued, to supply the want ever since. In this connection it is only necessary to mention Seymour's "Native Law and Custom" (1911), Whitfield's "South African Native Law" (1929), and Stafford's "Native Law as Practised in Natal" (1935).

(d) It is probably better to classify the South African books listed in the preceding paragraph as Digests of Case Law with running commentaries thereon, rather than as textbooks. They certainly have not been planned along the lines of the orthodox law books.

To be useful, such case-law digests must be compiled from published Law Reports or duly approved cyclostyled copies of judgments of the British-established courts, in so far as the extracts are those concerning issues of customary law taken there on appeal from the Native Courts. The records of these latter courts themselves should be the primary source material for the Digests. This implies that the records must have been well kept, be reasonably detailed on essential points and properly scrutinised by some supervising officer or Judicial Adviser. Unfortunately, such records are very rare and, for the most part, never published. The ideal would be for each territory to make a selection of the more significant judgments and to have them published either separately or as an integral part of the current Law Reports.

The Digests of Case-Law seem to be more common in the South-East Asian countries than in the African ones, mainly because in addition to better-kept court records written sources of the customary law exist there.

Yet there are at least two great defects in Case-Law Digests generally. They are, at best, fragmentary evidence of the living law of the territory; and they tend to encourage too mechanical an application of the rules of law to disputes that may require for their proper resolution an understanding of the general principles of the operative customary law.

Summary of the Arguments

1. The desire for certainty is the primary reason for the reduction of customary law to writing, though some would add the fostering of uniformity among diverse bodies of customary law.

2. Because of the break-up of the traditional structure of African and Asian societies today, the importance of recording customary law is greater, since the old legal concepts and values are no longer valid for the new social and economic conditions.

3. Patient investigation and careful research are a necessary preliminary to the reduction of customary law to writing: law and custom must be distinguished, local variations of customary law must be noted, divergent accounts of customary law need to be checked, the questionnaire method must not be used alone, etc.

4. Five stated reasons why the legal textbook is preferable to codes, handbooks, and case-law digests: the attendant dangers of these other forms of recording customary law are fossilisation and fragmentation.

SIMON ROBERTS

The Recording of Customary Law: Some Problems of Method

One might gain the false impression from the previous essays that recording folk law is a fairly straight-forward operation. If one follows directions or utilizes a questionnaire, one should be able to elicit a series of folk laws from the members of a particular society. In theory, this may be so, but in practice it is not.

Professor Simon Roberts of the Law Department at the London School of Economics details some of the inevitable problems that arise in the attempt to record folk law. There is the discrepancy between ideal and real behavior; there is the matter of the incompleteness of written records of trials; there is the issue of the variations of folk laws among different informants. Professor Roberts discusses some of these problems based upon his own fieldwork and his knowledge of African folk law scholarship in general.

Lawyers have been widely engaged in the recording of customary law in Africa for more than a decade,[1] so it is perhaps surprising that serious disagreement still exists as to what exactly they are looking for and how best to find it. But this is the case; and doubts and disagreement seem to be multiplying rather than approaching resolution.[2] As some research into customary law has recently been undertaken in Botswana, and parts of it reported in this journal,[3] something can well be said about these problems and the arguments to which they have give rise.

The practical importance of the arguments about methodology was soon brought home to the writer of this note when he found himself in the field. In the course of investigating the nature of interests in arable land held under customary forms of tenure, I asked several elderly men whether payment was ever made where fields were transferred from one person to another. All were emphatic that such payments were "against the law" and never happened. However, I had already discovered,

---

Reprinted from *Botswana Notes and Records*, 3 (1971), 12–15, with permission. An appendix (pp. 16–21) surveying the history of recording customary law among the Kgatla, Malete, Tlokwa, and the Kwena is not reprinted here.

reading through the records of the Chief's Court of their tribe, that payment was permitted by that court provided that the land in question had been cleared for cultivation (the idea being that such payments were referable to the cost of improvements carried out on the land). Later on, as I got to know the area better, I found that it was quite a common practice for payment to be demanded even where interests in uncleared land were transferred (particularly where such land was favourably sited in relation to water supplies and centres of population), even though people knew that this was not permitted by the Chief's Court. So here were three methods of investigation—talking to informants, investigating actual decisions of the court and observing the day-to-day habits and practices of tribesmen—each revealing a different picture of the law. Each picture was true in a sense, as what the old men said was probably the traditional position, whereas the discrepancy between the court records and everyday behaviour could be explained on the basis that the courts had not caught up with generally accepted practice (a common enough phenomenon in any legal system). The lesson to be gained was that the picture of the law formed might well be heavily dependent upon the method of investigation used; a possibility the full implications of which I had not really considered.[4]

Previous investigations of Tswana customary law had been almost entirely carried out through interviews with informants. This method formed the basis of the research upon which Schapera's classic, *A Handbook of Tswana Law and Custom*, was written;[5] it was also used in later investigations carried out on behalf of the Botswana Government by A.C. Campbell and J.M. Walker.[6] This method was also relied upon in the pioneering recording exercises carried out in Kenya,[7] Swaziland[8] and Malawi[9] under the auspices of the Restatement of African Law Project of the School of Oriental and African Studies in London. However, other researchers, notably anthropologists, have investigated customary law through the examination of actual disputes. Some have used the technique of observing disputes while they are actually in progress,[10] while others have relied upon written records kept by customary courts.[11] Latterly, some lawyers have also been won over to this method.[12]

Recent arguments about the methods of recording customary law have been largely concerned with the respective merits of the two approaches, and rather damaging attacks have been made upon investigations based upon interviews with informants.[13] Such criticism has been made on two levels. First, it is said, such investigations tend to be directed towards obtaining a set of abstract rules, or "disembodied propositions" about the law, and fail to reveal the function which these rules have in the social system and the mechanics of their operation. These criticisms, which are also fashionably directed at rule-centred legal research in common law systems as well, seem well founded as far as much of the work so far produced by the Restatement of African Law Project (already referred to) is concerned. The restatements so far published do largely consist of abstract rules inadequately anchored to the social context in which they are alleged to apply, and they are also very weak as far as procedural aspects of the law are concerned. However, these defects are not inevitably inherent in research conducted through discussion with informants, a fact which seems to be overlooked by some critics of the Restatement of African Law Project.

The other kind of criticism levelled at investigation through interviews is that a defective picture of the law is obtained on account of the individual opinions and preconceptions of the interviewer or the person interviewed. First, there is the problem that the range and kind of information obtained is circumscribed by the questions asked by the investigator. Any questions the recorder asks must be determined by his preconceptions as to what the legal system he is investigating is like; where his training has been in another legal system and he has not had an opportunity to watch the one he is investigating for a long time at close quarters, the questions asked may well be wrong ones, or, at least, peripheral matters may be laboured and central ones utterly neglected. There are also wrong ways of asking questions; a fact well known and guarded against by investigators in some areas of the social sciences, but seldom given much attention by lawyers. Secondly, there is the risk of distortion on the part of the informant: he may tell you what he thinks you would like the answer to be; what he would like the answer to be; or, what the answer might have been in the past. Of all these problems, the one that worried me most was the problem of dating information obtained from informants. My impression was that most informants talked most easily about the past, and lapsed back into this tense despite continual reminders.[14] Of course, this difficulty was greatest where an informant considered that the present law had taken an unfavourable turn. An example of this may be cited from the context of the law of procedure. Older informants always said that a young married couple might not bring a matrimonial dispute before a ward court before referring it to their senior relations, who had also to be present at the ward court proceedings. Similarly, it was regularly said that a young woman who had been impregnated might not bring proceedings herself, but that this had to be done by her father or guardian. No doubt this was true in the past, but the most limited personal experience of court procedure today discloses that this is no longer the case.

It was my experience that both of the dangers stressed in the previous paragraph could be greatly reduced by an examination of actual disputes, as opposed to posing theoretical questions to informants. For this it is necessary to look to the customary courts as a primary source of information. This involves sitting in these courts, watching and listening, or finding out what happens in them by other means. While it is indispensable to spend some time watching and listening, it is certainly impossible in this way to obtain a comprehensive picture of the law within the time likely to be available to most investigators (except, perhaps, anthropologists). In view of this it is necessary to investigate actual disputes by building up accounts of them from discussion with informants or by examining the records of proceedings kept by the courts (where such records exist, as they do in many customary courts in Botswana). It is certainly possible to build up a picture of past disputes by talking to informants, and on the whole men's memories of the details of past litigation seem curiously extensive, but the method is laborious and there is always the fear that crucial features of a piece of litigation have been forgotten with time. A well-prepared contemporary written record, on the other hand, provides a starkly neutral account of what took place in court. Although such a record is open to interpretation by the investigator, it can in no way be influenced in form or content by his preconceptions.[15]

A picture of the law drawn from actual disputes can thus be value-free in the sense that no product of a rule-centred investigation could be. A further advantage derived from the use of court records is that a very general survey of the records of a particular court tells you immediately the kind of problems which *actually arise* for judicial solution in the community concerned. Without such help, the recorder is likely to worry about problems which, for one reason or another, do not much preoccupy the courts in that area. It is certainly very difficult to obtain such a perspective talking to informants.

Another important advantage of a customary court record is the insight which it can give into the procedural aspects of customary law. Most Chief's Court records in Botswana contain at least a summary of what was said by the parties and their witnesses, as well as questions asked by members of the court and the judgment delivered. The Headman who tried the case below traditionally introduces the appeal, states his judgment and gives an indication of why this failed to resolve the dispute; then the parties give their account of the matter, and the background is filled in by relations and other witnesses who explain the facts of the dispute as they see them and tell the court what they attempted in the way of settling the dispute at a lower level. Thus the record illustrates two crucial features of the customary judicial process; the involvement of the family groups of the respective parties and the importance attached to achieving reconciliation, or at least judgment acceptable to both sides.

Without an understanding of these fundamental aspects of the judicial process, the objectives and content of the substantive law are hard to grasp. All this, too, is difficult to pick up in conversation with informants.

Notwithstanding the value of customary court records, it is important to recognise the limits of their use. They cannot be used as precedents in the manner of those of the common law courts, simply because the customary courts themselves do not regard their previous decisions in this way. A single decision is simply an example of a technique of dispute settlement, from which it is possible to draw conclusions about the kind of factors which influence a customary court in reaching a decision in the type of dispute involved. Obviously, lines of cases all pointing in the same direction can help the observer to predict the course of future litigation; but the search for black letter rules may not be very fruitful. It is significant that abstract rules are seldom expressly formulated in the judgment, or discussed while a case is being heard.[16]

It is also obvious that the business of a particular court has to be followed through the records for a good many years before a broad picture of the law is obtained; and even then it may be found that considerable gaps exist. Discussion with informants has obviously to be fallen back on then (although this will probably be of limited value, because if the matter concerned has not been before the court within recent memory, the views given by informants will be opinions only). Similarly, particularly in the case of a poor record, the nature of the dispute and the relationship of the parties to each other may only become clear after the record has been discussed with informants who remember the dispute.

It is at this stage, when a particular record has been examined, that discussion of the case with informants who remember it is particularly valuable. Such informants will be able to fill in the details of pre-litigation negotiation, and explain the significance of the many tantalising asides which abound in customary court records, and which often lead away into other disputes and other areas of the law.

In conclusion it must be admitted that, in committing himself to a particular method of research, the investigator also commits himself to a particular view of the general nature of law. In taking the customary court records as a point of departure, one is taking the view (possibly an unfashionable one today) that law is simply what happens in the courts. Obviously such a conclusion is only a partial answer, because, as we have seen from my initial example, the decisions of a court may differ from the actual practice of tribesmen and, even more, from stated legal norms.

Notes

1. Impetus was given to this work by the initiation of the Restatement of African Law Project, in the School of Oriental and African Studies, University of London, and by the London Conference on the Future of Law in Africa, 1959.

2. Fresh life has been given to the discussion of these questions by two recent articles: Richard L. Abel, "Customary Laws of Wrongs in Kenya: An Essay in Research Method" *American Journal of Comparative Law* (Michigan) XVII, 573; William Twining, "Two Works of Karl Llewellyn—II" (*The Cheyenne Way*) *Modern Law Review* XXXI, 165.

3. J.M. Walker, "The Bamalete Law of Contracts" *Botswana Notes and Records* (Gaborone) I, 1969; Simon Roberts, "Kgatla Law and Social Change" *Botswana Notes and Records* (Gaborone) II, 1970.

4. One point which experience of this kind brings home is that questions of method are inextricably associated with fundamental questions as to the nature of African customary law; one's view of the latter tends to govern the choice of the former, and *vice versa*—the process may be subconscious.

5. The reason for this was that the recording of cases in the customary courts was only beginning as Schapera finished this book. In his Preface to the Second Edition (1955), he acknowledges the great importance of the body of case materials which was then building up. An article of his, "The Work of the Tribal Courts in the Bechuanaland Protectorate" *African Studies* (London) II, 1943, 27, deals expressly with the court records which had been kept in the Tswana customary courts prior to 1940. Schapera must be regarded as the first scholar working in Africa to perceive the crucial importance of this body of material.

6. Although Campbell relied mainly upon informants in preparing his account of baNgwaketse Family law, he also used Court Records to check the information he was given.

7. Restatement of African Law: Kenya. *The Law of Marriage and Divorce* by Eugene Cotran (London, Sweet & Maxwell, 1968); *The Law of Succession* by Eugene Cotran (London, Sweet & Maxwell, 1969).

8. N.N. Rubin, "The Swazi Law of Succession: a Restatement" *Journal of African Law* (London) IX, 90.

9. Restatement of African Law: Malawi. *The Law of Marriage and Divorce* by J.O. Ibik (London, Sweet & Maxwell, 1970).

10. E.g. Max Gluckman, *The Judicial Process Among the Barotse of Northern Rhodesia* (Manchester, 1955); Paul Bohannan, *Justice and Judgement among the Tiv* (London, 1957); P.H. Gulliver, *Social Control in an African Society* (London, 1963).

11. E.g. Schapera in some of his later work ("Contract in Tswana Case Law" *Journal of African Law* (London) IX, 142); Lloyd Fallers, *Law without Precedent* (Chicago, 1969).

12. E.g. Abel, in his research in Kenya, published in the article referred to in footnote 2, *above*; Roberts, in the Botswana Government's Programme for Recording Tswana Customary Law.

13. A pioneer of these attacks is W.L. Twining; see his lectures, *The Place of Customary Law in the National Legal Systems of East Africa* (University of Chicago Law School, 1964); also his article referred to in footnote 2, *above*. More recently, Abel, in his article referred to in the same footnote.

14. Many informants do not seem to regard modern developments taking place in the customary courts as part of customary law at all. Drawing attention to something I have seen in court or read in a court record, I have often received the answer: "It is true that happens today; but it is not the law".

15. A description of customary court records in Botswana is contained in the Appendix to this article. [Ed. Note: Not reprinted here.]

16. It is very rare indeed for a litigant in the Tswana courts to cite an abstract rule of customary law as a reason why the case should be decided in his favour; citation of previous decisions is strongly discouraged. A chief may, nonetheless, call upon experienced men in the court to advise him on an abstract rule, although such occasions seem rare.

MUNA NDULO

Ascertainment of Customary Law: Problems and Perspectives with Special Reference to Zambia

From a general consideration of ascertainment of folk law in a large area of Africa, we move to the study of the same issues in a single African country. Presumably each individual country has its own peculiarities arising from matters of ascertainment. The reader should note that in this essay a distinction is made between folk or customary law and common law. The latter refers to English common law that was introduced into Zambia. Curiously enough such imposed colonial law is typically referred to in the literature as "received" law. In our view, "received" would appear to be a euphemism for "imposed!"

Many of the studies of folk law in Africa refer to individual countries or more often to individual peoples. See, for example, R.E.S. Tanner, "The Codification of Customary Law in Tanzania," East African Law Journal, 2 (1966), 105–116; James Y. Obol-Ochola, "The Application of Customary Law in Uganda: Judicial Ambivalence, Indifference and Sabotage," Eastern Africa Law Review, 3 (1970), 175–179; Sebastian Poulter, "An Essay on African Customary Law Research Techniques: Some Experiences from Lesotho," Journal of Southern African Studies, 1 (1975), 181–193; Robert B. Seidman, "Rules of Recognition in the Primary Courts of Zimbabwe: On Lawyers' Reasonings and Customary Law," International and Comparative Law Quarterly, 32 (1983), 871–903.

It has always seemed that the problem of the ascertainment of customary law is a fascinating and important problem. It is a problem which has been discussed by many eminent jurists[1] but still remains as unresolved as ever. The fact that it remains unresolved justifies continued discussion of the subject. This paper discusses the topic under four heads. These are the application of customary law, the courts, the methods of ascertainment of customary law and the future of customary law.

Reprinted from *African Social Research*, 31 (1981), 67–76, with permission.

Applicability of Customary Law

All countries in Commonwealth Africa have a dual system of laws—customary law and common law. In the case of Zambia most of the common law is composed of received law applied to Zambia by virtue of the English law extent of application Act.[2] This Act introduced English law, the doctrines of equity, and the statutes of general application in England into Zambia.[3] The introduced law was subject to the qualification that it be applied so far as the circumstances of the territory and its inhabitants permit and subject to such qualifications as local circumstances may render necessary. In all countries the reception date was specified.[4] In some areas of the law special provisions apply which allow current English law to apply. For instance in the area of marriage law in Zambia section eleven of the High Court Act[5] declares that the law of probate and divorce in Zambia is the law in force in England at a given moment. This means that the statutory law of marriage in Zambia is based on the 1973 Matrimonial Causes Act of England and any later amendments thereto. This arrangement puts a country like Zambia in an embarrassing situation where it can be said to be legislated to by Britain, its former metropolitan power. However, in so far as this is a conscious choice, it can be said to be an example of the exercise of sovereignty by Zambia.

The pre-colonial law in most African countries was essentially customary in character, having its source in the practices and customs of the people. The colonial regimes recognised customary law at the outset.[6] Recognition of customary law in Zambia as in many other African countries was given by orders in council.[7] It was applied as the law in all native courts. In fact in most of pre-independence Africa, Africans were never involved in litigation, either original or on appeal (other than criminal proceedings) in courts other than the local courts and the courts of that system. In present day Zambia, customary law is recognised as applicable to the country by virtue of section 16 of the Subordinate Courts Act[8] provided such customary law is not repugnant to justice, equity or good conscience and is not incompatible, either in terms or by necessary implication with any written law in force in Zambia. The repugnancy clause with respect to customary law exists or where it does not now exist, existed in most of Commonwealth Africa.[9] The effect of this clause has been to declare certain customary practices permitted under some of the systems of customary law, repugnant and contrary to law.[10] In Zambia customary law is also impliedly recognised by the Local Courts Act.[11] For although the Local Courts Act nowhere recognises customary law expressly, it provides in section 12 (1) that African customary law shall apply to any matter before Local Courts

Ascertainment of Customary Law: Problems and Perspectives

in so far as such law is not repugnant to natural justice or morality or incompatible with provisions of any written law.

It is perhaps fair to say that during the colonial period, even though customary law was expressly recognised, the colonial administration and its laws tended to emphasize the superiority of common law over customary law. In some parts of Commonwealth Africa, Zambia for example, in criminal trials a customary spouse was not regarded as a wife or husband for the purposes of evidence rules and as a result she or he could be compelled to testify against her or his spouse whereas the common law counter part could not be so compelled.[12] There is also the fact that Europeans were exempt from customary law.[13] In Zambia Africans were not allowed to marry under the Marriage Act until 1963 and could therefore only contract customary marriage.[14] It has also to be remembered that the early missionaries, on the whole, tended to discourage their adherents from engaging in customary law activities.[15] This was mainly to contain the practice of polygamy.

The Courts

A dual court structure was characteristic of the judicial structure in pre-independence Commonwealth Africa. This was a consequence of the introduction of judicial institutions based on English models together with the continued recognition of the indigenous African courts. This meant distinct judicial systems with no connecting link at any level of the judicial hierarchy. English law has always been administered by the Subordinate Courts and the High Court and the Court of Appeal. Practice and procedure has always been in substantial conformity with the law and practice observed in English courts.[16]

The courts administering customary law have changed over the years. In Zambia prior to 1939, customary law was administered by chiefs and headmen using traditional court institutions. In 1939 the native Courts Ordinance[17] and the Barotse Native Courts Ordinance[18] were enacted. The first Ordinance applied to the whole of Zambia except the Barotse province (now Western Province) and the second Ordinance applied to the Western Province. Under the Barotse Native Courts Ordinance, traditional Lozi court institutions were left to operate very much on their own. On the other hand, the Native Courts Ordinance instituted a Native Court system. Under this Ordinance, the Governor had the exclusive right to establish Native Courts as he thought fit by warrant. These courts were manned by Chiefs and District Officers, who exercised both judicial and administrative functions. The warrant specified whether a native court was an urban native or a rural native court. The Governor had exclusive right to determine who sat in the native courts and to suspend or terminate the appointment of justices where he was satisfied that a justice is incapable of exercising the duties of his office in a proper manner or that there is some other sufficient reason for such suspension or termination.

The courts had jurisdiction in the trial and determination of any civil cause or matter in which both the parties were Africans. They also had criminal jurisdiction to such an extent as was prescribed to the court in a matter in which the accused was an African, except that the native court had no power to hear such criminal cases if a non-African was required by a party as a witness and except in cases where the governor had by order directed that any person or class of persons was not subject to the jurisdiction of native courts. The practice and procedure were left to be regulated in accordance with customary law. The records of the courts were reviewed by the commissioner of Native courts. These courts were reorganised and renamed the Local Courts in 1966.[19] Both the Native Courts Ordinance and the Barotse Native Courts Ordinance were repealed. The Local Courts are established by warrants issued by the Minister of Justice. Their jurisdiction is limited to civil claims of less than two hundred Kwacha and to criminal matters assigned to them by the Chief Justice. Members of the courts are appointed by the Judicial Service Commission. This discards the system under which traditional authorities exercised both judicial and administrative functions and replaces it with a system, with court members whose duties are entirely judicial. The change, it must be pointed out, was greatly resisted by the Chiefs and other traditional rulers. The practice and procedure of local courts is regulated by rules established by the Chief Justice.[20] Decisions of the local courts can be appealed against first to the Subordinate Courts and then to the High Court and to the Supreme Court. In addition the Local Courts Act provides for the appointment of a Local Courts Advisor and offers to advise and review the work of local courts.[21]

Development in courts concerned with customary law has been dealt with at some length because the discussion demonstrates how the process of integrating these courts into the main court system has been undertaken. The process described above is fairly close to the processes that have gone on in other African Commonwealth countries. There are of course differences in names of courts and dates of the changes. Ghana was in 1960 the first African country to make any reorganisation in Commonwealth Africa of its court system.[22] In its 1960 Courts Act it made provision for a Supreme Court, High Court and inferior courts including local courts. On achievement of independence or soon after, other African countries made similar changes.[23] This is because the policy of most of these countries is to create unified systems of justice in their countries. It is government policy that the existing local courts presided over by justices should gradually be replaced by subordinate courts presided over by trained, but not professionally qualified magistrates. So far the efforts have concentrated on integrating the local courts with the common law courts, so that as far as is possible they are governed by the same Act and the removal of supervision of local courts by administrators. This as can be seen from the discussion above has been done by providing for appeals from local courts to the subordinate courts, High Courts and Supreme Court.

The role of administrators has not been done away with completely as the office of the Local Courts Advisor can be said to be semi administrative and semi judicial but then his administrative work relates to the local courts themselves. Legal practitioners are uniformly not allowed in these courts in Commonwealth Africa.[24] This is largely because local courts justices do not receive any legal training. This is desirable unless and until these courts are staffed by professionally qualified magistrates.

The Method of Ascertainment of Customary Law

While Customary law was recognised and continued to be the primary law, it did not stand on the same footing before the Subordinate Courts and the High Court as did received law. It was not accepted that the courts could take judicial notice of such law in the same way that they did of the statute and received law. The general attitude of the courts then was to regard customary law in much the same way as foreign law and to require proof of its content. It was, however, quite early accepted that when a particular customary law rule has become notorious it may be judicially noticed. This was accepted in *Angu v Attah*,[25] a privy council decision in a case which originated from West Africa.

A number of problems contributed to the existence of the problem of ascertaining Customary law. There was the contemptuous attitude towards customary law during the colonial period of European lawyers who generally regarded it as not law.[26] The Judges in the superior courts were largely ignorant of customary law and often had little or no legal interest in it either. This necessitated special methods of discovering the law applicable. This is particularly so in the absence of books on customary law. To some extent as has been observed, the very nature of customary law itself, unwritten, flexible and changing in response to new conditions and attitudes, required a continuous ascertainment in some areas of customary law.[27]

As a solution to the problem of ascertainment, *Angu v Attah*[28] suggested the calling of witnesses. Many African Commonwealth codes suggest assessors.[29] It is for instance provided in the Zambian legislation that a Subordinate Court or High Court may call an 'assessor' to attend the proceedings and advise on matters concerning Customary law, as well as customs and usages.[30] The issue with the use of assessors is whether in fact it precludes the calling of witnesses by the parties and dispenses with the need to prove customary law. In a Zambian case, *The People v Chitambala*,[31] the Court had assessors and each of the parties had his own expert witnesses. It is objectionable on political and legal grounds that the indigenous law of any country and a law which controls and regulates the greater majority of the people of the country should be a question of fact needing proof while the received law in the same country does not require proof and is a question of law. As Nkrumah observed on the occasion of the opening of Ghana University Law School:

> There is a ringing challenge to African lawyers today. African law in Africa was declared foreign law for the convenience of colonial administration, which found the administration of justice cumbersome by reason of the vast variations in local tribal custom. African law had to be proved in courts by experts. But no law can be foreign to its own land and country, and African lawyers particularly in the independent African states, must quickly find a way to reverse this judicial travesty.

Efforts to solve the problem have included passing legislation declaring that customary law is a question of law. This was done in Tanzania and Ghana.[33] But as McClain points out this does not solve the problem of ascertainment of such law.[34] The better judicial policy is of course to regard Customary law as a question of law and as capable of being judicially noticed on the same footing as common law, but that where there is difficulty in ascertaining it, be it for the reason that the judge is not knowledgeable about customary law or for any other reason, it is noticed after inquiry. Any other view would undermine the status of customary law.

Whereas the problems of ascertainment have so far tended to be associated with Superior Courts it appears that it is a question of time before the problem affects the local courts. Presently in the local courts Customary law is assumed to be in the breasts of the local court justices, that is to say within their general knowledge. There has never been any question of proving the law by evidence. This, however, cannot remain true for the future. It is in fact almost the price of progress in the professionalisation of the courts. An increasing number of young people are going to run the local courts in future. The solutions to both the problem in the superior courts and the new problem is going to be the same since the problem is really one of lack of knowledge of customary law. It can conveniently be discussed under the next heading, since a satisfactory solution to this problem will determine the future place of customary law.

The Future of Customary Law

Little attention has been given to the future of customary law by most governments in Commonwealth Africa. Like all generalisations this is not quite correct as a great deal has been done in some countries, though few in number.[35] The lack of progress it would appear is due to the fact that it was generally recognised that priority should be given to improving the working of local courts and to the integration of the local courts system within the main structure of the court system. There is urgent need to study this problem and plot a course for the future of customary law, if it is to develop on sound lines. The first step that needs to be taken now is the ascertainment and authoritative restatement of customary law. Efforts have been made in West Africa, Kenya and Malawi.[36] It is a truism to say that little can be done with any branch of the law without knowing it. Many problems stand in the way of ascertainment.

For instance, a person charged with ascertainment may find lack of rules for dealing with different situations. He may be confronted with the problem of deciding which norms are legal and which are merely social, moral or religious. One will find differences between laws of different ethnic groups. The task may prove particularly difficult in the towns, where to a large extent, in areas where customary law does not provide rules, new rules have been developed.[37] For courts members in the urban areas import into their judgments their experience of the whole way of life of the people, their habits and customs, their ethical code and system of knowledge. This in itself is good as it is changing customary law to meet changing conditions. Also to assist in the recording of customary law the law reporting councils of the various countries could be encouraged to reach out at some of the local court cases or those that go on appeal and report them as a way of restatement. The phrase 'reach out' is used because in the ordinary course of events and using normal law reporting criteria, these may not qualify as they do not break new ground. But they are important in that they record customary law decisions which have never before been reported.

The ascertainment and recording of Customary Law should be prepared in consultation with the elders of each community, so as to insure that it reflects their common authority. For there is no doubt that they still remain the single most learned part of the community in Customary law. After the ascertainment of the law, it should be unified. Most customary laws display great similarity. In discussion, frequent references to differences in custom which distinguish one ethnic group from another are made; but the custom invariably cited on these occasions, while often important in the context of a particular case, are rather badges of identity than statements of any legal rule. The object of unification ought to be one central or general system of law, which would apply to everyone. Unification may take place at two levels. It may take place at a low level. This will mean retention of the basic dualism of the legal system. This can be done by the internal unification and standardization of each component. At a higher level, it can take the form of replacing the systems of law by a single system. It is this second level which is suggested here. Integration should be approached with caution. The exercise would be hardly worth the effort if the result is not made to reflect the actual pattern of social behaviour. Family law touches upon deeply entrenched customs and habits, which cannot be changed by a stroke of the legislative pen. In spite of what has been said, however, it might be possible to introduce a single, integrated body of law which would make uniform regulations where possible and at the same time allow for dualism where necessary. Major problems must be recognised in unification; there is a danger of the introduction of too many legal technicalities and too much common law into the body of customary law and native courts procedure. In a unified system procedure in courts should reflect some of the values of customary law procedures. For instance in divorce proceedings, a court tries reconciliation before considering divorce. This saves the irreparable damage that can be done when there is speedy recourse to courts. The proceedings are simple and informal. Simplicity has the big advantage of making legal actions cheap. In developing countries where the majority of the people are poor, inexpensive legal procedures are a necessity if courts are to play a meaningful role in the life of the ordinary man. There is universal agreement that local courts are readily accessible to people, they are understood by them and do not impose on the state an excessive burden. The importance of these courts is underlined by the fact that they handle the greater majority of litigation in most African countries. Some other steps can be taken towards the solution of the aspect of the problem of ascertainment which can be ascribed to lack of knowledge. There is need to make our teaching programmes in law school cater not only to the needs of the Superior Courts but also to those of the local courts. Customary law must be introduced into the curriculums in every law subject at Universities. The training of the lay magistracy has to be looked at too. Presently lay magistrates and local court justices receive no training at all in Customary Law prior to their beginning of service.[38] Whatever training is received is not on substantive law. This would be easy to introduce as the inferiority complexes that troubled many an African lawyer and led them to believe that African law is inferior have been replaced by black consciousness. The relevance of this is that it is now respectable to teach Customary law.

Conclusion

This has been a largely descriptive paper whose main purpose has been to give information on the problems of customary law. It shows clearly that African law has an important role to play in the life of the peoples of Zambia and yet its problems are largely neglected. The government has paid attention only to the court systems rather than to customary law itself, particularly the issue of its development. Integration of the laws or courts alone should not be the only goals. It is time concern was shifted to include the restructuring of the law to meet development needs. The rules existing in customary law reflect the social, political and economic structures in the society at the time they developed. Where these have changed it should adapt. There are urgent questions to be answered such as discrimination based on sex, land usage, succession and rights of children.

The work to be done is gigantic. This is largely because, as pointed out in the paper, little has been done to define problems and issues. There is therefore little prior work that can be used to build on. Surprisingly even development studies have shown lack of interest in the nature of customary law. And yet being part of the general law of the land it forms one of the tools that policy makers daily employ to reach development goals. A legal system of a country should reflect the structure of the society in which it operates at the very least and at best it should in addition lead society in the creation of new social relationships that are more in tune with the modern desires and goals of the society. The law has to be changed for the sake of its own survival and legitimacy, otherwise it becomes irrelevant to the needs and aspirations of the people it is supposed to serve.

Notes

1. For example, Allott, A. (1960), *Essays in African Law*; Elias, O. (1965), *Nature of Customary Law*; Allott, A. (1967), *New Essays in African Law*; Gluckman,

M. (1967). *The Judicial Process among the Barotse of N.R.*, and White, C.M. (undated), *Principles of Customary Law.*

2. Chapter 4 of The Laws of Zambia.

3. *Ibid.*, §2.

4. In Zambia it is specified as 17 August, 1911, *ibid.*

5. The High Court Act, chapter 50 of the Laws of Zambia, § II Penal Code, chapter 146 of the Laws of Zambia § 18.

6. Royal Chapter of Incorporation of the British South African Company, 29 October, 1889, article 14. This ordinance stated quite clearly that 'in the administration of justice to the peoples or inhabitants careful regard shall be had to the customs and laws of the class or tribe or nation to which the parties respectively belong...'.

7. Northern Rhodesia Proc. No. 1 of 1913 article 5 reads: 'Nothing in this proclamation shall deprive the High Court of the right to observe and enforce the observance, or shall deprive any person of the benefit of any law or custom existing in the territory and such law or custom not being repugnant to natural justice, equity and good government'.

8. Chapter 45 of the Laws of Zambia.

9. Ghana and Tanzania have removed the repugnancy clause.

10. R v Ndhlovu, 5 N.R.L.R. 298 and R v Matengula 5 N.R.L.R. 148.

11. Chapter 54 of the Laws of Zambia.

12. This was done by defining wife and husband in terms of common law marriage. See Criminal Procedure code, Chapter 7 of the Laws of Zambia, 1965 ed § 2.

13. This is presently the position in Zambia to some extent; see § 16, Subordinate Courts Act, supra.

14. See Marriage Ordinance (Amendment) of 1963.

15. A. Phillips, *Survey of African Marriage and Family Life*, 1945, p. 347.

16. High Court Act, supra, § 9.

17. Native Courts Ordinance, Chapter 158 of the Laws of Zambia, 1965 Ed.

18. Barotse Native Courts Ordinance Chapter 160 of the Laws of Zambia, 1965 ed.

19. The Local Courts Act of No. 20 of 1966. Now Chapter 54 of the Laws of Zambia.

20. *Ibid.*, § 14.

21. *Ibid.*, § 3.

22. See 1960 Courts Act.

23. Uganda's African Courts Ordinance was substantially amended in 1961 and 1962; Tanganyika by the Local Courts (Amendment) Ordinance, 1961; The Local Courts, (Minister of Justice and Regional Local Courts Officer) Act, 1962 and finally the Magistrates Courts Act, 1963 coming into force in 1964, moved rapidly towards a complete reorganisation of the Judiciary; Kenya with a 1962 amendment to African Courts Ordinance 1951, moved away from the parallel system; Nyasaland's local courts ordinance, 1962 introduced basic changes as did Sierra Leone Local Courts Act, 1963 and Zambia in 1966 with the 1966 Local Courts Act.

24. In Zambia this is done by § 15 of the Local Courts Act, supra.

Ascertainment of Customary Law: Problems and Perspectives

25. /1916/ A.C. 74.
26. Some Africans did the same as T. Elias observed in the Nigerian Legal system 1963.
27. W. McClain (1964), 'Recent changes in African local courts and Customary Law', *10 Howard Law Journal*, pp. 209–212
28. Supra.
29. In Zambia both the local Courts Act, supra and the High Court Act, supra allows assessors.
30. Local Courts, Act, supra, § 61.
31. 1969 Z.R., 142.
32. K. Nkrumah, in address at the formal opening of both the Accra conference on legal Education and the Ghana Law School.
33. Ghana Courts Act, of 1960, § 67 and Tanganyika Local Courts (Amendment) Ordinance.
34. McClain, supra, pp. 215–216.
35. Kenya, and Malawi have carried on a Restatement of Customary law with the assistance of the School of Oriental and African studies University of London.
36. In West Africa several books appear on Customary law some of them quite early in the history of West Africa, e.g., *Fanti Customary Law* in 1896 by Ghanaian Lawyer, J.M. Sarbah.
37. A.L. Epstein has some very illuminating cases in his book Juridical Techniques and the Judicial Process, A Study in Customary law, *No. 23 the Rhodes Livingstone Paper.*
38. 1965 Government of the Republic of Zambia Annual Report of the Judiciary and the Magistracy.

OBEID HAG ALI

The Conversion of Customary Law to Written Law

The idea that one can simply write down unwritten folk law is based upon a number of unstated premises. The first premise is that it is possible to extrapolate from words or behavior abstract legal axioms. The second premise is that the culture of the recorder is irrelevant. Both these premises are analyzed in the following critical essay. The so-called restatement project in African folk law is the subject of discussion in this essay by Sudanese Advocate Obeid Hag Ali. The notion that one can isolate abstract legal axioms from their cultural contexts is called into question and the propensity of English lawyers to perceive African folk law in terms of English legal culture is also delineated.

For a succinct description of the African law restatement project in which sixteen countries in British Africa involving several hundred different bodies of folk law were to be studied, see William Twining, "The Restatement of African Customary Law: A Comment," Journal of Modern African Studies, *1 (1963), 221–228.*

The recent attempts to codify customary law in Africa can best be appreciated if they are tested against the accepted anthropological standards. In part one of this article a general survey of the major developments of Social Anthropology in this century is given in the hope that it sheds light on those accepted standards.

The attempts to convert customary law to written have been carried out by some outstanding English Lawyers who have recently been interested in the study of tribal law. Part two of this article consists of an examination of their treatment of it in order to see whether (and why) their treatment is any different from that of the anthropologist. One lawyer, namely, Mr. E. Cotran, will be identified with the typical English Lawyer envisaged by this article. His work in the restatement of customary law in East Africa[1] represents one of the early adventures of the English Lawyer in the neighbouring discipline of Social Anthropology.

Reprinted from *The Sudan Law Journal and Reports* 1971, pp. 147–161, with permission.

The process of codification which is going on at present in the Sudan purports to take into account the indigenous customs of the people, their religious and cultural background. It is hoped that the Law Commission finds this discussion useful.

Part (I)
Major Developments in Social Anthropology:

An Historical Layout:

Until the first decade of this century, anthropology was dominated by theories which purported to rationalize and systematize the study of simple societies and put an end to the chaos created by the works of earlier amateur writers. The evolutionary theory which was originally concerned with biological evolution was extended to cover cultural evolution. The anthropologists of that period focussed their attention on investigating how simple societies developed to their present state. Then came the historical school which, though rejecting some Darwinian assumptions, shared a common ground with evolutionism, in that it was mainly concerned with the origins and development of tribal institutions.

Both the evolutionists and historians groped into the history of tribal societies, which was mainly unrecorded and made use of the method of interviewing informants—a method which became, more or less, a standard tool for investigating tribal societies. This way of collecting rules and trying to account for their existence in terms of their historical evolution had at least two serious consequences. Firstly, it diverted attention from investigating the actual operation of these rules in tribal life and the picture ultimately projected was, therefore, unsatisfactory. Secondly, it concealed the erroneous assumption that behaviour conformed to the standard postulated by the norms collected. Deviations, that is, were not investigated or accounted for.

Anthropology later came to be influenced by the jurisprudential thought of the time. The analytical positivist movement, which was led by Bentham and Austin, focussed attention on law as a *corpus juris*, and aimed at its logical systematization and (for Bentham) reform. The obsolete laws which provoked Bentham and caused him to direct his tremendous intellectual capabilities towards criticising those laws and calling for their reform, the investigation of the "nature" of law which led Austin to limit its scope, prevailing doctrines such as *stare decisis* and the supremacy of Parliament, all these had the effect of conveying an image of law as consisting of a hard, crystallized body of rules. Anthropologists of the time were, also, concerned with rules and in pursuing that concern, took too much for granted, thereby giving a false picture of tribal societies and the individuals who comprised them.

The first quarter of this century witnessed a movement in England, which was motivated by dissatisfaction with that state of affairs. It was a constructive revolution which aimed at establishing social anthropology as a separate science, defining its subject-matter and providing it with the tools necessary for dealing with that complex subject-matter and describing it in a more complete and scientific way. This movement came to be known as "functionalism."

On the theoretical side, the functionalists had a wider and deeper conception of tribal life. Unlike previous theories, their starting point was not the "clan," but the individuals and the institutions that operated within the clan. In his quest for truth, a functionalist usually investigated one "culture." This culture was then, according to the theory, broken down into its constituent institutions which were assumed to have functions essential for tribal cohesion and order. This assumption was a hypothesis which a functionalist would have to verify. Correlations between tribal institutions were thought and proved to be so essential in the study of tribal cultures, that previous studies which singled out certain institutions for separate investigations, were thought hopelessly erroneous or were even ridiculed. A "culture," to the functionalists, was a "functioning whole," and they spared no effort in emphasising this integrated "wholeness".

The theory indicated the method to be used. In order to investigate the "functions" of tribal "institutions" and in order to correlate those functions and see how they contributed to social equilibrium, the anthropologist had to be in the field. Different field techniques were then devised. The anthropologist had to live in close contact with the people he was trying to study, learn their language, gain their confidence, observe intimately, and participate in their activities. In a word, he was supposed to convey the picture as seen from within.

Although descriptive, aspiring to accuracy, and paying attention to variations, functionalism was still norm-oriented. Tribal institutions were properly investigated, their functions recorded, correlations, variations from norms (civil as well as criminal) law in the observance, as well as in the breach, all were adequately covered, but this was done for the purpose of collecting norms. Having done that the functionalist would try to join the English jurisprudential tradition and provide his own *definition* of law in the light of his experience "abroad". The breakthrough was, therefore, not fully conceived and some friendly relations with the past, and with the prevailing English legal tradition were still maintained.[2]

The influence of the American realist movement, itself a product of American social, political and legal processes and structures, was, through Llewellyn, brought to bear on the study of tribal law. This influence came to have a profound effect on subsequent studes of tribal law. Contact was made in a successful collaboration between law and social anthropology.[3] Like functionalism, the realist influence supplied both theory and a method of investigation. Both theory and method were part of Llewellyn's general philosophy of law. The quest for a stipulative definition of law is turned into a quest for the jobs that law performs to keep a society cohesive and going, a quest for the characteristics of law. The anthropologist is required to address himself to how the law-jobs get done and not merely to concentrate on abstract norms even if they are functionally" observed. Law is no longer only a body of rules backed by sanctions of any kind. To Llewellyn it is much more than that. It includes "law-men", "law-ways" and a variety of other things that go far into life. Rules are only one constituent part occupying a peripheral place and they get their force and life when they are put to the test in concrete cases and worked upon by the "law-men."

In addition to this sort of microscopic testing of substantive rules, the authors of *The Cheyenne Way* hoped to isolate and emphasise certain aspects largely neglected by the functionalists. The study of cases of trouble, they believed, brings out the human element in the law more clearly. It shows in more detail the juristic methods employed by the law "specialists," in order to achieve their social aims, as well as the factors that work upon them and influence their "decisions." It also brings out the rules of procedure and the way they are used. All these are no less part of the law than substantive rules.

In order, therefore, to see the "institution of law" and all its constituent sub-institutions at work, and in order to see how the law-jobs get done in any society , the anthropologist is required to concentrate on cases of trouble, but without abandoning his functionalist field techniques. Those should be used to supplement the trouble-case method whenever necessary. Thus the two movements meet to supplement each other at the methodological level, if no further.

The influence of *The Cheyenne Way* was profound and the trouble-case method has ever since become a standard tool for the study of tribal law. One of the few scholars who has not employed this method is Mr. E. Cotran. His Restatement of the Personal Customary Law in East Africa will be examined, in the light of the above discussion, in Part II of this article.

Part (II)

The last two decades have witnessed the introduction into the anthropological vocabulary of the three controversial terms "restatement", "recording" and "unification" of African customary laws. A few remarks about the history of those concepts and the causes that gave them a place in anthropological literature may help to put Cotran's work in perspective.

The Restatement Project initiated by a panel of English lawyers in the School of Oriental and African Studies (S.O.A.S.) of the University of London, was caused by a growing anxiety about the future of African customary laws. The initiators of the Project believed that African customary laws were rapidly disappearing and that it was high time that those laws be recorded. The attainment of independence by many African countries in the last two decades, the rapid development of those countries, their tendency towards more industrialization, more education, and population mobility within each country, the hastening of these tendencies as a result of certain directed policies and their contact with each other and with the rest of the world, were all seen as symptoms of the imminent death of African customary laws. The Conferences that were held[4] and the Restatement Project that followed, were all geared towards training and providing a "rescue team" to save the dying African customary laws. Cotran was a member of that team.

The S.O.A.S. activities coincided with an interest on the part of some of the new rulers of the independent African countries. After the departure of the colonial rulers those African leaders succeeded to states which were, in many respects, loose and disunited. As many, if not all, of these countries consisted of several tribes, each having different social features and different customary norms, the African leaders came to realize that one important element of unity lay in the harmonization, unification and eventually the codification of those customary norms. The task was thought to be urgent for the elimination of the factors of disunity. This realisation was probably also prompted by a dilemma which faced these rulers. On the one hand, tribalism was seen as indicative of backwardness. On the other, there was, in the wake of colonial domination, a reaction in favour of maintaining the indigenous culture. Unification of customary norms may well have been seen as a way out of dilemma : the unified laws would be drawn from the indigenous culture yet would tend away from tribalism.

These leaders wanted to use the instrument of law for the purpose of achieving certain national objectives. In order to do this, they had to have one unified legal system in each of their respective states. But those states had gone through periods of transformation, first from traditional life to colonial rule and then to independent statehood. The result was conflict of cultures and legal systems. On the one hand there were the legal systems of a non-formalized kind whose rules had not, and have not up until now, been the subject of sustained juristic study or elaboration; with them, in some countries, was and still is, the Islamic legal system, whose rules are believed to emanate from God, and which have been closely worked upon over the centuries, by jurists of great sophistication and learning. These two systems confronted—and still do—other legal systems evolved in a completely different continent, with formalized rules which were formulated and refined by judicial, legislative and scholarly labours over a long period of time.

The African leaders were therefore faced with the problem of having different legal systems in each of their countries—a situation which was thought intolerable and inconsistent with the unification and construction of their newly born nations. But they were independent and had the power to frame their own policies; this meant positive intervention by governments to unify their different customary laws into a single system. This single and unified legal system was seen as one of the strongest cohesive forces that would help bring about a social change directed towards the attainment of specific social goals, a sense of nationhood.

This is the background against which Cotran's Restatement of the customary personal laws of Kenya should be seen.[5]

In 1960, the Kenya Government decided to undertake the task of ascertaining and restating the customary law of the various tribes in Kenya. Cotran, then a research officer with the Restatement Project, was seconded by S.O.A.S. to the Kenya Government to act as Officer in Charge of the investigation. Having finished investigating the customary criminal offences,[6] he started his second stage which "consisted in the restatement of the customary personal laws of the Kenya tribes relating to marriage, divorce and succession."[7] A Commission was appointed in 1967 "to consider the existing laws relating to marriage, divorce and matters related thereto ... (and) to make recommendations for a new ... uniform law of marriage and divorce applicable to all persons in Kenya, which will replace the existing law on the subject comprising customary law, Islamic law, Hindu law and the relevant Acts of Parliament and to prepare a draft for the new law; (and) to pay particular attention to the status of women in relation to marriage and divorce in a free democratic society."[8]

These terms of reference show the seriousness of the task with which this Commission was entrusted. Cotran was a member and secretary of the Commission and his restatement of the customary laws relating to marriage and divorce was heavily relied upon. It was not our purpose to collate tribal customs," the Commission says, "This task had previously been undertaken ... by Mr. E. Cotran a Commissioner and our Secretary assisted by local law panels."[9] It seems quite clear, therefore, that Cotran's Restatement was accepted by the Commission, *in toto*, as representing the customary laws of the different tribes in Kenya, not only at the time it was recorded, but also at the time the Commission submitted its final draft Bill which was to become law if and when passed by Parliament. This conclusion seems to be affirmed by the type of questionnaire[10] which the Commission drafted and sent to some selected personalities and organizations throughout the country and which would yield, at best, dry and rigid rules (if not mere opinions). The questionnaire, in whose drafting the Secretary no doubt took part, reveals the frame of mind of the Commission, including Mr. Cotran. If this conclusion is right, then the Restatement,[11] on which a significant part of the bill is based, should be the subject of serious scrutiny.

A glance at the Restatement shows a remarkable departure from the intellectual traditions of modern anthropologists. This departure could be seen in the methods Cotran used, his conception of the operation of customary laws in tribal life and in his objectives. On the other hand, it seems clear that he wanted to strike a balance between the often mutually irreconcilable demands of scholars and politicians.[12] Investigation of this threefold departure, in the light of the anthropological tradition, may clarify the advantages of each over the other, and show whether Cotran's claims are justifiable.

For the purposes of Cotran's investigation, Law Panels were established, each representing one of fifteen ethnic groups. These panels, we are told, consisted of persons having special knowledge of customary law. They comprised mainly presidents and members of African courts, chiefs and tribal elders. In addition, the panels, it is affirmed, "had the widest representation possible of local opinion by having local authority members, young persons to demonstrate the modern developments in customary law, and in a few instances, women representatives."[13] Meetings were held with each of these panels, and by means of questions and discussions and after consideration of all available literature, a restatement of the customary laws of the ethnic group represented on the panel was made.

"The restatement for each group was carried out according to a uniform plan with uniform headings and sub-headings", e.g. capacity and consent, the formation of marriage, marriage consideration and so forth.[14] This means that each one of those headings and sub-headings was investigated separately. As some of the tribes were grouped together, variations were noted or neglected and a unification within those tribes was suggested according to whether or not the variations were thought to be significant. Fifteen decisions delivered by The Court of Review (which was apparently made up of professional judges) were appended to the volume[15] and were said to have been *"noted, where appropriate in the text."*[16] Vernacular terms were also used where translation was not considered desirable.

The trouble-case method is thus neglected. The appended decisions do not, it is submitted, convert the method used by the author into a "case-method", for the simple reason that they show nothing about the practices and techniques of the different indigenous tribunals engaged in the settlement of disputes relating to marriage and divorce in Kenya. In fact they are used as *authorities*, in the same way that English textbook writers cite decisions of higher courts for the purposes of authenticating a certain statement or illustrating a specific rule or set of rules. One example from the Restatement will clarify this point. Under the heading of *Effect of Termination of Betrothal on Issue*, the following rule is stated:[17]

> "The natural father of the child has no claim or rights over the child if he does not marry the girl."

In case 4,[18] which was cited to illustrate this rule, the natural father claimed what he had paid for the maintenance of his child. The Court of Review found that there was no valid marriage according to Masai customary law because of non-payment of the bride price and held, therefore, that the applicant was entitled to be repaid the cost of maintaining the child.

This surely is not the way trouble-cases are used by anthropologists whose handling of cases is essentially descriptive. Nor does the use of vernacular terms, which are used as alternatives to what are taken as their English equivalents, add any more scientific colour to the Restatement than what it would have had otherwise. This is so because the whole approach was designed to collect "rules". The method used was, in effect, the old 19th century "question-and-answer" method which is incapable by its very nature, of yielding more than "rules," and even if we accept the author's word that great care was taken to record the customary laws as accurately as possible and as they were, not as they ought to be,[19] the question is not "are they accurate?" but "will they work?"[20] This, it is suggested, was the right question to which the author of the Restatement should have addressed himself, if he was to satisfy the practical needs of the Kenya Government.

This leads to the second objection to the Restatement which relates to its author's conception of tribal law, and indeed about "law" generally. The author seems to assume that the rules of customary law are the only decisive factors in the judicial process of tribal societies. Hence his endeavours to be as accurate as possible in collecting those customary rules. But the customary practices or procedures, the judicial personnel, their attitudes, the ways and techniques by which they arrive at a settlement that contributes towards social harmony, are no less part of the customary law than abstract rules of substance. In short, customary rules cannot be divorced from their social context and still purport to give a complete picture of tribal law. Insofar as the Restatement fails to take account of this essential part of the customary law, it is difficult to see how it can purport to reflect an objectively descriptive, and scholarly acceptable account of customary personal laws in Kenya.

To press and clarify this point further, let us look at the essentials as provided by the author of a valid Kamba marriage. He found that one of those essentials is that "the parties *must* have the *capacity* to marry, and the capacity to marry each other"[21] In another context we are told that in order to be capable of marrying each other, the parties must obtain the consent of the family of the bride. Consent of the bride's family, that is, is one of the fundamental rules relating to capacity. It is, therefore, "essential to the validity of the union",[22] so that if a girl marries a man without the consent of her family, then the union is not a valid marriage, even if such consent is unreasonably withheld, or even if the "bride price" is left with the bride's family before the completion of the union, or even if the couple produce children. But invalidated by whom and at whose initiative? If the author is to answer such simple questions then, it is suggested, he will have to go into areas completely neglected by his method, and he will have to to reformulate his question or questions. He might well arrive at answers that neutralize or even invalidate his stated rule rather than the union. Whatever people may think about their social norms, discussed and stated in the abstract, they are not usually so dogmatic about them when they are faced with actual situations; ways are invented by which tolerations are allowed and in order to see those ways, one will have to go beyond the norm and examine the situation, the social setting in which it arises and the social machinery which deals with it. In short, the reactions of all the individuals concerned to the alleged breach will have to be looked at very carefully.

This is not an *a priori* argument, because the existence of such machinery and such reactions could be detected from the author's study itself, if not provided by common sense. In his discussion of the "machinery for divorce"[23] in the Kamba tribe, the impression is given that divorce is seriously frowned upon, and the elders will not grant a divorce until they have exhausted all methods of reconciliation and if the spouses have children then divorce becomes more difficult. It is true that this relates to dissolutions of marriages which are valid according to the people's *standards* of validity, but it does show their attitude towards the preservation of the family and the *factors* that they take into account before breaking a family apart. If this is their attitude when the spouses do not wish to live together, one would, other factors being absent,[24] expect the elders to be much more reluctant to order the dissolution of the union when the couple not only want to live together as husband and wife, but are also tied to each other by the children of their union. The standards that they seek to defend are usually vague, uncertain and flexible. The factors that they have to take into account are determinate, "living" and their effect is appreciated. Is it not possible that when those factors are weighed against the standards, ways are found by which the flexible uncertainty of the standard is manipulated in order to avoid harsh conclusions?

In the example given above the person likely to seek dissolution of such a union is probably the father of the girl and the people who may withhold recognition of the union are the bride's family and probably society generally. An enquiry along these lines would involve examination of the kinship system and the extent of its influence within the tribe and the degree of deference which is accorded to that system generally within the tribe. This is relevant because the girl's disobedience to her family's wish is probably a breach of a rule relating to the kinship system, and the possibility of the union being recognized or not, being invalidated or not, may, and probably will, turn on the relative strength of two conflicting tribal policies: breach of kinship rule on the one hand and the hardships that result from "invalidation" to the couple and their children on the other. Gulliver's findings on the neighbouring Arusha tribe lend support to this argument. The age-group system is seen, in Arusha, as more influential than the kinship system. The councillors, the negotiations and the give-and-take that are fundamental mechanisms in Arusha indigenous tribunals, leave no room for dogmatism. In the study under consideration no such social picture is given and we are left to speculate, but the constant contact between these neighbouring African tribes, coupled with the fact that the Nuer, on the other neighbouring border of Kenya, have a similar social structure,[25] lend further support to the argument.

On the practical side, the Restatement claims to provide a guide for the courts. But the magistrates who preside over these courts need to know the standards that indigenous "judges" work with, and the values they try to achieve, together with the procedures that traditional "judges" employ. These could equally provide guidance to the courts and could be assimilated (to the same extent as substantive rules) in the legal system that the Kenya Government has as the end view. To ignore these important aspects of the judicial process—indeed *the* complementary half of the law—is to provide the Government with a distorted picture of the customary laws, which picture would militate against the attainment of the Government's practical objectives.

The Restatement is full of English legal concepts, but even if we accept that this problem is met by the use of vernacular terms, the precision and comprehensiveness with which the rules are phrased would deprive the customary norms of their essential characteristics. Customary norms and standards, it is submitted, are too flexible and uncertain to be encompassed in such precise phraseology. It is this flexible uncertainty that gives them life and endurance. To deprive them of this flexibility, which manifests itself in different forms, e.g. principles, policies, ideologies, and to divorce them from the human manipulation and the techniques that manipulation involves, is to deprive them of life.

Cotran's tendency to divorce "rules" from their cultural context, may be explained in terms of his English conceptual background. The Restatement, which consists, for the most part, of bare and nicely phrased rules, with the ingredients of each rule systematically and separately discussed, is the work of a typical English lawyer.[26] The English lawyer's concept of law—as exemplified by Cotran and his colleagues in the Restatement Project—is to a very large extent influenced by the Austinian theory and the subsequent positivist versions of it, like those of Kelsen and Hart. They all tend to think of law as a system of rules emanating from one point at the top of a pyramidal structure, which point is called "sovereign", "grundnorm" or master rule, by the three jurists respectively. To those jurists, whose cumulative influence has moulded present-day English lawyers the body of that pyramid is filled with rules varying in strength and precedence and extending to the base of the pyramid. That base consists of the terminal points of numerous chains of rules which could be traced up to the top of the pyramid. These are positive rules, in the sense that they exclude questions of morality, policy, judicial legislation and other considerations, except to the extent that these questions are provided for by the "top" of the pyramid. These factors are considered to operate as isolated exceptions. Hence it is not unnatural for Cotran, working in this ethos, to focus his attention on the hard, crystallized body of that pyramid—the rules. Policy is for the legislature and judicial manoeuvre is confined to the three sides of this pyramid and there it is primarily controlled by the individual constituent rules.

Llewellyn, on the other hand, and to some extent the anthropologists who have been influenced by legal realism, have a wider conception of law. To Llewellyn law is an institution which is as broad as life and which "for some purposes one will have to follow life pretty far (to get its) bearing".[27] By conceiving of the institution of law as having jobs to do in each society and investigating *how* those jobs are done, and by using more scientific methods and avoiding misleading terminology, they have come closer to seeing the realities of tribal life. The functionalists also had a broad view of tribal life, and although they were criticized for not paying attention to matters of procedure, their perception of tribal societies as consisting of several functioning institutions and their close investigation of those institutions together with their functions, allowed them to convey a more penetrating picture of tribal realities. Their conceptions about the nature of law, questionable as they may be, could be said to have been drawn from, rather than guided, their field studies. Cotran appears to have proceeded in the opposite direction.

Cotran's departure from anthropological tradition may also be explained in terms of his objectives. He wanted something which could be used by the courts as a guide[28] and probably something that could be used as a basis for a uniform law of marriage and divorce. This last probability has, in fact, been transformed into reality and the Restatement, so the Commission thought, spared it the trouble of investigating those customary laws in any thorough and rigorous way.[29] The objectives that motivated Cotran's efforts, distinguish his work from that of modern anthropologists. This distinction is described by one writer in the following terms:[30]

> "Anthropologists are interested in what is happening, in describing a changing situation in order to understand the implications that follow from change. They are not (with few exceptions) directly concerned with the practical problems confronting new nations; that is, they are not seeking, to arrive at one truly national law'.... The administrative legal specialist is principally concerned with policy questions, which *ipso facto* seems to mean that they do not carry out depth studies."

This passage is applicable to the Restatement under consideration. The picture given is not penetrating enough to be descriptive of the one seen by the individual Kenya tribes. The effects of culture contacts to which those tribes have been subjected are not discussed or accounted for. The social change which characterizes the African societies, the result of factors such as population mobility and urbanisation, can hardly be seen in those rules and customs contained in the Restatement. The understanding of such a change is particularly important for practical purposes. If a government accepts or creates instruments of change (like the Restatement and the codification that is to follow it) without understanding, anticipating and providing for the consequences of such an action, it will only create more problems or aggravate the existing ones. The understanding of the change that has already been going on, its scope, nature and direction, would have enabled the Government to predict the nature and direction of the change that codification based on the Restatement might produce. It would also have helped the

Government to anticipate the problems that might arise and provide for them in advance.

Anthropologist have generally addressed themselves to many of these problems. The Restatement contains no indication that any of these problems were ever considered. There are other differences between the Restatement and the modern anthropological approaches: for instance, while the anthropologist would content himself with one tribe and study it in depth, Cotran attempted to study fifteen tribes, and if we count the other ethnic groups that were included with those, the number jumps to forty-four. It is humanly impossible for one man to provide depth studies for such a vast number of societies in a period of about five years, and should a government, so interested in such a project, employ only one man?

In view of all these objections, it is hard to avoid the conclusion that the Restatement is, in effect, a return to the pre-Malinowski era.

Notes

1. E. Cotran, *Restatement of African Law: Kenya*, Vol I, *The Law of Marriage and Divorce* (1968).

2. See for example, B. Malinowski, *Crime and Custom in Savage Society*. London: Kegan Paul, Trech, Trubner and Co. 1926, see also Radcliffe-Brown, A.R., *The Andaman Islanders*, Glencoe, Illinois, The Free Press, 1948. Malinowski and Radcliffe-Brown can properly be considered as the founders of modern Anthropology. Apart from their writings they trained a good number of field-workers, who later used the functionalist concepts and methods to give a penetrating picture of tribal life.

3. K.N. Llewellyn and E.A. Hoebel. See their *The Cheyenne Way, Conflict and Case Law in Primitive Jurisprudence*. Norman: University of Oklahoma Press, 1941.

4. E.G. The London Conference on the Future of Law in Africa, December 1959—January 1960. For its Report, see A.N. Allott (ed.) *The Future of Law in Africa*, London: Butter-worth, 1960, and the Dar es Salam Conference on Local Courts and Customary Law in Africa. A report of this conference was published by University College, Dar es Salam (1964), see also Allott in his introduction to Cotran, *Restatement of African Law : Kenya*, Vol. 1, *The Law of Marriage and Divorce* (1968) pp. VII–IX.

5. For more details see A.N. Allott, "Towards the Unification of laws in Africa 14 I.C.L.Q. (1965) p.366: W.L. Twining, *The Place of Customary Law in The National Legal Systems of East Africa* (1964); Twining, "The Restatement of African Customary Law: A Comment vol. *I The Journal of Modern African Studies* (1963) p.p. 221–228 and E. Cotran, "The Unification of Laws in East Africa," Vol. I *The Journal of Modern African Studies* (1963) pp. 209–220. See also Cotran's

"The Place and Future of Customary Law in East Africa" *East African Law Today* (1966) pp. 72–92.

6. E. Cotran, *Report on Criminal Offences in Kenya* (1963).

7. See Cotran in *Supra*, note I, preface, p.xi.

8. See *The Report of the Commission on the Law of Marriage and Divorce*, (1968).

9. *Ibid.* p. 2, para. 5.

10. *Ibid.* p. 128ff.

11. *Supra*, note 1. The term will hereafter be used to refer to the Restatement under consideration.

12. See his articles in *supra*, note 5.

13. See *supra*, note 1, pp. xi and xii.

14. *Ibid.* pp. xii, xiii and xiv.

15. *Ibid.* p. 182 ff.

16. *Ibid.* p. xv (my emphasis).

17. *Ibid.* p. 157.

18. *Ibid.* p. 185. It may even be doubted whether the case is good legal authority for the rule, as the case concerns a duty owed by the natural father rather than "a claim" of "rights".

19. *Ibid.* preface, p. xv.

20. See Twining, *The Place of Customary Law*, supra, note 5, p. 45, whose criticism of Cotran's Restatement of the Customary Criminal Offences in Kenya, it is submitted, still holds good on this point, with regard to the present Restatement.

21. *Supra*, note 1, p. 28, rule iv (a), (my emphasis).

22. *Ibid.* p. 23.

23. *Ibid.* p. 31.

24. Other factors going to support the norm may be either general (e.g. a belief on the part of the tribe that some supernaturally imposed affliction may result from a condonation of the union) or confined to the case in hand (e.g. the wealth and power of the bride's father). The point here is that even factors which go to support the norm are not considered.

25. See E.E. Evans-Pritchard, *The Nuer*, Oxford: The Clarendon Press. 1956. Allowance should be made for the fact that Evans-Pritchard's study of the Nuer was made in the 1940s.

26. Cotran is here considered as an example of the English lawyer because of his working methods and the way in which his work is presented. It closely resembles an English textbook. The idea of the Restatement of African customary law is shared by other equally able English lawyers, see, for example A.N. Allott (ed.) *supra*, note 5.

27. K. Llewellyn, *Jurisprudence : Realism in Theory and Practice*, Chicago: University of Chicago Press, (1962), p.4.

28. *Supra*, note 1, preface p. xvi.

29. *Supra*, note 8.

30. See L. Nader, "The Anthropological Study of Law", in *"The Ethnography of Law"*, (supplement to vol. 67 (2) *American Anthropologist* (1965). p. 14. but cf. K. Gough "Anthropology : Child of Imperialism", *Monthly Review*, April

1968. Published in U.S.A. and reproduced in "Third World Study Group", October 1968. See also Richards A.I : "Anthropology on the Scrap Heap?" 1961 J.A.A. 3.

ROBERT J. GORDON

The White Man's Burden: *Ersatz* Customary Law and Internal Pacification in South Africa

The colonialist mentality that intruded upon early attempts to ascertain folk law in Africa has already been commented upon by various African scholars, but few of these scholars have objected to the recording and study of local folk law systems on the grounds that it constituted part of an insidious plot to ensure white supremacy. This argument is now made in the context of racist South Africa where apartheid unfortunately continues to hold sway. This essay by anthropologist Robert J. Gordon of the University of Vermont puts the many attempts to ascertain African folk law in a new perspective in which ideological considerations play an important role.

For other discussions of folk law in South Africa, see B.v.D. van Niekerk, "Some Thoughts on Custom as a Formative Source of South African Law, "The South African Law Journal, 85 (1968), 279–288; T.W. Bennett and T. Vermeulen, "Codification of Customary Law," Journal of African Law, 24 (1980), 206–219; Digby Sqhelo Koyana, Customary Law in a Changing Society (Cape Town: Juta & Co., Ltd, 1980). T.W. Bennett, The Application of Customary Law in Southern Africa: The Conflict of Personal Laws (Cape Town: Juta, 1985); M.W. Prinsloo, "Restatement of Indigenous Law," The Comparative and International Law Journal of Southern Africa, 20 (1987), 411–420. B. Kuper, "Bibliography of Native Law in South Africa 1941–1961," African Studies, 23 (3–4), (1964), 155–165.

For earlier attacks on folk law serving as an unwitting aid to racist segregation, see C.C. Saunders, "The Recognition of African Law: The Cape in the Nineteenth Century," African Perspectives (1979) (2), 89–95; Raymond Suttner, "The Social and Ideological Function of African Customary Law in South Africa," Social Dynamics, 11 (1984), 49–64.

Reprinted from *Journal of Historical Sociology*, 2 (1989), 41–65, with permission of Basil Blackwell Ltd.

Informa, a mass circulation journal of the South African Department of Development-Planning, aimed at blacks, headlined a recent article 'Do We Know Each Other?' (*Informa* November 1987:14–15). To answer this question they approached a Government ethnologist. African blacks, he said, are not simply whites with black skins. On the contrary, each black nation has its own language, culture, cultural heritage and culture-pride. To negate this was to insult blacks. He then proceeded to elaborate on this uniqueness along two lines: the political unit which is the tribe and has at its apex a chief. Secondly, he maintained that there was a close relationship between traditional life styles and indigenous law and cited examples from the latter to substantiate the claim of blacks' alleged uniqueness. In short, he framed the *locus criticus* of 'difference' by examining indigenous law. His discourse was by no means exceptional. One of the more noteworthy contributions to emerge from the 'golden age' of applied anthropology in Africa involved the study of 'customary law'. Since then, for a number of complex reasons, some of which are alluded to in this paper,[1] such studies have been in decline. A powerful exception has however been in South Africa where studies of indigenous or 'Bantu Law' constitute a sizeable industry although still largely a white preserve. Starting as a mere trickle in the late sixties, studies of 'customary law' by Afrikaner anthropologists (or *volkekundiges*) have within the last two decades become the major stuff from which doctoral dissertations are manufactured. At the University of Pretoria, the major producer of volkekunde doctorates, a clear pattern is discernible: budding volkekundiges literally cut their teeth on an MA which typically deals with the political and judicial organization of some group and then move on to do their doctorate on some aspect of the 'private law' of that 'people', generally the laws of inheritance and succession[2]. This is in sharp contrast to the situation at the black 'tribal' universities where white law teachers complain about their charges' indifference, if not hostility, to 'Bantu Law', a situation they very much regretted 'because Bantu law is one of the great cultural heritages of the blacks ... (but fortunately) the torch is being carried by a very few dedicated white academics' (Lupton 1974:79–83; see also Verloren van Themaat 1969: Sachs 1973:119; Hartman and Kriel 1984). Is this simply a case of minimal employment opportunities or is it that black law students know something which their white professors do not understand? What is the nature of jural volkekunde and what role does its discourse play in contemporary Southern Africa?

Jural Volkekunde as 'Text'

To justify their enterprise, most volkekundiges, like Vorster, follow the "Restatement of African Law" ideology which was popular especially among expatriate lawyers in Africa a few years ago and suggest 'that reliable sources on current customary law (are) necessary for law reform as part of a comprehensive program of economic and social reform' (Vorster 1985:42). To be sure, there are problems with the volkekundige approach. In a review of a book containing an article by a prominent jural volkekundige, a critic worried that they saw

> Bantu law as governed by a discrete code of neatly ordered norms whose weight in judicial decision-making can be specified *in vacuo*. . . . In adopting an apparently atheoretical stance, (they) convey the impression that Southern Bantu law represents a set of clear principles which determine social action and the institutional means of coping with deviations. Apart from representing an extreme view of jural determinism . . . this does violence to the data . . . Myburgh has not simply presented a set of uncontroversial ethnographic facts: he has selected, organized and imposed interpretations upon them which are open to doubt (Comaroff 1975:150–151).

An extensive literature, both theoretical and African, has developed in recent years which has led to a substantial revision of what we know as 'customary law'. Both the assumption that 'custom' gradually evolves into law and the orthodox notion of some ancient, pre-colonial oral customary law based on equilibrium (balance) with reconciliation and compromise being the chief judicial strategies has been convincingly debunked. Similarly, characteristics which ostensibly distinguish 'customary law' from 'Western law' like strict liability, group responsibility and self-help are shown to be largely figments in the imagination of some academics and local elites (Gordon and Meggitt 1985:190–209). The recording of 'customary law' is to fabricate it since two of its key characteristics—namely the fact that it is unwritten and that it is administered by insiders or members of the same 'moral community'—are invalidated in the recording process. Once 'law' is recorded it escapes community social control and can be manipulated by outsiders and insiders because it can be applied in other contexts[3]. In a powerful but neglected essay, Stanley Diamond argued that law incorporates elements of diverse customs into its rules and thereby deceived people into believing that law supported their interests (Diamond 1971). Recorded customary law in such cases is 'used like a prostitute to lure traditional groups into the marketplace consciousness and activity of modern capitalism' (Kidder 1983:91). It is now generally accepted, at least by the 'revisionists', that 'customary law' as it emerged in the colonial era was not the product of some authentic communal tradition but was rather a tool developed by local indigenous elites and colonizers to control resources. Institutionalization of customary law was thus part of a process for redistributing power (Scaglion 1983; 1985; Moore 1978; 1986; Colson 1974; Chanock 1978; 1985; Snyder 1981).

Despite the fact that some of the 'revisionists' are literally working in their backyard (especially Comaroff 1974; Comaroff and Roberts 1981), volkekundiges with few exceptions (e.g., Vorster 1983) studiously ignore the revisionist critique. This is not a matter of simple academic ignorance. Hund and van der Merwe have recently argued that these developments are disregarded because the key volkekunde concept of the 'jural community' constitutes the very cornerstone of the 'homeland' doctrine of separate development or Apartheid (Hund 1984; Hund and van der Merwe 1986:37) because the argument that group rights are more important than individual rights provides pseudo-scientific justification for the proposition that blacks are 'more primitive' than whites[4.]

Were one to ask volkekundiges why they ignore these revisions of the nature of 'customary law', their response is typically that the revisionists are practicing sociology or history and not anthropology and thus can be ignored (see e.g., Coertze 1973). Or they make a distinction between legal anthropology and their own particular project, indigenous law, which is 'concerned with the explanation of legal phenomena in jural terms' (Vorster, personal comment). Implicit in such a dichotomy is a strongly held belief in the validity of their own version of what legal or jural anthropology is.

Jural Volkekunde was profoundly influenced by at least three factors which only minimally influenced South African (English) social anthropology, namely their strong Germanic roots, the influence of F.D. Holleman, a retired professor of Indonesian Adat Law, and the fact that a number of volkekundiges were trained in Roman-Dutch Law.

The pioneering volkekundiges of the twenties, like Eiselen and van Warmelo studied in Germany and not in Britain. This was not only because of the bitterness engendered by the Anglo-Boer war but also because in terms of the study of African languages and cultures Germany led the world. In terms of 'primitive law' there was nothing comparable to German ethnological jurisprudence and the *Zeitschrift für vergleichende Rechtswissenschaft*. Works like Post (1887), Steinmetz (1903) and even Meinhof (1914) were impressive. To summarize the position of German ethnological jurisprudence at that time: they believed that law which is created by the *Volksgeist* (spirit of the people) is manifested among all peoples of the world in the form of legal rules which can be described by using European legal terminology. This position is still held by jural volkekundiges (Vorster 1987)[5]. In an effort to record the law of non-literate peoples, Kohler, one of the major figures in this school, mounted a questionnaire blitz which made Lewis Morgan's efforts of thirty years earlier look petty. Since there were many German missionaries in Southern Africa who responded to these questionnaires, Kohler's ideas came to be seen as important in this periphery of German kultur.

Kohler's concept of law was much wider and more precise than the rather simplistic and often tautological formulations of later Anglo anthropologists like Radcliffe-Brown (Schott 1982:42–43). Thus in his pioneering 4 volume study of Venda law, van Warmelo, who was much influenced by the German ethnological jurisprudence approach, was able to anticipate the famous debate between Gluckman and Bohannan on appropriate legal terminology by presenting both the recorded native text and his own interpretation of it. Van Warmelo's study is remarkable as it is based on over 18 years of intermittent fieldwork and makes a strong plea for a thorough knowledge of the indigenous language. Van Warmelo is a figure of mythic proportion in volkekunde, yet his sensitive, careful and sustained legal studies have yet to be replicated.

A second important formative influence was the retirement to South Africa of the prominent South African-born Indonesian Adat law judge and scholar, F.D. Holleman just prior to the Second World War. After study and service in Indonesia Holleman had held the Chair in Adat law at the University of Leiden before moving to Stellenbosch where he trained or profoundly influenced most of the second generation of jural volkekundiges (N.J.J. Olivier personal comment). Myburgh, whom Hund and van der Merwe see as the major representative of Jural Volkekunde studied under Holleman at Stellenbosch and worked under van Warmelo in the Department of Native Affairs. He is certainly an important figure because apart from his almost continuous consulting with the Department of Native or Bantu Affairs, as Professor at the University of South Africa he was responsible for developing correspondence courses in 'Native Law' which many judicious clerks in Native Affairs took as part of their legal studies. But to attribute Myburgh's notion of 'jural communities' to an elaboration of some neo-Calvinist doctrinal notion of sphere sovereignty (Hund and van der Merwe 1986:37), is probably to assign greater intellectual depth to Myburgh than is warranted. In developing this notion Myburgh was undoubtedly influenced by Holleman's work on *Bantoeregsgemeenskappe* (1952) which in turn was derived from his study, not of Calvinism, but of Indonesian 'Adat Circles'[6]. In sum then, the Germanic and Holleman influences gave Jural Volkekunde a decided unilineal evolutionary and positivistic slant[7].

A third factor of substantial importance in shaping the study of 'native law' at both English and Afrikaans Universities in South Africa was the fact that many of the experts were qualified in both anthropology and law. The South African legal system is one of those oddities based on the Roman-Dutch system so that an interest in 'native law' meant a natural gravitation towards Roman law in which the scholarship of von Savigny towered. Dugard has pointed out that a number of jurisprudential strains have greatly influenced the legislative and judicial strategies of *Apartheid* and these are reflected to a remarkable degree in volkekunde. These strains are

> the imperative theory of law, historical jurisprudence, and anti-humanism (which) have been expressly invoked on occasions to justify legislative or judicial action, but in the main they have operated silently and organically to produce a State premised on legislative supremacy and judicial subordination, in which the notion of legally protected individual rights plays no part (Dugard 1986:115).

The imperative theory emphasizes the role of the 'volkswil'-the will of the people, as epitomized in White South Africa by parliament which ties in well with von Savigny's and Kohler's idea of law as an expression of the *Volksgeist*. At the same time as an avowedly nationalistic 'purist movement' was defining itself in South African jurisprudence in the thirties, volkekundiges like Eiselen and Coertze were also struggling to properly assign the superorganic 'will of the people' (see e.g., Moodie 1975:272–73)[8].

Given this genealogy it is not surprising that the volkekunde study of indigenous law is solidly in the tradition of German essentialist-philosophical historical anthropology which remains firmly based in an ethnocentric European historical consciousness dressed up in universalizing concepts (Medick 1987:80)[9]. This *weltanschauung*, in tandem with the comparatively higher social status assigned to the law profession in South Africa, allows Jural Volkekundiges to snugly dismiss revisionist attacks as intemperate and not worthy of note or even rejoinder (see e.g., Myburgh 1981).

In the construction of their studies of indigenous law, volkekundiges typically only spend a few months in the field where assisted by interpreters and extensive questionnaires-cum-checklists, they would attempt to record the 'old' Bantu law before it vanished (Coertze, 1971; Ethnological Section 1969:i; Prinsloo 1983). For example, for his doctorate, Prinsloo, a leading contemporary Bantu law expert did only 53 days fieldwork, 46 of which were devoted to interviews. He does not acknowledge any black assistance in his acknowledgements and when he refers to blacks in the text he does so by first name: hardly the style of a fieldworker who respects his informants! (Prinsloo 1983). Field work, the *sine qua non* of good anthropology, is seen as ritually polluting (Gordon 1988). The best way to study law is through in-depth interviews with male elders supplemented by the observation and annotation of court cases. The 'extended-case method' was not encouraged because court cases are generally believed to be extraordinary events and thus non-representative of social life (Vorster 1983; Holleman 1973). Lack of extensive fieldwork enables them to ignore much of the problematic which has concerned other scholars like Moore and Pospisil. An important aspect of this *problematique* is pithily encompassed in Holleman *fils'* reflections on his six years fieldwork. In asking questions he found that:

> The answer would usually come without hesitation, sometimes framed in an attractive old legal maxim. Moreover the informants would unanimously agree to this. I would then happily write down this 'rule of law'. The trouble would start when I asked them to tell me about actual cases in which this point had occurred. I then found to my annoyance that, although there were cases in which a 'correct' decision had been given by a tribal court, there were sometimes even more cases in which the court had apparently ignored the law and given quite a different kind of judgement (Holleman 1958:35).

Minimal fieldwork allows volkekundiges to avoid such enriching quandaries and allows their research to serve as self-fulfilling or reinforcing of their basic postulates which can be rather crudely summarized as pertaining to some mythical golden age which is the opposite to 'Western law', 'Western law', they see as individualistic, abstract and rational while 'Bantu law' is ostensibly emotional or irrational, concrete and especially group or communally-oriented. Volkekundiges conclude overwhelmingly that the individual 'as such' is of less importance than the individual within a group context *(binne groepsverband)* and that 'the exercise of judicial power is one of the most important functions which the political-administrative authority structures exercise within the tribe' (Hartman and Kriel 1984:20). The key difference is that Bantu law is allegedly 'unspecialized' while 'Western law' is highly 'specialized'. This reified postulate ties in well with the unacknowledged ethnocentric ahistoric Parsonian evolutionary model in which change is explained in terms of a series of mystical burps of varying intensity.[10] A legal ethnography is not, of course, merely a random set of responses to practical problems, it also provides a map of what society should be, at least in the eyes of the consumers of such ethnographies.

The purpose of this paper then is to understand this recent growth spurt of Jural *Volkekunde*. This is a question of some interest as the almost hermetical academic isolationism of volkekunde (see e.g., Gordon 1988) would easily lead an outside observer to conclude that as an academic discipline volkekunde is bound to the same fate that befell 19th century phrenology. Yet this is clearly not the case and in order to appreciate why this should be, I intend to treat jural volkekunde as a 'text' and specify, if you will, both pre-text, that is the recognition of 'customary law' and attendant implications and context, the relationship between these jural texts and their chief users, the Department of Development Administration (in the splendour of its many names).

The first step in trying to understand the resurgence of 'jural volkekunde' is to look at the source of funding of these research efforts. Not surprisingly one finds that most of the sponsorship is by courtesy of the Ministry of Constitutional Development and Planning (née Cooperation and Development [1978-84]; Department of Plural Relations and Development [1978]; Department of Bantu Administration and Development [1958-77]; Department of Native Affairs [1911-57]). An important question is why the government finds such elaborate (re)statements of 'customary law' attractive at the present time. Also at issue here is the question of bureaucratic timetables. Current rationalization stresses the fact that the State has followed the recommendations of the Hoexter Commission on the Court structure and abolished the special (Native Affairs) Commissioners courts and now allows indigenous law to be applied in all magistrates courts (Prinsloo 1987). This is clearly a *post hoc* rationalization. The evidence led before the Hoexter Commission shows the Department of Bantu Administration arguing strongly in favor of maintaining its Commissioner's Courts on the grounds that such courts required specialist knowledge of 'Bantu law'. Moreover, when it became clear that the Department was going to lose its special Commissioner's Courts, it stopped funding indigenous law research.

The Hoexter Commission Report summarized a number of criticisms which had been made over the years:

> judicial dualism smacks of apartheid and is a waste of much-needed manpower. It was noted that the amalgamation of judicial and administrative powers in the commissioners' hands had not been conducive to a high standard of justice. But aside from this, the use of commissioner's courts for the prosecution of criminal offences (mainly, of course, influx control measures) had caused Africans to view these courts as instruments of oppression (Bennett 1985:49).

It is in this context that the Department's generous sponsorship of research has to be seen.

The Re-creation of 'Customary Law' in South Africa

The history of state recognition of 'Native law' is long and complex (see Holleman 1956:233; Bennett 1985). In the South African case the key pioneering figure was Theophelius Shepstone who moved from the Cape to Natal and played a key role there in a variety of roles ranging officially from Native Agent to Secretary of Native Affairs. Shepstone saw himself as paramount chief and administered his version of 'tribal law directly' or through the chiefs.

> As early as April 1846 he was hearing between six and ten cases a day, the majority of long standing, and dealing with disputes over cattle, lobolo, or assaults. The peasantry, believing that the government had deputed him to be their special superintendent and judge, readily received his decisions. His only warrant was their consent and the governor's tolerance (Simons 1968:19).

Citing experience in West Africa and India, a Royal Instruction of 1848 regularized Shepstone's practice by recognizing the (Lt) Governor as Paramount Chief (in practice delegated to the Secretary for Native Affairs) who wielded absolute executive, legislative and judicial powers with regard to 'natives'. The Instruction further stipulated no interference with the traditional powers of chiefs 'except', according to that well-known incantation, 'insofar as they might be repugnant to the general principles of humanity recognized throughout the whole civilized world'. Eventually in the face of opposition from an unusual alliance of liberal clerics and settlers, concerned at the power he had, Shepstone was forced to develop a Natal Native Code. A variant of his Natal model was bequeathed to the Transvaal during Shepstone's brief interregnum as Administrator there.

To rapidly skim a complex history, well analysed elsewhere (see e.g. Bennett 1985; Dubow 1986), when the four British Colonies formed a Union in 1910 the status of 'customary law' was variable. It was only in 1927 that the situation was rectified. As one account by a foremost 'native law' expert described this achievement:

> Lawyers and even legislators are capable of learning, however slowly. In time the work of the anthropologists created a mental climate that encouraged a new respect for Native customs and, above all, for Native law, And so, in the year 1927, Parliament gave a qualified recognition to Native law throughout the Union and an unqualified recognition to the central institution of Native law, the practice of *lobolo* (Lewin 1940:42).

Section 11(1) of the Native Administration Act (1927) provides that:

notwithstanding the provisions of any other law, it shall be in the discretion of the Courts of Native Commissioners in all suits or proceedings between natives involving questions of customs followed by Natives, to decide such questions according to the native law applying to such except insofar as it shall have been repealed or modified: provided that such native law shall not be opposed to the principles of public policy or natural justice: provided further that it shall not be lawful for any Court to declare that the custom of lobolo or bogadi or other similar custom is repugnant to such principles (Brookes 1934a:213).

To apply this 'native law and custom' a special series of segregated courts was promulgated: Courts of headmen and chiefs, Native Commissioners Courts and Native Appeal Courts (Sections 9–21). The Minister of Native Affairs could authorize any chief or headman to hear civil cases between blacks according to 'native law'. Later the Minister also gave these tribunals criminal jurisdiction. The Commissioners Courts served both as courts of appeal from the chiefs' and headmens' courts and as courts of the first instance. In civil cases involving blacks they had the discretion to apply either Roman Dutch or native law. Appeal from this court lay to the Native Appeal Court. Recognition of indigenous law was only partial. In Natal it was based on the Native Code of 1878 while elsewhere it was developed as it was discovered from assessors, reported cases, textbooks and special (anthropological-legal) studies. Recognition presupposes ascertainment of the law to be recognized. 'Native Law' was thus those perceived aspects of abstracted indigenous law which have been recognized by the courts as well as certain additions and amendments which the courts might have made[11].

The rationale for these special tribunals is generally in terms remarkably similar to debates in other colonial situations (e.g., Morris and Read 1972 for East Africa and Fenbury 1978 for Papua New Guinea). They were to afford

> the native a simpler and less expensive method of procedure, and also ensure that cases arising out of native law and customs are heard by officials experienced and learned in such laws and customs, and, in so far as chiefs' courts are concerned, to accord a measure of recognition to purely native institutions (May 1949:243).

The legislators' intention was to enhance flexibility, and provide a simple and convenient procedure stripped of technicalities and legal niceties in order to make the courts accessible to the majority. Thus the use of lawyers was prohibited in chief/headman's courts and discouraged, indeed excluded, in 'administrative matters', in commissioner's courts (May 1949;Suttner 1986). Among matters the state defined as 'administrative' were influx control offences and appeals from the chief/ headmen and commissioners courts. Lawyers are not entitled 'as of right' to appear in appeals or to peruse documents (Horrell 1964:315). The rationale for such a prohibition was that it would not only promote contact between officials and blacks, but would also deter lawyers from charging exhorbitant fees. Specifically it tried to recreate the atmosphere of a *lekgotla* (traditional court)(Suttner 1986).

Generally, assessments of the operation of the 'Native Law Courts', be it from a liberal or government perspective, have all been critical (see e.g. Suttner 1968; 1984; Holleman 1956). Even before the legislation was effectively implemented, strictures emerged even from the ostensible beneficiaries. In 1928 a Convention of Paramount Chiefs and Chiefs forcefully made the point that:

> If it is the policy of the Government that the Bantu people should be governed by means of their own law and customs, we feel it our duty, as guardians of our people to point out that this should be in accordance with Native Law, and not with the wishes of the White race. It is our firm conviction that the policy underlying the Native Administration Act is a violation of the Bantu system of government (cited in Brookes 1934a:107;Rubin 1956:5).

In a similar vein Mr J. Mohapeloa complained that

> although Native law was administered, chief were reduced to the position of stipendiaries. Tribal divisions and tribal chiefs were ignored. Districts were divided into locations without respect to tribes, and each location was under a headman nominated by the people and appointed by the Transkei Government. Some of these headmen were traditional chiefs but they did not possess their former powers, and they were no longer guardians of the land (cited in Lacey 1981:111).

White liberals too were worried. Edgar Brookes stridently condemned the 'licensed and irresponsible despotism of the Supreme Chief' as not only contrary to both constitutional law and native Law and that 'to apply (the Act) in the name of Bantu Law is surely adding insult to injury' (Brookes 1934a:107). These remarks suggest then that other factors than simply the narrow recognition of 'native law' were at play.

Other Ingredients in the Ideological Package

Most importantly, the 1927 Native Administration Act must be seen as simply one part of a large number of associated laws popularly but inaccurately, known as 'the Hertzog segregation bills' (Davenport 1977; Brookes 1934a; Cell 1982) which arose out of the State's efforts to deal with the processes of urbanization and industrialization and culminating with the removal of Africans from the common voters roll in 1936. While this wider political economic movement is important, the recognition of 'customary law' can also be seen as part of a more specific ideological package enshrined in the Native Administration Act which sought to establish a flexible but consolidated system of administration for blacks throughout the country.

Customary law was not simply recognized out of some gesture of liberal goodwill, nor, contrary to Rubin, was the object of the Native Administration Act simply the establishment of a uniform system of customary law (Rubin 1965:203). On the contrary, the recognition of 'customary law' was an integral embellishment to what was clearly the major intent of the act. Section 1 of the Act declares that:

> The Governor-General shall be Supreme Chief of all the Natives in the Union and shall in respect of all Natives in any part of the Union be vested with all such rights, immunities, powers and authorities as are or may be from time to time vested in him in respect of Natives in the province of Natal.

In Parliament preceeding passage of the Act, the Minister of Justice pointed out that the intention was that

> The Supreme chief gets the power in the fullest sense of the word that a chief would have if there was one chief for the whole of the natives. I regard it as of the very greatest importance that those powers should be conferred upon the Governor-General, not only in respect of natives who are living under the tribal system, but also over detribalised and exempted natives... who, in many cases, are the principal agitators in South Africa today. If you have the power to remove them from one place where they do mischief to a place where they do not mischief, what a useful provision that would be (cited in Welsh 1968:90–91).

The advantages of government by proclamation have been enumerated as:

> First, it has flexibility and elasticity, enabling the administration to differentiate... between people who have advanced more than others...; secondly, it enables detailed regulations to be enacted for the guidance of both officials and the natives...; thirdly, it enables changes to be made rapidly...; fourthly, it removes details of native administration from the

arena of party politics; and lastly, it is admirably suited to the native temperament... (May 1949:314).

The far-reaching power to govern blacks by proclamation and banish by edict provided the state with a convenient and flexible instrument of domination. A theory of 'tribal despotism' loosely based on how whites believed 'tribal law' and especially Shaka behaved was used to justify this absolutist model of the Supreme Chief (Welsh 1968). Apart from making blacks liable to 'collective responsibility', Section 10 of the Native Administration Act gave the Supreme Chief immunity from the jurisdiction of any court to question or pronounce upon his actions. This intermeshing is well illustrated by Section 5(1) of the Act which allows the Supreme Chief to banish any of his black subjects without recourse to a court hearing. It was and is used especially on people whose presence the Commissioners felt might give rise to dissension, 'for offences against community discipline—offences which for technical reasons cannot be levelled in the (Magistrates) Courts' (Hepple 1956:9–11).

All Native Commissioners were regarded as the deputy or representative of the Supreme Chief/Governor-General and did the actual governing of blacks while chiefs and headmen were to assist them. Chiefs and headmen were not necessarily hereditary but appointed by the Supreme Chief who could revoke their appointment at any time and for any reason. As a reward, chiefs and headmen were paid both an annual allowance as well as bonuses which were often equivalent to their salary depending on the manner in which they performed their duties. In addition, they qualified for a special bonus based on their assistance with tax collection (May 1949:308). From the Government's point of view appointed chiefs and headmen have no duties or powers except for those prescribed in the Government Gazette. These regulations are 'thoroughly European-conceived, and all Bantu concepts are completely ignored' Holleman complained (1956:241). Since the State had already appropriated the allocation of land which had been the basis of chiefly power, these chiefs were largely powerless. Eventually chiefs were given powers of banishment which their forefathers lacked as well as limited land redistribution powers (Davenport 1977:336–7) and the Supreme Chief doctrine came a full circle and re-created a chieftainship in its own image. Tribes were created by the government for its own administrative convenience.

This Act provided the administrative and ideological edifice upon which the Nationalist Government was later to build its so-called Independent Homelands or Bantustans. In 1951 the Bantu Authorities Act was passed establishing a hierarchy of authorities starting with local tribal authorities and moving up to regional authorities and finally area authorities which were to be the nascent independent states. Ostensibly this legislation purported to restore the power of the chiefs and bolstered tribalism and tribal authority since it was supposedly based on the principles of Bantu customary law. Chief duties, prescribed by proclamation, were to keep order and to inform the Commissioner of any unrest or dissatisfaction 'or any other matter of serious import or concern to the Government' (Hill 1964:9).

In trying to persuade blacks to accept this new form of control a special propaganda section was set up under a senior Native Commissioner (an ex-volkekundige). It is easy to see why Bantu Authorities were unpopular not only amongst ordinary people but chiefs as well: They were under the thumb of the Commissioner who could appoint, remove or nominate members to the authority[12].

Expediting Bantu Law Re-creation: The Department of Native Affairs

The recognition of 'customary law' occurred within a specific socio-intellectual milieu. It has to be seen within the context of the reorganization of the Department of Native Affairs in the mid twenties. It is now generally accepted that the Department was reorganized as a response to the massive African urban proletarianization which was then occurring. 'The threat posed by these developments to white hegemony was to be met by a distinct shift in government policy: the revival of traditional institutions' (Bennett 1985:46; Evans 1986). In arguing for this shift, white officials were not alone. On the contrary, they were supported by indigenous leaders who were fearful of the crisis of social dissolution they were witnessing (Chanock 1985).

In 1926 a full ministerial portfolio of Native Affairs was created and in trying to create its own area of expertise and jurisdiction the fledgling department was involved in a fierce rivalry with other governmental departments, most notably Justice and Lands (see especially Dubow 1986; Evans 1985 on this). The act was an attempt to enhance the authority of Native Commissioners *vis-à-vis* their local rivals for power and prestige, the Magistrates, by investing them with proclamatorial power from the Governor-General. The rivalry between Native Affairs and Justice was still evident in the 1984 Hoexter Commission hearings. The Hoexter Report provides various examples: for example, in 1957 Native Affairs Commissioners Courts were empowered to hear any offence committed by a black in an area which had a commissioner. When the Justice Department objected, Native Affairs justified this action by arguing that 'they were acting on behalf of the State President as Paramount Chief of all the Blacks in so-called White areas and were in those areas further therefore obliged, at places where the volume of work warranted this, to establish commissioners' offices which had to undertake the administration of justice in respect of the Blacks' (South Africa 1979:386–9). Both arguments point to the importance of delimiting a discourse which combines a utopian and pragmatic image of black politico-legal organization seen as fundamentally different to that of whites.

Administrative and legislative matters affecting blacks were reallocated to the department especially during the Verwoerdian era. After 1951 one of its major functions was to set up and control the various Bantu Authorities. This enterprise often called for a great deal of inventiveness:

> If, after a great deal of persuasion, a tribal authority is accepted, effective use is made of this by a ceremonious installation of the chief at which compliments and presents and staffs of office are exchanged, cattle slaughtered for a feast, and much kaffir beer drunk, all photographically recorded for the Press and for the official journal of the Department of Bantu, Administration and Development (Marquard 1962:12)

Other efforts to bolster the power of the government-defined 'traditional rulers' included an effort to extend their jural control to the urban areas. Indeed, the requisite legislation has been in place for some time but vociferous opposition to this proposal from the legal profession and a few liberal scholars (see e.g. Rubin 1956; Lewin 1958; Simons 1956) managed to prevent it from being implemented. By the 1980s, however, as the black townships become increasingly 'ungovernable', this proposal has received ominous reconsideration (Prinsloo 1977; 1987).

Undoubtedly, the major beneficiaries from the recognition of 'Bantu law' were the Native Commissioners because the dual court structure gave them increased organizational flexibility and hence power. While there was little change in substantive law, the administrative policy of the state as implemented by the commissioners ensured that more and more blacks were obliged to use their courts rather than the magistrates courts. Here they exercised a power out of proportion to the narrow legal definition of their courts because not only did chiefs/commissioners courts combine what is usually separated in western legal systems, namely legislative, executive and judicial powers (see Gordon and Meggitt 1985), but lawyers are also discouraged from appearing in them. In addition, commissioners had the discretion to apply either Native law or Roman-Dutch law. Moreover their courts were not courts of record. Even judgments of commissioners in cases of appeal from chiefs courts were not written. They were required only to give reasons for judgment when there was a further appeal to the Bantu Appeal Court.

From the fragmentary evidence available (Suttner 1985; 1986) it would appear that commissioners favor Bantu Law over Roman-Dutch Law and that the version which they apply is a frozen rigid form of what they believe to be the original customary law. An Afrikaner legal specialist complained that when applying Bantu law commissioners always looked for precedent and carefully tabulated rules and were very concerned with technicalities (Verloren van Themaat 1969:79). It is perhaps thus no accident that this model is powerfully reflected in Jural Volkekunde.

Generally, even armed with the 'repugnancy clause' to effect change, the Native Courts have refused to play a reforming role. The Native Appeals Court, for example, held that its task was to find the Native law, not make it. This conservatism is part of a policy of 'retribalization' in which the male dominated redistributive system is undergirded (Suttner 1984). In this exercise Jural Volkekundiges have played an important role in their recording of law by virtue of the fact that the very language they use leads to both mystification and deception in their effort to create an illusion of authority. Rather than creating more precise statements their language creates ambiguity (Edelman 1972:139), an asset for the commissioners. Recording of law is never neutral but involves the imposition of alien forms of law and the systematic downgrading and exclusion of existing historical norms. As critical legal theorists would argue, the law thus represented is almost unknowable because the record law exists only in a language spoken only by the rulers. Indeed, the provocative question recently raised by White as to whether legal language distorts or limits one's humanity, must in this case clearly be answered in the affirmative (White 1985). Moreover, by casting the whole legal discourse in positivistic terms the judiciary was able to apply the harshest laws with an easy conscience.[13]

In carving out an organizational niche for itself the Department of Native Affairs underwent rapid growth. While the size of the civil service trebled between 1930 and 1960 (Marquard 1962:113) the growth of Native Affairs was even more spectacular. From a personnel strength of some 1211 (including 419 whites) in 1926 (Dubow 1986) it grew to some 4056 (including 1760 whites but excluding the Bantu Education component) in 1953 (South Africa 1956:170). By 1958 the department was split into the Departments of Bantu Administration and Development (BAD) and Bantu Education and five years later the Minister of Bantu Administration was provided with two deputy ministers to assist in overseeing what was termed by a government commission a 'public service within a public service' (South Africa 1979a:200).

The Department of Native Affairs (and the State) was not the only beneficiary of the recognition of native law. An influential segment of the white polity also benefitted. The doctrine of 'communal responsibility' was selectively incorporated into other legislation. For example, the Stocktheft Act provides that if the spoor of stolen stock is traced to a kraal and it is impossible to trace the actual thieves then the whole kraal is held responsible. Since over 90% of all stocktheft cases heard in court involved blacks stealing from whites the advantage of this provision for the white farmers was substantial. The doctrine was also incorporated into the Native Service Contract Act 1932 (May 1949:324), again, an arrangement which benefitted the conservative but politically powerful white farmers.

Far from being manned by enlightened progressive officials determined to carry the White Man's Burden proudly the Department of Native Affairs was in fact a sumphole of white racism. Until 1924 the Department constituted something of a marginalized *corps d'élite* (Walker 1949) but then the Prime Minister, Hertzog, saw it as an opportunity to create employment for poor whites and numerous educated blacks were forced out and replaced by Afrikaners. There was very little opportunity for educated blacks in the department. In 1946 out of some 136 black matriculants who applied for positions within it, only eight were hired (Walker 1949:162–3). Even in the field of ascertaining Bantu law, blacks are consulted only minimally. The Bantu Appeal Courts are empowered to sit with black assessors, but in the nineteen years between 1960 and 1978 the three Appeal Courts only used assessors nine times (Buchner 1982). Clearly special skills were not required to administer blacks or their law. For promotion, Schapera complained:

> Officers of the Native Affairs Department must speak the two official languages of the country, and pass the Civil Service Law Examinations; but they are apparently not required either to speak the languages of the peoples with which they are most directly concerned, nor is any special knowledge demanded from them of the Native laws and customs which they have to administer (Schapera 1939:102).

In the two year Lower Civil Service Law Diploma, Bantu law was only an optional single course. Indeed, as Schapera showed, officials who took time off to study for a Diploma in Bantu Studies at one of the six South African Universities offering it, were discriminated against, losing three years of seniority. A cursory survey of Annual Reports of the Department of Native Affairs shows that very few officials took advantage of the financial bonus to study a black language. This racism is not restricted to the Department of Native Affairs, but is deeply embodied in the very structure of South African society. Despite the fact that 'Bantu law' is of critical importance to over 70% of the population, even in the law schools of liberal English-speaking universities it is hardly taught at all (Suttner 1986).

No wonder that Brookes lambasted the Department for possessing 'more than ordinary lack of imagination and much 'red tape' and... inflexible regulations' (Brookes 1934:253). In 1944 Oliver Walker, a journalist, was seconded to the Department of Native Affairs to prepare a series of booklets for distribution in the US and Britain. Significantly, in his reminiscences of his experiences he entitled his chapter on the Department 'The Native—Is he Human?' Not only was he struck by the often open racism but officials had 'no goal, no set plan, no conviction,' about the future of blacks (Walker 1949: 159), perhaps the ultimate expression of power.[14]

Bureaucracies everywhere are notorious for their conservatism but in the extensive South African civil service which employs over 26% of the economically active white males, and the Department of Native Affairs in particular, the situation was exacerbated by the fact that many of them owe their jobs directly to Apartheid and the 'civilized labour policy' in the first instance. Many whites with low educational qualifications have or had jobs based on the control of blacks—a situation which is rife with opportunity for graft by lower-level officials (Lipton 1985:317). Like the South African Police, Bantu Affairs tends to draw recruits from the lower middle-class less-educated Afrikaners: precisely that group which would be most threatened by black advancement (Frankel 1980)[15]. This then is the context in which the contemporary rise of Jural Volkekunde must be understood. Greenberg has recently dissected the ideological struggles within the South African state and the role of ideology in legitimation and control. Officials in the various guises of the Department of Native Affairs have generally shown a remarkable degree of ideological conservative consistency (Greenberg 1987:123–176). In the battle for competing ideologies it was natural that volkekundiges and bureaucrats should form an alliance (Gordon 1988). One of the results of that liaison is to be found in the efflorescence of Jural Volkekunde.

Conclusion

While the form of that State-recognized intellectual edifice known as 'customary' or 'indigenous' law persists, its tenacity conceals a transformation in its operation as well as a transfiguration of its ideological underpinnings. An approximate periodization of intellectual readings of this process would be something like this. The initial recognition of 'native law' by Shepstone in the 19th century was not simply 'a veneer covering total subordination' but was rather derived from a shrewd appreciation of the strength of the pre-colonial indigenous social formations (Guy 1982; Bennett 1985:41). By 1927 and stretching through to the late sixties academics commonly held that the only reason why the State had not suppressed indigenous law was the belief that indigenes were not yet 'civilized' enough to share the benefits of 'ordinary' law (Holleman 1956:238; Verloren van Themaat 1968). Later, a more economistic interpretation was to become fashionable. Suttner has argued that the recognition of Bantu law served two main functions: ideologically it helped to incorporate blacks as tribal subjects and thus tried to disrupt the formation of national consciousness, more important, though, was its 'function' of consolidating the tribal family-centered redistribution system and hence subsidizing capitalism (Suttner 1986:119–143). In like vein, liberals have pointed to the well-known fact that in the past Commissioners Courts, which pre-eminently processed Pass Law infringements, were a key labor supply source for white employers (Lever 1978). Native law has served to channel blacks into these recruiting forums, but even with native law as an ostensible legitimating device not surprisingly these courts were correctly seen as oppressive instrumentalities of the State. But this has changed in recent years with large scale unemployment now the norm. Instead there has been a major increase in 'forced removals' (Lipton 1985:74). One of the key pieces of legislative ideology used to justify removal is precisely the notion of the State President as Supreme Chief.

As the process of internal pacification changes, the role of a distinctive different 'customary law' remains of crucial authorizing importance. As the rulers went through the ideological contortions known as the verligte-verkrampte conflict in the early seventies the conservatives in the Department of Bantu Administration sought ideological sustenance from their natural cohorts, the volkekundiges who were increasingly displaying a similar conservatism. They made ideal bed-mates and could reciprocally reinforce each other's projects. Thus in 1982 the former head of Native Affairs urged the strengthening of influx control and objected to the granting of property rights to blacks in urban areas on the grounds that 'private property is not indigenous to Bantu law and customs' (cited in Lipton 1985:323). There is now also a strong move to enhance the policing of townships by legalizing rightwing *makgotla* vigilante groups in the townships on the basis of 'traditional politico-legal structures'.

South Africa, until recently, had one of the lowest ratios of police to population in the world (Frankel 1980), yet its policing was one of the most effective. This is because its policing activities were embedded in a dense social institutional network in which the Department of Native Affairs was a key carceral organization concerned with the administrative sequestration of blacks. In Giddens' (1985) terms, the Department was a decisive component in the 'internal pacification' of South Africa. The Department was crucially involved in internal pacification. It used a number of techniques including coercion, co-optation, dependency and less successfully, legitimacy. Co-optation was derived from the restructuring of various control devices so that a new unity between political and civil society was achieved which was dominated in its totality by the State. The use of 'Bantu Law' is acknowledged by the State to be an essential part of its strategy of co-optation of chiefs and other petty political figures into the control apparatus. One very common ploy in such situations, is the informalization of adjudication, in South Africa under the label of 'Bantu Law'. The benefits of 'informal justice' however, as Abel argues, are vague. What informal justice does, is to render conflict conservative and disguise the expanding coercive centralizing dominance of the State (Abel 1981). Volkekundiges thus find themselves lending support to an illusion of popular justice which disguises direct class action or a new form of state-controlled adjudication which is not accountable via the usual democratic representative processes.

While in other parts of the world the State might recognize 'customary law' in an effort to enhance its legitimacy (Gordon and Meggitt 1985), in South Africa it has had the effect of buttressing its illegitimacy[16]. As Skocpol (1979) has shown generally, and Adam and Moodley (1986) specifically for South Africa, modern regimes can ignore popular feeling indefinitely as long as they have the support of strategically placed key groups, in this case lodged in the Native Affairs Department and its subaltern chiefs and headmen.

In order to ensure compliance and in-group cohesion, Adam and Moodley argue, the ethnic state must exercise power legally. Authorization or legality replaces legitimacy as the key concern. In such circumstances 'divorced from substantive ideals with universal content, normative regularity becomes a reified faith in procedures' (Adam and Moodley 1986:129; Adam 1971:48). As Eiselen, pioneer volkekundige and 'architect of apartheid', put it: 'Once any measure becomes law, it is the duty of every citizen ... to obey that law ... anything else was nothing less than bare-faced incitement and thus a matter for the police' (cited in Evans 1986:265; see also Adam 1971: 48–9). Small wonder that studies of indigenous 'administrative law' are a major topic of concern for volkekundiges (e.g., Myburgh and Prinsloo 1985).

The Native Administration Act of 1927 was an attempt to coordinate the authoritative resources of the State with regard to controlling blacks.

A key component of the exercise of power is what Giddens terms 'surveillance activities' which he says:

> refer to two connected phenomena. First, to the accumulation of 'information'-Symbolic materials that can be stored by an agency or collectivity. Second, to the supervision of the activities of subordinates by their superiors within any collectivity. It is important to distinguish these as it is to emphasize the potential connections between them. The garnering and storage of information is a prime source of time-space distanciation and therefore of the generation of power. Power is also generated by the supervisory activities of superordinates, since supervision is one medium of co-ordinating... (Giddens 1981:169).

Volkekundiges contributed to the sequestration of blacks and at the same time provided a condition for the stability of the routine. Power is at its most durable and intense when running silently through the repetition of institutionalized practices (Giddens 1985:9). Volkekundige statements of Bantu Law serve as grids which officials can use to justify, sort, order and reorder the elements of power they have. Contrary to Foucault, disciplinary power does not depend primarily upon information-retaining surveillance, but rather on a set of documents which legalizes officials' autonomy. Moreover the availability of Jural Volkekunde texts absolve the officials from enquiring into the current social practices of blacks (Bennett 1985:23), a situation which might conceivably provoke some empathy which could have seditious undertones in the eyes of the more staunch proponents of Apartheid. It is in this sense, that we can understand the resurgence of studies of 'indigenous law' in South Africa. From its inauspicious beginnings as a negotiated concession, 'indigenous law' has been transubstantiated into a powerful means of control. Could it be that black law students in South Africa know something which their learned white professors do not?

Notes

1. I would like to thank Tom Bennett, Diana Wyllie and Saul Dubow for comments on this paper and Professors Louis Vorster of the University of South Africa and Bill Davies of Rhodes for responding to my letters requesting information. Obviously they are not responsible for any of the opinions expressed in this paper. This paper germinated in a National Endowment of the Humanities Summer Seminar on Anthropological Approaches to Law led by Larry Rosen (1984) and was polished in a 1988 History of Science seminar led by Everett Mendelsohn. In 1969 Raymond Suttner provoked my first foray into publishing on 'Bantu Law'. At present he is restricted after being held without trial for

two years in South Africa. I would like to dedicate this paper to him. He has finally convinced me.

2. See the bibliography in Hartman and Kriel 1984 as well as recent issues of the *South Africa Journal of Ethnology*.

3. On the dramatic implications of written law, see Goody 1986:127–170.

4. All Afrikaans ethnology textbooks teach that as cultures develop they change from a group to an individual focus (Coertze 1973; van der Wateren 1978).

5. For a case study of the disastrous consequences for Australian Aborigines of such an approach, see Gumbert 1984.

6. An assessment of Holleman pere's pioneering work has yet to be done. He was clearly one of the most original legal anthropologists of all time.

7. See also Hund and V.D. Merwe's 1986: 32–5 discussion of positivistic fictions which is however more formulaic than substantive.

8. Such was the zeal of the linguistic purists in literature that while many anglicisms were exorcised from Afrikaans, numerous germanisms were invented. Brink 1983:99.

9. Medick 1987 also provides a useful critique of this approach.

10. See also the useful summary statement by Bruwer in the Standard Encyclopedia of Southern Africa 1970:112–114.

11. In official discourse indigenous, customary or native law has undergone several transformations to Bantu and black law. My usage reflects that of the period.

12. For a discussion see Mbeki 164; Hill 1964.

13. Generally on the role of legal positivism in South Africa, see Dugard 1978.

14. Fragmentary anecdotal evidence tends to support Walker's analysis. Lewin, a liberal 'African law lecturer', for example, mentions that in the '40s when he wrote an advisory pamphlet for blacks on their legal rights, at least one Native Commissioner took it to the police to inquire whether such material could be freely circulated (Lewin 1947:83)!

15. For more on Bantu Affairs conservatism see Welsh 1982:96–109; Adam and Giliomee 1979.

16. As when it decided that 'the creation of a debt in European fashion, as is alleged by the plaintiff, is a thing unknown' or 'that is is foreign to Native custom in the circumstance to exact payment for board in this fashion' (Lewin 1940:45).

Bibliography

Abel, R. 1981 Conservative Conflict and the Reproduction of Capitalism: The Role of Informal Justice, *International Journal of the Sociology of Law* 9(3).

Adam, H. 1972 *Modernizing Racial Domination*. Berkeley: University of California Press.

Adam, H and H. Giliomee 1979 *Ethnic Power Mobilized.* New Haven: Yale University Press.
Adam, H. and K. Moodley 1986 *South Africa Without Apartheid.* Berkeley: University of California Press.
Bennett, T.W. 1985 *Application of Customary Law in Southern Africa.* Cape Town: Juta.
Brink, A.P. 1983 *Writing in a State of Siege.* New York: Summit.
Brookes, E. 1934 Native Administration in South Africa. In I. Schapera, ed., *Western Civilization and the Natives of South Africa.* London: Routledge and Kegan Paul.
Brookes, E. 1934a *The Colour Problems of South Africa.* London: Kegan Paul.
Bruwer, J.P. 1970 Bantu Law. In *Standard Encyclopaedia of South Africa.* Cape Town: Naspers.
Buchner, J.J. 1982 Inheemse Gewoontereg: Regskepping deur die appelhowe vir kommissarishowe. *De Rebus* April.
Cell. J W. 1982 *The Highest Stage of White Supremacy.* New York: Cambridge University Press.
Chanock, M. 1978 Neo-traditionalism and the Customary Law in Malawi. *African Law Studies* 16.
Chanock, M. 1985 *Law, Custom and Social Order: The Colonial Experience in Malawi and Zambia.* Cambridge: Cambridge University Press.
Coertze, P.J. ed. 1973 *Inleiding tot die Volkekunde.* Johannesburg: Voortrekker.
Coertze, R.D. 1971 *Die Familie-, Erf-en Opvolgingsreg van die Bafokeng van Rustenburg.* Pretoria: SABRA.
Colson, E. 1974 *Tradition and Contract.* Chicago: Aldine.
Comaroff, J. 1974 Chiefship in a South African Homeland. *Journal of Southern African Studies* 1(2).
Comaroff, J. 1975 The Case for a General Ethnography: Southern Bantu Perspectives. *African Studies* 34(2).
Comaroff, J. and S. Roberts 1981 *Rules and Processes.* Chicago: University of Chicago.
Davenport, T.R.H. 1977 *South Africa: A Modern History.* Johannesburg: Macmillan.
Diamond, S. 1971 The Rule of Law vs the Order of Custom. In Robert Wolff, ed., *The Rule of Law* New York: Simon & Schuster.
Dubow, S. 1984 'Understanding the Native Mind': Anthropology, Cultural Adaptation, and the Elaboration of a Segregationist Discourse in South Africa, c. 1920–36. UCT African Studies Seminar.
Dubow, S. 1986 Holding 'A Just Balance between White and Black': The Native Affairs Department in South Africa c. 1920–33. *Journal of Southern African Studies* 12(2).
Dugard, J. 1978 *Human Rights and the South African Legal Order.* Princeton: Princeton University Press.
Dugard, J. 1986 The Jurisprudential Foundations of the Apartheid Legal Order. *The Philosophical Forum Quarterly* XVIII(2–3).
Edelman, M. 1972 *The Symbolic Uses of Politics.* Urbana: University of Illinois Press.

Ethnological Section, eds. 1969 *Ethnological and Linguistic Studies in honour of N.J. van Warmelo*. Pretoria: Government Printer.

Evans, I.T. 1986 *The Political Economy of a State Apparatus: The Department of Native Affairs in the transition from Segregation to Apartheid in South Africa*. Ph.D Dissertation, University of Wisconsin, Madison.

Fenbury, D. 1978 *Policy Without Practice*. Canberra: Australian National University.

Fitzpatrick, P. 1983 Law, Plurality and Underdevelopment. In D. Sugarman, ed. *Legality, Ideology and the State*. London: Academic.

Frankel, P.H. 1980 South Africa: The Politics of Police Control. *Comparative Politics* 12(4).

Giddens, A. 1981 *A Contemporary Critique of Historical Materialism*. London: Macmillan.

Giddens, A. 1985 *The Nation-State and Violence*. Berkeley: University of California Press.

Goody, J. 1986 *The Logic of Writing and the Organization of Society* New York: Cambridge University Press.

Gordon, R. 1988 Apartheid's Anthropologists: Notes on the Genealogy of Afrikaner Volkekundiges. *American Ethnologist* 15(4).

Gordon, R. and M. Meggitt 1985 *Law and Order in the New Guinea Highlands*. Hanover: University Press of New England.

Greenberg, S. 1987 Ideological struggles within the South African state. In Marks, S & S. Trapido, eds. *The Politics of Race, Class and Nationalism in Twentieth-century South Africa*. London: Longmans.

Gumbert, M. 1984 *Neither Justice Nor Reason: A legal and anthropological analysis of Aboriginal Land Rights*. New York: Queensland University Press.

Guy, J. 1982 The Destruction and Reconstruction of Zulu society. In Marks, S. & R. Rathbone, eds., *Industrialization and Social Change in South Africa*. London: Longmans.

Hartman, J.B. and J.D. Kriel 1984 Inheemse Regsisteme as Volkekundige Studieterrein. In *Suid-Afrikaanse Tydskrif vir Ethnologie* 7(1).

Hepple, A. 1956 Banishment as a Weapon of Administration. In *The Forum*. October.

Hill, C. 1964 *Bantustans: The Fragmentation of South Africa*. London: Oxford University Press.

Holleman, F.D. 1952 Bantoeregsgemeenskappe. mimeo, Stellenbosch.

Holleman, F.D. 1956 The Recognition of Bantu Customary Law in South Africa: A Case Study. In Afrika Instituut, *The Future of Customary Law in Africa*. Leiden: Universitaire Pers.

Holleman, J.F. 1950 An Anthropological Approach to Bantu law. *Rhodes-Livingstone Journal* 10.

Holleman, J.F. 1958 *African Interlude*. Cape Town: Nasionale Pers.

Holleman, J.F. 1973 Trouble-Cases and Trouble-less cases in the study of customary law and legal reform. *Law and Society Review* 7(4).

Horrell, M. ed 1964 *A Survey of Race Relations*. Johannesburg: SAIRR.

Hund, J. 1982 Legal and Sociological Approaches to Indigenous Law in Southern Africa. *Social Dynamics* 8(1).

Hund, J and H.W. van der Merwe 1986 *Legal Ideology and Politics in South Africa*. Lanham: University Press of America.
Kidder, R. 1983 *Connecting Law and Society*. Englewood Cliffs: Prentice-Hall.
Lacey, M. 1981 *Working for Boroko*. Johannesburg: Ravan.
Lever, H. 1978 *South African Society*. Johannesburg: Jonathan Ball.
Lewin, J. 1940 Native Law and its Background. *Race Relations* 7(3).
Lewin, J. 1947 *Studies in African Native Law*. Oxford: Blackwell.
Lewin, J. 1958 Tribalism Coming to Town. *Africa South* 3(3).
Lipton, M. 1985 *Capitalism and Apartheid*. Totowa: Rowman & Allanheld.
Lupton, M.E. 1974 The Construction of a law Curriculum—with special reference to a University for Blacks. *Speculum Juris* (9).
Marquard, L. 1962 *The People and Policies of South Africa*. London: Oxford University Press.
May, H.J. 1949 *The South African Constitution*. Cape Town: Juta.
Mbeki, G. 1964 *South Africa: The Peasants Revolt*. Harmondsworth: Penguin.
Medick, H. 1987 'Missionaries in the Row Boat'? Ethnological Ways of Knowing as a Challenge to Social History. *Comparative Studies in Society and History*.
Meinhof, C. 1914 *Afrikanische Rechtsgebrauche*. Berlin: Berlin Missionary Society.
Moore, S.F. 1978 *Law as Process*. Boston: Routledge & Kegan Paul.
Moore, S.F. 1986 *Social Facts and 'Fabrications'*. New York: Cambridge University Press.
Moodie, D. 1975 *The Rise of Afrikanerdom*. Berkeley: University of California Press.
Morris, H and J. Read 1972 *Indirect Rule and the Search for Justice*. London: Oxford University Press.
Myburgh, A.C. 1981 Inheemse Reg as Reg. *Tydskrif vir Hedendaagse Romeins-Hollandse Reg* 44(3).
Myburgh, A. and M.W. Prinsloo 1985 *Indigenous Public Law of Kwandebele*. Pretoria: van Schaik.
Post, A.H. 1887 *Afrikanische Jurisprudenz*. Leipzig: Schulzersche Hof.
Prinsloo, M.W. 1977 Stedelike Inheemsregtelike Howe. *Journal of Racial Affairs* 28(1–2).
Prinsloo, M.W. 1981 *Die Inheemse Administratiefreg van 'n Noord-Sothostam*. Pretoria: University of South Africa.
Prinsloo, M.W. 1983 *Inheemse Publiekreg in Lebowa*. Pretoria: van Schaik.
Prinsloo, M.W. 1987 Toekomstige Ontwikkelinge in die Inheemse Reg. *Tydskrif vir Hedendaagse Romeins-Hollandse Reg* 50(1).
Roberts, S. 1985 The Tswana Polity and 'Tswana Law and Custom' Reconsidered. *Journal of Southern African Studies* 12(1).
Rubin, L. 1956 Fewer Rights and More Tribalism. *The Forum* June.
Rubin, L. 1965 The Adaptation of Customary Family Law in South Africa. In *African Law: Adaptation and Development*. H & L Kuper eds. Berkeley: University of California Press.
Sachs. A. 1973 *Justice in South Africa*. Berkeley: University of California Press.
Scaglion, R. 1983 *Customary Law in Papua New Guinea: A Melanesian View*. Port Moresby: Government Printer.

Scaglion, R. 1985 The Role of Custom in Law Reform. In *Essays on the Constitution of Papua New Guinea*. R. de Vere et al eds. Port Moresby: Tenth Independence Anniversary Advisory Committee.

Schapera, I. 1939 Anthropology and the Native Problem. *South African Journal of Science* XXXVI:89–103

Schott, R. 1982 Main Trends in German Ethnological Jurisprudence and Legal Ethnology. *Journal of Legal Pluralism* 20.

Simons, H.J. 1956 Tribal Worship. *Africa South* 1(4).

Simons, H.J. 1968 *African Women: Their Legal Status in South Africa*. Evanston: Northwestern University Press.

Skocpol, T. 1979 *States and Social Revolutions: A Comparative Analysis of France, Russia and China*. Cambridge: Cambridge University Press.

Snyder, F. 1981 Colonialism and Legal Form—the Creation of 'Customary Law' in Senegal. *Journal of Legal Pluralism* 19.

South Africa 1956 *Summary of the Report of the [Tomlinson] Commission for the socio-economic development of the Bantu Areas within the Union of South Africa*. Pretoria: Government Printer.

South Africa 1979 *[Hoexter] Commission of Enquiry into the Structure and Functioning of the Courts*. Pretoria: Government Printer.

South Africa 1979a *[Riekert] Commission of Inquiry into Legislation affecting the utilization of manpower*. Pretoria: Government Printer.

Steinmetz, S.R. 1903 *Rechtsverhaltnisse von eingeborene Volkern*. Berlin: Springer.

Suttner, R.S. 1968 Towards Judicial and Legal Integration in South Africa. *South African Law Journal* LXXXV(IV).

Suttner, R.S. 1984 African Family Law and Research in South Africa Today: Prospects and Problems, mimeo.

Suttner, R.S. 1985 The Social and Ideological Function of African Customary Law in South Africa. *Social Dynamics* 11(1).

Suttner, R.S. 1986 African Customary Law—Its Social and Ideological Function in South Africa. In T. Lodge, ed., *Resistance and Ideology in Settler Societies*. Johannesburg: Ravan.

Turner, V. 1975 Symbolic Studies. B.J. Siegal, ed. *Biennial Review of Anthropology*. Palo Alto: Stanford University Press.

van der Wateren, H. 1978 *Kultuur: Kleed van die Mens*. Pretoria: NG Kerkboekhandel.

van Warmelo, N.J. in collaboration with W.M.D. Phophi 1948–9 *Venda Law*. 4 volumes. Pretoria: Government Printer.

Verloren van Themaat, R. 1968 Die bepaling van Rigting by die Regsopleiding van die Bantoe. *Tydskrif vir Hedendaagse Romeins-Hollandse Reg* 31.

Verloren van Themaat, R. 1969 Legal Education for the Bantu of South Africa. *Comparative and International Law Journal of Southern Africa* 2.

Verloren van Themaat, R. 1970 Ontwikkeling in verband met die Reg en Regspleging van die Bantoe: Oorsig vir 1969. *Tydskrif vir Hedendaagse Romeins-Hollandse Reg* 33(4).

Vorster, L.P. 1983 *Volkekunde en Inheemse Reg*. Inaugural Lecture, University of South Africa. Pretoria.

Vorster, L.P. 1985 Indigenous Law and development. *Development Southern Africa* 2(1).
Vorster, L.P. 1987 *Indigenous Law/Study guide 1 for IHR100–N*. Pretoria: University of South Africa.
Walker, O. 1949 *Kaffirs are Lively*. London: Victor Gollancz.
Welsh. D. 1968 The State President's Powers under the Bantu Administration Act. *Acta Juridica*.
Welsh, D. 1992 The Policies of Control: Blacks in the Common Areas. In R. Schrire, ed. *South Africa: Public Policy Perspectives*. Cape Town: Juta.
White, J.B. 1985 *The Legal Imagination*. Chicago: University of Chicago Press.

The Expression of Folk Law in Folklore, Symbol, and Ritual

Individual folk laws may or may not be said to exist as abstract entities. More often than not, folk laws are manifested through a variety of cultural expressions. Folk laws may be phrased in proverbial form, e.g., as maxims. They may be the basis of popular fictions, e.g., as found in legends or folksongs. They may be explicit in different types of traditional rituals, e.g., ordeals and oaths. They may be exemplified through the use of culturally accepted symbols.

Because folk law can be expressed in so many ways, the study of folk law has had to take account of this diversity. For the most part, it has been folklorists who have sought to identify "legal antiquities" as a kind of survival in contemporary ballads and children's games. Many of these identifications are admittedly highly speculative. In contrast the common use of symbols in folk law is much easier to document. The same holds for the widespread occurrence of such ritual processes as ordeal.

The investigation of the symbols, metaphors, and rituals underlying the actual practice of folk law is surely one of the most fascinating facets of folk law scholarship.

HERMANN BALTL

Folklore Research and Legal History in the German Language Area

To the extent that folk law falls under the rubric of folklore in general, e.g., as analogous to folk medicine or to folk art, it should not come as a surprise to learn that German scholars have been among the most active in its study. Here we should be careful to distinguish the research carried out by German anthropologists or ethnologists from that resulting from the efforts of German folklorists. The German folkloristic tradition goes back to Jacob Grimm (1785–1863) and his teacher Savigny (1779–1861), who is generally credited with founding the so-called historical school of jurisprudence, and this folkloristic tradition has functioned largely independent of German ethnological jurisprudence (which may be said to have begun with Post).

The following essay by Hermann Baltl of the Institut für Österreichische Rechtsgeschichte [Institute for Austrian Legal History] at the University of Graz, seeks to survey some of the highlights of folk law research achieved by scholars in the German-speaking world, e.g., Germany, Austria, and Switzerland. Baltl tends to prefer the term 'legal archaeology' for the study of folk law, a term that betrays his basically historical bias. See, for example, his earlier essay, "Rechtliche Volkskunde und Rechtsärchaeologie als wissenschaftliche Begriffe und Aufgaben," Schweizerisches Archiv für Volkskunde, 48 (1952), 65–82.

It should be noted that several major twentieth-century folklorists, e.g., Corso from Italy, Saintyves from France, were interested in folk law. It is also fair to say that most of the research carried out by folklorists has been totally ignored by scholars in jurisprudence proper. Some basic survey essays of these folkloristic efforts include: Eberhard von Künssberg, "Rechtsgeschichte und Volkskunde," Zeitschrift für Deutschkunde, 36 (1922), 321–335; P. Saintyves, "Le Folklore juridique," Revue de Sociologie et d'Ethnologie, 12 (1932), 65–108; Walther Steller, "Volkskunde und Rechtskunde," Zeitschrift für Volkskunde, 42 (1932), 117–137; Rene Maunier, "Folklore Juridique," Archives de Philosophie du droit et de Sociologie 7 (3–4) (1937), 7–20, see also Maunier, "Le Folklore juridique," in Travaux du Ier Congrès International de Folklore *(Tours:*

Reprinted from the *Journal of the Folklore Institute*, 5 (1968), 142–151, with permission. The essay was originally translated from German into English by Stephen Wedgwood.

Arrault, 1938), pp. 185–191; and his book Introduction au folklore juridique *(Paris: Les Editions d'art et d'histoire, 1938; Claudius von Schwerin, "'Volksrechtskunde' und 'Rechtliche Volkskunde',"in* Studi di Storia e Diritto in Onore di Enrico Besta, *Vol. II (Milano: Dott. A. Giuffre, 1939), pp. 517–536; Karl Siegfried Bader, "Über das Verhältnis von Rechtsgeschichte und Volkskunde,"* Angebinde John Meier zum 85. Geburtstag *(Lahr: Moritz Schauenburg, 1949), pp. 31–41; Leon Halban, "Znaczenie Zwyczajow Prawnych i Ich Badanie," [The Importance of Legal Customs and Their Investigation]* Lud, *39 (1948–1951), 148–180; Raffaele Corso, "L'Ethologia Giuridica,"in* Problemi di Etnografia *(Napoli: Conte Editore, 1956), pp. 34–48; Gerhard Hafström, "Volkskunde und Rechtskunde,"* Folk-Liv, *21–22 (1957–1958), 39–48; Karl-S. Kramer, "Problematik der Rechtlichen Volkskunde,"* Bayerisches Jahrbuch für Volkskunde *(1962), 50–66; and Kramer,* Grundriss Einer Rechtlichen Volkskunde *(Göttingen: Verlag Otto Schwartz, 1974); and Luigi M. Lombardi Satriani, "Per il diritto folklorico: Note per una delimitazione teorica,"* Etnologia: antropologia culturale, *1 (1974), 14–34; and Karl Siegfried Bader, "Rechtliche Volkskunde in der Sicht des Juristen und Rechtshistorikers," in Konrad Köstlin and Kai Detlev Sievers, eds.,* Das Recht der kleinen Leute: Beiträge zur Rechtlichen Volkskunde *(Berlin: Erich Schmidt Verlag, 1976), pp. 1–11.*

For Savigny's views of folk law, see Frederick Charles von Savigny, Of the Vocation of Our Age for Legislation and Jurisprudence *(London: Littlewood, 1831) which was first published in German in 1814. For an appreciation of Savigny, see Hermann Kantorowicz, "Savigny and the Historical School of Law,"* Law Quarterly Review, *211 (1937), 326–343. For Savigny's influence upon the Grimm brothers, see Hans Fehr, "Die Brüder Jacob and Wilhelm Grimm und Friedrich Karl v. Savigny,"* Zeitschrift für Schweizerisches Recht, *N.F. 72 (1953), 437–443. For Jacob Grimm's decision to abandon legal studies in favor of more general folklore research see Wilhelm Schoof, "Jacob Grimms Abkehr von der Rechtswissenschaft,"* Zeitschrift für Schweizerisches Recht, *N.F. 82 (1963), 269–282. For an older work reviewing Jacob Grimm's contribution to jurisprudence, see Rudolf Hübner,* Jacob Grimm und Das Deutsche Recht *(Göttingen: Dieterich-sche Verlagsbuchhandlung, 1895). For more modern scholarship, see Werner Ogris, "Jacob Grimm und die Rechtsgeschichte,"in* Jacob und Wilhelm Grimm: Vorträge und Ansprachen in den Veranstaltungen der Akademie der Wissenschaften und der Georg-August-Universität in Göttingen *(Göttingen: Vandenhoeck & Ruprecht, 1986), pp. 67–96.*

Our field of investigation includes everything of a legal nature which has impressed itself on and has found continued application in popular life, and everything of a popular nature which has been carried over into law. One must remember, of course, that in former times no sharp distinction was made between actual legal norms in the modern sense and other elements, such as customs, symbols, and instruments, which were felt to have equal validity.[1] This means that the task of folklore research, "to recognize the general underlying patterns of human organization and the expression of these patterns among every people,"[2] will be especially evident, in all its complexity, in this field of inquiry. The objects of investigation are the legal norms themselves, the customs determined by law, the instruments employed in legal life, symbols which have a legal meaning, folk tradition insofar as it has legal relevance, *Sagen*, Märchen, other traditional narratives, literature, art, and the names of persons, places, and institutions.

Rules and forms may have been impressed by the folk on the nucleus of the legal norms, or else they may have been carried over from the legal realm to the popular. This point may be illustrated with the examples of ordeals, which have legal applications as well as a role in folk tradition. The actual forms of customary law, together with those customs which have been inspired by law, belong to the area of legally determined customs. The "instruments" of legal life include all objects: not only the instruments of punishment and execution, which stand in the foreground of popular interest, but also the building used for legal purposes, e.g., city halls, courthouses, prisons, palaces, castles, and other seats of legal authority. The badges of authority are also included, and here we touch on the realm of symbols such as boundary markers, weights and measures, and the utensils, such as chests and coffers, employed in the guilds. Folk tradition, so far as it is connected with law, often contains these elements. Games, including children's games, dances, *Sagen* and Märchen can often also be included. This last area provides many fruitful insights into older forms of legal thought. For example, the motif of the corrupt king who is banished can be related to the right of rebellion. Narratives describing disloyal administrators, adultery and its punishment, and the appropriation of lands also have obvious legal connotations. Literature and art often contain relevant references, and the names of regions, localities, institutions, and persons can, either overtly or covertly, reveal legal themes.[3]

In all the areas outlined here, and this is by no means a complete accounting, where legal history and folklore research come into contact, the material with which both disciplines must work has been growing, and continues to grow. From the standpoint of society, investigation cannot limit itself to problems of the *vulgus in populo*, but must extend to include all social levels, in other words, the entire folk. Because of the multiplicity of source materials and the wide range of society, quite understandably there has arisen a desire for greater order and clarity in system, terminology, and methods. These matters will now be considered.

As Jacob Grimm, under the influence of romanticism, began to collect "materials pertaining to the physical side of German legal history, without regard for the practices and systems of today," the collective designation "German legal antiquities" seemed to arise almost spontaneously. The venerable age, either real or imagined, of the objects treated was decisive, as was their striking quality, picturesqueness, and sometimes their strangeness and scurrility. In general the antiquarian spirit prevailed and there was no attempt at systematic division. Indeed, the concept of "legal antiquities" was extended broadly to include all older legal institutions. Even the old books of law were treated as legal antiquities.[4] In many works of the nineteenth century a connection with *iurisprudentia picturata* and *iurisprudentia symbolica*, the precursors of our subject, was visible.[5] The work on the *Deutsches Wörterbuch*, begun at this time, and on other dictionaries, helped bring much material to light. The Grimm's collection of fairy tales and folktales, the editing of the *Monumenta Germaniae Historiae* after 1826, and the early editions of the *Weistümer* (judgments) supplied more and more evidence of the close relationship between folklore research and legal history. The jurist Andreas Michelsen took up the problem of house and property markers,[6] and raised the question of the significance of these signs in legal history. In particular the use of *festuca notata* in the transfer of property provided an exemplary instance of productivity for both folklore research and legal history.[7] Carl Homeyer also studied these marks and progressed from these to a study of the personal brand.[8] Collections of house and property marks, editions of ancient court practices and legal customs, and collections of objects employed in legal life were published sporadically.

The extensive foundation of source materials available at the end of the nineteenth century was further enriched through related disciplines like philology, art history, archeology, and numismatics. Out of this recognition, and with the growth of folklore as a separate science, the area of contact between folklore research and legal history gradually became defined. In 1886 and 1887 the French journal *Mélusine* published a study of children's customs with legal content under the title "Folklore juridique des enfants."[9] In this way the term "legal folklore research" gradually came into use as a collective designation, at first especially for the study of legal customs, then for legal language-geography, and also for the expression and instruments of the law itself.[10] Meanwhile, largely through the efforts of Karl von Amira, who in 1905 had already disclosed important sources with his treatment of gestures in the illustrated manuscripts of the *Sachsenspiegel*, the term *Rechtsarchäologie* (legal archeology) was coined[11] and exemplified in Amira's studies of the legal symbolism of the mace and of Germanic death penalties.[12] Amira defined the task of legal archeology as the investigation of legal instruments, activities, and symbols.[13] As an essential prerequisite to this investigation he called for the critical description and cataloguing of these sources.

Initially, the term "legal folklore research" gained greater currency. Eberhard von Künssberg, who has done excellent work in the whole field, was the first to employ this term generally as an expression for "research in the border area between folklore... and legal history."[14] One of Künssberg's works, published in 1936 in the monograph series *Volk: Grundriss der deutschen Volkskunde in Einzeldarstellungen*, was entitled *Rechtliche Volkskunde*. Based on extensive knowledge, this was probably the first book devoted to this young field of research. Works by other authors followed. In addition to legal folklore research, there was renewed discussion of legal antiquities or "legal monuments," now focused on "objects employed in legal life,"[15] and even "legal tokens" which included customs as well as artifacts.[16] Finally, in 1943, there appeared the already mentioned work of Claudius von Schwerin, which, in recognition of Amira, bore the title *Rechtsarchäologie*. In view of this development a clear distinction between the materials is desirable, as is clarification of the terminology.

It should be remembered that legal folklore research, if it wishes to remain true to its name, must stand in direct connection with research in folklore. This means that legal folklore research must present itself as a study, oriented toward folklore, of the legal institutions which are created, influenced, or developed by the folk, or of the forms of popular life which have their origin in law. It is certainly correct that a sword of judgment, a gallows, an official building, an inscription, a boundary stone, or a ceremonial chest may to a great extent be created or determined by the folk, just as a custom, piece of furniture, or Märchen can be influenced by the law. However, the multiplicity of perspectives from which these objects can be viewed—art history, religious history, philology, economic history, or, directly, legal history, to mention a few—thereby becomes even greater, unless one is to identify folklore research altogether with cultural history in general. One also must consider what attitude is to be taken toward such important signs of authority in legal life as crowns and thrones, and more modest objects such as seal presses, handcuffs, and voting urns, whose forms are determined purely by their purpose. These elements have only a tenuous connection with folklore. It would also be interesting to consider the consequences of applying this broad extension of folklore to other disciplines, for example art history or archeology.

Claudius von Schwerin called for the limitation of legal folklore study to the investigation of popular legal customs, because inclusion of the articles and practices of official legal life oversteps the framework of folklore.[17] Schwerin's demand, however, seems too extreme and too exclusively directed by the legal point of view. Thus there exists the evident danger that legal folklore research, the most usual designation, may be extended too broadly and become a vague collective term for all phenomena and objects in the study areas bordering on legal history, general cultural history, and folklore, yet, if it does not do so, it may suffer from being too closely confined.

One simple solution to this problem is a subdivision in such a way that the investigation of articles, instruments, and tools used in ancient legal life would become the task of legal archeology, while customs of a legal or legally influenced sort, as well as relevant materials in language and religion, would become the province of legal folklore research. This division requires no separation of the objects under investigation and involves no special research. It does not overlook the "necessity of constant mutual intrusion and comparison," and fully recognizes the close interrelation of the sciences concerned.[18] This distinction is merely an attempt to gain terminological clarity in an area which has become difficult to survey, and thereby to aid research itself.[19] Special questions on the history of symbols would be the concern of legal symbolism.[20] All of these branches would help formulate a cultural history of law.

Following this discussion of the history, development, and systematic organization of our field, a general summary of the sources and approaches remains to be sketched. Written and unwritten sources stand in a fairly equal balance. A source may be an action, story, document, instrument, name, or pictorial representation, and each individual source will possess different meanings and applications.[21]

As far as the investigation of material objects is concerned, legal archeology in our sense of the term, the attentive observation of cities, markets, palaces, castles, and churches, is of particular interest. Despite great losses much material in this area has been preserved, both in dwellings and the open air, and most museums possess such objects. A collection primarily devoted to legal artifacts was built up by the late Hans Liebl and left to the Niederösterreichisches Landesmuseum in Vienna. The Liebl collection contains, under the somewhat old-fashioned heading of legal antiquities, instruments of punishment and execution as well as other artifacts.[22] The collections in the Bayerisches Landesmuseum in Munich are well known, as are the prisons and torture chambers, preserved or restored in individual fortresses. An extensive collection of materials concerned particularly with courts and prisons as well as places of execution was put together by L. Riedberg in Dessau, and is now at the Institut für österreichische Rechtsgeschichte in Graz. By way of publications the series *Arbeiten zur rechtlichen Volkskunde*, edited by Karl Frölich, should be mentioned, as well as the study of pillories by Grete Bader-Weiss and Karl S. Bader,[23] and Horna's book on pillories in Czechoslovakia, newly translated into German.[24]

Representations in painting and sculpture have been fruitful in both the secular and ecclesiastical spheres of legal folklore research.[25] Representations of justice and court proceedings obviously belong to our area of discussion, and one can find many references to these articles in handbooks and topographies of art.[26]

Popular sources are available for the study of legal customs, in addition to legal data, e.g., books of precedents, land registers, and the legal records of cities and provinces. The *Sachsenspiegel*, for example, provided Amira with the material for a fundamental study. Märchen, *Sagen*, other traditional narratives, and even *belles lettres* are also useful sources. Other interesting source materials include the *Aberrecht* (vulgar law) and superstitions.[27] In recent times the symbols of the state, such as crowns, thrones, seats, and badges of authority—objects bearing a close relation to legal archeology—have become a prominent research subject through detailed investigations by Percy Schramm and others.[28] The insignias of the universities have also been treated in recent years.[29] Customs, instruments, and badges of guilds are often described in publications for regional and provincial studies and folklore journals. Here, too, one can find information concerning the badges of various professions, for example, tavern signs, which often express the laws of the public house or brewery.

Studies of the legal meanings of names may be based on record books, registers of place-names, and dictionaries. Of particular importance are the *Deutscher Sprachatlas* and the *Deutsches Rechtswörterbuch*, a dictionary of older German legal language. Proverbs are treated in the *Deutsches Sprichwörterlexikon*.[30] Inscriptions are often directly influenced by law, such as those on city halls, courthouses, or legal articles.

The *Atlas der deutschen Volkskunde* also refers to certain legally influenced customs, for example the manner in which the wedding party is ransomed, itself a reflection of bridal abduction, engagement practices, and boundary and inheritance customs.[31] The widespread existence of these and other forms is indicated on the atlas map. The *Österreichischer Volkskundeatlas* contains reports on servants' contracts and the *Atlas der schweizerischen Volkskunde* also includes pertinent material.[32] Karl Frölich proposed an *Atlas der rechtlichen Volkskunde für das deutschsprachige Gebiet* (Atlas of Legal Folklore in the German Language Area) and Claudius von Schwerin intended to edit a register of monuments "significant for legal archeology."[33] Unfortunately neither plan was carried out, except in fragmentary form. There are also special inventories of legal archeology for individual territories, for example Styria and Rhine-Hessia.[34] Similar work is being conducted in the Burgenland, a section of eastern Austria that borders Hungary. In addition, much matter is contained in folklore journals and those for legal history, provincial history, art history, and other fields.[35] In the *Volkskundliche Bibliographie* and the later *Internationale Volkskundliche Bibliographie* the pertinent literature is indexed. Sections I (Folklore in General), II (Settlement), III (Buildings), V (Signs), XI (Social Tradition), XVIII (Folktales), and XXII (Names) are of particular interest.

Finally one must take note of the individual institutes and scholars in legal history and folklore research who are particularly concerned with the study of the topics outlined here. Munich, with Karl von Amira, Claudius von Schwerin, and Karl Kramer must certainly be mentioned. In addition there is Zurich with the Forschungsstelle für Rechtssprache, Rechtsarchäologie und rechtliche Volkskunde (Research Center for Legal Language, Archeology, and Folklore), founded by Karl S. Bader in continuation of his earlier work. Finally there is Graz, where legal archeology and legal symbolism are now being researched and studied.[36]

The study of legal history has gained in knowledge and understanding from its contact with folklore research. Present-day Volkskunde looks beyond national boundaries, for it has learned to pursue basic types of materials and their evolution in a wide territorial area, an area which is not necessarily determined by one folk alone. It is well on its way to becoming *Völkerkunde*, the study of all peoples, without losing sight of its original national goals. The expansion of folklore to include law and its history is therefore a natural and welcome development.

Notes

1. Hermann Baltl, *Rechtsarchäologie des Landes Steiermark* (Graz, 1957), p. 12.

2. Karl S. Kramer, *Haus und Flur im bäuerlichen Recht* (Munich, 1950), p. 36. Insofar as law is concerned, legal history has the same goals.

3. A partial list of general and individual studies of the objects under consideration (with great differences in scope, system, and terminology) includes: Eberhard von Künssberg, *Rechtliche Volkskunde* (Halle, 1936) and *Rechtsgeschichte und Volkskunde* (Cologne, 1965); Karl Fröhlich, *Stätten mittelalterlicher Rechtspflege auf südwestdeutschem Boden* (Tübingen 1938) and the series of which this last mentioned work is the first volume, *Arbeiten zur rechtlichen Volkskunde*, Vols. I–V; Karl von Amira and Claudius von Schwerin, *Rechtsarchäologie* (Berlin, 1943); Karl S. Bader, "Über das Verhältnis von Rechtsgeschichte und Volkskunde," in *Angebinde J. Meier zum 85. Geburtstag* (Lahr, 1949), pp. 34–35; Eugen Wohlhaupter, *Die Rechtsfibel* (Bamberg, 1956); Hermann Baltl, "Rechtsarchäologie und rechtliche Volkskunde als wissenschaftliche Begriffe und Aufgaben," *Schweizerisches Archiv für Volkskunde* XLVIII (1952), 65 ff., and *Rechtsarchäologie*

des Landes Steiermark; Karl von Amira, *Die Handgebärden in den Bilderhandschriften des Sachsenspiegels* (Munich, 1905), *Der Stab in der germanischen Rechtssymbolik* (Munich, 1909), and *Die germanischen Todesstrafen* (Munich, 1922); Hans Fehr, *Das Recht im Bilde* (Zürich, 1923), *Das Recht in der Dichtung* (Bern, n.d.), and *Die Dichtung im Recht* (Bern, 1936); and Jacob Grimm, *Deutsche Rechtsaltertümer* (Leipzig, 1899). This last work has a fundamental importance for this field of study.

4. Cf., for example, Heinrich Zöpfl, *Altertümer des deutschen Reiches und Rechtes* (Leipzig, 1860); Eduard Osenbrüggen, *Rechtsaltertümer aus österreichischen Banntaidingen* (Vienna, 1863); Heinrich G. Gengler, *Deutsche Stadtrechtsaltertümer* (Erlangen, 1882) and *Rechtsdenkmäler* (Erlangen, 1875). For the reproduction of legal sources, see Emil F. Rössler, *Deutsche Richtenkmaler aus Böhmen und Mähren* (Prague, 1845).

5. Concerning these early works, see the studies of Amira and Schwerin cited in n. 3.

6. Andreas L. J. Michelsen, *Die Hausmarke, eine germanistische Abhandlung* (Jena, 1853).

7. Andreas L. J. Michelsen, *Über die* festuca notata *und die germanische Traditions-symbolik* (Jena, 1856). Concerning house and property marks, see Karl Ruppel, *Die Hausmarke* (Berlin, 1939), esp. pp. 10ff.

8. *Über die Heimat nach altdeutschem Recht* (= *Sitzungsberichte der Königl. Akademie Berlin*, 1852). See also Herbert Meyer, *Das Handgemal* (Weimar, 1934).

9. Claudius von Schwerin, "Volksrechtskunde und Rechtliche Volkskunde," *Studi di storia e diritto in onore di Enrico Besta* (Milan, 1939), II, 517ff.

10. See also Hermann Baltl, "Rechtsarchäologie und rechtliche Volkskunde als wissenschaftliche Begriffe und Aufgaben," pp. 68 ff.

11. *Mitteilungen des Instituts für österreichische Geschichtsforschung*, XI (1890), 523.

12. Munich, 1909, 1922.

13. *Grundriss des germanischen Rechts*, 3rd ed. (Strassburg, 1913), pp. 15ff.

14. *Jahrbuch für historische Volkskunde*, I (1925), 69.

15. See, for example, Eberhard von Künssberg in *Handwörterbuch der Rechtswissenschaft* (Berlin, 1927), IV, 650ff.

16. See Wilhelm Funk, *Alte deutsche Rechtsmale* (Bremen, 1940).

17. Claudius von Schwerin, "Volksrechtskunde und Rechtliche Volkskunde," pp. 518, 523, 535.

18. This viewpoint counters the exposition of Berent Schwineköper in *Zeitschrift der Savignystiftung für Rechtsgeschichte, germanistische Abteilung*, LXXV (1958), esp. 479ff. In addition, see Hermann Baltl, *Rechtsarchäologie des Landes Steiermark*, pp. 13ff. and p. 22.

19. Oswald Menghin, in *Zeitschrift der Akademie für deutsches Recht*, VI (1939), 190ff., rightly confirms that many objects which were studied in folklore research were able to contribute little to the discipline, e.g., "coats of arms and seals, many insignia, the buildings of higher legal culture, and the like." Thus Menghin's suggestions to consider legal archeology as "a branch of legal history which studies the localities and objects of former times which have a basic connection with legal life" comes very close to the division suggested here.

20. See Eugen Wohlhaupter, "Rechtssymbolik der Germanen," *Handbuch der Symbol-forschung* (Berlin, 1941).
21. See also Karl S. Kramer, *Haus und Flur im bäuerlichen Recht*.
22. Hans Liebl, *Altertümer der österreichischen Strafrechtspflege* (Vienna, 1951). See also Hermann Baltl in *Kulturberichte aus Niederösterreich*, first series (1952) and *Österreichische Zeitschrift für Denkmalpflege*, V (1951), 128.
23. Freiburg, 1935.
24. Graz, 1965.
25. J. Braun, *Tracht und Attribute der Heiligen in der deutschen Kunst* (Stuttgart, 1943) and O. Wimmer, *Handbuch der Namen und Heiligen* (Innsbruck, 1956). The representations of saints are often interesting, not only from the point of view of legal history, but also specifically for legal archeology studies.
26. R. Simon, *Abendländische Gerechtigkeitsbilder* (Frankfurt, 1948); Georg Troescher, "Weltgerichtsbilder in Rathäusern und Gerichtsstätten," *Wallraf-Richartz Jahrbuch*, XI (1939). See also H. Bergner, *Handbuch der bürgerlichen Kunstaltertümer in Deutschland* (Leipzig, 1906) and *Österreichische Kunsttopographie* (Vienna, 1907 ff.).
27. See Eberhard von Künssberg, *Rechtliche Volkskunde*, pp. 69 ff.
28. Percy E. Schramm, et al., *Herrschaftszeichen und Staatssymbolik*, 3 vols. (Stuttgart, 1954–1956).
29. Walter Paatz, *Sceptrum universitatis* (Heidelberg, 1953) and Franz Gall, *Die Insignien der Universität Wien* (Graz, 1965).
30. Jacob and Wilhelm Grimm, *Deutsches Wörterbuch* (Leipzig, 1854 ff.); *Deutscher Sprachatlas* (Marburg/Lahn, 1927–1956); *Deutsches Rechtswörterbuch*, revised Richard Schröder and Eberhard von Künssberg (Weimar, 1914 ff.); *Deutsches Sprichwörter-lexicon*, ed. Karl F. Wander (Leipzig, 1867–1880; Aalen, 1963). Concerning the linguistic geography of law, see Eberhard von Künssberg, *Rechtssprachgeographie* (= *Sitzungsberichte der Heidelberger Akademie der Wissenschaften, phil.-hist. Klasse* Abh. 1, 4) (Heidelberg, 1926–1927).
31. See also Herbert Schlenger, *Methodische und technische Grundlagen des Atlas der deutschen Volkskunde* (Berlin, 1934).
32. *Österreichischer Volkskundeatlas* (Linz, 1959ff.) and *Atlas der schweizerischen Volkskunde* (Basel, 1950ff.).
33. Karl Frölich, *Hessische Blätter für Volkskunde*, XXXVI (1937), 84ff. See the foreword in Claudius von Schwerin, *Rechtsarchäologie*.
34. Hermann Baltl, *Rechtsarchäologie des Landes Steiermark*. See also Otto Höfel, *Rechtsaltertümer Rheinhessens* (Würzburg, 1940).
35. See for example, *Zeitschrift für Volkskunde*, *Rheinisches Jahrbuch für Volkskunde*, *Deutsches Jahrbuch für Volkskunde*, *Österreichische Zeitschrift für Volkskunde*, *Schweizerisches Archiv für Volkskunde*.
36. In this connection the folklore scholar Leopold Kretzenbacher has made many worthwhile contributions, e.g., *Die Seelenwaage* (Klagenfurt, 1958).

PAUL G. BREWSTER

Traces of Ancient Germanic Law in a German Game-Song

In the nineteenth century, folklore was defined almost exclusively in terms of survivals. These survivals were supposedly from the long distant past where full-fledged forms prevailed. Through a kind of degenerational or devolutionary process, these forms became in time mutilated fragmentary remains of the original primitive sources. The task of the nineteenth-century folklorist was essentially historical reconstruction of the past. From the mysterious survivals still to be found among European peasants could be reconstructed the presumed original archetype from which these survivals were thought to derive.

In the following essay, Paul G. Brewster, America's foremost student of traditional games, begins with a text collected from his own mother. In his attempt to find evidence of ancient folk law from the text we find considerable speculation, which is typical of most studies of this kind. For representative discussions of survivals, see Margaret Hodgen, The Doctrine of Survivals *(London: Allenson, 1936), and Aurelio Rigoli,* Il Concetto di Sopravvivenza nell Opera di Pitrè *(Caltanissetta: Edizioni Salvatore Sciascia, 1963).*

There is a vast literature—most of it in German—dedicated to discovering "legal antiquities" in nearly every genre of folklore. For sample investigations of folksong, see Wilhelm Heiske, "Rechtsbrauch und Rechtsempfinden im Volkslied," Deutsches Jahrbuch für Volkskunde, *2 (1956), 73–79; Wolfgang Suppan, "Rechtsgeschichte im Volkslied—Rechtsgeschehen um das Volkslied," in Gernot Kocher and Gernot D. Hasiba, eds.,* Festschrift Berthold Sutter *(Graz; Leykam-Verlag, 1983), pp. 353–379. For alleged legal survivals in folktales, see Alice Eisler, "Recht im Märchen,"* Neophilologus, *66 (1982), 422–430; Gerhard O.W. Mueller, "The Criminological Significance of Grimms' Tales," in Ruth B. Bottigheimer, ed.,* Fairy Tales and Society *(Philadelphia: University of Pennsylvania Press, 1986), pp. 217–227. See also the doctoral dissertation by Jens Christian Jessen,* Das Recht in den Kinder- und Hausmärchen der Gebrüder Grimm *(Kiel, 1979). For survivals in legend, see Hans Fehr,* Das Recht in den Sagen der Schweiz *(Frauenfeld: Huber, 1955); and Louis Carlen, "Rechtliches*

Reprinted from *Southern Folklore Quarterly*, 2 (1938), 135–143, with permission of the University Press of Kentucky.

in französischen Sagen," in the interesting journal edited by him, Forschungen zur Rechtsärchaologie und Rechtlichen Volkskunde, 6 (1984), 143–165.

It is a commonplace that in folktale, folksong, and, to a lesser degree, in other types of folklore as well, there survive traces of many customs, practices and rites long since discontinued. Perhaps one of the most interesting of these is the early system of trial and punishment, which one finds frequently occurring in folksong, particularly in the traditional ballad. There come to mind at once "Sir Aldingar" (Child, No. 59), "Young Waters" (Child, No. 94), "The Maid Freed from the Gallows" (Child, No. 95), and the "The Lord of Lorn and the False Steward" (Child, No. 271), as well as "Lady Diamond" (Child, No. 269), "Lady Maisry" (Child, No. 65), and "The Cruel Brother" (Child, No. 11), in which the punishment lacks legal sanction.

Games and game-songs of children, too, have preserved for us something of the stern, hard rules of society in an early day, of summary vengeance meted out to violators of the code by kinsmen jealous of their honor, and of harsh penalties imposed by more lawful, though often arbitrary and prejudiced, judges for infractions of commonly accepted standards of conduct. Certain versions of "Judge and Jury," particularly the German and the Swiss, illustrate admirably the way in which the tradition of the severity of ancient law has been perpetuated in the play of children.[1] The "thief" of the Swiss version flees, but is captured after a long chase. He is borne back in triumph to the king, who orders that he be beheaded, and the sentence is duly carried out in mimicry. "Oranges and Lemons"[2] and some versions of "King and Queen"[3] also preserve as a feature the king's power of life and death over his subjects.

The text of the German game-song upon which the present study is based was obtained from the writer's mother, Mrs. Nancy E. Brewster, who played the game more than fifty years ago at the little Lutheran parochial school in Stendal, Pike County, Indiana. Known locally as "Ännchen sass auf einen Stein,"[4] the game was introduced into the community by a young German girl, Marie Sundermann, who had recently come over from Germany and who spoke no English whatever.

"Ännchen sass auf einem Stein"[5]

(musical notation)

Ach, Ännchen sass auf einem Stein, einem Stein, einem Stein; die Ännchen sass auf einem Stein, einem Stein.

2. Sie Kämmte sich ihr gold'nes Haar, usw.
3. Da kam der böse Bruder Karl
4. Dann fing sie an zu weinen
5. Das Messer war in Tasche[6]
6. Er stach das Messer in ihr's Herz
7. Das Blut es schot aus Ännchen
8. Dann kam der Bruder Benjamin
9. Ännchen war ein Engelein
10. Der Karl er war ein Teufelein.

The game was played as follows: The players formed a circle, with Ännchen seated on a stone in the center. While those forming the ring marched around her singing verses, the three actors carried out in pantomime the action of the song. Ännchen sat combing her golden hair, seemingly unaware of the approach of the wicked brother Karl. As soon as he came to her in the center of the ring,[7] however, she began to weep. He then pulled a knife from his pocket, stabbed her, and fled through the circle of players. Some of the latter rushed to the aid of Ännchen, who was now lying on the ground. At this point the good brother Benjamin appeared on the scene, lifted her from the ground, and carried her out through the circle. Since boys and girls were not permitted to play together, the parts of the brothers Karl and Benjamin were taken by girls.

Apparently this was once, and perhaps still is, a very popular game among German children. Dr. Schläger writes regarding it: "Das Spiel stellt vielleicht die verbreiteste aller Kinderballaden dar und ist in unzähligen Abänderungen bekannt..."[8]

All the different versions of the game-song seem to have their ultimate origin in the ballad "Ritter Ulinger (Ulrich)," which tells of the murder of a maiden by a robber knight. The details of the old ballad have been best preserved in the dramatic game-song "Anna und der Fähnrich,"[9] a summary of which follows.

Seated on a broad stone, Anna is combing her hair,[10] when a lieutenant comes riding up. He notices that she is weeping, and inquires the cause of her grief. She replies that she is weeping not for riches or goods but because she must die that day.[11] He draws his sword and stabs her through and through. Then follows the query of an unidentified speaker, "Wovon ist dein Schwertchen so roth?" to which the slayer replies, "Ich habe gestern Abend zwei Täubchen geschlacht."[12] The song concludes:

> Zwei Täubchen geschlagtet, das kann es ja nicht sein
> Die wunderschöne Anna wird das Täubchen wohl sein."

In some of the oldest texts known, the heroine, realizing her peril, calls her far-distant brother to her aid and is rescued by him.[13] Still earlier is the story form in which the maiden herself kills the would-be abductor.[14] Our present version seems to be based upon one of the most common forms of the old song, "Ulrich und Ännchen," in which the summoned brother arrives too late to prevent the slaying, and can only avenge the crime.[15]

In the Indiana text, as we have seen, the *dramatis personae* are three: Ännchen and the brothers Karl and Benjamin. The Lewalter text has Anna, her brother, the hunter, and the witch-mother.[16] Böhme's first text has the same characters.[17] The second, a version from Upper Alsace, contains only two, the heroine and her brother Karl.[18] Jöde's No. 27A has three principal characters, Anna, the hunter, and the good fairy.[19] Besides these there are the aunt, the uncle, the grandmother, and other relatives who come to her chamber inquiring the reason for her tears.[20] The B version contains four characters: Anna, her brother (unnamed), the hunter, and her mother.[21]

In "Bertha im Walde," another dramatic game-song derived from the "Ritter Ulinger" ballad, a brother appears in answer to the call of his imperiled sister, but, although he arrives before the murder, he is powerless to prevent it. The heroine, menaced by a robber, asks and gains permission to give three cries before she is slain. She cries first to her father, next to her mother, and then to her brother Rudolf. All of them are in another part of the same wood, and at each cry the one summoned comes and kneels down, begging that the maiden's life be spared. At the conclusion, however, the robber seizes and stabs her.[22]

Why, in every instance save one, is the heroine represented as sitting on a stone?[22] In other words, what is the part played by the latter? What is the true cause of the heroine's grief? What is the real identity of the slayer? Is he brother or lover? Why is the heroine killed? These four questions naturally and inevitably are in the mind of the student of folksong, and arriving at any satisfactory answer is rendered more difficult by the interlocking of the four. In the following pages each question will be considered separately insofar as is possible; however, the intrusion of one or more of the others can hardly be escaped. Owing to the lack of a sufficient number of variants for a thorough study, no attempt will be made to reach a definite conclusion, but it is hoped that the reasons and possibilities advanced may prove suggestive.

As for the role played by the stone, there are, it seems to the present writer, two possible interpretations. The *Breitenstein* was a favorite trysting-place for lovers,[24] and it was here, too, that the banns were published.[25] The fact that the maiden was sometimes left waiting at the stone by a truant lover or faithless fiancé gave rise, explains Dr. Schläger, to the folk phrase "auf einem Stein," used as a designation of abandonment. As illustrations of the phrase employed in this sense he cites the forfeit rhyme

"Ich steh auf einem breiten Stein:
Wer mich lieb hat, holt mich ein."[26]

and the *Märchen* "Königssohn Johann." The story of the latter is, briefly, as follows:

The maiden Jettchen (Harriet, Hetty), is sitting on a broad stone awaiting the coming of the prince again to take her away. However, when he returns to his parents, he forgets all about her. One day when he leaves his window open, a white dove flies in and sings:

"Johann hat Jettchen vergessen
Auf einem breiten Stein."[27]

The use of a stone as a trysting-place appears also in British tradition. The famous "Stone of Odin," of Stennis (Stenhouse), Orkney, is perhaps one of the most notable examples. Some idea of the sacredness with which it was invested by the peasantry will be gained from the following story:

A young man had seduced a girl under promise of marriage, and she proving with child, was deserted by him. The young man was called before the session; the elders were particularly severe. Being asked by the minister the cause of so much rigour, they answered, You do not know what a bad man this is; he has broke the promise of Odin. Being further asked what they meant by the promise of Odin, they put him in mind of the stone at Stenhouse, with the round hole in it; and added, that it was customary, when promises were made, for the contracting parties to join hands through this hole, and the promises so made were called the promises of Odin.[28]

So highly venerated was the stone that when, in 1814, a sacrilegious farmer (originally from the south) used it in building a cowhouse, residents of the district made several attempts to burn his house over his head.[29]

Lady Gomme also mentions this stone in commenting upon the simplicity of the marriage ceremony in the game-song "Isabella."

> The marriage ceremony is of the simplest description—the clasping of hands and the kissing within the circle probably implying the betrothal at a spot sacred to such functions, similar to the Standing Stones of Stenness. Whatever may have been the original intention of these stones, they came in more recent times to be the resort of lovers, who joined their right hands through the hole in the altar stones in the belief that this ceremony would add solemnity to the betrothal...[30]

The child in the center of the ring in "Merry-Ma-Tansa" may, too, she thinks, be a priest or priestess of "the stones."[31]

Dr. Schläger gives it as his opinion that the murdered girl in "Bertha im Walde" is the bride of the slayer.[32] If he is right in this conjecture, it is possible that the brothers and the hunters of the other versions are in reality faithless lovers or cruel husbands. But let us pass on to the second interpretation.

The stone upon which the heroine sits has been explained by Böhme as being a large stone under the village linden trees or in the marketplace.[33] On this stone, in ancient times, judges and other magistrates met to hear cases and to hold trials, and from it proclamations were read to the assembled folk.[34] From it, too, the prisoner was led away to prison or to death, or left as a free man if any of the onlookers could be sufficiently interested in his case.[35] The judgment stone, *Gerichtsstein*, was used not only in the prosecution of criminal cases but in the trying of civil ones as well. Here confiscated goods were burned, and convicted offenders condemned to remain fastened for an hour or more to the stone, in the manner of the New England stocks.[36]

The antiquity of the stone,[37] the standing upon it of the judge or his deputy during a court session, and the solemn leading of the convicted person around it three times served to create in the minds of the folk a peculiar reverence.[38] Besides the ritualistic nature of the judicial proceedings held there, the primitive belief that contact with the stone gave to the person or persons touching it a certain mysterious or magic sanctity invested the *Gerichtsstein* with awesomeness.[39]

Dismissing for the moment the possibility that the killing of the heroine was done by her lover or fiancé from motives of jealousy or some other violent passion, let us consider the act briefly not as a murder but as an execution.[40] It is interesting to note in this connection that in only one of the versions considered is there the slightest evidence of motivation on the part of the slayer, and that this meagre bit of evidence supports our present theory.[41] The brother has just asked the weeping sister the cause of her sorrow, and she has replied that she must die. He then asks

"Ach, warum musst du sterben?"

to which she answers

"Weil ich den Vater nicht gehört."

However, in each of the three versions of Böhme, in the single version of Lewalter, and in the two of Jöde the heroine knows of her impending doom, as her lament "Ich muss sterben!" indicates. It is only in the Indiana version that this detail is missing.[42]

Instead of Ännchen's being slain by a faithless lover or by a robber knight or would-be ravisher, is it possible that the murderer may in truth have been the brother and that her offense was the disobeying of his, or the father's, wishes (perhaps in the matter of choosing a husband) or incontinence? As has already been noted, these, with the almost unpardonable crime of loving a foreigner,[43] are the usual offenses for which ballad heroines are condemned to death and executed by other members of the family.

If it was a case of refusing to bow to the wishes of a brother, we have a connection between the German game-song and "The Cruel Brother" of English balladry. If the charge was incontinence, the resemblance to "Laidy Maisry" is at once apparent. It is possible, too, that in Ännchen sass auf einem Stein" we have an analogue to ballads of brother-sister incest such a "Lizie Wan" in which the brother takes the sister's life in order to prevent the father's learning of the illicit relationship.[44]

It would seem reasonable to suppose that the happy ending given in some versions is a late development, and that the original close was tragic. The crux of the whole matter is the reason for Ännchen's weeping. Does she weep for a faithless lover, who later returns and stabs her to death? If this is the case, how account for her knowledge that she is to die? Can it be accounted for by saying that it is premonition? Does she weep because she has become lost from the others of her family (as in "Bertha im Walde") and because she fears death at the hands of robbers known to live in the wood? Or is the stone on which she sits an execution stone, upon which she must atone with her life for a crime, real or assumed, the punishment being meted out by her own brother?

Notes

1. W. W. Newell, *Games and Songs of American Children*, 1911 ed., p. 123.
2. Alice B. Gomme, *The Traditional Games of England, Scotland, and Ireland*, II, 25 f.
3. Newell, *op. cit.*, p. 120.
4. Other variants bear the titles "Ach, Anna sass am Breitenstein,'" "Maria sass auf einem Stein," and "Anna am Breitenstein und der Jäger."
5. The air of the Indiana text is identical with those in Böhme, *Deutsches Kinderlied und Kinderspiel*, p. 546, and in Lewalter, *Deutsches Kinderlied und Kinderspiel*, p. 84. For these references and for those to Meier which follow, I am indebted to Professor Archer Taylor.
6. The *im Tasche* of stanza 5 should be in *der Tasche* or perhaps the more rhythmical in *Tasche; in ihr Herz* seems to be called for in 6, and the *schot* of stanza 7 should be *schoss*.
7. At the beginning of the game, those forming the circle held hands. Later, however, they stood with hands at their sides, thus facilitating the entrance and the exit of the brothers.
8. Lewalter, *op. cit.*, p. 335.
9. Böhme, *op. cit.*, pp. 545–546.
10. It is interesting to note that here the heroine "kröllte ihre *schwarzbraunen* Haare" instead of the usual golden locks. An Upper Alsace version given by Böhme (p. 546) describes her hair as "krauses."
11. The premonition present in the old song has been lost. In one version of the original ballad the maiden sees her predecessors hanging in the fir tree under which she is sitting. See Lewalter, *op. cit.*, p. 336.
12. This is reminiscent of the mother's question and the son's reply in "Edward:"

> "Why dois your brand sae drap wi bluid?"
> "O I hae killed my hauke sae guid."

13. Lewalter, *op. cit.*, p. 336.
14. *Ibid.*, p. 336.
15. Lewalter, *op. cit.*, p. 336. "Das Lied von der wunderschönen Anna beruht auf der häufigsten Form des alten Liedes, Ulrich und Ännchen, wo der herbeigerufene Bruder zu spät kommt und nur die Untat rächen kann." The avenging of the murder has, however, disappeared from our version, which ends with the arrival of the good brother and his bearing Ännchen from the ring.
16. *Ibid.*, p. 84.
17. *Op. cit.*, p. 546.
18. *Ibid.*, pp. 546–547.
19. *Ringel Rangel Rosen, 150 Singespiele und 100 Abzählreime, nach mundlichen Überlieferung gesammelt von Fritz Jöde.*
20. Cf. the procession of relatives in "The Maid Freed from the Gallows" and "The Noble Sibilla." In none of these cases do the relatives offer any assistance.

21. For the references to Jöde and for copies of versions in his collection I am indebted to Miss Anne G. Gilchrist, of Lancaster, England.
22. Böhme, *op. cit.*, p. 547.
23. The sole exception is Jöde, No. 27A, in which the heroine sits "im Kämmerlein."
24. Lewalter, *op. cit.*, p. 335. Schläger is here quoting Böhme.
25. *Ibid.*, p. 335.
26. With references to Simrock and to Frischbier. Cf. also Meier, "Der blaue Stein zu Köln, "*in Zeitschrift des Vereins für Volkskunde*, NF II (1930), 33.
27. Lewalter, *op. cit.*, p. 336.
28. G. F. Black, *County Folk-Lore*, III (Orkney and Shetland Islands), 2 London, 1903. Published as volume XLIX of *Folk-Lore*.
29. *Ibid.*
30. *Op. cit.*, I, 256.
31. *Ibid.*, I, 374.
32. Lewalter, *op. cit.*, p. 336. "So konnte der eigentliche Sinn sein, dass der Jäger oder Fähnrich seine verlassene Braut mordet."
33. *Op. cit.*, p. 547.
34. *Ibid.*
35. Cf. Meier, "Alter Rechtsbrauch im Bremischen Kinderspiel," in *Festschrift zur Vierhundertjahrfeier des alten Gymnasiums zu Bremen*, p. 230. "Ein Gefangner musste hier dreimal feierlich um den Stein geleitet und das Volk befragt werden, ob jemand für ihn bürgen wolle, ehe man ihn in Haft führte."

In ancient Cologne the condemned was stood upon the *blaue Stein* three times by the beadle, was thrust against it thrice with the words

"Ich stussen dich an de blae Stein;
Do kus ze Lebdag no Vadder un Moder nit mih heim."

and then led out into the public square, where the death penalty was inflicted. [Meier, "Der blaue Stein zu Köln," in *Zeitschrift des Vereins für Volkskunde*, NF II (1930), 33].

36. Meier, "Alter Rechtsbrauch im Bremischen Kinderspiel," in *Festschrift zur Vierhundertjahrfeier des alten Gymnasiums zu Bremen*, p. 230. See also Banks, *British Calendar Customs*, I (Scotland), 98 for a discussion of similar customs in early times in Edinburgh, Aberdeen, and other of the larger towns.
37. See Meier, "Der blaue Stein zu Köln," in *Zeitschrift des Vereins für Volkskunde*, NF II (1930), 32, 37.
38. Meier, "Alter Rechtsbrauch im Bremischen Kinderspiel," in *Festschrift zur Vierhundertjahrfeier des alten Gymnasiums zu Bremen*, p. 231.
39. *Ibid.*
40. This does not mean, of course, a legal execution but rather a death penalty imposed by the family and inflicted by one of the other members, in this instance a brother. Thus, in "The Cruel Brother" the bride meets her death at the hand of a brother, whose authority in the matter of her marriage has been slighted. The heroine of "Andrew Lammie," who would marry against the wishes of her relatives, is beaten to death, a brother dealing the death-blow.

The usual penalty for incontinence was burning, as in "Lady Maisry." See Child, *ESPB*, II, 113 and note.

41. Böhme, *op. cit.*, pp. 546–547 ("Anna am Breitenstein und der Jäger"). An excellent treatment of the whole subject of ancient legal procedure as preserved in the games of children in Eberhard Frh. v. Künssberg, "Rechtsbrauch und Kinderspiel, Untersuchungen zur deutscher Rechtsgeschichte und Volkskunde," in *Sitzungsberichte der Heidelberger Akademie der Wissenschaften*, Heidelberg, 1920.

Motivation is lacking also in the following Dutch version, kindly furnished me by Miss Gilchrist. It was obtained by her from Dr. Arnold Bake, whose niece, as a girl living on the Isle of Walcheren, learned it from a girl from Vlissingin.

1. Maria zat op de witte steen, witte steen, witte steen,
2. Daar zat ze zoo te weenen, *etc.*
3. Daar kwam haar lieve moeder aan
4. Maria, waarom weent gij zoo?
5. Omdat ik morgen sterven moet
6. Daar kwam de booze Fred'rik aan
7. Die nam een mesje uit zijn zak
8. Dat stak hij in haar borstje
9 Toen hebben we haar in kistje gelegd
10. Toen hebben we haar begrewin

42. Both the question and the answer have been lost. It will be noted, too, that the girl taking the part of Ännchen does not begin to weep until the arrival of the wicked brother Karl. Does she recognize in him the expected executioner?

43. It should be borne in mind that Maisry's offence consists in part, at least, in having given her love to an Englishman rather than to a man of her own country" (L. C. Wimberly, *Death and Burial Lore in the English and Scottish Ballads, University of Nebraska Studies in Language, Literature, and Criticism*, No. 8, p. 20, note).

44. The fact that extant texts contain no lines supporting such a theory does not necessarily disprove it. It is quite natural that objectionable lines or phrases would be omitted by older persons singing in the presence of children, and by the children themselves as unintelligible to them. Many such changes and omissions have resulted from the transition from ballads to game-songs.

On the general subject of ballads of incest, see Schutte, *Die Liebe in den englischen und schottischen Volksballaden* (Halle diss., 1906), p. 85 f. Family relations in general are treated by Georg Baldow in his *Ehe und Familie in den englisch-schottischen Volksballaden* (Halle diss., 1908).

A.F. CHAMBERLAIN

Legal Folklore of Children

Part of the study of legal survivals in folklore includes investigations of children's folklore. It is true that children constitute an authentic folk group with its own special traditions. For example, in Anglo-American children's folklore, if a child discovers a "lost" object and wishes to claim it, he or she may say, "Finders, keepers; losers, weepers." The folk legal principle inherent in this rhyme is explicit. Also to be found in Anglo-American children's folklore is the equivalent of an oath. A child may swear to be telling the truth by concluding with the formula: "Cross my heart and hope to die." Another traditional "legal" formula found in Anglo-American children's folklore is one employed to reserve a particular desired object or privilege. In American folklore, a child may say, "Dibs" to ensure precedence or possession, while in English folklore a child would probably say "Bags" in the same context. For variations of these and other children's formulas, see the chapter entitled "Code of Oral Legislation," in Iona and Peter Opie, The Lore and Language of Schoolchildren *(London: Oxford University Press, 1959), pp. 121–153.*

Still another children's folk legal custom—one also practiced by adults—concerns the division of a piece of pie or pizza into two parts. In order to ensure a fair and equitable division, one of two individuals cuts the item in question whereupon the other individual has the right to choose his "half" first. If the two portions are not equal, it is the divider who presumably ends up with the smaller share.

Alexander F. Chamberlain (1865–1914) earned the first doctorate in anthropology awarded in the United States. This was in 1892 at Clark University under the direction of Franz Boas (1858–1939). Much interested in folklore, Chamberlain edited the Journal of American Folklore *from 1900 to 1907, wrote more than one hundred book reviews for that journal, and taught folklore at Clark University. He was particularly interested in child development and published* The Child and Childhood in Folk Thought *(1896). In this brief review of early European scholarship on children's legal folklore, Chamberlain gives a sample of this type of research.*

The early studies of children's folk law are those cited by Chamberlain, e.g., Giuseppe Pitré, "Folklore giuridico dei fanciulli in Sicilia," Archivio per lo studio delle tradizioni popolari, *9 (1890), 538–541, but the major work on the*

Reprinted from *Journal of American Folklore*, 16 (1903), 280. By permission of the American Folklore Society. Not for sale or further reproduction.

417

subject is Eberhard von Künssberg's Rechtsbrauch und Kinderspiel, *2nd printing (Heidelberg: Carl Winter, 1952). See also Giovanni Antonucci, "Il diritto dei fanciulli," Folklore Calabrese, 9 (1923), 87–94.*

To Pitré's little study, "Folk-lore giuridico dei fanciulli in Sicilia" (Palermo, 1890), and Gaidoz and Rolland's "Le Folk-lore juridique des enfants" (*Mélusine*, Tome III, pp. 156–159), dealing respectively with the "legal folk-lore" of Italian and French children, has now been added the contribution of A. de Cock, "Rechtshandelingen bij de Kinderen," just begun in "Volkskunde" (Vol. XV, 1902–1903, pp. 193–199) devoted to the same subject among children in Flemish Belgium, etc., the first part treating particularly of the "finding right," or *droit de trouvaille*, and the "law of presents."

The "law of finding," still in full force among Flemish children (and more or less among Dutch, German, Italian, French, etc.) is briefly this:

If one boy has found something belonging to another (marble, knife, piece of money, toy, etc.), he hides it in his closed hand, and cries repeatedly: "Who's lost it? I've found it!"

If one of the others says "I," the first asks at once, "What is it?" Now it does not suffice for the loser to answer simply, e.g., "A knife." He must describe it exactly, before he can rightly receive it. If the object found is claimed by no one, the finder asks, "Can I have it?" and the answer is a unanimous "Yes." With this the legal proceedings are over. Several curious variants of the formula are in vogue. In Schelle the rime runs

> "Pirrewirrewit!"
> Whose thing is this?
> Pirrewirrewat!
> Whose thing is that?"

If no one puts forward satisfactory claims, then the finder opens his hand crying, "Whoever first says ikkepik gets it!" And so the matter is decided.

When two find something at the same moment, it belongs to the one who first speaks the appropriate formula: "Finding is holding!" etc.

A French finding-rime is quite suggestive:

> "Qui a perdu? J'ai trouvé
> La bourse à monsieur l' curé;
> Si je le dis trois fois
> Ce sera pour moi."

The "trois fois" appears in Languedoc as, "Piu, piu, piu." Another French phrase is "J'y retiens part" (or *de part*, or simply *pie*).

A common "law of presents" is the formula

"Once given, stays given;
Taking away is stealing!"

This warns against our "Indian giving," for which penalties are prescribed, one of them, with Dutch, Flemish, German and French children being thus expressed:

"Once given, taken away,
Go to Hell three times."

Some of the variants are less cruel or less theological.

De Cock has made a valuable contribution to an interesting subject.

JOHN C. MESSENGER, JR.

The Role of Proverbs in a Nigerian Judicial System

Of all the folklore genres it is almost certainly the proverb which is considered to be the most relevant to the study of folk law. In some cases proverbs have the force of law and serve as the ratio decidendi, *that is, the basis for the decision. In Anglo-American jurisprudence some proverbs are cited in their Latin form, e.g.,* Caveat emptor *(Let the buyer beware). See James Williams, "Latin Maxims in English Law,"* The Law Magazine and Law Review *4, series 20 (1895), 283–295. Of course, there are also many English legal proverbs, e.g., "Possession is nine-tenths of the law" and "A man's home is his castle." See Donald F. Bond, "English Legal Proverbs,"* Publications of the Modern Language Association, *51 (1936), 921–935; Archer Taylor, "The Road to 'An Englishman's House . . .'",* Romance Philology, *19 (1965–1966), 279–285; Marcia Speziale, "Is a House a Castle?",* Connecticut Law Review, *9 (1976), 110–135;*

Legal proverbs can be found in many countries. See J.-L.-Alexandre Bouthors, Les Proverbes, Dictons, et Maximes du Droit Rural Traditionnel *(Paris: A. Durand, 1858); for a discussion of more than three-thousand German legal proverbs, see Eduard Graf and Mathias Dietherr,* Deutsche Rechtssprichwörter *(Aalen: Scientia, 1975); see also Leonhard Winkler,* Deutsches Recht im Spiegel deutscher Sprichwörter *(Leipzig: Zentralantiquariat Der Deutschen Demokratischen Republik, 1977); for a theoretical analysis of the way in which German legal proverbs articulate principles of law, see Wilhelm Weizsäcker, "Rechtssprichwörter als Ausdrucksformen des Rechts,"* Zeitschrift für vergleichende Rechtswissenschaft, *58 (1956), 9–40, For Italian folklorist Raffaele Corso's consideration of Italian legal proverbs, see his "Proverbi giuridici Italiani,"* Archivio per lo studio delle tradizioni popolari, *23 (1906–1907), 484–506; 24 (1907–1909), 41–53. 109–130; or "Proverbi giuridici Italiani,"* Revista italiana di Sociologia, *20 (1916), 531–592.*

Nowhere in the world are proverbs more a part of legal process than in Africa. In the following essay by John Messenger, Professor of Anthropology at Ohio State University, one can see how proverbs are used as precedents in actual cases to sway the judge in favor of one side or the other. Other examples of African legal proverb

---

Reprinted from *Southwestern Journal of Anthropology*, 15 (1959), 64–73, with permission.

studies include: Bruno Gutmann, "Das Rechtsleben der Wadschagga im Spiegel ihrer Sprichwörter," Zeitschrift für Eingeborenen Sprachen, *14 (1924) 44–68; I. Schapera, "Tswana Legal Maxims,"* Africa, *36 (1966), 121–134; Wilhelm Möhlig, "Sprichwörter als Quelle des traditionellen Rechts in Afrika,"* Zeitschrift für Vergleichende Rechtswissenschaft, *78 (1979), 221–237; Kwesi Yankah, "Proverb Rhetoric and African Judicial Processes: 'The Untold Story,'"* Journal of American Folklore, *99 (1986), 280–303; and J. Olowo Ojoade, "Proverbial Evidences of African Legal Customs,"* International Folklore Review, *6 (1988), 26–38.*

For dozens of additional references on legal proverbs generally, see the entries under "law" and "legal" in Wolfgang Mieder, International Proverb Scholarship *(New York: Garland, 1982) and the same author's* Supplement I *(New York: Garland, 1990) and* Supplement II *(New York: Garland, 1993).*

The Anang, in common with other African peoples, possess a rich folklore tradition, comprising most importantly tales, proverbs, riddles, and song verses. Proverbs are by far the most numerous and the most frequently employed of these forms of verbal art, and are used in all manner of situations—as a means of amusement, in educating the young, to sanction institutionalized behavior, as a method of gaining favor in court, in performing religious rituals and association ceremonies, and to give point and add color to ordinary conversation. Neighboring Ibo gave the Anang their name, the term denoting "ability to speak wittily yet meaningfully upon any occasion," and not a little of Anang eloquence, admired by Africans and Europeans alike, stems from their skillful use of maxims. This paper recounts a number of proverbs collected during court hearings, places them within their cultural and juridical contexts, and assesses their use as rhetorical devices affecting the course of justice in Anang tribunals.

Second largest of the six Ibibio-speaking tribes of southeastern Nigeria, the Anang possess no centralized political organization but are divided into twenty-eight sub-tribes, called *imɑn*, each of which is a group of villages ruled, to a limited degree, by a hereditary chief whose duties are mainly of a religious nature. The members of an *imɑn* share certain distinctive cultural traits and express a consciousness of unity; in addition, the meat of a particular animal is forbidden to them.

Politically preëminent is the community, or *obio*, rather than the sub-tribe, and a hereditary leader and a council of elders direct its affairs and perform important social and religious functions. The largest social grouping is the patrilineage, known as *ɛkpuk*, composed of both nuclear and extended families inhabiting a continuous tract of territory in the village. Each family lives in a compound surrounded by forest, bush, and land belonging to the head and farmed by his wives and children.

British rule over the Anang was established during the decade following the first contact of these two peoples in 1903. Native and Magistrates' Courts were gradually introduced which officially superseded the indigenous ones,[2] and continual action has been taken by the colonial government to eradicate the latter, an effort that has met with only partial success. Two of the five types of traditional courts, called *esop*, have been abolished, but the other three still flourish in many communities. This paper treats only the indigenous judiciary, and the maxims under discussion were transcribed during proceedings conducted by these illegal bodies.

With the breakdown of *imɑn* political forms as the result of acculturation, the highest Anang court no longer exists. This was an *esop* composed of the chief of the sub-tribe and the heads of the communities within the village group. It convened two or three times a year to try the most heinous crimes—murder, failure to observe the food taboo, and the theft of objects used for religious sacrifice. Market courts as well no longer exist, for Anang markets are not numerous and thus can be policed easily by the British authorities. At one time, the leaders of *obio* contiguous to a market made up the tribunal and conducted hearings involving traders from their own and other *imɑn*. The crimes usually tried by this body were theft and usurping another's trading position.

The traditional courts still active are those serving the village, patrilineage, and family. Only a few *obio* tribunals continue to meet, and these sporadically, whereas patrilineage and family *esop* function in most communities as they did in the past. All try cases involving crimes not subsumed under Native Law and Custom, a state of affairs unofficially favored by some District Officers because they feel it allows the Anang to maintain a certain cultural equilibrium in a period of rapid change.

The head of the family and, if they reside in the compound, his adult brothers and sons form the family court, which convenes in the house of the compound leader at sunset on the day an offense is committed. The crimes most commonly tried are quarreling among wives, cruelty toward wives, disobedience of children, and petty stealing within the family group. The patrilineage *esop* meets weekly in a court building located in a small square central to the area inhabited by the kin-group. Presided over by the *ɛkpuk* head, this body consists of family leaders and sometimes old men who do not hold this position but who have high prestige. Most of the cases brought before the tribunal can be tried either here or in the village court, depending upon whether the principals are from the same or from different patrilineages. Chief among the offenses in this category are theft, assault with a deadly weapon, adultery, and causing an unmarried girl to become pregnant.

In the past most Anang adjudication took place in the community *esop*. It was composed of *ɛkpuk* heads presided over by the village leader, and met once each week in the compound of the latter or in the court house serving his kin-group. Certain of the offenses which fell within its jurisdiction have just been mentioned; others of importance which could not be brought before other tribunals were: refusal to bear arms in inter-village warfare, striking parents or old people, performing sexual intercourse in the bush, practicing evil magic or witchcraft, and refusing to refund bride wealth following divorce. Today, in those communities where this *esop* continues to meet, the personnel of the court remains unchanged, and many of the crimes listed above still are tried, as well as some formerly falling within the province of the *imɑn* tribunal.

Village court procedures are much the same as those of other judicial bodies. Usually only older men and women attend the sessions, the former far outnumbering the latter, and children are barred except when they are principals or serve as witnesses. Women seldom speak out except when asked to furnish evidence, although a very old woman of high social standing might act as a character witness or advise the judges as to a proper verdict. Once the presiding member has introduced the case under consideration, the plaintiff stands before the justices, termed *ɛkpɛ ikpɛ*, and pays a small "utterance fee," used to purchase palm wine for the court members following adjournment. He states his grievance, without benefit of a lawyer, in a speech that may last as long as an hour, following which he surrenders the floor to the defendant who proceeds in like manner. When the *esop* itself initiates a case, the chief justice speaks as the plaintiff. The *ɛkpɛ ikpɛ* and those in the audience pay rapt attention to the litigants as they deliver their talks, and outbursts of applause mark the course of a well-presented accusation or defense. Listeners are especially appreciative of an original or little known proverb that captures their imagination and is cleverly introduced at a crucial moment.

The presiding member maintains strict control over the hearing, preventing interruptions when the principals are addressing the tribunal and allowing neither to dwell upon irrelevant matters. Both are then questioned at great length, first by one another, next by the *ɛkpɛ ikpɛ*, and finally by elders in the room, and at this time each may call forth material and character witnesses to buttress his position. When the chief judge decides that sufficient evidence has been introduced, he seeks the opinions of important old men as to the innocence or guilt of the defendant and retires with his colleagues to ponder a decision, returning with them to announce the verdict they have agreed upon.

The court may call a diviner to uncover hidden facts if it lacks sufficient evidence for a conclusive decision, or it may consult an oath swearer if it is apparent that one of the litigants or witnesses is falsifying his testimony. Often confronting a person with one of these dreaded specialists is enough to induce him to present additional evidence or to alter his statement. If an oath is sworn, a trial must be postponed until the results of the oath can be ascertained. Periodically, *ɛkpɛ ikpɛ* are required to swear in public before a powerful oath administrator that they will neither accept bribes nor allow personal bias to influence their decisions.

The death penalty for a crime no longer can be exacted, but prior to the advent of the British those tried before the sub-tribal *esop* and found guilty were executed or, more commonly, sold into slavery. Lower tribunals were limited to levying fines and flogging convicted felons, this being the condition prevailing in the village court today. Fines are paid in cash or in domestic animals, both of which are shared by the justices. When a compensatory fine is ordered, there is usually a small accompanying punitive one that reverts to the members of the tribunal. As legal offenses are considered infractions of divine law, a guilty party, in addition to rendering a fine or being flogged, must perform a sacrifice before a particular shrine to placate the deity.

Now that we have examined in broadest outline the structural and procedural forms of the judiciary, let us discuss those factors which facilitate or hinder the administration of justice by the Anang courts. The strongest force acting to ensure equitable decisions is the belief of these people that their legal system is an instrument utilized by the deity, known as *abɑssi*, to punish those who have failed to conform to his divine moral code. It is held that a miscarriage of justice in the courts can result in an aroused *abɑssi* chastising not only the culprit, but also his relatives and even his fellow villagers. Thus, not only is the guilty one eventually forced to pay for his crime, but many innocent parties may suffer as well. Another supernatural sanction having great efficacy is the oath sworn by *ɛkpɛ ikpɛ*, for the oath spirit, at the behest of the deity, will quickly and ruthlessly attack any court member who engages in corrupt practices or who fails to act impartially during a hearing.

Democratic procedures certainly are evident in the conduct of a case. As we have noted, both plaintiff and defendant are given ample time to present their positions, and are forbidden to dwell upon extraneous issues that might unduly influence the justices. All aspects of the case are probed by the tribunal members as well as by interested elders through extensive questioning of the principals and witnesses. Pertinent evidence is examined with great care, the *ɛkpɛ ikpɛ* often traveling afar to view at first hand the site of a crime. Occasionally an authoritarian chief justice fails to call for opinions on a verdict from the audience and dominates his colleagues when a decision is considered, but most often he seeks the judgments of at least a dozen elders, as well as agreement among the members of the *esop*.

Most apparent of the shortcomings of the Anang judiciary is the willingness of some judges to accept bribes and the tendency of others to express bias, especially when kin are involved. The people readily admit that the Native Courts are corrupt,[3] but they insistently hold that the *ɛkpɛ ikpɛ* of the indigenous tribunals have always been inviolate. It became evident that there is some discrepancy between the ideal and the real in this are after several months were spent in the field during which numerous hearings were attended and informants queried. Bribery and partiality are occasionally manifested, and probably were in the past despite the spiritual sanctions against them. The reasons for this are threefold: first, a very few have unorthodox religious beliefs and doubt the avenging propensities of *abɑssi*; second, there are those whose pecuniary motives are so strong that they are willing to risk the consequences of immoral practices; and third, some possess charms procured at great expense from workers of evil magic which they believe can thwart supernatural retribution. Evidence also suggests that at times justices are prompted to declare the guilt of an individual when testimony fails to warrant it in order to share the fine, a condition that may have been more commonplace in the past when it was possible to sell convicted criminals into slavery for enormous profits. It is difficult to know how effective religious sanctions were half a century ago.

Anang justices of long standing were unconscious of and only slowly came to realize the influence of proverbs upon decision-making in courts. As the Anang take every opportunity to display their eloquence and constantly employ adages, it appears that such verbal expression is taken for granted and its impact thus not evaluated. Proverbs were collected which seemed to affect verdicts in particular trials; it must be admitted, however, that the *ɛkpɛ ikpɛ* did not always agree with the researcher as to whether they had been unduly influenced by maxims in these trials, therefore only those hearings in which at least one justice admitted being swayed are reported on the following section.

During a case in which a chronic thief was accused of robbery, the plaintiff aroused considerable antagonism toward the defendant early in the trial by employing the following proverb: "If a dog plucks palm fruits from a cluster, he does not fear a porcupine."[4] A cluster from the oil palm tree contains numerous sharp needles that make handling it extremely hazardous, therefore a dog known to pick palm fruits certainly would be unafraid to touch a porcupine. The maxim implies that the accused is the logical suspect since he was a known thief and lived close to the person who was robbed, and many in the audience regarded the trial as a mere formality. His guilt came to appear doubtful, however, in the light of evidence produced during the proceedings, and just before the *ɛkpɛ ikpɛ* were to retire he presented an adage that was instrumental in gaining his acquittal: "A single partridge flying through the bush leaves no path." Partridges usually travel close to the ground in coveys and can be followed by the trail of bent and broken grass they leave behind. In using this proverb the accused likened himself to a single bird, without sympathizers to lend him support, and called upon the tribunal to disregard the sentiments of those in attendance and to overlook his past misdemeanors and judge the case as objectively as possible.

In another case the precept "Something happened to the smoke which caused it to enter the bush and become mist" was employed by a person accusing a former friend of assault with a machete during a heated argument. The plaintiff wanted the court to know that he disliked bringing charges against the defendant in light of their former close association, but was compelled to do so because of the severity of the attack. He compared himself to smoke which rightfully belongs in the compound but which has been forced out into the bush by the wind to become mist. Witnesses were introduced to support the accusation, and later the defendant claimed that they had been bribed by his opponent to testify in the latter's behalf. The accused attempted to show the justices that, although posing as a friend, the plaintiff was in reality a jealous enemy who had chosen this means to discredit him, ending his exposé with the adage "A leopard conceals his spots." Under ordinary circumstances a leopard resembles a large bush cat, but once angered it extends its limbs and arches its back revealing the distinguishing spots. The animal attempts to hide its identity by making itself as small as possible when stalking an intended victim. Thus the plaintiff was pictured as a dangerous foe hiding his true motives under the guise of friendship. The court was sufficiently impressed by this accusation in reverse to demand that the plaintiff and his supporting witnesses swear oaths as to the veracity of their claims, a demand they were afraid to comply with. When calling upon the specialist to administer the oaths, the presiding member appraised the case with the proverb "If an animal resembles a palm fruit cluster, how can it be butchered?" By this he meant that at this point in the hearing the evidence was so inconclusive that the *ɛkpɛ ikpɛ* would be unable to reach a verdict, just as an animal possessing the needles of a cluster would be difficult to handle. The chief judge admonished the plaintiff and his supporters with the maxim "If you visit the home of the toads, stoop" when they expressed their unwillingness to take oaths, thereby forfeiting the case. This adage is similar in meaning to our "When in Rome, do as the Romans do" and is frequently used by a presiding member when pronouncing a decision by which he emphasizes the necessity of conforming to the divine moral code, in this instance not bearing false witness.

In still another case a boy accused of impregnating an unmarried girl denied his guilt and accused a young man of having committed the act and boasting of it to other men in the *obio*. Not only did the girl contradict the defendant's plea, but the young man whom the latter had accused asserted his innocence. As the trial progressed, the case came to rest upon the girl's claim that the boy was guilty, especially after a number of witnesses admitted hearing the young man boast of his sexual exploits with her, exploits that she emphatically denied. The girl's relatives testified that her honesty was above reproach, and an oath might have been called for had not two witnesses spoken out using proverbs which influenced the judges to rule against the boy. The father of the boy, when called upon as a character witness, seemed reluctant to support his son, admitting that he often had punished the boy for sexual practices and telling lies. In light of this, he told the court, he considered his son capable of having committed the act for which he was accused and ended his testimony by using the precept, "The *nsɑsɑk* said she was ashamed of the small size of her offspring." Smallest of the birds in the region, the *nsɑsɑk* is thought by the Anang to be ashamed of its diminutive size. Naturally, they claim, the mother of the species is even more ashamed of its fledgling since it is far smaller than she. In employing this maxim, the father revealed his lack of faith in his son's claims and the great shame he left at making the admission publicly. The proverb which finally persuaded the judges to declare the boy guilty was used by the girl's father when he was called upon as the last witness. He denounced the accused after telling the *ɛkpɛ ikpɛ* that her word was to be trusted absolutely, highlighting his speech with the proverb "The *ɛkɛnuk* tried to eat as much as the *ɔkɔnɔ* and his stomach burst." There are several types of rats in the area; one, the *ɛkɛnuk*, is only two or three inches in length, while another, the *ɔkɔnɔ*, is almost two feet long. The girl's parents likened the boy to the small variety and a married man to the large one; the youth is about to suffer for an act that only a married man is eligible to perform with his spouse.

Upon one occasion the misuse of a proverb by a defendant was instrumental in causing his conviction. A man accused of being an accessory in a theft became incensed at the manner in which evidence was turning against him as the trial proceeded. After a particularly damning piece of evidence was introduced by a witness with the precept "When the fire burned the dog, it also burned the hunter holding the rope attached to the neck of the dog," the accused pleaded his innocence with the maxim "The snail is bleeding." Since a snail, lacking blood, cannot bleed when wounded, the defendant was asserting that he could not be punished for a crime which he had not committed. He continued by berating his opponent, the witnesses who had testified against him, and finally the members of the tribunal, saying that if the latter convicted him they would be guilty of misconduct. He employed the proverb "Overeating destroys the soul" in condemning the justices, implying that they would be going beyond what the evidence indicated and would thus invite the punishment of *abɑssi* were they to rule against him. The *ɛkpɛ ikpɛ*, already disturbed by the inflammatory remarks directed at them, admitted that this precept consolidated their opinion as to his guilt. Once the verdict was announced, the accused in an emotional outburst admitted his involvement in the crime, claiming that he was not responsible for his conduct but was the unwilling victim of fate, and uttering the adage "The crayfish is bent because it is sick" to support his contention. In its natural condition a crayfish is elongated, but when trapped by fisherman and dried on a rack over the fire it curls up as a sick person might; the felon compared himself to the animal, compelled to do something against his wishes by a force over which he exerts little control.

These cases should suffice to illustrate the vital role played by proverbs in the dispensation of justice by Anang tribunals. In conclusion, it might be pointed out that adages play the same role in the Native Courts as they do in the indigenous ones, with like effect, and government officials appear as unaware of this obstruction to justice as the *ɛkpɛ ikpɛ* themselves. Before either judiciary can be considered equitable, Anang elders and colonial administrators must cope with this problem as well as with others, such as corruption, which are more obvious. It may be that the influence of proverbs is becoming less pervasive now that many justices in the tribe are aware of it. If this is so, it represents another example of the unpremeditated effect of anthropological research upon indigenous custom. There have been several instances of primitive peoples incorporating into their folklore tales related to them by anthropologists, and it is known that traditional theologies have been altered when inconsistencies in dogma were revealed by researchers. It may be that Anang judges will come to weigh more consciously the impact of maxims in arriving at their verdicts, for they pride themselves on the objectivity of their judiciary.

Texts of Proverbs[5]

If a dog plucks palm fruits from a cluster, he does not fear a porcupine.
ɛbuɑ   ɑmɑ   ɛbɛk   oyop   kɛ   ifɛrɛ   ibɑkɛ   ɛdiɔŋ
dog   who   plucks palm fruit from   cluster   fears not porcupine

A single partridge flying through the bush leaves no path.
ikpɔŋ   ɑsɑsɑ   ɑmɑ   ɔfuɔrɔ   ɑfɑŋ   ɛsidɛ
lonely   partridge who   after flying   path   closes

Something happened to the smoke which caused it to enter the bush and become mist.
ŋkpo ɑkɑnɑm   nusŋ   ikɑŋ ɛnyɛ oduk   ikɔt   ɑkɑpɑ   otukubɛ
something happened fly   fire it   entered bush   turned into mist

A leopard conceals his spots.
ɛkpɛ   ɛdidip   nkɛmɛ
leopard   conceals   spots

If an animal resembles a palm fruit cluster, how can it be butchered?
unɑm   ɑmɑ   ɛtiɛ nte   ifɛrɛ   oyop   ebɑk   diɛ
animal   who   resembles   cluster palm fruit   butcher   how

If you visit the home of the toads, stoop.
ɛkpɛdɛ ɑkɑ   iduŋ   ikwɔt   ɛsɔsɔrɔ   kɛnɛ   ɛsɔsɔrɔ
if you go   village   toads   stoop   follow   stoop

The nsɑsɑk said she was ashamed of the small size of her offspring.
nsɑsɑk   ɛkɛbo   kɛbut   ntok   ɛyɛn   imum
nsɑsɑk said   in shame   small   child   mute

The ɛkɛnuk tried to eat as much as the ɔkɔnɔ and his stomach burst.
ɛkɛnuk   ɛkɛbo   idiɑ   nte   ɔkɔnɔ   ɛkpɑ   obomo
ɛkɛnuk said   eat   as   ɔkɔnɔ   stomach   burst

When the fire burned the dog, it also burned the hunter holding the rope attached to the neck of the dog.
ikɑŋ   ɑmɑtɑ   ɛbuɑ   ɔfuɔrɔ   ɑtɑ   ɑkɑmɑ   uduk   ɛbuɑ
fire   burned   dog   fly   burn   holder   rope   dog

Overeating destroys the soul.
ukɑk   ɑdiɑ   ɛdɛ   uwot   ukpɔŋ
filled   eat   is   killings   soul

The crayfish is bent because it is sick.
ikifɔnɔfɔn   obu   ɛnyɛ   ɔmukhɔ   ɛkuŋ
ill   crayfish   it   bends

Notes

1. This paper is a lengthened revision of one delivered in 1957 before the Central States Anthropological Society, and is based upon research conducted in Nigeria during 1951–1952.

2. Most cases are tried in the Native Courts, the members of which are Anang elders, usually village and partrilineage heads, who have been assigned their position by the District Officer. They are sworn to uphold Native Law and Custom as delineated by the British—a body of statutes embracing both European and Anang concepts of morality—and their decisions are subject to review by the District Officer or appeal to the Magistrates' Courts.

3. The Anang attribute corruption in these *esop* to the fact that oath swearing in them was discontinued in 1947, as the result of missionary pressures, and salaries paid sitting members are low.

4. The linguistic data for this proverb and those to follow are found at the end of the paper, in the order of their citation.

5. The Anang consonants are as follows: b, d, f, h, k, kp (labio-velar plosive with no Indo-European equivalent), m, n, ŋ (as ng in sing), ny (as gn in agneau), p, r, s, t, w, and v. Its vowels are as follows: α (as o in hot), *e* (as e in met), e (as a in hate), i (as ee in meet), ɔ (as au in author), o (as oe in hoe), and u (as u in rule). There is no a (as a in hat) nor i (as i in hit). Long consonants and vowels are shown by doubling the letter (as in αbαssi). Anang (Ibibio) is a tonal language, and I have employed eight tonal designations; however, they are unnecessary in a paper such as this.

HARRY L. LEVY

Property Distribution by Lot in Present-Day Greece

One area of human activity that is typically governed by folk law is that of inheritance or property distribution. In the following essay, classicist Harry L. Levy discusses a customary means of dividing family property found in both classical and modern Greece. He discovered the modern version of the custom when he accompanied his wife, anthropologist Ernestine Friedl, on her fieldwork to the village of Vasilika during 1955–1956.

As it happens, Greek folklore scholarship is marked by a tendency to seek continuities (or survivals) of classical Greek culture in contemporary Greece. See, for example, John Cuthbert Lawson, Modern Greek Folklore and Ancient Greek Religion *(Hyde Park: University Books, 1964), first published in 1910, and Loring M. Danforth, "The Ideological Context of the Search for Continuities in Greek Culture,"* Journal of Modern Greek Studies, *2 (1984), 53–85, and especially Michael Herzfeld,* Ours Once More: Folklore, Ideology and the Making of Greece *(Austin: University of Texas Press, 1982).*

For more detail about the village of Vasilika, see Ernestine Friedl, Vasilika: A Village in Modern Greece *(New York: Holt, Rinehart and Winston, 1962). For an entrée into modern Greek folklore scholarship, see Julia E. Miller,* Modern Greek Folklore: An Annotated Bibliography *(New York: Garland, 1985). For an interesting discussion of the concepts of custom and law in contemporary Greece, see Michael Herzfeld, "'Law' and 'Custom': Ethnography of and in Greek National Identity,'* Journal of Modern Greek Studies, *3 (1985), 167–185.*

Reprinted from the *Transactions of the American Philological Association,* 87 (1956), 42–46, with permission.

The division of a paternal estate by lot among the surviving sons is a trait of Greek culture attested from Homeric times downward. In the fictitious autobiography which Odysseus narrates to the swineherd Eumaeus, he speaks of his pretended half-brothers, the legitimate sons of the Cretan Castor, as having divided their father's property (ζωὴν ἐδάσαντο) after his decease, and as having cast lots for the shares thus formed (ἐπὶ κλήρους ἐβάλοντο, *Od.* 14.208–9). The same trait is of course reflected in Poseidon's words to Iris in the fifteenth *Iliad*. He reminds her that Cronos' three sons had divided all their patrimony (πάντα δέδασται) and that each had then received his share through the casting of lots (παλλομένων, *Il.* 15.187–92).[1]

In classical times, the distribution of inherited property by lot occurred in two different ways. If the brothers agreed amicably on a fair division into the appropriate number of shares, they proceeded to cast lots for the portions thus divided, either in private or in the presence of a trusted friend. It is this method which Plutarch (*Moral.* 483D) praises as conducive to fraternal friendship and harmony. If, on the other hand, they could not agree as to what constituted a just division, they might, in Athens at least, appeal to a government official (in the case of Athenian citizens, the eponymous Archon), to appoint apportioners (δατηταί).[2] These would then divide the property equally, and lots would be cast to determine which share was to fall to each brother.

A striking echo of the custom which we have been describing occurs in Aeschylus' *Seven against Thebes*. The duel of Eteocles and Polynices over their patrimony, a struggle which ended in the death of both, is ironically conceived of by the poet as a form of division by lot, with the steel of their swords as the grim divider. In the end, the division turns out to be perfectly equal: each receives enough of the paternal lands to furnish him with a grave. The theme recurs at intervals throughout the latter part of the play. The language is everywhere patterned on expressions normally appropriate to the division of inheritance by lot: the steel is a property-divider, χρηματοδαίτας (729), who has cast the divisory lots, διαπήλας (731), and has left the brothers without the share in the broad acres, ἀμοίρους (733). The brothers are said to receive property by lot, λαχεῖν κτήματα (789–90, cf. 816–17, 906–10), and their graves are their portion, τάφων πατρῴων λάχαι (914). If instead of λάχαι, portions, the word λαχαι, excavations, is read, the word-play on λάχαι makes the point scarcely less evident.[3] Finally, the word δατητάς itself occurs in verse 945.

I have enlarged on this passage because, while Aeschylus is obviously familiar with the system of distributing inheritances by lot and expects his audience to be equally familiar with it, it is apparently only here and in the Plutarch passage cited above that we find in classic Greek literature an explicit mention of this procedure. The custom is, however, amply attested by papyri dating from the first four Christian centuries,[4] by an inscription of uncertain date from Mylasa in Caria,[5] and by numerous Coptic documents from the eight Christian century.[6] Among the latter are extant ostraca which were actually used for the casting of lots. Some of these list the property included in the share on one side of the sherd, the name of the person to whom the lot fell on the other.[7] For Byzantine times, I suggest that the use of the word συνήθως by Eustathius, the twelfth-century bishop of Thessalonica, in his commentary on *Odyssey* 14.209, points to the persistence of the custom in his own age and locality. There is other evidence from the same general period.[8]

In view of this long history, stretching from the Homeric to the Byzantine epoch, it was with considerable interest that I discovered what appears to be the persistence of the trait in present-day Boeotia. In the little village of Vasilika at the foot of Mt. Parnassus, where my wife and I devoted the academic year 1955–56 to an ethnographic study of the small community, the casting of lots is regarded as a normal way to divide τὰ πατρικά among the surviving sons. Within the last few years, the procedure has been used by two of the forty-odd families of the village.

Taken by itself, this fact provides an interesting instance of the survival of customary law alongside of statutory law—for our method of property distribution, I am informed, appears nowhere in the Roman codes, though nothing in those codes would have prevented its continuance, on an extra-legal basis, as a form of voluntary agreement.[9] Nor is it recognized—and again, neither is it prohibited—by the contemporary Greek Civil Code. The cultural trait has survived, passed down from generation to generation, through the centuries of Roman, and later of Turkish domination.[10]

But is not merely a matter of survival as a formal and fossilized relic. The trait has been elaborated by our villagers, or their forebears more or less remote, into a social mechanism peculiarly Greek in its character and operation, and in the attitudes surrounding it.

Let us take the case of three brothers living as tenants in common in the house and on the land left by their father. Each has brought home a wife; the three couples live together in the paternal house, and work the family fields together. With the advent of children, the house becomes crowded, and numerous petty irritations lead to a decision to divide the inheritance. Now each conjugal family needs a house of its own: the old house will do for one, so that two others must be constructed. Before setting out to make any division either of fields or of movable property, the three brothers cooperate in building two new houses on suitable plots of the family land, and in refurbishing the paternal house to bring it as nearly as possible up to the same standard as the houses being newly built. In this building program, which in present-day Greece requires several years of slow if steady progress, all brothers work with exemplary cooperativeness. In view of the strong sense of individuality and the suspiciousness as regards the motives of others which are predominant traits of the Greek personality, modern as well as ancient, and particularly in view of the feelings which led up to the decision to divide the inheritance, one may well ask, "Whence this disinterested pooling of effort during years of labor?" The answer lies in the mechanism which we have been describing, extended now to cover not only the property which the father left, but the houses which are newly coming into being. During the course of construction, no one of the three families can possibly know which house is to be its own. This question will ultimately be decided by the inexorable operation of chance. In the meantime, then, it is to the interest of all that the three houses be made as nearly equal in value as possible, and that all be equally desirable. Thus is enlightened self-interest harnessed for the common good of the entire family. Even if the old house cannot quite be brought up to the standard of the new, there is honest effort to improve it as much as possible. Only when the houses are ready is a division of the fields into shares agreed upon. Then lots are cast separately for fields and for the houses, since except for the little plot on which each house stands, the family fields are scattered here and there in the village domain. As in the case of the Coptic ostraca, the description of the property constituting the share is written on the lot itself; the writing is then concealed, and the lots are distributed at random by a disinterested party. The outcome of the lottery is eagerly awaited, particularly as regards the houses. The families which draw new houses are overjoyed, the recipients of the refurbished paternal homestead accept it with resignation.

There is general agreement that this is one good way to divide family property, if it must be divided, μὲ ἀγάπη, with love. In this the remarks of the villagers parallel those of their old neighbor Plutarch (for Chaeronea is just five miles from Vasilika), who states that the division of family property by lot is the method which provides an occasion of friendship and harmony (*Moral.* 483D). Similarly the Byzantine Eustathius speaks of the process as contributing to ungrudgingness and justice (*ad. Od.* 14.209). This is not the only parallel between ancient and modern Greek thought on the subject. Our villagers, while agreeing that lots provide a very good way of accomplishing the division, speak of the division itself as a rather lamentable necessity, for it means a breaking up of the family unit. Note Plutarch again: he urges that, even as they divide the property, the brothers deem it to be the care and management that they are dividing, while allowing the use of possession ἐν μέσῳ κεῖσθαι κοινὴν καὶ ἀνέμητον ἁπάντων (*Moral.* 483D). Surely this paradox of a division which is not a division is a sign of Plutarch's feeling of repugnance at the idea of division itself.

One more possible point of similarity. The words in which the wife of the brother who had drawn the old house expressed her resignation—τί νὰ κάνονμε; "What can we do?"—are typical of our villagers' rather good-natured fatalism in the face of adverse circumstances over which they have no control. I suggest that in their use of lots to divide inheritances our villagers are voluntarily placing a situation beyond their control so as to avoid the responsibility for a deliberate and rational choice. The suggestion that the wide-spread ancient Greek use of lots represented a voluntary submission of man to the will of the gods has been put forward by Ehrenberg.[11]

Sterling Dow, in his discussion of the Athenian allotment machine, the κληρωτήριον,[12] mentions the ancient Greeks' suspicion of human nature, their fascination with luck, and their penchant for machine-like institutions. All these are illustrated in the development and the operation of the procedure which we have been discussing. I particularly suggest that the cultural descendants of the ancient Greeks, these villagers of Boeotia, have displayed a social inventiveness worthy of those who contrived the Athenian mechanism of the *antidôsis*, and to a similar end: that the forces of personal self-interest themselves might be harnessed to produce the very equity of which, if not thus harnessed, they would be most destructive.

Notes

1. E. Buchholz, *Die Homerischen Realien* (Leipzig 1881) 2.95, who cites Eustathius *ad Od.* 14.211. Cf. also J. D. Zepos, Ἀρχεῖον Ἰδιωτικοῦ Δικαίου 10 (1943) 262-63. I am indebted to Dr. Peter Topping and to Miss E. Dimitrakopoulou of the Gennadeion Library, Athens, for bibliographical assistance.

2. E. Caillemer in *DarSag* s.v. "Datêtai," 27–28. See also *id.*, *Le droit de succession légitime à Athènes* (Paris 1879) 198–204; L. Beauchet, *Histoire du droit privé de la république athénienne* (Paris 1897) 3.454, 645, 651, 653.

3. See Verrall's edition (London 1887) *ad loc.*, which he numbers 898.

4. F. Preisigke, *Wörterbuch der griechischen Papyrusurkunden* 1 (Berlin 1925) s.v. κληροω (2).

5. R. Dareste, B. Haussoulier, Th. Reinach, *Receuil des inscriptions juridiques grecques*, Série 1 (1891–95) 244, B, 2–3.

6. W. C. Till, *Erbrechtliche Untersuchungen* [= Akademie der Wissenschaften (Wien), Phil.-hist. Kl., Sitzungsb., 229, Abh. 2 (1954)] 20–21, 128 (KRU 41), 131 (KRU 42), 140 (KRU 45–46) (KRU, as cited by Till = *Koptische Rechtsurkunden des achten Jahrhunderts auf Djême* [Theben], ed. Walter E. Crum [Leipzig 1912]); A. Steinwenter, *Das Recht der koptischen Urkunden* [= Müller-Otto, *Handbuch*, 10 Abt., 4 Teil, Bd. 2 (1955)] 51–52; H. Kreller, *Erbrechtliche Untersuchungen* (Leipzig 1919) 88. I am indebted to Prof. A. A. Schiller of Columbia for the reference to Steinwenter's work.

7. Cf. Till (above, note 6) 20.

8. Cf. A. P. Christophilopoulos, Σχέσεις γονέων καὶ τέκνων κατὰ τὸ Βμζαντινὸν δίκαιον (Athens 1946) 62: ἀμπέλιον... ὃ ἔλαχεν κἀμοῦ ἐμ....ἐκ πατρικοῦ κλήρον, from a Cyprian codex now in the Vatican.

9. Personal communication from Prof. Adolph Berger of the École Libre des Hautes Études, New York.

10. On the survival of Greek law, see Christophilopoulos (above, note 8) 52, 156; G. Michaélidès-Nouaros, *Contribution à l'étude des pactes successoraux* (Paris 1937) 209–10; K. D. Triantaphyllopoulos, *Laographia* 5 (1915) 239–48; P. I. Zepos, *Greek Law* (Athens 1949) 12. Traces in Turkish law of the custom of dividing inheritance by lot may perhaps represent a borrowing by the Turks from their Greek subjects; if the custom was a trait of Turkish culture prior to the capture of Constantinople, it may be assumed that it served to reinforce the Greek pattern. For the Turkish law referred to, see J. Leonides and Ph. Tsellentes, Ὁδηγὸς ἐπὶ τῆς διεξαγωῆς τῶν κυριωτέρων κτηματικῶν ὑποθέσεων (Constantinople 1903) 58.

11. *RE* s.v. "Losung" 1464.36–37.

12. *HSCP* 50 (1939) 1.

DURICA KRSTIĆ

Symbols in Customary Law

Folk law is full of symbols. A handshake as a sign of a bargain struck would be one instance; the image of blind justice holding a balance is another. This last configuration is actually a blend (and confusion) of two separate symbols: blindness to show the impartiality of justice who cannot see the litigants, and a scale to measure the weight of arguments pro and con. The confusion comes from the fact that a blind judge could not possibly see the results of the balance with respect to which side outweights the other. For an extended consideration of the iconography of justice, see Dennis E. Curtis and Judith Resnik, "Images of Justice,"The Yale Law Journal, 96 (1987), 1727-1772. For a brief glimpse of the same iconography in cartoon form, see Cathleen Burnett, "Justice: Myth and Symbol," Legal Studies Forum, 11 (1987), 79-94. Ernst von Moeller, "Die Augenbinde der Justitia," Zietschrift für christliche Kunst, 18 (1905), 107-122, 141-152. See also Andrew Simmonds, "The Blindfold of Justice,"American Bar Association Journal 63 (2) (1977), 1164. For a folklorist's historical account of the conceptualization of justice, see Alexander H. Krappe, "Observations on the Origin and Development of the Idea of Justice," University of Chicago Law Review, 12 (1944), 179-197.

 The following survey of folk law symbols from the perspective of a specialist in Yugoslav customary law, Durica Krstić of the Institute for Balkan Studies in Belgrade, provides an interesting view of this unusual facet of folk law scholarship. For further discussion of folk legal symbols, see Bernhard Rehfeldt, "Begriff und Wesen der Rechtssymbolik," Studium Generale, 6 (1953), 288-295; Leopold Kretzenbacher, "Rechtssymbolik in Sozialbrauchtum Südosteuropas," Südost-Forschungen, 31 (1972), 239-266. For a survey of symbolic acts of property acquisition in classical antiquity, see Norbert Strosetzki, "Antike Rechtssymbole," Hermes, 86 (1958), 1-17. For a discussion of the key as a folk law symbol, see Lizzie Carlsson, "Nyckeln som rättslig symbol, Rig, 25 (1942), 80-99; for a consideration of the hand in folk legal symbolism, see Ernst Pfleging, "Handen. Den äldsta rättsymbolen," Ord och bild, 60 (1951), 436-442. For an account of the foot as a legal symbol, see Léon de Lantsheere, "Le pied et la chaussure comme symboles juridiques," In Mélanges Charles de Harlez: Recueil de Travaux d'Érudition (Leyden: E.J. Brill, 1896), 149-161. For additional sources concerned

Reprinted from *Balcanica*, 12 (1981), 117-130, with permission.

with legal symbols, see Manfred Lurker, Bibliographie zur Symbolkunde *(Baden-Baden: Verla Heitz, 1968), 189–198.*

Introductory Remarks

The symbols as a category in law have not been adequately treated in Yugoslav literature on the history of law, or otherwise. Moreover, this subject-matter is not of a particular interest in the contemporary legal thinking, although the literature on symbols outside the law is rather abundant.[1] To a degree this is also true of the systematic theoretical approach to the subject of customary law, where the symbolism is particularly present. However, during the last decade customary law has been studied in the Institute of Balkan Studies of the Serbian Academy of Sciences and Arts and corresponding results have been published.[2]

This marginal question related to the law and neighbouring fields, however, deserves greater attention of scholars along the lines of history of law and of contemporary Balkan studies, as well as, more particularly, of the customary law.

The area of study of symbols is remarkably large since it includes quite a number of branches and activities, beginning with ethnology, anthropology, psychology, philosophy, religion, and law and up to the theories on human behaviour and usages which are formed, for instance, in trade, in family relations, as well as in some other areas. The symbols in law, or legal symbols, both in their forms as objects and as actions which are intended to transmit to others a message with specific meaning, however, if treated more closely, provide first of all the possibilities of various associations between some basic issues of origin of legal rules, while taking into consideration many related fields of human knowledge. Contemporary studying of symbols in the area of law, i.e., of customary law, in addition to the above, may prove useful in finding out some specificities in the formation of legal consciousness in the region of the Balkans, although at the same time one should emphasize the fact that with symbols of legal character there are many more general elements, common to entire mankind, i.e., the ones connecting different cultures, growing over different geographical spaces.

The second relevant element while speaking of symbols in law gives insight into deep roots of certain legal rules and aspects of legal behaviour which are expressed without the support of written law and which make up the contents of the entire complex of customary law. Studying of symbols may accordingly point at some specific common elements of law, of the morals and, in the historical perspective, of religion—which is also a subject worthy of more intensive elaboration.

In addition, studying of legal symbols—and this is the third aspect of relevance for the subject-matter discussed—may provide additional material for the field of legal ethnology, which we consider a *sui generis* history of the unwritten law. In such a way, the answers could be obtained concerning the foundations of some rudimentary legal institutions, which in course of time have developed into solutions which one might find even in contemporary written law.

These considerations of the reasons for studying symbols in law in general, and in Yugoslav customary law in particular, are aimed at renewing the interest in research into this neglected and little known matter which in such a way may become one of the elements in the mosaics of the general cultural and legal history of the peoples of the Balkan Peninsula.

Roots of Symbolism in Law and the Beginnings of Corresponding Research

Deep are the roots of symbols and early the beginnings of their use in society in general, and within the realm of law in particular, and this is witnessed already in early sources. Moreover, the law in a way even began to express its contents through symbolical actions, which took place earlier than any form of state community. Naturally, the term "law" is used here in its widest sense, since quasi-legal and "ante-legal" rules of behaviour of people did exist much prior to creation of state power.

In its external manifestations the law did not always dress its substance into the oral form, i.e., into the words and speech, or later on while developing through history, into written text. In order for the primitive and not yet sophisticated minds of undeveloped intelligence in the early stages of development of mankind to grasp the meaning of legal rules, the law had a need, just as the case was with religion, for conspicuous pictures, i.e., representations. These representations used artistic and physical signs which addressed themselves to the eyes of people and to their imagination. These things or animals, or other living creatures, assumed the term of "symbols", i.e., of "legal symbols". Whereof the origin of at present neglected branch of scholarly interest within the history of law, which developed in the middle of the nineteenth century particularly in France and Germany, and which was known as the "symbolism of law".[3]

The subject of legal symbolism as mentioned above was not formed as a separate branch of study in the history of law of the Yugoslav countries, so that it did not provoke adequate attention even of such scholars interested in customary law, as well as general culture of people, as was Valtazar Bogišić, except for his elaboration of particular legal customs and usages, as a result of his well-known survey published in the last quarter of the nineteenth century.[4] In the twentieth century, however, particular attention was dedicated to symbols in law by Slovene legal writer Metod Dolenc.[5] Legal symbols are otherwise mentioned in the studies by M. Kostrenčić,[6] A. Solovjev,[7] I. Jelić,[8] A. Hudovernik,[9] F. Marolt, [10] Jakob Kelemin,[11] M. Barjaktarović and some others.

Historical and Theoretical Foundations of Studying Symbols in the Sphere of Law

An insight into the ancient past of mankind permits the conclusion that religion, fine arts and law—these primeval creations of man which engaged his capacities, were characterized by the great use of symbols and poetic fictions. Thus, according to Jakob Grimm and Creuzer, first legal rules, in order to be memorized more easily, had been sung and put into unwritten verses. In those times people were able to conceive ideas on morals and religion, as well as to communicate in the sphere of relative abstractions primarily through figural representations and pictures, which affected the sense of sight, as well as through pantomimes.[12] Along these lines one may even speak of common primeval beginning of sculpture, religion and law, although this does not mean neglecting production and other social and material conditions which were in essence instrumental in the formation of legal orders. Priests, namely, in almost all nations of the world were the first artists, creators, and legislators. They were therefore the first to make use of symbols, both in form of material objects and of symbolical actions, and thus to dress into visible forms for inexperienced eyes of barbarians the sensitive body of first intellectual notions. Moral and religious thoughts, instead of being expressed openly, were enveloped in the forms of symbols. In such a way the picture itself much more easily found its way into the soul of man, while permeating the spirit by means of senses. The symbol and the dogma in such a way became identical.[13]

According to basic theoretical conceptions of legal symbolism—as expressed by French scholar M. Chassan—the symbol as such and in itself contains the meaning invoked by the representation (or picture) of an object or an action which are used as symbols. From that aspect symbolical form is not always entirely arbitrary, since it is not absolutely foreign to the idea which it expresses through the picture. However, since this form never entirely represents the pure idea of a particular right, as it frequently contains a series of elements having no connection at all with the idea, and as one and the same representation may often be expressed by means of various ideas—the relationship which unites the symbol with the idea is in many cases rather arbitrary. This very element makes a symbol, and especially the one belonging to the undeveloped category of symbols, in essence an ambiguous one. As far as legal symbol in its narrow sense is concerned (i.e., without the ingredient of morals and religion), however, there was a need for such form of representation of legally relevant rules or notions to be in as direct as possible a relationship with the object it had to represent, so that it could correspond to the level of consciousness and capacities of understanding of people from the early stages of development of mankind. If it were not so, people would not understand the symbol and receive the message, and the purpose of the symbolical language could not have been realized.

It was therefore necessary for the symbols in law, already at the time of their origination, to be simple, clear and specific. This, however, according to Chassan, was characteristic of the undeveloped application of legal symbols. To a degree the application of legal symbols in course of prehistory and history was developed, their original meaning gradually faded away, and while mixing during millennia and centuries with habits and usages, with religious symbols and practices, i.e., rites—assumed new meanings and some kind of solemn and consecrated character. In such a way, while becoming related to beliefs and even to superstitions, and merging frequently with mythological tradition, legal symbols assumed a more precise and stronger meaning, which in a specific way affected both laymen and scholars.[14]

This simplicity of legal symbols, both regarding their meaning, i.e., contents, and their form, is characteristic particularly for primeval symbols which, on the other hand, could not be said for many a religious symbol, with which the emphasis is on mysteriousness and sublimity.

Legal symbolism—according to Chassan's synthesis which he constructed after studying all relevant theoretical works in the fields of law and ethnology, as well as literary and historical works—is found in judicial practice of the times past, but is also represented in legal customs, in usages, then until the present time in emblems, signs, trade names, brands, trademarks, tokens, labels and the like. Legal symbolism may be also found in legal analogies, in myths, in legal formulas and concise legal formulations, as well as rather frequently in legal fictions, which are characteristic for some branches of contemporary law.[15]

In its most developed form, however, a legal symbol informs a man on a specific right belonging to him, or it solves some legal difficulty, or dispute at the court. In a simple sense, a legal symbol has to represent in a fictitious way some physical object or, which is more frequent, an abstract idea belonging to everyday life. Thus, for instance, a clod of soil represents a field or an acre; a tile or a key—a building; a hat means man's person; the hair style is the symbol of freedom and power, while the sceptre above which there is an open hand is the symbol of general justice; a sword is, however, a representation of criminal justice. A symbol was accordingly a figural embodiment of an action affecting everyday life.[16]

Independently of its connection with religion and law, the symbol has been related to plastic arts too which—while always striving towards the aesthetical and representing it to our senses, as well as attempting at idealizing the real and realizing the ideal—assumed gradually an eloquent and energetic simplicity. Both sculpture and painting do this in allegories and symbols which, however, are much more refined than legal symbols. And in spite of the paradox in saying so, one is able to find here the distant relationship between the fine arts and the law whose traces may be followed even until our days through the relics of various symbols, in spite of their losing the original meaning. In quite an elaborated theory on legal symbols, set forth by M. Chassan, their general character is emphasized, as well as their long rule, particularly in the field of customary, i.e., unwritten law. In religion, in law, in the fine arts, the same physical signs are almost always common for these three areas, although their meanings may be sometimes different.[17] According to that theory, it is possible to distinguish the category of legal mythology which may be a general one—as expressed for instance in the Nordic Saga, where law is only partially mentioned—and the legal mythology in its proper sense. After this, there follow the categories of trade mark, of legal formula and particularly of legal fictions which were always dear to law. In its "childhood", namely, the law "played" with emblems which in fact were material fictions, while in its more developed and more "mature" stage, these were replaced by intellectual fictions, which were incorporated into the intimate poetics of law, which was characteristic for its ancient beginnings, as far as external expressions and forms of law, were concerned. Thus the uttered symbol, i.e., the one expressed by words, is frequently only a transformation of the onetime real symbol.[18]

Legal symbols may further be classified according to their origin, then in terms of their relationship towards the object or the idea represented by them, according to their nature and, finally, according to their form. Specific classification of legal symbols is further elaborated along the following scheme: according to their origin legal symbols are either of a general character (i.e., common to all of mankind) since they are so general that they belong to all peoples of the world, as they are addressed primarily to the sense of sight and to man's feelings—or of a national character, or specific for individual cultures, i.e., regions. According to the object, there are four kinds of symbols, namely: the ones in relation to the object which is represented (for instance, when a part of something serves to designate a whole—*pars pro toto*—a key symbolizes the entire building, the clause in contemporary construction contracts); then in relation to an action (placing arms over the grave of an assassinated, as a sign for a need of vendetta in the Albanian unwritten law, or placing a blood-stained shirt on a conspicuous spot in the house, as well as burying it to mark the same intention;[19] in relation to a person (gloves, hat, portrait—this kind of symbol was rather frequently used by the courts); and finally, in relation to representing with the aid of a solemn form or particularly strict ceremony (for instance, a festive dinner with strict procedure of speaking and sitting, as a sign of peaceful settlement of a dispute otherwise leading to a bloody revenge according to Albanian and Montenegrin customary law; a glass of wine to symbolize a concluded contract, etc.).[20]

According to their nature, legal symbols are divided into several kinds, namely: silent or pantomimic, and uttered ones or audible; simple and composite ones; pure and mixed legal symbols (the latter ones were particularly in use as judicial symbols). As to their form, the symbols may be natural and artificial. Natural ones encompass parts of the nature, usually soil—which since the earliest times was a sacred element, then water, fire, animals, particularly domestic ones. Also a man, as a symbol of God, as well as his blood and hearth.[21]

The Survey of Most Frequent Legal Symbols in World Customary Law

Already in the ancient Great Collection of Legal Customs of France[22] it is found that the sign for acquiring a title of a personal estate is the so-called heredity taking of a piece of turf. Thus, soil, grass, straw (particularly within the sphere of private law and the law of contracts), a branch and a whole tree—all had specific legal meanings in the customary law, both in its unwritten and written forms (i.e., collections where oral tradition from the area of law was gathered). A branch, for example, served to ensure the transfer of ownership of real property as far as accessories attached to such property were concerned.

According to the old French customs also a dowry to a girl could consist only of a flower wreath, as a symbol of honesty and purity, or of only one walnut. Women in Normandy wanting to be hired as servants (a kind of labour law!) held in their hands bunches of flowers while waiting in the market-place, and the potential employer would only ask them about the price of the flowers.[23]

Fruits as symbols of fertility and abundance are known in many areas of the world, and especially with the Vlachs in the marriage ceremony, when hazelnuts are thrown at the newlyweds. The same custom is found in Russia too and the meaning is—"multiply yourselves and be fertile". In the island of Corsica walnuts, hazelnuts and other fruits are thrown in front of the newlyweds, while in the Balkan Peninsula the same is done with wheat.

The category of significant symbols include also fire, in its various forms: torch, bundle of twigs in flames and the like. Fire symbolizes occupation, ownership, family and war. Water, on the other hand, is seldom a symbol in the West, but in the East it is found as such, particularly in marriage relations. Thus, water is poured over the hands of the newlyweds. In the customs of Slavic peoples water played an important role as a symbol, particularly in the area of customary criminal law, due to the general belief that water "does not accept anything impure and sinful". This is the basis of the ancient custom of submerging a culprit into deep water,[24] as a kind of ordeal, and if the criminal rises to the surface—he is not guilty. This is also the explanation of the old saying which evokes that kind of ordeal in Serbia, Slovenia and in other areas of South East Europe: "give me the luck—and you can bind me in a sack".[25]

Furthermore, the cock is a symbol of a house, a home, i.e., family (today too the figure of the cock is often found over the chimney of houses), as well as a sign of the intention to stay and to subsist in the specific place.[26] Out of other animal symbols, one may mention the bees, as the symbol of new cities, and a white horse—the sign of domination, of suzerainty; a conqueror usually entered the city riding on a white horse, and each first of January the Roman consul in a white toga rode on a white horse to the capitol and to the temple of Jupiter.

Parts of the human body too had symbolical meaning in the former law. Thus, a hand or an arm were the signs of power and of authority. Whereof, already in Roman law, the institution of *emancipatio, manumissio*; furthermore, a wife falls *in manu mariti*, i.e., under the full authority of the husband. In the Middle Ages the transfer of property was effected in a solemn way by using the symbol of a hand. The hand was, namely, laid down on the movable property in the case of sale and it was lifted from it by the seller. The hand is, as is known, also the symbol of alliance, friendship, fraternity and is universally accepted as such, particularly the right hand, or both hands clasped together, which meant peace among the peoples. A hand open towards the sky signifies the oath.[27]

The foot also is a legal symbol. Putting a foot on the ground means taking possession over it. Whereof the term in Roman law possessio, which originated from *pes-sitio, quasi pedum positio*. Sexual organ has been a symbol too. According to Herodotus, Egyptian king Sezostris at his conquests erected columns all over the territories taken; when he took a country without battle, he would carve on such columns female sexual organs to indicate the weakness and submissiveness of peoples conquered in such a way. In the heroic age, again according to Herodotus, only those belonging to the heroic class have been considered men, while plebeians were treated as females and "weak and feebleminded creatures". Accordingly, sex was also a symbol of belonging to a particular social class. Some authors see in that a trace of explanation for maenads and amazons, while others go even further when claiming that the term *mulieres* in the Code of the Twelve Tables did not mean females, but members of the lower class, i.e., slaves who were not even allowed to drink wine, as a sign of possessing the rights of citizen.

The heart has a character of a symbol even in the criminal law of modern times. Thus according to the nineteenth century French Criminal Procedure Act, the president of the jury when announcing the verdict had to put his hand on his heart. Blood as a spoken symbol was a sign of the high justice and also of kinship, which is at present in use in the family law of all countries. In taking an oath it has figured as a real symbol—when blood of two persons was mixed mutually in order to become blood (adopted) brothers, as well as when it was, even, drunk for that purpose (the old custom of Arabs, Scythians, old Scandinavians, Albanians etc.).

There exists quite a number of combined symbols, such as the following: a hand holding a sword, sceptre or a stick of commanding and justice; a ring on the finger, as a symbol of highest authority (the case of Venetian doge, Normandian dukes, bishops in the Catholic Church and the like), as well as, naturally, of matrimonial fidelity; a boot on the foot; a toque over the hair; a hat or a crown on the head; belt around the waist; a veil over the face etc.

From among the symbolical objects which are particularly important and in general use at present is the flag, which started as a token of towns and areas, to be distinguished from a sword which was a symbol of investiture of kings, dukes, and knights. In contemporary public and private international law, for instance, one should mention the well-known institution of the law of a flag of a ship or an aircraft—as a sign of their belonging to a particular state ("citizenship" of a ship).

Wheel in the criminal law field was a sign used to stigmatize a criminal who is going to be executed; such a criminal, namely, carried the wheel on his back. In the Middle Ages (not in Antiquity, since that type of garment did not exist) the glove has been a way of expressing the transfer of property and the procedure of investiture, particularly with peoples of German origin. Thus the rules of the ancient collection Saxonian Mirror permitted judges while sitting in the courtroom to wear gloves, since a bare hand was a symbol of sincerity and loyalty. The ring was, as already mentioned, a sign of fidelity, even in religion—the bishop "united" with his Church. Among the Romans the ring was a symbol in transferring ownership—the one who received it became successor of the one giving it. However, ring-fetters around the neck of a convict were a conspicuous symbol from the area of criminal law. A toque, a cap, helmet and hat in Rome were all the symbols of honour and freedom, and that meaning was carried over into the Middle Ages. Thus, as a sign of his power, the king stayed with his hat on, while all the others were bareheaded. The debtor came to the court bareheaded (today too), while a member of the jury who is taking oath is also without a hat and standing, but the president of the court receiving the oath is sitting with his hat on. At the moment of arrest, the hat of a man was taken off, the same action being used also as far as a veil of a woman was concerned; they lost thus in a symbolical way their honour, as well as the right to protection.

Well known symbols are also the crown and the mitre (ceremonial headdress of a bishop symbolizing his apostolic authority). Belt was a symbol during marriage ceremony; on the first night of the marriage the husband took off his wife's belt; in defeat and taking prisoners, belt is also taken off the enemy (also today); belt is a symbol of transferring property too, of dissolution of a community, of expressing respect in feudal relationships, as well as of investiture of public functionaries. The bed is a symbol in marriage law; it is thus said "children from the first or second bed"; a broken bed meant the divorce.[28] The list of symbols in law and of their explanation would be rather long if one should extend one's survey to wider areas of the world and to various periods. However, the above summary listing suffices to underline the significance of symbols in the history of law and, particularly, in customary law. It provides also some material and a stimulus for eventual further and deeper study of contemporary relics and transformations of symbols even in the written law of the present times, as well as in the legal practice. The same attention should be given to symbolical actions, but due to the scope of an article, it was not possible to treat them here in more detail.

Legal Symbols in Yugoslav Law

Almost until the period between the two world wars Yugoslav peoples made use of various symbolical sentences and sayings, in order to describe in a pregnant and concise manner some legal institutions in their customs and usages which they met in their everyday life and work.[29] In many a branch of law there existed legal symbolism in various degrees. Many of these symbols to be found while studying the legal past of Yugoslav and other Balkan peoples, However, these symbols were not of an autochtonous character, since they were assimilated and adopted from the customary law of other peoples, which only meant that the symbols in law were of a more universal character. However, their significance and influence in the legal practice of people were not at all less intensive due to that.

While treating the subject of sources of law in his textbook or encyclopedia of law, F. Taranovski touches upon the category of legal symbols which he relates to customary, i.e., unwritten law: "The norms of customary law are preserved directly in the memory of people and at the initial stages of social development they are manifested only through those actions where they are realized. Actions in which norms of customary law are effected and put into practice are followed by special rites (ceremonies), so that in such a way they are transformed into legal symbols. Such symbols are, for instance, shaking hands and 'cutting through' at the sale of goods; using a clod of soil and saying 'let it be successful' for designating the transfer of property over land, etc. All these and other similar ceremonies represent not only the form of concluding legal transactions, but also a symbolic expression of a norm of customary law which regulates these legal transactions and corresponding legal relations. Together with the development of capacity for abstract thinking, the norm of customary law becomes distinguished from the legal action itself and finds its expression as a judgment which rather frequently appears in the form of sayings, which are suitable to be memorized. Thus, for instance: people are tied for tongue, and oxen for horns; warrantor—payer, my home—my freedom; ring given—wedding concluded etc."[30]

In addition to symbols and symbolical actions which were used by Yugoslav peoples, in current use are also legal proverbs which are sometimes sarcastic. These are relics of ancient penalties which were often cruel. However, this phenomenon is also outside the scope of the present article.

Symbols and symbolical actions were present, first of all, in the field of public law. Thus, with Slovenians, the well-known inauguration of the king in the Field Gosposvetsko. The judges had a special judging mace which was different according to different judicial districts (relevant data originate from the sixteenth century). The judge held that mace while pronouncing his verdict. Similar symbols are also noted in the eighteenth century in the area of the Slovenian place Žužemberk, where judges elected by the people had maces (corresponding category are the judges elected in the present time as umpires) while adjudicating in disputes over woods and pastures, as well as over real property.

Public activity of Slovenians, according to M. Dolenc (rolls from the surroundings of Škofja Loka) was formerly full of symbolical actions and ways of expression, which were, for instance, visible in the common processions. These processions had in the late sixteenth century also the character of marking and repeated determining of land boundaries (so-called surrounding of land boundaries—*obhod*), and not only of religious ceremony. Corresponding data are found in the area of Kostanjevica, in Dolenjska area in Slovenia (seventeenth century). During such processions joint lunches have been organized. Similar collective meals, by means of which returning from mountain pastures is marked, existed still in the seventies of the twentieth century in Montenegro ("*zdig*"). This custom of procession, with torches, is known in German ethnologic literature as *Umreiten*.[31]

In public places and markets in the north-western parts of our country, during market days there existed the practice known as "market or police justice", and the corresponding symbol was the displaying in the marketplace of the sword and a shield. That legal symbol too most probably is not of an autochtonous character, but is assimilated from the German customary law practice, where it is known under the terms *Schilder, Fahnen, Rolandsäulen*.

One symbol is found also in the documents of the Montenegrin Great Court (at the end of the nineteenth century), and it relates to symbolical payment by means of a drink in the tribe of Kuči. The corresponding formulation was: ". . . only those who will labour this land shall be bound to give to their tribe at the end of each year a drink, as a sign that the land was not theirs, but common property".[32]

There are many symbols also in the area of family law in Yugoslav countries. Thus, as is known, growing a beard means the sign of masculinity, and the corresponding proverb is—"God created first of all the beard to himself. Therefore, plucking or singeing somebody else's beard was a severe violation of honour. The penalty for such an act was provided for by Dušan's Code in articles 97 and 98, and a corresponding institution was termed "*mehoskubina*".[33] In Germany a man with long hair was considered a free man *("Lass mich ungeschoren")*. A kind of revival of this old custom in many countries of the world in the middle of our century is the long hair of young people.

In the relations between husband and wife there existed the institution of morning gift (*Morgengabe*—in German customary law) which formerly entered the written law too,[34] and according to which all that was given or promised to the wife on the first morning after the wedding was considered an irrevocable gift. Furthermore, obtaining the keys of the house by the newly married woman meant her authority as a housewife. Moreover, the wife could be present when the husband sold valuable objects from the house.

The symbol of household and of a community is, as is known, the fire-place, so that in the customary law of some Slavic countries the smoke was used as a designation of the number of households—"a village numbers fifty smokes".

Long ago people have noticed that the welfare and cohesion of the household depended also on the continuity of work of hired house help. They were sometimes compensated by payment in kind. According to unwritten rules, they were not allowed to leave their work posts whenever they wanted to. Therefore in Slovenia it was symbolically said that such person had to stay in the household at least a year, "even if he had to serve as a saw-horse." The one not behaving like that and leaving "at Christmas Eve" would be given only "a sleeveless sheepskin coat". On the other hand, and in a way related to the above, was a customary law rule which protected the hired household worker—noted down by M. Dolenc in Gorenjska and Notranjska in Slovenia, and according to which the one who became exhausted on someone else's possession had a right to just compensation.[35] This right inspired famous Slovenian writer I. Cankar to write his novel "Servant Jernej and his Right".

Compulsory sale of land and of other real property or movables due to insolvency is known as "the sale on the drum" (i.e., auction), which is only a verbal symbol and a relic of the former custom of making public announcements by using a drum. There are also symbolical signs by means of which trespassing is prohibited, i.e., two crossed twigs (a similar road sign for marking an open railroad crossing exists today too). In the customary law of Montenegro there exists even today so-called *zabjela*, i.e., peeled off branch pinned in the ground to mark the prohibition to enter a private property. A similar role is played also by the seal across the door of a house or a church, and unauthorized removal is punishable.

In the unwritten law of contract too there exist symbols of symbolical actions which are rather generally known. Thus contracting parties when entering into a contract on sale shake hands and (in the past) even kiss each other for the success of the transaction. This ceremony is known in Slovenia as *zaključek*((conclusion) or *dokonček* and it is widely in use all over the Balkan Peninsula. Also drinking a glass of beverage means, today too, that a transaction was successfully accomplished. Formerly the judges too had a right to such a drink, but this was expressly prohibited later on. According to medieval German law the glass of drink amounted even to an essential element of the contract on sale (*Lit*). Earnest-money is also a symbolical institution which exists in the contemporary law of contract too. According to former customary law in the Balkans there was a possibility for a party negating a contract to repay the entire earnest-money amount, which was done as a sign of accepting the dissolution (even in the sphere of the law of marriage).

Valtazar Bogišić in his survey of legal customs recorded the following specific understanding of each other in the unwritten law of marriage: "When a young man and a girl are asked whether they would like to be married, they would express themselves through symbols; for instance, the affirmative youth was looking in front of himself and smiling, while the girl also looked in the same manner and shed a few tears; when they disagreed, they would again look ahead and barely uttered through set teeth that they did not agree with the proposal."[36]

While writing on the topic of land boundaries in Serbia, M. Barjaktarović particularly elaborated from the ethnological-juridical aspect the issue of some legal symbols. Thus a cross—and not only as a symbol of Christianity—was used to mark off a boundary between fields. The same role is played by a boundary stone (in Montenegro a similar term is *kiljan*, although with some additional meaning), which sometimes was followed by "additional witnesses", in fact by several smaller stones. The same way is found in the well-known collection of Albanian unwritten law—the Code of Leka Dukadini.[37]

Conclusions

This summary review of various symbols, both objects and actions in customary law and in the law in general points to the category of phenomena of legal character which are related to many spiritual creations and activities of man. It also shows that between the law and these creations there exists a connection which is not at first visible. Contemporary research of legal symbols in terms of Balkan studies, and particularly if realized in an interdisciplinary way, would undoubtedly provide additional contribution to the clarification of the complex of customary law. In such a way a relatively blank space would be filled out in our historical-legal studies. Symbols, although their origin is difficult to ascertain, are older than customary law. Their study could therefore also contribute to better understanding of unwritten law rules which have been developing throughout the centuries in our countries.

And through that it would be possible to better understand even the history of our written law. In the final analysis, the benefit of such a study of legal symbols could also be found by the legislator, since in such a way he could acquire further knowledge of our legal tradition, which would help him in the search for best solutions, as far as legislating on a local level is concerned.

Notes

1. E. Cassirer, Philosophie der symbolischen Formen, Berlin 1923–1931; E. Kasirer, *Jezik i mit*, Novi Sad 1972; B. Malinoswki, *Magija, nauka i religija i druge studije*, Beograd 1971; M. Veber, *Privreda i društvo*, Beograd 1976; S. Trojanović, *Psihofizička izražavanja kod Srba, poglavito bez reči*, Srpski etnografski zbornik, knj. 52, Beograd 1935; I. Ivić, *Čovek kao animal symbolicum*, Beograd 1978; V. Pavićević, *Sociologija religije sa elementima iflozofije religije*, Beograd 1980; C. Morris, *Foundations of the Theory of Signs*, Chicago 1938; K. Lévi-Stros, *Divlja misao*, Beograd 1975; K. Jung, *The Symbolism of Spirit*; B. Bettelheim, *The Uses of Enchantment*, 1975

2. The Institute organized two symposia (the reports are published) and published monographs and articles on the subject.

3. M. Chassan, *Essai sur la Symbolique du droit, précédé d'une introduction sur la poésie du droit primitif*, Paris 1847; Reyscher, *Symbolik des germanischen Rechts*; J. Grimm, *Poesie im Recht*; J. Grimm, *Deutsche Rechtsalterthümer*, 1828; Creuzer, *Symbolik*.

4. Undoubtedly Bogišić did know of all mentioned works and publications, which is visible from the survey of his library in Cavtat, as well as from his marginal notes.

5. M. Dolenc, *Simbolična pravna dejanja in izražanja med Slovenci* (posebni odtisk iz Slovenskega pravnika, let. LII, Nr. 9–10, 1938).

6. *Bezujetje*, Mjesečnik 1913, 550–556.

7. *Privatno-pravni ugovori XVI veka iz Poljičke župe*, Arhiv za pravne i društvene nauke, 1934, 398–415, as well as the remaining works in the area of history of law of Yugoslav peoples written by this well-known author.

8. I. Jelić, *Krvna osveta i umir krvi u Crnoj Gori i Severnoj Albaniji*, Beograd 1926.

9. A. Hudovernik, *Pravni običaji slovenski*, Slovenski pravnik, 1883, 2–7.

10. F. Marolt, *Tri obredja iz Zilje*.

11. *Staroslovenske pravde*, Gl. Muz. Dr. 1935, 47, 48.

12. Creuzer, *Symbolik*, introduction, chapter I, quoted according to Chassan, 11.

13. Creuzer, *op. cit.*

14. J. Grimm, Poesie im Recht, parag. 10—quoted according to Chassan, 13.

15. M. Chassan, *op. cit.*, 19.

16. J. Grimm, *Deutsche Rechtsalterthümer*, 109.

17. Chassan, *op. cit.*, 15.
18. Chassan, *op. cit.*, 41.
19. S. Dučić, *Život i običaji plemena Kuča*, 128.
20. D. Krstić, *Pravni običaji kod Kuča*, 157.
21. The above classification of legal symbols is stated, with minor changes, according to the above mentioned work by M. Chassan, 50–65 and *passim*.
22. *Grand coutumier de France*.
23. Chassan, *op. cit.*, 85.
24. The motive to be found in literary work by Slovenian author Ivan Tavčar (1851–1923), *Visoška hronika*.
25. M. Dolenc. *op. cit.*, 24.
26. In 1463 Flemings, as allies of Frenchmen, brought to the walls of besieged Calais all their belongings, including their cocks, expressing thus their intention to remain there until the town surrendered. Quoted according to Chassan, *op. cit.*, 103.
27. Collection of French Customary Law of Town of Reims even treats the term "hand" as equal to term "oath". Quoted according to Chassan, *op. cit.*, 119, footnote 1.
28. Major part of data on symbols and symbolical actions in this section of the article is taken from mentioned systematic work on legal symbols by M. Chassan.
29. M. Dolenc, *op. cit.*, 1.
30. T. Taranovski, *Enciklopedija prava*, Beograd 1923, 181.
31. C. Pützfeld, *Deutsche Rechtssymbolik*, 1936, 46 and 90.
32. Order of the Montenegrin Great Court, Nr. 1165 of June 1, 1891, State Archives, Cetinje, fasc. 144/1891.
33. The penalty was severe: if a noble was insulted the perpetrator's hands were to be cut off.
34. Paragraph 1232 of the Slovenian General State Law of 1853.
35. M. Dolenc, *op. cit.*, 17.
36. Written down by archimandrite N. Dučić in 1898 in the survey on customary law. Bogišić's Library, Cavtat.
37. M. Barjaktarović, *O zemljišnim medama u Srba*, SAN, Posebna izd., *knj. CCIII, Etnograf. inst., knj. 4, Beograd* 1952, 57, 58.

CLINTON BAILEY

A Note on the Bedouin Image of 'Adl as Justice

Each culture has its own set of symbols, the majority of which cannot be understood without reference to its particular cultural setting. In the following brief essay, Clinton Bailey of Jerusalem University draws from his fieldwork experience collecting Bedouin poetry in Sinai since 1970 to elucidate the subtle metaphorical nuances of a single symbol, the camel saddlebag. His insightful explication of the traditional imagery involved should serve as a reminder of just how difficult it is for members of one culture to penetrate the symbolic code of another culture. For some of the results of Bailey's fieldwork, see Bedouin Poetry from Sinai and the Negev: Mirror of a Culture *(Oxford: Oxford University Press, 1991).*

For more detail about Bedouin folk law, see L. Bouvat, "Le Droit coutumier des tribus Bédouines de Syrie," Revue du Monde Musulman, 43 (1921), 27–45; Omar Effendi el-Barthuthi, "Judicial Courts among the Bedouin of Palestine," Journal of the Palestine Oriental Society, 2 (1922), 34–65; Austin Kennett, Bedouin Justice (Cambridge: Cambridge University Press, 1925); Joseph Chelhod, Le droit dans la societé bedouine (Paris: M. Riviere, 1971); Aharon Layish, "Challenges to Customary Law and Arbitration: The Impact of Islamic Law upon Settled Bedouin in the Judaean Desert," Tel Aviv University Studies in Law, 5 (1980–1982), 206–221; Larry W. Roeder, Jr., "Trial Law and Tribal Solidarity in Sinai Bedouin Culture," Anthropos, 84 (1989), 230–234. *For a more complete general discussion of Bedouin folk law scholarship, see* Frank H. Stewart, "Tribal Law in the Arab World: A Review of the Literature," International Journal of Middle East Studies, 19 (1987), 473–490.

Writing on the term *'adl* in the *Encyclopaedia of Islam*, Emile Tyan presents it as a noun meaning "justice" and an adjective meaning "rectilinear and well-balanced" and states that the two meanings do not correspond exactly. Through contact with Bedouin culture, however, one encounters a number of indications that the two meanings not only correspond quite closely, but that the images "rectilinear and well-balanced" lie at

---

Reprinted from *The Muslim World*, 66(2) (April, 1976), 133–135, with permission.

the root of the term ʻadl as "justice." This seems natural when we consider that *lex talionis* may itself be a product of nomadic existence in the desert. As justice in its Islamic context, however, ʻadl, according to Tyan, has come to mean obeisance to the moral and religious laws of Islam, a meaning far removed from the Bedouin principles of balance and compensation. It is therefore of interest to view the term ʻadl as it was perhaps perceived in the desert, before being adapted to Muslim legal terminology and divorced from its original context.

The rectilinear image of justice appears in the jurisprudential terminology of several languages; in French we have the concept *droit*, and in English the idea of "right." Often, too, the concept of injustice embodies the image of "something twisted," as the French *tort* (from old French, *tortus*; cf. torture) and the English "wrong" (cf. to wring). The Bedouin image of ʻadl is also rectilinear, but specifically in the sense of flat, even or well-balanced. It corresponds, in this respect, to the underlying concept of the English word "law," which stems from the old Teutonic root *lag* (to lie). Because the image is of "something lying flat," however, the contrary image of "twisted" is hardly applicable; instead, the Bedouins have conceived of wrong or injustice in the "tilting" or "inclining" action. The opposite of ʻadl, balanced, is thus *māyil*, tilted.

The imagery of balanced and tilted derives, in particular, from what the camel carries on its back: either large woolen saddlebags (*khurj*) that protrude on both sides of the saddle or the load itself. One Bedouin poet, for example, in praise of his she-camel's saddlebags, says: *wa khurjhā, fīh ʻadl wa lā mīl* (her saddlebags are straight not inclined). Another poet uses the second conjugation verb *ʻaddal* for "to straighten out" a camel's load that is tilting: *in mālit al-aḥmāl, bi 'īdī ʻaddaltahā* (when the loads tilt, I balance them with my hand).

The use of the word "to tilt" as meaning "to wrong, or be unjust" is heard in everyday Bedouin conversation. If a Bedouin wants to say that someone has done him wrong, he may express it as, "so-and-so has tilted (been unjust) in regard to me": *fulān māl ʻalay*. This expression is also found in the Bedouin proverb, *idhā mālit ʻalayk ad-dinyā, mīl ʻaʻdhrāʻak* (if the world leans on you [i.e., wrongs you], lean on your arm [i.e., resort to force]). In presenting an actual legal claim, a Bedouin may say, "so-and-so has tilted (been unjust) in regard to my right": *fulān mīl ʻalā ḥaggī*. By the same token, a Bedouin may see his right, itself, as tilted or out of balance: *ḥaggī māyil*.

The use of saddlebag imagery for justice is clearly indicated in the wording of a poem that has enjoyed wide currency in the Bedouin world. In it the poet asks God to grant him the ten things that made life a success, one of which is "power wielded on horseback with which to balance the tilted right of a protégé" (one who has sought protection):

A Note on the Bedouin Image of 'Adl as Justice

al-khāmsih, 'izwih min fawg al-amhār
a'addil bihā, law māl ḥagg aṭ-ṭanīb.

Here we have the same verb, 'addal, which was used to balance tilted camel loads (*in mālit al-aḥmāl*) presently employed to balance someone's tilted rights.

The use of saddlebag and camel-load imagery to make the concepts of justice and injustice palpable to the Bedouins is highly appropriate. All Bedouins understand that one cannot survive in the desert without a camel and that for a camel to be of service his load must be balanced and not tilted. This essentialness of the camel is closely paralleled by another sine qua non of existence in the desert: a Bedouin's need never to be remiss in the defense of his rights. These, basically defined, are: not to be killed, not to be maimed, not to have one's honor maligned, and not to have one's possessions taken.

In the absence of law enforcement agencies in the desert to protect these rights, a Bedouin's own reputation for relentlessness in the redress of wrongs committed against him is his primary guarantee of security. This reputation, in itself, serves as a deterrent to other members of a naturally contentious society, who are often tempted to violate each other's rights in order to survive. If a Bedouin should once neglect to redress a wrong, however, whether slight or grave, he would lose this reputation and henceforth be considered easy prey. Then, like an unevenly loaded camel, he, too, could barely go on in the desert; "He would have no future," Bedouins say.

Thus, even a Bedouin who is in fact attempting to rectify a wrong feels that his life, too, is "out of balance" so long as he has not yet succeeded. He fears lest ultimate failure be attributed to a lack of resolve. Only the actual redress of a wrong, through either retaliation or retribution, will bring him relief. This is what constitutes the balancing of the load that enables his life in the desert to proceed.

A Bedouin, who had to take vengeance for the murder of a son, captured this image of justice as 'adl in the concluding lines of a poem that he composed when, according to the legend,[1] sitting in a mountain retreat, he watched his son's murderer being buried on the morrow of the night of revenge. The earlier lines of the poem relate some details of the act: how the avenger appeared disguised as a beggar, how he waited for the murderer (Salih) and killed him, and how a black slave helped him escape. At the end of the poem comes an expression of relief, for he has shed the burden of care: he has made a counterpoise ('adīl) for his sideheavy saddlebag (*il-khurj ith-thigīl*).

1. I was your guest before Salih came your way;
   Salih alighted at your camp just today.

2. I sat without shame and ate unrestrained,
   And among dregs I was myself disdained.
3. A reed of *'awarwar* my defense against mongrels
   With which I beat every hound that howls.
4. But a dagger of the *Ijbārah* lay at my waist,
   You could hear it scraping within its case.
5. I plunged it in twice, perhaps even thrice,
   Quickly; I had no time on hand.
6. I plunged it in twice, perhaps even thrice;
   Jets from a rain cloud for a droughty land.
7. Thank God for the slave at the edge of the waste
   Diverting the dogs in an adverse direction.
8. Morning found me hiding in a steep mountain crag;
   Only wild beasts had ever repaired here before me.
9. I retired encumbered but arose feeling light;
   My sideheavy saddlebag has now been put right.[2]

Notes

1. The complete story, as narrated to me by 'Id Imfarrij of the Tarabin Hasablih tribe in Sinai, appears in both Arabic and English in Clinton Bailey, "The Narrative Context of the Bedouin Qasidah-Poem," in *Folklore Research Center Studies*, III (Jerusalem, 1972), 67–105.

2. *Sawwayt lil-khurj ith-thigīl 'adīl.*

JOHN N. HAZARD

Furniture Arrangement as a Symbol of Judicial Roles

It is one thing to speak of symbols of a culture, symbols which are consciously recognized by members of that culture, and quite another to refer to the possible symbolic significance of cultural features which may or may not be recognized as such by those same members of the culture. In the following essay by a professor of public law at Columbia University, we find fascinating speculations about the semantics of courtroom space. How the furniture is arranged, along with the relative positions of the participants in the judicial process as it is commonly found in European contexts are imaginatively interpreted. While it may be difficult to prove the validity of all the speculations vouchsafed beyond the shadow of a doubt, the essay is surely thought-provoking.

The scientific study of spacial relations is termed "proxemics." In this instance, proxemics is combined with implications for national character analysis. For a contrasting picture of an African "court" setting, see J.D. Krige, "Some Aspects of Lovhedu Judicial Arrangements," Bantu Studies, 13 (1939), 113–129. For a more general though brief comparison of diverse judicial arrangements, see Stuart S. Nagel, "Culture Patterns and Judicial Systems," Vanderbilt Law Review, 16 (1962), 147–157.

For an introduction to "proxemics," see Edward T. Hall, "Proxemics," Current Anthropology, 9 (1968), 83–108, and O. Michael Watson, "On Proxemic Research," Current Anthropology, 10 (1969), 222–224. Although it is by no means clear that the term "proxemics" has become widely known, there is no question that the investigation of interpersonal spatial relations is a most challenging subject.

Walk into an empty courtroom and look around. The furniture arrangement will tell you at a glance who has what authority. In nearly every country, judges now look down on their courtrooms from a raised platform, and when the bench is collegial, the presiding judge has a chair whose back protrudes several inches above the rest. This is so even

---

Reprinted from *ETC.: A Review of General Semantics*, 19 (1962), 181–188, with permission.

in the Soviet Union where the judge has been elevated above his 1917 role when he was wise friend and conciliator to his village. Today, he sits with his colleagues even in the lowest court upon a platform rather than around a table with the parties. His dignity is enhanced not only by his elevated chair but by the attendant's cry, "All stand," as he and the lay assessors file into the room to take their places. Only a robe is missing to command respect. And in the People's Republic of Poland, after the "October" of 1956, even the robe was redraped on judicial shoulders, with its purple piping in traditional designation of the majesty of the law. The portrait of power was further enhanced at that time by encircling his neck with a great gold seal and chain of office in traditional Polish fashion.

The judge's commanding seat catches first attention, but the eye soon wanders to the other furniture. In a British or American courtroom, the jury box stands out to the right of the enclosure behind the "bar". Between it and the judge's bench on a raised platform somewhat lower than that of the judge stands the chair waiting for the witness, facing outward into the room so that all can hear, including the press for whom a gallery or at least a bench is often reserved to give meaning to the concept of "publicity" characteristic of the common law concept of "due process."

Compare the assize court in the canton of Geneva, and you will find the jury, but in a different place. It is in no box separated from the judge, but arranged on two rows of chairs to the judge's left behind the great semi-circular bench that extends the width of the room. One scarcely needs to be told that the judge retires with the jury in this Swiss canton, and that he shares with the jurymen the decision on guilt and punishment. At the eastern end of Europe there is no jury box at all, for the Soviet legal procedure relies on two lay assessors in every type of case, both criminal and civil, to share with the judge the decision on matters both of fact and law. This is so in all of the Eastern European states that have adopted the Soviet legal system, and has been accepted even in Communist China.

Witness stands in continental Europe traditionally face in toward the judge rather than out toward courtroom. The assembled public sees only the back of the witness's head when he testifies and hears little of what he says unless he raises his voice. In Geneva the press is aided because the press bench is placed along the right hand wall below the great semi-circular bench of judge and jury but forward of the public's seats. Reporters may hear and see everything and perform their critical democratic function of informing the wider public of what transpires. In the Eastern European courtrooms there are no special press galleries, unless the defendant happens to be an American U-2 pilot and the affair

Furniture Arrangement as a Symbol of Judicial Roles

a cause célèbre. Soviet concepts of "due process" require no participation of a press independent of the state and prepared to sound the tocsin if injustice is done. If the press is present, it is because the court has a case with a public message which the judges believe the public should hear.

The Prosecutor's Seat is placed in a wide variety of positions in various legal systems. In the American courtroom the casual visitor will note no chair that can be quickly identified as one of special dignity. The district, state's or United States' attorney, as he is likely to be called, will sit in a chair placed on the other side of the center aisle from the chair of the defense counsel and inside the "bar." This chair has no ornate carved seal on its back, but is whatever standard model the janitor chooses to set at the table. Both prosecutor and defense counsels are placed on the same level, without benefit of elevation above the courtroom's floor, and the prosecutor is not farther forward or on the side to provide his voice with a more effective sounding board than that of his opponent.

This location of equality with that of the defense is suited to the prosecutor's standing in a legal system that reveres the adversary procedure under which the prosecutor is in theory as well as in fact a state's attorney charged with presenting the strongest possible case for the state and expecting to be countered with the strongest possible case for the defense so that there are created conditions like that of an ancient tournament. The judge becomes under this system the arbiter to assure conformity to the procedural rules that have evolved over centuries to constitute the rules of fair play, and the jurymen will decide the issues on the basis of those facts the judge permits them to hear. The humble location of the state's attorney's chair indicates to the jury that his word is no more weighty than that of counsel for the defense.

Consider the contrast offered by Geneva. The prosecutor in the assize court sits at the left end of the great semicircular bench at the middle of which sits the judge in frock coat, flanked by his jury at the other end. The prosecutor's seat places him well above the level of the chairs of the counsel for defense, the accused and the witness stand, all of which are on the main floor. He carries by virtue of his location a certain majesty, not wholly distinguishable from the majesty of the judge. He is above the battle, and the procedural codes place a special responsibility upon him accordingly. He is required to be impartial, to be more than a state's attorney. In some countries, as in France, he is technically an arm of the magistracy.

The nonpartisan position of the prosecutor adheres even in the Soviet Union, where the procedural codes require the prosecutor to act in protection of legality even against a judgment in his favor by the court but too severe in its sentence. Look at the Cour Correctionelle in Paris' Palais de Justice, and you will find "Le Parquet" on a raised platform to the left of the judge's bench, less elevated and somewhat in front of the judges but quite unrelated to the position given the "avocat" who must plead for the defense. The continental prosecutor has such an unfamiliar position to the Anglo-American attorney, that it has often been suggested that he be called by his title in his own language to avoid confusion caused by a term that has other connotations for the common law trained mind.

While placing a special burden upon the prosecutor and treating him as more than an attorney for the state than is usual in Western Europe, the Soviet procedural codes espouse the adversary proceeding while retaining elements of the inquisitorial procedure of Western Europe as well. Thus, the Soviet prosecutor's chair is on the main floor at the same level as defense counsel, but it is usually placed at a desk on the left side of the room permitting the prosecutor to put his back to the wall and face the witness and the parties without rising. This seat puts him at an advantage over the defense counsel, and his dignity is further enhanced by a special uniform of office. This might create in the accused's mind an image of greater dignity than the judges, for they wear the clothes of the average Soviet man of the street.

The prosecutor's special position in continental Europe once created a struggle over furniture arrangement in the People's Republic of Poland that illustrates the problem with exceptional clarity. Before the Gomulka reforms of 1956, attempting to overcome some of the extreme Soviet influences upon communist Poland, the prosecutor sat at the left end of the same bench as the judges, and to the untutored defendant, he must have looked like a fourth judge, albeit seated around the corner from the other three. This made for too much dignity in the eyes of the reformers of 1956, and they hit upon a solution of some novelty. They brought in the carpenters to cut a narrow slit in the table at the prosecutor's end, so that today the Polish prosecutor sits at the same level as the judges above the rest of the room, but his table is physically distinct from that of the judges. He is almost but not quite as authoritative as the men and women charged with reaching the decision. His status is clearer than before, but he still has special dignity. He wears a black robe like a judge, except that his is piped with red in preservation of the traditional color of the medieval inquisitor for the Church, from whom his office is descended.

The Polish defense attorney, since the reform, also wears the black robe of his office, as does the barrister of the English court, but he has no specially designed wig as does his English counterpart to mark his position and difference from the judge and Crown's attorney each with his distinctive wig. The defense attorney's mark in Poland is the green piping that runs along the hem of his garment giving his robe a bit of color down the front.

Bitter conflict over the location of the prosecutor's chair has raged in Germany since the war. Perhaps under the impact of common law thinking, there has been a demand in some German states for a change in the prosecutor's place from the exalted traditional seat at the end of the bench with the judges to a position on the main floor no more prestigious than that of defense counsel. This movement has had its effect in one state as has the demand that the witness' chair face out toward the courtroom rather than in toward the judges' bench.

Next, there will be in many European criminal courts one more chair that would not appear in the American or English courtroom at all. This is the chair reserved for the attorney of the "civil plaintiff." Having no differing standards of proof for civil and criminal cases, the continental jurists have no difficulty in deciding the rights of the victim to damages at the same time as they determine the guilt of the accused. In consequence, the victim, or his survivor in the event of his death, is in the courtroom not solely as a witness, but as a party, and his attorney may rise to question witnesses or plead arguments if he believes that the prosecutor is failing in his duty.

Last, but not inconsequential among the participants in the trial, is the court secretary, for on him falls the task of preparing the record without which no appellate system can have validity, unless the appellate judges are authorized to recall witnesses and retry the case. The American courtroom is characterized by the early entrance of the court stenographer with his silent stenotype machine. He takes his place just under the judge's nose at a table placed where everything from the bench, the witness stand, and the tables for state's attorney and defense can be heard. He is expected to record every word spoken by any participant, and to reproduce it during the night in neatly typed pages made available to all concerned on payment of costs. His chair and his silent machine with endless strips of stenographic paper symbolize the determination of American courts to record everything.

Contrast Geneva or Cambridge, England. The court secretary will be sitting below the judge with a heavy desk typewriter. He will sit motionless while the testimony proceeds, but when the witness finishes, he cocks an ear to the bench without turning around and types swiftly and noisily what His Honor dictates as the substance of the testimony. Then he will strip his machine and place the page before the witness who has remained in place to affix his signature in verification. No English court wants to be burdened with a record of hundreds of pages of all that has been said, for this seems to the British to be cumbersome, wordy and confusing.

In the Soviet courtroom the secretary presents a sharp contrast. Usually a young woman, the secretary sits at the end of the bench in the People's Court with foolscap, ink pot, and pen to record what she can catch and thinks important without benefit of dictation by a judge, except in the unusual and complicated instance. It is no wonder that the U.S.S.R. Supreme Court has had to remand a case for retrial in some instances because of the inadequacy of the record for appellate purposes.

When considering the making of court records it is well to consider the bench to which the British assize judge mounts in majestic scarlet robe and wig following the blaring of trumpets from the courthouse steps as his carriage rumbles up from his temporary lodgings. That bench is completely clean of papers. There is no record of prior proceedings. The judge begins his hearing with a *tabula rasa*. Not so on the continent. Every judge who mounts the bench on the other side of the English Channel will have before him several volumes of "dossier" awaiting verification at the trial. In these volumes stands another symbol of a basic difference between the procedures of the common and civil law.

Civil Law Systems, including the Soviet, provide for preliminary review of the case, not as a grand jury would hear a United States attorney in New York, merely to determine whether there is likelihood of adequate evidence to proceed to trial, but to determine to the best of the preliminary investigator's opinion whether conviction can be expected to occur. The continental preliminary investigator is a magistrate charged with a special function like that of the judge's at the trial, to determine "objective truth," to create within his own mind a sense of "intimate conviction" of guilt. In consequence a continental trial in most countries, even in the words of some distinguished continental experts, is a verification of the work of the preliminary investigator, or the *juge d'instruction*, as he may be called.

By procedural codes the trial judges, where the "instruction" has occurred, must verify in open court by rehearing the witnesses and looking at the material evidence anew everything on which a finding of guilt is to be rested. In fact, there are times when to a common-law-trained mind, the judges violate "due process," for they permit reading of the testimony at the preliminary investigation when a witness who has testified before cannot return for reasons that seem like nothing more than inconvenience. In France, the trial judge will even read the preliminary record of testimony of a defendant who refuses to speak at the trial.

Furniture Arrangement as a Symbol of Judicial Roles

Perhaps in the light of the situation it is not facetious to suggest that while comparative law scholars are currently concerned with exhaustive examination of what is meant by the rule of law in various legal systems, a comparison of furniture arrangement in the courtroom merits a chapter in their study.[1]

Note

1. A first attempt to move in this direction has appeared in Sybille Bedford's *The Faces of Justice: A Travellers Report* (New York, 1961).

CARL BOCK

The "Ordeal of Water" in Nineteenth-Century Thailand

Not all judicial process, especially customary judicial process, takes place indoors in courtrooms. In many parts of the world, the process consists of some sort of ordeal which the complainant or defendant, or their proxies, must undergo to prove their guilt or innocence.

One form of ordeal involves being submerged in water for a prolonged amount of time. The following traveler's account of such an ordeal in late nineteenth-century Thailand provides a graphic description of this ritual. Travelers' accounts must be read with caution as they are not always accurate, but on the other hand, some travelers spend as much time with the people they visit as do modern anthropologists and folklorists. In this instance, Carl Bock (1849–1932), author of The Head-Hunters of Borneo *(London: S. Low, Marston, Searle & Rivington, 1881), claims he spent fourteen months in Siam and Lao. He is aware of the difficulties of a foreign visitor obtaining information, but as he phrases it, "What I saw, however, I have described with fidelity; what I heard I have recorded as it was stated to me."*

From other accounts of water ordeal, which is a very old form of ordeal—a version is found in the Code of Hammurabi—there is every reason to believe that this description is reasonably accurate. For a late nineteenth-century inventory of forms of ordeal in Thailand in which the ordeal of water is but one of nearly a dozen different types, see G.E. Gerini, "Trial by Ordeal in Siam and the Siamese Law of Ordeals," Asiatic Quarterly Review, N.S. 9 (1895), 415–424; 10 (1895), 156–175. The types include ordeal by fire (pp. 419–421), ordeal by diving (pp. 421–424), and ordeal by swimming across or against the stream (p. 156).

On the morning of the 14th of January my friend Pra Udon informed me that an appeal in a law-suit of some importance was about to be tried between two Phyas, who both claimed the ownership of a number

---

Reprinted from *Temples and Elephants*: The Narrative of a Journey of Exploration Through Upper Siam and Lao (London: Sampson Low, Marston, Searle & Rivington, 1884), pp. 233–241.

Carl Bock

of slaves. The defendant in the case said he had lost the "title deed" to the "property" in question, the document having, according to his statement, been burnt during an attack on his house by Ngiou raiders. The judges before whom the case was first tried had been unable to agree upon the evidence brought before them, and "granted a case" for a superior court, in which the Water-Spirit was the presiding genius! In other words the disputants were ordered to settle their case by what in former times in this country would have been called the "ordeal of water"; that is to say, they were to dive into the river, and whoever remained under water the longest would be adjudged the winner of the cause. This, I was told, was a very ancient custom in Lao, but it was not often that this mode of settling a dispute was resorted to, and great importance was consequently attached to it. The present trial derived additional significance from the position of the two litigants, and from the value of the stake at issue; for each party, before appealing to the Water-God, was obliged to deposit the sum of 2000 rupees, which would go, together with the slaves, to the winner; while the defeated suitor, besides losing the slaves and this considerable forfeit-money, would himself become a slave for life.

The people consequently turned out in force on the day appointed for the "hearing" to witness the trial, the scene of which was the Meping River. Early in the morning both banks of the stream were lined with thousands of spectators. Among the crowd were all the numerous Chows and officials of every grade, the more important of whom were easily distinguishable by their great state umbrellas—large canopies of red, yellow, or blue silk or cotton cloth, supported on bamboo handles encased in silver, and towering often as high as six or eight feet in the air. From the amount of wagering that went on on all sides, I am afraid that, had the scene been England instead of Lao, many of these gorgeous umbrellas would have been seized by the police as illegal "betting-places." Besides their umbrella-bearers, the most important personages were attended by numbers of slaves, bearing the usual array of gold or silver betel-boxes, teapots, spittoons, decanters, and other "insignia of office," some single pieces of which were worth perhaps 6000 or 7000 rupees.

There was no pushing or apparent excitement among the crowd, but every one seemed to take a deep interest in the proceedings, an interest which was increased by the frequent giving and taking of "the odds." I was invited to stake a few rupees on one or other of the litigants, but preferred to keep myself free from partisanship.

In the thick of the leading members of the company stood the two Phyas most directly interested in this novel trial; but, as time went on and they made no sign of divesting themselves of their robes and of preparing for the dive, I inquired whether they would—in sporting

The "Ordeal of Water" in Nineteenth-Century Thailand

parlance—don "the buff" or dive in full dress. The reply was that the diving would be done by proxy, each Phya having provided himself with a "champion," who would do his best to prove his master in the right. At that moment there was a stir amid the umbrellas, and two natives came forward with an offering of flowers which they laid before the Chow and his council of Phyas, each making an oath at the same time that he firmly believed in the justice of the side which he represented. The two men then walked into the river, each with a rope round his waist, which was held by a third man, to prevent them from being carried away by the swift current. Each man bore some flowers on his head, and a string of leaves round his neck, as a sort of mute appeal for the favour of the Water-Spirit.

Amid a breathless silence the two swarthy figures stood awaiting the word to dive; then a splash, and they were lost to view. I carefully timed the duration of the dive, and sixty seconds, that seemed like an age, so still was the vast crowd, passed without a sign of either of them. One minute and a half! Two minutes! Surely the swift current of the river must have carried them beyond our sight, and, while we were watching the point at which they had entered the water, vainly expecting to see them emerge, they were being whirled away down stream! A few moments later and a great shout greeted the reappearance of a dark, round object above the water, and the trial was over. It was the head of the losing diver, who had remained under water exactly two minutes fifteen seconds. The man who held the ropes then gave the signal to the other competitor to come up: but he made no sign, and the cry ran round that he was dead! No, at last he emerges from the water, evidently exhausted, but with a "record" several seconds better than his opponent. A general rush took place to see if the "right man" had won—the right man being, of course, he upon whose staying powers each individual in the crowd had staked his money!

But as in horse-racing the first horse sometimes turns out not to be the winner, the judge's verdict being reversed on an objection lodged with the stewards, or, to take a more appropriate parallel, just as the verdict of the "twelve good men and true" is apt sometimes in the home of trial by jury to be upset by a "demurrer," an "application for a new trial," an "appeal," or some other incident calculated to add to the glorious uncertainty of the law—so here the jubilations of those who had backed the possessor of the strongest lungs, and of his fortunate employer, were destined to be cut short. The umpires came to the conclusion that one of the divers had entered the water a moment before the other, and so the appeal was fruitless, and the matter would have to be remitted to the "court for the consideration of Crown cases reserved"—otherwise to the chief himself as the fountain of justice.

What sort of a fountain of justice the Chow Hluang of Chengmai was, may be gathered from what happened a few days afterwards. I have already said that Phya Radjasena, the Siamese commissioner, has been recalled from his post at Chengmai because of the complaints of the people about his mode of administering the law. It is not for me to defend any more than it is for me to blame Phya Radjasena, but the following narrative will show either that the notions of the people as to the due ordering of justice must be rather confused, or that some one else besides Phya Radjasena is worthy of degradation on the same plea. But tastes differ.

It appears that one evening, while the third Siamese commissioner was riding through the city of Lampoon after dusk, the elephant on which he was seated was stabbed by some person and seriously injured. Now it so happened that, just previously to this, a brother of the chief of Lampoon, while gambling in a native "hell" in that city, had had a quarrel with the followers of this commissioner, who at once attributed the deed to the prince in question. The Chow was generally credited with being a scapegrace—though, if he was worse than his brethren and fellow Chows, he must have been bad indeed!—so he was denounced to the Phya Radjasena and to the Chow of Chengmai, whose anger was aroused by the fact that the injured elephant belonged to himself: so the young prince was selected to pay the extreme penalty of the law, first for offering an indignity to the Siamese representative; second, for injuring the Chow's elephant; third, for his general bad character; and fourth, because a scapegoat was wanted on whom injured justice could avenge itself for the wrongs inflicted by others equally worthy of punishment, but against whom no suitable pretext could be found. The Chow of Lampoon made inquiry into the matter before allowing his own brother to be executed, and succeeded in establishing his innocence of this particular crime; but the Chow of Chengmai was inexorable, and the young prince was condemned to die, his brother making the stipulation that he should not be "disgraced" by having the condemned man's body brought back to Lampoon, but that he should be buried at that place of execution near the temple of Tawangtang, outside the city walls.

Early on the morning of the 17th of January, I heard that the execution was to take place that day, and at once started for the scene of the dreadful ceremony. The town was already half deserted, nearly every one having gone to witness the tragic spectacle, for, although executions are common enough in Chengmai, it is not every day that a prince is beheaded; so I hastened to walk across the rice-fields to the scene of execution. It was only an hour's walk, but before I had got half-way I met an unusually large train of elephants—some fifteen or twenty beasts, all fine tuskers—besides several hundred men on foot, and a few on horseback, who were returning from the scene, the execution having already taken place. I did not turn back, however, and on arriving at this Laosian Aceldama I found two natives just digging a shallow grave, by the side of which lay the headless trunk—most beautifully tattooed—of a fine-built youth, who but a few minutes before had been in the full enjoyment of health, and whose corpse a few minutes later would be rolled ignominiously into a shallow trench, surrounded by many similar graves of dishonour. On examining the body I found the executioner had missed his first stroke, and left a deep gash in the left shoulder. The head, which lay face downwards close by, was that of a really handsome youth of about two and twenty years of age. The face bore a calm expression, with no trace of the agony which the first blow of the executioner's axe must have occasioned.

The execution-ground was full of graves—not the long, narrow mounds to which the eye is accustomed in Europe, but—a series of shallow depressions, which in the rainy season would be filled with water, each marking the last resting-place of some "criminal," whose body, hastily covered beneath a few inches of earth, had returned to its original dust, leaving the soil to fall in as it crumbled away, or when, as perhaps was more likely, it was filched by vultures.

Scattered around in all directions were a number of logs of wood which, roughly shaped, as they were, somewhat in the shape of a cross, might at first sight almost have been mistaken for gravestones—many of them uprooted, but a few still standing—in a desecrated Christian churchyard. They were, however, rather in the shape of the letter Y than of a cross; and a pool of blood, in which stood one of these forked crosses, close by the dead Chow's body, plainly indicated that they were the execution-blocks upon which the doomed man lays his head to enable the executioner to do his bloody work.

The victim is made to walk to the field of execution with these worse-than-Caudine forks attached to his neck by ropes, led by the gaoler, who, when the fatal spot is reached, stretches him prone on the earth in such a manner that his head is lifted from the ground and firmly held between the projecting arms of the *crux*.

How many graves represented the spilling of innocent blood—blood, that is, innocent of the particular crime for which the Laosian goddess of justice had exacted retribution—it would be hard to say. Judging from this last addition to the roll of decapitated victims, I should say the percentage of really just sentences carried into execution would be very small indeed.

I might give other examples of the way in which the law is administered in Lao; but one more will suffice. We have just seen how a prince could be put to death at the wish of his chief, ostensibly for an offence which he had never committed; and the following instance will show how, on the other hand, a guilty man may be spared when the caprice of the Chow so ordains it. Only a short time before the events above narrated, a Lampoon man had entered a house in Chengmai in order to violate a young girl who he knew was alone. The girl's screams attracted the attention of a man, who, on coming to the rescue, was stabbed to death by the offender. Next day the murderer was caught and identified by the girl, and condemned to death, but, being in favour with the chief of Lampoon, he was not only pardoned, but set at liberty, the consent of the chief of Chengmai being purchased by the payment of a "fine" of six rupees.

Sometimes, however, it would seem that the conscience of the native administrators of the law is touched, and atonement is made, not only by offerings to Buddha, but in a more practical way.

A few days after the execution of the Lampoon prince, I was invited by the Chow Hluang to dine with him and the principal chiefs and officials of Chengmai. Among the first topics of conversation was the probable result of the appeal from the undecided trial by ordeal in the recent Water-Spirit case. The Chow was quick to tell me that neither of the Phyas interested in the slaves in dispute would be able to make good his title to them, since he had liberated them all. This, I thought, was a novel mode of cutting the Gordian knot, and I complimented the chief on his astuteness. But he added that he had liberated not only these particular slaves, but all the other slaves in Chengmai, and had paid the value of them, amounting to several thousand rupees, to their owners—an act, I was assured, utterly unparalleled in the history of Chengmai. This I was quite prepared to believe: and the whole proceeding seemed so completely out of harmony with the ordinary course of Laosian traditions that I felt sure there must have been some unseen motive at work. Then I thought of the dead body of the Lampoon prince, and wondered whether all this generosity might not have been prompted by a desire to make amends in some way for a manifest miscarriage of justice. So I delicately broached the subject, to see if I could find any indication in his manner or his words of the chief's feelings on the point. He was evidently unwilling that the matter should be mentioned, and resolutely kept the manumission of the slaves in the forefront of the conversation.

Some days afterwards I was assured by one of the Phyas that the liberation of the slaves was really, as I had suspected, an act of contrition for what the chief felt to be a flagrant breach of Buddha's laws, and a desire to make atonement for the spilling of innocent blood.

THEODOR REIK

The Euro-American Trial as Expiatory Oral Ordeal

For those readers who may tend to regard ordeal as a kind of primitive judiciary process, the following essay by psychoanalyst Theodor Reik (1888–1969) may come as a surprise. Reik argues that the modern Euro-American trial process is, in fact, a form of ordeal insofar as the "crime" is re-enacted by the accused not in deed, but in words. After this ordeal of reenactment, the guilt or innocence of the accused is presumed to emerge. In this interpretive context, one could then imagine the attorneys for the plaintiff and the defendant acting as their proxies, the court battle being fought by them. Not everyone will find Reik's thesis convincing, but if it has any validity at all, it would demonstrate the structural and psychological continuity of rituals such as ordeal used in a wide variety of traditional judiciary processes.

There were earlier attempts to see vestiges of ordeal in contemporary trial procedure. See, for example, H. Goitein, Primitive Ordeal and Modern Law *(London: George Allen & Unwin, 1923), p. 269. For a consideration of ordeal in a biblical context, see Meredith G. Kline, "Oath and Ordeal Signs,"* Westminster Theological Journal, *27 (1964–1965), 115–139; 28 (1965–1966), 1–37. For perhaps the classic nineteenth-century account of ordeal, see Henry Charles Lea,* The Ordeal *(Philadelphia: University of Pennsylvania Press, 1973), first published in 1886. For more modern treatment, see Robert Bartlett,* Trial By Fire and Water: The Medieval Judicial Ordeal *(Oxford: Clarendon Press, 1986).*

The Oral Ordeal

We shall choose a few African examples from our rich ethnological material. In Atakpame poison is made from the bark of the *iroko* tree which is sacred to the fetish and may be touched by fetish people only. The poison is given to the suspect to drink with the words: 'You have

---

Reprinted from Theodor Reik, *The Unknown Murderer* (New York: Prentice-Hall, 1945), pp. 145–159, 253–254.

killed,' He answers: 'You kill by your accusation.' If he vomits he is considered innocent. Otherwise he dies and is buried there and then after his heart has been cut out.[1] The Beronga in South-east Africa add to the poison the fat of a man who has died of leprosy as well as a powder made from his bones. If the accused shows certain symptoms he is held guilty. Compiègne[2] describes how in Jombe the fetish priest makes a furrow about ten steps in front of the suspect to whom he hands the poison. He has to swallow it in one draught and advance at a given sign. If he falls in a fit before reaching the furrow his guilt is proved. His death-agonies are shortened by the furious throng which tear him to pieces. But if he succeeds in passing the furrow he is considered innocent. Most African tribes believe in the innocence of the man who brings up the poison, and in the guilt of him who retains it or on whom it acts as a purgative. In Papabella an infusion of Casca rind is used for the ordeal. Anyone who does not bring it up is hacked to pieces by the natives or roasted over a slow fire. According to Johnston[3] everybody who is held responsible for a death undergoes this ordeal. The Masai drink a mixture of blood and milk.[4] In ancient Greece bull's blood[5] was drunk as an ordeal. The Israelites took the dust of the golden calf mixed with water, a kind of collective ordeal. Similarly, in India, a suspect had to drink water in which the images of the 'terrible gods' had been soaked. While drinking he turned to the gods and said: 'I have not done this deed.'[6] In Madagascar a strong poison, *tanghin*, was used for the ordeal.[7] The accused had to eat some rice, then the accuser put his hand on the other man's head and began the adjuration of the poison: 'Listen, listen carefully! Manamango! You are only a simple seed, quite round. Without eyes you see clearly, without ears you hear and without a mouth you talk. Through you God shows his wishes.' It is hard to estimate the number of the victims of *tanghin*; according to what the people say one person in five dies from its effects. In the last century about a tenth of the inhabitants of Madagascar underwent this ordeal; this means from forty to fifty thousand deaths in one generation through the ordeal, or fifteen hundred to two thousand deaths per year. A French official tells us of the Neyaux on the Ivory Coast where similar ordeals decrease the population, since each death causes four or five others. When a chief died, fifteen people followed him by ordeal. The French Government had the greatest difficulty in suppressing the ordeal, since the inhabitants were absolutely convinced of its justice, and if innocent, willingly subjected themselves to it.[8] The same deep belief prevails among the natives of Calabar; this makes them appeal voluntarily to the ordeal to prove their innocence. According to a missionary, the Rev. Hugh Goldie,[9] a small tribe, the Uwet, in the hills of Calabar has become almost extinct through the consistent use of the ordeal by poison. On one occasion the whole tribe drank the poison to prove themselves innocent.

What is the significance of the oral ordeal? What does the belief mean—if there is any meaning in it—that he who retains the poison or magic substance is guilty while he who brings it up is innocent? So far there has been no satisfactory explanation; yet the psycho-analytic technique of interpretation refuses to think a custom absurd merely because it may seem so at the first glance. It looks for a hidden sense, a psychological connection that has been lost to consciousness. If we apply those principles of interpretation here the result is amazing. Originally, and to this day unconsciously, the poison or other substance which is taken must stand in a connection with the crime which it attempts to solve. It is not difficult to guess this relation. In a murder case the magic substance comes from the murdered person, is perhaps a part of his body or blood, or replaces these. If this view is correct the first explanation of the latent sense of the oral ordeal emerges. It is, whatever else it may be besides, a repetition of the crime (practised on a substitute) for the purpose of detection. Let us accept this suggestion provisionally, grotesque and improbable though it may seem. The suspect is made to take a piece of the murdered man's body. This means that if the suspect is guilty the flesh or blood of the murdered man will take vengeance on him by causing his illness or death; but if he is innocent he will vomit up what he has swallowed as something with which he has nothing to do. What is the special relation between the nature of the crime and the eating of a piece of the dead man? Our understanding of the unconscious principles of the mind carries us to a conclusion which alone will satisfy the archaic law of talion. If the suspect succumbs to the ordeal of eating a piece of the dead person his crime must have consisted in eating that person. This result seems less strange when we remember that for primitive man killing and eating was the same thing—that the murderer actually ate his victim. Our conclusion is, therefore, that the oral ordeal referred originally to cannibalism.

This origin of the oral ordeal has become lost to consciousness with the increasing secular repression of cannibalistic tendencies, but its effect points to its primary motive even in its later stages of development. We recognise the psychologic connection behind the magical one, since the deed which has to be expiated is repeated on a substitutive material in the later development of the ordeal. It is from this point that we can carry out hypothesis back into an earlier prehistoric time. We can see that the oral ordeal as met with nowadays in half-savage peoples is a later and weakened development of an original, much cruder trial. Originally the suspect had really to eat a piece of the murdered man's body or to drink some of his blood. Does not this remind us of the

Christian Eucharist? Does not the mediæval use of the Holy Communion as an ordeal signify a return to an earlier form? In the belief that he who eats of the Lord's body in a sinful state shall die, the cannibalistic nature of Holy Communion is clearly recognisable.

An objector might reply that the oral ordeal is by no means restricted to murder, and that in those other cases the supposed operation of the law of talion could not hold good. Let us choose an example from South-West China, from the Lolo tribe[10] where, according to Colborne Baber, the oral ordeal is in frequent use. If anything valuable is stolen and the thief cannot be discovered the medicine man collects the people together and gives each one a handful of rice to eat. An interval of solemn chewing follows. The chewed mass is spat out. The presence of a blood-stain in it infallibly proclaims the thief. It is said that the gums of the guilty man bleed, and that he then confesses to the theft. Here, as in numerous other cases, there is no corpse and the ordeal stands in no visible connection to the nature of the misdeed. But our inferences refer to the origin of the custom and we cannot tell what changes it has undergone through the psychological mechanisms of displacement and generalisation. The rarer the crime of cannibalism became, as a result of repression, the easier would it be to displace the oral ordeal on to the detection of other offences. Cultural changes helped this process of displacement. The oral ordeal appears in cases of other serious crimes besides murder or manslaughter; the original eating of a piece of the corpse and drinking its blood are replaced by other substances, which later on are only hinted at symbolically. But the figure of the murdered man still lurks in the background. The Bukongo in giving the casca bark to the suspect believe 'that he will bring up the devil and spew him out.'[11] "Most African tribes regard the tree from whose bark the substance used in the oral ordeal is prepared as a fetish tree. In Angolo the taking of poison is called *nuam kissi*, the swallowing of the fetish. The primary meaning of the oral ordeal is almost symbolically expressed in what happens in Loango when a serious theft is committed. A banana is placed in the mouth of the fetish who is supposed to assist in the discovery of the criminal. The suspect has to extract this with his mouth and eat it. If he is guilty his body will swell and he will die. Does not this correspond to the original picture of the guilty man eating a piece of the fetish, the sacred thing?[12] And the fetish undoubtedly stands for the dead chief.

Our investigation, which, it is true, has dealt only with a representative example of this second group of clues, has led to a surprising result. The difference between the clues observed on the dead man's body and the clues observed on the suspected man's body is not of any fundamental significance. An analysis of the oral ordeal has shown that its essence lies in the incorporation of a part of the murdered man by the supposed culprit. The oral ordeal may be regarded as the most significant example of a proof made upon the body of the suspect. Its most important element is still the effect of the mystical, magic substance. The effect of that substance on the suspect's body showed us the way to an analytic interpretation. The substance gives every indication of something alive and active, though it may be only a piece of dead flesh, or its substitute. We suggest that the presence of this element as the earliest and most essential factor can be ascertained in most ordeals, whether they consist of hot water, fire or hot oil. It is not for us to trace in every single group of ordeals this latent connection which has become unconscious.[13] An expert in the comparative history of law should, with the help of the analytic method, be able to bring us nearer to a solution of this interesting problem.[14] We have come to regard the interpretation of magic clues originating in the dead man's body as an early form of criminal detection. The culprit is discovered through contact with the dead man's body or with a part of it; it is immaterial whether this contact takes place by means of the ordeal at the bier, or the bone oracle or the ordeal by poison. The ordeal furnishes the clue. We have supposed that the clues appeared at first on the dead man's body and then transferred themselves to the body of the suspect. This happens in a way that can best be compared to the process of infection. We should venture to differentiate the special kinds of infection according to the development of the different groups of ordeals. But our interest in the problem is, for the present, exhausted, since we have realised that even in the disguised form of the oral ordeal, the dead man is alive enough to bring his murderer to justice.

Venturing farther into prehistoric times, we assume the existence of a period when the taboo of the dead was even more effective. The ordeal at the bier is undoubtedly connected with a taboo of this kind. In touching the man who is dead but whose soul has not yet fled, the murderer experiences the mysterious effect of that taboo. The solution of crime and its punishment, the production of evidence and the execution of justice are here still the same thing. The ordeal discovers the guilty man and expiates his guilt. Both happen in a magic way.

No Expiation Without Repeating the Deed

The analytic investigation of the ordeal by poison led us to the prehistoric original ordeal showing a single form of the proof which later became so differentiated. We found that the oral ordeal consisted in the suspect having to commit his cannibalistic crime again in an indirect way and on a substitutive object. But how can it be that the perpetrator is made to commit his crime over again as an expiation of it? Does this not make a thesis of a paradox, elevate what is contradictory to a scientific hypothesis? On the other hand, it cannot be denied that all the elements which we have discerned in the oral ordeal constituted a repetition of the deed. Has, then, our interpretation gone astray?

We must keep in mind that the main part of the ordeal lies in the production of evidence and not in the execution of punishment. The ordeal is meant to show whether the suspect is guilty by making him commit the crime again on a substitute. This is without doubt the original character of the ordeal. But it cannot be denied that it is at the same time a penal procedure: it ends with punishment. But we doubt whether punishment is the primary aim, the essence of the ordeal. Once again a symptom exhibited by obsessional neurotics offers itself for comparison. It is what Freud has called the unconscious tendency to annul or undo the act. The term is justified; but the presence of a tendency to expiation or penance is so marked that it would deserve to be included in the nomenclature. This tendency shows itself in small unobtrusive actions or movements that are seemingly absurd or ridiculous. The patient has to walk round a certain object in a certain way, or stretch out his right hand and touch something or gaze at his reflection in a mirror, and so on. He has a compulsion to do these things and would feel anxiety, or at least great uneasiness, if he omitted to do them. Analysis leads to the conclusion that these actions are meant to undo or expiate former acts or movements, to paralyse their effect. Through our technique it becomes possible to recognise the latent significance of such behaviour and the nature of the acts the patient wishes to undo. Here is an example: a patient, a young woman, had to see about a hundred times in one day whether the water tap was turned off and did not drip. She could not explain her symptom, but it became clear when it was put into relation with her sexual life. That act, so often repeated, replaced symbolically another precaution which should prevent her becoming pregnant before marriage. The mechanism of displacement had so radically distorted the meaning of her action that it remained unknown to her consciousness. At the beginning of treatment the symptom strengthened, as is usual, before it became finally explained and disappeared. At the same time as it became intensified it changed its character. It had appeared as a precautionary or defensive symptom; the tap had to be closed, no drop must flow out. But now the patient's need for conviction became so intensified that she kept opening the tightly shut tap again and again to make quite sure it was closed. The suppressed impulse had come more and more strongly to the fore in the defence mechanism until it pushed the latter aside and remained victor in the substitutive displacement. The character of annulling an act is first seen clearly in the displacement; the symptom appears as a reaction to the sexual act. The defensive symptom already contains what is being defended against, and becomes more and more apparent as a mixture and compromise between the impulses of warding off and the impulses that are being warded off—only, in the end, to give satisfaction to the forbidden set of impulses. This development of obsessive symptoms has a special, typical character; the symptoms begin with a strong defence against the instinct, and end, while apparently increasing this defence, with a victory of the instinct itself, with the repetition of the deed, in a changed form.

The development of the ordeal seems to find its psychological parallel in the genesis and change undergone by those symptoms of obsessional neurosis. Originally, to be sure, the ordeal was more in the nature of expiation than punishment; it probably developed out of the cleansing and expiation ceremonies which primitive tribes use after a taboo has been violated. It started as an expiation for the crime; but the tendencies that were operative in the crime must have come more and more to expression until the ordeal became a distorted repetition of the crime done on a substitute. Here a correction of our former hypothesis must be made in the sense that the oral ordeal cannot have been a very primitive phenomenon. Precisely this return of the repressed in the midst of the repressing forces proves that it must have been a later development. For the primary impulses emerge in a very distorted and generalised form. From this point the penal institutions can develop no further. Other institutions will henceforward carry on the old conflict between the defence against and the breaking through of forbidden instincts.

The oral ordeal as a repetition of the crime commanded by the community reminds us in many respects of an element in primitive religion—the solemn killing and eating of the totem animal. In spite of the important differences between the two, the totem feast has the character of a collective ordeal. Its collectiveness is one of the differences; it is true that there are cases where whole tribes or villages subject themselves to an ordeal. Again, in the totem meal, all commit the crime once more; but the community sanctions it and so the crime becomes a duty. Like war, it is a crime ordered by society, and it probably awakened the same feelings in our ancestors as the order by the state for mass murder does in us. By participating in the killing and eating of the flesh and blood of the totem animal all have repeated the old deed and satisfied the instincts which come to expression in the act. This satisfaction sanctioned by the community differs essentially, nevertheless, from the original one. It unites the participants with the totem and among themselves, and guarantees future abstinence. This collective ordeal, if the name is permissible, already exhibits all the features of compromise as we have come to know them in the oral ordeal, but it is without a doubt a sacred repetition of an otherwise forbidden deed. This characteristic still appears in the Christian Eucharist.

We have traced the ordeal by poison from the Middle Ages back to its prehistoric days, to the totem meal; let us now follow its later development until it gives way to other institutions. An essential part of its latent significance, namely the repetition of the deed for its detection and expiation, is still recognisable in the latest and most varied developments of the ordeal, though that repetition may no longer have the same dramatic and plastic expression. The progressive distortion of the original meaning will take on more abstract forms. A survival of the ordeal in modern penology is the oath. The oath substitutes the word for the original action and only reminds us dimly of the latter by a movement of the hand. And that earlier dramatic repetition of the crime has now to be enacted in the spoken word only, and receives a modest expression suited to our present-day culture. Examinations, production of evidence, explanations of the accused, reports of the experts, pleading of the counsel, all these are fragments which make up the whole—the repetition of the crime through the word. Culture has partly changed the function of this repetition; it has become a means of producing evidence and is now more complicated, difficult and time-robbing, so that it is distributed among many people. But the main part is still played by the accused. He is as it were the hero of the tragedy and he must undo his crime. This, paradoxically expressed, can only be done by repeating it, by showing how it came about that he did it. The psychological effect of confession is better understood when we realise that it is a repetition of the crime in its palest form, in words. With this repetition a kind of undoing of the deed, in a magical sense, has been achieved. But this endeavour to undo by word and gesture, may be insufficient unless there is a strong affective reaction. Yet it remains an endeavour to master the deed mentally. Such an effect may seem strange. Perhaps it becomes clearer by a description of what happens when such a repetition, in the magical sense, does *not* follow. As this repetition consists in the partial coming to consciousness of the genesis and the significance of the crime, repentance or expiation is impossible without it. A thorough consciousness of guilt and an effective tendency to expiation is possible only when the instinctual satisfaction in the crime has become conscious in its whole depth. A condition of its becoming conscious is the recollection and its translation into words, as well as the affective re-living of the whole. Without a repetition of the instinctual satisfaction experienced the deed is lost to consciousness like hieroglyphics in the earth of Egypt. In analytical practice we observe that the phantasied repetition of what the patient feels as criminal and sinful is a pre-condition of the mental upheaval that leads to the overcoming of pathogenic experiences. Here the inner re-living of the deed combines with the 'cathexis' of verbal images to bring about therapeutic success.

Without such a re-living of the deed and the gratification contained in it a consciousness of guilt is impossible, and this consciousness is a necessary condition of expiation. Without it the word 'expiation' or 'punishment' loses its sense or descends to the level of a purely formal or mechanical legal term. It would be as though an untrained animal were to be punished for its natural behaviour; the animal must first be aware of what its behaviour implies before the punishment can have any sense—if, indeed, it ever does have sense.

The word 'deed' must not mislead the psychologist. The culprit has committed the deed; but it would often be better to say that the crime happened through him. It is only possible for him to take cognisance of the participation of his ego in the crime if he remembers it affectively, that is to say, if he re-enacts the deed on a representational substitute. The problem is to lead the criminal to a recognition of his guilt in the psychological sense ('Do you recognize that you are guilty?') and not in the legal sense ('Do you admit being guilty?').

We regard modern criminal procedure as the most recent development of the ordeal. It contains—for a new purpose, to be sure, in order to find out the truth—a reconstruction of the crime, just as the ordeal does. But while the ordeal carried out the repetition of the deed on a concrete substitute, modern criminal procedure attempts to achieve it, in the form of language and logical inference, on an ideational one; and in this procedure circumstantial evidence is perhaps the most important element of such a reconstruction.

As a kind of a postscript to the history of the ordeal it may be mentioned that when the public expresses its pleasure or displeasure in court, the judge admonishes it sternly, usually adding: 'You are not in the theatre.' This is to emphasise the serious character of legal procedure. But not every judge knows how near to each other originally were the two institutions he separates so strictly. We have said that the ordeal was a representation of the deed, an expiation in dramatic form, an annulment by repeating it in a plastic displacement. But the content of ancient tragedy is nothing else than the reproduction of a serious crime, the rebellion against the gods, its solution and expiation. This is true, not only of the oldest Greek drama, but also of *Œdipus Rex* and of the Passion plays of the Middle Ages.

In the ordeal and its modern substitute the individual expiates his crime. In the theatre the mass identifies itself with an individual representative, as Aristotle puts it, 'in terror and pity' and so deals with the emotion psychologically.

Notes

1. Muller in *Globus*, Bd. 81, S. 280.
2. De Compiègne, *L'Afrique Equatoriale*, Paris 1875, p. 309, 320.
3. J. H. Johnston, *The Congo*.
4. *Encyclopedia of Religion and Ethics*, Vol. IX, p. 526 ff.
5. Compare Frazer, *Pausanias*, 1898, Vol. IV, p. 175.
6. From the *Encyclopedia of Religion and Ethics*, Vol. IV, p. 508.
7. *Encyclopedia of Religion and Ethics*, Vol. IX, p. 526 et seq.
8. *Gouvernement Général de l'Afrique Occidentale Française. Notices publiées par le Gouvernement Général à l'occasion de l'Exposition Coloniale de Marseille. La Côte Ivoire.* Corbeil, 1901, pp. 570–2.
9. *Calabar and its Mission*, 1901, p. 34 *et seq.*
10. 'A Journey in West Issu-ch-uan,' *Royal Geographical Society, Supplementary Paper*, 1886, I, p. 70.
11. Peschuel-Losche, *Volkskunde von Loango*, 1907, S. 434 *et seq.*
12. Nausea, that is, the giving back of what has been eaten, is the forerunner of confession. It is, so to speak, a primitive form of repentance. The man who 'keeps' the portion of corpse he has eaten, is guilty.
13. Psycho-Analysis can interpret many forms of ordeal, hitherto unexplained, by the factor of symbolism. Thus, for instance, the Latuka in Africa make a woman suspected of adultery grasp a red-hot spear-point. (Fr. Stuhlmann, *Mit Emin Pascha ins Herz von Afrika*, 1894, S. 781.)
14. According to ancient and primitive thought, divination (by means of which the priest-magician finds an unknown murderer) is accomplished by touching. The dead man's ghost descends into the priest; the magician is possessed.

Codes of Folk Law

At the great risk of oversimplification, we may distinguish two basic approaches to the study of folk law. The first approach is predicated upon the assumption that folk law exists in the form of rules or behavioral proscriptions. In the situation where the society in question has no written language, the task of the student of folk law is to record these rules and proscriptions. Within this rule-centered approach, one finds either a conviction that the rules belong to some kind of system or the alternative that the rules are more or less independent, belonging to no holistic coherent pattern. Analysts persuaded that an overall system or pattern exists are wont to speak of "codes" of folk law. Others are content merely to record rather than "codify" unwritten folk law. Some of the earliest recorded "codes" of folk law, e.g., from the Near East, turn out to be not codes at all in the strictest definition of the concept of code. Rather they are enumerations of sets of "rules," often seemingly in no particular order. Still, for the rule-oriented student of folk law the discovery or formulation of codes or pseudo-codes remains a desideratum.

The second basic approach to folk law is concerned with process, not product. Rules of law are not without interest, but the primary goal is to understand how a cultural legal system works in particular cases. The case approach to folk law will be the subject of the next section of this volume. Of course, one can study both cases and codes, if one so chooses. For example, one might seek to extrapolate "laws" from a series of specific cases in a culture.

In any event, archaeological research in ancient Near Eastern cultures unearthed tablets containing what appeared to be sets of "laws." Presumably these "laws" were orally transmitted for considerable time before they were recorded on these tablets. Since the Judeo-Christian bible also contains such sets of laws—the Decalogue (Ten Commandments) would be an example—much of the initial scholarship was concerned with the relationship, if any, of Sumerian and Babylonian law codes to biblical law.

ALBRECHT GOETZE

Mesopotamian Laws and the Historian

The study of ancient Near Eastern law is truly a fascinating one, but one that requires a combination of great linguistic expertise and a fair amount of luck. The luck is necessary to find fragments of legal records among the materials from archaeological excavations. Rarely does one find a complete tablet or inscription. Hence much of the linguistic reconstruction of the contents of such fragments becomes a matter of educated guesswork and dispute. However, even to make such educated guesses, one must be conversant with a number of ancient languages in their written forms.

Notwithstanding all the difficulties attending the discovery and translation of specimens of ancient Near Eastern law, we are fortunate to have a number of early "codes." The best known is surely the Code of Hammurabi or Hammurapi, usually abbreviated CH. Hammurabi was a king of Babylonia who ruled during the second millennium B.C. There is disagreement on exact dates but the CH is presumed to have come into existence some time in the 18th century B.C. and it almost certainly contains laws borrowed from earlier compilations. It may come as a bit of a surprise to learn that the stone upon which the CH was inscribed was discovered only at the beginning of the twentieth century, in 1901 in Susa, Iran.

Another important contribution to our knowledge of ancient Near Eastern jurisprudence consists of the laws of Eshnunna, usually abbreviated LE or CE, which were discovered in 1945 and 1947 on two tablets excavated at Tell Harmal on the outskirts of Baghdad. The first English translation of LE was that of 1948 by Professor Albrecht Goetze of Yale University, author of this essay. The LE is thought to be older than CH.

The existence of a number of ancient codes permits comparisons to be made and this is most important for the present context. If we have only one instance of a law, we cannot know for certain that the law was traditional. (Folklore, it must be remembered, is always manifested in multiple existence.) If, however, we have two or more instances of a given law, then we can more reasonably infer that the law was a traditional or folk law.

Reprinted from the *Journal of the American Oriental Society,* 69 (1949), 115–119, with permission. The final pages, pp. 119–120, of this essay, which was a presidential address delivered at the Society's annual meeting in New Haven on April 6, 1949, were not reprinted here.

For Professor Goetze's translation of LE, see The Annual of the American Schools of Oriental Research, *31 (1956). For additional consideration of this code, see Reuven Yaron,* The Laws of Eshnunna, *2nd Revised Edition (Jerusalem: The Magnes Press, 1988). For a useful survey of evidence of ancient folk law, see Rafael Taubenschlag, "Customary Law and Custom in the Papyri,"* Journal of Juristic Papyrology, *1 (1946), 41–54. For other surveys of law in the ancient Near East, see P. Koschaker, "The Scope and Methods of a History of Assyrio-Babylonian Law,"* Proceedings of the Society of Biblical Archaeology, *35 (1913), 230–243; E.A. Speiser, "Early Law and Civilization,"* Canadian Bar Review, *31 (1953), 863–877; R.A.F. Mackenzie, "The Formal Aspect of Ancient Near Eastern Law," in W.S. McCullough, ed.,* The Seed of Wisdom: Essays in Honour of T.J. Meek *(Toronto: University of Toronto Press, 1964), pp. 31–44.*

It should perhaps be noted that some individual ancient laws have received more attention than others. One such law concerns the penalties for the owner of an ox which gores someone. See, for example, A.Van Selms, "The Goring Ox in Babylonian and Biblical Law," Archiv Orientální, *18 (1950), 321–330; Reuven Yaron, "The Goring Ox in Near Eastern Laws,"* Israel Law Review, *1 (1966), 396–406; J.J. Finkelstein, "The Goring Ox,* "Temple Law Quarterly, *46 (1973), 169–290; B.S. Jackson, "The Goring Ox Again,* Journal of Juristic Papyrology, *18 (1974), 55–93. Finkelstein's study was later separately republished as* The Ox That Gored, Transactions of the American Philosophical Society, *Vol. 71, Part 2 (1981).*

The study of cuneiform tablets, in over a century of patient research, has opened up a new world which in terms of time covers several millennia—all of them before the beginning of the Christian era—and, as far as subject matter is concerned, every conceivable kind of human pursuit. Students of the Ancient Near East, when faced with cuneiform inscriptions, could not avail themselves of a stream of living tradition leading from the present back to the past. Everything that man may have known about them at some remote day, had long since been forgotten; what remained of the glory of the ancient empires lay buried in the ground. Thus modern scholars had to decipher the script anew, philologists had to reconstruct unknown languages, excavators had to search for the remains of forgotten civilizations, before the historian could begin to piece together into a more or less comprehensive picture the innumerable details which slowly emerged. Even today our knowledge of ancient Mesopotamia is still fragmentary. Only too often we lack reliable information, or must laboriously obtain it by fitting a fragment picked up here to another fragment recovered there.

Mesopotamian Laws and the Historian

The outsider, who from his schooldays remembers Gilgamesh and the Epic of Creation, Hammurapi, Assurbanipal, and Nebuchadrezar, imagines that one has only to set to work on any mound in Mesopotamia and there will appear libraries of tablets inscribed with the literature of the ancients. This is an illusion. Not only does it require hard work and some kind of a sixth sense to find anything worthwhile, but libraries have been found so far only a very few times. For the most part, what is dug up—a small batch here, another one there—are the modest documents of daily life, the letters, deeds and contracts, the business notes and accounts which were kept in shops, in offices and in private houses. In consequence, cuneiformists are compelled to pay much attention to legal matters. From contracts, briefs and protocols, and from the formulae used, they try to reconstruct the laws that were valid in the country, the institutions that these laws regulated and the government which enforced them. Thus, law and the history of law play a large role in cuneiform studies. I propose to sketch here the stages through which research in the law of the Ancient Near East has moved and to reflect on its development and future.

The first period, a period of pioneering, covers the last decades of the nineteenth century. It was a scientific achievement of no mean proportions when the first legal documents were recognized as such, and when the first attempts at their interpretation were made. With that step taken, progress depended on the availability of a sufficiently large body of material. It was provided by numerous excavations, at first in the palaces of the Assyrian kings of the 9th to 7th centuries B.C., then later in the mounds of Babylonia. Soon material accumulated not only from the period of the Neo-Babylonian kings like Nebuchadrezar and Nabonidus (6th century B.C.), but also from the time of Hammurapi, i.e., the first third of the second millennium B.C., a time which then seemed very remote since its true age was at first obscured by an inadequate knowledge of history and chronology.[1]

The second period begins with a discovery which marks an epoch in more than one respect: the recovery of the stela inscribed with the laws of Hammurapi, king of Babylonia. Excavated in Susa by a French expedition led by J. de Morgan during the winter of 1901–2, it was speedily published by Père Scheil, who served as the epigraphist of that expedition.[2] Here we obtained not only a carefully written text of considerable length composed in a grammatically consistent and beautifully translucent language, which since then has been recognized as the classical form of Babylonian, but also for the first time a legal code which in about 280 sections presented the norms according to which the numerous contracts previously recovered were drawn up. It became now possible to compare these norms with the legal practice; they did not always coincide.

The find stimulated the further publication of contracts and the more detailed study of legal institutions.[3] One may justly call this period of research the Babylonian phase; Hammurapi and his law formed its focal point.

Quite naturally the discovery also started comparative research. In those days Mesopotamian archaeology and 'Assyriology,' as it then was called, were intimately tied up with Biblical research. Nothing was therefore more natural than to raise the question as to the relationship between Hammurapi's law and the Jewish laws, or, admitting the results of Biblical criticism, rather between Hammurapi and the various codes embedded in the Pentateuch, in particular the oldest among them, the so-called Covenant Code.[3a] Pan-Babylonianism was then en vogue and therefore it is hardly surprising to find the opinion dominant that just as, e.g., the story of creation and that of the deluge had come to the Jews from Babylon, so also Babylonian laws were the source from which the Israelites drew inspiration. Although there is little merit in this all too simple and naive solution of the problem, there was nevertheless considerable merit in posing it. It has remained alive ever since.

Undisturbed by such theories cuneiformists pursued their work. In a third period of research it led to an altogether unexpected widening of our horizons. The first World War had passed and the coming of the peace saw a renewal of the archaeological and the philological work on an unprecedented scale. Not only were several legal codes excavated before the war published, but entirely new provinces of research were now opened for the first time. The publication of a tablet with Sumerian laws of pre-Hammurapi date by A. T. Clay in 1915[4] may be taken as an early indication of a general trend; it was followed in 1919 by H. F. Lutz's copies of a few more Sumerian fragments which, as we have learned, belong to the code of Lipit-Ishtar, a king of Isin about 150 years before Hammurapi.[5] In 1920, O. Schroeder presented us with copies of the Middle Assyrian lawbook,[6] and a year later F. Hrozný acquainted the scientific world with a code composed in Hittite, a language of Ancient Asia Minor then in the process of decipherment. The last mentioned document led far away from the Semitic world and Mesopotamia. Indeed, it was one of the principal inferences to be drawn from the Hittite discovery that Mesopotamian civilization, early in the second millennium, had spread to Anatolia. It was by no means the only startling discovery of those years. Other varieties of cuneiform tablets testifying to the same process of diffusion became now either known for the first time or available in quantity. The 'Cappadocian tablets,' mostly from Kül-tepe in Asia Minor, are witnesses of the trade activities of early Assyrian merchants;[8] the 'Nuzu tablets' from the vicinity of Kerkuk[9] introduced to historians the Hurrians, then 'a new factor in the history of the Ancient East.'[10] The Old Babylonian documents from Susa demonstrated[11] vividly what became of Old Babylonian civilization when it was transplanted to Elam, Babylonia's neighbor toward the southeast. In this manner new provinces were added to the old ones. It was no longer adequate to speak of Babylonian civilization and Babylonian law. Only the term 'cuneiform law' was now wide enough to cover all that had been gained.[12]

With this new material at the scholars' disposal, the Code of Hammurapi invited re-examination. Two questions in particular posed themselves almost automatically. First, a comparative question: what is the relationship of the new codes to that most extensive and most authentic of all codes, the Code of Hammurapi? Are they prototypes or descendants of it, or do they represent an independent development of legal thought? The second question, not independent of the first, concerns the background of the Hammurapi code; it is this: what does the new evidence teach us with regard to the genesis of that famous code?

Any study of relationships is fraught with difficulties. Identical conditions may lead to parallel but nevertheless independent results. Moreover, in the field of law, the possibilities for variation are limited, particularly when the political and the economic conditions are similar. In such circumstances interdependence can be proved only by very specific coincidences; general similarities are not enough. When the various codes are scrutinized with such methodical considerations in mind, they do indeed reveal coincidences of the nature which assure interrelationship. But this interrelationship is probably indirect rather than direct.

The Code of Hammurapi was also subjected to internal criticism. A scholar of the rank of P. Koschaker[13] observed that it exhibits features of uneven style, of superfluous duplication and of outright contradiction. These betray, he concludes, its composite nature. An acute observation of such features leads to an analysis of the text which we possess; glosses and interpolations can be recognized. Of course the legislation of Hammurapi cannot be divorced from his main political achievement, which is the re-establishment of a unified empire on Mesopotamian soil. This empire comprised the basically Sumerian states of the south, only 250 years prior to the king's time the core of the empire of Ur. It also included the basically Akkadian north which had held the leadership under the great kings of the Akkad dynasty between 2400 and 2200 B.C. Finally it extended up the two rivers to both Mari and Nineveh, ancient centers of civilization. A centralized government, the existence of which is demonstrated by ample sources, could only function under a uniform law. It can be expected to reflect in its domain the process of adaptation and amalgamation through which the empire was created and consolidated.

Quite recently a more direct approach to this problem—essentially a historical problem—has become feasible, and again by a new increase in the comparative material at the scholars' disposal. During the last few years two new codes of law, both of pre-Hammurapi age, have emerged, one in Sumerian, the other in Akkadian. The new Sumerian code proves to be the work of Lipit-Ishtar, king of Isin; it embodies—or rather embodied when complete—the law valid in Isin, his capital. The Akkadian code represents the city law of Eshnunna, the main center of civilization in the Diyala region east of Baghdad, and, leading back almost to the Third Dynasty of Ur, is probably still older than the code of Lipit-Ishtar. The Lipit-Ishtar code was discovered by F. R. Steele in the University Museum in Philadelphia;[14] the discovery of the Laws of Eshnunna is the fruit of my own happy association with the Iraq Department of Antiquities during my term as Annual Professor of the American Schools of Oriental Research in Baghdad for the first five months of 1948.[15] Here then we have come into the possession of two law codes, one valid in a Sumerian city, the other in an Akkadian city; both of these were later incorporated into Hammurapi's empire. Here then are two city laws precisely of the kind which Hammurapi must have utilized when he undertook the harmonization and unification of the laws found in his realm. In consequence, we are now in a position to check to some extent on the methods which he employed to achieve his goal.

Let me illustrate this by a few selected examples. Our purpose will be served best by subjects which are dealt with in all three codes. Such a subject is, e.g., engagement and marriage. The three texts are as follows:

Lipit-Ishtar § 29:[16]

'If the son-in-law enters the house of his father-in-law and "does" his bride-money, but afterward they make him leave and give his wife to his companion, they will give back to him the bride-money which he brought and his companion will not obtain that wife.'

Laws of Eshnunna § 25:[17]

'If a man enters(??) the house of (his) father-in-law and his father-in-law accepts him into servitude, but gives his daughter to another man, then the girl's father will return the bride-money which he received in the double amount.'

Hammurapi § 160:[18]
'If a man has a gift brought to the house of his father-in-law (and) gives the bride-money and the girl's father says, "My daughter I shall not give to thee," then he shall double everything that had been brought to him and return it.'

The two Akkadian versions have essential features in common. The girl whose father rejects her first suitor is obviously considered free to marry whomever her father selects for her as soon as the bride-money (*terḫatum*) is repaid in the double amount. In the Sumerian version it is paid back in the same amount in which it had been received; however, the girl is not allowed to get otherwise married; obviously she is legally the young man's wife. In other words, in the Akkadian versions we encounter an institution which is equivalent to our engagement and can be broken off; in the Sumerian version engagement (if this term can at all be used) is as binding as marriage itself. However, there are also resemblances between the Isin and the Eshnunna versions—i.e., the two older versions; if I understand the texts correctly, they both envisage the son-in-law serving for the bride-money in the house of his father-in-law (much as Jacob served in the house of Laban). Nothing of the kind is found in the Code of Hammurapi; there, on the other hand, a 'gift' (*biblum*) appears, which is unknown in the other laws. The transaction has become rather impersonal and businesslike. One may say that the provisions of the Hammurapi code follow essentially Akkadian custom, but that apparently the patriarchal conditions which are still discernible in the earlier versions have been eliminated. They probably had become outmoded with the advance in the social and the economic structure which the country experienced in the Old Babylonian period.

If thus we observe, with Hammurapi, a trend toward modernization, it is the more striking to see him retain a feature as archaic as the *jus talionis*. Phrased abstractly it states that anybody injuring his fellow-citizen is to suffer the corresponding injury himself, or as it is put in the Covenant Code (Ex. 21:23 ff.): 'Life for life, eye for eye, tooth for tooth, hand for hand, foot for foot, burning for burning, wound for wound, stripe for stripe.' Hammurapi's conservatism is particularly surprising, since the Laws of Eshnunna, considerably before his time, had made it possible for the offender to buy himself free,[19] and the Hittite Code follows the same practice.[20] The various lists encountered in the respective sections, partly enumerating parts of the body and partly kinds of injuries, offer interesting material to the comparativist. Let it suffice here to emphasize the fact that the 'biting of the nose,' which vexes the reader of the Hittite Code, reappears now in the Laws of Eshnunna;[21] personally I would suspect that also the *næfæš* of the

Covenant Code, poetically translated 'life' in the English Bible, would find its prosaic explanation in an analogous fashion. From the point of view of method it should be remarked that such specific points of contact make the assumption of a genetic relationship inevitable.

The case of the goring ox is also interesting for the investigation of relationships. I cite in the following the texts of the Covenant Code, the Laws of Eshnunna, and the Code of Hammurapi (in all of them, incidentally, the case of the apparently peaceful ox which unexpectedly runs wild preceded the text cited):

Ex. 21:29:
'If the ox were wont to push his horn in time past, and it hath been testified to his owner, and he hath not kept him in, but that he hath killed a man or a woman, the ox shall be stoned and his owner also shall be put to death.'

Laws of Eshnunna § 54:[22]
'If an ox is known to gore habitually and the authorities have forewarned its owner, but he did not have his ox dehorned(?), if it gores a man and causes his death, then the owner of the ox shall pay two thirds of a mina of silver.'

Code of Hammurapi § 251:
'If the ox of a man is known to gore habitually and the authorities have forewarned him, but he did not blunt its horns (and) did not pen it up, if it goers a man and causes his death, he shall pay half a mina of silver.'

The coincidences are obvious; in the original Semitic texts they are even closer than the translations offered show. In all three documents the premises are virtually identical. The punishment is of the same kind in the two Akkadian codes, clearly archaic in the Covenant Code. There the ox is stoned as though it were a murderer, and its owner likewise is put to death.

Numerous other examples might be added. Wherever one looks, from Asia Minor to southern Mesopotamia, the same crimes and offences are described often in a surprisingly similar phraseology; everywhere the transgressor is threatened with similar or even identical punishment. There is no doubt, then, that we deal with a phenomenon which can no longer be understood as a parallel development caused by more or less identical standards of civilization. There must be more to the problem.

Here the point is reached where the problem definitely assumes proportions which go beyond the strictly philological and the narrowly juridical; it becomes a problem for the historian. Indeed, there begins to emerge the great task with which future investigators will find themselves confronted to an ever increasing extent: the integration of various approaches into an over-all interpretation of that particular period. After all, law is only one among many other phenomena of human civilization. It can be properly understood only when it is seen against the background of the civilization in which it grew.

Notes

1. The names that stand out in this period are those of J. Oppert, V. and E. Revillout, C. H. W. Johns, N. Strassmaier, F. Peiser, B. Meissner.
2. *Mémoires de la Délégation en Perse* IV (1902).
3. The material which had been published up to 1923 is translated in Kohler (Koschaker)-Ungnad, *Hammurabi's Gesetz* III (1909), IV (1910), V (1911), VI (1923); the respective publications are quoted there in full.
3a. For the various theories which have been advanced with regard to this problem see M. David, De Codex Hammoerabi en zijn verhouding tot de wetsbepalingen in Exodus (*Tijdschrift voor Rechtsgeschiedenis* 17, 1939, 73–98).
4. *Yale Oriental Series, Babylonian Texts* I (1915) No. 28.
5. University Museum of the University of Pennsylvania, *Publications of the Babylonian Section* I/2 (1919) Nos. 100, 101, 102.
6. *Keilschrifttexte aus Assur verschiedenen Inhalts* (1920) Nos. 1–6, 143, 144, 193.
7. *Keilschrifttexte aus Boghazköi* VI (1921) Nos. 2–26.
8. For a presentation of the significant facts and a bibliography see A Götze, *Kleinasien* (1933) 64–76.
9. An up-to-date summary of the results obtained is lacking and can hardly be expected at the present moment. The archaeological evidence is presented in R. F. S. Starr, *Nuzi* (1937–1939); cf. also R. H. Pfeiffer, *Smithsonian Report for 1935* (1936) 535–558 and A. Parrot, *Archéologie mésopotamienne* (1946) 394 ff. (and the bibliography on p. 436 f.).
10. Chiera and Speiser, *AASOR* 6 (1926) 75–92.
11. V. Scheil, *Mémoires de la Mission en Perse* XXII, XXIII, XXIV, XXVIII.
12. Cf. P. Koschaker, Keilschriftrecht in *ZDMG* 89 (1935) 1–39; M. San Nicolò, *Beiträge zur Rechtsgeschichte im Bereiche der keilschriftlichen Rechtsquellen* (1931).
13. *Rechtsvergleichende Studien zur Gesetzgebung Hammurapis* (1917).
14. *AJA* 51 (1947) 158–164; 52 (1948) 425–450.
15. *Sumer* 4 (1948) 63–102.
16. *AJA* 52 (1948) 442f.
17. *Sumer* 4 (1948) 78f.
18. The latest translation is that of W. Eilers, *Die Gesetzesstele Chammurabis* (1932).
19. *Sumer* 4 (1948) 84 ff.

20. F. Hrozný, *Code Hittite* (1922) 6ff.
21. *Sumer* 4 (1948) 84 f. (§ 42).
22. *Sumer* 4 (1948) 88 ff.

RAYMOND WESTBROOK

Biblical and Cuneiform Law Codes

Having been introduced to several of the codes of folk law found in the ancient Near East, we may now turn to a consideration of why these codes may have been formulated in the first place. Were they intended to be commemorative celebrations of particular rulers? Were they the by-products of schoolboy scribal or literary exercises? In the following essay by Raymond Westbrook of the Hebrew University of Jerusalem, it is imaginatively proposed that these codes were part of the scientific writing of the time and that by listing sets of precedents or rules covering a variety of possibilities, it was intended to offer a kind of reference work to be consulted by judges.

For a useful survey of the whole subject of codes, including those of modern times, see Jean Louis Bergel, "Principal Features and Methods of Codification," Louisiana Law Review, 48 (1988), 1073–1097. See also M.D.A. Freeman, "The Concept of Codification," The Jewish Law Annual, 2 (1979), 168–179. For an earlier consideration, see Torgny T. Segerstedt, "Customs and Codes," Theoria, 8 (1942), 3–22, 126–153.

1.—The Law Codes

A particular genre of Ancient Near Eastern literature is the so-called "law code". To date, nine separately identifiable law codes have come down to us, in whole or part. Seven of them are in the form of cuneiform documents:[1] Codex Ur-Nammu *(CU)*, Codex Lipit-Ishtar *(CL)*, Codex Eshnunna *(CE)*, Codex Hammurabi *(CH)*, the Assyrian Laws *(AL)*, the Hittite Laws *(HL)* and the neo-Babylonian Laws *(NBL)*. The other two are to be found in the Bible, *Ex.* XXI, 1–XXII, 16 is part of the Covenant Code and has long been recognized as an independent source.[2] Likewise in Deuteronomy the remains of, or extracts from, an independent legal source can be discerned, especially in Chapters XXI–XXV, in spite of being

Reprinted from *Revue Biblique*, 92 (1985), 247–264, with permission.

heavily re-worked for their present purpose and interspersed with a great deal of hortatory and other non-legal material.[3]

All nine codes are remarkably similar both in form and content, They are predominantly formulated in a casuistic style (albeit in varying degrees), that is to say, a particular set of circumstances is given, followed by the legal ruling appropriate to that case,[4] The subject matter is problems of practical law: in many cases the same or related problems are considered by different codes, and in some cases whole paragraphs have been copied by one code from another.[5]

This similarity is evidence at least of a common type of intellectual activity. The purpose of this study is to examine whether this factor can help to explain the nature and purpose of these "codes".

2.—The Law Code as a Royal Apologia?

Our starting point is the classical (and most complete) example of the genre, Codex Hammurabi. It has long been recognized that the term "code" as applied to it by Scheil in the *editio princeps* is a misnomer; *CH* lacks the comprehensiveness that would make it a law code in the same sense as the Code Napoléon, for example. Thus, G.R. Driver and J.C. Miles wrote:

"The Laws must not be regarded as a code or digest, but as a series of amendments to the common law of Babylon...",[6] a statement expanded a few pages later to: "a series of amendments and restatements of parts of the law in force..."[7] There was no doubt in the learned authors' minds, however, that they were dealing with a source of positive law, any more than there had been in the earlier commentaries of D. H. Müller[8] or P. Koschaker.[9]

Doubts on this point were expressed by B. Landsberger, who pointed out that Codex Hammurabi is never cited as authority in judgments, nor does it state that the judges must in future decide according to these laws.[10] Since Landsberger's article two cases have been found which appear to refer to the text of a *narûm*, but they are too obscure to resolve the question of practical application.[11]

These doubts were taken up by J. J. Finkelstein in an entirely new approach to the problem.[12] Finkelstein pointed out, firstly, that Codex Hammurabi could not have been compiled except in the last years of Hammurabi's reign, after he had accomplished all of the conquests enumerated in his prologue, and secondly, that the Code concluded with an epilogue addressed primarily to posterity, especially to future kings.[13] He concluded that the Code's purpose was not legislative at all. It was representative of a literary genre, namely the royal *apologia*, and its primary purpose was to lay before the public, posterity, future kings, and, above all, the gods, evidence of the king's execution of his divinely ordained mandate: to have seen "the Faithful Shepherd" and the šar mīšarim.[14]

Finkelstein applied his theory to two earlier law codes, Codex Ur-Nammu and Codex Lipit-Ishtar, both of which had prologues and epilogues in the same spirit, and concluded that Hammurabi was following a traditional genre of royal inscription. Our question is whether this understanding of Codex Hammurabi can be used to explain the general phenomenon of law codes in the Ancient Near East: was there a literary, rather than legal, tradition shared by the monarchs of that region?

The answer must be in the negative. The prologue and epilogue, which are vital to the purpose of the royal inscription, are missing in the cuneiform codes later than Codex Hammurabi, and probably also in Codex Eshnunna (which slightly antedates it).[15] Since we possess copies of these codes that originally provided a complete version of the text, and not an extract (with the possible exception of the Neo-Babylonian Laws), there is no reason for them to have omitted the prologue and epilogue if they existed. We must therefore agree with S. Paul in concluding that this traditional literary pattern was not continued after Codex Hammurabi, if indeed it existed at all outside the central Mesopotamian cultural sphere represented by the three codes that were modelled upon it.[16] Paul does claim to see in both Deuteronomy and the Book of the Covenant the same tripartite division of legal corpus within a prologue-epilogue frame[17], but the two Biblical codes are in a literary context too different from that of their Mesopotamian counterparts to allow any meaningful comparison. The content and purpose of the framework bear no relationship to that of the Mesopotamian codes: by no stretch of the imagination can the chapters following the legal corpus (however widely defined) in Exodus and Deuteronomy be described as an *apologia* of the lawgiver; there is therefore no evidence from their present textual context that the codes originated in a royal inscription. If, in the alternative, it is suggested that the Biblical structure is patterned on that of the Mesopotamian codes, the additional difficulty is faced that there exist other models for the Biblical version to copy, in particular Ancient Near Eastern treaties.[18]

If the activity of writing law-codes could be engaged in without the addition of a prologue and epilogue to the legal corpus, it suggests that a royal *apologia* was not the primary purpose in the composition of the latter. This is confirmed by the remarkable dichotomy in style between the Mesopotamian codes' prologues and epilogues and their central legal corpus. It has even been suggested[19] that they were formulated by two different sets of authors: the legal corpus by jurists and the prologue and epilogue by Temple or Court poets. It seems to us evidence rather that the legal corpus already existed as an independent unit with an independent purpose and was sometimes inserted into a frame, as in Codex Hammurabi, in order to be applied to a new purpose, that of the royal *apologia*. This is a recognized process in the case of the Biblical codes, which were inserted into a religious-historical framework.[20]

3.—The Law Codes as a Scribal Exercise?

The nature and purpose of the central legal corpus is the subject of the theory proposed by F. R. Kraus in respect of Codex Hammurabi.[21] Kraus begins with Hammurabi's own definition of his laws: *dīnāt mīšarim*[22], which he translates *"gerechte Richtersprüche"* (just judicial decisions).[23] The legal corpus is therefore *prima facie* a list of the king's decisions in his capacity as a judge.[24] Closer examination, however, reveals that by no means all the "judgments" recorded in the Code are real. They are organized in groups wherein a single case is expanded by logical extrapolation, i.e., various theoretical alternatives are considered and the appropriate solution given by *a priori* reasoning.[25] For example, paragraphs 229–231 read:

229. If a mason builds a house for a man and does not reinforce his work and the house that he built collapses and kills the owner of the house, that mason shall be killed.
230. If it kills a child of the householder, they shall kill a child of that mason.
231. If it kills a slave of the householder, he shall give slave for slave to the householder.

Similar gradation of penalties occurs elsewhere in the Code, in paragraphs 209–11, for example. We are therefore in the presence of a type of academic method. Now, this same method is found in a seemingly unrelated group of texts—the omen collections. For example, in the omen series *šumma izbu* a typical sequence is:[26]

5. If a woman gives birth, and the right ear (of the child) is (abnormally) small, the house of the man will be scattered.
6. If a woman gives birth, and the left ear (of the child) is (abnormally) small, the house of the man will expand.
7. If a woman gives birth, and both ears (of the child) are (abnormally) small, the house of the man will become poor.

The connection, according to Kraus, is that the law codes and omen collections are both representatives of a particular type of literature, namely scientific treatises. Divination was regarded as a science by the Mesopotamians and the compiling of omens the equivalent of scientific research. By the same token, the casuistic style in which both texts are couched was the "scientific" style par excellence—transferring the concrete individual case to the sphere of the impersonal rule.[27]

This scientific activity is the work of the scribes, and takes place in the scribal schools. Codex Hammurabi itself exists in the form of school copies already in the Old Babylonian period. It borrows extensively, often verbatim, from the text of the earlier codes of Ur-Nammu and Lipit-Ishtar (as one would expect if it were a literary genre), which in turn exist in the form of Old Babylonian school copies. Likewise, both extant copies of Codex Eshnunna are school texts.[28] In Kraus' view, therefore, it is Hammurabi the scribe rather than the judge who is represented by the legal corpus of his code. It is a work of theoretical literature designed to illustrate his wisdom—"wise" *(emqum)* being a typical epithet of the scribe)[29]

The notion of the law-codes as an activity of the scribal schools provides a ready explanation for their appearance among the Hittites, in Assyria, and as far afield as Israel. Cuneiform scribal schools existed throughout the Ancient Near East in the second millennium, including the cities of Canaan prior to the Israelite conquest.[30] They were not merely places for learning the cuneiform script; such schools were the universities of the Ancient Near East where the cultural and literary inheritance, both Babylonian and local, was preserved and developed. Codex Hammurabi itself continued to be copied and re-copied in scribal schools both in Babylonia and elsewhere for more than a millennium after its promulgation.[31] It would be no surprise, therefore, to find similar codes compiled from the local law by Canaanite or Hittite scribes who were inspired by contact with Hammurabi's *magnum opus*.

Attractive as this picture is, in our view it requires correction in one important respect: Kraus' basic assumption that the intellectual activity of collecting legal decisions, expanding them by the addition of logical variants and formulating them in scientific style resulted in a work of pure science, a monument to scribal wisdom and no more.[32] Our reasons for questioning this assumption emerge from a closer examination of the parallel adduced by Kraus himself—the omen series.

4.—Law Codes and Omen Series: Practical Application

The omen series were compiled for a very practical purpose: to be used as reference works by diviners when they sought to determine the significance of an ominous feature (as in extispicy) or event. For example, if a lamb were born with but a single horn, the diviner *(bārû)* would consult the series dealing with unusual births, *šumma izbu*, select and excerpt the pertinent omens and prepare a report. Then, if necessary, an appropriate ritual would be performed in order to expiate the evil effects of a bad omen. Presumably the report would usually be presented orally, but in the library of Assurbanipal have been preserved a number of written reports from diviners to an Assyrian king, upon which our knowledge of this procedure is based.[33] The diviner did not directly cite the name of the series that he was consulting, but would differentiate his sources by drawing a line between omens from different tablets of the series, or else by placing them on opposite sides of the tablets.[34] There is evidence of the consultation of omen series as far back as the Old Babylonian period.[35] The activity of compiling the lists of omens together with their meanings was therefore not merely a scribal exercise; it was "applied science".

We suggest that the compiling of lists of legal decisions basically served a similar purpose. They were a reference work for consultation by judges when deciding difficult cases. In view of the association of most of the law codes with a king, it is reasonable to suppose that it was the king as judge, or at least the royal judges, that these lists were intended to serve. The royal courts, as supreme courts, would be called upon to decide difficult points of law and would therefore be most in need of precedents to assist them.[36]

There is no direct evidence from cuneiform sources for the consultation of law codes as there is for the omen series.[37] This is not a decisive consideration, nor even surprising, for three reasons. Firstly, the selection of cuneiform sources available to us is notoriously arbitrary, depending on the fortunes of the archaeologist's spade, and argument from silence is therefore inappropriate. Secondly, the interpretation of omens played a far more important and common role in Mesopotamia than did lawsuits. The king consulted diviners because, like the rest of his subjects and perhaps more so, he was a potential victim of the divine judgment signified by the omens, he needed the advice of the diviners before undertaking any significant act, and irrespective of his own initiative whenever a natural phenomenon of ominous portent occurred. On the other hand, the king was never party to a law-suit, only the judge in a restricted number of cases, and his need for consultation of legal precedents, whether personally or through experts, would be much more circumscribed. Inevitably, the number of recorded omens would be far greater than that of legal precedents, and in fact in the library of Assurbanipal omen series formed by far the largest category of texts.[38] This in turn would affect the chances of finding material evidence of their application. Finally, there is the question of oral and written procedure. Direct evidence for the consultation of omen series exists only for a short period of time covering two neo-Assyrian kings,[39] and only due to the fortuitous circumstance that the diviners in question did not live in the palace, so that consultation was by letter.[40] It would require equally unusual circumstances for consultation of legal reference-works during or at the conclusion of a trial to be by letter and not orally.

The cuneiform sources do, however, provide some indirect evidence of the use of law-codes that we have postulated. Firstly, there is the archaeological evidence concerning the Assyrian Laws. This vast collection, originally numbering 14 tablets, is, as we have noted, not a royal inscription. Nor is it a school text. Most of the tablets recovered were found in a gate-house identified as the "Gate of Shamash", which is the normal location of the courthouse in Mesopotamia (Shamash being the god of Justice), and already E. Weidner referred to them for this reason as a legal library for judges.[41]

Secondly, there is the nature of the Hittite Laws. These are likewise neither a royal inscription nor a school tablet. They are part of the royal archives, but more interesting than their location is the historical development that they betray. The collection was recopied over several centuries, and the later copies still retain some archaic language.[42] On the other hand, there is evidence of an updating not only of language[43] but also of the substantive law. In some cases this is implied and in others in the form of an express reference to an amendment.[44] And a fragment of an even later version (*K Bo* VI 4) substitutes new penalties for those of the principal text. Regular changes to keep abreast of developments in the law would not have been necessary if the text were merely academic,[45] as a comparison with the subsequent fate of Codex Hammurabi shows.

As we have seen, Codex Hammurabi continued to be copied for more than a millenium after its promulgation, both within and outside of Babylonia. The copies are remarkably faithful to the original; certainly no changes whatsoever were made to the substantive law. The reason is that it became a piece of canonical literature, a part of the scribal school curriculum that was copied for its own sake.

This illustrates the difference between school texts and scientific texts. The local scribes saw no reason to alter Codex Hammurabi because for them it was only a scribal exercise and not part of their positive law. Their own law codes, however, had a practical purpose and therefore had to reflect the local law, which meant also regular amendment to take account of changes in the law. This is not to say that "foreign" codes copied in the scribal schools were not without influence. The codes under discussion contain many similar provisions, because the societies themselves and therefore their substantive law were so similar.

An earlier law code therefore provides an obvious model when drafting one's own, particularly in terms of the legal problems to be addressed, but its provisions are not binding. It has rather what modern lawyers from independent systems with a common tradition call "persuasive authority", as, for example, with United States precedents cited in English courts.[46] The process of adoption is selective. Thus the Sumerian codes of Ur-Nammu and Lipit-Ishtar exist in school copies in the Old Babylonian period and some of their provisions re-appear in Codex Hammurabi in almost verbatim translation.[47] Other paragraphs of Codex Hammurabi, however, depart fundamentally from their parallels in the earlier Codes, for example, where physical injury is punished by talio instead of monetary compensation.

Again, the later codes did not reproduce the provisions of Codex Hammurabi verbatim, but a curious use of terminology illustrates how they took note of it as a source. The dowry that a bride brings from her parent's house is consistently called *šeriktum* in Codex Hammurabi, and the gifts that she receives from her husband, *nudunnûm* (paragraph 172). This terminology does not reflect the documents of practice, where *šeriktum* does not appear at all, gifts from the husband have no special appellation and the *nuddunnûm* in all periods refers to the dowry. All the evidence points to an innovation which was not taken up in practice.[48] Nonetheless, the Assyrian Laws in their discussion of questions of marital property use the same scheme—*širku* for dowry (A 27) and *nudunnû* for gift from the husband (A 29, 32)—suggesting a conscious imitation of Codex Hâmmurabi, although the laws in which these terms appear are not directly parallel to the provisions of the earlier code. The same tradition even makes its way into the Neo-Babylonian Laws (8–13), with this difference, that the author of the later code found the traditional scheme too illogical and simply reversed it—*nudunnû* for dowry, as in practice, *šeriktu* for gift from husband, the latter use being a complete innovation. Again, the content of the laws in which these terms appear are not the same as in the earlier codes.

Finally, the practice of selective adoption can be seen in the relationship between the cuneiform and the Biblical codes. Codex Eshunna exists as a school text and in some form must have reached the Israelite cultural sphere, since *Ex.* XXI, 35, concerning the ox that gores another ox, is virtually a translation of *CE* 53. However, whereas *CE* 54 imposes a monetary penalty on the previously warned owner of a goring ox that kills a man, *Ex*, XXI, 29 in the same circumstances requires the death penalty.

To summarize: in our view the Ancient Near Eastern law codes derive from a tradition of compiling series of legal precedents in the same manner as omens, medical prognoses and other scientific treatises.

Biblical and Cuneiform Law Codes

The purpose of these series to act was as reference works for the royal judges in deciding difficult cases. Probably this began as an oral tradition and only gradually became a systematic written corpus.[49] The clearest examples of such series are the Assyrian Laws and the Hittite Laws; the other law codes are evidence that such series could be adopted to other purposes. Three types of secondary purpose appear from the extant codes: (1) royal inscriptions designed to praise the king's activity as a judge *(CU, CL, CH)* which were characterized by the addition of a prologue and epilogue, (2) school texts *(CU, CL, CH, CE, NBL)*, which would take on independent existence as part of the scribal curriculum, and (3) part of a religio-historical narrative (Covenant and Deuteronomic Codes) where the deity replaces the king as the source of the law.

The final piece of evidence for this thesis comes from an unexpected source, but in order to evaluate it we must first analyse the process by which the law codes were created.

5.—Law Codes and Omen Series: The Cycle of Creation

The example given earlier in which the diviner, when called upon to interpret the ominous significance of an unusual birth, would select the pertinent omens from the series *šumma izbu*, is but one step in the cycle of creating precedents and applying them.

The first step theoretically will be the case where a birth occurs for which there is no precedent—a mare gives birth to a hare. If the diviner interprets this, whether by analogy with known omens or some other process of logic, as meaning that the king will flee from the battlefield, and in the event the king in question does flee, the diviner's decision will then become a precedent for future omens of the same kind.

The second step is for the omen to pass through what we may call the "first stage of generalization". This stage is evidenced in the cuneiform sources by the "*tamītu*" texts.[50] These are answers put to a god, e.g., *tamīt alāk ḫarrāni*, "a *tamītu* concerning going on a campaign". In most cases the name of the person for whom the question was being put is replaced by "so-and-so, son of so-and-so" *(annanna apīl annanna)*. W. Lambert explains: ... "the suppression of the names suggests the reason for the handing down of these documents which at first glance would seem to have no practical use after they were originally employed by the appropriate priest. Just as in law a case once decided can become a precedent so that future parties having the same problem can find the answer without recourse to the expensive and time-consuming processes of the law, so the *tamītus*, once answered, were preserved in case any one should wish to find the gods' answer to that particular question again".[51]

The third step represents the second stage of generalization, whereby the anonymous precedent is put into casuistic form, and the fourth step is the compilation of lists of these casuistic rules with the addition of their logical variations by analogy so as to form a series. This "scientific" treatment is necessary because in Mesopotamian eyes it makes the series universally applicable (by exhausting all possible alternatives) and therefore authoritative.[52]

The fifth step is then one already familiar to us, namely consultation of the series by the diviner who excerpts the relevant omens. If the occurrence contains some new element not directly covered by the existing omens, then the new omen may itself become a precedent, undergo the two stages of generalization and be taken up into an omen series, thus repeating the cycle.

The above cycle will have a familiar ring to lawyers, for it accurately reflects the development of general legal rules from individual cases in legal systems where judge-made law predominates. The only difference is that in the modern systems the process of generalization consists in creating abstract principles of law rather than variants of the precedent. It is reasonable to suppose, therefore, that the same process took place in moving from individual judgment to law code and back again. A decision of the king (or royal judge) in a difficult case would be turned into a casuistic rule of general application and, expanded with the necessary variants by extrapolation would eventually become part of a canon of such rules, which in turn were consulted in deciding new cases, and where a new decision was made it eventually would be added to the canon, and so forth, Accordingly, Hammurabi could speak truthfully in his Code of the just decisions that *he* had made, for the central part of that Code represents those parts of the received canon of legal rules that he chose to adopt and apply in his own court, supplemented by his own judgments (and perhaps the logical variants thereof).

The cuneiform sources are not, however, so forthcoming with evidence of the legal steps described above as they are with the omen literature. The only step recorded is the first one—the king of his judges giving judgment in a particular case—without any indication of the decision's value as a precedent.[53] Even in the few full trial reports that exist, the *ratio decidendi* is not given.[54] Bottéro refers to one decision of Hammurabi that appears to be based on the same principle as an article of his code.[55] According to *CH* 32: "If a merchant ransoms a soldier who is taken prisoner on a royal campaign and brings him back to his city, if there are the means for redemption in his house he shall redeem himself. If there are not the means in his house for redeeming himself, he shall be redeemed from (the resources of) his city temple. If there are not the means in his city temple, the palace shall redeem him...".

The following order is given by Hammurabi in a letter: "Speak to Luštamar-Zamama and Belanum: Thus says Hammurabi. (As to) Sin-Ana-Damru-lippalis, the son of Maninum, whom the enemy took: give his merchant ten shekels of silver from the temple of sin and redeem him".

From the name of the prisoner it could be assumed that the temple of Sin was his city temple. What then is the connection between the king's order and *CH* 32? Was it the precedent from which at least part of the legal rule was constructed? Or was it given in application of the rule? Indeed, were the conditions for redemption laid down in the rule, namely the lack of funds in the soldier's household, fulfilled in this case? No answer can be derived from the laconic terms of order. To find evidence of the intervening legal steps we must turn to our one non-cuneiform source: the Bible. The process in question is illustrated not by the Biblical law-codes themselves but by the reports made of five difficult cases, four of which were decided by recourse to a special procedure (the oracle) and one by the special order of a military leader.

The first case that we wish to consider is reported in *Num.*, xv, 32–37. A man was found gathering wood on the Sabbath. The case must have been without precedent, for he was held while Moses consulted God. The decision was that the man was to be executed by stoning. As it stands the report is no more informative than Hammurabi's order. The grounds for the decision and the fact that it is intended as a precedent are indeed implicit, but neither received express mention.

The second case is reported in two places. In *Num.* xxxi, after a war against the Midianites, Moses is ordered by God to divide the spoils of war between those who went out to battle and all the "congregation" (`edah, vv. 25–28), As in the previous case, there is no specific indication that this decision is to serve as a precedent for future battles. However, the same principle at least (of division between combatants and non-combatants)[56] is the ratio of the decision attributed to David in *I Sam.* xxx. The background here is a victory over the Amalekites. The victory was achieved with only part of his forces, the rest being left behind at Nahal Besor (vv. 9–10), but David decides nonetheless that the spoil is to be divided equally between those who actually took part in the engagement and those who remained behind. The decision in this report is formulated in terms of an anonymous rule:

"... For as his share is who goes down into the battle, so shall his share be who stays by the baggage; they shall share alike" (v. 24). Furthermore, we are expressly informed that this ruling had the force of precedent: "And from that day forward he made it a statute *(ḥoq)* and an ordinance *(mišpaṭ)* for Israel to this day" (v. 25). The terms *ḥoq* and *mišpaṭ* are, of course, familiar from the Biblical law-codes.

The third case is even more explicit. In Num. XXVII, 1–11, the daughters of Zelophehad, who died without sons, approach Moses and claim a share of their father's estate. Following the same procedure as in the case of the man who gathered wood on the Sabbath, Moses consults God and the specific decision is given to share Zelophehad's estate among his daughters (v. 7). There then follows a re-formulation of that same decision as a casuistic rule, with the addition of possible alternatives: "... If a man dies, and has no son, then you shall cause his inheritance to pass to his daughter. And if he has no daughter, then you shall give his inheritance to his brothers. And if he has no brothers, then you shall give his inheritance to his father's brothers. And if his father has no brothers, then you shall give his inheritance to his kinsman that is next to him of his family, and he shall possess it. And it shall be to the people of Israel a statute and ordinance *(ḥuqat mišpaṭ)* ..." There thus begin to emerge some of the steps in the creation of a code that we have already seen in the case of the Mesopotamian omen series and postulated for the cuneiform law codes.

The problem of inheritance when a man dies leaving daughters but no sons could not have been a rare one, and in fact we find exactly the same solution in a Sumerian fragment probably belonging to Codex Lipit-Ishtar:[57]

"If a man died and he had no son, (his) unmarried daughter [shall become] his heir..." The extra condition of being unmarried fits the case of Zelophehad's daughters perfectly, since in a postscript to the story (*Num.* XXXVI) we discover that they were unmarried and had to marry within the clan in order to preserve the family estate. Without wishing to enter into the intricacies of Biblical compositional history, it seems to us that if this rule had already entered the law-codes as early as the reign of Lipit-Ishtar, then it must have been in a canon of legal rules in the Israel as well. If, therefore, as is claimed, the story is the projection back to the time of Moses of an incident designed to explain a later political phenomenon[58] the technique must have been to take the well-known rule from a code and present it as an early precedent, the association being obvious to the contemporary reader familiar with the way that law codes developed from precedents.

The fourth example adds another element. In *Num.*, IX, 6–14, the oracle is consulted by Moses in the case of persons who were unable to keep the passover on the appointed day. The divine decision is that they are given a second date, but far from being specific to the persons concerned, it is formulated directly as a general casuistic rule: "If any man of you or of your descendants is unclean through touching a dead

Biblical and Cuneiform Law Codes

body, or is afar off on a journey, he shall still keep the passover.... In the second month on the fourteenth day in the evening they shall keep it..." (v. 11–12). The intermediate steps between case and Code are obvious to the reader and can therefore be omitted. The actual wording of the casuistic introit *'iyš 'iyš kî*... is in fact already known in Codex Eshnunna[59] and employed throughout the Neo-Babylonian Laws (*awīlum ša*...) But there is, as we mentioned, an additional element. Verse 13 goes on to consider the opposite case: "But the man who is clean and is not on a journey, yet refrains from keeping the passover, that person shall be cut off from his people..." Here is the technique familiar from all the law-codes and identified by Kraus as the universal thought-process of Mesopotamian science. It is not at all necessary to the decision in this particular case, but has been added as the drafters of the codes added theoretical examples. And v. 14 adds a further variant, concerning the applicability of the passover law to the *gēr*. We have thus seen in these four examples: (1) the initial decision, (2) the first stage of generalization (anonymity), (3) the second stage of generalization (casuistic form), (4) the creation of a code (academic variations). The picture is completed by our final example: the case of the man who in the course of a fight cursed in God's name (*Lev.* XXIV, 10–23).

The case begins with the now familiar pattern of oracular consultation, specific decision (vv. 10–13) and execution in the particular case: "Bring out of the camp him who cursed; and let all who heard him lay their hands upon his head, and let all the congregation stone him" (v. 14). There then follows the repetition of the same decision in the general casuistic form (vv. 15–16): "... Whoever curses his God shall bear his sin. He who blasphemes the name of the Lord shall be put to death; the sojourner as well as the native, when he blasphemes the Name, shall be put to death". Thus far the pattern is the same as in the earlier examples. The ruling continues, however, with the following variants: "He who kills a man shall be put to death. He who kills a beast shall make it good, life for life, When a man causes a disfigurement in his neighbour, as he has done it shall be done to him; fracture for fracture, eye for eye, tooth for tooth; as he had disfigured a man, he shall be disfigured. He who kills a beast shall make it good; and he who kills a man shall be put to death" (v. 17–21). The relevance of these variants is not all apparent. Only the vaguest association of ideas would link them to the actual decision in the case which concerned the using of God's name in a curse. On the other hand, if we consider all the circumstances of the case; namely that there was a fight between two men, then the reference to rules on unlawful death or wounding is understandable. In a modern context, a lawyer giving an opinion on the case—*prior to the decision*—would naturally wish to cover those aspects as well. In the Ancient Near Eastern context, the method involved becomes clear if we refer once again to our Mesopotamian parallel, the practice of the diviner (*bārû*) when consulted on an ominous event. It will be recalled that the diviner's report consisted of omens excerpted from the omen-series. But, as Leichty points out:[60] "It is interesting to note that the *bārû*- priest never filed just one omen as a report, but rather attempted to include all omens which might in some way pertain to the case". The very same technique has been used in our passage in Leviticus, and just as the *bārû*-priest would excerpt quotations from *šumma izbu* or some other omen-series, so excerpts from a law-code have been quoted here—to all appearances from that same collection upon which the present Covenant Code is based. In the light of the cuneiform material then, the Biblical source can be seen to provide the missing piece of evidence that the law codes were applied in practice. And thus the cycle is completed.

Notes

1. There are also various fragments too small to be of use in this discussion. Note that the so-called "Sumerian Family Laws" in *ana ittišu* are not normative provisions at all, but contractual formulae (ed. B. Landsberger, *MSL* I, Rome 1937). Also to be excluded are the "Sumerian Laws" of *YBC* 2177. As J. J. Finkelstein points out, they are a scribal exercise executed by a student, which combines various legal phrases and contractual formulae with normative provisions (*ANET*, p. 525). The two types of material are never combined elsewhere: there is a strict separation by the scribes between the lexicographical tradition as exemplified by *ana ittišu* and the law-code tradition.

2. See e.g. O. Eissfeldt, *Einleilung in das Alte Testament* (3rd ed.), Tübingen, 1964, pp. 33–37.

3. The Priestly Code in Leviticus and Numbers has for the most part a different subject-matter from the two Biblical codes mentioned or the cuneiform codes. It is more aptly compared with cuneiform series concerning priestly functions such as *Šurpu*. See M. J. Geller, *The Šurpu incantations and Lev. v. 1–5*, in *JSSt*, XXV, 1980, pp. 181–192.

4. The casuistic style is usually introduced by a conditional beginning "If . . .", but other forms are possible. See R. Yaron, *"Forms in the Laws of Eshnunna,"* in *RIDA*, IX, 1962, pp. 137–153.

5. E.g. CL 29 and CH 160, CE 53 and Ex. XXI, 35.

6. *The Babylonian Laws*, Oxford, 1952, Vol. I, p. 41.

7. *Op. cit.*, p. 45.

8. *Die Gesetze Hammurabis*, Wien, 1903.

9. *Rechtsvergleichende Studien zur Gesetzgebung Hammurapis*, Leipzig, 1917.

10. *Die Babylonischen Termini für Gesetz und Recht*, in *SDIOP*, II, pp. 221–222. On the meaning of ṣimdal šarrim, see now M. de J. Ellis, in *JCS*, XXIV, 1972, pp. 74–82.

11. Cited by F. R. Kraus, *Ein Zentrales Problem des Altmesopotamischen Rechtes: Was ist der Codex Hammurabi?*, In Genava, VIII, p. 292.

12. *Ammi-Saduqa's Edict and the Babylonian "Law Codes"*, in *JCS*, XV, 1961, pp. 91–104.

13. *Op. cit.*, p. 101.

14. *Op. cit.*, p. 103.

15. A date-formula appears to precede the laws. The end of both extant copies is not preserved.

16. *Studies in the Book of the Covenant in the Light of Cuneiform and Biblical Law*, Leiden, 1970, p. 11 n. 5.

17. *Op. cit.*, pp. 27–36.

18. See M. Weinfeld, *Deuteronomy and the Deuteronomic School*, Oxford, 1972 pp. 146–157.

19. J. Klima, *Gesetze*, in *Reallexikon der Assyriologie*, p. 244.

20. *Op. cit.*, note 18 above, pp. 283–296.

21. *Op. cit.*, n. 11 above.

22. Col. xxiv, Rev. 1–2.

23. *Op. cit.* p. 285. First proposed by B. Landsberger, *op. cit.*, note 10 above, p. 223.

24. Although they translated the phrase "just laws" (*op. cit.*, Vol. II, p. 95), Driver and Miles in fact noted that these laws resembled English case-laws rather than statute (*op. cit.*, Vol. I, p. 52).

25. *Op. cit.*, p. 289. In other passages, the composition of the Code is more complex, although the same principle obtains: See R. Westbrook and C. Wilcke, *AFO*, XXIV, 1974–1977, pp. 111–121.

26. Tablet III, 5–7. E. Leighty, *The Omen Series Šumma Izbu*, TCS, IV, New York, 1970, p. 54.

27. *Op. cit.*, pp. 288–290. The same argument by J. Bottero, *Le "Code" de Hammurabi*, in *Annali della Scuola Normale Superiore di Pisa*, XII, 1982, pp. 409–44 at pp. 426–435, using the example of the medical texts, another form of scientific treatise. Bottéro points out that Babylonian science sought to achieve exhaustive treatment of a subject by listing examples not only of the commonly observed and the exceptional, but also of the possible.

28. *Op. cit.*, pp. 293–4.

29. *Op. cit.*, p. 290.

30. See H. Tadmor, *A lexicographical Text from Hazor*, in *IEJ*, 27, 1977, pp. 98–102.

31. See J. Laessoe, in *JCS*, IV, 1950. pp. 180–182; J. Nougayrol, in *CRAI*, 1951, pp. 42–47, *JA*, 1957, pp. 339–366, *JA*, 1958, pp. 143–155; J. J. Finkelstein, in *JCS*, XXI, 1967, pp. 39–48, *RA*, LXIII, 1969, pp. 11–27.

32. To be fair, Kraus does hint at their possible use "... gibt es ein Handbuch, so greift man zu ihm" (*op. cit.*, p. 290), but no specific application is suggested.

33. E. Leichty, *op. cit.*, note 26 above, pp. 7–11. For reports based on excerpts from an astronomical omen series, see S. Parpola, *AOAT*, V/I, Nos. 324–326.

34. Leichty, *op. cit.*, p. 8.

35. Leichty, *op. cit.*, pp. 7–8 citing an Old Babylonian letter.

36. On the role of the royal courts as a final court of appeal in difficult cases, see M. Weinfeld, *Judge and Officer in Ancient Israel and in the Ancient Near East*, in *Israel Oriental Studies*, VII, 1977, pp. 65–76; W. F. Leemans, *King Hammurapi as Judge*, in *Symbolae David*, Vol. II, Leiden, 1968, pp. 107–129.

37. See note 11 above. An express, if later reference to the use of a law code by royal judges is found in a land which so far has yielded no law codes, namely Egypt. According to the Greek Historian Diodorus Siculus (I 75 (6)), at a trial in Egypt all the laws lay before the judges, written down in eight books. E. Seidl claims that this account is confirmed by a picture in the tomb of Rekhmireh, a vizier of the eighteenth dynasty, which shows the vizier sitting in judgment with forty leather scrolls before him (*Einführung in die Aegyptische Rechtsgeschichte*, Gluckstadt, 1957, p. 19).

38. The omen series *šumma izbu* alone, as preserved in the library of Assurbanipal contains more than two thousand omens, arranged in a series of twenty-four tablets. Leichty, *op. cit.*, p. 2.

39. S. Parpola, *Letters from Assyrian Scholars to the Kings Esarhaddon and Assurbanipal*, AOAT, V/2, 1983, p. XVII.

40. Leichty, *op. cit.*, pp. 9–10.

41. *Das Alter der mittelassyrischen Gesetztexte*, in *AFO*, XII, 1937, pp. 46–54.

42. A, Goetze, *Kleinasien* (2nd ed.), München, 1957, pp. 110–111.

43. See H. Hoffner, *The Old Hittite Version of Laws 164–66* in *JCS*, XXXIII, pp. 206–209.

44. E.g. Paragraph 94: "If a free man steals in a house, he shall give (back) the respective goods; they would formerly give for the theft 1 mina of silver, now he shall give 12 shekels of silver". (Translation: A. Goetze, in *ANET*, p. 193). See also V. Korošec, *La codification dans le domaine du droit Hittite*, in *RIDA*, IV, 1957, pp. 99–100.

45. "KBO VI 4 schleppt die veralteten Bestimmungen nicht mehr mit; der Text gibt nur das geltende Recht." A. Goetze, *op. cit.*, note 42 above, p. 111.

46. Compare G. Cardascia's theory of the "reception" of Codex Hammurabi, drawing on the analogy of the Continental law experience: *La transmission des sources juridiques cunéiformes*, in *RIDA*, VII, 1960, pp. 47–48.

47. See note 5 above.

48. See the discussion by the author in *Old Babylonian Marriage Law* (Diss. unpubl.) University Microfilms, Ann Arbor, 1982, Vol. II, pp. 257–268.

49. On the analogy of the omen literature: see Leichty, *op. cit.*, note 26 above, p. 23.

50. W. G. Lambert, *The "Tamītu" Texts*, in *La Divination en Mésopotamie Ancienne (XIVth Rencontre Assyriologique)*, Paris, 1966, pp. 119–123.

51. *Op. cit.*, p. 121.

52. See Bottero, *op. cit.*, note 27 above, pp. 431–433. In the alternative, precedents might be compiled first and then turned into casuistic form—there are some examples of large tablets containing a number of collected *tamītu's*, Lambert, *op. cit.*, pp. 119–120.

53. See Leemans, *op. cit.*, note 36 above, and the examples given therein.

54. A possible exception is the trial report edited by T. Jacobsen, *An Ancient Mesopotamian Trial for Homecide* in *Toward the Image of Tammuz*, Cambridge, Mass., 1970, pp. 193–214. The legal issue appears to be whether a wife who is informed by her husband's assassins of his murder but keeps silent is herself guilty of murder. The case was remitted by the king to the Assembly of Nippur, and the report contains a debate before the Assembly, followed by the Assembly's reasoned decision as to her guilt. The report exists in duplicates from the reign of king Rim-Sin of Larsa and in later copies (unpublished) from the time of Samsu-iluna (Jacobsen, *op. cit.*, p. 196). This suggests that it had value as a precedent, although of course it may merely have been a cause célèbre. The same legal issue does not occur in any of the extant law codes. It is interesting to note that according to Jacobsen, the later copies of the report also contain reports of a number of other trials before the Assembly of Nippur (*loc. cit.*).

55. *Op. cit.*, note 27 above, p. 421.

56. The two rulings differ as to the details of the division: David's decision gives an equal share to each, whether warrior or not, the order in Numbers is to divide the spoil equally between two groups of presumably unequal size.

57. Edited by M. Civil, *New Sumerian Law Fragments*, in *Studies in Honour of Benno Landsberger*, *AS*, XVI, 1965, pp. 4–5.

58. N. H. Snaith, *The Daughters of Zelophehad*, in *VT*, XVI, 1966, pp. 125–127. The character of the precedent as a source of law was recognized by J. Weingreen, *The Case of the Daughters of Zelophehad*, in *VT*, XVI, 1966, pp. 518–522.

59. *CE* 12, 13, and 19. It is also found in the Edict of Ammi-saduqa and in the Assyrian Laws, paragraphs A 40 and B 6. See R. Yaron, *The Laws of Eshnunna*, Jerusalem, 1969, p. 65.

60. *Op. cit.*, note 26 above, p. 8.

SHIH-YÜ YÜ LI

Tibetan Folk-Law

From the ancient Near East, we move through space and time to Tibet. In this interesting essay, we have both a description of contemporary folk law as well as a translation of a set of rules issued in 1733. The disparity between modern practice and details of the eighteenth-century code demonstrate the difficulty in extrapolating law from codes in general. A law may be "on the books" so to speak, but may or may not actually be observed or enforced. Still, the existence of a law in a code is itself not without interest.

Tibetans inhabit three major regions, Tibet proper, Khams, and A-mdo. Tibet is the region so marked on the maps; Khams is the province marked as Sikang; A-mdo does not exist as a political entity, but is divided into a number of Hsien (counties) in the north-western part of Szechwan, the south-western part of Kansu, and the area inhabited by Tibetans in Ts'inghai or Kokonor. My four years' field experience of Tibetan culture was in A-mdo on the Kansu-Ts'inghai border. My study of Tibetan folk-law, therefore, is based on conditions in A-mdo. The appended translation of "Rules of Punishment for Tibetans" (promulgated by the Manchu Imperial Court in 1733) applies mainly to Tibetans in A-mdo and secondarily to those in Tibet and Khams.

As Tibet, Khams, and A-mdo have a culture different from Chinese and other cultures, folk-law, like other aspects of Tibetan culture, irrespective of its predominance in any particular region, is always traced to Tibet's culture hero, King Srongtsan Gampo, who married in A.D. 641 the Chinese Princess Wench'eng. And however different it may appear to us, it is supposed to have its origin in the "Sixteen Articles of Law" of Srongtsan Gampo. These sixteen articles are as follows:—

1. Take refuge in the Buddha, in the Dharma (law), in the Sangha (monks).
2. Practise persistently the Dharma of these Three Treasures.

Reprinted from the *Journal of the Royal Asiatic Society of Great Britain and Ireland*, 1950, Parts 3 & 4, 127–148, with permission. Copyright © 1950 Cambridge University Press.

3. Observe filial piety.
4. Preserve morality.
5. Respect the aged and the noble.
6. Get rid of selfishness in friendly relations.
7. Give assistance to neighbours and the helpless.
8. Rectify the mind without being influenced by gossip.
9. Imitate the behaviour of the superior ones (monks).
10. Go to no extremes in taking food and in personal conduct.
11. Never forget the favours done by others.
12. Use standard measures for outgoing and incoming goods.
13. Harbour no grudge against anybody.
14. Phrase words so as to please others.
15. Pay no attention to the words of women and those of bad company.
16. Be patient and determined, for neither the code of the mundane world nor that of the supramundane world is easy.

These sixteen articles of law remind us of similar codes reported from Korea and Japan[1] about the same time, when the T'ang dynasty had its widest contact with non-Sinitic cultures. Whether or not they have a common origin in the outflow of Chinese culture is not our concern here, but the coincidence is worth noticing for further comparative study.

1. Historical Background of Tibetan Folk-law in A-mdo

In comparison with Tibet and Khams, A-mdo is more semi-independent and disunited because it has never been under direct rule either of the Chinese government or of Lhasa. Even in the heyday of the Manchu dynasty it was only during active military operations that any direct control was possible. Lacking unified rule, A-mdo consists of more or less unrelated tribal communities and monasteries. The people under tribal or monastic control are predominantly nomadic and secondarily sedentary.

Only within a "we-group" are the rules of morality observed. In dealings with an "other-group" justice can be maintained only if a wronged party can enforce it. Even then responsibility is not individual but collective. For example, when A of tribe X has done some injury to B of tribe Y, it is not A who is accountable to B individually; rather it is X that is accountable to Y collectively. Suppose A kills B and Y is strong enough to demand redress, all the members of X will have to contribute towards an appropriate "life-price" to be paid to Y; A as an individual does not have to pay the whole of it. If X declines to pay for loss suffered by Y from the death of B, blood feuds will result. Then an agreement may or may not be reached between tribes X and Y. Without agreement feuds will start afresh if either tribe is strong and bellicose. When agreement is reached the deaths in both tribes should cancel one another. The balance will have to be paid for in terms of "life-prices" to the tribe that suffered more deaths. As one individual may have a greater social value than others, the "life-price" for him, as we shall see, may be higher.

Recurrent feuds are not uncommon, and outside people who live among Tibetans without tribal protection of their own are easily abused without possibility of redress. Under the Tibetan system of folk-law a person wronged will take direct action himself, employ a mediator, or resort to litigation.

2. Direct Action

Direct action is the logical result of the lack of government protection. The ignorance and incompetence of officials expected to introduce reforms may partly explain the present lack of government protection. But historically the cause of it goes deeper. For during the Manchu dynasty the policy was to divide one ethnic group against another and to split groups into as many units as possible to remove the possibility of united revolt. It was unlawful for the Chinese to study Tibetan or Mongolian and for Tibetans and Mongols to study Chinese. As we may see in the ruling of Article 59 in the appendix mentioned above, the travel of Tibetans among faraway tribes was also restricted. Having been long denied the opportunity of wholesome cross-culture contact, Chinese and Tibetans alike need more time to correct a situation caused by an undesirable policy.

Direct action may be divided into (*a*) preparatory self-defence and (*b*) the handling of affairs afterwards.

(*a*) Even walking on the street Tibetans always carry swords and rifles. Travelling on open plains they go in large caravans for mutual protection, accompanied by fearsome mastiffs. These precautions are against possible attack and robbery. Robbers are seldom professionals. Any Tibetan may be a robber. For robbery is accepted as a way to acquire prestige. In the social scale of Tibetan life to be born an aristocrat or a Living Buddha is desirable; but this cannot be secured by individual effort. The only way to gain prestige by one's own effort is to become a lama with both religious and scholastic distinctions or to become a robber with all the glory of a warrior. The popularity of the lamas is proverbial. Robbery too is attractive. And it is encouraged by the insurance of collective responsibility, the idea that it is not wrong to harm another tribe, the urge of a poverty due to primitive economy and the not uncommon practice of giving alms to a monastery as a means of acquiring merit. On thus bankrupting oneself there is ironical comment in Buddhist teachings. In fact, robbery may not only be due to religion but make a man more religious. As a Buddhist, a robber will certainly repent of his sin of robbery, and he will more frequently attend the monasteries for purifying ceremonies. Of course he has to pay. He may even give up everything and take to robbery again.

So to deter robbers travellers are equipped for self-defence. As a rule, when two caravans approach from opposite directions they will try to ascertain the names and business of one another. Should mutual friends be discovered nothing will go wrong. Should there be no mutual friends they keep a respectable distance when passing. For it is not uncommon for the stronger party, on discovering the weakness of the other, to start a sudden attack, even though it was not originally meant to be a marauding party. Here is a vicious circle common in international politics. Unless you are well prepared you do not feel safe. Once you are well prepared, strength may tempt you to become involved in warfare under some pretext or other.

(*b*) Now suppose fighting starts among these Tibetans. What happens? If the defeated party is too weak to demand redress or the attacking party is not identified, no action is taken. Otherwise one of three courses may be followed.

(i) The tribe to which the attacking party belongs may be approached for compensation. Should it refuse peaceful settlement there will be fights on an inter-tribal scale. (ii) If it is conciliatory, compensation in terms of "life-prices" may be arranged through mediation. (iii) A third course is followed when both parties belong to the same chieftain or monastery authorities. For the aggrieved party will appeal to the chieftain or the monastery for a trial. Mediation and litigation are both contrary to the spirit of Article 33 of the ruling of the Manchu Imperial Court, as they are not handled by central authorities but "privately" by chieftains or monasteries.

There are other occasions for direct redress besides robbery. If one's field is damaged by another family's cattle, the cattle may be seized by the watchman of the crops or by the owner of the field. As a watchman comes from each family in turn he gets no pay. If he seizes animals their owner has to pay for damage they have done and the payment goes to the watchman. If the proprietor of the field gets hold of the animals the owner of the animals pays him directly.

Pastures to the nomads are what fields are to the agriculturist. Tribe A cannot pasture animals in places belonging to tribe B and vice versa. Should this rule be broken the trespassing animals will be taken by the tribe that has right to the land and their owners will have to pay for the trespass before they can be claimed. Chinese authorities have constantly erred by concluding that, as nomads roam about, there is no proprietorship of grasslands. The Manchus were better informed, as we may see from Article 7.

A caravan travelling through tribal territories inevitably presents a gift to the chieftain whose tribe claims the pasture-land by way of "grass money", to acknowledge his tribal authority and to pay for grass consumed. It is also a gesture to solicit his protection. No tribesman will then attack the caravan, and in case of attack the chieftain will help identify the marauders and be useful in mediation.

The caravan maintains order among its members. For example, every day there is a chosen leader for the road. On the second day the unit that led on the first will be the last in the train; the unit that was second on the first day will take the lead, and so on for the succeeding days. Any breach of the order will be punished by the representatives of the different units. The exact fine is determined at a conference at the end of the day. Absence of any representative from this conference entails loss of the right to speak. The keeping of watch over animals and goods at night is arranged in a similar manner. Nobody would dare to go against the ruling of a caravan council, which would entail expulsion from the party. Expulsion means loss of group protection and consequently starvation.

Direct redress or compensation may also accompany divorce and adultery. For Tibetans marriage and divorce are largely matters of mutual consent. On separation any rich wedding gifts should be returned to the family that gave them. If the family of a divorced woman is very poor, compensation is expected. The settlement of these cases involves a great deal of bargaining. A third party may arbitrate. Article 58 in the appendix may be read together with this as a recognition of Tibetan folk-law.

In the case of adultery, husband and wife may just separate. If the husband is particularly jealous and strong he may kill his wife and her lover on the spot and then take refuge for a while till their families have calmed down. Or the woman may be tortured by the cutting of her hair, her face, the tip of her nose, or a combination of these. In A-mdo particularly separation without further ado is more usual than not. Article 9 in the appendix is no doubt due to a mixture of Tibetan and Chinese influence.

3. Mediation

The most important matter for mediation is the settlement of "life-prices". The official explanation of this system stresses the value of human life. To have one person killed is bad enough. Why kill another to maintain justice? This explanation and actual practice differ from area to area, nor does it accord with capital punishment as promulgated by the Manchu Imperial Court. But by and large in A-mdo the family or tribe of a murdered person are generally content with his "life-price".

The exact amount of such a price for a commoner was sixty strings of copper coins, each string containing twenty-five coppers. With the money price becoming less dependable, the "life-price" is paid in kind, namely the equivalent in animals, a combination of horses and cattle (v. Article 39 in the appendix). As a horse is more valuable than a cow, for every horse there must be two cattle.

The "life-price" for a woman is only half that for a man. And different walks of life make a great difference. For instance, the "life-price" of the steward of a small monastery at Khagya is more or less the total of the following:—

(a) price of his head: horses, *dso* (mongrel-breed of the yak-bull and common cow), yaks, cows, to make a total of 40;
(b) price of his two hands: 80 animals;
(c) price of his legs: 80 animals;
(d) price of his body: 7 ingots (one ingot is equal to 50 taels of silver).

Of course the price for a Living Buddha is much higher, according to his rank.

Before the discussion of any "life-price" begins the following must be handed over as a preliminary peace gesture:—

(a) weapons used in the killing;
(b) horses used by the killer;
(c) one yak for the purpose of carrying the dead to the place to feed the vultures (a form of burial);
(d) an equal weight of butter to balance the dead body on the yak for transportation.

Theoretically the "life-price" for a robber killed in robbery is only half the usual amount, unless his tribe or family is strong enough to demand more. If a party is strong and persuasive there is much in its favour. When the value of a dead person admits of arguments there is no end of bargaining and even the threat of armed force. If arguments are even, the only way out is to swear an oath in the temple of the Protector of the Faith. Once an oath is sworn the balance will be entirely in the favour of the swearer. Even the Manchu Imperial Court had to take cognisance of such oaths, as illustrated by Articles 12, 13, 14, 19, 22, 23, etc., in the appendix.

If a person is killed unintentionally, in theory there is no compensation. But in practice half of a "life-price" is always demanded. If persons are injured in a fight the less injured should pay for the cost of medicines and for any religious performance for the cure of the more seriously injured (*v.* Articles 28, 29).

Very curious to any outsider is the folk-law for mastiffs that guard a tent. If one is attacked and hurt by them there is no redress. But if they are hurt seriously by a person in self-defence then he must pay for the injury. For it is the duty of the dogs to guard against intrusion and their life is as valuable as a human life. It is natural for them to attack an intruder (cf. Article 30).

4. Litigation

A monastery official or chieftain may fine a person for any breach of custom. For instance, no commoner may have the eaves of his house made of shales or his door painted; no woman may wear trousers or put on Chinese stockings and shoes. Any offender will be heavily fined by the monk in direct charge of the people (gñerpa). Failure to appear in statute labour or to contribute one's share of fuel and fodder to the traditional authority is similarly punished.

To start a lawsuit a Tibetan has first to offer enough presents to the judge. For a Tibetan official is not to serve but to be served by his people. During the hearing of a case the judge remains silent, while the two parties keep on reciting historical happenings that have led to the suit. This recitation may go back for generations and continue for many days. When the hearing is concluded and the judge is about to proclaim his decision, "mouth-opening money" (kha-hbyed-rdsas) of one to twenty silver dollars should be paid to him or his proxy (gzug-pa). One convicted of homicide would be sentenced to pay the "life-price" as given above, a penalty with an element of compulsion not following arbitration. In suits as to property rights and the like winner and loser have both to pay fines to the authority for the trouble caused to the judge.

After the sentence the parties involved should pay "conclusion money" or "mouth-closing money" (gzu-tshar) to balance the "mouth-opening money".

In addition to the fixed amount of the fine there is usually a demand for so many *Khathos*; each *Khatho* may range from 40, 60, to 80 strings of copper coins. The fixed fine cannot be changed. But the number and the size of *Khathos* is open to bargain. This system of *Khatho* accompanies not only litigation but also mediation.

Fines and presents go to the authority, either a chieftain or monastery. "Mouth-opening" as well as "mouth-closing" money and the *Khathos* are put together to be equally divided between the proper authority and the judge.

Besides fines there are the punishments of incarceration in a pit or of exile from the community. A criminal may be fettered and manacled and kept in a pit, both before trial and afterwards by sentence of the court or for failure to pay a fine. An exiled criminal wears a paper hat, puts on woman's clothes, and receives so many stripes before he is driven out.

The examples and rules here cited represent the norm. As is any other branch of culture, there are all sorts of deviations from the norm in Tibetan folk-law. The "Rules of Punishment" promulgated in 1733 by the Manchu Imperial Court may be taken as an attempt to standardize this folk-law by removing authority from the local chieftains and monasteries. Many sections try to reconcile this law with legal conceptions prevalent in other parts of China. As those "Rules" were at least sporadically observed during the Manchu dynasty, it is not without interest to compare them with folk-law existing to-day.

Rules of Punishment for Tibetans

(announced in 1733 by the Manchu Imperial Court)

1. Failure to Participate in Military Expedition when Ordered.

The punishment for *Ch'ienhu* (chieftains over 1,000 families) is a fine of 50 *dso* (*dso*, Tibetan name for mongrel-breed of the yakbull and common cow); for *Paihu* (chieftains over 100 families), 40 *dso*; for centurions, 30 *dso*; and for elders in direct command of tribal forces the penalty provided by military law. For failure to appear at an appointed place and time the punishment for one day's delay is a fine of 7 *dso* for a *Ch'ienhu*, 5 *dso* for a *Paihu*, and 3 *dso* for a centurion. Delay for more than one day is punished by fines calculated on the same basis.

2. Failure to Muster for Attack when Enemy Forces Come.

When enemy forces come to a territory all chieftains and elders in charge should take cattle, sheep, and other properties to a safe spot and order their military forces to appear at the place invaded. Failure to do so is fined on the same scale: 50 *dso* for *Ch'ienhu*, 40 *dso* for *Paihu*, and 30 *dso* for centurions. As soon as these forces have gathered where the territory is encroached upon, their leaders shall devise means and tactics to surround and attack the invaders. Should the elders in direct charge of tribal forces under these chieftains fail to appear, similar fines are levied against them accordingly.

3. Tribal Desertion.

All other tribes in the neighbourhood shall send forces, in appropriate proportion as for military operations, to drive back the deserters. Failure to do so is fined similarly : 50 *dso* for *Ch'ienhu*, 40 *dso* for *Paihu*, and 30 *dso* for centurions.

4. Group Desertion with Arms.

When an armed group of less than twenty people desert their tribe, the other tribesmen should pursue them. Should the deserting group be larger than twenty people, neighbouring tribes shall co-operate in the pursuit by sending people in proportion to the number of deserters and by equipping their pursuers with rations, horses, etc. Failure in such a matter is punished by fines in terms of *dso* : 15 for *Ch'ienhu*, 10 for *Paihu*, and 5 for centurions. At the same time the reasons for such desertion should be reported to higher authorities. Failure to report same is punished by fines in terms of *dso*: 7 for *Ch'ienhu*, 5 for *Paihu*, and 3 for centurions.

5. Pursuing Deserters.

When deserters are pursued, if their leader is killed all his forces and properties belong to the pursuers. If deserters have taken other people's horses away with them half of the booty shall go to the pursuers. If deserters escape the properties taken from them in the pursuit go not to the pursuers but to the masters of the deserters. If the deserters have taken other people's horses and have left their wives and other properties behind the loss should be made good out of the latter. If nothing is left behind there can be no compensation for the loss and the masters of the deserters shall be held responsible for other people's loss.

6. Failure to Attend an Appointed Meeting.

Failure so to attend after due notice is to be fined in terms of *dso*: 13 for *Ch'ienhu*, 10 for *Paihu*, and 5 for centurions. Delay beyond the appointed date is punished by fine according to the number of days, on a similar scale in terms of *dso*.

7. Pasturage Trespass.

Trespass upon the pasturage of other tribes is punished by fine in terms of *dso*: 7 for *Ch'ienhu*, 5 for *Paihu*, and 3 for centurions. If the trespass is committed by commoners the fine is 1 *dso* for one family.

8. Going beyond one's tribal Allotment for Pasturage.

Such roaming is punished by fine in terms of *dso*: 50 for *Ch'ienhu*, 40 for *Paihu*, 30 for centurions, and 10 for elders immediately in charge. In the case of commoners, anybody who sees the offence is entitled to seize their livestock and other properties.

9. Adultery.

For a commoner committing adultery with a commoner's wife the fine is 5 "nines" (nine animals, of horses, *dso*, and cows in various combinations being the unit; see Article 39; 5 "nines" means five times so many animals). The adulteress should be handed to her husband to be put to death. Unless she is killed, her husband cannot get the benefit of the fine, which should be handed to the elder in charge. One guilty of flirting with another woman is fined 3 "nines".

10. Depriving a Commoner of His Betrothed.

For depriving a commoner of his betrothed by marrying her, an elder in charge of the community shall be fined 3 "nines"; a commoner 1 "nine". The girl thus married should be returned to her original fiancé.

11. Whipping in lieu of Payment of a Fine in Animals.

In the case of inability to pay a fine in so many head of cattle 25 strokes count for one head, 50 for two, 75 for three, 100 for four.

12. Oath in lieu of Delivering Animals and Fine for Perjury.

If unable to meet a fine in animals the criminal should on his request be taken by the elder in charge to a man of standing to take an oath to this effect. But after the oath, should it be discovered that he did have the required animals, he should pay the number fined as well as 1 "nine" to the person before whom the oath was taken.

13. Discovery of Stolen Animals.

If the original owner discover his stolen animals, should the thief say that among them there are others given by other people, the latter must be brought to testify. Failing such evidence, the thief should swear an oath. After this oath the original owner may take back whatever belonged to him, without fining the thief.

14. The Sheltering of Robbers by Tribal Chiefs Implying Partnership.

For this crime the *Ch'ienhu* shall be fined 5 "nines", *Paihu* 4 "nines", centurions 2 "nines". For actual robbery the fines are respectively 5 "nines" and 3 "nines" for *Paihu* and centurions. In case robbery or the harbouring of robbers is not confessed, the paternal uncles of those suspected should be required to swear an oath. If such uncles are dead their sons should swear. When chieftains have actually committed robbery they should be deprived of their rank and the people in their charge transferred to other authorities. This being done their property shall not be confiscated (see Articles 17, 50).

15. On Discovering Lost Horses in a Military Expedition.

When lost horses are discovered in a military expedition under government authorities and it is proved that the horses their owner has at the present are other than those he lost, he should be compensated and get back the original animals.

16. To Testify to the Commission of a Crime from Personal Grudge.

For doing this in order to take advantage of a person by getting more animals, *Ch'ienhu* are fined 2 "nines", *Paihu* 1 "nine", and centurions 5 animals. The animals so got should be returned to their owner.

17. Failure to Reveal Robbers.

For failure to reveal robbers to proper authorities in order to protect the criminal the fine is 3 "nines" for *Ch'ienhu*, 2 "nines" for *Paihu*, and 1 "nine" for centurions (cf. Articles 14, 50).

18. Refusal to be Searched.

To search for theft is to look for evidence and witnesses. If a person refuses to be searched, theft is considered proved.

19. On Discovering Suspicious Traces.

When responsibility for territory is handed over and suspicious traces are discovered within three days' pasturage, the person who has handed over responsibility should swear an oath.

20. *Theft of Domestic Animals.*

For the theft of such domestic animals as dogs and pigs, the fine is 5 animals (v. Article 39); for the theft of fowls, a three-year old cow. The animal stolen should be returned. (Tibetans do not keep fowls as domestic animals. This item must be either an oversight on the part of the Manchu authorities or a reference to dealings with non-Tibetan neighbours).

21. *Theft of Other Articles.*

For the theft of gold, silver, sable, otter-skin, hides, money, cloth, food, etc., there should be a return of equal value. Fines for these thefts are to be regulated according to the value of the goods—3 "nines" for a two-and-half years' old cow; 1 "nine" for a sheep; and a three-year-old cow for any animal of less value than a sheep.

22. *Other Suspicious Traces.*

When any other suspicious trace is within one arrow's distance of the residence of the suspect he should swear an oath. When it is beyond that distance no oath is required.

23. *On the Secret Slaughtering of Animals.*

When somebody has killed another's animals and removed them, the guilty person should pay in compensation their exact value. When it is within the range of suspicion the elder in charge should swear an oath. Refusal to swear is to be taken as a proof of guilt and the offender is fined.

24. *On Informing the Proper Authority of Other Person's Crime.*

One who does this voluntarily is entitled to get half the value of the fine imposed.

25. False Report of Theft.

One falsely reporting the theft of animals discovered to be hidden is fined 3 "nines". This fine is to be divided equally between the elder in charge and the person falsely charged (cf. Article 61).

26. Making Fire to Burn Wild Animals out of Their Lairs.

Whoever discovers anyone making a fire to drive wild animals out of their lairs as a form of hunting may fine the hunter 1 "nine". Damage to other animals because of such fires should be compensated similarly. Loss of life should justify a fine of 3 "nines". For fires caused by carelessness anyone in sight is entitled to fine the guilty 5 animals (v. Article 39). Full compensation is to be paid for animals killed by such careless fires. For the loss of one human life the fine is 1 "nine" (cf. Article 39).

27. On the Careless Handling of Arms.

Fines for the careless handling of arms without justifiable causes are: 2 "nines" for *Ch'ienhu*, 1 "nine" for *Paihu*, 7 animals for centurions, 5 animals for lesser centurions, and 3 animals for lesser elders and commoners.

28. Injury in Personal Fights

The fine for injury to the eye, hand, foot, etc., in personal fights is 3 "nines"; if the injury is slight enough to be cured the fine is 1 "nine". There is the same fine for injury caused by abortion. For injury caused by stick, whip, and fists the fine is 5 animals. There is no fine when the fight is mutual. If teeth are broken the fine is 1 "nine". When hair is torn off the fine is 5 animals (cf. Article 68).

29. Death Caused Unintentionally.

When death is caused from unintentional injury, such as in play, the family of the victim shall receive a fine of 3 "nines" from the person who caused it.

30. Injury to Other People's Animals.

When an animal is injured to death, one is fined 1 "nine", in addition to paying the full value of the beast to its owner. If a horse is shot and killed unintentionally, two horses should be given in compensation. If the horse be injured but does not die, the compensation is a two-year old cow.

31. On Reporting Loss of Animals to Community Elders.

One should report three days after the loss of animals to the community elders, who will try to recover them and receive one sheep for every horse, yak, or *dso*. Anyone riding such a lost animal shall be fined three animals. One who falsely claims possession of such an animal is to be fined 3 "nines" ; for a mistaken claim the fine is 1 "nine". The finder of stray animals is entitled to their keep. Should one try to hide them, however, the fine is 1 "nine".

32. Catching Stray Animals.

A passer-by cannot seize a stray animal. Should he do so he is to be fined for theft. So for every twenty sheep kept overnight the fine is one sheep. For any number above that the amount of fine is increased proportionately.

33. On the Private Settlement of Crime.

A criminal and the tribe in which he takes refuge cannot settle a crime privately. For disobedience to this rule a *Ch'ienhu* incurs a fine of 3 "nines" ; a *Paihu*, 2 "nines" ; a centurion, 1 "nine" ; a lesser centurion, 7 animals ; a lesser elder or commoner, 5 animals. On discovering the criminal the tribal authority should have him sent to the tribe in which the crime was committed for proper trial. Failure to send him after two days incurs a fine of one three-year-old cow for every day, to be exacted from the guilty tribe. If there is failure to deliver ten days after settlement, the fine for *Ch'ienhu* is 7 *dso*, *Paihu* 5 *dso*, and centurions 3 *dso*. If the animals delivered as a fine are forcibly taken back by the guilty party he shall be fined double the original amount. Failure to settle a case shall be reported to higher authorities.

34. Failure to Give Hospitality.

For refusal to give shelter to travellers, who in consequence starve or freeze to death, an offender in addition to responsibility for the loss of life is to be fined 1 "nine". If the traveller does not die, the offender is fined one two-year old cow.

35. Contagious Disease.

A traveller with contagious disease may not sell personal articles to a landlord. For any such sale he is fined : a sale which results in the death of the purchaser justifies a fine of 3 "nines" ; if the purchaser falls ill, the fine is 1 "nine" ; if he does not, the fine is one animal.

36. Insult to Tribal Authorities.

A commoner who insults a *Ch'ienhu* to his face is fined 2 "nines" ; a *Paihu*, 1 "nine" ; a centurion, 7 animals. If insult behind his back is proved, the fine should be on the same scale. Insult to a lesser centurion justifies a fine of 5 animals ; to a lesser elder, 3 animals.

37. Failure to Appoint an Elder for Every Ten Families.

For every ten families an elder shall be appointed. Failure by the *Ch'ienhu* to do this incurs a fine of 7 *dso* ; by a *Paihu*, 5 *dso* ; by a centurion, 3 *dso*.

38. On Unjustified Ula Service.

For officers with proper permits, free transportation by horses and yaks called *ula* and a supply of barley and peas for fodder should be offered in accordance with the stages. For failure to supply fodder a fine has to be paid in cattle. Failure to supply ula is fined 3 "nines". Should horses be hidden to avoid this service the fine is 1 "nine". If people without proper permits make such demands the tribal elders shall arrest them and hand them over to the authorities at Siningfu for punishment. Should the tribal elder maltreat certified officers the fine is 3 "nines". If a commoner maltreats such officers the fine shall be 1 "nine".

39. Official Proportion of a Fine in Different Animals.

One "nine" means a combination of nine animals such as 2 horses, 2 *dso*, 2 cows, 2 three-year-old cows, 1 two-year-old cow. "Five Animals" means 1 *dso*, 1 cow, 1 three-year-old cow, and 2 two-year cows. The person who comes to demand these fines is entitled to receive as his fee 1 three-year-old cow from the guilty. In places where horses are not plentiful *dso* may be offered in their stead.

40. On Returning Home from an Expedition without Awaiting Proper Turn.

In a military or hunting expedition each band should await its proper turn to withdraw. A *Ch'ienhu* who returns home without awaiting his proper turn is to be fined 7 *dso* ; a *Paihu*, 5 *dso* ; a centurion, 3 *dso*; anyone accompanying them, his own riding horse.

41. Military Discipline.

For defeat in a military expedition *Ch'ienhu*, *Paihu*, and centurions are to be deprived of their respective rank. A commoner shall suffer capital punishment and the loss of his family and property. Anybody, whether chieftain or commoner, who advances to defeat an enemy is to be rewarded. When a chieftain of any tribe is about to lose a fight, any elder coming to his assistance to save the situation shall be rewarded by being given fifty families to rule which formerly belonged to the chieftain he rescues from defeat. In a joint undertaking, when others are still engaged in fighting, those *Ch'ienhu*, *Paihu*, and centurions who withdraw first shall be stripped of their titles and become commoners, and their subjects shall be given as a reward to those who continue to fight. When a tribe loses half its forces and cannot advance the tribal chieftain is not punished for defeat. But defeated elders shall be stripped of their titles and become commoners and their subjects shall be given as a reward to elders undefeated. Should one tribe be ready and start to fight while other tribes are not ready at the proper time, the tribe first ready shall be rewarded for merit. In advancing to meet enemy forces in the open those *Ch'ienhu*, *Paihu*, centurions, and lesser elders who do not observe the order of advance, or seeing the enemy forces not strong advance rashly without ascertaining the real situation, shall have their riding horses taken away and shall not get any share of the victor's booty. All forces should keep the order of march, slow or fast, in accordance with the demand of the situation. For hiding behind another column, or leaving one's own column to join another, or standing by without assisting those busily engaged in fighting, capital punishment, confiscation of one's family, the loss of titles, or fine is the penalty, according to circumstances. When all columns are together, any question as to whether one was ahead or another behind shall not be investigated. When enemy forces are retreating, mounted soldiers should be sent in pursuit, but the leaders in charge, whose duty is to keep the flags in order to direct the operation, should not go ahead in pursuit. If the pursuing force meets with an ambush or enemy reinforcements these leaders should rally other soldiers for the attack. All commanders shall instruct their subordinates to keep their place in any military advance by punishing any uproar, anybody going back for things forgotten, or any drunkard. Anybody seeing this sort of disorder may arrest the guilty and report to the commander in charge to receive a reward of one *dso*. Those who cause a fire shall be beheaded. Those who steal saddles, reins, and the like shall be whipped. During a military march by night no shout or bugle-blowing is allowed. Any disobedience of this sort shall be punished. Those who keep secretly in custody an enemy's wives shall bring upon their commander a proper punishment. No monastery shall be destroyed or looted. Orderly travellers should be cared for and the disorderly killed. The clothes of captives shall not be taken away. Married couples shall not be separated. No commander or commoner shall allow captives to keep watch over horses, and anyone violating this rule shall be punished as if the horses were stolen. A commander shall make every effort to maintain peace and order, to pacify the natives, and to keep his subordinate officers from doing any doing any harm to the common people. To keep this rule brings upon him reward if a memorial is sent to the Imperial Court, but violation of this rule for self-aggrandisement shall be heavily punished. When anybody falls in battle and another pulls him to safety on his horse, there shall be a reward from the person thus saved. The reward differs according as the saviour is a *Ch'ienhu* or a *Paihu*, etc. *Ch'ienhu* gets 10 *dso*; a *Paihu*, 8 *dso*; a centurion, 5 *dso*; lesser elder or a commoner, 2 *dso*.

42. Failure to Arrest a Fugitive (from Justice or Military Service).

For seeing a fugitive and allowing him to escape without arrest, a *Ch'ienhu* is deprived of 7 families in his domain; a *Paihu*, of 5 families; a centurion, of 3 families; a lesser centurion is fined 4 "nines"; a lesser elder or a commoner, 3 "nines". Should one get killed in an attempt to arrest a fugitive, one's family gets the benefit of a slave and 3 "nines" from the fugitive, if he has any. Failing this the tribal chief in charge of the fugitive shall pay a fine of 3 "nines" to the victim's family.

43. Supplying a Fugitive with a Horse.

Any tribal chieftain, whether in direct charge or not, who supplies a horse to a fugitive to facilitate his escape shall be deprived of his titles and his subjects. Lesser centurions and elders shall have their titles taken away and their family property confiscated. A commoner shall suffer capital punishment and confiscation of his family property.

44. On Capturing Fugitives.

When a fugitive is captured his master shall pay the captor a two-year-old cow and give the fugitive 100 stripes. A person who harbours a fugitive shall be fined 1 "nine", to be given to his master; the family head of the person who has given this refuge shall be fined 1 "nine", to be given to his immediate elder of ten families.

45. On Delivering an Arrested Fugitive.

When a fugitive is arrested irrespective of the tribe in which the arrest has been made, he should be sent to Siningfu within two days of arrest. Any delay beyond two days on the part of a *Ch'ienhu* shall bring upon him a fine of 7 *dso*; a *Paihu*, 5 *dso*; a centurion, 3 *dso* (cf. Article 64).

46. On Killing a Fugitive without Reporting to the Proper Authorities.

Should an outside fugitive be killed without report to the proper authorities, a *Ch'ienhu* shall be deprived of 7 families in his domain; a *Paihu*, of five; a centurion, of three. If a tribesman reveals the offence, a *Ch'ienhu* shall be fined 7 *dso*; a *Paihu*, 5 *dso*; a centurion, 3 *dso*; and these animals shall be given to the informant, who shall be free to choose any other tribe to live in. Should a chieftain not confess, his paternal uncle should swear to his innocence. Should a lesser elder or a commoner kill the fugitive the principal criminal shall be beheaded, together with a fine of 3 "nines"; his partners shall each be fined 3 "nines"; and these animals shall go to the elder, who gives the information. If an informant is not a tribal elder, half the fine goes to the government and half to the informant. If a tribal elder kills a fugitive, the principal criminal shall be hanged and his partners shall be deprived of their titles and be each fined 3 "nines".

47. Robbery by Tribal Chieftains.

For robbery a *Ch'ienhu* shall, in addition to the return of things robbed, be fined 50 *dso*; a *Paihu*, 40 *dso*; a centurion, 30 *dso*. If the person robbed is also hurt with weapons, he should receive half a "life-price", namely 2 "nines"; and the chieftain is also fined in addition, as indicated above. Such a fine goes to the person robbed, whether injured or not. When robbery involving murder is committed by a lesser elder or a commoner in partnership with others, the robbers, irrespective of dominant or secondary roles, shall be beheaded, and their families and properties confiscated for the benefit of the victim's family. Should a lesser elder or a commoner in co-operation with several partners try to rob and should this be discovered, so that a party start to drive the robbers away and any of the pursuers gets hurt in the fight, the robbers, irrespective of dominant or secondary roles, shall be beheaded and their families and properties be confiscated for the benefit of the injured. If a lesser elder or a commoner starts a robbing party in co-operation with others without hurting any person, the leader of the party and his friend who has given him the idea shall be hanged and their families and properties shall be confiscated; their followers shall each receive 100 stripes and be fined 3 "nines" for the benefit of the family robbed (cf. Article 67).

48. On Stealing Four Kinds of Animals.

When horse, camel, sheep, or cattle are stolen by anyone, whether master or servant, he shall be hanged. When the theft is committed by two people, one shall be beheaded; when by three, two shall beheaded; when by many, two of the leaders shall be beheaded. The rest shall be given 100 stripes and be fined 3 "nines". When a thief is captured by a householder or any other person he may be beheaded and his wife, children, and property be confiscated for the benefit of the victim of the loss. When there is any doubt as to identity, the suspect shall swear an oath. If he swears, it shall be proof of his innocence, and there shall be no punishment. If the suspect refuses to swear, he shall be beheaded, his wife shall not be enslaved, but his livestock shall be confiscated for the benefit of the victim of the loss. If a master voluntarily reports the theft of his servant, he is held to be innocent. The thief is beheaded, his wife is not enslaved, but all his livestock shall be handed over to the victim of the theft.

49. Non-participation in the Pursuit of a Detected Criminal.

For such non-participation resulting in the criminal's escape a *Ch'ienhu* shall be fined 5 "nines"; a *Paihu* 4, "nines"; a centurion, 3 "nines".

50. On Harbouring Robbers after Denial on Oath.

When after his denial on oath evidence of looting is discovered in a tribal chief's place and he does not admit harbouring, his paternal uncle should swear to his innocence. Failing such an oath a *Ch'ienhu* shall be fined 5 "nines"; a *Paihu*, 4 "nines" ; a centurion, 2 "nines"; and elder of ten families, 1 "nine".

51. On Loot Taken from a Robber by Another Person.

When loot is taken from a robber by another, the original owner shall pay him a reward of one animal for every 2–10 animals recovered. Should only one animal be recovered no reward is required. If an owner would escape payment by saying that his animals were not stolen or robbed, his immediate tribal elder shall affirm on oath the truth of his plea and quit him of liability to pay. Failing an oath the reward must be paid. If a person falsely claims a reward for recovering from a robber animals he only found, he shall be punished for theft.

52. On the Custody of Thieves in the Hands of Their Tribal Chiefs.

When thieves are captured they shall be given to their tribal chiefs for custody. Their immediate elders of ten families shall be fined one *dso*.

If these elders voluntarily reveal a theft they shall be rewarded with the fine exacted from the thieves.

53. On the Escape of Criminals from Custody.

Should a criminal to be beheaded escape from the custody of a lesser centurion the fine is 3 "nines"; if from the custody of lesser elders, 2 "nines" and the deprivation of titles; if from a commoner, he gets 80 stripes. If the criminal is not to be beheaded, a lesser centurion shall be fined 2 "nines" for his escape; a lesser elder, 1 "nine"; a commoner shall get 60 stripes. When an escaped criminal is captured by anybody, the fine to be exacted from the custodian shall be his captor's reward. If a fugitive criminal is not captured the fine exacted from his custodian shall be given to the tribal chief.

54. On Forcibly Removing a Criminal from Custody.

When a criminal to be beheaded is taken by force from custody by a group of people, the leader shall be beheaded and his partners shall each be fined 1 "nine". For forcibly freeing lesser criminals a leader shall be fined 3 "nines" and his partners each 1 "nine".

55. On Arson for a Personal Grudge.

Should a tribal chief set fire to property to cause death for personal vengeance he shall be hanged, and his family with the exception of his wife shall be confiscated for the benefit of the victim's family. Should the guilty be a commoner he shall be beheaded and his family similarly confiscated. If the fire caused the death not of man but of animals a guilty chief shall be deprived of titles and his family similarly confiscated. Should the guilty person be a commoner he shall receive 100 stripes and his family be similarly confiscated.

56. On Torturing Slaves and Servants.

When a slave or a servant is tortured with shots of arrows, cuts of a sword, or mutilation of ear or nose, the guilty *Ch'ienhu* shall be fined 4 "nines"; a *Paihu*, 3 "nines"; a centurion, 1 "nine"; a lesser elder or commoner, 7 animals. If a slave or a servant is tortured to death, punishment shall be meted out according to the scale for wilful murder.

57. *False Claim of Horses.*

Whoever falsely claims the horses of a traveller as his own stray animals shall be fined 5 animals to be given to the traveller.

58. *On Divorcing a Wife.*

When a wife is divorced all her dowry, except articles worn out during cohabitation, shall be returned to her.

59. *On Restricting Travelling among distant Tribes.*

No Tibetan should travel far beyond the frontier into the territory of Mongolian, Mohammedan, and other barbarian tribes for the purpose of trade or visits to relatives. Knowing this rule and doing nothing to stop such travel, a *Ch'ienhu* in charge shall be fined 50 *dso*; a *Paihu*, 40 *dso*; a centurion, 30 *dso*; a lesser centurion, 2 "nines" being deprived of his titles; an elder of ten families shall be fined 1 "nine" and suffer 100 stripes. The leader of the party shall be hanged and his property confiscated. Other members of the party shall each receive 100 stripes and be fined 3 "nines". The confiscated properties go to the treasure of the government. Failure of frontier guards to arrest such a party, if reported, entails loss of titles and property for their commander; his subordinates shall each receive 100 stripes and be fined 3 'animals'. Their property also goes to the government treasury. The person who reports such a misdeed to the authorities shall be rewarded with half the animals exacted as fines and shall be free to choose a place to live in.

60. *On Arresting an Escaped Slave.*

When a slave has escaped to other territory and is arrested there, a captor who sends him back to his master shall receive as reward half the things found with the slave. The other half goes to the master, and the slave shall receive 100 stripes.

61. On Secretly Reporting the Whereabouts of Lost Animals.

When there is a secret report of the whereabouts of lost animals which are later found at the spot stated, the informant shall be tried as a thief (cf. Article 25).

62. On Serious Crime not Confessed.

When a crime involving capital punishment is not confessed by a suspect and there is insufficient evidence to convict him he should swear an oath.

63. On the Murder of a Master by a Slave.

When a master is murdered by a slave, the murderer shall be put to death by mutilation.

64. On Forwarding an Arrested Criminal.

The transfer to the proper authority of an arrested criminal from another territory entitles the person performing the task to a piece of brocade and six pieces of cloth (cf. Article 45).

65. On Importing Arms from Chinese Territory.

When a customs officer finds arms bought from Chinese territory without report to the proper authority, the offender, if a *Ch'ienhu*, shall be fined 3 "nines"; if a *Paihu*, 2 "nines"; if a centurion, 1 "nine"; if a lesser centurion, 7 animals; if a lesser elder, 5 animals; if a commoner, he shall receive 80 stripes. The arms thus discovered shall be confiscated by the government.

66. On Stealing the Animals of a Lama.

The thief who has stolen the animals of a lama shall have his family property confiscated by the government.

67. On the Killing of his Pursuer by a Thief.

Should a thief kill his pursuer he shall be fined 9 "nines" (cf. Article 49).

68. On Killing in Personal Fights.

When one kills another in a fight the offender shall be fined 9 "nines" (cf. Article 28).

Note

1. Though the eight-item regulations in Korea are attributed to Chitze in 1121 B.C., the most frequent contact between China and Korea was in the seventh century A.D. Of the eight items, only three are mentioned by Ma Tuanlin in his famous study of *Institutional History* (Wenhsien T'ungk'ao): capital punishment for murder, compensation in grain for injury, slavery for theft. But Japanese histories attribute "Seventeen Articles of the Constitution" to Prince (taishi) Shotoku in the seventh century A.D.; they may be summarized thus: (1) harmonious relations among men; (2) refuge in the Buddha, Dharma, and Sangha; (3) obedience to imperial orders; (4) propriety among ministers; (5) just litigation without greediness; (6) punishment and reward to deter the wicked and encourage the good; (7) proper division of labour to suit individual qualities; (8) early attendance at the court and late adjournment; (9) sincerity as the basis of righteousness; (10) tolerance for individual differences; (11) discernment of merit and demerit in making rewards and punishments; (12) no unauthorized taxation by officials; (13) as colleagues know each other's duties, there should be no neglect of affairs if an official is ill or absent on leave; (14) no jealousy among officials toward one another; (15) friendly co-operation as a result of unselfishness; (16) timely employment of people in order not to hurt their occupation; (17) consultation with the many in affairs of importance.

JOSEPH MINATTUR

The Nature of Malay Customary Law

One of the most important chapters in the history of the study of folk law concerns the traditional law found in Indonesia and Malaysia. This law, called adat, *has been thoroughly documented and examined by a series of Dutch legal scholars, some of whom were discussed in an earlier section of this volume.*

In the following essay, the reader will find a eloquent sample of adat. *A notable characteristic of folk law which has not yet been adequately treated concerns its poetic features. Jacob Grimm in his 1816 essay "Von der Poesie im Recht" was one of the very first to point out the poetic features of folk law. However, such features as alliteration, assonance, and internal or end-rhyme rarely survive translation. That is why it is crucial to study folk law in its original language. Actually, poetic features may be a misnomer. In all probability, there was a functional mnemonic reason for such features. It is easier to remember something in rhyme than the same thought in prose. With a written language, such mnemonic aids were no longer needed but were presumably retained for purely esthetic reasons. In any case, many of the adat examples cited in this essay bear the unmistakable marks of maxims or proverbs.*

For other considerations of Malay folk law, see R.J. Wilkinson, Law, Part I. Introductory Sketch, Papers on Malay Subjects *(Kuala Lumpur, 1922), pp. 1–48; Haji Mohamad Din Bin Ali, "Malay Customary Law/Family," Intisari: The Research Quarterly of Malaysia, 2(2) (1965), 33–45; Ahmad B. Mohamad Ibrahim, "Islam Customary Law/Malaysia,"Intisari, 2(2) (1965), 47–73; M.B.* Hooker, ed., Readings in Malay Adat Law *(Singapore: Singapore University Press, 1970);* Hooker, Adat Laws in Modern Malaya *(Kuala Lumpur: Oxford University Press, 1972);* Hooker, "Adat and Islam in Malaya," *in G.W. Bartholomew, ed.,* Malaya Law Review Legal Essays *(Singapore, 1975), pp 164–187.*

Richard Winstedt and P.E. de Josselin de Jong, "A Digest of Customary Law from Sungai Ujong," Journal of the Malayan Branch of the Royal Asiatic Society, *Vol. 27, Pt. 3 (1954), 5–71.*

Reprinted from the *Malaya Law Review*, 6 (1964), 327–354.

Introduction

Malay customary law is called *adat*, a word borrowed from Arabic. *Adat*, in general, means right conduct; and in common usage, it stands for a variety of things all connected with proper social behaviour.[1] Thus it will connote rules of etiquette and the ceremonies prescribed for a particular occasion such as marriage as well as those customs which have "legal consequences".[2] It is in this last sense that the word is generally used in this paper. It has been said:

> A social norm is a customary mode of behaviour—it is what people in a given society are expected by their fellow members to do, not only because such behaviour is usual but also because it is deemed good. The man who upholds the norms will be rewarded by his fellows—with approbation, honours and the like; these are positive sanctions. The man who does not uphold the norms will be punished by negative sanctions. These may take many different forms ranging from minor social sanctions, such as ridicule and refusal to interact with him, to the most extreme—that of ostracism by the community. Economic sanctions such as refusal to cooperate in economic activity and political sanctions such as the depriving of an elected person of one's support and vote may be applied. Legal sanctions are those in which force may be used by a recognised authority.[3]

Attempts have been made to redefine law so that the definition may cover customs which have legal consequences. "A social norm", writes Hoebel, "is legal if its neglect or infraction is regularly met, in threat or in fact, by the application of physical force by an individual or group possessing the socially recognised privilege of so acting".[4] S. Roy would define law as "a body of rules of human conduct, either prescribed by long established usages and customs or laid down by a paramount political power."[5] Sir Arthur Goodhart defined it as "any rule of human conduct which is recognised as being obligatory".[6] Dr. T. O. Elias attempted to improve upon the definition by suggesting that "the law of a given community is the body of rules which are recognised as obligatory by its members".[7]

Writing of Sumatra more than 150 years ago, William Marsden stated:

> There is no word in the language of the island which properly and strictly signifies law; nor is there any person or class of persons among the *Rejangs* regularly invested with legislative power. They are governed in their various disputes, by a set of long-established customs (*adat*) handed down to them from their ancestors, the authority of which is founded on usage and general consent. The Chiefs, in pronouncing their decisions, are not heard to say, "so the law directs," but "such is the custom."[8]

It may be that *adat* will weld the society as sweetly and well by any other name such as *sadachara*[9] or "native law and custom".[10]

Adat Melayu (Malay Custom)

Malay community may be classified under two different groups: one following *adat temenggong* and the other, *adat perpateh*. *Adat perpateh* is adhered to by the Malays inhabiting Negri Sembilan and certain parts of Malacca, especially Naning. Malays in other parts of Malaysia are supposed to follow *adat temenggong*. Though both the *adat* originated from tribal organisations in the past, it is in *adat perpateh* that the remnants of tribal structure are clearly evident at present. To cite one instance, consider exogamy. Marriage between persons belonging to the same clan is regarded as incestuous and is strictly prohibited. Another characteristic of *adat perpateh* is that it adheres to matriliny while *adat temenggong* favours patriliny.

The two *adat* are believed to have been called after two legendary law-givers, Parapatih nan Sa-batang and Kei Tamanggungan. According to the *terombo* (song of origin), familiar to the present day followers of *adat perpateh*, these law-givers held sway over different parts of Minangkabau in Sumatra, Parapatih ruling over the hilly inland region and Tamanggungan governing the coastal region. According to legend, they were half-brothers. Why Parapatih insisted upon matriliny and exogamy for his followers, while his half-brother was inclined to patrilineal descent and endogamy is not known. A legend narrated by Willinck[11] may explain the prevalence of exogamy in *adat perpateh* society, but it does not indicate why it is not followed in *adat temenggong* society. According to the legend, Parapatih, when young, went on a long journey. On his return he married Putri Zamilau, without knowing that she was his half-sister. Later when it was discovered that they were blood relations, Parapatih and Tamanggungan, horrified by the incestuous connection, decided to divide the Minangkabaus into two groups, Koto-Piliang and Bodi-Chaniago, and ruled that no one should marry within his own group. In general it is the *adat perpateh* group which seems to follow its *adat* strictly and therefore it is not unlikely that when the *adat temenggong* group gradually gave up exogamy, the other group adhered to it.

The adherence to matriliny seen in the *adat perpateh* society may also be due to its general tendency to stick to its *adat*. Assuming that matriliny was indigenous to Minangkabau, it is not improbable that the system gained strength from the South Indian settlers who followed a similar rule of descent. But the possibility of its having been introduced into

Minangkabau[12] by South Indians cannot be absolutely ruled out. It could be that the South Indians in Minangkabau were those who followed matriliny in their own native land and they either introduced the system into the country of their adoption or incorporated it with the indigenous system.

As it is the *adat perpateh* society which follows its *adat* scrupulously, when one speaks of Malay *adat*, one is more inclined to think of *adat perpateh* than of *adat temenggong*. Wilkinson wrote in 1908:

> The difference between the adat perpateh and the adat temenggong is visible in these days of British administration. Whenever a miscarriage of justice occurs in Perak, Pahang and Selangor, the Malays take it very calmly; but in the Negri Sembilan the whole population is excited by any non-recognition of the local adat.[13]

This paper concerns itself more with *adat perpateh* as representing Malay customary law than with *adat temenggong*. The digests dealing with *adat temenggong* are "mixed with relics of Hindu law and overlaid with Muslim law."[14] Thus the Malacca Laws (*Undang-Undang Melaka*) though entitled *Risalat Hukum Kanum* (A Tract on Customary Law) is a digest "grafting the Islamic Law of the new Sultanate [of Malacca] on to the earlier law of a Hindu court."[15] One is, therefore, on surer ground in dealing with Malay customary law when such rules of *adat perpateh* as could be gleaned from traditional sayings are selected for discussion.

Basic Laws

It is arguable that even the Austinian definition of law would cover the fundamental rules of the Malay customary law, as they were laid down by the two law-givers, Parapatih and Tamanggungan; they were rules (if one gives credence to their legendary origin,) "set by political superiors to political inferiors."[16] But it may be conceded that the Malays follow their *adat* not merely because it is believed to have been laid down by the law-givers, but also because it is expressive of an instinctive sense of right, of the common consciousness of the people (*Rechtsuberzeugung*).

What the law-givers proclaimed for the observance of their followers may be regarded as the basic rules of the *adat*. Tamanggungan laid down:

> Who casts the net shall jump to drag it in;
> Who commits an offence shall compensate;
> Who owes shall pay; who slays shall be slain.[16a]

The Nature of Malay Customary Law

Parapatih declared:

> A debt adhered to the tribe [clan] of the debtor;
> A mortgage becomes a lien on the tribal land;
> Who wounds shall pay smart-money, who kills shall give restitution.[17]

These by no means seem to have constituted all the rules of conduct followed by the Malay society and generally contained in *kata pesaka* (traditional sayings) or *perbilangan* (customary sayings). According to tradition, these were the laws first formulated. The rest of the customary laws may be regarded as springing from them.

The history of the development of this customary law is not a secret to the Malay. For, as the *perbilangan adat* (customary saying) puts it,

> The old men know tradition,
> The young men hear report.[18]

And the law of the tradition is:

> The pattern becomes the mould;
> The example becomes the type;
> Precept passing into usage,
> Practice passing into custom,
> The custom handed down by our forefathers from generation to generation:
> Transplanted it withers,
> Uprooted, dies.[19]

Here in a few words is summarised the development of traditional or customary law (*kala tua*) which may be distinguished from the custom of the country (*resam negri*) expressed in such sayings as:

> Duty gives and receives again,
> Courtesy repays kindness.[20]

Adat Law and Custom

From the sayings it is not always easy to distinguish between the customs that have legal consequences and those that do not have such consequences. Here again what ascribes legal consequences to a custom is the law of tradition; if, according to tradition, the pattern has become the mould which the clansmen will be interested in maintaining intact with whatever coercive powers they may possess for the purpose, one may assume that that pattern has passed from custom into customary law. It is obvious that when it is said:

> Clansmen of a clan, tribesmen of a tribe,
> With kin both far and near;
> To those afar we hearken,
> Those near we mark and obey.[21]

the hearkening (*di-dengar-dengarkan*) cannot be enforced.

But the rule of exogamy contained in "Our boys we wed to other clans"[22] should not be broken, for a breach would bring in its train dire consequences on the offender. Again, the saying

> A stranger weds into our clan.
> For every stranger that weds into our clan
> A share is set with just consent:[23]

contains a rule of law which will be enforced by the community.

The sayings handed down from generation to generation are known to every one so that in fact ignorance of law cannot be an honest or valid excuse. According to a derisive saw, dull-witted may be the people of Minangkabau, who have no footing on the sea, but they and their kinsmen in Malaysia are smart enough to know and remember their *adat*.

The sayings are simple and can be easily memorised. This memorable quality does not always make for easy comprehension. Thus the pithy saying

> Pound rice in a mortar,
> Cook rice in a pot.[24]

is explained to mean that complaints should be made to the proper court.[25] It is also supposed to imply that punishment must fit the crime.[26] A third explanation given is to the effect that a person should attend to his business in the proper manner.[27]

There is probably no harm if a saying signifies many things, provided all of them are in conformity with the accepted social norms.

In spite of a variety of meanings attributable to some of them, the interpretation of these saws appears to be less difficult than the interpretation of a statute in a common law court; for the interpretation of the saying along with the significance of the metaphor or other figure of speech contained in it is handed down from generation to generation. This recourse to what one might regard as the preparatory work to the enunciation of the rule makes the saying not unduly difficult of understanding.[28]

Constitutional Structure

Adat perpateh appears to envisage a hereditary constitutional monarchy. The ruler of Negri Sembilan, the *Yang di-Pertuan Besar* (one who is acknowledged as the great lord) is, in theory, elected by the *Undangs* of Sungei Ujong, Jelebu, Johol and Rembau. But as Wilkinson observes: "Nowadays the choice of a *Yamtuan*[29] is a foregone conclusion; his election is a mere form".[30] In 1934 when Muhammad Shah died, his son Abdul Rahman succeeded him. All that the *Undang* of Sungei Ujong declared in this connexion on behalf of the four electors at the installation ceremony was that "... This day we have installed Tuanku Abdul Rahman, son of the late Yang di-Pertuan Besar Muhammad Shah, on the Lion Throne of the Kingdom of Negri Sembilan."[31] Neither the matrilineal principle nor the rule of primogeniture is accepted in relation to the succession to the throne. It is up to the electors to choose a younger son of the late *Yang di-Pertuan Besar* in preference to the eldest, if the latter is found unsuitable for the position; but no *Yang di-Pertuan Besar* is elected from outside the royal family.[32] The democratic principle, however, appears to be maintained in the tradition that the *Yamtuan* should marry a woman who is one of his subjects and not of royal descent.[33] The opinion is sometimes expressed that the royal consort should be a member of the Ayer Kaki family of the Batu Hampar clan, the family to which Raja Melewar's wife belonged.[34] But no such rule is considered obligatory at present.[35]

The principle of election is recognised in the choice of the *undang*, the *lembaga* and the *buapa*. The *buapa* is to be elected by the members of his *perut* and approved by the *lembaga* who can dismiss him at will.[36] In the election of the *lembaga*, the principle of *giliran* or *pesaka bergelar*[37] is followed, that is, every *perut* in turn has the right to supply the *suku* chief. The principle thus postulates, as de Moubray puts it, "that each *perut* should have its equality in this matter ensured by being placed as it were on a roster."[38] In Rembau and Naning, the *lembagas* elect the *undangs* by unanimous vote from different *perut*, off shoots of the original Malacca house.[39] In Jelebu, Johol and Sungei Ujong, there are electoral colleges for the election of the *undangs*. Though the principle of election, direct or indirect, is recognised, one finds that the choice for the electors is strictly circumscribed, and, in some instances, as, for example, in the case of the election of the *Undang* of Sungei Ujong, the electors themselves generally have to be members of certain specified families.

No election or dismissal of a *lembaga* is valid until confirmed by the *undang*.[40] A *buapa* may be dismissed at will by the lembaga.[41] In spite of the democratic elements evident in the *adat perpateh* society,[42] one cannot be oblivious of the hierarchical pattern, based on blueness of blood and ancient lineage, in the general social structure.

> A king has his royal annals,
> A chief his genealogical tree,
> A tribal headman [*lembaga*] his song of origin.[43]

This need not be a matter of surprise when one considers that the *adat* originated in a tribal organisation, with its paramount chief, subordinate chiefs, headmen and elders.

This hierarchical set up is evidenced by the saying:

> The king rules his world;
> The chief rules his province;
> The lembaga rules his clan;
> The elder rules his own people;
> The peasant rules his house.[44]

Another saying describes the dignity attributed to the king and the chief:

> The king has majesty, the chief honour;
> The king decrees, the chief orders;
> The king rules the world, the chief rules the clan.[45]

The nature of the jurisdiction of the various dignitaries is expressed in the *perbilangan*:

> The Raja is the fount of equity;
> The Chief carries out the law;
> The cord for arrest is the tribal headman's,
> The execution creese is the territorial chief's,
> The headman's sword is the Raja's—
> He can stab without asking leave of any suzerain,
> He can behead without reporting it to any suzerain.[46]

In spite of his being able to wield the headman's sword (or the sword of execution) he has only limited powers as may be seen from the fact that

The king does not own the soil nor can he levy taxes;
he is the fountain of justice and may levy definite fees for his maintenance.[47]

As a Jelebu saying puts it, "The highroads with their stepping stones belong to the prince and the bulbuls."[48] Any attempt on his part to levy taxes would cause him to be expelled, or in the picturesque language of the traditional saying, he would be cast out upon "a waveless sea and a grassless field."[49]

Under the *keadilan* (the fountain of justice) the jurisdiction of the various chiefs and headmen was well-defined and carefully graded. "In itself", wrote Wilkinson, "the gradation of official powers is no protection of the liberty of the subject. Its effectiveness in Negri Sembilan lay in the fact that the higher authorities were like our own appellate or assize courts: they could not initiate an attack on an individual. If the peasant committed a petty offence, he was judged by his own people: the chief could not interfere. If he was charged with a graver crime, he was heard by his own people and if a *prima facie* case was made out against him, he was handed over to the higher authorities for trial. . . . The (territorial) chief could not proceed against any one except the tribal headman [*lembaga*], nor was he strong enough to attack any single *lembaga* unjustly in face of opposition that such a proceeding would arouse among the rest."[50]

The other members of the hierarchical order also had their allotted position and sphere of influence:

Disputes among their families
Are the province of the elders.
When a husband disputes about the property
Acquired by his own and his wife's joint labour
It is the province of his family.
Within the four threshold beams of his house
Is a husband's province.[51]

Land Tenure

The importance of landed property to an immigrant people like the Minangkabau settlers in the Malay Peninsula cannot be exaggerated, especially when they were given to the felling of trees and the tilling of soil rather than to commercial business. In spite of all the acquisitiveness one might expect of them, the Minangkabau settlers seem to have been guided by a remarkable sense of justice in the acquisition and apportionment of land. According to the customary sayings current in Jelebu,

> When the first clod was upturned
> And the first creeper severed,
> And the first tree felled—
> Our custom and system of entail were not yet established.[52]
> When holding was dovetailed into holding,
> When our stretches of rice-field were made,
> When the shoots of our plants swayed in the breeze,
> When our betel palms grew up in rows
> Then were established our custom and system of entail.[52a]

In determining rights to property, the social position of a person and his lineage are of significance. It is recognised that

> The highroad with its stepping stones
> Belongs to the king.[53]

and

> Stretches of rice-field
> Old betel-nut palms
> Ancestral coconuts
> Belong to the tribal headmen [*lembaga*]
> The path over the knolls in the swamps
> Belongs to the tribal headmen [*lembaga*]
> The Sakai path with its tree-trunk bridges
> Belongs to the clan that owns the soil.[54]

While the land cleared and cultivated by the immigrants was regarded as belonging to them, the aborigines and their heirs whose lands the immigrants had taken possession of also had rights recognised under the *adat*.

> Ravines and valleys
> Hills and hill-bases
> Belong to the territorial tribe and their chief.[55]

The *adat* attempted to be fair to the birds and fishes too.

> The high way with its stepping stones,
> Hills and hill-bases,
> Lonely forest,

> Deep ravines,
> Broad plains,
> Sloping water-courses,
> Belong to the birds,
> Deep pools
> To the fishes.[56]

While the king shared with the birds the highroad with its stepping stones, the *waris* and their chief shared with them the hills and the hill-bases.

As Wilkinson observes, ownership of land was based on real working tenure. The *adat* "did not allow a land lord to lock up valuable land at his own discretion or to exact a heavy tax from would-be workers. To use a homely metaphor, it allowed the dog-in-the-manger to levy toll on the cows to the extent of the value of the manger to the dog, while English law allows toll to be levied to the extent of the value of the manger to the cows."[57]

The *adat* expected its adherents to take good care of their property, for

> Rice-crops unfenced become waste grass,
> Buffaloes unpent become wild cattle.[58]

The conditions of entail are also laid down. When the land bears clear evidence of occupation, it is considered heritable.

> Idle fallow, land with stubble,
> Land with tree-stumps left by the feller,
> Land that has been levelled—
> These can be inherited.[59]

And the inheritance under *adat perpateh* is in the female line.

> Our heritage comes from our women,
> Men wear the insignia of hereditary office,
> The inheritance belongs to the woman,
> The man cherishes it.[60]

As a measure of social security envisaged to prevent a member of the clan ending up landless and homeless, certain restrictions on the alienation of ancestral property were contemplated under the *adat*.

The woman's nearest of kin can approve or prevent;
The full members of the woman's clan elect to find the money;
If there are full members of her clan, they can subscribe to save the tail;
If there are next of kin, they can bar the sale;
If the property in question has an owner already, the sale cannot proceed;
The tribal headman can quash the sale.[61]

Husband's Position

Contrary to popular belief, this system of inheritance does not mean that the husband is under a petticoat government in the *adat perpateh* society. His high position in the family is guaranteed to him under the *adat*.

> Within the four threshold beams of his house
> Is a husband's province.[62]

His importance in the home is again acknowledged in the saying

> Slaves can offend against the masters,
> Pupils against their teachers,
> Children against parents,
> Wives against husbands.[63]

This clearly indicates that wives are expected to be obedient and faithful to their husbands. It is also said

> Warder of the wife is the husband.
> Warder of the husband his wife's family.[64]

Because the wife's family happens to be his warder, a husband may occasionally find himself in certain unenviable situations:

> When a man marries and goes to his wife's family,
> If clever, he will be a friend in council;
> If a fool, he will be ordered here and there.
> A tall man, he will be as a sheltering buttress,
> Prosperous he will be as a laden branch that gives shade.
> The married man must go or stay as he is bid.[65]

It is also said,

> A bridegroom among his wife's relations
> Is like a soft cucumber among spiny *durian*;
> If he rolls against them, he is hurt,
> And he's hurt, if they roll against him.[66]

If he follows the customs of his wife's family and makes himself useful, he may find his life among his wife's relations not too unhappy, though,

> If a fool, he will be ordered about
> To invite guests distant and collect guests near.[67]

but,

> If he is strong, he shall be our champion.[68]

A fool's position may hardly be better elsewhere.

The husband among his wife's relations is naturally expected to observe the customs of their family:

> When you enter a byre, low;
> When you enter a goat's pen, bleat;
> Follow the customs of your wife's family.
> When you tread the soil of a country and live beneath its sky,
> Follow the customs of that country.[69]

It would not be fanciful if one assumed that the position of the man in a matrilineal society should be more than enviable. Though matrilocal residence of the wife and the customary requirement that the husband should live in the wife's home may bring in certain problems of human relations, especially in his association with the in-laws, one cannot overlook the fact that he has his 'province', his sphere of influence and power within the four threshold beams of his house, and that he also has a cherished place in his own family and clan. In his capacity as uncle or brother, he may be the manager of the family and it is not unlikely that he is or he becomes an elder or chief in his clan.

Even when he suspects a shade of unfairness, he should be philosophical enough to console himself with the thought that

> The hap of this life goes by turns,
> A while to him, anon to me,[70]

This is specially relevant. If his wife's male relations forget that "courtesy repays kindness" (*Berbudi orang berbahasa kita*) the relatives of their own wives may be equally forgetful of the adage.

If the wife's relations exercise some control over him, it seems to be justified for two reasons. The well-being of the family is mainly their concern, and it is their responsibility to see that the husband of their sister or niece contributes to that well-being. Further, they have taken upon themselves a good deal of responsibility for him. For the *adat* stipulates

> To unravel disputes,
> To pick up the fallen and search for the lost,
> To pay debts and receive dues
> Is the business of a man's wife's family.[71]

For this extreme solicitude envisaged in the requirement about picking up the fallen and searching for the lost, the price he pays in the inconvenience of his being ordered about, if he be a fool, is small in comparison with the value of the benefits he receives. *Noblesse oblige*. All that the *adat* seems to enjoin on him in return, apart from attending to his duties in his new surroundings, is that he should pay due regard to the customary law of marriage which stipulates:

> Two familiar spirits in one household,
> Two ladders to one sugar-palm,[72]
> Sprouts without seed[73]
> Are offences against morals.
> Custom looks for signs of guilt;
> When custom declares the offence proved,
> It is not a peccadillo to be mildly corrected.
> Nor can recourse be had to religious law
> For this crime of taking two brides when a man has been given one.[74]

Whatever discomforts he may consider himself to be put to by his wife's relations, the *adat* prescribes a fair distribution of property between the husband and the wife, if a divorce is decided upon.

> What a man has got by his wife remains with her clan,
> What the husband brought goes back to him;
> Property in partnership is split up,
> The common property acquired by a man and wife's joint labour is equally divided;
> Any loss or profit on the wife's estate is a matter for her clan;
> The man's person is restored to his own clan.[75]

The husband's absence of independence among his wife's relations does not seem to deprive him of his rights to a fair share when there is a division of property. After all,

What is the custom of the land?
Duty gives and receives again.[76]

Administration of the *Adat*

The Malay, in general, is not a litigious person. When he happens to be a litigant, he appears to be unhappy about it. It is said,

Victory—a defeated foe,
defeat—a bowed head,
agreement—a joining of hands.[77]

What he likes to do when conflicts arise is expressed in the saying:

The injured is made whole,
The tangled is made straight.[78]

The injured is made whole by applying the customary remedy which in most cases, especially in *adat perpateh society*, consists in awarding compensation.

In a tribal society such as the one envisaged by the *adat*, arbitration plays a very important role. Petty disputes were referred for arbitration to the village elder. Only when arbitration failed or when the dispute was serious enough to require stronger measures were the services of the *lembaga* sought. He could make an arrest and if found necessary or expedient, hand the offender over to the *undang* who could command the use of the execution creese.

Small matters are the place for arbitration,
great for the application of custom,
the most weighty for ancient ancestral right.[79]

Though no doctrine of judicial precedent, as applied in common law jurisdictions, is recognised under the *adat*, the phrase *menchari adat* (search for the custom) is significant in that a search for a precedent remedy is usually made. The saw is

A day of loss is a day of search,
The hurt is healed, the wound is stanched.[80]

The judges are usually the village elders or the chiefs of the clans who uphold the norms of their society. As they are not bound by precedent, though a precedent may have great persuasive value, it is not difficult for them to reinterpret the *adat* in the light of modern needs. The sayings in which the *adat* rules are couched may be reinterpreted in such manner as to suit present day conditions. As interpretation of *perbilangan* has not been developed into an esoteric science, there will be no serious objection to reinterpretation which is intended to keep pace with the times. One could therefore argue that customary law needs no modification. Whatever modification is necessary is being made in the application of the *adat* by those who are interested in upholding the norms of their community. Until the *adat* rules are written down and the meanings of words and phrases quibbled over by lawyers conversant with the interpretation of modern statutes there will be no need for the modification of these rules, as they are easily adaptable to the demands of rapid social changes.[81]

Though a search is made for a precedent, there may be a few cases for which no precedent can be found. In such a situation, the procedure followed by the *Rejangs* in Sumatra is described by Marsden.

> It is true that, if any case arises, for which there is no precedent on record (of memory), they deliberate and agree on some mode that shall serve as a rule in future similar circumstances. If the affair be trifling, that is seldom objected to; but when it is a matter of consequence, the *pangeran or kalippah* (in places where such are present) consults the *proattins* or lower order of chiefs who frequently desire time to consider of it, and consult with the inhabitants of their *dusun*. When the point is thus determined, the people voluntarily submit to observe it as an established custom . . .[82]

This procedure in its essentials seems to have been adopted in Malaysia too, though no case is known where the inhabitants of a *mukim* were consulted before laying down a principle for its decision; but, it may be assumed that the elders or chiefs who act as judges are aware of the common consciousness of the people. When once the law is 'discovered', it is applied in the same way as

When a coat is ready, it is put on,
When a mould is there, the metal is poured in.[83]

A good judge is he who is killed in the art of the wriggling lizard,[84] and not one who will automatically apply a precedent remedy without taking trouble to make a cautious and thorough inquiry. Like the wriggling lizard which climbs slowly from the foot to the top of a tree, the judge should proceed carefully and cautiously, not unwilling to retrace his steps when his line of inquiry has been found wrong.

> Astray at the end of the track—
> Back to the start of the track,
> Astray at the end of the talk—
> Back to the start of the talk.[85]

A method of inquiry that is discountenanced by the *adat* is that of insufficient discrimination and is described as the judgment of the thrusting fish trap *(hukum serkap)*, for, a cone-shaped trap when thrust down in shallow water may enclose indiscriminately a myriad catch of fish.[86]

Under *adat perpateh*, circumstantial evidence is preferred to oral evidence tendered by witnesses.

> Change a sarong behind the house,
> Change a word behind the tongue.[87]

It is easier to commit perjury than to change clothes; no built-up privacy is required for the feat.

> Customary law requires signs of guilt,
> Religious law calls for witnesses.
> When religious law meets circumstances obscure,
> It throws wide its net to catch the offender...
> 'There is a clear case' says custom,
> When there is evidence of guilt and information laid,
> When a man is chased from the scene of the crime and is found panting,
> When there are hacks and cuts;
> If evidence be at hand, it requires to be shown it,
> If it be not at hand, it requires it to be related.[88]

When there is no such clear case, circumstancial evidence is relied upon and becomes more significant. In relation to the laws of theft, twelve circumstances are forbidden.[88a] They range from being found with booty snatched or stolen by force to being found with fluttering heart. In this reliance placed on circumstantial evidence, it is probable that mere coincidence will be mistaken for cause and effect.

> The branch breaks as the hornbill passes.[89]

The purpose of the *adat* in accepting circumstantial evidence may have been that men should be encouraged to walk warily, avoiding suspicious proximities.[90] After all, *adat* is approved behaviour, apart from its being customary *law*.

What is contemplated under the *adat* is perfect, even-handed justice.

> The quart measure that is full,
> The gallon measure that is true,
> The weight that is just,
> The scales that are even.[91]

The compensation to be paid for a wound would vary according to the intensity of the provocation and also according to the place where it was inflicted—in the language of the *adat*, whether it "grows on the hill, on the slope or in the valley." (*tumboh di-bukit, di-lereng, di-lembah*) that is, on the head, on the body or on the leg.[92]

The saying

> It is forbidden by custom
> To conceal and abet.
> It is approved by custom
> To bring to light and compare facts.[93]

indicates the high sense of civic duty the Minangkabau settlers possessed. To conceal and abet would be socially dangerous acts and the *adat* forbids them in the interests of social justice and general well-being.

Restitution rather than retribution was the keynote of the humane administration of criminal justice under the *adat*.[94] But this statement should not be taken to imply that all offences were compoundable. Incest was punishable by death and was usually punished with outlawry and confiscation of property.[95]

The requirement in the *adat* that there should be absolute unanimity for every decision and every election may have been induced by the concept of *laras*, (harmonious, belonging together).

> The greatness of men lies in taking counsel together;
> ...As a bamboo conduit makes a round jet of water,
> So taking counsel together rounds men to one mind.[96]

The imposition of a decision of the majority might leave the minorities discontent, while a unanimous decision would make every one feel a sense of harmony, a feeling of belonging together. This requirement of unanimity was probably desirable and certainly effective during the days of close-knit clan organisations.

Conclusion

One of the versions of the *terombo* has the line:

Adat sentosa di-dalam negeri.[97]
(Custom brought peace on the land).

This appears to have been the purpose of the *adat*—to bring peace and harmony induced by a sense of justice. And this purpose was achieved by letting covenants develop into customs.

What in the beginning are covenants
Grow up into customs;
Custom is lord over covenants.
Water proceeds along water-ways,
Sanction proceeds from covenant;
A country grows up with its customs.[98]

This growth is accelerated by the scrupulous observance of the traditional injunction:

Each shall get his share and portion;
Take ye not the goods of others;
Squander not the children's birthright.[99]

In its pursuit of justice and fair play, the *adat* considers itself to be in harmony with religious law. It declares:

Customary law hinges on religious law,
Religious law on the word of God.
If custom is strong, religion is not upset;
If religion is strong, custom is not upset.[100]

If there is any difference between the two, it is only a difference in emphasis:

Our customary law bids us
Remove what is evil
And give prominence to what is good;
The word of our religious law

Bids us do good
And forbids our doing evil.[101]

If the difference, according to the followers of the *adat*, is so negligible, can there be any serious conflict, in their view, between religion which is ideal law and custom which is real law?[102] If there is no major conflict, why should they be persuaded to forsake their *adat* and adopt a tantalizing hybrid, *adat ketemenggongan?* The Mapillas of North Kerala, a *Sunni* Muslim group, are not regarded any the less Islamic in their life because of their adherence to matriliny. They are predominantly matri-local too.[103]

In the same way as covenants grow up into customs, covenants can destroy custom.[104] An enactment, passed by a majority of votes, can effectuate the destruction more easily still. But it will be harder to retrace one's steps and resurrect the *adat*.

It may be suggested that customary law should be regarded as the common law of the people in those spheres of their lives where it is applicable. To equate "native law and custom" with local customs in England and to treat them as facts to be proved in court does not seem fair, because they deserve to be regarded as common law rather than as local customs. That it is not such a fantastic suggestion as might appear to some may be shown from a decree issued in 1708 by Johan van Hoorn, Governor-General of the Dutch East Indies. He ordered that all civil and criminal matters in the Preanger districts should be decided in the courts of the regents who would render justice according to the local laws. The Dutch officials had only the duty to see that the local laws and customs were faithfully applied and justice impartially administered.[105] Commenting on the decree, a Dutch historian said, "In the Preager there were continuous conflicts between the Batavian and the regency courts but the principle had been stated that the native law would not be superseded by western law."[106]

When the westerner looks at the customary law of the east, he may see it blurred; the kathi, trained in the ways of religion and immersed in Arabic culture, may find it far too worldly for his sympathetic understanding; and one does not learn the rules of Naning games in London's Lincoln's Inn Fields. The only persons who can be expected to have a clear understanding and a proper appraisal of customary law are the traditional leaders of the community. They are interested in maintaining the norms of their community and to them should be entrusted the administration of customary law. They will know how to reinterpret it to keep pace with social changes, changes which their own community has accepted as being relevant to it. Speaking of Yoruba customary law P.C. Lloyd says,

The Nature of Malay Customary Law

Customary law is constantly being reinterpreted to satisfy the needs of a commercial economy; one would use the word *reinterpreted* and not *changed*. Many modern transactions, such as sale, were not illegal a century ago and legal to-day—a century ago they were inconceivable to most Yoruba ... each generation sees its own problems, though the law may remain basically unchanged.[107]

Adat is

Uncracked by the sun,
Unworn by the rain.[108]

Notes

1. Dictionaries give the following meanings, among others, for *adat*: custom, customary law, customary behaviour, proper behaviour, courtesy.

2. C. Snouck Hurgronje, *De Atjèhers* (The Achinese), Vol. I, (Leyden, 1893), at p. 357. To connote the *adat* that has legal consequences, he used the expression "*adatrecht*" in Dutch, which means "*adat law*".

3. P. C. Lloyd, *Yoruba Land Law*, (London, 1962), at p. 14.

4. E. A. Hoebel, *The Law of Primitive Man*, (Cambridge, Mass., 1954), at p. 28.

5. S. Roy, *Customs and Customary Law in British India*, at p. 4.

6. Quoted in T. O. Elias, *The Nature of African Customary Law*, (Manchester, 1956), at p. 53.

7. *Ibid.*, at p. 55.

8. William Marsden, *The History of Sumatra*, (3rd ed., 1811), at p. 217.

9. A Sanskrit word used by text writers to mean approved usage.

10. A term used by British colonial administrators. No distinction was made between law and custom, and as P.C. Lloyd remarks, "it was perhaps not intended to be made." (*op. cit.*, at p. 15).

11. G. D. Willinck, *Het rechtsleven bij de Minangkabausche Maleiers*, (Leyden, 1909), at p. 121.

12. Despite all legends concerning the origin of the name Minangkabau, it is probable that it originally meant the portion (or division) of land allotted to *Menoki* (Malayalam, literally, a superintendent). *Menoki* was also a baronial title in North Kerala. *Menokibhagam* (the chief's or superintendent's portion) could easily have been corrupted to *Minangkabau*. See also the *bau* or *bu* endings in place names like Rembau, Jelebu which may once have been *Rem* (Rama?) *bhaga*, *Jalabhaga*. *Lembaga* originally seems to have meant a territorial division. *Bahagian* in Malay vocabulary indicates that the Sanskrit *bhaga* was not unknown to the Malay world.

If this etymological interpretation be correct, it is possible that the baron and his kinsmen who occupied the fenced area (Pagar Ruyong) and its surroundings followed matriliny, while their local tenants or dependents followed the (indigenous) system of patriliny. It could as well be that while the baron and his kinsmen followed matriliny, those who adhered to patriliny were those of the chief's followers who, though they also came from South India, were given to following the rules of patrilineal descent in their own country. It was only certain sections of the Kerala community (for example, the Nayars, and certain groups of Tiyas and Mapillas) which followed matriliny.

13. Wilkinson, *Law: Introductory Sketch*, in *Papers on Malay Subjects* (Kuala Lumpur, 1908), at pp. 19–20.

14. Winstedt, *The Malays: A Cultural History*, (6th ed., 1961), at p.91.

15. *Ibid.*, at p. 99. See also Haji Mohd. Din bin Ali, "Two Forces in Malay Society", Intisari, Vol. I, No. 3, at p. 15, where he says in regard to the inheritance of Malay holdings in the "Islamic-cum-Temenggong States": "Take away the Hukum Shara and the residual adat which is Temenggong would be beyond recognition. (*ibid.*, at p. 19). He also says: "At present the amalgamation of Islam and the Adat Temenggong is so complete that it is well nigh impossible to separate one from the other." (*ibid.*, at p. 20).

16. *Austin's Jurisprudence*, (1911 Edition), Vol. I, at p. 87.

16a. *Siapa menjala, siapa terjun,*
Siapa salah, siapa bertimbang,
Siapa berutang, siapa membayar;
Siapa bunoh, siapa kena bunoh.

The translation quoted is that of A. Caldecott, "Jelebu Customary Songs and Sayings", Journal of the Straits Branch of the Royal Asiatic Society, (hereinafter abbreviated as J.S.B.R.A.S.), Vol. 78, p. 3, at p. 17. Most of the translations of *perbilangan* in this paper are those of A. Caldecott, J. L. Humphreys, Parr and Mackray, Wilkinson and Winstedt.

17. *Hutang nan berturut, chagar bergadai;*
Chinchang pampas, bunoh beri balas.

This again is from Caldecott's "Jelebu Customary Songs and Sayings". Some versions of the *teromba* (for instance, the one familiar to the people of Naning) contain many more rules. See J. L. Humphreys, "A Naning Recital", J.S.B.R.A.S., Vol. 83, at p. 1. See also Haji Mohd, Din bin Ali, "Two Forces in Malay Society", Intisari, Vol. I, No. 3, at p. 15. I prefer the Jelebu version as laying down the basic law. The various rules given in the Naning version appear to be either elaborations of the basic principles or mere matters of procedure. See below, the section on administration of the *adat*.

18. *Pebilangan pada nang tua-tua,*
Perkhabaran pada nang kechil-kechil.

19. *Berlukis berlambaga,*
Berturas berteladan;
Nang di-ucha di pakai,
Nang di-pesar di-biasakan,
Turun-menurun dari-pada nenek moyang:
Di-anjak layu,
Di-chabut mati.

20. *Shariat palu-memalu,*
Berbudi orang berbahasa kita.

21. *Bersuku berwaris,*
    Jauh pun ada, dekat pun ada
    Jika jauh di-dengar-dengarkan,
    Jika dekat di-pandang-pandangkan.
22. *Yang jantan di-semendakan ka-orang.*
23. *Menerima pula orang semenda.*
    Tiap-tiap menerima orang semenda itu,
    Di-tentukan pula dengan benar dengan muafakat:
24. *Menumbok di-lesong*
    Menanak di-periok.
25. See J. L. Humphreys, "A Collection of Malay Proverbs," J.S.B.R.A.S., Vol. 67, at p. 108; also Winstedt's "Notes to Caldecott's Jelebu Customary Songs and Sayings", J.S.B.R.A.S., Vol. 78, at p. 29.
26. Winstedt, *op. cit.* footnote 25 *supra*, at p. 29.
27. Wilkinson, *Law: Introductory Sketch*, (Kuala Lumpur, 1908), at p. 17.
28. Differences in interpretation as well as differences in the text do occur in different areas; this may be because there are variations in the custom between one area and another.
29. A colloquial term for *Yang di-Pertuan*.
30. Wilkinson, *Sri Menanti*, in *Papers on Malay Subjects*, 2nd series (Kuala Lumpur, 1914), at p. 39.
31. J. J. Sheehan, "Installation of Tuanku Abdul Rahman", J.S.B.R.A.S., (1939), at p. 237.
32. See the Laws of the Constitution of Negri Sembilan, Article VII (3) which reads "No person shall be elected Yang di-Pertuan Besar of the State unless He . . . is a lawfully begotten descendant in the male line of Raja Radin ibni Raja Lenggang.".
33. P. E. de Josselin de Jong, *Minangkabau and Negri Sembilan*, (Leyden, 1951), at p. 151.
34. Wilkinson, *op. cit.* footnote 30 *supra*.
35. *Ibid.*
36. Winstedt, *op. ct.* footnote 14 *supra*, at p. 14.
37. The Minangkabaus call it *adat sansako*.
38. G. A. de C. de Moubray, *Matriarchy in the Malay Peninsula*, (London, 1931), at p. 106
39. Winstedt, *op. cit.*, at p. 85.
40. *Ibid.*, at p. 84.
41. *Ibid.*, at p. 82.
42. According to customary sayings in Jelebu, "If a chief dies, election by the common voice is required. A family by common consent can elect or dismiss its elder; elders by their common consent and with the support of the enfranchised members of the clan can elect or dismiss the headman of a clan. The headmen of clans by common consent can elect or dismiss an undang. The chiefs by common consent and with the support of the lembagas can elect or dismiss the king."

(Ganti mati berkebulatan
Kebulatan anak buah membuat atau memechat buapa
Buapa bulat, waris-nya rapat, membuat atau memechat tua;
Kebulatan tua, boleh membuat atau memechat undang;
Undang bulat, lembaga rapat, waris sedia, membuat atau
    memechat raja.
(Caldecott, "Jelebu Customary Songs and Sayings", *op. cit.*, at pp. 34–37.

43. *Raja bersejarah,*
    Penghulu bersalasilah,
    Lembaga berteromba.
44. *Raja menobat di-dalam alam;*
    Penghulu menobat di-dalam luak;
    Lembaga menobat di-dalam lingongan-nya;
    Ibu bapa menobat pada anak buah-nya;
    Orang banyak menobat di-dalam teratak-nya.
45. *Raja berdaulat, penghulu berandika,*
    Raja bertitah, penghulu bersabda;
    Raja berkhalifah, penghulu bersuku.
46. *Raja sa-kedilan;*
    Penghulu sa-undang;
    Tali pengikat daripada lembaga;
    Keris penyalang daripada undang;
    Pedang memanchong daripada keadilan,
    Tikam, ta' bertanya,
    Panchong, ta' berkhabar.
47. *Ada-pun Raja itu tiada mempunyai negeri dan tiada boleh menchukai kharajat, melainkan, berkeadilan sahaja serta permakanan-nya.*
48. Winstedt, *op. cit.*, at p. 88.
49. *Ibid.*
50. Quoted in Winstedt, *op. cit.*, at p. 89.
51. *Anak buah yang berchalun*
    Ibu bapa yang punya
    Orang semeda yang gadoh bersuarang,
    Anak buah yang punya.
    Lingkongan bendul yang empat,
    Orang semenda yang punya.
52. *Sa-bingkah tanah terbalek,*
    Sa-helai akar yang putus,
    Se-batang kayu rebah—
    Adat dengan pesaka belum di-adakan.
52a. *Tetekala*
    Kampong sudah bersudut,
    Sawah sudah berjingang
    Puchok sudah meliok,
    Pinang sudah berjijir
    Adat dengan pesaka di-adakan, ia-itu.

53. *Jalan raya titian batu*
    Raja yang empunya.
54. *Sawah yang berjinjang*
    Pinang yang gayu
    Nyiur yang saka
    Lembaga yang punya.
    Jalan paya titian permatang
    Lembaga yang empunya.
    Jalan Sakai titian batang
    Waris yang empunya
55. *Gaung guntong,*
    Bukit bukan,
    Waris dan penghulu yang punya.
56. *Jalan raya titian batu,*
    Bukit bukau,
    Rimba yang sunyi
    Gaung yang dalam
    Lapan yang lebar
    Bandar yang sundai,
    Si-barau barau yang punya.
    Lubok dalam si-kitang kitang yang punya.
57. Wilkinson, *Law: Introductory Sketch* (Kuala Lumpur, 1908), at pp. 28–29.
58. *Padi ta' berpagar lalang*
    Kerbau ta' berkandang seladang
59. *Pesaka*
    Yang bersesapan, yang berpirami,
    Bertunggul, berpemarasan.
60. *Terbit pesaka ka-pada saka,*
    Si-laki-laki menyandang pesaka;
    Si-perempuan yang punya pesaka,
    Orang semenda yang membela.
61. *Sah batal ka-pada sa-kadim;*
    Kata berchari ka-pada waris-nya;
    Tinggal waris menogkat;
    Tinggal sa-kadim melintang;
    Tinggal harta bertuan ta' jadi;
    Tinggal tua batal.
62. See footnote 51 *supra*.
63. *Salah hamba ka-pada tuan*
    Salah murid ka-pada guru
    Salah anak ka-pada bapa
    Salah bini ka-pada laki.
64. *Kunchi bini laki*
    Kunchi semenda tempat semenda.
65. *Orang semenda bertempat semenda.*
    Jikalau cherdek, temen berunding;
    Jikalau bodoh, di-suroh di-arah.

Tinggi, banir tempat berlindong;
Rimbun, dahan tempat bernaung;
Orang semenda pergi karna suroh,
Berhanti karna tegah.

66. *Orang semenda dengan orang tempat semenda*
    Bagai mentimun dengan durian,
    Menggolek pun luka, kena golek pun luka.
67. *Jikalau bingong di-suroh arah,*
    Menyeput nan jauh, mengampongkan nan dekat.
68. *Jikalau kuat di-bubohkan di-pangkal kayu.*
69. *Masok kandang kerbau, menguak;*
    Masok kandang kambing, membebek;
    Bagai-mana 'adat tempat semeda, de-pakai
    Bila bumi di-pijak, langit di-junjong,
    Bagai-mana adat negeri itu di-pakai.
70. *Dunia berganti-ganti,*
    Sa-kali di-orang sa-kali di-kita.
71. *Kusut menyelesaikan,*
    Chichir memungut, hilang menchari
    Utang membayar, pintang menerimakan
    Oleh tempat semenda.
72. These two lines signify a man's union with another woman of the same clan as his wife during the wife's life.
73. A euphemism for bastards.
74. *Pelesit dua sa-kampong*
    Enan sa-batang dua sigai
    Mata tumboh tiada berbeneh
    Sumbang ka-pada tabiat.
    Adat menuju ka-pada tanda
    Bila 'Sah' kata adat tiang
    Tanggal ta' boleh di-patoh lagi,
    Salah ta' boleh di-hukum
    Ia-itu suatu di-beri, dua di-ambil.
75. *Dapatan tinggal,*
    Pembawa kembali
    Kutu di-belah
    Suarang di-ageh
    Rugi laba pulang ka-tempat semanda
    Nyawa darah pulang kapada waris.
76. *Nama mana resam negeri?*
    Shariat palu-memalu.
77. *Menang berkechudang*
    Alah berketundokan
    Sa-rayu berjabat tangan.
78. *Burok di-baiki*
    Kusut di-selesaikan.

79. *Dudok dengan aturan kechil nama mepakat;*
   besar nama Adat: gedang, bernama pesaka sembah.
80. *Sa-hari hilang sa-hari di-chari*
   Sait di-ubat, luka di-tasak.
81. See the observations of P. C. Lloyd, *Yoruba Land Law*, (London, 1962), at p. 17.
82. William Marsden, *The History of Sumatra*, (3rd ed., 1811), at p. 217.
83. *Baju sudah di-sarongkan*
   Lembaga ada di-tuangi.
84. *Malim biawak bengkong.*
85. *Sesat ka-hujong jalan—*
   Balek ka-pangkal jalan;
   Sesat ka-hujong kata—
   Balek ka-pangkal kata.

In some versions of the *terombo* these lines are included among the laws declared by Parapatih nan Sa-batang.

86. J. L. Humphreys writes: "I regret to say that this proverb is commonly used, not without a certain aptness, to describe some phases of English justice, especially the summary trial and conviction of batches of prisoners, such as gang-robbers, hawkers or gamblers." (J.L. Humphreys, "A Collection of Malay Proverbs", J.S.B.R.A.S., Vol. 67, at p.111).
87. *Beraleh kain ka-balik rumah,*
   Beraleh chakap ka-balik lidah.
88. *Adat bertanda, hukum bersaksi;*
   Adat yang tiba ka-gelap menjala.
   Sah, kata adat.
   Apa-bila tertanda, terbeti;
   Terkejar, terlelah;
   Terpakok, terpauk;
   Dekat, tertunjokkan;
   Jauh, terkatakan.
88a. *Undang-undang churi,*
   Pantang dua-belas.
89. *Enggang lalu, ranting patah.*
90. *Tergesek kena miang,*
   Tergegan kena embun
   (Rub against the stem of a bamboo and you itch,
   Shake it and you are sprayed with moisture.)
91. *Chupak yang pepat,*
   Gantang yang piawi,
   Bongkal yang betul
   Teraju yang baik.

Caldecott has the marginal note "We seek for perfect justice" for these lines; but he adds in a footnote that Malay casuists distinguish four points in these four lines: (i) if the bench of judges be full (ii) if the judges have full authority (ii) if the weight of evidence is sufficient (iv) if the judges are just. (A. Caldecott, "Jelebu Customary Songs and Sayings", *op. cit.*, at pp.28–29).

92. See J. L. Humphreys, *op. cit.*, at pp. 107 – 108.
93. *Kepantangan adat,*
    Di-lindong di-endapkan
    Kepejatian adat,
    Di-terang di-bandingkan.
94. For wounding smart-money is the penalty,
    For slaying substitution of a person to the dead person's clan.
    The children of the murderer are invited to the feast of atonement,
    And one of his kin given to the clan of the murdered man.

    (*Chinchang pampas; bunoh beri balas,*
    Anak di-panggil makan,
    Anak buah di-sorong 'kan balas.
95. Parr and Mackray, "Rembau", J.S.B.R.A.S., Vol. 56, p. 78.
96. *Kelebehan umat dengan muafakat,*
    Bulat ayer karna pematong,
    Bulat manusia karna muafakat.
97. See Caldecott, "Jelebu Customary Songs and Sayings", *op. cit.*, at p. 17.
98. *Tetekala kechil bernama muafakat*
    Tetekala besar bernama adat:
    Si-raja adat kapada muafakat
    Ayer melurut dengan bandar-nya,
    Benar melurut dengan pakat-nya,
    Negeri bertumboh dengan adat-nya.
99. *Berumpok masing-masing*
    Berharta masing-masing.
    Harta orang jangan di-tarek
    Untok anak jangan di-berikan.
100. *Adat bersendi hukum*
     Hukum bersendi kitabullah.
     Kuat adat, ta' gadoh hukum,
     Kuat hukum, ta' gadoh adat.
101. *Pada adat menghilangkan yang burok,*
     Menimbulkan yang baik;
     Pada shara menyuroh berbuat baik;
     Meninggalkan berbuat jahat.
102. *Adat yang kawi,*
     Shara yang lazim.
103. See Schneider and Gough (Ed.), *Matrilineal Kinship*, (Berkeley, 1961), at p. 415 *et seq.*
104. *Hüang adat karna muafakat.*
105. B.H.M. Vlekke, *Nusantara*, (The Hague, 1959), at pp. 222–23.
106. *Ibid.*, at p. 223.
107. P.C. Lloyd, *Yoruba Land Law*, at pp. 11–12.
108. *Tak lekang dek panas*
     Tak lapok dek hujan.

See Tunku Hussain bin Tunku Yahya, "Uncracked by the Sun" *Intisari*, Vol. I, No. 3, at p. 45, from which the translation of these two lines is taken.

EDWARD WESTERMARCK

Customs Connected with Homicide in Morocco

Folk law is also to be found in abundance in the Maghreb, the Arabic cultures of north Africa. Finnish anthropologist Edward Westermarck (1862–1939) carried out extensive fieldwork in Morocco, about nine years in all. Publications resulting from that fieldwork include: Marriage Ceremonies in Morocco *(1914),* Ritual and Belief in Morocco, 2 vols *(1926), and* Wit and Wisdom in Morocco *(1930), an annotated collection of some 2,013 Moroccan proverbs.*

Westermarck was also a generalist. He is perhaps best known for his ambitious The History of Human Marriage *(1891),* The Origin and Development of Moral Ideas, 2 vols *(1906–1908), and* Ethical Relativity *(1932). For details of his life, see his autobiography* Memories of My Life *(London: George Allen & Unwin, 1929). For an overview of his contributions to philosophy, sociology, and anthropology, see Morris Ginsberg, "The Life and Work of Edward Westermarck," in* Essays in Sociology and Social Philosophy, *Vol. II,* Reason and Unreason in Society *(London: William Heinemann, 1949), pp. 61–83.*

The following paper was found in manuscript after Westermarck's death and was published posthumously as the first essay in the Transactions of the Westermarck Society *in 1947, a society obviously named in honor of this unusual scholar. The article is replete with engrossing ethnographic detail about such matters as the blood feud or vendetta, and is an excellent example of the rule-centered approach to folk law.*

For other considerations of customs connected with homicide in the Arab world, see J.N.D. Anderson, "Homicide in Islamic Law," Bulletin of the School of Oriental and African Studies, *13 (1951), 811–828; T. Canaan, "Der Mord in Sitten und Gebrauchen bei den Arabern Jordaniens,"* Zeitschrift des Deutschen Palestina-Vereins, *80 (1964), 85–98; and A.K. Irvine, "Homicide in Pre-Islamic South Arabia,"* Bulletin of the School of Oriental and African Studies, *30 (1967), 277–292.*

Reprinted from *Transactions of the Westermarck Society*, 1 (1947), 7–38, with permission.

The following notes were made by me during my travels in Morocco before the country was occupied by France and Spain. The Sultan was recognised as its sovereign ruler, although in large parts of the country, especially among the Berber-speaking tribes and the Arabic-speaking mountaineers of Northern Morocco, the so-called *Jbâla*, his power was only nominal. The Mohammedans of Morocco are chiefly of Berber race, and before the arrival of the Arabs the Berber language was spoken throughout the country; but since it has largely been superseded by the language of the immigrants.

My notes refer mainly to the following Berber-speaking tribes: the *Ait Yúsi*, *Ait Waráin*, and *Ait Sáddĕn* living south of Fez, the *At Ubaḫti* living near Ujda, the *Ait Wäryâgär* in the *Rîf*, the *Iglîwa* in the Great Atlas, the people of Aglu on the coast of *Sūs*; and to the Arabic-speaking tribes of the *Ulâd Bu'ăzîz*, the *Ḥiáina*, and the *Jbâla* of *Andjra* and the *Jbel lä-Ḥbîb*.

The blood feud has been a custom among all Berber tribes from time immemorial and continued to be so even after their conversion to Islam, in accordance with the Koranic rule, "O Ye who believe! Retaliation for the slain is prescribed for you".

Among the *Ait Yúsi* it is the custom that when a man has killed another, both he and all his grown-up male relatives on the father's side who live in the same or any neighbouring village run away to another village either inside or outside the tribe. An attempt to postpone the feud (*lḫú^{dd}jaṯ*; among the *Ait Sáddĕn* called *lä'ḏáuṯ*, from the Arabic *'ădáwa*, "hostility") is then made by some influential men who are not related to the homicide. On the day of burial they go to the grave which has been dug for the slain man, either before he is buried or shortly afterwards, and sacrifice there a sheep as *'ār* on his family; or they slaughter a sheep at some distance from the grave and then take it there while the blood is still gushing from the wound. This sacrifice, called *támăgruṣt n ṯnḏalṯ*, "the sacrifice of the grave", which is made at the expense of the homicide or his family, is intended to be a means of coercion. As an act of *'ār* it implies the transference of a conditional curse to the dead man's family for the purpose of compelling them to do what is asked of them: if they refuse they are cursed and are supposed to meet with some calamity. If no sheep is available another method of *'ār* is resorted to: three or four of the men descend into the grave while the scribes are making recitations on behalf of the deceased before he is buried, and remain there until an agreement with his family is reached. They require the latter to promise to refrain from all persecution within a certain region for a certain length of time. The nearest relative or relatives of the dead man at first refuse to do so, or grant a respite of a couple of days only; but the men persist in staying in the grave, other people intervene, and at last a period within which no vengeance is to be taken is agreed upon. Similar bargaining for the postponement of hostilities also takes place when a sacrifice is made.

In neither case, however, is a mere promise held to be sufficient. The dead man's family must produce an acceptable security for its fulfilment. A trustworthy man becomes by mutual agreement *báb umur*, or guarantor of the compact. Should any member of the dead man's family break the truce (*lhĕna*) by killing the homicide or one of his relatives, the *báb umur* would have to pay a fine of a hundred and twenty ewes. Should he be seen taking aim at the enemy but be prevented by someone else from firing off his gun, the fine would be sixty ewes. Should he discharge his gun without being seen aiming at anybody and without killing anybody, it would be thirty ewes. The *báb umur* would exact the fine from the party who broke the truce; but in any case he would himself be responsible for the payment of it. Should he fail to pay he would be disgraced for ever. His grave would be dug at a market-place or a high-road: he would be a socially dead man and avoided by everybody. He would be unable to get a wife. At weddings the women would sing lampoons about him. He would no longer be called by his own name, but be referred to as the *am'äiwŭrṯ*, or "traitor". It is not necessary that the guarantor should be a man: instead of a *báb umur* there may be a *läll umur*, or female guarantor, with the same liabilities and the same punishment in store for her if she fails to fulfil her duty. For her also a grave would be dug and called the grave of the *ṯam 'äiwŭrṯṯ*, or "traitress".

The promise of the injured party to refrain from taking vengeance, and the security given for it, only implies that the homicide and his relatives are safe for the time being if they keep at a certain distance from the dead man's village, whereas they may be attacked with impunity if they cross the stipulated border. This border is also preserved in the new agreement which is apt to follow on the first one. Shortly before the time agreed upon expires the homicide or his relatives ask a shereef or a few other influential men to go to the dead man's village and put *'ār* upon his kindred by sacrificing a sheep or cutting the sinews of a bullock's hocks as *am'árqab* (in Arabic *t^s'argîba*) which is the most awful of all *'ār*- sacrifices[1] at their house or tent or outside the mosque of the village. Then negotiations are opened with a view to extending the truce, and if they are successful a *báb umur* is again appointed. The same ceremony may be repeated on subsequent occasions, until the relatives of the deceased at last relinquish their revenge altogether, accepting *ddīṯ*, or blood-money in its place. If they are few in number and weak, they may be willing to do so before long. But it is scarcely considered proper to come to an agreement of this kind until a year has passed after the perpetration of the crime.

Before blood-money is accepted the relatives of the homicide may on their own behalf make terms with the family of his victim in order to prevent their vengeance from being wreaked upon them. They commission the shereef or the other men employed as negotiators to arrange about the so-called *abĕrra* or *ttĕbrît*, from the arabic *tebrîya*, which each of them has to pay as the price of their safety. It may amount to two Moorish dollars or ten, or even a hundred dollars if they are well off and the injured party appears implacable; and it may be paid either with money or with a silver ornament or with a gun. After it has been paid the relatives of the homicide go to the family of the deceased, accompanied by the shereef or the other negotiators, kiss the head of each member of the family, and entertain them with a meal, of which everybody present partakes. When they arrive there the women of the household cry and complain of the agreement that has been made. The women generally play an important part in the negotiations, and not on the side of peace. When their relative was killed they scratched and tore their faces and breasts in a terrible manner—more so than on an ordinary death in the family; and they cut off their right plait (*aškkuš*), or their left one as well, as they would otherwise do only when they have lost somebody who is very dear to them. If the proposal to pay *abĕrra* seems to them to have been made too early, they say that it cannot be accepted before their wounds have healed. The *abĕrra* is taken by the male members of the dead man's family—his father, brothers, and sons—not by more distant relatives; and *báb umur* again assumes responsibility for their faithfulness to the agreement.

The life of the homicide himself is made safe only by the payment of *ddīt* and the guarantee given by one or more *idbäb imurr* (plur. of *báb umur*). If he is too poor to pay his share of the *ddīt*, he tries to raise the necessary sum by putting '*ār* on people or in other ways, and if he fails he will probably leave his tribe for ever. When the *ddīt* has been paid he goes, accompanied by a shereef or a few other men of importance, and some relatives, to the family of his victim with a dagger between his teeth and his hands behind his back, kisses the men of the family and other male relatives of the deceased who are present, as also his mother, on the head, and says: Ḥna *mttéibin lĕlláh, ay äitma rằbbi aiġīfiqăddĕrn[?]*, "We are repentant for the sake of God; O brothers, God laid it upon me according to his decree." Then a meal is served with *áfttäl* (the Arabic *sĕksu*) and meat of an animal slaughtered for the occasion; and henceforth the homicide can go wherever he likes without running the risk of being killed. As to the dagger between the homicide's teeth, which figures so frequently in Morocco among the ceremonies of reconciliation, I have been told that it stamps him figuratively as a dead man. But it is in no case a mere symbol: it is *'ăr*.

Ddīt and *abĕrra* are not the only expenses he or his relatives have to pay in order to come to a satisfactory agreement with the enemy. A *rršūt* (from the Arabic *réšwa*), or "bribe", must be given to the persons who were asked to prevail upon the family of the deceased to accept *abĕrra* and *ddit* instead of taking vengeance. It is offered secretly, and its amount varies according to the circumstances. Moreover, if the people are loyal to the Sultan and his government, a *dd'äirt* (in Arabic *d'äira[?]*), or a fine, is paid to the governor of the district. Again, if the tribe is in a state of rebellion and there is consequently a chief who has been elected by the people themselves, a so-called *amġar n-túg^ya, dd'äert* is given to him in order to induce him not to assist the other party; but the amount of it is never very considerable.

Among the *Ait Waráin* a person who has killed another and wishes to atone for it by paying blood-money (*ddiyt*) asks some shereefs to negotiate with the nearest relatives of his victim. If these have agreed to accept the compensation, he goes to their house, accompanied by the shereefs and the schoolboys of the village, with a dagger between his teeth and hands behind his back, repeats a phrase similar to that used among the *Ait Yúsi*, and puts the dagger on the ground in front of them. He also slaughters a bullock, or sacrifices it as *t'arqībt* by cutting the sinews of its hocks, and pays the *ddiyt* agreed upon. But it may be that the relatives of the deceased, in spite of the previous agreement, kill the homicide without ceremony when he appears before them. In order to induce them to accept *ddiyt* he may, in addition to the other preliminaries, send his wife to put *'ăr* on them by sacrificing an animal or by sucking the breast of the principal avenger's wife.

If the homicide is unable to pay the sum required, he goes with a dagger in his mouth to the market and the various villages of the neighbourhood, asking for money contributions by repeating the phrase, *Lfdiyt lílláh*, "Ransom for the sake of God". As this is *'ăr* the people cannot easily refuse to help him. In a similar manner a poor man collects blood-money among the *Ait Sáddĕn*, saying, when he enters a house or tent. *Lĕfdît n răbbi*, "The ransom of God". But he can only make such an appeal with hope of success if he has committed his deed without premeditation, not if he is known to be a bad character. Besides the *ddiyt* paid to the injured party, the so-called *lḥaqq*, always amounting to ten dollars, must, among the *Ait Waráin*, be paid to the *amġar n-túg^ya*, or native chief.

Among the *At Ubáḫti* the homicide and the other persons living in the same tent run away immediately on the commission of the deed, in order to escape the blood feud. Other relatives, who remain in their village, pay to the slain man's family and to the *aiṯ arbʿäin*, or native government, a so-called *ṣṣálāḥ*, amounting to about twenty or thirty dollars, and will then be left in peace. When a year has passed, arrangements are made for the payment of blood-money, or *ddíyiṯ*, which enables the homicide and those who fled with him to return in safety. If the culprit and his family are too poor to pay it, the former walks about from village to village with a dagger between his teeth, to collect the necessary sum; and in this way he may collect so much money that he is not only able to pay the *ddíyiṯ* required, but can even set aside something for his own use. But a fine, called *dd'ǟrăṯ*, amounting to thirty dollars must also be paid to the *aiṯ arbʿǟin*.

Among the *Aiṯ Wāryâgär* it occurs that the homicide, when persecuted by the relatives of his victim, takes refuge in somebody's house and seizes hold of the handmill, which is *ʿār* upon its owner, the mistress of the house. The pursuers must then stop firing, and the inhabitants of the house are obliged to protect him and take him back to his own home. Yet it is considered a cowardly act thus seek refuge with others. The hostilities may be checked through the mediation of a shereef who induces the parties to make peace. In such a case the injured party receives a *ddíyiṯ*, or the homicide and the principal avenger give to each other a sister or daughter in marriage. But neither the payment of blood-money nor the exchange of women is a guarantee of a lasting peace; revenge is often taken a few months afterwards. In such a case the *ddíyiṯ* must be returned, whereas, if there has been an exchange of women, the husband may or may not divorce the wife who has thus been given him. But if he does not divorce her, he takes care not to eat any food prepared by her unless she herself also partakes of it, for fear of being poisoned. Although blood-money has been accepted, however, not even the relatives of the homicide are safe.

In the same tribe, if a village has been beaten in a blood feud with another village and desires to make peace, some of its men go in the night to the enemy's village taking with them a sheep or a goat, which they kill outside the yard of the mosque and then throw into the yard. When the dead animal is found there in the morning by the people of the village, they understand from whom it has come and send the schoolmaster to the enemy, who now expresses a wish to put an end to the hostilities. Some men from a third village are called to act as peace-makers, and blood-money is paid for the act which was the cause of the feud. The animal thus sacrificed as *ʿār* is only eaten by scribes who are not natives of the village in which it was killed, no native partaking of its meat.

Among the *Igdmiūn*, in the Great Atlas region, a person who kills another tries to make his escape. When the *amzwug*, as such a fugitive is called, has stayed away for a year, he comes back and kills a bullock as *'ār* on the tribe to induce some of its leading men to act as mediators and prevail upon the family of his victim to accept *ddīt*. If the homicide does not succeed in running away he has to pay a fine, called *dd'āert*, to the governor.

Among the *Iglíwa* a man who has killed a tribesman takes refuge with the neighbouring *Infdŭak (Ftŭâka)*, who are sure to shelter him because there is *tada*, or brotherhood, between them and the *Iglíwa*.[2] When a year has passed the people with whom he has been staying go with him to the family of the deceased, kill an animal as *'ār* on them, and make their *protégé* appear before them with his hands tied and a dagger between his teeth. If they forgive him, as is usually the case, they remove the dagger and loosen his bonds, but "forgiveness" only means that they will not seek after his life, whereas they may kill him if he gets in their way; and this is the case even though they accepted *ddīt* for their pardon. If they find the homicide in their neighbourhood, one of them ascends the top of the village, and cries out loudly that if he does not leave the tribe he will be killed. Unless the sheikh of the district pleads for the homicide, the governor will probably confiscate all his animals and all movable property found in his house.

In Aglu a person who is guilty of homicide flees at once to another tribe and places himself under its protection. His relatives then pay *ddīt* to the family of the deceased, (if the latter was a man) and puts *'ār* on them. This, however, will only prevent the injured party from taking revenge on any of them, but does not entitle the homicide to return; if he appears outside the territory of the tribe to which he has fled for refuge, he is at any time liable to be killed. Yet there are cases in which he is pardoned by his enemy and can return. A holy man may go to the family of the deceased and ask them to forgive him, promising to help them to a place in paradise on the day of resurrection; and if his promise is of no avail he may resort to threats, which are always fearful when uttered by a man possessed of *baraka*, or holiness. If they consent to pardon the culprit the holy man goes and fetches him from the tribe to which he fled, and takes him to their house with his hands tied behind his back. When he arrives there a dagger is put between his teeth. One of the family removes it and throws it on the ground, and also unlooses his hands. And when he has thus received their pardon, the holy man admonishes him henceforth to keep away from their place and not to speak badly about them.

In Aglu the expenses connected with an act of homicide are not restricted to the payment of blood-money to the injured party. When the tribal authorities, or *inflas*, are informed of the deed, they at once go to the house of the homicide and claim the so-called *linṣaf*, and receive in addition a handsome *lmunt* (the Arabic *mûna*), or lot of provisions. If the culprit has not the necessary means, his family must pay for him, and if they also are too poor to do so they have to borrow the money from others. The *linṣaf* amounts to seventy dollars if a man has been killed and a hundred dollars if the victim was a woman; but in the latter case no *ddīt* is paid. If revenge is taken upon the homicide at once, before he has had time to escape, no *ddīt* is paid in either case, but both parties are obliged to give *linṣaf* to the *inflas*.

Among the Arabic-speaking tribe of the *Ulâd Buʿăzîz* a homicide who succeeds in escaping to another tribe can only return, after the lapse of two or three years, if *díya* is offered to and accepted by the family of the victim and *d'äira* is paid to the governor; and a homicide who is caught by the authorities and put in prison can only be released on similar conditions. In order to induce the injured party to accept bloodmoney some shereefs are asked to act as negotiators, and a cow or a bullock is given them to be used for an *ʿār*-sacrifice. But though the payment of blood-money will exempt the relatives of the homicide from the danger of being killed, and though his own life will not be sought after, he is still liable to be slain by any man of the dead person's family who happens to meet him in some uninhabited place. If he is killed the avenger will be put in prison, but is easily released if he pays a comparatively small sum of money to the governor. The amount of the *d'äira* is fixed by the latter in accordance with the means of the homicide, but is smaller than the *díya*.

In the *Hiáina* a homicide, if caught by the authorities, is put in prison, but is often released after some months if *d'äira* is paid to the governor. Yet he and his relatives are still exposed to the injured party's revenge (*ṭulb*). They may save themselves from it by means of paying compensation or by running away to another tribe, but in the latter case the relatives of the homicide cannot return as long as he himself remains alive. It may also happen, however, that the governor who has accepted *d'äira*, instead of releasing the prisoner, is bribed by the injured party to send him to the prison in Fez. In such a case no revenge will be taken, but the culprit will have to stay in prison forever unless his family can induce the other party to pardon him. They may go to the house of the latter secretly at night and sacrifice a sheep as *ʿār* outside the door; and on the following day they go there again, accompanied by some shereefs. The family of the deceased are requested to send a letter to the governor to tell him that they no longer have any objection to the release of the prisoner. If they have been induced to do so, not only through the persuasions of the shereefs but also by the money offered them, the governor is prevailed upon by similar means to reclaim the prisoner from Fez. When the latter is back again among his own people, he goes, accompanied by the shereefs, to the family of the man he killed with his hands behind his back and a knife between his teeth, and says: "Here I am, if you want to kill me, kill me". The reconciliation is sealed by a common meal, and the homicide kisses the head of everybody present. He afterwards sends his unmarried daughter or some other girl of his family to his former enemies to be married to one of them, thus effectively preventing them from exacting revenge in the future.

Among the *Jbâla* of the *Jbel lä-Ḥbîb* it is nowadays the custom that if a man kills another the *šēḫ* of the district comes with his soldiers and burns his house, confiscates his animals and other property, and, if they catch him, put him in prison for some years, releasing him only after *ḍ'äira* has been paid. If he is not caught, his village will have to pay *ḍ'äira* because he was allowed to escape. The dead man's family will nevertheless try to avenge his death by killing the culprit or some of his relatives, and they are allowed to do so on condition that they pay *ḍ'äira* to the *šēḫ*. No *díya* is taken by them. But in former days it was different. When the homicide had been put in prison, his family sent holy men to the injured party to ask for forgiveness, and if their request was refused a bullock or a sheep or a goat was sacrificed as *'ār* outside the dead man's house, and his friends had to accept *díya* and forgive. In Andjra, also blood-money was formerly accepted by the injured party, but this is seldom the case nowadays, the only satisfactory means of reconciliation being inter-marriage between the two families. The community of the homicide must generally pay a hundred dollars as *ḍ'äira*, though if "the *šēḫ* is kind to the village" the fine may be reduced by one-half; and if the culprit belongs to another village than his victim, the village of the latter must also pay something to the *šēḫ*. If the homicide is caught by the authorities he is generally put in prison and kept there for a year, after which the injured party may kill him if they pay *ḍ'äira*. Though the *ḍ'äira* in all these cases, both in Andjra and the *Jbel lä-Ḥbîb*, is given to the *šēḫ* of the district, the latter has to hand over some of it to the governor of the tribe, who resides in Tangier.

The amount of the blood-money is either variable or fixed. Among the *Aït Yúsi* the *ddīt* generally varies between 200 and 500 dollars, according to the agreement made in each case; but in one quarter of the tribe, the *Aït Árrba'*, it is fixed by custom once for all, being 300 dollars if a man and 150 dollars if a woman was killed, provided that both the culprit and his victim belonged to this quarter. In other parts of the tribe the *ddīt* for a woman is likewise smaller than that for a man; if a man and a woman of the same kin are killed, the *ddīt* for the latter is only one-half of the sum paid for the former. There are people who accept only money for *ddīt*, but not infrequently it also consists of fruit-trees, land, or animals, or even a girl. It may be that the family of the deceased demand that the homicide shall give his daughter or sister or niece in marriage to the nearest relative of his victim. She is then valued at a certain price, which is deducted from the sum-total of the *ddīt*. She is married with the usual ceremonies; and if her husband dies she becomes the wife of some other relative of the person who was killed. This was the custom even in those days when a widow generally, on the death of her husband, passed back into her father's power, a custom which no longer exists. It is still preserved in the neighbouring tribe of the *Ait Sáddĕn*, where nevertheless a woman who has been given in marriage as part of the *ddīt* makes an exception to this rule. Among the *Ait Sáddĕn* the *ddīt* was formerly everywhere 300 dollars, but in one section of their tribe it was not long ago raised to 500; it may be paid with cattle, sheep, or grain as well as with money. Among the Ait Waráin the regular amount of the *ddiyt* is 400 dollars if a man and 200 if a woman has been killed, but the shereefs who act as mediators commonly contrive to reduce it by one-half. It frequently occurs among them that only one-half of the *ddiyt* for a man is paid with money or animals, and that a marriageable girl is substituted for the other half; but she must not be taken in marriage by the principal avenger, although she may be given in marriage to his son. Among the *At Ubáhti* the *ddíyīt* is 100 dollars both for men and women, unless a shereef has been killed, in which case it is 1000 dollars. It is not the custom among them to give a woman away in marriage as part of the compensation. In the *Rīf* the blood-money varies in different tribes: among the *Ait Wäryâgär* it is 40 dollars, in another tribe it is only 30, but in a third as much as 100. In Aglu, Mássa, and Tíznit in *Sūs* the blood-money amounts to 70 dollars if a man has been killed; whereas in Aglu at least, no *ddīt* is paid if the victim is a woman. Among the *Ulâd Bu'āzîz* the amount of the *díya* is fixed by the family of the slain person, according to the means of the homicide; a poor man may get off by paying 100 dollars, which is said to be the minimum, whereas a wealthy person may have to pay 2000 or 3000. On the other hand the sex of the victim does not seem to influence the amount of the *díya*. In the *Ḥiáina* it is 100 dollars, or the daughter or sister of the culprit is given in marriage to some members of the slain man's family, not merely as compensation but also to serve as a safeguard against revenge in the future. In the latter case the marriage is celebrated with little ceremony; but if the new wife gives birth to a son, a great feast is held on the seventh day. Among the *Jbel lä-Ḥbíb* the *díya* which was formerly paid amounted to 1200 *mét^{s}qal*.

In the payment of the blood-money the homicide is supported by his relatives. Among the *Ait Yúsi* only a third part of it is paid by himself and the other male members of the family—his father, brothers, and sons—while two thirds are paid by the other men, more distantly related to him on the father's side, who belong to his *ljma't* or kin, whether they live in his own village or not. So also the latter receive two thirds of the *ddīt* paid for the killing of one of their kinsmen, whereas only one third of it goes to his father, brothers, and sons. But if a woman is killed the more distant relatives receive no portion of the *ddīt*, because the *ljma't* is considered to suffer no loss through the death of a woman. If she was unmarried the whole *ddīt* is given to her nearest male relatives, her father or brothers; the same is the case if she was married but childless; but if she was married and left behind sons it is divided between them and their father, and if she left behind daughters only it is taken by the widower provided that he is their father. Among the *Ait Waráin* the *ddiyt* is taken by the principal avenger or avengers, mentioned below; but some portion of it is also given other male members of the kin, if only in order to prevent their killing the homicide after *ddiyt* has been paid, as they might do if not properly appeased. Among the *Ulâd Bu'azîz*, if a person is found dead in a strange village or in an uninhabited place, the village or, in the latter case, the neighbouring villages will have to pay *díya* to his family, as well as *d'áira* to the governor.

The efforts to evade revenge are made with variable success. Among the *At Ubáḫti*, I was told, the injured party always accept *ddíyit* if it is offered them. Among the *Ait Yúsi* the acceptance of *ddīt* entails no disgrace and is actually encouraged by the tribe, as it wants to preserve peace among its members; but if the homicide belongs to another tribe the acceptance of *ddīt* is out of the question. Yet in spite of all negotiations it may be that the offer of *ddīt* may be refused. If the dead man's son is opposed to accepting it, his will is decisive; but a grown-up brother also has a strong voice in the matter, stronger than that of an old father. Moreover, if a son is still a child or not yet born when a peaceful settlement is made, he may later on avenge his father's death, although in such a case the *ddīt*, once accepted, must be returned. Among the *Ait Waráin* it happens quite frequently that the *ddiyt* which is offered is refused by the injured party on the plea that they would not stay their stomachs with the blood of their own people even though they died of hunger. It is the father of the deceased, if he is still alive and they lived in the same house, who decides whether *ddiyt* is to be accepted or revenge to be taken. Among the *Ait Sáddĕn ddīt* is only accepted by people who are not strong enough to avenge the death of their relative. The *Ait Wäryâĝär* consider it shameful not to take revenge, and, as we have seen, neither the acceptance of *ddíyit* nor an exchange of women is a guarantee of a lasting peace. The *Iglíwa* likewise consider it mean to take *ddīt*, which is only done by poor people. Among the *Ulâd Bu'azîz* revenge is the rule; to take *díya* is a cowardly act and equivalent to selling a relative. Among the *Beni Atusen*, another Arabic-speaking tribe, I was told that *díya* is not accepted for intentional homicide.

The duty of exacting revenge is incumbent on the kinsmen of the person who was killed, and by preference on certain relatives according to the degree of the relationship. Among the *Ait Waráin* the principal avenger is his father, if they lived together in the same house and he is not too old. Otherwise the sons of the deceased, particularly the eldest son, have in the first place to avenge his death. If in such a case several relatives together undertake an avenging expedition, the eldest son shall fire first; and if he is too young to take part in the expedition the homicide, if caught, is brought to him, a loaded gun is put in his hands, and he shoots the enemy or else, on the persuasion of his mother, accepts *ddiyt*. A son who was not yet born when his father died may later on take revenge on the culprit. Other relatives are avengers in the following order: brothers, paternal uncles, and paternal cousins. Relatives on the mother's side may become avengers in default of paternal ones, or, like anybody else, if appealed to by '*ār*. If a married woman is killed, it is her husband who in the first place avenges her death. I was told of a newly married wife who was killed by three vagabonds when she, in the company of her husband, went to see her parents shortly after her marriage; she was a little ahead of him when it happened. He killed one of them on the spot, and took the other ones with him and handed them over to his parents-in-law the words, "I killed one and brought these to you, one for each of you". Then the father-in-law slew one of them, whereas the other one saved his life by sucking the breast of his wife.

Among the *Aiṯ Yúsi* any one belonging to the *ljma'ṯ*, or kin, of the deceased may avenge his death, whereas relatives on the mother's side have nothing to do with the blood feud, unless they at the same time happen to be related on the father's side; for otherwise they belong to another *ljma'ṯ*, even though they live in the village of the deceased. But strangers who have settled down in the village take part in its blood feuds, because they are reckoned as adopted members of the *ljma'ṯ* by which the village is principally populated, and they are therefore also exposed to the blood feud if any member of the village has committed homicide. Among the *Aiṯ Sáddĕn* all the inhabitants of the slain person's village, including strangers residing there, must likewise in the case of a blood feud help to avenge his death, and so must his relatives on the father's side living in other villages.

Among the *Ait Wäryâgär* the duty of avenging a person's death devolves in the first place on the man who is most closely related to him on the father's side. If, for example, he has a son and a brother, they go together to take revenge, but the son is the first to fire. The whole village, however, consisting of relatives on the father's side, joins in the feud. Maternal relatives only take part in it if they live in the same village, in which case they are paternal relatives as well, or if there is an outbreak of the feud while they are travelling together with the proper avengers; but in such circumstances other friends travelling with them would also lend them assistance.

In Andjra a son and a brother are both the principal avengers, but in default of either, revenge will be taken by any relative on the father's side however remote, even if he has never seen the person who was killed. Maternal relatives are not avengers, and a brother-in-law only if there is no paternal relative. Among the *Ulâd Bu'âzîz*, who likewise include among the avengers the remotest paternal kinsmen, a maternal relative may also kill the homicide if he meets him alone in an uninhabited place, but not if he finds him together with other people, and the same is true of a brother-in-law. If a person who is killed has no avenger but his widow gives birth to a son after his death, the latter will, when grown-up, have to avenge the death of his father. In the *Ḥiáina* maternal relatives act as avengers in default of paternal ones.

The duty of an avenger does not compel him to take vengeance with his own hands or with the assistance of certain people only: he may engage anybody he pleases to help him to accomplish his aim. Among the *Aiṯ Yúsi* it is not unusual to hire some one to kill the culprit. When I asked whether this was not considered a somewhat disreputable manner of taking revenge, the answer was that the principal thing is the destruction of the homicide or one of his kinsfolk. In the *Ḥiáina* it seems to occur still more frequently that the avenger hires a substitute, who is generally satisfied with a pay of fifteen or twenty dollars. In other cases the assistance of strangers is obtained by putting *'ār* on them. Among the *Aiṯ Yúsi*, for example, if the *ljm'aṯ* is not strong enough to take revenge for the murder of one of its members, it may appeal to others for help by means of sacrifices. Among the *Ait Waráin* it is a common thing for powerless avengers to make similar appeals. Among the *Aiṯ Wäryägär* a person who has to avenge the death of a relative may induce the owner of a house in which he takes refuge to assist him in his task by offering him a sum of money, which, if accepted, is looked upon as *'ār*. Various other methods of using *'ār* for a similar purpose will be mentioned in another connection. In the *Ḥiáina* a man who is too weak to act as an avenger and too poor to hire a substitute walks about from house to house and from village to village with a knife between his teeth, or sends his mother or wife or sister to walk about in the same way. This also is *'ār*, but his object is not to induce those on which it is put to slay the homicide, but to compel them to give money with which he can hire a man to do so. This custom is called *l-fédya*, or "ransom".

The general rule is that attempts are made to take vengeance on the homicide himself, and on one of his kinsmen only if the former cannot be caught; he is not lost sight of behind the veil of common responsibility. Among the *Aiṯ Yúsi* it is the custom that if he is killed, a formal reconciliation between the parties takes place at a saint's tomb or in the house of some influential man. The same is also generally the case when not the homicide himself but some other member of his *ljama'ṯ* is killed. But then the feud may still be continued: revenge may be taken in return upon the avenger or on one of his kindred, if he comes near the other party's village or is accidentally encountered on the road. This, however, is likely to happen only in the beginning; after some time has passed the parties are in most cases formally reconciled, if they have not been so before, even though the homicide remains alive. Among the *Aiṯ Sáddēn* it is the custom that if he escapes and one of his kinsmen is killed instead, he pays as compensation a reduced *ddīṯ* to the family of the latter; but this is not the custom the *Aiṯ Yúsi*. If a child causes the death of a person, the *Aiṯ Yúsi* do not admit revenge to be taken on another child in its place, though it may be taken on a grown-up person if the child itself has not been killed.

Among the *Ait Waráin*, if the injured party refuse to accept the *ddiyt* offered them, the homicide generally runs away to another tribe, but his relatives—even the nearest—may in such a case remain where they are without incurring any risk. On the other hand, if he does not run away, and only then, one of them may be killed in his stead. There is another rule, however, which applies to a woman who has killed somebody by poison and has run away for fear of revenge because her victim, before dying, accused her of her crime. Then some other member of her family will be killed, quite contrary to the rule which is followed when a man runs away after committing murder. For a woman is not supposed to be able to escape without the assistance of her family, who thereafter become implicated in her crime. The blood feud stops as soon as the culprit or one of his kinsmen has been slain, unless there has been more than one victim on either side, because each lost life requires its equivalent. After revenge has been taken the parties are formally reconciled by the aid of some shereefs.

Among the *Aṯ Ubáḫti*, if *ddíyīṯ* is not offered, the homicide who has run away exposes his relatives to the blood feud; and when one of them has been killed the matter ends. So also among the *Aiṯ Wäryâgär*, if the manslayer runs away and consequently cannot be caught, revenge is taken on one of his kinsmen. But even if he himself is killed the feud is not at an end: his death has also to be avenged. This leads to incessant feud and universal insecurity. People do not go out when it is dark except for the purpose of killing somebody; nobody likes to leave his village unless in company, and, as my informant put it, the men eat with their guns in their hands, even in their own houses. Women and children, however, are not exposed to the blood feud unless they have themselves been guilty of homicide or the enmity develops into rage. When there is a feud between different villages, the women therefore go out first to see if the enemy is lying in wait for the men.

Among the *Iglíwa*, when a person has been killed, a fight is likely to ensue at once between the families though other people try to stop it; and some relative of the culprit or his wife may have to atone for his crime. But this can happen only in the very beginning, in the heat of passion; and the only person whose life is sought after is the homicide himself.

Among the *Ulâd Bu'ăzîz* a kinsman may be killed if the homicide cannot be got at, though only if no *díya* has been paid. The blood feud should be at an end when one life has been taken, in accordance with the principle *rōḥ fi rōḥ* "a life for a life". But this rule was not strictly followed under the anarchical conditions which prevailed at the beginning of the present century when I made my notes: a murder committed by a man belonging to a neighbouring tribe, the *Ulâd Fraj*, led to a feud in which twenty-five men from the *Ulâd Bu'ăzîz* and forty men from the *Ulâd Fraj* lost their lives. In the *Ḥiáina*, where revenge likewise is taken on a kinsman of the homicide only when he himself escapes, the act of vengeance calls forth fresh revenge unless the feud is brought to an end by the offer of a girl. Among the *Jbel lă-Ḥbíb* revenge is, as usual, by preference wreaked upon the culprit and upon one of his kinsmen only if he himself cannot be caught.

Although the homicide is generally the person who is in the first place searched for by the avenger, there are cases in which he in any circumstances goes scot-free, because, unless blood-money is accepted, vengeance *must* be taken upon somebody else, in strict accordance with the law of talion. Thus among the *Aiṯ Yúsi*, if a man kills a woman, not he but one of his kinswomen is to be killed, and if a woman kills a man, not she but a man belonging to her kin shall die. So strictly is this rule observed that if a woman who is with child is killed in a fight between tribesmen, her body is cut open so that it can be ascertained whether the child in her womb is a boy or a girl and the vengeance, or the blood-money, can be regulated according to its sex. Among the *Ait Waráin*, also, it is the rule that if a woman is killed the avenger for preference kills another woman in return, according to the principle, "You have killed my wife or sister or daughter, I will kill yours". Among the other tribes of whose customs I have spoken there is no such rule.

Among the *Aiṯ Ubáḫṯi*, if a man has killed a woman he, and not any woman of his family, is subject to the law of revenge, and if a woman has killed a man her own life is sought after. Among the *Aiṯ Wäryâgär* a husband who kills his wife is liable to be killed by her brothers, and a woman who poisons her husband will be killed unless she runs away, and in such a case some one of her brothers is likely to have to atone for her crime. Among the *Ulâd Buʿāzîz* there would be no revenge if a woman committed homicide, though *díya* would have to be paid; but I was told that women are like Jews, who never kill anybody. A woman is scarcely considered responsible for her actions; if she is guilty of theft, for instance, her husband, or if she has no husband, her father or brother or son is put in prison, and only if she has no guardian or near male relative is she herself punished. In the *Ḥiáina* a woman who kills any one by magic—the only form of homicide committed by women—escapes all punishment, but her father or brothers are caught by the governor and are only set free after the payment of a fine.

Revenge may be taken even for manslaughter which has been committed on strong provocation. Among the *Aiṯ Yúsi*, if a married man finds another man with his wife and slays the adulterer, the kindred of the latter are allowed to avenge his death, though they may perhaps content themselves with accepting one half of the ordinary *ddīt*; and the killing of a robber, even when he is caught at night, leads either to vengeance or to payment of the full *ddīt*. So also among the *Aṯ Ubáḫṯi* a person who kills a thief either in the daytime or in the night has to run away and pay *ddíyīt*, as in other cases of homicide. In Andjra it happened that a man who was suspected of intending to commit robbery was killed at night in the neighbourhood of a village where I was staying. Nobody knew who killed him, but a fine was nevertheless exacted by the authorities on the tribe from the nearest three villages—twenty dollars from the very nearest, fifteen from the next one, and twelve from the farthest one. But no *díya* was paid to the family of the slain man on account of his supposed evil intention.

Accidental homicide is treated differently by different tribes. Among the *Aiṯ Yúsi* it is attended with the same consequences as intentional homicide, even when committed by a child. It is argued that otherwise lack of intention might easily be pleaded as an excuse for voluntary manslaughter or wilful murder; for who can define what is accident and what is not? Among the *Ait Waráin* revenge may also be taken for accidental homicide, but not when *ddiyt* is offered. If the involuntary slayer is an intimate friend of the family of the person whom he has killed the matter will probably be settled by his sucking the breast of the latter's mother or of some other woman of his family and paying a smaller compensation than usual for the loss inflicted. Among the *Aiṯ*

Waryâgär, if a person kills another accidentally, there is no revenge, but the ordinary *ddíyĭt* has to be paid or the manslayer has to give his sister or daughter in marriage to the brother or son of his victim. If he is too poor to pay the sum required he goes, after the Great Feast has passed, from village to village asking the inhabitants to help him by giving him the skins of the sacrificed goats, which he then sells to get the money he wants. Among the *At Ubáḫti* no difference is made between accidental and intentional manslaughter, unless the deceased has declared before his death that the act was unintentional and therefore forgiven by him. If he makes such a declaration his words are taken down by one of the *ait arb'äin*, or native authorities, the manslayer and his family do not run away, nor do they pay *ddíyĭt*, but *dd'äirăt* is claimed by the *ait arb'äin*. In Aglu accidental homicide is likewise treated as wilful murder unless the involuntary manslayer is expressly pardoned by his victim before he dies. If he is thus pardoned by the latter he can remain in the tribe and no *ddĭt* is paid, but the usual *linṣaf*, or fine, must be given to the *ait arb'äin*; for, as my informant said, he was forgiven not by the tribe but by the dead man only, who had nothing to do with the *linṣaf*. Among the *Iglíwa* the involuntary homicide, even though pardoned by his victim, is not pardoned by the family of the latter, and has to run away; but they will make no effort to catch him and reconciliation is easy. Among the *Ulâd Bŭ'azîz* there is neither revenge nor the payment of blood-money if a person who has been wounded declares in the presence of witnesses that it happened by accident; but the man who caused his death must pay a small fine to the governor, unless he escapes and remains away for a year or two. The same is the case if the person dies at once and his family have no doubt that the death was inflicted by mere accident; only greedy people would exact blood-money in such circumstances, and revenge would be out of the question. In the *Hiáina* and in Andjra, too, no revenge is taken for homicide by misadventure, but *d'äira* is exacted by the governor. Among the *Jbĕl lä-Hbíb* an involuntary manslayer is pardoned by the family of the man he slew if he was pardoned by the dying man, but hardly otherwise. Among the *Ait Yúsi*, on the other hand, the last wish of the wounded person can in no case prevent a feud. My informant's sister's son had been killed by a man belonging to kin of his maternal uncle. Before he died he expressly forbade his kinsmen—that is, relatives on the father's side— to take vengeance on his maternal uncle (my informant) or any of his brother's sons; but nevertheless one of the latter was killed. This again shows that homicide is looked upon not merely as an offence against the individual, but as an offence against his kin.

Among the *Ait Yúsi* there may be a feud also in the event of an act that does not immediately lead to a person's death. If someone who was wounded by another but has recovered, at any time afterwards falls ill and dies and before his death declares that his illness was due to the wound he received, the person who inflicted it is treated as a manslayer, and it matters not how many years have passed since the infliction of the wound. The same applies to anybody who beats a pregnant woman if she subsequently gives birth to a still-born child. Among the *Ulâd Bu'azîz* the offender is in similar circumstances at all events compelled to pay *díya* to the woman's husband, as well as *d'äira* to the governor.

The law of revenge may or may not apply to killing in war. In Andjra and among the *Aiṭ Sáddĕn* and the *Ulâd Bu'azîz* there is no revenge; I was told that if a person is killed in war, it is just as if a dog were killed. Among the *Aiṭ Wäryâǧär*, on the other hand, there will be revenge, to be exacted according to the same rules as those observed in other cases of revenge. This is possible owing to the fact that the members of the same village keep together in the fight. Moreover, it is the custom for a warrior who has shot another to cry out that he has done it, and that if the other one is going to rise he will fire again and kill him. Among the *Aiṭ Yúsi* killing in war is likewise attended with the same consequences as any other kind of homicide if the war is intratribal; but the case is different if it is carried on with another tribe. If a person is killed by a member of a strange tribe, there will be a feud not merely between his kinsmen and those of the manslayer, but between the two tribes, and in this case the rule of a life for a life is not observed: peace may be concluded though the number of lives lost on one side is not equal to that lost on the other. It is brought about by the leading men of both tribes who, after some preliminary negotiations, agree to meet on a certain day at a certain place. There they exchange their cloaks (*ízĕnnar*, sing. *ázĕnnar*) or, if they have no cloaks, their turbans or the cotton kerchiefs of their wives; and if the meeting is held in a village they have a meal in common. These proceedings are acts of covenanting which lay restraints on those who perform them in accordance with certain native beliefs.[3] To partake of a common meal is a frequent method of sealing a compact, because he who breaks it thereby exposes himself to the other party's conditional curses which are embodied in the eaten food; it is said that "God and the food will repay him". The exchange of cloaks or turbans or kerchiefs, again, is due to the idea that the promisee will be able to avenge a breach of faith on the part of the promisor owing to the magical connection between a thing and its owner. This also underlies another custom that may be mentioned in this context. When the *Aiṭ Yúsi* are going to fight another tribe, the man who has been elected chief secures the cloaks of the leading men of the tribe as a pledge for their appearance at a certain place on the day and the hour fixed by him; and if any of them fails to appear, he blackens the cloak of the delinquent and sends it to different parts of the tribe to be shown to all the people. The blackening of the cloak of the faithless man is not merely a means of disgracing him, but is supposed to cause him misfortune, black being a colour that contains *bas*, or evil.

There are cases of homicide, besides those mentioned above, in which no vengeance is taken nor blood-money paid, namely when a person has been killed by a member of his own family. In explanation of this I was told that the family does not like to lose another member in addition to the one it has already lost.

Among the *Aiṯ Yúsi* a son who has killed his father or mother—such cases are by no means rare—runs away, not to return for a few days, if he has grown-up brothers, and then nothing is done to him; but if he has no grown-up brothers he may not have to leave his home at all. If a man slays his brother there is, for the moment at least, no question either of revenge or blood-money, unless the brother has a grown-up son; but if he has a son who is still young, the fratricide may later on have to pay for his deed with his life. A Berber from the *Aiṯ Sáddēn* mentioned a case in which a man in his tribe who had slain his brother was at last killed by the son of the latter, although the son was not yet born when his father died. The same informant told me that while he was among the *Aiṯ Nḏēr*, living in the same neighbourhood, he was present on an occasion when a man killed his paternal uncle who lived together with him in the same tent; the murderer then married the uncle's widow, and his neighbours believed that he had committed his deed for this very purpose. He could not, however, have done this with impunity if the uncle had had a grown-up son. Among the *Aiṯ Yúsi* there will be revenge if a person kills his paternal cousin; and if a husband kills his wife her kindred will avenge her death on a woman of the husband's kin, or blood-money has to be paid to them.

Among the *Aiṯ Waráin* a person who kills his father or brother is not subject to revenge if he has one brother only; he simply leaves his home and stays away for a short time. But if he has several brothers, and especially if the dead father or brother was dear to them and the homicide is a bad character, they will slay him. I asked a Berber from this tribe what would happen if a father killed his son, but the answer was that he had never heard of such a case. If a person kills his paternal cousin, the brothers of the latter will take revenge on him; and if a husband kills his wife her kinsmen will avenge her death.

Among the *Aṯ Ubáḫti* a person who has killed his father or mother runs away, unless he is caught before he has time to escape; and in the latter case he will be killed by the *aiṯ árb'äin*. *Ddíyīt* is out of the question, but the parricide is not allowed to return until *dd'airat* is paid to the *aiṯ árb'äin* and *ṣṣåláḥ* to the villagers. In any case he has to stay away for a year; and when he dies he is buried outside the cemetery. Again, if anybody kills his brother he does not leave the village, but runs to the tent of another family. He is not killed, but the *aiṯ árb'äin* burn his tent and confiscate his animals. Most of these are given to his relatives, but some of them are taken by the other members of his village and the rest kept by the *aiṯ árb'äin* as *dd'ärăṯ*.

Among the *Aiṯ Wäryägär* a son who kills his father may be killed by his uncles, or he runs away, or is compelled to leave the village. If a father kills his son, he is not exposed to revenge, nor does he leave his home, but he is looked down upon; it is said that he must have been cursed by his own parents. If a man kills his brother, there will be no revenge and he may even remain in the village, although he will be treated with disrespect; but there have also been cases in which fratricides have committed suicide. If a man kills his half-brother, he will be subject to revenge, unless he leaves the village never to return. If a person kills his cousin or second cousin living in the same village, he will run away or his family will see that he leaves the place. They also make apologies and promise to kill him if he comes back; they prefer doing it themselves so as not to have to avenge his death if he is killed by the other party. If the homicide and his victim, though they live in the same village, are only distantly related, it depends on the circumstances whether there will be revenge or not; if the village is involved in many feuds with other villages, the two families will come to terms. If there is a blood feud inside the village or between neighbouring villages, it is often carried on from the houses, the combatants firing at each other through the windows or from the roofs. We have in another connection noticed rules relating to uxoricide and matricide among these Berbers.

Among the *Iglíwa* it sometimes happens that a person kills his brother. He then runs away—otherwise he would be imprisoned—and is not allowed to return until he has paid a fine (*ḍḍ'aert*) to the authorities. But there is no question of either revenge or *ddiṯ*.

Among the *Ulâd Bu'äzîz*, I was told, a parricide would run away; but my informant had never heard of such a case. If a man has killed his brother he leaves the tribe and visits remote villages and markets with a dagger between his teeth in order to collect *ṣadâqa*, or "alms", from the people. On his return he buys food with the money he has thus received and entertains with it a large number of scribes, even as many as two hundred, whom he has invited to his tent to recite there the whole Koran and call down blessings on him. He does all this whether he is rich or poor, and when he walks about he must have no money with him; the main thing for him is to be freed of his sin through the alms given him and all the money he has collected must be spent on the scribes. He pays no *díya*, but he must give *d'äira* to the governor, and this is to be paid with his own money. The governor, in addition, exacts *d'äira* from the village of the fratricide. A similar method of removing bloodguiltiness is also sometimes resorted to by other manslayers.

In the *Ḥiáina* a man who has killed his father tries to escape, but if he is caught, he is imprisoned by the governor and has to remain in prison till his death. If a father kills his son, both he and all his family run away for fear of the governor. If a man kills his brother, the son of the latter, if he has one, will try to avenge his father's death. Otherwise there will be no revenge, but the fratricide runs away to escape imprisonment.

In certain circumstances revenge may have to be suspended. Among the *Aiṯ Yúsi* it is the custom that if they are at war with another tribe, the *amġar n-ṯúgʸa*, or native chief, who is appointed on such an occasion, decrees that any blood feud inside the tribe shall lie dormant for the time being. So also among the *Ait Waráin*: all intratribal feuds stop in case of war with another tribe. Persons who a short while previously were enemies may be seen walking together side by side or giving powder to each other. But after the war is finished the blood feud will be resumed again.

Among the *Ait Waráin* revenge is at all times prohibited at a market; should anybody there be guilty of homicide, whether in revenge or otherwise, the sheikh and his assistants would burn his house or tent and confiscate his animals. Among the *Aiṯ Wäryâġär* revenge is not only forbidden at a market, but must not even be taken on any one who is on his way to or from a market. If a person starts for it on the day before it is held and returns to his home on the third day, he is thus protected all that time. When the marketplace is filling with people the man whose office it is to measure the grain sold there cries out from the top of a shop in the centre of the place: "There is only one God and Mohammed is the prophet of God; may God beat the infidels, may God curse the Jews; O tribesmen, obey the commandment of the sheikh; if anybody kills another at the market, he will be shot as though he were a target, and his people will have to pay a thousand dollars". And this is no empty threat. For every market-place—there are three such places, with weekly markets in the tribe—five *imġárĕn*, or sheikhs, are elected by the people of the district, one of them, who is simply called *ámġar*, "sheikh", being their head. They must be brave men with large families in order to command respect, and they are chosen for life, though liable to be displaced if found fault with. Their duty is to maintain order at the market and to act as leaders in war; but their authority does not extend beyond this, and there is no other form of government in the tribe. If anybody is killed at the market, either in revenge or otherwise, these men have to see that the homicide is caught, tied up, and shot by the people at the place where the butchers are selling their meat. His family and village have besides, to pay a fine of a thousand dollars, called *lḥaqq ne ssōq*, "the fine of the market", of which one fifteenth part is kept by the *ámġar*, two fifteenths are divided between the other *imġârĕn*, and the remaining four fifths are entrusted to some reliable and wealthy man to serve as a fund for buying bullocks to be sacrificed as '*ăr* upon other tribes whose assistance may be wanted in case of war, as well as for bribing their sheikhs. The same fine must be paid if a person can be proved to have killed anybody who is on his way to or from a market. My informant had himself been guilty of an offense of this kind. He once killed a rival who had married the girl promised to him by her father, while the man was on his way to the market. He succeeded in making his escape; but if he had been caught he would have been killed and his village would have been obliged to pay the fine of a thousand dollars.

Certain magical rites are practised by homicides with a view to evading the consequences of their deed. Among the *Aṯ Ubáḫti* the homicide steps seven times over the dead body in order to escape detection. Among the *Ait Yúsi* he thinks he may save his life by stepping three times over the grave of his victim on the night after the burial, among the *Aiṯ Sáddĕn* by stepping over it three times in the same direction within three days of the burial, among the *Aiṯ Wäryâġär* by stepping over it three times before forty days have passed after the burial. But among these tribes he is also in great danger of being killed by the relatives of the deceased, who expect him to come to the grave. The *Iglíwa* have another method by which the homicide hopes to escape revenge. On the night after the burial he goes, accompanied by friends, to the grave and takes from it some earth, which he gives to the women of the household. They make use of it in a secret manner, not known to my informant, with a view to appeasing the enemy. In the *Ḥiáina* a homicide makes use of the destructive force attributed to the ground on the 17th of the May—the first day of summer—called *mūt l-arḍ*], "the death of the ground". He hires a woman is living with the avenger of his victim to give the latter a drink mixed with earth taken from underneath his (the homicide's) threshold in order to kill the avenger's courage. An old man from the same tribe told me that a homicide is sometimes troubled in the night by the soul of his victim, appearing to him in his dreams. He tries to stay these unwelcome visits by burning incense, but if he fails he has recourse to another procedure which is sure to prove effective. He goes during the night to the grave of the murdered man, steps over it three times, and thrusts into the head part of it a peg used for the tying of animals, saying: *Rṣa' yā hăd l-míyit^s ma rṣa' l-ût^{s}ed fi l-arḍ* "Remain quiet, O this dead one, as long as the peg remains in the earth."

The relatives of the slain man, again, may make use of magic if they do not know who has killed him. The following rite is practised among the *Ait Waráin* if a person is found dead with his blood on the ground. One of his family takes an earthenware pot which has not been used before, makes a fire there, removes the blood from the ground, and puts in into the kettle to boil. While it is boiling he addresses the dead person three times, saying: "O So-and-so, O So-and-so, O So-and-so"! Then the blood answers, mentioning the name of the culprit. This is done in the night, and nobody else must be present. The same method of finding out an unknown homicide is practised among the Arabic-speaking neighbours of the *Ait Waráin*, the *Ulâd l-Ḥajj*.

In various tribes compurgation is used as a means of establishing the guilt or innocence of a person accused of homicide. In the *Hiáina* the conjurators are selected by the accused, who may have to resort to *'ār*-sacrifices to get the necessary number. This is twelve if they are men; but women are also accepted, though in the proportion of two women to one man. Among the *Aiṯ Sáddĕn* the conjurators, called *imggílla*, are fifty, out of whom ten, called *imnqqarn*, are chosen by the accuser. If any of these refuses to swear, the suspected person is considered guilty of the crime; hence it frequently happens that the accuser induces by bribery some kinsman of the latter to refuse to act as conjurator. This holds good of the *Aiṯ Yúsi* as well. Among the *Ait Waráin* the conjurators are sixty, and the accused may bring whomever he likes to act in the conjuration. It is he who swears first, moving his hand towards the shrine or mosque at which the accuser wants the oaths to be taken and then the others swear in the same manner. Among the *Aṯ Ubáḫti* the *imjílla* are fifty—the accused person and those he brings with him according to his own choice; and here also *'ār*-sacrifices are made to prevail upon unwilling persons to act as *conjurators*. The oaths are taken on the Koran. Among the *Aiṯ Wäryâgär*, who require the number of conjurators to be no more than four, compurgation only leads to a suspension and not to an abandonment of the blood feud, which will anyhow sooner or later break out when a person has been killed and someone is suspected of being the perpetrator of the deed. The custom of compurgation may be traced to the kinship organisation: to the collective responsibility of kindred and to their duty of mutual assistance. As an act of homicide exposes not only the manslayer himself but also his kindred to the blood feud, so also homicide exposes them to the danger involved in perjury; and the larger the number of conjurators, the greater the havoc. This explains why young boys are also accepted as conjurators; they are valueless as witnesses, but their perjury reduces the strength of the kin. Compurgation was known to the ancient Arabs, who also seem to have required fifty conjurators in the case of homicide.[4] But considering its prominence among many Berber tribes in Morocco and Algeria[5], and its close connection with a social system undoubtedly indigenous, it is highly probable that it is a custom rooted in Berber as well as Arab antiquity. There are traces of it in ancient Greek legislation;[6] it occupied an important place in the jurisprudence of most Teutonic peoples and the Welsh;[7] and it is found among many other peoples as well, especially in the Indian Archipelago.[8]

In these cases the oath serves to confirm a denial of guilt, but oaths are also used to confirm a promise. In many cases the avenger makes a vow, silent or loud, to refrain from certain acts until revenge has been taken—not to have his head shaved, not to wash or change his clothes, not to have matrimonial intercourse, not to slaughter an animal, or not to go to the market.[9] Among the *Aiṯ Wäryâgär* the women of the family in such a case also refrain from wearing silver ornaments round the head or the neck and from painting themselves with henna, and boys and unmarried men, who otherwise make use of henna at the feast of the *mūlûd* and at weddings, refrain from doing so if their father has taken a vow of this kind. Such vows, however, are not always strictly observed. Among the *Aiṯ Sáddĕn*, for instance, a man who has sworn not to have his head shaved may after some three or four months be persuaded by his friends to break his vow, or he may do so on his own. In the *Hiáina*, I was told, some shereefs may come with a barber and induce him to have his head shaved; then he will sleep with his wife on the following night, and as soon as possible hire another person to kill the enemy, but he will not try to do it himself. Yet there are people who say that a man who breaks a vow of this kind will become mad. Among the *Aiṯ Wäryâgär* an avenger of blood sometimes takes the vow that he will eat the liver or the tongue of his enemy; he then goes to the enemy's grave after he has killed him. cuts off a piece of his liver or tongue, and puts it into his own mouth, the vow being considered to be fulfilled through this act of symbolical cannibalism.

Among the *Aiṯ Yúsi*, again the avenger after killing the enemy, in many cases drinks a little of his blood or cuts off a small piece of his flesh and eats it. He then says: *Bĕrrḏăġ ulinû ḏikk ay arûmi, allâh*, "I cooled my heart with you, O Christian, Allah"; the last word is an expression of great satisfaction. Among the *Ait Waráin* the avenger may likewise, after accomplishing his task, further gratify his passion by licking the blade of his dagger, dripping with the enemy's blood, or by sucking some blood out of the dead body. Among the *Jbâla* of Andjra and the *Jbel lä-Ḥbíb* it also frequently occurs that the avenger licks the blood off his dagger, and I heard of the same practice in Dukkâla. In Andjra

I was told of a case in which a man, after taking revenge, bit off a piece of his victim's body, sucked the blood from it, and then spat it out. This was said to be done merely in a fit of passion, whereas the licking of the blood from the dagger was also represented as a means of acquiring courage. I heard the story of a man who killed many people and, in order to become brave, licked the blade of his dagger after stabbing his first victim. Among the *Ait Waráin* it occurs if a man kills somebody whom he admires for his bravery, he eats a little piece of his liver in order to get his courage. The avenger may also torture his victim before killing him. Among the *Aiṯ Wäryăgär* it sometimes happens, in the case of a much hated enemy, that the avenger, after catching him, cuts off his penis, puts it into mouth, and then shoots him. Among the *Jbel lä-Ḥbíb* the enemy, if caught alive, is not infrequently tied up and compelled to eat his own penis or a piece of his own flesh, which has been cut off by the avenger, before he is put to death.

Everywhere in Morocco it is the custom to pile a small cairn of stones upon the spot where a person is found killed. Such a cairn is called in Arabic *kàrkōr-l-măǧdōr* (or *măǧdōr*), "the cairn of him who was secretly killed", or (in *Andjra*) *l-maqtᵇla ḏe l-măǧdōr*, "the place of him who was secretly killed". The Berbers of the *Aiṯ Yúsi* call it *agʸrur* (meaning "cairn") *umăǧdōr*. In some parts of the country travellers passing such a cairn often add a stone to it (*Hiáina, Andjra, Aiṯ Wäryăggär, Aglu*). Among the Ait Waráin some passers-by throw a stone on the cairn, others do not, but a near relative of the murdered person always does so when passing the place before his death has been avenged. Among the *Aiṯ Yúsi* I saw two cairns of this consisting of a few stones only; it is not the custom among them to throw stones on such cairns, but if the relatives of the murdered man find his cairn upset, they restore it and at the same time add a few new stones. In Andjra travellers often throw a myrtle sprig instead of a stone. Both there and elsewhere such a cairn is decidedly smaller than the cairn of a saint.

As to the meaning of these practices I have heard different opinions expressed by the natives. Some people maintain that the object of the cairn is merely to warn travellers to be on their guard against robbers. According to others the stones put at the place are meant to confer blessings on the murdered person. The throwing of the stone is often accompanied with some such phrase as: *Ălláh iráḥmăk yā hād l-măgdōr*, "May God be merciful to you, O this *măgdōr* (*Hiáina*); *Ălláh iráḥmăk yā flăn*, or, if the name of the dead one is not known, *yā grīb*, "May God be merciful to you, O So-and so", or, "O stranger" (Andjra); *Šuf hāḏ l-méskīn fein qátᵇluh, alláh iráḥmu*, "Look where they killed this poor fellow, may God be merciful to him" (*ibid.*). Among the *Ulăd Buʿăzîz* the person who passes such a cairn says, without adding a stone to it:

Áhna fîn mät flän mskīn, lláh iráhmu, "Here it is that So-and-so died, poor fellow, may God be merciful to him". But a scribe from the *Hiáina* told me that the throwing of the stone on the cairn, in spite of the invocation which accompanies it, is really meant to keep off *l-bas*, "the evil"; and exactly the same explanation was given me by a man from the *Shāwîa*—the person who passes the cairn puts a stone on it in order to prevent the *bas* of the murdered man from affecting him, by making it stay where it is. This explanation is supported by the fact the stones are in the first instance laid so that they cover up the blood, and also by the general belief that the place is haunted.

The soul (*rōh*) of the murdered man is there (*Ulâd Bu'ăzîz*) and passers-by may hear him groan (*Ait Yúsi*). A Berber from the *Ait Waráin* told me that once when he passed a cairn of this sort he saw a partridge coming out of it and then running to and from in front of him. He got a fright and took to his heels, but the partridge continued to run ahead until it suddenly disappeared in a pillar of smoke, from which he heard groaning. The partridge was the soul, of *lähiäl*, of the murdered man, which may appear in the shape of all sorts of animals or birds. The same man said that there is a place on the border between the *Ait Sáddĕn* and *Ait Warain*, where many men were killed in a fight some years ago and there are many cairns there in consequence. He who passes the place in the night hears the voices of the dead warriors repeating the last words they uttered before they died, and he throws a stone there. In the *Hiáina lä-hiäl l-măğdōr* is said to be, not the soul of a murdered man, but a *jinn*, or spirit, who haunts an uninhabited place where somebody has been killed, even though it happened long ago. It appears in the shape of an animal, such as a he-goat, horse, donkey, dog, cat, or hare; but if the person who sees it knocks a knife against a stone, or if he wears a certain charm, it will take to flight. In Andjra I was told that the place where a person has been murdered is *meskûn*, or haunted by *jnūn*. A scribe from the *Ait Wäryăgär* denied that it is *meskûn*, but admitted that his people are afraid of it.

At the same time there is curative power in the cairn of a murdered person. Among the *Beni Ahsen* I was told that a person suffering from fever may cure himself by sleeping on such a cairn, and I heard the same in Dukkâla, Andjra, and Amzmis in the Great Atlas. In the *Hiáina* a person troubled with headache or some other complaint goes to *kárkor l-măğdōr* and rests his head on it, and, before leaving the place, throws two or three stones on the cairn, asking God to be merciful to the murdered man; and if the patient is too ill to go there himself, a stone is brought from the cairn and his body is touched with it, after which the stone is carried back to its former place.

When the murdered person is a stranger or one who has no family, he is in many cases buried on the spot where his body is found and a cairn is, as usual, piled there. The *Ulâd Bu'azîz* use such a cairn for medicinal purposes. If a person has fever, a vessel filled with water is placed on it and left there overnight, and on the following morning the patient is washed with the water. It is also the custom among them to take a child suffering from whooping-cough to such a place in the morning before sunrise, and to touch its throat with a knife pretending to slaughter it. He who holds the knife says to the whooping cough: *Qtĕlnak ki tĕqtĕl bād l-măgdōr*, "We killed you as this *măgdōr* was killed". Among the *Ait Waráin* a murdered stranger is buried at the place where his body is found, and a ring of stones, called *rutt úñgrīb*, or "the *rằuḍa* (ring of stones) of the stranger", is made over his grave. Persons suffering from fever go and lie down inside the ring and leave there a hot loaf of bread if they feel hot and a cold loaf if they feel cold, thus ridding themselves of the *bas*. My informant said that if he had to visit such a place he would enter the ring, kiss the head part of the grave, rub himself with some of its earth and eat a little of it, put a loaf of bread on the grave, sleep there for a while, tie a piece of his turban to the stones or to a stick, add a stone to the ring, and then go away. In the *Hiáina*, if a person is badly troubled with *lä-ryāḥ (jnūn* as disease spirits), some earth is brought from the grave of a person who has been secretly murdered, this earth is mixed with pounded coriander seed and water, and the mixture is drunk by the patient on three consecutive days after sunset. In Andjra earth from such a grave, mixed with water, is sprinkled on the joints of a person who has been hurt by *jnūn*.

A homicide is haunted by *jnūn (mejnûn* or *meskûn)*, and unclean. Poison oozes out for ever from underneath his nails *(Andjra, Hiáina, Ait Waráin)*; hence anybody who drinks water in which he has washed his hands will fall dangerously ill *(Andjra)*, and those who may have to eat with him from the same dish will take care to avoid any portion of the food which he has touched with his finger *(Ait Waráin)*. Indeed, people refuse to eat together with a homicide *(Hiáina)*—members of the Därqâwi brotherhood are particularly careful in this respect; food partaken of in his company is indigestible (Andjra). The meat of an animal which he has killed is bad to eat *(Andjra, Ulâd Bu'azîz, Aiṯ Waráin, Ait Sáddĕn)*. When the heart of such an animal is cut, its inside is found to be black with blood *(Ait Waráin)*. It is a common rule that a homicide must not perform the sacrifice at the Great Feast with his own hands (Fez, *Hiáina, Ulâd Bu'azîz, Beni Aḥsen, Aiṯ Yúsi, Aiṯ Ndĕr, Demnat, Iglíwa, Aglu)*; but this rule is not universal *(Andjra, Aiṯ Wäryâgär, Aiṯ Sáddĕn, Ait Waráin)*, or though it be admitted in theory it is not always followed in practice. Among the *Amanūz* in *Sūs* a *fqī* who has committed homicide may kill his own animal but cannot conduct the service at the feast. In the Ḥiáina a homicide is not allowed to butcher an animal, nor to skin one, nor to cut up its meat, and at a market he must keep at a little distance from the meat offered for sale by the butchers; when the governor wants to squeeze money out of the butchers he sends a homicide to them, who can punish any obstinacy on their part simply by touching the meat to make it unsaleable. A homicide is not allowed to go into a vegetable garden or an orchard nor to tread on a threshing floor or to enter a granary, nor to go among the sheep, nor to visit a mosque (Ḥiáina). It is a widespread belief that if a homicide comes to a place where people are digging a well, no water will appear, or the water which has already appeared will run away (Ḥiáina, Andjra, Aglu). I remember how conscientiously a servant of mine who in his younger days had killed several persons avoided passing such a place. In Andjra I was told that even a man who had killed somebody in war is *meskûn*; but elsewhere the taboos just mentioned refer to private slayers alone.

A manslayer is unclean because all blood that has left the veins is unclean and haunted by *jnūn*. But his uncleanliness is also due to his sin. This is obvious from the general view that it is neither sinful nor polluting to kill in war. Among the *Aiṯ Wäryâġär* an ordinary manslayer is neither considered unclean nor is he blamed for his deed. They admit that murder was forbidden by the Prophet and that a murderer will go to hell; but if he says his prayers and gives alms and invites scribes to his house to recite the Koran he is likely to get rid of his sin, and, besides, a Rifian is not much afraid of hell. Whatever religion may say on the matter, a man who has not taken anybody's life before he is married is not considered a man. When a young fellow has for the first time killed a person, he goes to the next market at the head of his family, dressed in his best clothes and wearing a new bag; and he wears it not on his left side as usual, but on his right, to announce to all people what he has done and to show that now he is a man. This is done whether the homicide took place in revenge or not. And as it is glorious to kill, so it is also glorious to fall in a fight; only he who dies by being shot is really a man. But though ordinary homicide is approved of, it is considered very bad to kill a scribe without sufficient reason because of his knowledge of the Koran, and it is also considered bad, though not equally bad, to kill an unoffending shereef on account of his holy parentage; and if a man who has committed either of these crimes slaughters an animal, its meat will be difficult to digest. This also indicates that the taboos imposed upon manslayers have something to do with the moral side of the matter.

On the other hand homicides also act as doctors. Among the *Ulâd Buʿâzîz* and in Andjra whooping-cough is cured by a homicide feigning to cut the throat of the patient; among the former this is done in the morning before sunrise. In Andjra, if a person suffers from pain in some particular part of the body, a homicide thrusts his dagger three times towards the affected part without touching it; and if a person is generally ill and confined to bed, he pretends to stab the patient all over his body, at the same time reciting something from the Koran. Pretended stabbing by a homicide is a very widespread cure for stinging pain, in Arabic called *náḥṣa, nógza, bäb*, or *bîbän*, among the *Iglíwa nnaḥst* or *nnogzt*, among the *Ait Waráin táuwurt*, among the *Aiṯ Wäryâgär ḏauwort*. In the last-mentioned tribe ashes are put on the part of the body where the pain is felt, and the homicide then pretends to stab it with his dagger seven times, every alternate time touching the flesh. In the *Ḥiáina* he thrusts his dagger three times towards the chest without touching it and he does so in the morning before breakfast; or he rolls up a small piece of calico, sets light to it, and then touches the affected part of the body with it. In the same tribe, if a woman has been struck by *jnūn*, her husband calls a homicide to cure her by stepping three times over her body. In *Sūs* a person who has a sty (*ilḍ*) is cured by a homicide pretending to stab it seven times. The curative power attributed to a homicide is obviously due to an association between the idea of killing a man and that of killing an illness: a person who has killed a man must also be able to kill a disease. And the curative power attributed to a place where a person has been murdered or to his grave is easily accounted for by a kindred association: contact with such a place has a destructive influence on the illness owing to the destruction of the person.

Notes

1. See my book *Ritual and Belief in Morocco*, i (London, 1926), p. 528.
2. *Cf* my book *Marriage Ceremonies in Morocco* (London, 1914), p. 57 *sqq*.
3. See my *Ritual and Belief in Morocco*, 564 *sqq*.
4. J. Wellhausen, *Reste arabischen Heidentums* (Berlin, 1897), p. 187 *sqq*.
5. A. Hanoteau and A. Letourneux *La Kabylie et les coutumes kabyles* (Paris, 1873), ii. 372 *sq*., iii. 29.
6. R. Hirzel, *Der Eid* (Leipzig, 1902), p.6.
7. H. C. Lea, *Superstition and Force* (Philadelphia, 1892), p. 34 *sqq*.
8. R. Lasch, *Der Eid* (Stuttgart, 1908), p. 100 *sqq*.
9. See my *Ritual and Belief in Morocco*, i. 515.